The Resource Guide
for Christian Counselors

The Resource Guide
for Christian Counselors

Edited by
Douglas R. Flather

Baker Books
A Division of Baker Book House Co
Grand Rapids, Michigan 49516

© 1995 by Douglas R. Flather

Published by Baker Books
a division of Baker Book House Company
P.O. Box 6287, Grand Rapids, MI 49516-6287

Printed in the United States of America

Library of Congress Cataloging-in-Publication Data

Flather, Douglas R., 1960–
    The resource guide for Christian counselors / Douglas R. Flather.
      p.   cm.
    ISBN 0-8010-5249-1 (pbk.)
    1. Pastoral counseling—Bibliography. 2. Pastoral counseling—Directories. I. Title.
Z7820.F57   1996
[BV4012.2]
016.2535—dc20   95-37639

Contents

Preface to the Print Version

Just browse through any Christian bookstore and you'll see it.

Over the course of the past few years, the Christian community's interest in "Christian" counseling has blossomed. As you might expect, publishers have responded. It seems there are hundreds of books, Bible studies, videos, support group materials, and self-help books on everything from abstinence to xenophobia!

I believe this is good. It's good because we live in a world full of hurting people. A dramatic percentage of them will seek help from the church—the Body of Christ. This too is good. It's good because God wants His people to "weep with those who weep," to "bear one another's burdens," and to "bind up the broken-hearted." Thousands of Christians are responding to God's call to be instruments through which He effects healing and wholeness. The question is not whether you, the reader, will be involved in the process, but rather whether you will do it skillfully and biblically. Consider this scenario:

Someone comes to you for help with a problem. This person is wrestling with feelings of anger, but can't seem to put a finger on the cause. You've listened compassionately. You are praying for this person faithfully. You are both familiar with Scripture on the subject, but you wonder if there is anything available that might enhance the application process. You might:

- be a **Lay Counselor.** For years you struggled with a problem of your own. Then, God brought several caring Christians into your life. Not only did they tenderly and patiently minister to you, but they came across a book about someone who, with the Lord, overcame the very same struggles you faced. Now you wonder if there's a book like that on anger.

- be a **Pastoral Counselor.** You took a few counseling courses in seminary. Little did you know then just how much of your time with the church would be dedicated to this task. In addition to your sessions with the counselee, you wonder if there might exist any Bible study workbooks they might use during the week to reinforce your ministry.

- be a **Clinical Christian Therapist.** You studied counseling psychology at a state university. As a committed Christian, you constantly seek to integrate scriptural principles into your counseling practice. You now wonder if anyone has done any work comparing scriptural principles on dealing with anger with rational emotive therapeutic techniques.

The fact is, all of the above resources exist—and many more. The problem for most of us is finding them. Trying to sort through the mass of available materials can be overwhelming. When looking for something specific, most of us experience the frustration of not knowing where to begin, whom to trust, or how to find out.

The *Resource Guide for Christian Counselors* fixes the problem! The purpose of this project is to expose counselors to the vast sea of Christ-centered counseling resources presently available.

Our goal is to place at your fingertips virtually everything that has been produced within the Christian Counseling and Recovery movement. You'll be able to access and evaluate printed materials, national professional and support organizations, and information clearing houses for scores of counseling issues. In other words, we will show you what is out there. What you do with it is up to you.

You'll begin learning how to use this guide in the introduction that follows.

Acknowledgments

Many thanks to the publishers, authors, and information providers that supplied the information and resource samples during the research process.

Thanks also to the editorial and production staff at Baker Books. Their patience and careful work have taken this project from an idea to a finished product.

Finally, thanks to my exceptional wife Tami, for her willingness to sleep night after night under the soft glow of the computer monitor. Her support and encouragement have enabled me to make this small contribution to the field.

Introduction to the Print Version

How to Use the *Resource Guide for Christian Counselors*

This guide can be one of the most important enhancements to your counseling ministry or practice. It is arranged so you will be able to locate and evaluate resources that can greatly reinforce your ability to help hurting people. As mentioned in the preface, there is a substantial body of materials (at all levels) that you can learn from, adapt, and in many cases immediately apply to specific counseling cases you encounter.

How Resources Are Arranged

We've organized the resources by broad topics. Perhaps the first thing you should do is scan the contents page. Then browse, page by page, through a few chapters to get a feel for the types of information in each.

Generally, the resources in each chapter are presented in alphabetical order, based on the author's last name. Organizations and information clearing houses follow. We've tried to provide you with as much meaningful information about the resources as possible. In addition to basic descriptive and bibliographic information, we've sought to give you the author's professional and academic background, and even the contents. Occasionally, you'll find a resource is missing some information. In these cases, the publisher was unable to provide us with the material by press time.

Choosing Resources That Are Right for You

Now that you have the *Resource Guide,* finding resources should be much easier. But you might now encounter a new problem—deciding which ones to use! Here are a few suggestions that might help.

1. Decide exactly what you are looking for in a resource. Are you facing a new problem and need to know what the issues are? Are you after specific counseling tech-

niques? Perhaps you want something to give to a client to read during the week. Or, maybe you are writing a paper and want an alternative view. Determining what you need will help you focus your search.

2. Carefully read the product description. We asked the authors to tell us what distinguishes their work from similar works on the market.

3. Note the size of the entry. Is it a 350-page book or a 24-page booklet? Which are you or your client more likely to read?

4. Check the author's background. Consider where the person received training. Is the author actively involved in private practice, ministry, or education? Is the author a counselor or someone who personally recovered from the issue? Be aware that some authors approach issues from a clinical perspective while others take a more spiritual angle. Depending on the counseling issue, this can make a big difference.

5. Where we could, we've given you the entire contents. This will give you a tremendous overview of the entry.

6. Consider the level or audience for which the resource was produced. After the number of pages, you'll find the following:

a. *for counselors.* These works are produced at a professional level for people providing counseling services. They assume a broad knowledge of the behavioral sciences, often contain clinical/technical language, and tend to be written at an undergraduate level or above. Listed here you'll find resources on theory, technique, and professional organizations.

b. *for counselees.* These are the resources you will recommend and/or work through with your clients. Self-help, general trade, inductive Bible studies, fill-in-the-blank workbooks, devotional and meditation books, anecdotal/biographical titles, and books written for children are examples of resources written for counselees.

c. *for both counselors and counselees.* Here you will find support group materials and yet another type of resource—"crossover titles." A number of publishers produce counseling resources aimed at both audiences. These titles often approach an issue in depth, but avoid confusing clinical language. Literally the best of both worlds, such titles are particularly helpful to counselors who might lack formal training.

d. an organization. Sometimes calling an organization, specialty ministry, hotline, or information clearing house is the best place to start looking for help.

7. Finally, don't be afraid to try something new. Occasionally you should look into something from a publisher or organization that may not be tied to your particular church, background, or clinical orientation. For instance, if you are a Baptist, see what the Presbyterians or Catholics have to offer. If you are primarily dynamic in approach, look into what the cognitive people have to say about that issue. It could be very helpful. Remember, no matter where you are on the theological or clinical continuum, God is working and people are being helped both to your right and to your left.

Disclaimer

As you pore over the entries in this project, you will not find any one counseling methodology or approach advocated. In fact, some of the resources confront the same issues from very different angles. You'll find a great deal of diversity even within the field of Christian counseling. *Consequently, it is necessary to point out that the entries herein are not necessarily endorsed by either the editor or Baker Book House. Most of the entries are produced by people and groups that are distinctively Christian. Some come from sources that are loosely affiliated with Christianity, but share Judeo-Christian values. A few are not Christian at all, but might be of interest to some individuals under special circumstances.*

Updates

Finally, the *Resource Guide for Christian Counselors* is intended to be a constantly growing and improving resource. We look forward to providing you with regularly updated editions. (Be sure to send in the business reply card in the back of the book so we can keep you up to date.) We look forward to hearing your suggestions and comments. Our goal for this project is to help you help others toward wholeness in Christ even more effectively! May God richly bless you in your practice or ministry.

The Editor

1. Addictions and Compulsive Behaviors

General Works on Addictions

Hand-Me-Down Genes and Second-Hand Emotions *Overcome the Genetic & Environmental Predispositions That Control Your Life,* Stephen Arterburn

Oliver Nelson (a division of Thomas Nelson), 1993, $17.99, cloth, 320 pp., for both counselors and counselees

Description A myth-shattering handbook that counselors, pastors, and laypeople can use to "break the cycle" of addiction in themselves, their families, and others. Will help to identify key symptoms of addiction and break denial, overcome shame and paralyzing guilt, take steps to free oneself from negative predispositions.

Author Stephen Arterburn is founder of New Life Treatment Centers, Inc., a nationwide treatment program for emotional problems and addictive disorders.

Contents *Part 1:* Depression *1.* Could it be predisposition? *2.* The valley of the shadow of death *3.* The causes of depression *4.* Freeing ourselves from depression *5.* Freeing our children from depression *Part 2:* Suicide *6.* The seeds of destruction *7.* The larger picture of suicide *8.* The case for predisposition *9.* Freeing ourselves from risk *10.* Freeing our children from suicide *Part 3:* Obesity *11.* The dilemma of obesity *12.* The case for predisposition *13.* Freeing ourselves from obesity *14.* Freeing our children from obesity *Part 4:* Alcoholism *15.* Alcoholism: Dispelling the myths *16.* The case for predisposition *17.* Freeing ourselves from alcoholism *18.* Freeing our children from alcoholism / *Conclusion:* Principles for living life on purpose

Finding the Freedom of Self-Control
William Backus

Bethany House Publishers, 1987, $7.99, paper, 173 pp., for both counselors and counselees

Description Dr. Backus focuses on the misbelief that instant gratification of desires leads to happiness. He shows the reader that a biblical picture of a happy, free person is one who has learned self-control through honestly facing his bad habits and changing his behavior according to the truth of God's Word. Dr. Backus shows the reader how to understand self-control, apply truth to misbeliefs about self-control, control bodily urges to overindulge, break the pattern of old habits, and build new habits of self-control. He emphasizes that power to change comes from God and not self. The Word of God exhorts and instructs the new man, empowered by the Holy Spirit, in how to walk to please God. The author illustrates the principles with case histories and dialogues to help the readers visualize and apply truth.

Author William Backus is a licensed clinical psychologist and an ordained Lutheran clergyman. He is founder and director of the Center for Christian Psychological Services, St. Paul, Minn., and an associate pastor of a large Lutheran church.

Contents *1.* How to understand self-control *2.* How God gives self-control *3.* Self-control and the truth *4.* How to stop putting it off until tomorrow *5.* How to control your temper *6.* Does your sex drive manage you? *7.* Self-control and our daily bread *8.* How to break a habit

Are You Having Fun Yet? *How to Bring the Art of Play into Your Recovery,* Carmen Renee Berry

Thomas Nelson Publishers, 1992, $8.99, paper, 160 pp., for both counselors and counselees

Description This guide helps people who are beating their addictions discover joy in the recovery process. Restore fun and zest in life by following seven proven steps to joy and personal fulfillment.

Author Carmen Renee Berry is a noted lecturer, author, and workshop and retreat leader. With more than ten years of experience in the area of child sexual abuse prevention and treatment, Berry specializes in overcoming childhood trauma, burnout prevention, integration of spirituality and recovery, and the use of bodywork in the recovery process. She holds two master's degrees in social work.

Contents *1.* Rekindle your hope in the possibility of play *2.* Embrace the perspective of abundance *3.* Enlarge the limits of your enjoyment comfort zone *4.* Acknowledge the value of play *5.* Open yourself to your inner child *6.* Insist on safety for you and your inner child *7.* Accept responsibility for your own enjoyment *8.* Discover your own enjoyment style *9.* Explore new ways to play with your inner child *10.* Invent new ways to enjoy life as an adult *11.* Share the celebration *12.* Notice the nurturance available

When Addiction Comes to Church

Helping Yourself and Others Move into Recovery, Melinda Fish

Chosen Books, 1990, $8.99, paper, 286 pp., for counselees

Description Uses interesting case studies woven with biblically based teaching and a creative writing style to help the reader recognize addictive behavior in himself and his Christian friends. It fully explains the addictive cycle; what happens when addiction is left untreated in a Christian; the physical, emotional, and spiritual issues for a Christian addict that need to be addressed including: denial, perfectionism, hidden anger, breaking ties with the addictive environment, overcoming guilt, and choosing healthy relationships. Other sections include how to stop the abuse one receives from an addict and how to find an appropriate support and recovery system including group therapy, counseling, and a supportive local church.

Author Melinda Fish is copastor of Church of the Risen Savior, Trafford, Pa., author of three books, pastor's wife, mother of two children. She holds a B.A. from the University of Texas at Austin and is a frequent speaker at churches, retreats, seminars, and women's groups across the United States and abroad.

Contents *1.* Addiction: the root of so much misery *2.* What is addiction? *3.* The addictive environment *4.* The tornado of addiction *5.* In the church: addiction by mouth *6.* Action addictions *7.* The addict: a slave and oppressor *8.* People addiction: the counterfeit agape *9.* "I can't be an addict—I'm a Christian" *10.* Leaving Egypt—cold turkey! *11.* The wilderness—pathway to emotional healing *12.* The role of fear in addiction *13.* Rage in addiction: healing hidden anger *14.* The addict's particular battle: overcoming perfectionism *15.* Restoring fellowship with God *16.* Choosing healthy relationships *17.* Conquering relapse *18.* Possessing the land / *Appendix 1:* How to start a Christian support group / *Appendix 2:* A Christian's 12 steps / *Appendix 3:* A daily personal inventory

Healing Life's Hidden Addictions

Overcoming the Closet Compulsions That Waste Your Time & Control Your Life, Archibald D. Hart

Servant Publications/Vine Books, 1990, $9.99, paper, 276 pp., for both counselors and counselees

Description Dr. Hart explores fascinating new research on addictive behaviors and the most effective way to overcome them. In addition to offering sound medical and psychological advice, he probes deeply into the spiritual dynamic at the heart of addiction and points to the path of grace, the way of lasting recovery.

Author Dr. Archibald D. Hart is dean of the Graduate School of Psychology and professor of psychology at Fuller Theological Seminary.

Contents *Introduction:* The addiction controversy *Part 1:* Understanding hidden addictions *1.* What are hidden addictions? *2.* Addictions and cravings *3.* Is there an addictive personality? *4.* The addictive cycle *5.* Obsessions and compulsions *Part 2:* Varieties of hidden addictions *6.* Lifestyle addictions *7.* Codependency: addiction to helping *8.* Religious addiction *9.* Addictions to sex and love *10.* Addiction to adrenaline: hurry sickness *11.* Addiction to food *Part 3:* Healing for hidden addictions *12.* Overcoming your hidden addiction *13.* A theology for self-control

Structured Intervention *How to Deal with the Addict in Your Life,* Ken Howard

Morehouse Publishing, 1993, $39.95, video, 50 minutes, for both counselors and counselees

Description A simple, basic outline developing "structured intervention," the first step necessary for recovery from chemical and/or alcohol dependence. Hosted by Ken Howard and endorsed by the National Council on Alcoholism and Drug Dependence.

Too Much Is Never Enough *Behaviors You Never Thought Were Addictions. How to Recognize and Overcome,* Gaylen Larson and Marita Littauer

Pacific Press, 1993, $8.95, paper, 128 pp., for counselees

Description A Christian's guide to recognizing and overcoming addiction. It speaks to the person whose life is out of balance with too many good things and offers concrete help for those who need to know when enough is enough.

Authors Gaylen B. Larsen, a licensed and ordained minister with a Ph.D. in clinical psychology, is the director of the Alpha Counseling Centers, which specialize in treating addictions and co-dependency. Marita Littauer serves as the national women's advisor of the Alpha Counseling Centers and is the director of corporate marketing for CLASS Speakers, Inc. She is the daughter of popular author Florence Littauer.

Contents *Part 1:* Discovery / *Introduction* / *Section 1*— Identifying the problem *1.* What is addiction? *2.* When does addiction become sin? *3.* To what do people get addicted? *4.* Why some people get addicted and some people don't *5.* How do addictions happen? *6.* What about healing? *7.* How do you know if you need help? *Part 2:* Recovery *Section 2*—Open your eyes *8.* Do you have a problem? *9.* Do you need professional help? *Section 3*—Learn all you can *10.* What is your addiction? *11.* What set the addictions up? *12.* Where did your problem come from? *Section 4*—Get support *13.* Are your friends contributing to your problem? *14.* How can you evaluate your friends? *15.* Why do you need a support group? *16.* What support group is best for you? *Section 5*—Get objective feedback *17.* Do you have blind spots? *18.* How do you measure progress? *19.* Who should give feedback *Section 6*—Allow time for healing *20.* How long will it take? *21.* How can you know when it's over?

Behind Our Sunday Smiles *Helping Those with Life-Controlling Problems,* Jimmy Ray Lee

Baker Book House, 1991, $9.99, paper, 178 pp., for counselors

Description A counselor teaches pastors and lay leaders how to identify hidden addictions and despair among church members and to stimulate the entire congregation to concerned love.

Author Jimmy Ray Lee is president of Turning Point Ministries and founder of Project 714, both based in Chattanooga, Tenn. A former pastor, he serves on the national board of Teen Challenge.

Contents *1.* Introduction to life-controlling problems *2.* Ways to help hurting people *3.* Helping families with dependencies *4.* A local church model

The Compulsive Woman *How to Break the Bonds of Addiction to Food, TV, Sex, Men, Exercise . . . ,* Sandra Simpson LeSourd

Chosen Books, 1987, $9.99, paper, 317 pp., for counselees

Description A firsthand look at the nightmare of addictive-compulsive behavior, with guidelines for recovery.

Author Sandra Simpson LeSourd is a lecturer on chemical dependency and compulsive behavior.

Contents *Book One*—Illness and recovery *1.* Facing off *2.* The violated childhood *3.* The dysfunctional home *4.* Into the fast lane *5.* The cultist *6.* Why live? *7.* Breaking the cycle *8.* Do it now *9.* The pain in change *10.* Intervention *11.* Facing truth *12.* Anger and male dependency *13.* Deception and other little monsters *14.* Learning to like yourself *Book Two*—Handbook of special helps *1.* Listings of self-help programs *2.* Helps for families and friends *3.* The spiritual dimension

The Not-So Compulsive Woman *20 Recovery Principles to Pull You Out of the Pit,* Sandra Simpson LeSourd

Chosen Books, 1992, $14.99, cloth, 206 pp., for counselees

Description Combining humor and vivid anecdotes, with insights from her own experience, the author presents 20 solid principles for overcoming compulsive-addictive behavior.

Author Sandra Simpson LeSourd is a lecturer on chemical dependency and compulsive behavior.

Contents *1.* Seek the prayers of others *2.* Say no *3.* Trust God's love for you *4.* Accept yourself *5.* Smell the flowers *6.* Obey the inner voice *7.* Give yourself away *8.* Be vulnerable *9.* Be reconciled *10.* Identify your real needs *11.* Expect the best *12.* Seize the moment *13.* Forgive those who have hurt you *14.* Talk about it *15.* Celebrate *16.* Be honest *17.* Like yourself *18.* Confess your wrongdoing *19.* You are loved! Believe it! *20.* Reach out / *Appendix:* Support organizations

How to Say No to a Stubborn Habit
Erwin W. Lutzer

Victor Books, 1979, $8.99, paper, 143 pp., for counselees

Description Every day we face the oldest human dilemma—the choice between good and evil. Erwin Lutzer discusses biblical strategies for resisting evil.

Author Erwin Lutzer is senior pastor of Moody Memorial Church in Chicago. He is a graduate of Dallas Theological Seminary.

Contents *1.* Why so much temptation? *2.* The ground rules *3.* Putting your past behind you *4.* Getting God's perspective *5.* The freedom of living at the cross *6.* The power of the Holy Spirit *7.* The renewing of your mind *8.* Living with your feelings *9.* The taming of your will *10.* The intercession of Christ and believers *11.* Resisting satanic activity *12.* Trapped again *13.* Writing the last chapter

When Good Things Become Addictions
Gaining Freedom from Our Compulsions,
Grant L. Martin

> Victor Books, 1990, $8.99, paper, 192 pp., for counselees

> **Description** Offers hope, encouragement, and steps to freedom, all from a biblical perspective. An opening chapter describes the addictive cycle and how one gets "hooked" into it. Also describes various applications of the 12-step system of recovery.

> **Author** Grant L. Martin (Ph.D., University of Washington), a licensed psychologist and marriage and family therapist, is a counselor with CRISTA Counseling Service, where he has served for over 18 years. He is also an adjunct professor in the graduate counseling program at Seattle Pacific University. Widely published, he is vice president and executive board member for the Christian Association for Psychological Studies (CAPS).

> **Contents** *1.* Introduction to addictions *2.* Romance addiction *3.* Relationship addiction *4.* Sexual addiction *5.* Eating addiction *6.* Power addiction *7.* Religious addiction *8.* Activity addiction *9.* Steps to recovery / *Resource agencies*

The Search for Freedom *Demolishing the Strongholds That Diminish Your Faith . . . ,* Robert S. McGee

> Vine Books, 1995, $8.95, paper, 232 pp.

> **Description** Helps Christians understand and overcome strongholds such as insecurity, fear of abandonment, lust, addiction, poor self-esteem, and anger through the CROP principle (Confession, Repentance, Obedience, and Praise).

> **Author** Robert McGee, founder of Rapha, is a professional counselor, lecturer, and the author of several books.

> **Contents** *1.* How freedom is lost *2.* Stuck with childhood patterns *3.* Childhood behaviors *4.* Emotions of childhood *5.* Understanding the enemy within *6.* A closer look at strongholds *7.* Messages from the past; help for the present *8.* Getting to the root of the problem *9.* Hearing God's voice *10.* Prayer paves the way *11.* The path to freedom *12.* Avoiding common failures and setbacks *13.* Where do I go from here?

Dealing with Desires You Can't Control
Mark R. McMinn

> NavPress, 1990, $1.95, paper, 23 pp., for both counselors and counselees

> **Description** What do you do when all your efforts to resist temptation only seem to make it stronger? When the harder you try to ignore it, the more overwhelming it becomes? You acknowledge your temptations and learn how to properly manage them. In *Dealing with Desires You Can't Control,* Mark McMinn honestly discusses the source of our temptations. He explains why trying harder doesn't really work, and by looking at biblical principles regarding temptation management, he clearly demonstrates the pathway to genuine maturity.

> **Author** Mark McMinn is professor of psychology at George Fox College in Newberg, Oreg. He received his Ph.D. in psychology from Vanderbilt University in 1983 and is a licensed psychologist in Oregon. He is the author of three other books dealing with counseling.

Making the Break *First Steps in Overcoming Eating Disorders, Pornography, Drugs, Alcohol,* David Partington

> Harold Shaw Publishers, 1991, $6.99, paper, 112 pp., for both counselors and counselees

> **Description** If you think you have a compulsive dependency problem, then you probably do—so say the experts. But you're not alone. An estimated four in ten people are somewhere on the slide into dependency, longing to be free from their secrets, lies, fears, and bondage. *Making the Break* won't snatch away your problems. No book can do that. But these pages hold the secrets to the first steps toward freedom. As you learn to identify your self-destructive patterns, *Making the Break* will help you break the cycle—and break free to a more fulfilling life.

> **Author** David Partington, director of Yeldall Christian Centers (a group of addiction counseling clinics), draws on his own experience to aid sufferers and those who care about them.

> **Contents** *1.* Always on your mind *2.* The slide into dependency *3.* Who's to blame *4.* Making the right choices *5.* Practical steps and spiritual breakthroughs *6.* Breaking free *7.* Helping someone break free / *Resources*

Addictive Lifestyles *Breaking Free,* Richard Peace

> Serendipity, 1991, $6.95, paper, 109 pp., for both counselors and counselees

Description A 7- or 14-week course designed for anyone wanting to become a part of a support group. Groups discuss how it is possible for innocent activities and harmless substances to become addictive and develop into behaviors that seriously damage people's lives. This course is designed for anyone interested in learning about addictive behavior and is willing to approach the problem compassionately and with an open mind. For this group to be of value, each participant must be willing to look honestly at his or her way of life and to share openly their addictive patterns, real or potential, that he or she discovers.

Contents *1.* Our addictive society *2.* What is addictive behavior? *3.* Addiction to television *4.* Addiction to shopping *5.* Addiction to work *6.* Overcoming addiction *7.* Love, fear, and addiction

Fatal Attractions *Overcoming Our Secret Addictions,* Bill Perkins

Harvest House Publishers, 1992, $8.99, paper, 287 pp., for both counselors and counselees

Description What makes harmful things so attractive? Why do we allow them to have such power over us? From the beginning of history people have struggled with "fatal attractions," secret thoughts and actions that pull them away from God and each other. Sex, food, compulsive habits . . . these and a multitude of other cravings quickly turn into addictions that destroy people's lives. In *Fatal Attractions,* author Bill Perkins shows how these addictions develop and then lays out a step-by-step plan for finding freedom. A study guide is also included.

Author Bill Perkins is the senior pastor of the South Hills Community Church in Portland, Oreg. A graduate of Dallas Theological Seminary, Perkins is the writer for Moody Bible Institute's *Today in the Word* daily devotional guide. He also writes a daily two-minute radio spot that is broadcast on the Moody network. He has appeared on nationally broadcast radio and television shows and has addressed audiences in the United States and Canada. The Fatal Attractions Seminar has helped thousands understand and overcome their own destructive behavior.

Recovery from Addictions Dale Ryan and Juanita Ryan

InterVarsity Press, 1992, $4.99, paper, 60 pp., for both counselors and counselees

Description This Bible study is part of a series of 16 volumes on various recovery themes. Each book contains studies on six biblical texts. Leader's notes are provided for group study.

Authors Dale Ryan is the executive director of the Recovery Partnership, the parent organization to the National Association for Christian Recovery. Juanita Ryan is a counselor in private practice in Hacienda Heights, Calif.

Contents *1.* Admitting our powerlessness *2.* Admitting our lives are unmanageable *3.* Believing God's power is greater *4.* Being restored *5.* Turning our wills over to God *6.* Turning our lives over to God / *Leader's notes*

Running in Circles *How to Find Freedom from Addictive Behavior,* Gary Steven Shogren and Edward T. Welch

Baker Book House, 1995, $8.99, paper, 106 pp.

Description More than a self-help strategy for beating addiction. The authors—a psychologist and a pastor—show that spiritual and relational dynamics involving idolatry and estrangement from God's kingdom underlie all addictions. They do not believe true addicts are helped merely with self-discipline. Nor do the authors think addicts are helpless victims of low self-esteem, disease, or societal injustice. Here's practical, biblically sound counsel on how to understand and overcome addiction.

Authors Gary Steven Shogren has served as pastor and now teaches at Biblical Seminary in Philadelphia. Edward T. Welch is a licensed psychologist and director of the Biblical Counseling and Educational Foundation in Philadelphia.

Contents *1.* A kingdom of slaves: how to know if you are enslaved *2.* The real nature of the kingdom of slaves: disease, low self-esteem, or what? *3.* Finding freedom in the kingdom of God: acting out the gospel *4.* Counterattacks of the dark kingdom: danger to spot *5.* Living at peace in the kingdom of God: getting back together *6.* Ongoing life in the kingdom of God: recovery tools

Addictive Behavior *A Short-term Structured Model,* Gary Steven Shogren and Edward T. Welch

1995, $17.99, cloth, 196 pp.

Description At the root of any physical or emotional dependency there lies a spiritual problem. Based on this presupposition the authors help counselors understand addictions. Written for students or practicing pastoral counselors, each problem is adapted to the five-session Strategic

Pastoral Counseling model developed by David G. Benner. A companion book of the Strategic Christian Living series, *Running in Circles,* is available as a counselee handout or self-help resource.

Authors Gary Steven Shogren has served as pastor and now teaches at Biblical Seminary in Philadelphia. Edward T. Welch is a licensed psychologist and director of the Biblical Counseling and Educational Foundation in Philadelphia.

Contents *1.* A kingdom of slaves: how to know if you are enslaved *2.* The real nature of the kingdom of slaves: disease, low self-esteem, or what? *3.* Finding freedom in the kingdom of God: acting out the gospel *4.* Counterattacks of the dark kingdom: danger to spot *5.* Living at peace in the kingdom of God: getting back together *6.* Ongoing life in the kingdom of God: recovery tools

God, Help Me Stop *Break Free from Addiction and Compulsion,* Claire W.

Zondervan Publishing House, 1993, $8.99, paper, 128 pp., for counselees

Description Here is a presentation of the 12 steps of Alcoholics Anonymous as applied to any addictive behavior such as alcoholism, overeating, smoking, compulsive gambling, or sexual addiction. Part of the God, Help Me series from Zondervan. These self-help books are designed not only to explain the recovery process, but to guide and support the reader throughout that process. Emotional and spiritual healing are promoted through Bible verses, questions for reflection, writing assignments, and the personal examples of the author and other people who have experienced recovery.

Author Claire W. draws on her Ph.D. training in clinical psychology and her work as a counselor as she writes for Christians in recovery.

Counseling for Problems of Self-Control
Richard P. Walters

Word Publishing, 1987, $15.99, cloth, 215 pp., for counselors

Description Part of the Resources for Christian Counseling series from Word. Dr. Walters gives examples to help both the therapist and counselee to recognize the problem and come to grips with its origin.

Author Richard Walters is minister of counseling at First Presbyterian Church in Boulder, Colo.

Contents *Part 1:* Foundations *1.* A survey of the problem *2.* An illustration of the problem *3.* The beginnings of the problem *4.* Resolving the problem *5.* Crisis management in disorders of self-control *6.* Counseling and the problem: see and hear *7.* Counseling and the problem: understand *8.* The IDEAS diagram: an aid to understanding *9.* Counseling and the problem: turn *10.* Counseling and the problem: be healed *11.* What to do when counseling is not wanted *12.* What to do when friends or family interfere *Part 2:* Resolving root problems *13.* Sinful human nature: Eric's impulsiveness *14.* Physiological influences: Chuck's idleness *15.* Deficits: Keely's adultery *16.* Wounds: Cheryl's perfectionism *17.* Discrepancies: Howie's pornography *18.* Results of personal sin: Nina quit drinking, but . . . *Part 3:* The only sufficient answer *19.* Christian maturity: when? *20.* Christian maturity: how? / *Appendixes 1.* How to cope with anger *2.* How to stop unwanted thoughts *3.* Scriptures displace unwanted thoughts *4.* How to break habits *5.* Ways to be accountable for your actions *6.* Accepting God's view of your worth *7.* How to resist temptation

Winning the War Within *How to Stop Doing What You Don't Want to Do,* Peter Wilkes

Description Peter Wilkes, drawing from biblical resources, counseling experience, and psychological understanding, answers questions with fresh insights into the inner workings of how we are made. He then takes us through a step-by-step process for understanding the pieces of our individual personality puzzles. This sets the stage for us to develop concrete strategies for change.

Author Peter Wilkes is pastor of South Hills Community Church in San Jose, Calif., where he carries on an extensive counseling ministry.

Contents *1.* Doing what we don't want to do *2.* Which I is me? *3.* Three Freds and two Janes *4.* The Apostle Paul looks at personality roles *5.* Self and the Christian *6.* Resolving your inner tensions *7.* Starting the inner journey *8.* Seeking help *9.* Breaking bad relationships *10.* Blaming, choosing, and responsibility *11.* Pleasing people, pleasing God *12.* Cultivating a forgiving spirit / *Appendix 1* Interpreting Romans 7 / *Appendix 2* Ego-state theory

Beating a Bad Habit or Addiction

Abbey Press, 1993, $.50 each, paper, 8 pp., for counselees

Description Part of the New CareSteps series from Abbey Press. Each CareStep pamphlet (three panel) is filled with insightful advice and quotes from respected leaders in the helping professions. Very useful during the early stages of recovery. The underlying message in all CareSteps pamphlets is the emphasis on using all one's resources—emotional, physical, mental, social, and spiritual, to cope with life's biggest challenges. This title emphasizes acknowledging the problem, getting necessary help, preparing to be uncomfortable, being cautious of substitutions, and never giving up.

Drawing on Faith to Fight an Addiction

Abbey Press, $.50 each, paper, 8 pp., for counselees

Description Part of the CareNotes series from Abbey Press. CareNotes are short booklets that help readers identify issues and begin the process of seeking resolution. Anecdotal and uplifting. Beautiful photographs grace the covers. Over 20 million CareNotes have been sold in just over five years. Can be used as an alternative to a greeting card or in conjunction with pastoral care visits.

Edge TV—Addictive Behaviors

NavPress, 1992, $24.95, video with leader's guide, for both counselors and counselees

Description For youth workers who want to steer their group away from "church appropriate" discussions and get them talking about what's really going on in their lives. *Edge TV* (a video magazine for church youth groups) is the place to start. Created in partnership with Youth Specialties and IMS Productions, each episode of *Edge TV* is packed with high-energy visuals, no-holds-barred drama, startling interviews, Christian music videos, captivating humor—and an honest approach to Jesus Christ that will get kids asking some very interesting questions.

Getting an Addicted Loved One into Treatment

Abbey Press, $.50 each, paper, 8 pp., for counselees

Description Part of the CareNotes series from Abbey Press. CareNotes are short booklets that help readers identify issues and begin the process of seeking resolution. Anecdotal and uplifting. Beautiful photographs grace the covers. Over 20 million CareNotes have been sold in just over five years. Can be used as an alternative to a greeting card or in conjunction with pastoral care visits.

Journal of Ministry in Addiction and Recovery

The Haworth Pastoral Press, biannually, $20.00, a reference or academic work

Description A new journal that seeks to provide a forum for networking (sharing ideas about addiction and recovery) and to provide a multidisciplinary approach to ministry. It offers pastoral caregivers and others in the addiction field innovative approaches to treating a variety of addictive behaviors. Representative articles: Addiction and dualistic spirituality: shared visions of God, self, and creation; The twelve step program and Christian spirituality; Spirituality in treatment programs for addicts; Grief issues in alcoholism and addiction; Do clergy encourage codependency?; Let God be God: a theological justification for the anonymity of God in the 12 step program.

Substance Abuse Addictions

Is Your Teenager an Alcoholic? Christine Adams

Ligouri Publications, 1992, $.75, paper, 24 pp., for counselees

Description Explains the disease of alcoholism, details its signs and symptoms, and tells what parents can do to help their teen arrest this life-threatening addiction. Also includes a "self-test" to help teens determine if they need help.

Alcohol and Substance Abuse, Second Edition *A Handbook for Clergy and Congregations,* Stephen Apthorp

Morehouse Publishing, 1985, $12.95, paper, 240 pp., for counselors

Description Shows clergy and laity how to be pastoral problem solvers, not practitioners, through intervention and referral. Since families are the first line of prevention and churches have access to half the families in America weekly, Dr. Apthorp focuses on what the church family can do. He offers unique strategies to prevent problems before they begin and deal with chemical problems after they've begun. This is a how-to handbook with specific descriptions and suggestions.

Author Stephen P. Apthorp received his training in the problems of alcohol and drug abuse at the Johnson Institute and Hazelden Foundation in Minneapolis and through doctoral studies at Andover Newton Theological Seminary in Boston. He heads his own educational/prevention consulting organization called ASAP (Alcohol and Substance Abuse Prevention) in Tucson, Ariz.

Contents *1.* The minister's dilemma *2.* The clergy as catalyst *3.* A program for chemical health *4.* Prohibition or prevention? *5.* Alcoholism—sin or sickness? *6.* The misuse and abuse of illicit drugs *7.* Illegal drug abuse *8.* The cry for help *9.* Creating a treatment network *10.* Theological perspectives, spiritual foundations

Prelapse, Relapse, and True Recovery
Daniel T. Budenz

CompCare Publishers, 1992, $3.95, paper, 102 pp., for both counselors and counselees

Description Author and chemical dependency expert Dr. Daniel Budenz states that relapse is always preventable—if you know the danger signs. In this booklet, he uses his 20 years of experience to explain why relapse happens and how anyone can practice "relapse prevention."

Never Too Late *A Message of Hope for Older Alcoholics and Their Families and Friends,* Cecil Carle

CompCare Publishers, 1989, $5.95, paper, 109 pp., for counselees

Description The late Cecil Carle began his AA program at the age of 70. Twenty years later he wrote his book, explaining his story and sharing why seniors are especially vulnerable. Myths about older drinkers and crucial information about the AA process of recovery are included.

Author Cecil Carle was a retired member of the motion picture industry, a writer, and a grateful member of AA.

Understanding and Counseling the Alcoholic Howard Clinebell

Abingdon Press, $13.95, paper, for counselors

Alcoholism and Codependency Alexander DeJong

Tyndale House Publishers, 1994, $7.99, paper, 128 pp., for both counselors and counselees

Description This question and answer book written by a recovered alcoholic will help anyone afflicted by alcoholism.

Beating the Chemical Cop-Out Charles Dickson

New Hope, 1992, paper, $1.95, 21 pp., for counselees

Description Designed to be shared between young adults, *Beating the Chemical Cop-Out* will help you understand the reasons for abuse and what drugs are doing to your friend. But he doesn't have to become another statistic. With you as his friend and Christ as his pattern, he can deal with changes, readjust his life, and move on toward some life goals.

Author Charles Dickson is a counselor and teacher in Hickory, N.C.

Problem Drinking *How to Help a Friend,* Charles Downs

Harold Shaw Publishers, 1990, $7.99, paper, 110 pp., for counselors

Description A pastor who is an alcoholic in recovery addresses the questions surrounding alcohol abuse. Those who struggle in relating to an alcoholic will welcome the heartfelt encouragement and advice, background information, and thorough resource section.

Author Charles Downs (a pseudonym) is an alcoholic in recovery. As a pastor and committed friend to those who struggle with addictive lifestyles, Downs has found meaning and fulfillment in living alcohol free.

Contents *1.* Jilian's story *2.* Doug's story *3.* Why doesn't my friend stop drinking? *4.* My friend is acting strange *5.* How can I help? *6.* What about me? *7.* The journey of recovery *8.* End of the story / *Resources* / 12 step groups / Treatment centers

God Is for the Alcoholic *Revised and Expanded,* Jerry Dunn

Moody Press, 1986, $10.95, paper, 236 pp., for both counselors and counselees

Description Three broad sections deal with various aspects of alcoholism and ways individuals in contact with alcoholics can deal with this problem.

Author Jerry Dunn is a recognized authority on alcoholism. He has lectured extensively on this subject at special conferences for pastors, medical students, and doctors. Pastor Dunn was executive director of People's City Mission Home,

Lincoln, Nebr., before his retirement in 1979. He is currently a lecturer and consultant on alcoholism.

Contents *Part 1:* Understanding the problem *1.* The complexity of alcoholism *2.* The seven steps to alcoholism *3.* The seven steps to alcoholism, part 2 *4.* Completing the cycle *5.* The family of the alcoholic—hindrance and help *6.* What God says *Part 2:* Ways others can help the alcoholic *7.* Tap the resources of prayer *8.* Present the gospel *9.* Provide fellowship *10.* Rely on God's help *11.* Plan to be long-suffering *12.* Practice firmness *13.* Helping the teenager *14.* Groups that take action (MADD, SMART, SADD) *Part 3:* Five ways the alcoholic can help himself *15.* Transfer your dependency to God *16.* Talk with God daily *17.* Give yourself *18.* Live a step at a time *19.* Keep a personal inventory

Are You Becoming an Alcoholic? Father Frank

Ligouri Publications, 1989, $.75, paper, 24 pp., for counselees

Description This self-examination booklet answers the questions: What is alcoholism? What signs indicate alcoholism? It also explains how Alcoholics Anonymous can help.

Three Compulsions That Defeat Most Men Vincent Gallagher

Bethany House Publishers, 1993, $8.99, paper, 157 pp., for both counselors and counselees

Description A straightforward book for men on overcoming the three most common pitfalls: workaholism, substance abuse, and sexual compulsions.

Author Vincent Gallagher is a Christian counselor with Life Counseling Services, a large Christian counseling center located in suburban Philadelphia. He earned his master's degree in counseling at Denver Conservative Baptist Seminary in Denver, Colo.

Contents *1.* Waiting for the miracle worker *2.* New way of looking at life *3.* Well meaning advice—but wrong *4.* I'm just a hard worker *5.* Sex drive or overdrive *6.* What's so bad about a little drink? *7.* The real need *8.* Looking to God *9.* Looking to self *10.* Looking to others *11.* Growing in spiritual health *12.* Retaking our manhood

Seeing Yourself through God's Eyes June Hunt

Zondervan Publishing House, 1990, $6.99, paper, 96 pp., for counselees

Description A 31-day devotional for recovering addicts to help them see their worth in God's eyes.

Author June Hunt, host of the daily radio broadcast *Hope for the Heart,* is committed to unraveling the difficult "heart" issues of life with biblical hope and practical help.

Understanding Alcoholism *Answers to Questions People Ask,* Carolyn Johnson

Zondervan Publishing House, 1991, $8.99, paper, 208 pp., for both counselors and counselees

Description Written to help people who know and care for someone suffering from alcoholism. Four in ten people are affected by someone's alcoholism. These spouses, children, parents, and friends of problem drinkers ask questions like: "Is alcoholism really a disease?" "How can you tell a heavy drinker from an alcoholic?" and "What should you or shouldn't you do about someone's destructive behavior?" *Understanding Alcoholism* answers these questions and more.

Author Carolyn Johnson is a recovering alcoholic. She is a homemaker and freelance writer. Her articles have appeared in *Home Life, Family Life Today,* and *Virtue.* Her other published works are *How to Blend a Family* and *Forever a Parent.* In eight sections, the author deals with typical questions asked by various segments of people. Highly readable. Chapter summaries are included.

Contents *1.* Is it really a disease?—society asks . . . *2.* Why do you want to die?—psychologists ask . . . *3.* Where did we go wrong?—parents ask . . . *4.* How can you do this to me?—spouses ask . . . *5.* Is Daddy home yet?—children ask . . . *6.* Where do we turn for help?—families ask . . . *7.* How can we help?—the Christian community asks . . . *8.* You have it licked now, don't you?—people keep asking . . .

Understanding Alcoholism *A Starting Point for Families,* Ted Lawson

Ligouri Publications, 1991, $1.95, paper, 64 pp., for counselees

Description This book explains how to recognize alcoholism and addresses special problems faced by spouses and children of alcoholics. Explores several treatment/recovery options. Also available on audio cassette. Call Ligouri for details (800-325-9521).

Contents *1.* The disease *2.* The alcoholic *3.* The spouse *4.* The children *5.* Life-giving options / *Conclusion / Glossary / Appendix 1:* Are you an alcoholic? *Appendix 2:* Are you codependent? *Appendix 3:* Do you need AlaTeen?

Still Married, Still Sober *Hope for Your Alcoholic Marriage,* David MacKenzie and Elsie MacKenzie

InterVarsity Press, 1991, $8.99, paper, 180 pp., for counselees

Description The authors tell how their marriage was almost destroyed by alcoholism and offer hard-won counsel for others who face this problem. They discuss many issues including how to confront the alcoholic, rebuild the damaged marriage, and lessen the pain on the children.

Authors David MacKenzie pastors St. Christopher's Episcopal Church in Portsmouth, Va. He and his wife, Elsie, have counseled dozens of couples trapped in alcoholic marriages. Coauthor Beth Spring is a contributing editor to *Christianity Today.*

Contents *1.* Alcoholic and married *2.* Hurtling toward bottom *3.* What a spouse endures *4.* What the alcoholic endures *5.* Finding help *6.* Rebuilding a marriage relationship *7.* The alcoholic parent *8.* Going the distance / Afterword / Appendix: The myth and the reality

Conquering Chemical Dependency *A Christ-Centered 12-Step Process,* Robert S. McGee

LifeWay, 1992, $9.95, paper, 225 pp., for both counselors and counselees

Description Part of the LifeWay Support Group Ministry commissioned by the Southern Baptist Convention. This title helps individuals understand the painful problem of chemical dependency and learn a 12-step, Christ-centered process to achieve recovery from alcohol and other chemical addictions. Designed for both individual and discovery-group study. The book provides self-paced, interactive study, and resources for the 12 weekly sessions. A leader's guide is also available ($4.95) that provides administrative guidance and suggested activities for the weekly discovery-group sessions.

Author Robert McGee is founder and president of Rapha, a health care organization that provides in-hospital and outpatient care, with a Christ-centered perspective, for adults and adolescents suffering from psychiatric and substance abuse problems.

Contents About the author / *Introduction* / *Unit 1*—Beginning the search *Unit 2*—The performance trap *Unit 3*—Justification *Unit 4*—Approval addict *Unit 5*—Rec-onciliation *Unit 6*—The blame game *Unit 7*—Propitiation *Unit 8*—Shame *Unit 9*—Major obstacles in growth *Unit 10*—Our source of change *Unit 11*—Renewing our minds *Unit 12*—The trip in

Conquering Chemical Dependency—Workbook *First Steps to a Christ-Centered 12 Step Process,* Robert S. McGee

LifeWay, 1993, $9.95, paper, 160 pp., for both counselors and counselees

Description A 64-page workbook to help learners begin to understand about chemical addiction and the 12-step process toward recovery. A companion to the book of the same title.

Author Robert McGee is founder and president of Rapha, a health care organization that provides in-hospital and outpatient care, with a Christ-centered perspective, for adults and adolescents suffering from psychiatric and substance abuse problems.

Overcoming Chemical Dependency *Rapha's Twelve Step Program,* Robert S. McGee and Pat Springle

Rapha Resources, 1991, $12.99, paper, 225 pp., for counselors

Description Comments in a more biblically overt manner on the famous 12 steps conceived by Alcoholics Anonymous. The workbook format applies biblical truth for effective and lasting change.

Authors Robert McGee is founder and president of Rapha, a health care organization that provides in-hospital and outpatient care, with a Christ-centered perspective, for adults and adolescents suffering from psychiatric and substance abuse problems. Pat Springle is currently senior vice president, Church and Family Resources for Rapha, Inc. He served on the staff of Campus Crusade for Christ for 18 years. He is the author of several other recovery-oriented works.

Rapha's 12-Step Program for Overcoming Chemical Dependency Robert S. McGee

Rapha Resources, $9.99, paper, for counselors

Description This clinically tested, biblically based, self-paced program leads the chemically dependent to acknowledge their powerlessness, make sound judgments, understand the part their families may have played, depend upon God to resolve their boundary and responsibility issues, handle guilt, and more.

Author Robert McGee is founder and president of Rapha, a health care organization that provides in-hospital and outpatient care, with a Christ-centered perspective, for adults and adolescents suffering from psychiatric and substance abuse problems.

Taking Control *New Hope for Substance Abusers and Their Families,* Frank B. Minirth, Paul D. Meier, et al.

Baker Book House, 1988, $7.99, paper, 174 pp., for counselees

Description Explains how use becomes abuse, the church can recognize and help addicts, parents can raise children free of substance abuse, and addresses other issues associated with substance abuse.

Authors Psychiatrists Frank Minirth and Paul Meier are senior officers of the Minirth-Meier Clinic in Richardson, Tex., where coauthors Walter Byrd, Don Hawkins, and Sigfried Fink have also served.

Contents *1.* The problem we refuse to face *2.* From use to abuse *3.* Types of drugs *4.* From sin to genes *5.* Putting the parts together *6.* Curing the addict—step-by-step *7.* Curing the whole addict *8.* The Romans road to recovery *9.* Abusers and their families *10.* Abusers and the church *11.* Preventing addiction in the next generation / *Appendix:* Addictive personality disorders

Alcoholism *Coping with Your Family's Problem,* Kathleen Ross

InterVarsity Press, 1993, $.99, paper, 32 pp., for counselees

Description Kathleen Ross discusses the challenges faced by children and others who live with an alcoholic. Offers practical counsel, including "letting go of family secrets," talking about personal and family suffering, and seeking support from others.

Author Kathleen Ross (pseudonym) is a woman living in the Midwest who has experienced the difficulties of growing up with an alcoholic parent.

I Know the World's Worst Secret *A Child's Book about Living with an Alcoholic Parent,* Doris Sandford and Graci Evans

Gold 'n' Honey Books (Questar), 1993, $7.99, cloth, 24 pp., for counselees

Description Part of the Hurts of Childhood series from Gold 'n' Honey. The series was developed for children ages 5–11 who have experienced deep and tragic hurts. The books deal gently and compassionately with children's delicate feelings when they're forced to handle burdens far too big for them to carry.

Counseling for Substance Abuse and Addiction Stephen VanCleave, Walter Byrd, and Kathy Revell

Word Publishing, 1987, $15.99, cloth, 217 pp., for counselors

Description The authors probe social factors which make drugs a popular means of escape. They emphasize the spiritual dynamics and effective methods of therapy. Part of the Resources for Christian Counselors series from Word.

Authors Stephen Van Cleave, M.D., is medical director of a drug treatment program in San Antonio, Tex. Walter Byrd, M.D., is director of the substance abuse program at Garland Memorial Hospital, Garland, Tex. Kathy Revell, R.N., is nursing director of the Garland program.

Contents *1.* Nobody starts out to be an addict *2.* What you don't know could kill you *3.* The equal opportunity destroyer *4.* If drugs are so bad, why do people keep using them? *5.* Helping is not helping *6.* Addiction is a family affair *7.* The road to recovery *8.* Picking up the pieces *9.* What really works in treatment *10.* Working with substance abuse families *11.* Questions and answers about drug abuse / *Appendixes 1.* Glossary of terms *2.* Drugs of abuse: slang terms *3.* Resources *4.* Signs of teenage drug abuse *5.* Michigan alcoholism screening test *6.* Drug abuse screening test *7.* A chart of alcohol addiction and recovery *8.* The progression and recovery of the family in the disease of alcoholism

Drugs or Alcohol *When You Want to Get Back in Control*

Abbey Press, 1993, $.50 each, paper, 8 pp., for counselees

Description Part of the CareNotes for Teens series from Abbey Press. CareNotes are 5 x 7 booklets designed to offer strength and help to (young) people in crisis. Each CareNote gently introduces an issue, then encourages a person to take appropriate steps toward resolution. Over 20 million CareNotes have been sold.

Stepping Stones *A Journal*

CompCare Publishers, 1985, $8.95, cloth, 128 pp., for counselees

Description Each page of this journal has a short inspirational saying, and space to write the day's date and an important stepping stone toward any goal—whether it be sobriety, weight loss, or some other aspect of personal growth. Tastefully designed with an ivory linen cover and gold embossed words. Over 250,000 sold.

Al-Anon/AlaTeen Family Group Headquarters

Al-Anon/AlaTeen Family Group Headquarters. An organization

Description Though not a Christian organization, this group provides information to family and friends of alcoholics and substance abusers. Maintains a national referral service to local support groups for families.

Alcohol and Drug Abuse Hotline

Alcohol and Drug Abuse Hotline. An organization

Description Though not a Christian organization, this hotline provides national help and referral service for alcohol and drug treatment hospitals and individuals.

Alcoholics Anonymous *General Service Office*

Alcoholics Anonymous. An organization

Description Founded in 1935, A.A. is a fellowship whose members share experience, strength, and hope with each other so they can solve their common problem and help others achieve sobriety. Alcoholics Anonymous's sole purpose is to help alcoholics recover through the 12 steps of A.A. Alcoholics Anonymous is not allied with any sect, denomination, political group, organization, or institution. For information call 212-870-3400, or see Alcoholics Anonymous in your local telephone directory. Write Alcoholics Anonymous, Box 459, Grand Central Station, New York, N.Y. 10163.

Alcoholics for Christ

Alcoholics for Christ. An organization

Description An interdenominational, nonprofit Christian fellowship. Provides literature, referral to Christ-centered treatment centers, and limited crisis phone counseling. Assists in the establishment of Christ-centered support groups. Over 100 open group meetings throughout the United States.

Narcotics Anonymous

Narcotics Anonymous, World Service Office. An organization

Description Narcotics Anonymous is a fellowship of men and women who are recovering from the disease of drug addiction. The World Service Office provides literature and information about local chapters.

National Clearinghouse for Alcohol and Drug Information

National Clearinghouse for Alcohol and Drug Information. An organization

Description Though not a Christian organization, this group functions as a clearinghouse for information on alcohol and drug abuse.

National Drug Abuse Information and Referral Line

National Drug Abuse Information and Referral Line. An organization

Description Though not a Christian organization, this information networking service provides free information and referrals to a wide range of treatment centers and options.

Overcomers Outreach

Overcomers Outreach. An organization

Description Christian organization that assists in the establishment of various Christ-centered support groups.

Process Addictions/ Impulse Control Disorders

Sexual Temptation *How Christian Workers Can Win the Battle,* Randy Alcorn

InterVarsity Press, 1989, $2.99, paper, 32 pp., for counselors

Description In a world that makes sex an idol, we are fooling ourselves if we think society's lure will have no effect on us. Randy Alcorn, author of *Christians in the Wake of the Sexual Revolu-*

tion, explains how it is possible with God's help to live sexually pure lives.

Author Randy Alcorn codirects Eternal Perspective ministries. He is a graduate of Multnomah School of the Bible and a college and seminary professor as well as a frequent conference speaker.

When the Stakes Are Too High *A Spouse's Struggle to Live with a Compulsive Gambler,* Loraine Allison

Abbey Press, 1991, $6.95, paper, 92 pp., for counselees

Description Author Loraine Allison details the pain, deceit, humiliation, and insanity of this disease in her deeply personal account of the devastation reeked upon her family and others by compulsive gambling. She offers compulsive gamblers a way to break out of the cycle of addiction through the 12 steps of Gamblers Anonymous and offers codependents hope through Gam-anon.

Author Loraine Allison is the pseudonym of a writer who works in addiction recovery. She writes from her own experience as the wife of a compulsive gambler.

Contents *1.* The story *2.* The family *3.* The disease *4.* The pain *5.* The emotions *6.* The program *7.* The beginning *8.* The healing *9.* The relapse *10.* The message of hope *11.* The children *12.* Our higher power

A Way of Escape Neil T. Anderson and Russell Rummer

Harvest House Publishers, 1994, $9.99, paper, 236 pp., for counselees

Description *The Bondage Breaker* helped believers understand Satan's assault on their hearts and minds. Now *A Way of Escape* equips Christians to fight and win in one of the most sensitive and vulnerable areas: their sexual thoughts and actions. Compassionate, yet committed to the truth, Anderson and coauthor Russell Rummer guide people in practical, biblical steps that lead to breaking the power of sin and experiencing true freedom in Christ.

Authors Neil T. Anderson is the president of Freedom in Christ Ministries. He is a highly sought counselor and conference speaker. Coauthor Russell Rummer is a licensed marriage, family, and child counselor.

Contents *1.* There is a way out *Part 1:* Detours in the darkness *2.* The lure of a sex-crazed world *3.* Pathways

to sexual bondage *4.* The pimp in your mind *5.* The phony and the genuine *6.* The harvest of sinful deeds *7.* The dark dead end of bondage *Part 2:* The way of escape *8.* Beliefs that open prison doors *9.* Behaving must follow believing *10.* Rethink how you think *11.* Recovery in Christ / *Appendixes: A.* Steps to freedom in Christ *B.* Presenting a healthy view of sex and sexuality to your children

Hope and Recovery *A 12 Step Guide for Healing from Compulsive Sexual Behavior,* Anonymous

CompCare Publishers, 1987, $14.95/$9.95 book/workbook, paper, 327 pp., for both counselors and counselees

Description Written by people recovering from this often misunderstood addiction. Features a specialized 12-step outline, anecdotes, and discussion/reflection questions.

Contents *1.* Am I really out of control? *2.* There is help *3.* Accepting the help *4.* Threshold to self-knowledge *5.* From shame to acceptance *6.* Commitment to change *7.* Asking for grace *8.* The end of isolation *9.* Restoring relationships *10.* Maintaining the growth *11.* Spiritual intimacy with God *12.* Giving as its own reward *13.* Abstinence and sobriety *14.* Sponsorship *15.* Slips/relapse *16.* Telling others about our addiction *17.* The slogans *18.* The 12 traditions

What Everyone Needs to Know about Sexual Addiction Anonymous

CompCare Publishers, 1989, $5.95, paper, 45 pp., for both counselors and counselees

Description This book provides you with an introduction to the concepts of sexual addiction and codependency. Included are stories from the authors—addicts and codependents—showing how they came to recognize their powerlessness and how a 12-step program helped them heal and rebuild their lives.

Contents *1.* Sex addiction—what is it? *2.* Codependency to sex addiction: an explanation *3.* A message from the authors

Gentle Eating *Permanent Weight Loss through Gradual Life Changes,* Stephen Arterburn, Vivian Lamphear, and Mary Ehemann

Oliver Nelson (a division of Thomas Nelson), 1994, $17.99, cloth, 256 pp., for counselees

Description A safe, gentle, and effective method of weight loss that begins and ends with gradual life changes. Instead of drastic diet and exercise programs, readers learn to make simple, easy changes that gradually add up to a trimmer figure and a transformed lifestyle.

Authors Stephen Arterburn is the founder of New Life Treatment Centers, Inc., a Christ-centered treatment program for emotional problems and addictive disorders with treatment centers nationwide. Mary Ehemann is vice president of field marketing for the Dr. Fred Gross Christian Therapy Program. Vivian Lamphear, Ph.D., is a clinical psychologist, lecturer, and author in private practice in Los Alamitos, Calif. All three authors have lost excess pounds and have been able to keep them off more than ten years.

Counseling the Sexual Addict *Systems, Strategies, and Skills,* Patrick Carnes

CompCare Publishers, 1993, $60.00, cassette(s), 8 hours, for counselors

Description An in-depth workshop for therapists working with sexual addicts. Systems, strategies, and skills are presented on eight one-hour cassettes. Carnes explains the range of sexually addictive behaviors and tells how to help sex addicts integrate new beliefs. A companion workbook is available from the publisher for $3.95.

Author Patrick J. Carnes, Ph.D., C.A.S., is a nationally known speaker on addiction and recovery as well as the author of four books on recovery. He is the director of new programs for sexual addiction and trauma treatment at Del-Amo Hospital in Torrance, Calif.

Out of the Shadows *Understanding Sexual Addiction,* Patrick Carnes

CompCare Publishers, 1992, $11.95 (also available on cassette), paper, 180 pp., for counselors

Description Over 170,000 copies in print. The premier text in the field of sexual addiction. Counselors, addicts, and codependents will find help and hope in Dr. Carnes's explanation of this problem.

Author Patrick J. Carnes, Ph.D., C.A.S., is a nationally known speaker on addiction and recovery as well as the author of four books on recovery. He is the director of new programs for sexual addiction and trauma treatment at Del-Amo Hospital in Torrance, Calif.

Contents *Introduction*—A moment comes for every addict *1.* The addiction cycle *2.* The levels of addiction *3.* The family and the addict's world *4.* Coaddiction *5.* The

belief system *6.* Twelve steps to recovery *7.* The future is conditional

Can't Buy Me Love *Freedom from Compulsive Spending and Money Obsession,* Sally Coleman and Nancy Hull-Mast

CompCare Publishers, 1993, $12.95, paper, 240 pp., for counselees

Description Dedicated to people who have difficulty managing and worrying about money.

Authors Sally Coleman, M.A., N.C.A.C., is a staff psychotherapist and coordinator of addiction services at the University of Notre Dame Counseling Center. Coauthor Nancy Hull-Mast is a freelance writer with training in addictions and counseling.

Contents *Part 1:* The full closet/garage/refrigerator/house *1.* The plastic placebo *2.* Ginny's story *3.* Compulsive spending survey *4.* Getting to know more about yourself *5.* Phases of compulsive spending *6.* Inventory for spending phases *7.* Poverty addiction *Part 2:* The empty heart *8.* Ginny's story continues *9.* Money issues for relationships *10.* Families and money matters *11.* Grieving: a journey through pain and sorrow *Part 3:* The full heart *12.* Uncovering denial and other smoke screens *13.* Getting help *14.* Creating a recovery journal *15.* Going forward in recovery *16.* The eight freedoms *17.* Money success for children *18.* How to help someone who has a money addiction *19.* Ginny's story: conclusion

A Table before Me *Devotions for Overeaters Who Crave the Power of God,* Pauline Ellis Cramer

Pacific Press, 1992, $7.95, paper, 127 pp., for counselees

Description A book of love and encouragement for those who are overweight as well as for those who are struggling with feelings of low self-esteem. The author focuses on keeping one's life centered upon God as a key to overcoming compulsions. Anecdotal. Compulsive overeaters have been lectured, shamed, rejected, and ignored. What they need is a better self-concept and motivation with support. Written in a conversational style with 300–450 words per devotional. Each devotional has a central theme such as anger, fear, denial, or perfectionism. Each begins with a verse of Scripture followed by a personal experience and ends with a sentence prayer and affirmation.

Three Compulsions That Defeat Most Men Vincent Gallagher

Bethany House Publishers, 1993, $8.99, paper, 157 pp., for both counselors and counselees

Description A straightforward book for men on overcoming the three most common pitfalls: workaholism, substance abuse, and sexual compulsions.

Author Vincent Gallagher is a Christian counselor with Life Counseling Services, a large Christian counseling center located in suburban Philadelphia. He earned his master's degree in counseling at Denver Conservative Baptist Seminary in Denver, Colo.

Contents *1.* Waiting for the miracle worker *2.* New way of looking at life *3.* Well meaning advice—but wrong *4.* I'm just a hard worker *5.* Sex drive or overdrive *6.* What's so bad about a little drink? *7.* The real need *8.* Looking to God *9.* Looking to self *10.* Looking to others *11.* Growing in spiritual health *12.* Retaking our manhood

Silent Hunger *A Biblical Approach to Weight Management and Healing Compulsive Behavior,* Judy Halliday and Arthur Halliday

Fleming H. Revell, 1993, $8.99, paper, for both counselors and counselees

Description A doctor and counselor, leaders of the Thin Within Seminars, teach an effective and distinctively Christian approach to weight management and compulsive disorders.

Losing Your Shirt *Recovery for Compulsive Gamblers and Their Families,* Mary Heineman

CompCare Publishers, 1992, $12.95, paper, 191 pp., for both counselors and counselees

Description Presents a warm, nonthreatening approach to compulsive gambling. Defines the issues, shows how they affect family members, and describes how a 12-step program can end this "quiet disease."

Author Mary Heineman, C.S.W., C.A.C., is a certified New York social worker and a nationally certified compulsive gambling counselor.

Contents *1.* The degeneration of the compulsive gambler's marriage *2.* Dynamics in the compulsive gambler's marriage *3.* Meeting unmet needs, paying the cost: the afflicted *4.* Fighting a losing battle: the affected *5.* Recovery: on the steps *6.* Recovery: beyond the steps

The First Step for People in Relationships with Sex Addicts *A Workbook for Recovery,* Mic Hunter

CompCare Publishers, 1989, $3.95, paper, 123 pp., for counselees

Description This workbook contains 100 open-ended questions designed to guide the client through the vital first step of a 12-step recovery program (admitting a problem exists).

Author Mic Hunter, who has graduate degrees in human development, education, and psychological services, practices in Minneapolis, Minn.

Play Therapy Michael Joseph

Abbey Press, 1992, $3.95, paper, 80 pp., for counselees

Description Presents an eminently practical strategy to reclaim our birthright. Learning to discover the wonder of our inner child is not simply the domain of the rhetoric of recovery, but a response to the ancient wisdom call to "become as a little child." The 35 points contained within this wonderful book are guaranteed to facilitate your response to that call.

The Secret Sin *Healing the Wounds of Sexual Addiction,* Mark Lasser

Zondervan Publishing House, 1992, $8.99, paper, 256 pp., for both counselors and counselees

Description Golden Valley Health Center faculty member Mark Lasser traces the roots of sexual addiction in families and in cultures and details specific means for treatment and recovery.

Author Mark Lasser was trained as a pastor at Princeton Theological Seminary. He received his doctorate from the University of Iowa. He is affiliated with Christian Care Centers in Largo, Fla.

Contents *Part 1:* The secret sin—sexual addiction *1.* Sexual addiction and sin *2.* Building block behaviors of sexual addicts *3.* Types of sexual addiction *4.* Characteristics of sexual addiction *5.* Sexually addicted pastors *Part 2:* Roots of sexual addiction—the secret sin of the family *6.* Unhealthy families *7.* Family abuse *8.* How sex addicts cope with abuse *Part 3:* Healing the wounds of sexual addiction *9.* The twelve steps: a tool for healing *10.* Confronting the sexual addict *11.* Treatment for sexual addiction *12.* Recovery for couples *13.* Recovery for congregations

Love, Infidelity and Sexual Addiction *A Codependent's Perspective,* Christine A. McKenna

Abbey Press, 1992, $6.95, paper, 148 pp., for counselees

Description For persons with partners who are struggling with sexual addiction, this book offers hope and healing by dispelling the denial surrounding this disease. It provides a practical 12-step system of spiritual and emotional self-help. The author's spiritual approach is particularly fresh and inspirational.

Author Christine A. McKenna is the pen name for an established author in the area of addiction recovery with over 20 years' experience as a teacher and counselor.

Contents *1.* Introduction *2.* Sexual addiction *3.* Sexual coaddiction *4.* The shame-based family; the spiritually centered family *5.* Denial *6.* Signs of obsession *7.* Compulsive behavior *8.* Finding help: the solution *9.* A healthy relationship *10.* Forgiveness *11.* The primary relationship

Love Hunger *Recovery from Food Addiction,* Frank B. Minirth, Paul D. Meier, et al.

Janet Thoma (a division of Thomas Nelson), 1990, $17.99, cloth, 352 pp., for counselors

Description The successful ten-stage recovery process used by the Minirth-Meier Clinic. Includes 150 recipes, meal plans, and suggested activities.

Authors Psychiatrists Frank Minirth and Paul Meier are senior officers of the Minirth-Meier Clinic in Richardson, Tex. Dr. Robert Hemfelt is a psychologist who specializes in the treatment of chemical dependencies, codependency, and compulsive disorders. Dr. Sharon Sneed is a registered dietitian and a practicing nutrition consultant.

Contents *Part 1:* Understanding the problem: *1.* When is a binge a binge? *2.* I know I binge—I want to know why *3.* Feeding the hungry heart *4.* Understanding the addiction cycle *Part 2:* Ten pathways to recovery *5.* Path 1: preparing to succeed *6.* Path 2: eating for success *7.* Path 3: saying goodbye *8.* Path 4: grieving out the pain *9.* Path 5: exploring new vistas *10.* Path 6: trusting new directions *11.* Path 7: choosing new guides *12.* Path 8: joining a footpath society *13.* Path 9: maintaining your victory *14.* Path 10: dealing with relapse *Part 3:* Love hunger cookbook *15.* Cooking tips and meal plans *16.* Recipes

The Workaholic and His Family *An Inside Look,* Frank B. Minirth, Paul D. Meier, et al.

Baker Book House, 1981, $6.99, paper, 159 pp., for both counselors and counselees

Description Covering a subject of intense interest, the causes of workaholism are seen to be rooted in guilt. Despite severe consequences for the workaholic and his family, hope lies in God's grace.

Authors Paul D. Meier and Frank Minirth are vice president and president, respectively, of the Minirth-Meier Psychiatric Clinic, Richardson, Tex. Dr. Frank Wichern is director of counseling services and assistant professor of pastoral ministries at Dallas Theological Seminary. Bill Brewer is senior pastor of Richland Bible Fellowship. States Skipper, an ordained minister, is also a counselor in the Minirth-Meier Clinic.

Contents *Part 1:* Symptoms and causes of workaholism *1.* Personal evaluation *2.* An evaluation of the workaholic's family *3.* Portrait of the workaholic *Part 2:* Cures for workaholism *4.* Overcoming workaholism *5.* Tips for the workaholic's wife *6.* Resolving conflicts between the workaholic and his wife *Part 3:* The workaholic's belief system *7.* The guilt trip *8.* Legalism: the road to bondage *9.* Grace: the road to freedom

Slow-Down Therapy Linus Mundy

Abbey Press, 1993, $3.95, paper, 80 pp., for counselees

Description Offers 35 concrete ideas for helping you discover something you already possess—time, enough time. This delightful book will guide you to a more peaceful, relaxed use of time and help you celebrate the priceless prize time gives—the priceless prize called life. Format: a series of about 30 short sayings, proverbs, and admonitions accompanied by whimsical cartoons on every page.

A Woman's Place Is in the Mall *And Other Lies . . . ,* Karen O'Connor

Thomas Nelson Publishers, 1995, $12.99, paper, 240 pp.

Description This book is for women who have trouble with money whether from overspending, compulsive shopping, abusing credit, getting into serious debt, underearning, or finding themselves frequently broke.

16

Author Karen O'Connor is an author and speaker for self-help seminars and women's groups.

Contents *Part 1*—Money madness *1.* Secret shame *2.* How and why women feel crazy about money *Part 2*—Beliefs and behaviors *3.* A woman's place is in the mall: overspenders *4.* Born to shop: shopaholics *5.* Maxed out credit card abusers *6.* A dollar and a dream: compulsive gamblers *7.* The great cover-up: debt enablers *8.* Living on the edge: under-earners *9.* The can't say no: self-debtors *10.* Barefoot and broke: perpetual paupers *Part 3*—Ending the madness *11.* Telling and receiving the truth *12.* It's not about money after all *Part 4*—Discovering joy *13.* Building a support system *14.* Sanity, serenity, solvency: a way of life

Perfect Every Time *When Doing It All Leaves You with Nothing . . . ,* Paula Rinehart

NavPress, 1992, $10.00, paper, 200 pp., for counselees

Description Explores the internal dynamics of the performance cycle. Rinehart shares honestly from her own life and from the lives of other women who try too hard and do too much. With compassion and clarity, she'll help you listen more to the God-given desires within and less to the dictates of our culture, your past, or other people. Ultimately, you'll discover a restored enjoyment of womanhood, giving you the ability to receive from God and others, and to relax in a strength that's not your own.

Author Paula Rinehart is the author of the Starting Strong Bible study series for preteens, and coauthored the award-winning best-seller *Choices: Finding God's Way in Dating, Sex, Singleness, and Marriage.* She lives with her husband and two children in Raleigh, N.C.

Contents *Part 1:* Profiles of women who do too much *1.* A journey I never intended to make: an unnerving invitation to sanity *2.* Standing on our mothers' shoulders—reaching to the stars *3.* The push-ahead woman—when enough is never enough *4.* The indispensable woman: when you give until it hurts *5.* Ecstasy and agony: as the pendulum swings *Part 2:* The emotional roots of doing too much *6.* Mothers and daughters, shared identities, common quests *7.* A nightingale in a gilded cage: the hero and her dilemma *8.* The little girl in the cellar: why we hide *9.* Our greatest need: to discover an unreasonable love *Part 3:* The way change looks and feels *10.* Longings: making those important inner connections *11.* Relationships: enjoying intimate moments *12.* Embracing the journey: cultivating a spirit of adventure

Recovery from Workaholism Dale Ryan and Juanita Ryan

InterVarsity Press, 1992, $4.99, paper, 60 pp., for both counselors and counselees

Description This Bible study is part of a series of 16 volumes on various recovery themes. Each book contains studies on six biblical texts. Leader's notes are provided for group study.

Authors Dale Ryan is the executive director of the Recovery Partnership, the parent organization to the National Association for Christian Recovery. Juanita Ryan is a counselor in private practice in Hacienda Heights, Calif.

False Intimacy *Understanding the Struggle of Sexual Addiction,* Harry W. Schaumburg

NavPress, 1992, $10.00, paper, 205 pp., for counselors

Description False intimacy goes beyond behavioral symptoms and willpower-based solutions to provide biblical guideposts on the journey to restoration. With frank honesty and deep compassion, it offers hope to those whose lives or ministries have been impacted by sexual addiction.

Author Dr. Harry W. Schaumburg is a licensed therapist who has treated sexual addiction and sexual abuse problems for the past 13 years. He received his M.A. from New York University, his M.S. from the University of Wisconsin-Milwaukee, his D.Min. from New York Theological Seminary, and completed postgraduate work at Northwestern University. Currently he works with Christian leaders regarding problems of sexual misconduct and sexual addiction.

Contents *1.* What is sexual addiction? *2.* Sexually addictive behaviors *3.* What causes sexual addiction? *4.* Hope for those who are sexually addicted *5.* Responding to your sexually addicted spouse *6.* Preventing sexual addiction in your children *7.* Sexual addiction in the church *8.* The church as a healing community *9.* Healing for Christian leaders / *Appendix A:* Recommended reading / *Appendix B:* Ministry resources / *Appendix C:* Indicators of sexual abuse

The Food Trap *Breaking Its Hidden Control,* Pamela M. Smith

Creation House, 1990, $7.99, paper, 201 pp., for both counselors and counselees

Description Why do you eat? To escape from a stressful situation? To deal with anger? To ease the pain of loneliness? To reward yourself for a job well done? If so you may be another unsuspecting victim of the food trap. Learn what and when you need to eat in order to break a physical dependency on food. *The Food Trap* will give you the principles and practical helps you need to choose a lifetime of freedom.

Author Pamela M. Smith, R.D., is a nationally known nutritionist and culinary consultant. She is a frequent television guest and also runs a successful private practice.

Contents *Part 1:* Help me! *1.* Out of control *2.* Born to be free *Part 2:* Your body: designed to work for you, not against you *3.* Setting the stage *4.* The right thing at the right time *5.* More of the best, less of the rest *6.* Dents in your armor *7.* Stress: you can cut its cost *8.* Physical change: the challenges *Part 3:* Free at last *9.* Looking back *10.* Walking free *Part 4:* Practical tips for staying on track *11.* The practical side of changing behavior *12.* Eating free / *Appendix:* What about anorexia and bulimia?

The Thorn of Sexual Abuse *The Gripping Story of a Family's Courage and One Man's Struggle,* Beth Sterling

Fleming H. Revell, 1994, $8.99, paper, 178 pp., for counselees

Description Here is the powerful account of one man's bondage to sexual addiction and the courageous family who ministers to him. "Paul's" journey to recovery illustrates that healing both the offender and the victim is possible.

Contents *1.* How can we help? *2.* He hugs me "funny" *3.* Stranger in our midst *4.* A matter of trust *5.* Cheese and nonsense *6.* The friend with many faces *7.* Filthy rags *8.* Tears and forgiveness *9.* Sexual addiction—what is it? *10.* Child molestation *11.* The arraignment *12.* Excuses and symptoms *13.* Diagnosis *14.* Marie's search for herself *15.* The sentencing *16.* Rebuilding a marriage *17.* The treatment *18.* In recovery / *A professional perspective / Sources of help*

Am I Hungry . . . Or Am I Hurting? Carla Wills-Brandon

Recovery Publications, Inc., 1993, $12.95, paper, 256 pp., for both counselors and counselees

Description A popular therapist and recovery author offers a creative 26-week program to heal from food addiction—adapting/using the 12 steps. Includes her own story of recovery from a wide range of addictive eating disorders and helps readers explore their own issues with food, eating, exercise, and body image.

Author Carla Wills-Brandon is a well-known therapist and workshop leader who regularly appears on radio and TV. She is the author of five other recovery titles.

Contents *1.* Food is not the issue *2.* Breaking the myths about eating addictions *3.* Step 1: admitting our powerlessness *4.* Step 2: "came to believe . . ." *5.* Step 3: letting go *6.* Step 4: getting honest *7.* Step 5: letting go of our shame! *8.* Step 6: our defects of character run amok *9.* Step 7: time to move on *10.* Step 8: examining our relationships *11.* Step 9: taking responsibility for our behavior *12.* Step 10: the journey continues *13.* Step 11: time to explore *14.* Step 12: having had a spiritual awakening, where do I go from here?

When Someone You Love Has a Gambling Problem

Abbey Press, $.50 each, paper, 8 pp., for counselees

Description Part of the CareNotes series from Abbey Press. CareNotes are short booklets that help readers identify issues and begin the process of seeking resolution. Anecdotal and uplifting. Beautiful photographs grace the covers. Over 20 million CareNotes have been sold in just over five years. Can be used as an alternative to a greeting card or in conjunction with pastoral care visits.

Codependents of Sex Addicts

Codependents of Sex Addicts. An organization

Description A secular national, nonprofit group that seeks to assist those involved with the sexually addicted. Provides referral networking, group meeting directories, and written resources.

Debtors Anonymous General Service Board

Debtors Anonymous General Service Board. An organization

Description An information clearinghouse for resources on compulsive spending.

Gam-Anon/Gamateen

Gam-Anon/Gamateen. An organization

Description Though not a Christian organization, GA is a support organization that endorses the use of the 12-step model in treating problem gambling. Provides free information, support group starter kits, and referral network for existing support groups.

Gamblers Anonymous

Gamblers Anonymous. An organization

Description Formed for the express purpose of helping the compulsive gambler overcome his or her problem. Though not a Christian organization, utilizes a 12-step model. Provides a wide variety of written materials on the subject. Assists in the establishment of local chapters and provides referrals.

National Council on Compulsive Gambling, Inc., The

National Council on Compulsive Gambling, The. An organization

Description Established in 1972 to address the disease of problem gambling as defined by the American Psychiatric Association. Though not a Christian organization, furnishes information and referrals to local Gamblers Anonymous chapters and private therapists. Cosponsors the *Journal of Gambling Studies.*

National Council on Sexual Addiction

National Council on Sexual Addiction. An organization

Description A private, nonprofit organization dedicated to promoting public understanding, awareness, and recognition of sexual addiction and compulsivities. NCSA is a grassroots effort comprised of service providers, allied health professionals, educators, members of the recovering community, and other concerned citizens. Though not a Christian organization, they provide education, information, and referral services throughout the professional and lay communities.

National Sexual Addiction Hotline

National Sexual Addiction Hotline. An organization

Description Offers free information and referrals for sexual addicts.

Overeaters Anonymous

Overeaters Anonymous, Inc. An organization

Description Though not a Christian organization, this group assists in the establishment of support groups for those with compulsive eating disorders.

Pure Life Ministries

Pure Life Ministries. An organization

Description Provides a variety of materials and support for those involved in sexual addiction and their loved ones. Includes an intensive residency program at the Pure Life Ranch, extension materials, teaching tapes, Pure Life support groups in several cities, and a variety of written

resources. The following are several of the titles from their catalog: 1. *Sexual Idolatry* $8.50 2. *Conformed to His Image* $10.00 3. *The Walk of Repentance* $15.00 4. *Overcoming the Effects of Pornography* $3.00.

Sex Addicts Anonymous

Sex Addicts Anonymous. An organization

Description A fellowship of men and women who share their experience, strength, and hope with each other so they may overcome their sexual addiction and help others recover from sexual addiction or dependency. Also seeks healthy sexuality. Utilizes a 12-step method. Produces a wide variety of materials dealing with sexual addiction and related topics, including *The Plain Brown Wrapper* journal/newsletter. Call for a catalog. Estimated 200 local groups.

Sex and Love Addicts Anonymous

Sex and Love Addicts Anonymous. An organization

Description A fellowship based on a 12-step model that seeks to assist members in overcoming sexual compulsive behaviors. Assists in the establishment of new chapters and of locating existing ones (about 525 local chapters). Produces a variety of resources on sexual addiction. Integration of Christianity varies by locale.

Sexaholics Anonymous

Sexaholics Anonymous. An organization

Description Though not a Christian organization, provides a variety of services to the sexually addicted and those who care for them. Sponsors about 750 local 12-step groups. Information, counseling referrals, and printed resources.

Spender Menders

Spender Menders. An organization

Description Support group that assists those involved in compulsive spending.

Workaholics Anonymous

Workaholics Anonymous. An organization

Description A (secular) fellowship of people who assist in the development of support groups for this problem.

2. Adult Children from Dysfunctional Homes

Making Peace with Your Parents Joan Wester Anderson

Ligouri Publications, 1991, $.75, paper, 24 pp., for counselees

Description When there is continuing friction between parents and grown children, it affects other areas of the grown child's life. Readers will find concrete ways to reach out with faith and love to try to mend the relationship.

Adult Children of Alcoholics *Ministers and Ministries,* Rachel Callahan and Rea McDonnell

Paulist Press, 1990, $9.95, paper, 179 pp., for counselors

Description A comprehensive introduction to ministry to adult children of alcoholics and other adult children of dysfunctional families.

Authors Rachel Callahan (C.S.C.) is a clinical psychologist at the Consultation Center at Adelphi, Md., a center for psychotherapy, pastoral counseling, and spiritual development. Rea McDonnell (S.S.N.D.) is a spiritual director and pastoral counselor, also at the Consultation Center.

Contents *Part 1:* Focusing the issue *1.* Key concepts *Part 2:* The minister *2.* Family awareness *3.* Psychological self-awareness *4.* Spiritual self-awareness *5.* When the minister is an adult child *Part 3:* The ministry—public leadership *6.* Liturgical leadership *7.* Preaching *8.* Teaching *Part 4:* The ministry—helping relationships *9.* Listening *10.* Crisis intervention *11.* Pastoral counseling *12.* Spiritual leadership *13.* Spiritual direction *14.* Other one-on-one service *15.* Prayer *Part 5:* The church as a system *16.* The church: community of believers and codependents *17.* Church organization and addiction *18.* When church leaders care

Never Good Enough *How to Break the Cycle of Codependence & Addiction for the Next Generation,* Carol Cannon

Pacific Press, 1993, $10.95, paper, 256 pp., for counselees

Description Takes a look at the reasons behind addictive and codependent behavior. Experiences are told by the victims of those problems. Understanding that these behaviors can begin during childhood and that they are a no-fault disease, those struggling to win their battles can begin recovery.

Author Carol Cannon is the program director at the Bridge, which provides extended care for dependency disorders, specializing in the treatment of hidden addictions along with chemical dependency.

Contents *Part 1:* The impact of codependence on Christian families *1.* Will the real codependent please stand up? *2.* When "knowing better" isn't enough *3.* Sin, the ultimate addiction *4.* Anesthesia for wounded spirits *5.* Addiction as a no-fault disease *6.* Why conservative Christians are at high risk for addiction *Part 2:* Hidden addictions among Christians *7.* Officially approved addictions *8.* The abandonment of self *9.* Trying too hard to do the right thing *10.* Using religion as a mood modulator *11.* Confessions of a churchaholic *12.* The hurry disease *13.* The making of a martyr *Part 3:* The anatomy of a dysfunctional family *14.* Shattered dreams, wounded hearts, broken toys *15.* Shot down by friendly fire *16.* Robes of righteousness, coats of shame *17.* Who's in control—you or your feelings? *18.* Do Christians have to be boundariless to be selfless? *19.* What we didn't learn in kindergarten *20.* Can the church be a dysfunctional family? *Part 4:* Thrice born: recovery from codependence *21.* Pardon, your symptoms are showing *22.* Sanctified white-knuckling *23.* Healing for adult children of Pharisees and publicans *24.* When the Holy Spirit came to Akron *25.* Rejoicing in the Lord and in recovery

Secrets of Your Family Tree *Healing for Adult Children of Dysfunctional Homes,* Dave Carder, Earl Henslin, Henry Cloud, et al.

Moody Press, 1991, $17.99, cloth, 298 pp., for both counselors and counselees

Description Part of the Healing for the Heart series from Moody Press. Even the best families, including those in the Bible, have elements of dysfunction. This book takes the complex task of correcting and preventing destructive behavior and makes it understandable and reachable for families. Includes appendixes with support groups, recommended books, and other resources.

Authors Dave Carder (M.A., Calvary Bible College; M.A., Wayne State University) serves as assistant pastor for counseling ministries at the First Evangelical Free Church of Fullerton, Calif. With his wife he conducts marriage and family seminars. Earl R. Henslin (Psy.D., Biola University) is a licensed marriage, family, and child psychologist in practice in Fullerton, Calif. Henry Cloud (Ph.D., Rosemead Graduate School of Psychology) is codirector of the Minirth-Meier Clinic West and maintains a private practice in Newport Beach, Calif. John Townsend (Th.M., Dallas Theological Seminary; Ph.D., Rosemead Graduate School of Psychology) maintains a private practice in Newport Beach, Calif. Alice Brawand (M.A., Azuza Pacific University) has served 31 years with Wycliffe Bible Translators, 11 of them in counseling missionaries and pastors from Wycliffe's International headquarters in Dallas, Tex.

Contents *Part 1:* Dysfunctional families in the Bible *1.* David and his family tree *2.* Isaac and his family tree *Part 2:* Contributing factors in family dysfunction *3.* Passing the torch—the multi-generational transition process *4.* Guilt-ridden baggage—the role of religious shame *5.* Helping the helpers—dysfunctional families in "the ministry" *6.* Blest be the tie that binds: local church "family patterns" *Part 3:* Family health: how to do it right when you learned it wrong *7.* Learning to bond *8.* Learning to set boundaries *9.* Learning to achieve adulthood *10.* Learning about goodness/badness *11.* Jesus models healthy relationships *12.* Facing life's "unfair assignments" *13.* How the local church can help / *Appendix A:* Where ACDFs can find help / *Appendix B:* Patterns predicting pastoral infidelity / *Appendix C:* The 12 steps of Alcoholics Anonymous

Boundaries *When to Say Yes; When to Say No to Take Control of Your Life,* Henry Cloud and John Townsend

Zondervan Publishing House, 1992, $17.99, cloth, 256 pp., for counselees

Description This book presents a biblical treatment of boundaries, identifies how boundaries are developed and become injured. Shows Christian misconceptions of the function and purpose of boundaries, targets areas in our lives that have boundary conflicts, and gives a program for developing and maintaining healthy, biblical limits. Also available on audio and video.

Authors Dr. Henry Cloud and Dr. John Townsend are codirectors of the Minirth-Meier Clinic West, a group of treatment centers headquartered in Newport Beach, Calif. They both earned their Ph.D. degrees at Rosemead Graduate School of Psychology.

Contents *Part 1:* What are boundaries? *1.* A day in a boundariless life *2.* What does a boundary look like? *3.* Boundary problems *4.* How boundaries are developed *5.* Ten laws of boundaries *6.* Common boundary myths *Part 2:* Boundary conflicts *7.* Boundaries and your family *8.* Boundaries and your friends *9.* Boundaries and your spouse *10.* Boundaries and your children *11.* Boundaries and your work *12.* Boundaries and your self *13.* Boundaries and your God *Part 3:* Developing healthy boundaries *14.* Resistance to boundaries *15.* How to measure success with boundaries *16.* A day in the life with boundaries

Changes That Heal *How to Understand Your Past to Ensure a Healthier Future,* Henry Cloud

Zondervan Publishing House, 1992, $17.99, cloth, 256 pp., for counselees

Description This book focuses on four developmental tasks that all of us must accomplish to heal our inner pain and enable us to function and grow emotionally and spiritually. These tasks are bonding to others, separating from others, integrating good and bad in our lives, and taking charge of our lives.

Author Dr. Henry Cloud is a clinical psychologist and codirector of the Minirth-Meier Clinic West. He leads seminars and hosts a daily local radio program on issues related to psychological and emotional growth.

Contents Changing in him *Part 1:* Three ingredients of growth *1.* Grace and time *2.* Time *Part 2:* Bonding to others *3.* What is bonding? *4.* When we fail to bond *5.* Learning to bond *Part 3:* Separating from others *6.* What are boundaries? *7.* How we develop our boundaries *8.* Crossing over boundaries *9.* When we fail to develop boundaries *10.* Learning to set boundaries *Part 4:* Sorting out good and bad *11.* What is the problem? *12.* When we fail to accept good and bad *13.* Learning to accept both good and bad *Part 5:* Becoming an adult *14.* What is adulthood? *15.* When we fail to grow up *16.* Learning to become mature adults

Adult Children of Legal or Emotional Divorce *Healing Your Long-Term Hurt,* Jim Conway and Sally Conway

InterVarsity Press, 1990, $10.99, paper, 272 pp., for counselees

Description A book built upon ten years of research carried out by Jim and Sally Conway about adult children whose parents had divorced. The unique focus of the book is that research has shown that emotional divorce (where parents stay together, but there is no love) is as damaging in the life of the child, and ultimately the adult, as the legal divorce. The last half of the book focuses on areas the individual needs to work through in order to resolve the traumas of a dysfunctional home.

Authors Jim Conway holds five degrees in psychology and theology and is the author of many books. His wife, Sally Conway, holds an M.S. in human development. Together they own and operate Mid-Life Dimensions/Christian Living Resources, a nonprofit organization ministering to people at various stages of life through a variety of media formats.

Contents *Part 1:* Facts about adult children from legal or emotional divorce *1.* Who are these adult children from legally or emotionally divorced families? *2.* A growing national awareness *3.* What has the adult child lost? *Part 2:* Major problems for adult children of legal or emotional divorce *4.* Cheated out of life *5.* Damaged self-image and blurred boundaries *6.* Dysfunction breeds dysfunction *7.* Missing normal life development *8.* Distrust and role playing *9.* Unsuccessful marriages and fear of parenting *10.* The outside world *Part 3:* Steps for healing your damaged past *11.* Step one—deciding to be healed *12.* Step two—the spiritual link *13.* Step three—joining a recovery group *14.* Step four—remembering your past *15.* Step five—grieving your losses *16.* Step six—shaking off the victim mentality *17.* Step seven—forgiving the past *18.* Step eight—working on your problems *19.* Step nine—maintaining and enjoying your new life *Part 4:* Helping the helpers *20.* How to help adult children of divorce / *Appendix A:* How to start a support group / *Appendix B:* How to find a support group / *Appendix C:* Suggestions for choosing a counselor / *Appendix D:* Survey for adults whose parents have divorced

Adult Children and the Almighty

Recovering from the Wounds of a Dysfunctional Home, Melinda Fish

Chosen Books, 1991, $8.99, paper, 224 pp., for both counselors and counselees

Description Written from the unique perspective of having pastored a church, 90 percent of whose members are adult children of alcoholics. The book explores how the emotional issues created by the environment of the dysfunctional home inhibit the adult child's spiritual life.

Author Melinda Fish is copastor of Church of the Risen Savior, Trafford, Pa., author of three books, pastor's wife, mother of two children. She holds a B.A. from the University of Texas at Austin and is a frequent speaker at churches, retreats, seminars, and women's groups across the United States and abroad.

Contents *1.* Starving for love *2.* The family curse *3.* What makes a hurting home dysfunctional *4.* The hurting child *5.* Coming out of the womb *6.* Facing the damage *7.* Restoring the wounded soul *8.* Healing the child within *9.* Taking the sting out of shame *10.* Lord help me to trust *11.* Overcoming a timid spirit *12.* How to stop running on empty *13.* Taking the pain out of memories *14.* The giant step of forgiveness *15.* Inheriting the blessing

When Victims Marry *Building a Stronger Marriage by Breaking Destructive Cycles,* Don Frank and Jan Frank

Thomas Nelson Publishers, 1991, $9.99, paper, 208 pp., for counselees

Description Help and hope for couples struggling in their marriages due to victimization in their past. Specific steps to rebuild the marriage foundation and enhance intimacy.

Authors Jan Frank holds a master's degree in marriage, family, and child counseling and is the author of the best-selling *A Door of Hope.* Don Frank, her husband, is a high school teacher and gifted communicator.

Contents *1.a.* Faulty foundations—Jan *1.b.* Faulty foundations—Don *2.* Preparing the soil *3.* Who needs an architect? Or blueprints? *4.* Periodic inspections *5.* Plumbing check *6.* Repairing the foundation *7.* Framing the house *8.* Walls of support/walls of division *9.* Insulation vs. isolation *10.* Is the roof leaking? *11.* Homeowner's insurance *12.* Stumbling blocks to unity *13.* Dwelling in unity

The Twelve Steps—A Spiritual Journey *A Working Guide for ACA and Other Dysfunctional Families,* Friends in Recovery

Recovery Publications, Inc., 1987, $14.95, paper, 248 pp., for both counselors and counselees

Description A dynamic recovery workbook based on Bible truths, 12-step wisdom, self-understanding, and God's sustaining love—200,000 copies sold. Reflections and journal exercises.

Contents The twelve steps and your spiritual pilgrimage / *Introduction* / The twelve steps and related Scriptures / Very important guidelines for the reader / Common behavior characteristics of adult children / Step 1 / Step 2 / Step 3 / Step 4 / Step 5 / Step 6 / Step 7 / Step 8 / Step 9 / Step 10 / Step 11 / Step 12 / *Appendixes* /

Methods of study / Facilitator's guidelines / Meeting announcement / Group study format / Weekly writing exercises / Introduction to family group communication / Ongoing Christian step study / Self-help resources / Suggested reading

The 12 Steps—A Way Out *A Working Guide for ACA's and Other Dysfunctional Families,* Friends in Recovery

Recovery Publications, Inc., 1987, $14.95, paper, 128 pp., for both counselors and counselees

Description The original 12-step workbook for adult children—over 250,000 copies sold. Widely used by individuals and groups, this popular guide provides an effective 28-week program for adult children to confront their painful past, surrender to a higher power, and move toward a life of serenity and fulfillment.

Contents The twelve steps and our journey toward wholeness / *Introduction* / The twelve steps for adult children / Very important guidelines for the reader / Common behavior characteristics of adult children / Step 1 / Step 2 / Step 3 / Step 4 / Step 5 / Step 6 / Step 7 / Step 8 / Step 9 / Step 10 / Step 11 / Step 12 / *Appendixes* / Methods of study / Facilitator's guidelines / Meeting announcement / Group study format / Weekly writing exercises / Introduction to family group communication / Self-help resources / Suggested reading

The 12 Steps for Adult Children *From Addictive and Other Dysfunctional Families,* Friends in Recovery

Recovery Publications, Inc., 1989, $7.95, paper, 128 pp., for both counselors and counselees

Description The first book to focus on the 12 steps as they relate to adult children—more than 275,000 sold.

Contents The twelve steps and our journey toward wholeness / *Introduction* / The twelve steps and related Scriptures / Very important guidelines for the reader / Common behavior characteristics of adult children / Step 1 / Step 2 / Step 3 / Step 4 / Step 5 / Step 6 / Step 7 / Step 8 / Step 9 / Step 10 / Step 11 / Step 12 / *Appendixes* / Self-help resources / Suggested reading / Step study writing workshop

The Twelve Steps for Christians *From Addictive and Other Dysfunctional Families,* Friends in Recovery

Recovery Publications, Inc., 1987, $7.95, paper, 144 pp., for both counselors and counselees

Description A powerful, Scripture-based model for recovery, written especially for adult children—100,000 copies sold.

Contents Important information / The 12 steps and your spiritual pilgrimage / *Introduction* / The 12 steps and related Scripture / Common behavior characteristics of adult children / Step 1/ Step 2/ Step 3/ Step 4/ Step 5/ Step 6/ Step 7/ Step 8/ Step 9/ Step 10/ Step 11/ Step 12

Sometimes It's Hard to Love God *How Your Past Affects Your Relationship with God Now,* Dennis Guernsey

InterVarsity Press, 1989, $8.99, paper, 171 pp., for counselees

Description Designed to help readers overcome the inner barriers of family background, cultural values, and emotional makeup that can keep us from growing closer to God. Based on the Lord's prayer.

Author Dr. Dennis Guernsey is associate dean and director of the Institute for Marriage and Family Ministries at Fuller Theological Seminary in Pasadena, Calif.

Contents *1.* When we feel like spiritual failures *2.* When we're not what we pretend to be *3.* When our understanding of God is still that of a child *4.* When our earthly experiences are too painful *5.* When we have trouble with authority *6.* When our minds are confused *7.* When our lives are directionless *8.* When we don't know how to ask *9.* When we feel lonely *10.* When our world is confusing *11.* When we live with unforgiveness *12.* When we struggle with sin *13.* A closing hymn

Forgiving Your Parents *How Adult Children Can Heal Past Hurts,* Joan Lloyd Guest

InterVarsity Press, 1988, $1.95, paper, 32 pp., for counselees

Description This is a readable and anecdotal approach that looks at the sources of tension that adults have with their parents such as desires for approval, hurtful memories, misinterpretations, control issues, and family crises such as divorce. Offers a rationale for working through resentments with techniques such as detachment, seeking grace, and viewing history from the parents' perspective.

Author Joan Guest (M.A., Northern Illinois University; M.S.W., George Williams College of Social Work, Aurora University) is a licensed social worker and family therapist at a psychiatric

23

hospital. She has experience in both outpatient and inpatient settings and is also the author of *Forgiving Your Parents* and many magazine articles.

I Went to the Animal Fair *A Journey through Madness to Meaning,* Heather Harpham

NavPress/Piñion Press, 1994, $12.00, cloth, 159 pp., for counselees

Description A woman's journal reveals her search for herself, her past, and spiritual truth during her gut-wrenching discovery of an abusive past.

Author Heather Harpham is a speaker, writing instructor, regular magazine contributor, and the author of *Daddy, Where Were You?*

Contents *Part 1:* Hunting the ordinary animal *Part 2:* Tracking the suspects *Part 3:* Watching out for God

Strongest in the Broken Places *A Story of Spiritual Recovery,* Dan Harrison

InterVarsity Press, 1990, $7.99, paper, 144 pp., for counselees

Description Telling his own story of recovery from a dysfunctional childhood, Dan Harrison shows how God can bring us from anger to forgiveness, insecurity to affirmation, compulsiveness to balance.

Author Dan Harrison is director of missions for InterVarsity Christian Fellowship. Previously he served with Wycliffe Bible Translators.

Contents *Introduction:* A story of hope and healing *1.* How can God use me? *2.* Crippled children *3.* Second chances *4.* From criticism to affirmation *5.* From anger to forgiveness *6.* From workaholism to balance *7.* From guilt to acceptance *8.* Honor your father and mother *9.* Healing through marriage *10.* Breaking the cycle *11.* In weakness made strong *12.* The history of God's faithfulness

Growing Up Divorced *For Adults Who Once Suffered the Trauma of Parents' Divorce,* Archibald D. Hart

Servant Publications/Vine Books, 1994, $9.99, paper, 312 pp., for counselees

Description Hart examines the long-term effects of divorce, the damaging consequences that follow children of divorce, and ways to resolve past hurts that have shaped their lives.

Author Dr. Archibald D. Hart is dean of the Graduate School of Psychology and professor of psy-

chology at Fuller Theological Seminary in Pasadena, Calif.

Contents *Introduction*—The ACOD syndrome *Part 1:* Understanding your need for recovery *1.* Growing up in a divorced family *2.* Assessing the divorce damage in your life *3.* The "blended family" blues *Part 2:* Beginning your recovery *4.* Facing your unfinished business *5.* Resolving your hurt, anger, guilt, and shame *6.* Taking care of your ACOD self *7.* Rewriting your life script *Part 3:* Continuing your recovery *8.* Getting on with your life *9.* Building your own happy family *10.* Breaking the divorce cycle *11.* Success strategies for a life of recovery

Healing Adult Children of Divorce *Taking Care of Unfinished Business So You Can Be Whole Again,* Archibald D. Hart

Servant Publications/Vine Books, 1991, $16.99, cloth, 300 pp., for counselees

Description Dr. Hart knows from personal and professional experience what it means to be an adult child of divorce. In this book he offers not only psychological insight, but spiritual wisdom essential to meaningful growth, recovery, and true healing.

Author Dr. Archibald D. Hart is dean of the Graduate School of Psychology at Fuller Theological Seminary. He has written numerous books on psychology and recovery.

Contents *Introduction:* The ACOD syndrome *Part 1:* Understanding your need for recovery *1.* Growing up in a divorced family *2.* Assessing the divorce damage in your life *3.* The "blended family" blues *Part 2:* Beginning your recovery *4.* Facing your unfinished business *5.* Resolving your hurt, anger, guilt, and shame *6.* Taking care of your ACOD self *7.* Rewriting your life script *Part 3:* Continuing your recovery *8.* Getting on with your life *9.* Building your own happy family *10.* Breaking the divorce cycle *11.* Success strategies for a life of recovery

Healing the Scars of Emotional Abuse Gregory L. Jantz

Revell, 1995, $8.99, paper, 174 pp.

Description Examines the pervasive yet overlooked problem of emotional abuse—and why it is so common and damaging. This book will help you understand the effects of the abuse, give you insight into the problems of the abuser, and show you how to overcome the past.

Author Gregory Jantz, Ph.D., is executive director of THE CENTER for Counseling and Health Resources, Inc., with locations in Seattle and the Puget Sound region.

Contents *Part 1:* Understanding emotional abuse *1.* What is emotional abuse? *2.* Why is emotional abuse so common? *3.* Why is emotional abuse so damaging? *Part 2:* Types of emotional abuse *4.* Emotional abuse through words *5.* Emotional abuse through actions *6.* Emotional abuse through indifference *Part 3:* The effects of emotional abuse *7.* The effects on sense of self *8.* The physical effects *9.* The effects on relationships *Part 4:* Overcoming emotional abuse *10.* Recognizing your abuse and its effects *11.* Getting over the past and living for the future

Verbal Abuse *Healing the Hidden Wound,* Grace H. Ketterman

Servant Publications/Vine Books, 1993, $8.99, paper, 238 pp., for both counselors and counselees

Description Explores the kinds of family systems that perpetrate abuse. Ketterman explains what verbal abuse sounds like, and the kind of people most likely to be abused and become abusers. She helps readers determine if they are suffering from abuse and how to start on the road to recovery.

Author Grace H. Ketterman, M.D., is the medical director of the Crittenton Center in Kansas City, Mo., and author of several books.

Contents *1.* What is verbal abuse? *I.* Verbal abuse in the family *2.* Behind closed doors *3.* Young and impressionable *4.* Sibling rivalry gone awry *5.* The transgenerational triangle *II.* Verbal abuse outside the family *6.* Academic stress *7.* Profanity in the pews *8.* In the marketplace *9.* Living in an irate world *III.* Forms and effects of verbal abuse *10.* Guises and disguises *11.* The name game *12.* Permanent scars *13.* The making of an abuser *14.* Are you an abuser? *IV.* Combating verbal abuse *15.* Coping with the pain *16.* Abuse and addiction *17.* Doing something about it

Healing for Adult Children of Alcoholics Sara Hines Martin

Broadman, 1994, $11.95, cloth, 187 pp.

Description Assists both therapists and those they counsel with the difficult issues associated with ACOAs.

Author Sara Hines Martin (M.A., Georgia State University) is a counselor in private practice in Marietta and Acworth, Ga. She specializes in working with adult children of alcoholics. She teaches seminars internationally on ACOA topics.

Contents *1.* The way they are *2.* The way we are *3.* The root of the matter *4.* Codependency and the dysfunctional family *5.* Marital styles of adult children of alcoholics (ACAs) *6.* Parenting styles of ACAs *7.* Work styles of ACAs *8.* Physical and emotional health problems of ACAs *9.* The spiritual life of ACAs. *10.* Forgiving the alcoholic parent (and the sober one) *11.* Dealing with a drinking parent (and the sober one) *12.* To joy!

Breaking the Cycle of Hurtful Family Experiences Robert S. McGee, Pat Springle, and Jim Craddock

LifeWay, 1994, $9.95, paper, for both counselors and counselees

Description Part of the LifeWay Support Group Ministry commissioned by the Southern Baptist Convention. This title helps individuals understand how our parents, as primary role models, shape our view of God, our self-concept, and our relationships with other people. Designed for both individual and discovery-group study. The book provides self-paced, interactive study and resources for the 12 weekly sessions. A leader's guide is also available ($4.95) that provides administrative guidance and suggested activities for the weekly discovery-group sessions.

Authors Robert McGee is founder and president of Rapha, a health care organization that provides in-hospital and outpatient care, with a Christ-centered perspective, for adults and adolescents suffering from psychiatric and substance abuse problems. Pat Springle is currently senior vice president, Church and Family Resources for Rapha, Inc. He served on the staff of Campus Crusade for Christ for 18 years. He is the author of several other recovery-oriented works.

Contents About the author / Covenant / *Introduction* / Qualifications for leadership / Steps for starting a group / How to succeed as a leader / Get to know your group / Optional first group session: Getting started *Group Session 1:* The cycle begins *Group Session 2:* Substitutes for relationships *Group Session 3:* Stages of development *Group Session 4:* Emotional healing *Group Session 5:* Analyzing your family *Group Session 6:* Bonding with God *Group Session 7:* Getting to know God *Group Session 8:* Metamorphosis *Group Session 9:* Grieving and healing *Group Session 10:* Modeling God's character *Group Session 11:* Responding to your parents *Group Session 12:* Toward the future / Handout masters / Scripture memory verses / Church study course

Father Hunger Robert S. McGee

Servant Publications/Vine Books, 1993, $12.99, paper, 280 pp., for both counselors and counselees

Description *Father Hunger* describes the emptiness that so many people experience because they crave a father's love. McGee offers insight into the types of fathers we have and our responses to them, for better or worse. He understands what happens when our trust is violated and we try various methods to escape the pain.

Author Robert McGee is founder and president of Rapha, a health care organization that provides in-hospital and outpatient care, with a Christ-centered perspective, for adults and adolescents suffering from psychiatric and substance abuse problems.

Contents *I.* What is father hunger? *1.* Father hunger affects us all *2.* The powerful influence of a father *3.* Our longing for security and comfort *4.* A broader famine in our society *II.* What father hunger goes unfulfilled *5.* No father is perfect *6.* What we learn by watching our parents *7.* How trust in a father can be lost *8.* The child as victim *9.* Growing up with daddy *10.* What roles are children forced to play? *11.* Wrong ways to cope *12.* When women marry their fathers *13.* Hidden problems *III.* Relieving the hunger *14.* Mental snapshots of the past *15.* What do you expect from a father? *16.* New perceptions, new definitions *17.* Fathers and sons, fathers and daughters *18.* Getting on with your life *19.* Feelings about God the Father *20.* Facts about God the Father *21.* Change begins with you *22.* Starting over with your father *23.* New ways of relating to other family members *24.* Avoiding the father hunger in your kids *25.* God the Father wants to satisfy your hunger

Getting Unstuck *Help for People Bogged Down in Recovery,* Robert S. McGee and Pat Springle

Rapha Resources, 1992, $9.99, paper, 165 pp., for both counselors and counselees

Description Although recovery is now a well sought after process, many people feel stuck between hurt and healing. The authors offer hope for those who feel trapped in their recovery process. Usually what is hindering complete recovery is their long-buried emotional wounds— wounds they do not even know exist. Uncovering this unfinished business from the past and seeing how it affects the present can bring the sufferer out of the mud and onto the dry ground of wholesome recovery. Includes a small group leader's guide.

Authors Robert McGee is founder and president of Rapha, a health care organization that provides in-hospital and outpatient care, with a Christ-centered perspective, for adults and adolescents suffering from psychiatric and substance abuse problems.

Free to Forgive *Daily Devotions for Adult Children of Abuse,* Paul D. Meier and Frank B. Minirth

Janet Thoma (a division of Thomas Nelson), 1991, $7.99, paper, 372 pp., for counselees

Description Part of the Serenity Meditation series. Three hundred sixty-five inspirational messages written specifically for adult children of abuse. Brings the healing truths of Scripture into the recovery process.

Authors Psychiatrists Frank Minirth and Paul Meier are senior officers of the Minirth-Meier Clinic in Richardson, Tex.

Contents Dozens of short daily readings.

The Healing Journey for Adult Children of Alcoholics Daryl E. Quick

InterVarsity Press, 1990, $9.99, paper, 216 pp., for counselees

Description Uses a step-by-step approach (enhanced by inspiring stories and practical exercises) to help readers learn new ways of thinking, feeling, and acting that will replace destructive patterns learned in childhood.

Author Daryl E. Quick is a clinical psychologist at the Clackamas Family Counseling Service in Clackamas, Oreg. He earned the Ph.D. from Western Conservative Baptist Seminary.

Contents The journey begins *1.* Surviving the trauma *2.* Roadblocks on the healing journey *3.* The AAA recovery format *4.* Discovering our emotions *5.* The variety of feelings *6.* Healing emotions: the need for a comforter *7.* Healing emotions: grief *8.* Building awareness of our thoughts *9.* Renewing our minds: challenging our self talk *10.* Renewing our minds: more strategies *11.* Building awareness of our behavior *12.* Changing our behavior *13.* Recovering relationships *14.* The journey continues

Family Pain Randy Reynolds and David Lynn

Zondervan Publishing House, 1992, $4.99, paper, 96 pp., for counselees

Description Part of the Recovery Discovery series of workbooks. This title helps the many hurting people who want to experience God's grace and deliverance from the pain of growing up in a dysfunctional family.

Authors Randy Reynolds is director of Renewal Counseling in Tuscon, Ariz., and served as a pastor for more than 15 years. David Lynn is a pastoral counselor and author.

When I Grow Up . . . I Want to Be an Adult *Christ-Centered Recovery Workbook for Adult Children,* Ron Ross

Recovery Publications, Inc., 1991, $12.95, paper, 220 pp., for counselees

Description This empowering workbook introduces the value of the 12-step recovery process to Christians raised in dysfunctional families. Using Scripture and practical exercises for hurting individuals and groups, Rev. Ross encourages hurting Christians to draw upon the healing power of Christ.

Author Ron Ross is the director of the Florida Net Institute, a networking group; and he copastors Central Church in Titusville, Fla. He is active in support group ministry.

Contents How to benefit from this book / Invitation to Christ-centered recovery *1.* Who am I? *2.* Pain insulators *3.* Stunted growth *4.* Trusting our senses *5.* The healing touch *6.* Becoming childlike *7.* Becoming Christ-centered *8.* Becoming an adult *9.* Bringing our healing home *10.* Twelve step recovery / *Appendixes*

Recovery from Family Dysfunctions Dale Ryan and Juanita Ryan

InterVarsity Press, 1992, $4.99, paper, 60 pp., for both counselors and counselees

Description This Bible study is part of a series of 16 volumes on various recovery themes. Each book contains studies on six biblical texts. Leader's notes are provided for group study.

Authors Dale Ryan is the executive director of the Recovery Partnership, the parent organization to the National Association for Christian Recovery. Juanita Ryan is a counselor in private practice in Hacienda Heights, Calif.

Contents *1.* Learning to talk to others *2.* Learning to talk to God *3.* Learning to express feelings to others *4.* Learning to express feelings to God *5.* Learning to trust others *6.* Learning to trust God

Adult Children of Divorce *Haunting Problems and Healthy Solutions,* Karen J. Sandvig

Word Publishing, 1990, $10.99, paper, 215 pp., for both counselors and counselees

Description Traumatized in a variety of ways when their parents divorced, grown children have crossed into adulthood carrying unresolved shame, grief, anger, and judgmental attitudes. In a carefully researched book, the author provides practical advice that can help resolve persisting problems such as establishing emotional and relational boundaries, experiencing true intimacy, and developing a healthy trust in others. Sandvig provides help, hope, and wholeness for the adult child of divorce.

Author Karen J. Sandvig is a licensed, certified chemical dependency counselor and a frequent speaker and consultant on issues relating to dysfunctional families and codependency.

Contents *1.* Dealing with dysfunctional relationships *2.* Keeping up the pace *3.* The tendency of extremes *4.* Insecurity *5.* The great need for consistency *6.* The fear of abandonment *7.* Looking at lower self-esteem *8.* Loneliness is not just being alone *9.* Physical ailments and emotional drain *10.* The quest for control

Unfinished Business *Helping Adult Children Resolve Their Past,* Charles M. Sell

Multnomah Books (Questar), 1989, $9.99, paper, 200 pp., for counselors

Description Charles Sell combines personal experience with extensive research, detailing the traits common to adult children. Without accusing or attacking, he reveals the impact of our childhood families and provides a biblically-based resolution to inner conflict.

Author Charles Sell, Th.D., is professor of Christian education at Trinity Evangelical Divinity School.

Contents *Part 1:* Recovering the past *1.* Living now in the past *2.* Going back to the present *Part 2:* Resolving the past *3.* Checking behavioral reactions *4.* Appraising emotional harm *5.* Practicing dynamics of recovery *6.* Considering forgiveness *7.* Dealing with parents *8.* Coping with emotional problems *9.* Forming a better self-image *10.* Building intimacy skills *11.* Finished business?

Making Peace with Your Past *Help for Adult Children of Dysfunctional Homes,* Tim Sledge

LifeWay, 1992, $9.95, paper, 221 pp., for both counselors and counselees

Description Part of the LifeWay Support Group Ministry commissioned by the Southern Baptist Convention. This title leads adults to uncover and understand how their past affects their lives today. This 12-week course combines individual study with small group activities. Designed for both individual and discovery-group study. The book provides self-paced, interactive study and resources for the 12 weekly sessions. A leader's guide is also available ($4.95) that provides administrative guidance and suggested activities for the weekly discovery-group sessions.

Author Tim Sledge is a pastor who grew up with an alcoholic parent. From his experience of moving beyond his painful past, he developed a recovery ministry in his church.

Contents About the author / *Introduction* / Face-to-face support group covenant *Unit 1*—Discovering self-esteem *Unit 2*—Recognizing compulsive behavior *Unit 3*—Release from shame *Unit 4*—Overcoming the fear of joy *Unit 5*—Help for people who grew up too soon *Unit 6*—Perfectionism and procrastination *Unit 7*—Healing painful memories *Unit 8*—The advantages of a turbulent past *Unit 9*—It's OK to be yourself *Unit 10*—Forgiving the people who have hurt you *Unit 11*—Coming to terms with blessing *Unit 12*—Reflection and direction

Adult Children of Alcoholics *Help, Hope and Healing,* Fran Stein

Ligouri Publications, 1989, $.75, paper, 24 pp., for counselees

Description Helps adult children heal the heartache of growing up in an alcoholic home. Explains how and why it is important to acknowledge alcoholism's impact on their lives and offers hope and help.

Forgiving Our Parents, Forgiving Ourselves *Healing Adult Children of Dysfunctional Families,* David Stoop and James Masteller

Servant Publications/Vine Books, 1991, $12.99, paper, 336 pp., for counselees

Description Begins by exploring the family patterns that perpetuate dysfunction. Step-by-step you will begin to learn to construct a psychological family tree that will help you uncover family secrets and family habits that have profoundly shaped your adult identity. As you develop greater understanding of your family of origin, you will be able to take the essential step of forgiveness. When this happens, you will find yourself moving into a place of profound spiritual healing which will change your life forever.

Authors David Stoop, Ph.D., is the clinical director of the Minirth-Meier-Stoop Clinics in southern Calif. James Masteller, D.Min., is a marriage and family therapist with the Minirth-Meier Clinic in southern Calif.

Contents *Part 1:* Unpacking family baggage *1.* Family: who needs it? *2.* The family system *3.* My family and me *4.* The sins of the fathers *5.* Three-way relationships *Part 2:* The freedom of forgiveness *6.* Releasing others, releasing ourselves *7.* Forgiving, forgetting, denying, accepting *8.* Superficial forgiveness *9.* What's anger got to do with it? *10.* The blame game *11.* Confrontation, retaliation, reconciliation *12.* Forgiving my parents, forgiving myself

Making Peace with Your Father David Stoop

Tyndale House Publishers, 1993, $9.99, paper, 319 pp., for both counselors and counselees

Description Beginning with the significance of the father's role, Dr. Stoop explores how fathers influence their children's development. For adults who need to heal childhood hurts, he provides guidance for making peace with their fathers and learning to live productively. Ultimately, he points to the only truly good Father—God himself.

Author David Stoop, Ph.D., is a clinical psychologist and partner in the Minirth-Meier-Stoop Clinics.

God, I'm Still Hurting *Break Free from the Legacy of Family Dysfunction,* Claire W.

Zondervan Publishing House, 1993, $8.99, paper, 128 pp., for counselees

Description Times and places may change, but the painful experiences and feelings of childhood may be endlessly recreated in adulthood. This is a book for those who want to be free of the effects of growing up in a dysfunctional family. Part of the God, Help Me series from Zondervan. These self-help books are designed, not only to explain the recovery process, but to guide and support the reader throughout that process. Emotional and spiritual healing are promoted through Bible verses, questions for reflection, writing assignments, and the personal examples of the author and other people who have experienced recovery.

Author Claire W. draws on her Ph.D. training in clinical psychology and her work as a counselor as she writes for Christians in recovery.

Contents *Part 1:* Asking questions *1.* Do I have to keep hurting? *2.* What do I need to do? *3.* How do I get started? *4.* Can I do this on my own? *Part 2:* Looking at problems *5.* Hurting for love *6.* Hurting for approval *7.* Hurting for security *8.* Hurting for understanding *9.* Hurting for forgiveness *Part 3:* Finding solutions *10.* Growing free *11.* Living well *12.* Feeling good

Counseling Adult Children of Alcoholics
Sandra D. Wilson

Word Publishing, 1989, $15.99, cloth, 312 pp., for counselors

Description Dr. Wilson speaks of the special issues confronting Christians raised in alcoholic families, creating a context for change and facilitating the recovery process.

Author Sandra D. Wilson is counseling coordinator for Faith Evangelical Free Church in Milford, Ohio, and visiting professor at Trinity Theological Divinity School.

Contents *Part 1:* Understanding the alcoholic family *1.* Understanding alcoholism *2.* The alcoholic family system *3.* Children in the alcoholic family *Part 2:* Understanding adult children of alcoholics *4.* Characteristics of adult children of alcoholics *5.* Adult children and the alcoholic family *6.* Adult children and their concepts of God *Part 3:* Counseling adult children of alcoholics for recovery *7.* Revealing the secret: learning to share *8.* Renewing the mind: learning the truth *9.* Reclaiming the emotions: learning to feel *Part 4:* Counseling relational problems *10.* Counseling for an accurate identity *11.* Counseling for respectful relationships *12.* Counseling for healthy marital and parenting relationships *13.* Counseling for new family roles *Part 5:* Counseling spiritual problems *14.* Counseling biblical God-concepts *15.* Counseling for forgiveness *Part 6:* Final thoughts *16.* Problems, promise, privilege

Released from Shame *Recovery for Adult Children of Dysfunctional Homes,* Sandra D. Wilson

InterVarsity Press, 1990, $8.99, paper, 175 pp., for both counselors and counselees

Description Explains the patterns of thinking and feeling common to adult children of dysfunctional homes and helps readers start on their own journey toward recovery.

Author Dr. Sandra D. Wilson is counseling coordinator for Faith Evangelical Free Church in Milford, Ohio, and visiting professor at Trinity Evangelical Divinity School.

Contents *1.* My story—"half a loaf" *2.* Understanding shame and stumbling *3.* Shame in dysfunctional families *4.* Rules in dysfunctional families *5.* Abuse and shaming in dysfunctional families *6.* Abuse and shaming in Christian families *7.* Understanding consequences and change *8.* Released from shaming our flaws *9.* Released from shaming our feelings *10.* Released from shame-based dependency *11.* Released from shame-bound concepts of God and religion *12.* Released to forgive the shamers *13.* Released for potential and purpose

Breaking Free As an Adult Child of an Alcoholic

Abbey Press, $.50 each, paper, 8 pp., for counselees

Description Part of the CareNotes series from Abbey Press. CareNotes are short booklets that help readers identify issues and begin the process of seeking resolution. Anecdotal and uplifting. Beautiful photographs grace the covers. Over 20 million CareNotes have been sold in just over five years. Can be used as an alternative to a greeting card or in conjunction with pastoral care visits.

Adult Children of Alcoholics (ACOA)

Adult Children of Alcoholics (ACOA). An organization

Description An information clearinghouse.

National Association for Children of Alcoholics

National Association for Children of Alcoholics. An organization

Description An information clearinghouse.

National Association of Adult Children of Dysfunctional Homes

National Association of Adult Children of Dysfunctional Homes. An organization

Description A national information clearinghouse.

3. Aging

Alzheimer's Disease *A Call to Courage for Caregivers,* Martha O. Adams

Abbey Press, 1987, $5.95, paper, 152 pp., for counselees

Description This book is a timely resource for the millions of Americans suffering from Alzheimer's disease and those who care for them. It addresses worrisome questions from home care to the quagmire of legal concerns. Offering the honest narrative of her own mother's illness, the author gives light, love, and strength as she honestly explores our very human reactions to the tragedy and tension of living all the way through an Alzheimer's epic.

Author Martha O. Adams has worked as a public schoolteacher and religious educator for churches of many denominations. As the daughter of an AD-afflicted mother, she speaks and writes as an advocate for caregivers. She has published articles and poems in various magazines and journals and has authored two Abbey Press CareNotes.

Contents *Part 1:* The challenge *1.* Beginnings *2.* Progressive stages *3.* Maintaining communication *4.* Later stages *5.* Sexual and emotional needs *6.* Advanced stages *7.* Legal issues *8.* Support services *9.* Choosing a nursing home *Part 2:* The human response *10.* A growing serenity *11.* Relief through humor *12.* A call to sainthood *13.* Adaptation, detachment, and solitude *14.* Reaching out of solitude */ Poems / Helpful program resources / Helpful printed resources*

When Someone You Love Needs Nursing Home Care Martha O. Adams

Abbey Press, 1990, $.50 each, paper, 8 pp., for counselees

Description Part of the CareNotes series from Abbey Press. CareNotes are short booklets that help readers identify issues and begin the process of seeking resolution. Anecdotal and uplifting. Beautiful photographs grace the covers. Over 20 million CareNotes have been sold in just over five years. Can be used as an alternative to a greeting card or in conjunction with pastoral care visits.

Author Martha O. Adams has worked as a public schoolteacher and religious educator for churches of many denominations. As the daughter of an AD-afflicted mother, she speaks and writes as an advocate for caregivers. She has published articles and poems in various magazines and journals and has authored two Abbey Press CareNotes.

Caregiving for Your Loved Ones Mary Vaughn Armstrong

Chariot Family Publishing, 1992, $14.99, cloth, 240 pp., for counselees

Description This helpful book contains hope and encouragement for people who give continual care to an aging person and a comprehensive list of resources and organizations for the caregivers' consideration.

Preparing for Retirement *Financial Security in Uncertain Times,* Larry Burkett

Moody Press, 1992, $13.00, cloth, 280 pp., for counselees

Description A comprehensive handbook for retirees, present and future. Larry Burkett gives sound advice on the many financial aspects of retirement to help you make the best decisions as you approach retirement age.

Author Since 1976, Larry Burkett has directed Christian Financial Concepts, a nationwide, nonprofit organization dedicated to teaching biblical principles of handling money. He has published over 20 books on finances with a total distribution of over two million. He is heard daily on two radio broadcasts carried by over 1,000 outlets worldwide. Christian Financial Concepts also publishes a free newsletter that focuses on current economic issues.

Contents *1.* The facts about retirement *2.* Retirement realities *3.* Future problems *4.* When to start a retirement plan *5.* Who should retire? *6.* Retirement options *7.* Insurance decisions *8.* Reducing overhead in retirement *9.* Where to retire *10.* Investment ideas for retirees *11.* Where to invest *12.* Untapped income sources *13.* Social security benefits *14.* Military, ministers, and missionaries *15.* A retiree's budget *16.* Estate planning for retirees

Ministry with the Aging *Designs, Challenges, Foundations,* William M. Clements

The Haworth Pastoral Press, 1989, $14.95, paper, 275 pp., for counselors

Description A past runner-up for the Book of the Year Award by the Academy of Parish Clergy, *Ministry with the Aging* is a landmark volume that offers a unique and insightful look at meeting the needs of the elderly in our society. Each chapter is written by an eminent scholar.

Author William M. Clements, Ph.D., is director of Behavioral Science, Family Practice Residency Program at the Medical Center in Columbus, Ga. He is also associate professor and pastoral counselor at Emory University School of Medicine, Atlanta, Ga.

Contents *1.* The new context for ministry with the aging *2.* Age and aging in the Old Testament *3.* The elderly in the life and thought of the early church *4.* Cultural antecedents to contemporary American attitudes toward aging *5.* Christian theology and aging: basic affirmations *6.* Worship and aging: memory and repentance *7.* Aging: on the way to one's end *8.* Retirement *9.* Ethical aspects to aging in America *10.* Religion and the elderly in today's world *11.* The family relations of older persons *12.* Adults with parents in crisis: a personal account *13.* Education for ministry with the aging *14.* Death, dying, and the elderly *15.* Adult religious education and the aging *16.* Lay ministries with older adults

Alzheimer's *Another Opportunity to Love,* Grayce Bonham Confer

Beacon Hill Press of Kansas City, 1992, $3.95, paper, 64 pp., for counselees

Description Only from the heart of personal experience could anything be written that would inspire, encourage, and challenge families and friends of Alzheimer's victims. From her personal journal, Confer tells the story of her life with her husband, afflicted with this mysterious disease, offering words of wisdom and hope.

Author Grayce Bonham Confer is a graduate of the University of Illinois and a former schoolteacher. She is active with an Alzheimer's helpline in Calif.

The Golden Years *Riding the Crest,* William Cutler

Serendipity, 1990, $6.95, paper, 126 pp., for counselees

Description This is a 7- or 14-week course designed for forming a support group while discussing issues related to aging. This course is designed for anyone who is retired, or about to retire, over 65 years old, or who would like to be part of a support group with others dealing with common issues of aging. Intelligent use of Scripture, dialogue, and discussion throughout.

Contents *1.* Images of aging *2.* Retirement *3.* Problems of aging *4.* Personal health *5.* Friendship *6.* God in our lives *7.* The life to come

My Journey into Alzheimer's Disease *Helpful Insights for Family and Friends,* Robert Davis

Tyndale House Publishers, 1989, $7.99, paper, 140 pp., for counselees

Description A book of encouragement, of how one man of faith faced the oncoming darkness of Alzheimer's disease. This book is unique in that Dr. Davis wrote it immediately following the diagnosis of "Probable Alzheimer's." He speaks of the changes and losses he is experiencing early in the disease in 1987. His wife, Betty, then describes from her research the changes which they must anticipate. He speaks of the spiritual changes taking place as his brain has difficulty processing new material and making old connections. He tells caregivers to listen to the patient and to meet the patient's perceived needs. Robert Davis died March 8, 1993. He lost the ability to swallow but still knew his family and maintained a vital prayer life.

Author Robert R. Davis was pastor of the Old Cutler Presbyterian Church of Miami, Fla., prior to his diagnosis at the age of 53. In the 15 years of ministry there, the church grew from a mission church of about 150 to over 2400. Davis and his wife, Betty, are graduates of Taylor University in Upland, Ind. Robert also attended Toccoa Falls College and holds the B.A. and M.Div. degrees from United Theological Seminary.

Contents *1.* From sunlight to moonlight *2.* Called into sunshine and servanthood *3.* Though the darkness hide me *4.* The reaching power of Christ *5.* The joy of the unhooked yoke *6.* Alzheimer's: disease of the decade *7.* The abnormal changes so far *8.* Spiritual changes that bring confusion *9.* Death before death *10.* Life after life—from moonlight to Sonlight

Caring for Your Aging Parents *When Love Is Not Enough,* Barbara Deane

NavPress, 1989, $8.95, paper, 272 pp., for counselees

Description This book is a unique blend of practical advice and Christ-centered wisdom to help adult children minister to the needs of their aging parents without burning out in the process. It gives scriptural bases for self-care, setting limits on a parent's demands, and letting go of the attempt to control the parent's aging process. Indexed for quick reference. Appendix lists resources for caregivers.

Author Barbara Deane is a freelance writer for national magazines and an author, lecturer, and workshop leader on issues of caregiving and aging. A member of the American Society on Aging and the American Society of Journalists and Authors, she was cofounder of Christian Caregivers Support Group.

Contents *1.* The crucible of caring *2.* You can't "fix" old age *3.* The skills of active listening *4.* Is self-preservation wrong? *5.* Deliverance from the captivity of the past *6.* Counting the cost of caregiving *7.* Love and money *8.* Where to find the help you need *9.* Where can your parents live? *10.* Coping with the health problems of aging *11.* When your parent must be in a nursing home *12.* Walking through the valley of the shadow of death. / *Appendix:* Admissions agreement—Living will

Getting Ready for a Great Retirement *A Planning Guide,* Barbara Deane

NavPress, 1992, $10.00, paper, 249 pp., for counselees

Description if you are an adult today, you may spend as much as one-third of your life in retirement. The kind of planning you do now will determine if those are years of fulfillment or years of restlessness. The book goes well beyond the issues covered in most books on the subject, especially in addressing the spiritual issues of the postretirement years and the developmental tasks of the later stages of life. Extensive appendix of resources.

Author Barbara Deane is a freelance writer for national magazines and an author, lecturer, and workshop leader on issues of caregiving and aging. A member of the American Society on Aging and the American Society of Journalists and Authors, she was cofounder of Christian Caregivers Support Group.

Contents *Part 1:* Retirement: the first day of the rest of your life *1.* Getting to know me *2.* Letting go *3.* Planning to grow *Part 2:* Spending the gift of time *4.* Time for exploration and discovery *5.* Volunteering: finding yourself through giving yourself away *6.* Education and travel are wasted on the young *7.* If you need paid employment *8.* Where will you spend the rest of your life? *9.* Looking to the future *Part 3:* Caring for the important people in your life *10.* The postretirement marriage *11.* When you become the surviving spouse *12.* The enduring power of friendships *13.* Once a parent, always a parent *14.* Let your children know who you are *15.* Being there for your grandchildren *16.* The challenge of long-distance grandparenting *Part 4:* How to not outlive your money *17.* What you can't afford not to know *18.* Investing for an unknown future *Part 5:* When the spirit is willing but the flesh is weak *19.* Attitude is everything *20.* An ounce of prevention *21.* Strengthening your spiritual muscles

Caring for Those Who Can't *Caregiving for Your Loved One—And Yourself,* Carol Dettoni

Victor Books, 1993, $7.99, paper, 192 pp., for counselees

Description From her own experience and extensive research, the author discusses such issues as becoming medically knowledgeable, home care vs. nursing home, and finding other sources of support which can see caregivers and their families through this difficult time.

Author Carol Dettoni and her husband, John, are founders of Chrysalis Ministries, an international educational ministry for church leadership.

Contents *Part 1:* A family matter *1.* It can't be happening *2.* A week in the life of a caregiver *Part 2:* Taking charge *3.* What do I need to know? *4.* Planning ahead *5.* Some practical helps for caregivers *6.* Family, friends, church, and other support resources *Part 3:* Facing the future *7.* Home care, institutional care, and hospice care *8.* Facing death *Part 4:* Caring for the caregiver *9.* Take care of yourself *10.* The stages of caregiving *11.* Spiritual nourishment for the caregiver

Eldercare for the Christian Family *What to Do When a Loved One Becomes Dependent,* James W. Duncan Jr., Timothy Smick, et al.

Word Publishing, 1990, $14.99, cloth, 240 pp., for counselees

Description The four authors discuss the aging process and the challenges that confront the family of a senior adult who needs care. The book describes the role of the family in caretaking and clarifies the issues involved in understanding God's call to care for one another. Full of practical advice and spiritual help.

Authors Timothy Smick is cochairman of PersonaCare, Inc. James Duncan Jr. is cochairman of PersonaCare, Inc. J. P. Moreland is professor of philosophy of religion at the Talbot School of Theology, Biola University, La Mirada, Calif. Jeffrey A. Watson is senior pastor of Grace Bible Church in Seabrook, Md., and associate professor of counseling and gerontology at Washington Bible College.

Contents *1.* The sandwiched generation *2.* When someone in the family is sick *3.* The age of loss *4.* Getting assistance for the caregiver *5.* Housing and health care alternatives for the elderly *6.* Selecting a nursing home *7.* The eldercare connection *8.* When the going gets tough *9.* Tough decisions: cultivating the art of ethical decision making *10.* Ethical decisions at the end of life *11.* Talking with your elderly parents

Forget Me Not *Caring for God's Aging Children,* Elisabeth Elliot

Multnomah Books (Questar), 1989, $4.99, paper, 32 pp., for counselees

Description A series of short stories and anecdotes recounting life with the author's aging mother. Sensitively written.

Author Elisabeth Elliot is best known for her book *Through Gates of Splendor.*

Welcome to the Rest of Your Life *A Guide to Worry-Free Retirement,* Ted Engstrom

Zondervan Publishing House, 1994, $8.98, paper, 189 pp., for counselees

Description This book will help you discover the secrets for making your retirement worth all those years of learning and working. Ted Engstrom, one of the most trusted leaders in the church, shares insights into money management, personal health, service opportunities, and time management.

Author Ted W. Engstrom is president emeritus of World Vision International. He is the author of 40 books.

Contents *1.* Welcome to the rest of your life *2.* Exercising your options *3.* It's about time *4.* One for your money *5.* Voluntarism: the language of love *6.* Take charge of your health *7.* Legal and estate planning *8.* Living free *9.* The road last traveled

Alzheimer's *Caring for Your Loved One, Caring for Yourself,* Sharon Fish

Lion Publishing, 1992, $10.95, paper, 275 pp., for both counselors and counselees

Description Informed guidance and sensitive advice from a nurse, teacher, and daughter of a mother with Alzheimer's.

Author Sharon Fish, R.N., M.S.N., is coauthor of *Spiritual Care: The Nurse's Role,* a popular nursing textbook.

Contents *Part 1:* Something has gone wrong *1.* Bruised reeds and dimly burning wicks *2.* Searching for the truth *3.* Facing the facts *4.* What's happening upstairs? *Part 2:* Caring for your loved one *5.* When memory starts to fade *6.* Emotional fireworks *7.* Always on the move *8.* Baffling behaviors *9.* The struggle for safety *Part 3:* Caring for yourself *10.* People who help *11.* Get me out of here! *12.* Our tangled emotions *13.* Hot but not burned up *14.* Joy in the morning *Part 4:* Saying goodbye *15.* The difficult decisions *16.* Blowing out the candle / *Appendix:* Checklist for evaluating a nursing home

Beyond the Gold Watch *Living in Retirement,* Deborah V. Gross

Westminster/John Knox Press, 1994, $14.99, paper, 208 pp., for both counselors and counselees

Description Gross addresses many important questions about retirement. Helps readers customize a plan to maximize their resources and minimize their problems. Includes worksheets.

Author Deborah V. Gross, M.D., is a writer and psychiatrist in private practice in the Gulf Coast area of Mississippi.

Contents *Part 1:* Facts *1.* Why you need a plan *2.* Retirement in America: transition to later life *3.* Retirement and you: what to expect *4.* Aging, ageism, and attitude *Part 2:* Decisions *5.* What kind of later life do you want? *6.* To retire or not to retire: adjustment is the question *Part 3:* Planning *7.* Physical health *8.* Mental health *9.* Relationships *10.* Money

Caring for Your Aging Parents *6 Sensitive Studies for Women with Families in Transition,* Judy Hamlin

Victor Books, 1992, $4.99, paper, 64 pp., for counselees

Description Part of the Searching for Answers series from Victor. This study incorporates discussion on practical needs such as housing, medical care, insurance, finding emotional support for your own needs, identifying your concerns about caregiving, and discovering solutions for a growing issue among women.

Author Dr. Judy Hamlin (Ph.D. in adult education, University of Southern Mississippi) is an authority on small groups and women's ministry.

Contents *1.* You're not alone *2.* Identifying concerns *3.* "How to" help *4.* Emotional support *5.* Encouraging relationships *6.* Love attacks (children as caregivers) / *Leader's notes*

Now That Retirement Has Come A. F. Harper

Beacon Hill Press of Kansas City, 1988, $1.95, paper, 60 pp., for counselees

Description Covers various issues associated with making the transition to retirement.

Vintage Journey *A Guide to Graceful Aging,* Trish Herbert

The Pilgrim Press, 1994, $15.95, paper, 184 pp., for both counselors and counselees

Description Provides a practical guide to use in examining and evaluating one's journey through life. Enables the process of examining options and guides toward responsible planning.

Author Trish Herbert is a licensed psychologist and gerontologist. She is a cofounder of Journeywell, where she counsels and teaches about issues on aging and self-care for caregivers. She received her Ph.D. from the Union Institute in Cincinnati, Ohio.

A Survival Guide for Family Caregivers
Strength, Support, and Sources of Help . . . , Jo Horne

CompCare Publishers, 1991, $11.95, paper, 184 pp., for counselees

Description Covers assessing present and future needs, handling medical and legal complexities, and other issues.

Author Wisconsin writer Jo Horne and her husband, Larry Schmidt, are administrators of an adult day-care center in Milwaukee.

Contents *Part 1:* Basics *1.* What on earth is a caregiver? *2.* Walk around in their shoes *3.* Facing old age *4.* But doesn't Medicare pay for that? *5.* History lessons in attitude adjustment *6.* Riding the roller coaster *Part 2:* Specifics *7.* Help! Mom just walked out of the house naked! Caring for people with Alzheimer's disease *8.* Parenting our parents *9.* Grow old along with me: caring for a spouse *10.* The loneliness of the long-distance caregiver *Part 3:* Postscripts *11.* Guilt and those other terrible feelings

12. And the caring goes on . . . and on . . . and . . . *13.* You want me to do what? *14.* A chance to say goodbye

Aging Parents *How to Understand and Help Them,* Richard P. Johnson

Ligouri Publications, 1993, $3.95, paper, 78 pp., for counselees

Description A gerontological counselor helps adult children cope with the problems and meet the challenges of caring for their aging parents.

Too Late to Say Goodbye *My Experience with Aging Parents,* Ethel McIndoo

New Hope, 1988, $2.95, paper, 57 pp., for counselees

Description When Ethel McIndoo's mother developed Alzheimer's disease, McIndoo's world changed forever. This book describes how she coped with the ending of her mother's life. Suggestions for living with aging parents, written by Sr. Albert Meiburg, appear at the end of the book.

Author Ethel McIndoo has served as minister of childhood education, director of a day school, and as consultant in children's education in Tennessee and Alabama.

When Our Parents Need Us Most *Loving Care in the Aging Years,* David L. McKenna

Harold Shaw Publishers, 1995, $8.99, paper, 125 pp.

Description Your parents are entering their senior years. How can you, as a caregiver: Help them face retirement? Assist them in their financial decisions? Handle your own emotions while "parenting" your parents? Cope with physical changes? Encourage them to reflect on their spiritual lives? Dr. McKenna speaks powerfully from his own experiences with four aging parents, two of whom lived in his home. He offers comfort and guidelines for times of transition, and explores in everyday terms the biblical meaning of caregiving.

Contents *1.* Living with the inevitable: aging *2.* Honoring old age: self-worth *3.* Knowing when to step down: retirement *4.* Severing the symbols: independence *5.* Choosing between parents: alienation *6.* Recycling the generations: heredity *7.* Parenting our parents: roles *8.* Borrowing on trust: finances *9.* Handling our emotions: guilt *10.* Meeting our mortality: sickness *11.* Dealing with doubt: salvation *12.* Sightings of heaven: death *13.* Learning from

Jesus: caregiving / Rights and responsibilities of the Christian caregiver

When Parents Grow Old Joyce Althens Minatra

Here's Life Publishers (c/o Thomas Nelson), 1992, $9.99, paper, 186 pp., for counselees

Description Practical help to deal with the emotional and physical needs of aging parents. The author looks at the parent–child relationship, how adult children can be supportive, and how to preserve hope and dignity in difficult situations.

Author Joyce Althens Minatra is a speaker with CLASS and has been a guest on several television and radio shows.

Contents *1.* A critical time of life *2.* Dealing with decisions *Part 1:* The feelings *3.* Recognizing your feelings *4.* Dealing with feelings *5.* Recognizing your parent's feelings *6.* Dealing with your parent's feelings *Part 2:* The facts *7.* Knowing the physical needs *8.* Knowing the housing needs *9.* Knowing the finances *10.* Knowing your resources *Part 3:* The focus *11.* Refocusing personal needs *12.* Refocusing your parents *13.* Refocusing on caregiving *14.* Refocusing on the joy *15.* Refocusing on God's perspective of aging ones / *Epilogue:* When your loved ones are gone

Aging and Ministry Henri J. M. Nouwen

Ave Maria Press, 1973, $11.90, cassette(s), 1 hr. 44 minutes, for counselees

Description Father Nouwen discusses the basic options of aging: faced negatively as a time of segregation and desolation, or positively, with hope, humor, and vision. He looks at the realities of caring for the aging, the suffering, and the despairing.

Author Henri J. M. Nouwen has taught at the University of Notre Dame, Yale Divinity School, and Harvard Divinity School. He now lives and writes in Toronto, Canada, as a member of l'Arche, a community where people with mental handicaps and assistants share life together.

The Christian Guide to Parent Care Robert J. Rieske and Henry Holstage

Tyndale House Publishers, 1992, $9.99, paper, 286 pp., for counselees

Description This book is an excellent, accurate, and readable description of the processes of aging that should be extremely useful to adult children who are engaged in helping their older parents, or anticipating such a role in the near future. Through interesting examples and stories as well as a comprehensive review of the relevant scientific literature, the authors describe the personal and family changes that commonly occur in old age and the typical reactions to them. Caregivers are provided a wide variety of approaches within the family as well as descriptions and addresses of programs available from government and nonprofit agencies. The role of the church and the applicability of the Christian faith to these situations are included throughout so that a realistic and hopeful approach to the aging of family members is reached.

Authors Robert J. Rieske is a professor at Grand Rapids Community College and director of the Calvin College-Grand Rapids Community College Consortium on Aging. He writes and speaks on the topic of aging and has developed a wide variety of programs and projects to help improve the lives of older people. Henry Holstage is associate director of the Calvin College-Grand Rapids Community College Consortium on Aging and a professor of gerontology and sociology at Calvin College. He has authored many articles on the family and on aging.

Contents *Part 1:* 1. What's happening to American families? *2.* Understanding the aging process *3.* Physical changes and the aging process *4.* Mental health and aging *Part 2:* *5.* Planning ahead for the golden years *6.* Why does money grow short as people get older? *7.* How to help aging parents cope with finances *8.* How can Christians help older people? *Part 3:* 9. Should mom and dad leave their home? *10.* Should mom and dad move in with us? *11.* Other housing options for mom and dad *12.* Nursing homes: when and where? *Part 4:* 13. Dealing with frustration, anger, and guilt *14.* Honoring your parents as their years increase *15.* When you must say good-bye / *Appendix—* Organizations for caregivers

TLC for Aging Parents *A Practical Guide,* Betty Benson Robinson

Beacon Hill Press of Kansas City, 1992, $5.95, paper, 103 pp., for counselees

Description A guidebook covering the many difficult issues and decisions that accompany caring for aging parents. Strong scriptural content.

Author Betty B. Robinson serves as editor of *Parent Care,* a monthly newsletter for children of aging parents. She is a pastor's wife, dedicated church worker, and adjunct college professor.

Contents *1.* Pertaining to preparation *2.* Choosing to care *3.* Rebuilding relationships *4.* Dealing with decisions

5. Overview of options 6. Answers to anxieties—legal and financial matters 7. Observant to organization 8. Facing the feelings 9. Challenge of coping 10. Dealing with death

Caring for Your Elderly Parents *The Help, Hope, and Cope Book,* Patricia H. Rushford

Fleming H. Revell, 1993, $8.99, paper, 248 pp., for counselees

Description A guide for improving the quality of life for older persons. Readers will find detailed and practical help for aging on how to: understand the aging process; provide necessary care; find the right living arrangements; deal with guilt, denial, anger, and grief; develop healthy relationships with the elderly; deal with medical problems; prolong their independence; handle finances, insurance, and legal problems; and face death with hope and peace. A helpful tool for counselors, pastors, and health-care professionals as well as for adult children of aging parents. Offers detailed information and practical help for dealing with aging parents. Readers will find comfort and encouragement and learn to give the best possible physical, emotional, and social care for the elderly by addressing the many subjects included. Includes a resource chapter of articles, books, periodicals, and organizations that provide further information on the topic of aging.

Author Patricia H. Rushford, R.N., M.A. in counseling, has written numerous articles and 14 books on family-related topics. She is a contributing editor to *Christian Parenting Today* and adjunct professor at Western Evangelical Seminary.

Maria's Grandmother Gets Mixed Up
Doris Sandford and Graci Evans

Gold 'n' Honey Books (Questar), 1993, $6.99, cloth, 28 pp., for counselees

Description Part of the In Our Neighborhood series from Gold 'n' Honey. The series was developed for children ages 5–11 who have difficult issues to cope with. The books deal gently and compassionately with children's delicate feelings when they're forced to handle situations that are hard to understand.

And Then There Were Two *Empty Nesting after Your Kids Fly the Coop,* Cliff Schimmels

Harold Shaw Publishers, 1989, $6.99, paper, 141 pp., for counselees

Description A heartwarming, humorous look at life after the kids leave.

Author Cliff Schimmels is a former professor of education at Wheaton College. He has authored numerous books and is a widely appreciated speaker.

Letting Go and Moving On *Easing Retirement for Professional Men and Their Wives,* Dwight H. Small

Baker Book House, 1993, $9.99, paper, 214 pp., for both counselors and counselees

Description The dominant theme is the post-retirement disorientation crisis that professional businessmen face when leaving the highly productive world of work for the nonproductive world of unlimited leisure. Having reached a career pinnacle, one's long-established work patterns and close-knit circle of associates are abruptly left behind. What follows is a loss of status and familiar structured roles. High visibility, professional recognition, and acknowledged success no longer provide one's rewards. The author recounts lessons learned from his own crisis. Counsel includes spiritual and psychological help. Deals with the relinquished status derived from one's job role at retirement and the ensuing period of confused identity. A new identity must be formed using spiritual and psychological means, or one is apt to live in an idealized past.

Author Dwight Harvey Small is professor emeritus of sociology at Westmont College, Santa Barbara, Calif. He retired in 1982 after serving 12 years as teacher and counselor, and previous to that 27 years as a pastor. An author of numerous books on marriage, ethics, theology, and devotional life.

Contents 1. Blind-sided by status change 2. How the self is defined 3. Profile of a personal trauma 4. Losses can't make losers 5. No longer shackled by the past 6. Moving beyond yesterday 7. New life parameters 8. Learning to live with the unfinished 9. God's wounded healers 10. With eternity's values in view 11. Give me this mountain!

Glimpses of Grace *A Family Struggles with Alzheimer's,* Rosemary J. Upton

Baker Book House, 1990, $7.99, paper, 159 pp., for counselees

Description Rosemary Upton and her siblings couldn't believe that their vivacious, independent, and completely reliable mother was suffering from Alzheimer's disease. In diary-like form, Upton relates the pressures and frustrations of solving problems, the heartbreak of crucial decisions, and yes, even God's safety valve in difficult times—a sense of humor. Easy to read, it is a compassionate look at modern-day traumatic illness. A guidebook, a survival manual for families watching helplessly while their relative declines through the inevitable stages of Alzheimer's. The final chapter contains medical information in layperson's terms.

Author Rosemary Upton is a professional writer and an active member of ADRDA (an Alzheimer's Disease Association). She has both the bachelor of theology and master of biblical studies degrees. Her other published works include articles on social issues, radio commentaries, drama, short stories, and a novel.

Contents *1.* 1976—Wheels *2.* 1977—Finances *3.* 1977—Diagnostic consultation *4.* 1977—Role reversal *5.* 1978—Healing? *6.* 1978—Repetition *7.* 1978—Help, please *8.* 1978—Dealing with dementia *9.* 1979—A nursing home? *10.* 1979—Decision *11.* 1979—Life after *12.* 1980—Guilt *13.* 1982—Alzheimer's association *14.* 1983—Help and understanding *15.* 1983 and 1984—Euthanasia? *16.* 1984—Government awareness *17.* 1985—Neuropsychiatry *18.* 1985–86—God's grace *19.* 1989—Research / *Resources*

The Wrap-Up Years Clara Verner

Beacon Hill Press of Kansas City, 1990, $2.50, paper, 47 pp., for counselees

Description This veteran author tells the struggle she and her husband had regarding the decision to enter a nursing home. Uplifting, optimistic. Testimonies of others at "the home" are included.

Our Journey *Diary of a Caregiver,* Kenneth Vogt

Beacon Hill Press of Kansas City, 1992, $3.95, paper, 64 pp., for counselees

Description Stricken by the devastating disease called Alzheimer's, Ruby and Kenneth Vogt began to understand "in sickness and in health." As Vogt became the caregiver for his wife, he penned his most personal thoughts and feelings.

The Courage to Care *Helping the Aging, Grieving, and Dying,* Jeffrey A. Watson

Baker Book House, 1992, $10.99, paper, 186 pp., for counselors

Description *Courage to Care* integrates the biblical theology of aging, grief, and death with the significant findings from the behavioral sciences on the respective topics. *Courage to Care* includes powerful case studies, statistics, charts, graphs, discussion questions, endnotes, bibliography, and subject index. The author of *Courage to Care* is an accomplished pastoral practitioner with 14 years of experience in parish counseling, hospice, hospital/nursing home chaplaincy, and the training of clinical/pastoral caregivers. He holds theological degrees from both Protestant and Roman Catholic graduate schools as well as behavioral science credentials from a secular university. The Scripture is eloquent in its trilogy of metaphors: "The grass withers . . . the flower fades . . . but the Word of God stands forever." Dying mankind, like a withering meadow, is described through a historical/theological model in Part 1. Dying individuals, like fragile flowers, are described through a pastoral/psychological model in Part 2. But the ever enlivening Word of God, woven throughout the fabric of the whole book, points to true hope and life in Jesus Christ.

Author Jeffrey Watson is senior minister of Grace Bible Church in Seabrook, Md., professor of gerontology at Washington Bible College, consultant in bioethics and chaplaincy. He formerly did pastoral care at Prince George's Hospital and at the Joseph Richey Hospice. A graduate of Capital Bible Seminary, Catholic University, and Dallas Theological Seminary, he is an engaging seminar speaker.

Contents *Part 1:* Biblical caregiving *1.* Why should we face aging, grief, and death *2.* How the Old Testament helps us face aging, grief, and death *3.* How the New Testament helps us face aging, grief, and death *Part 2:* Personal caregiving *4.* The fear of death *5.* The grief of loss *6.* The pain of suicide *7.* The challenge of aging *8.* The mentoring of children *9.* The care of sufferers / *For further reading*

Mom and Dad Can't Live Alone Anymore *Making a Family Decision,* Eldon Weisheit

Lion Publishing, 1994, $10.95, paper, 240 pp., for both counselors and counselees

Description Examines the moral and ethical issues that arise when deciding how to deal compassionately with the changing needs of aging parents. Clarifies options, traditional and creative, for dealing with parents in need.

Author Eldon Weisheit is the author of more than 25 books for children and their families.

Contents *1.* The tables are turned on you *2.* The tables are turned on your parents *3.* Your decision needs a zip code *4.* Which floor? *5.* Level one: home care *6.* Level two: board and care homes *7.* Level three: assisted living *8.* Level four: nursing-care homes *9.* Living with your decision

Journal of Religious Gerontology

The Haworth Pastoral Press, quarterly, $32.00/year, a reference or academic work

Description Designed to 1. inform religious professionals about developments in the field of religious gerontology, 2. inform secular professionals who work with the elderly in religious institutions, and 3. focus traditional academic disciplines within religion on the phenomena of human aging. Sponsored by the National Interfaith Coalition on Aging.

Making Decisions about the Care of an Elderly Parent

Abbey Press, 1994, $.50 each, paper, 8 pp., for counselees

Description Part of the New CareSteps series from Abbey Press. Each CareStep pamphlet (three-panel) is filled with insightful advice and quotes from respected leaders in the helping professions. Very useful during the early stages of recovery. The underlying message in all CareSteps pamphlets is the emphasis on using all one's resources—emotional, physical, mental, social, and spiritual—to cope with life's biggest challenges. This title emphasizes evaluating the need for additional care, using family common sense, considering care options that are available, and choosing the best alternative.

Making the Most of Your Retirement

Abbey Press, $.50 each, paper, 8 pp., for counselees

Description Part of the CareNotes series from Abbey Press. CareNotes are short booklets that

help readers identify issues and begin the process of seeking resolution. Anecdotal and uplifting. Beautiful photographs grace the covers. Over 20 million CareNotes have been sold in just over five years. Can be used as an alternative to a greeting card or in conjunction with pastoral care visits.

When a Loved One Has Alzheimer's

Abbey Press, $.50 each, paper, 8 pp., for counselees

Description Part of the CareNotes series from Abbey Press. CareNotes are short booklets that help readers identify issues and begin the process of seeking resolution. Anecdotal and uplifting. Beautiful photographs grace the covers. Over 20 million CareNotes have been sold in just over five years. Can be used as an alternative to a greeting card or in conjunction with pastoral care visits.

Wondering What's Best for an Aging Parent

Abbey Press, $.50 each, paper, 8 pp., for counselees

Description Part of the CareNotes series from Abbey Press. CareNotes are short booklets that help readers identify issues and begin the process of seeking resolution. Anecdotal and uplifting. Beautiful photographs grace the covers. Over 20 million CareNotes have been sold in just over five years. Can be used as an alternative to a greeting card or in conjunction with pastoral care visits.

Alzheimer's Disease and Related Disorder Association

Alzheimer's Disease and Related Disorder Association. An organization

Description The ADRDA has hundreds of chapters and support groups nationwide to help caregivers. Provides information to families with loved ones with AD.

Alzheimer's Disease Education and Referral

Alzheimer's Disease Education and Referral. An organization

Description Though not a Christian organization, this group offers valuable assistance to those struggling to cope with Alzheimer's disease.

American Association of Homes for the Aging

American Association of Homes for the Aging. An organization

Description Though not a Christian organization, provides a free packet of caregiving brochures and information on housing options for seniors. Assists those involved in providing quality care for the elderly.

American Association of Retired Persons

American Association of Retired Persons. An organization

Description A support organization that offers tremendous help and support to the retired and those involved with them. Anyone involved or interested in issues associated with aging would do well to contact them for a general information packet.

National Institute on Aging Information Center

National Institute on Aging. An organization

Description Though not a Christian organization, an outstanding source for all types of information on issues related to aging.

4. Anger

What Do You Do When Anger Gets the Upper Hand? Jay E. Adams

P & R Publishing, 1975, $.25, paper, 9 pp., for counselees

Description Contrasts various ineffective methods of coping with anger with God's method as found in Scripture. Based on nouthetic techniques.

Author Dr. Adams is the author of numerous books on Christian counseling. He has served on a seminary faculty (Westminster Theological) and in the pastorate. He is founder of Christian Counseling and Educational Foundation in Laverock, Pa., and visiting professor of practical theology at two seminaries.

Anger and Personal Rights David Batty

Turning Point Ministries, Inc., 1992, $5.00, spiral, 88 pp., for both counselors and counselees

Description Part of the Group Studies for New Christians support group materials from Turning Point Ministries. A leader's guide is also available.

Secret Wounds and Silent Cries Dewey Bertolini

Victor Books, 1993, $7.99, paper, 156 pp., for counselees

Description Is there any release from the prison of bitterness? Once himself a captive of bitterness, this author proclaims "Yes." He recounts his 17-year struggle with the man who broke his emotional backbone, his father. The author tells how, through God's intervention, that relationship was significantly restored. This book provides a biblically based approach to winning a personal battle with bitterness, discussing such issues as: how bitterness starts, forgiving others, forgiving yourself, living with situations that can't be changed, and breaking the cycle of bitterness in the next generation.

Author Dewey Bertolini is a speaker and consultant for Scripture Press. He also serves as assistant to the president at Western Baptist College.

Contents *1.* The legacy of a loser *2.* Slow but certain suicide *3.* Forgive and forget? *4.* The moment of truth *5.* It ain't over 'til it's over *6.* A permanent ending *7.* Breaking the chains *8.* I'm glad you asked

Overcoming Hurts and Anger *How to Identify and Cope with Negative Emotions,* Dwight Carlson

Harvest House Publishers, 1981, $6.99, paper, 185 pp., for counselees

Description Helps you identify and cope with your feelings of hurt and anger. Dr. Carlson, a well-known psychiatrist and author, explains that you don't have to experience frustration and paranoia. Instead he teaches that only by confronting and learning to cope with your feelings and negative emotions can you experience liberation and fulfillment and achieve a more significant grasp of the concept of God's grace and mercy.

Author Dwight Carlson, M.D., is a specialist in both internal medicine and psychiatry. He has an active psychiatry practice and is assistant clinical professor at UCLA.

Contents *1.* The feelings of anger *2.* Mishandling anger *3.* Biblical principles *4.* How do you handle anger? *5.* Preparing to handle anger *6.* Handling your anger *7.* How to forgive and forget *8.* Practice what you know *9.* Preventing anger *10.* Ideal ways to handle anger

Good 'n' Angry *How to Handle Your Anger Positively,* Les Carter

Baker Book House, 1983, $7.99, paper, 166 pp., for both counselors and counselees

Description Assertive (nonaggressive) anger, used for positive ends, makes a positive ally, says the author, who counsels self-awareness and -control instead of repression and denial of God-directed emotions.

Author Les Carter is a Christian psychotherapist maintaining an active counseling practice at the Minirth-Meier Clinic.

Contents *Part 1:* Know what anger is *1.* To be or not to be *2.* Mirror, mirror, on the wall *3.* Stand up and be counted *4.* The two types of anger *Part 2:* Why anger gets out of hand *5.* I'm depending on you *6.* Out from under the heap *7.* Because I said so! *8.* On the treadmill *9.* The near-sighted syndrome *Part 3:* How people handle anger (or how anger handles people) *10.* Repress it, express it, or release it *11.* Hit and run *12.* Silent but deadly *Part 4:* Getting anger under control *13.* The importance of personal security *14.* The Bible and anger *15.* Love comes first *16.* Steps toward a life of composure *17.* How to argue fairly

The Anger Workbook Les Carter and Frank B. Minirth

Janet Thoma (a division of Thomas Nelson), 1993, $14.99, paper, 320 pp., for counselees

Description The only anger management program that offers interactive exercises to help anyone move beyond unhealthy anger toward inner peace. Understand how unmet needs feed anger and learn to identify the lifestyle patterns that indicate a problem with anger.

Authors Dr. Les Carter is a nationally known expert in the field of Christian counseling with more than 15 years in private practice. He is a psychotherapist with the Minirth-Meier Clinic. Dr. Frank Minirth founded the clinic in Dallas, Tex., one of the largest psychiatric clinics in the world.

Contents *Part 1:* Identifying your anger *1.* What is anger? *2.* Managing your anger *Part 2:* Anger thrives on unmet needs *3.* Why can't you just love me? *4.* Feeling controlled causes anger *5.* Myths that perpetuate anger *6.* Self-inflicted anger *Part 3:* How other emotions create anger *7.* How pride influences anger *8.* Fear's effect on anger *9.* Loneliness creates anger *10.* Anger reflects inferiority feelings *Part 4:* Applying new insights about anger reduction *11.* Managing a child's anger *12.* Being accountable

Counseling and Anger Mark Cosgrove

Word Publishing, 1988, $15.99, cloth, 198 pp., for counselors

Description Dr. Cosgrove challenges everyone to take responsibility for controlling anger in marriage, at home, at ourselves, and at God—affirming that Christ's life within the Christian makes all change possible. Part of the Resources for Christian Counselors series from Word.

Author Mark Cosgrove is chairman of the Department of Psychology at Taylor University, Up-

land, Ind. He has published four other books on the integration of psychology and Christianity.

Contents *1.* The fires within *2.* Defining anger and hostility *3.* The causes of anger *4.* How not to deal with anger *5.* Slow to anger: holding anger back *6.* Expressing anger properly *7.* Counseling and anger in marriage *8.* Counseling and anger in children *9.* Counseling and anger at self *10.* Counseling and anger at God *11.* Preventing anger

How to Deal with Anger Larry Crabb

NavPress, 1991, $2.00, paper, 24 pp., for counselees

Description Many people feel that anger is a bad idea. Others believe that anger must be vented, or it will lead to bitterness and resentment. So who's right? Larry Crabb maintains that neither approach is consistent with biblical teaching. In this booklet you'll learn how to identify what's really making you angry, and you'll discover four clear-cut ways to deal with your anger.

Author Dr. Larry Crabb (Ph.D. in clinical psychology, University of Illinois) is the founder and director of the Institute of Biblical Counseling. He is widely known for his work in the area of biblical counseling.

The Faces of Rage *Resolving the Losses That Lead to Anger, Guilt, Shame, Cynicism, Isolation,* David Damico

NavPress, 1992, $11.00, paper, 203 pp., for both counselors and counselees

Description Rage is more than unbridled anger. It's a response to a series of unresolved griefs or losses, which often manifests itself in subtle ways through guilt, isolation, compulsions, cynicism, superficiality, or the nagging feeling that our Christian life is less than victorious. This work explores the pitfalls of the rage-driven lifestyle and will bring you through the process of healing by showing you how to discover God as your true protector—rather than seeking safety in rage and its huge walls of emotional and spiritual resistance.

Author David Damico is the founder and director of Christian Assisted Recovery Environments, Inc., a lay organization committed to helping those who are struggling with unresolved losses.

Contents *Part 1:* Loss: why are we rageful? *1.* The nature of loss *2.* Eight significant losses *3.* Five ways we experience loss *4.* How unresolved loss visits the next generation *Part 2:* Avoidance: how do we protect ourselves with rage? *5.* The deadly dance of performance and control *6*. The furious battle against powerlessness *7*. The fearful escape from truth and self *8*. The ruthless defense against conflict *Part 3:* Resolution: how can we relinquish our rage? *9*. Confrontation: allowing truth to penetrate our defenses *10*. Conviction: facing the full impact of rage's rule *11*. Repentance: inviting God to rescue us *12*. Resolution: incorporating loss and transcending death *13*. Integration: crossing from grief to grace

Mistreated Ron Lee Davis

Multnomah Books (Questar), 1993, $8.99, paper, 200 pp., for counselees

Description It's so easy to let resentment take hold after you've been unfairly treated—whether at work, at church, or by friends or family. You can have freedom from bitterness when you believe God is in control. Davis shares stories of people who have overcome the hurt of mistreatment to help you find the way to healing, renewed self-esteem, and forgiveness.

Healing the Hurts of Resentment
Robert K. Drummond

Beacon Hill Press of Kansas City, 1991, $1.95, paper, 41 pp., for counselees

Contents *1*. What are resentment and jealousy? *2*. Where does resentment come from? *3*. How do you rid yourself of resentment and jealousy?

Reshaping a Jealous Heart *How to Turn Dissatisfaction into Contentment,* Alice Fryling

InterVarsity Press, 1994, $8.99, paper, 144 pp., for counselees

Description Practical, biblical advice for beating the green monsters of the heart (illustrated by candid stories of her own battle and followed up with study and discussion questions for readers). Addresses anger, ambition, fear, covetousness, and much more.

Author Alice Fryling is a homemaker, speaker, and writer who lives in Madison, Wis.

Contents *1*. Sometimes it's hard to love my neighbor *2*. There's mildew in my soul! *3*. If God can be jealous, why can't I? *4*. Why am I jealous when I don't want to be? *5*. Wishful thinking *6*. Does God know that life is unfair? *7*. Is it okay to be ambitious? *8*. Sometimes I'm afraid my life is not working *9*. If God loves me, why can't I have it all? *10*. Transforming jealousy into faith *11*. Finding freedom through repentance *12*. Letting God release us from the jealousy trap

Overcoming Frustration and Anger
Paul A. Hauck

Westminster/John Knox Press, 1974, $9.99, paper, 142 pp., for counselees

Description Discusses the causes, dynamics of, and solutions to anger. Utilizing a cognitive approach combined with Christian principles, Hauck teaches new ways of interpreting anger and expressing it.

Author Paul A. Hauck has been a full-time clinical psychologist in private practice in Rock Island, Ill., since 1968. He received his Ph.D. in 1953 from the University of Utah. In 1987 he was honored with the Distinguished Psychologist Award in Illinois. He travels widely, speaking and disseminating his views. He has over 30 articles published as well as 12 books. His writings have sold about 400,000 copies.

Contents *1*. After 30 years of fighting, a smile *2*. Should we avoid all anger? *3*. Who makes you mad? You do! *4*. Don't be a catastrophizer *5*. Watch that blame *6*. If not anger, what? *7*. Making it work

Overcoming Jealousy and Possessiveness
Paul A. Hauck

Westminster/John Knox Press, 1981, $9.99, paper, 140 pp., for counselees

Description There are three common errors people make which bring on jealousy. This book describes them thoroughly for readers to comprehend them quickly and then to apply them in their own interactions with people. Advice on coping with jealous feelings is offered.

Author Paul A. Hauck has been a full-time clinical psychologist in private practice in Rock Island, Ill., since 1968. He received his Ph.D. in 1953 from the University of Utah. In 1987 he was honored with the Distinguished Psychologist Award in Illinois. He travels widely, speaking and disseminating his views. He has over 30 articles published as well as 12 books. His writings have sold about 400,000 copies.

Contents *1*. The psychology of jealousy and possessiveness *2*. Ways to correct jealousy by yourself *3*. How to become a superlover *4*. Coping with jealous and possessive persons / *Summary*

Men at Peace Dick Brian Klaver

Thomas Nelson Publishers, $15.99, paper, 288 pp., for counselors

Description Based on Klaver's highly successful Men at Peace program, this nine-step strategy helps you explore the roots of your anger, take responsibility for your actions, and find serenity.

Anger Is a Choice Tim LaHaye and Bob Phillips

Zondervan Publishing House, 1982, $5.00, paper, 192 pp., for counselees

Description Best-selling authors tell us what we need to know to control the emotion of anger. They not only examine it from beginning to end, but they help us evaluate our own "Irritability Quotient" through the anger inventory and other exercises throughout the book.

Authors Dr. Tim LaHaye is president and founder of Family Life Seminars and is a Family Life leader. He has written many other books on counseling and family life issues. Bob Phillips, M.A., is a licensed marriage-family-child counselor in private practice. He is the author of six other books and is assistant director of Hume Lake Christian Camps.

Contents *1.* Anger—everybody's problem *2.* Meet the angry family *3.* Anger and body language *4.* Anger and your health *5.* Anger inventory *6.* The anatomy of mental problems *7.* Why do I get angry? *8.* Anger and your temperament *9.* Outside help for anger *10.* Is it ever right to be angry? *11.* Anger and forgiveness *12.* The other side of forgiveness *13.* How to deal with your anger

Bitterness Robert S. McGee

Rapha Resources, 1992, $2.50, paper, 56 pp., for counselees

Description Being hurt by others is an unavoidable part of life. The authors demonstrate the short- and long-term effects of this devastating feeling and how you can find freedom in forgiveness.

Author Robert McGee is founder and president of Rapha, a health care organization that provides in-hospital and outpatient care, with a Christ-centered perspective, for adults and adolescents suffering from psychiatric and substance abuse problems.

How to Check Your Anger Donald F. Miller

Ligouri Publications, $.75, paper, 24 pp., for counselees

Description Anger can be used for either positive or destructive purposes. This pamphlet contains suggestions for how readers can control this powerful emotion and use it the way God wants.

Dealing with Feelings of Anger Clyde M. Narramore

Narramore Christian Foundation, 1989, $19.99, video, for counselees

Description This video skillfully deals with many kinds of frustration and anger. Dr. Clyde Narramore and Mark McNear cover 13 penetrating points about anger and how to prevent it.

Author Dr. Clyde M. Narramore is a licensed psychologist and the president and founder of the Narramore Christian Foundation—a charitable, nonprofit educational, training, and counseling organization ministering primarily to the Christian community. He is also the founder of the Rosemead School of Psychology and author of 29 books.

Jealousy Clyde M. Narramore

Narramore Christian Foundation, $.35, paper, for counselees

Description One of the many booklets available from the Narramore Christian Foundation. Designed to be handed to a person beginning to come to grips with a problem in living.

Author Dr. Clyde M. Narramore is a licensed psychologist and the president and founder of the Narramore Christian Foundation—a charitable, nonprofit educational, training, and counseling organization ministering primarily to the Christian community. He is also the founder of the Rosemead School of Psychology and author of 29 books.

The Many Faces of Bitterness Clyde M. Narramore

Narramore Christian Foundation, $.35, paper, for counselees

Description One of the many booklets available from the Narramore Christian Foundation. Designed to be handed to a person beginning to come to grips with a problem in living.

Author Dr. Clyde M. Narramore is a licensed psychologist and the president and founder of the Narramore Christian Foundation—a charitable, nonprofit educational, training, and counseling organization ministering primarily to the Christian community. He is also the founder of the Rosemead School of Psychology and author of 29 books.

When Anger Hits Home *Taking Care of Your Anger Without Taking It Out on Your Family,* Gary Jackson Oliver and H. Norman Wright

Moody Press, 1992, $16.99, cloth, 249 pp.

Description Instead of a time bomb to be avoided, anger can be a valuable gift to use in accomplishing God's will. This helpful book clears up the myths about this least understood emotion and provides a step-by-step approach to constructively redirecting its power.

Authors Dr. H. Norman Wright is one of America's best known Christian marriage and family counselors at the Family Counseling and Enrichment Center in Tustin, Calif. He is author of more than 50 books. He has also served on the faculty of Talbot School of Theology and the Graduate School of Marriage Counseling of Biola University. Gary Jackson Oliver is a therapist at Southwestern Counseling Associates.

Contents *1.* The many faces of anger *2.* Anger in your family tree *3.* The myths of anger *4.* Made in God's image—anger included *5.* The gift of anger *6.* Where did all this anger come from? *7.* Feel the frustration *8.* Men and anger *9.* Women and anger *10.* Anger in marriage *11.* Angry parents, angry children *12.* When anger crosses the line *13.* What's your anger style? *14.* Making anger work for you

When You're Angry at God William Rabior

Ligouri Publications, 1984, $.75, paper, 24 pp., for counselees

Description Is it wrong to be angry at God? How can a person let go of such anger? This pamphlet answers these questions and explains that God accepts anger, even if it is directed at him.

When You're Angry at the Church
William Rabior

Ligouri Publications, 1987, $.75, paper, 24 pp., for counselees

Description Explores the reasons people become angry at the church. Helps readers judge whether or not their anger is justified and suggests healthy ways to reconcile themselves with the church.

Anger Shannon B. Rainey

NavPress, 1992, $5.00, paper, 67 pp., for both counselors and counselees

Description Anger can be very good or very harmful. What you do with it makes all the difference. In this IBC discussion guide, you'll explore anger and the role it plays in your life and relationships.

Author Shannon B. Rainey is a wife, mother, and counselor in private practice in Winston-Salem, N.C., working with adult individuals, married couples, and groups. She is a group leader and individual counselor for the Institute of Biblical Counseling's sexual abuse recovery seminars. She is also a conference and retreat speaker.

Contents *Session 1*—What is anger? *Session 2*—The symptoms of anger—what does anger look like? *Session 3*—The sources of anger—where does anger come from? *Session 4*—The functions of anger—what does anger do for me? *Session 5*—Styles of dealing with anger / *Healing from anger / Help for leaders*

Recovery from Bitterness Dale Ryan and Juanita Ryan

InterVarsity Press, 1992, $4.99, paper, 60 pp., for both counselors and counselees

Description This Bible study is part of a series of 16 volumes on various recovery themes. Each book contains studies on six biblical texts. Leader's notes are provided for group study.

Authors Dale Ryan is the executive director of the Recovery Partnership, the parent organization to the National Association for Christian Recovery. Juanita Ryan is a counselor in private practice in Hacienda Heights, Calif.

Contents *1.* Facing the hurt *2.* Feeling anger *3.* Grieving *4.* Letting go *5.* Choosing growth *6.* Finding purpose / *Leader's notes*

The Angry Man David Stoop and Stephen Arterburn

Word Publishing, 1992, $12.99, cloth, 183 pp., for both counselors and counselees

Description Here you'll learn to understand masculine anger, realize how it can destroy relationships, and learn how to detect and diffuse it. Men and the women who love them will gain practical answers for working through this volatile emotion.

44

Authors David Stoop, Ph.D., is the clinical director of the Minirth-Meier-Stoop Clinics in southern Calif. Stephen Arterburn is the founder of New Life Treatment Centers, now merged with the Minirth-Meier Clinics.

Make Anger Your Ally Neil Clark Warren

Focus on the Family, 1993, $9.99, paper, 205 pp., for counselees

Description Anger is a neutral force that offers magnificent possibilities for those who learn to manage it creatively. This positive, constructive book teaches the reader to master anger and transform its energy into a dynamic force for living a satisfying life.

Dealing with Anger

Abbey Press, $.50 each, paper, 8 pp., for counselees

Description Part of the CareNotes series from Abbey Press. CareNotes are short booklets that help readers identify issues and begin the process of seeking resolution. Anecdotal and uplifting. Beautiful photographs grace the covers. Over 20 million CareNotes have been sold in just over five years. Can be used as an alternative to a greeting card or in conjunction with pastoral care visits.

Dealing with Feelings of Jealousy and Envy

Abbey Press, $.50 each, paper, 8 pp., for counselees

Description Part of the CareNotes series from Abbey Press. CareNotes are short booklets that help readers identify issues and begin the process of seeking resolution. Anecdotal and uplifting. Beautiful photographs grace the covers. Over 20 million CareNotes have been sold in just over five years. Can be used as an alternative to a greeting card or in conjunction with pastoral care visits.

Expressing Anger in Healthy Ways

Abbey Press, 1994, $.50 each, paper, 8 pp., for counselees

Description Part of the New CareSteps series from Abbey Press. Each CareStep pamphlet (three panel) is filled with insightful advice and quotes from respected leaders in the helping professions. Very useful during the early stages of recovery. The underlying message in all CareSteps pamphlets is the emphasis on using all one's resources—emotional, physical, mental, social, and spiritual—to cope with life's biggest challenges. This title emphasizes identifying destructive expressions, assertiveness, taking time to stay calm, respecting the target of one's anger, keeping information flowing, and learning to use degrees of anger.

5. Anxiety

One-Day-at-a-Time Therapy Christine Adams

> Abbey Press, 1992, $3.95, paper, 80 pp., for counselees

> **Description** Written to help those who continually replay the past and project into the future. Helps readers focus on today. Encourages the reader to see himself as a child, happy and loved, and in control of his own life. It is a beautiful little book filled with reminders for revitalizing today, helping us come to know that God is very close to us—and God is now. Format: a series of about 30 short sayings, proverbs, and admonitions accompanied by whimsical cartoons on every page.

What Do You Do When Fear Overcomes You? Jay E. Adams

> P & R Publishing, 1975, $.25, paper, for counselees

> **Description** Contrasts fear and love and teaches how to restructure thought patterns in order to serve God and others with love.

> **Author** Dr. Adams is the author of numerous books on Christian counseling. He has served on a seminary faculty (Westminster Theological) and in the pastorate. He is founder of Christian Counseling and Educational Foundation in Laverock, Pa., and visiting professor of practical theology at two seminaries.

The Good News about Worry *Applying the Truth of the Gospel to Problems of Anxiety, Fear, and Worry,* William Backus

> Bethany House Publishers, 1991, $8.99, paper, 219 pp., for both counselors and counselees

> **Description** Fears, anxieties, and worries come in many shapes and with varying degrees of intensity. But the fact is that everyone has them. For many Christians, the biblical directive from Jesus and Paul, "Do not be anxious about anything . . . ," presents a major dilemma. If they are trusting God, why do they still worry and get nervous? Backus has written to show readers how their faith can effectively help them deal with worry and anxiety. Anxiety results from believing and acting upon misbeliefs. Avoiding anxiety perpetuates it. True faith is telling yourself the truth and doing it. Faith overcomes anxiety by removing the reason for avoidance and ending the reinforcement of worry.

> **Author** William Backus is a licensed clinical psychologist and an ordained Lutheran clergyman. He is founder and director of the Center for Christian Psychological Services, St. Paul, Minn., and an associate pastor of a large Lutheran church.

> **Contents** *1.* Does everybody get anxious? *2.* The real culprit: avoidance *3.* The classic double bind *4.* The "disguises" of anxiety *5.* The spiritual roots of anxiety *6.* Two personalities *7.* Real causes of anxiety *8.* How free do you want to be? *9.* Washing in the river *10.* Laying yourself open *11.* Breaking the spiral *12.* Exploding your myth beliefs *13.* Moving truth into your heart *14.* Accepting anxious feelings *15.* Lessening phobic anxiety *16.* Agoraphobia: fear of panic *17.* How to (almost) stop worrying

Helping Worriers *A Short-term Structured Model,* James R. Beck and David T. Moore

> Baker Book House, 1994, $17.99, cloth, 140 pp.

> **Description** Guides in retraining a worrier psychologically and spiritually. Shows how to help the worrier work out a strategic plan for trusting God. Written for students or practicing pastoral counselors, each problem is adapted to the five-session Strategic Pastoral Counseling model developed by David G. Benner. A companion book of the Strategic Christian Living series, *Why Worry?* is available as a counselee handout or self-help resource.

> **Authors** James R. Beck is associate professor of counseling at Denver Conservative Baptist Seminary. David T. Moore is senior pastor of Southwest Community Church.

Contents *Series Preface:* An introduction to Strategic Pastoral Counseling / *Introduction:* Counseling worriers *1.* Worry can get you down—the psychology of worry: an overview *2.* "Don't worry about it"—the encounter stage—session 1 *3.* The agony of worry—the engagement stage—session 2 *4.* Worrying about worry—the engagement stage—session 3 *5.* Acting on worry—the engagement stage—session 4 *6.* The last word on worry—the disengagement stage—session 5 *7.* A case history of a world class worrier

Why Worry? *Conquering a Common Inclination,* James R. Beck and David T. Moore

Baker Book House, 1994, $8.99, paper, 88 pp.

Description Worriers can be set free from their deadly habit of dread. In this guide they will find ideas they can put into practice to replace a joy-robbing, energy-draining attitude, with a new, healthy perspective. Contains helpful worksheets and interactive study questions.

Authors James R. Beck is associate professor of counseling at Denver Conservative Baptist Seminary. David T. Moore is senior pastor of Southwest Community Church.

Contents *1.* Don't worry about it *2.* The agony of worry *3.* Worrying about worry *4.* Acting on worry *5.* The last word on worry

The Doubting Disease *Scruples and Obsessive Compulsive Disorder,* Joseph W. Ciarrocchi

Paulist Press, 1995, $14.95, paper, 160 pp.

Description Brings together the most current information available today on religion and scruples, scrupulosity and obsessive-compulsive disorders.

Author Joseph W. Ciarrocchi is associate professor of pastoral counseling at Loyola College in Maryland. He is also a clinical psychologist whose treatment and research interests are in the area of compulsive behaviors.

Contents *Part 1*—Scruples: an orientation and overview *1.* Scrupulosity: an overview *2.* Scruples and obsessive-compulsive disorder *3.* Scruples: common and uncommon *4.* Scruples in the history of pastoral care *Part 2*—Changing scruples *5.* Targeting scruples and developing motivation *6.* Reducing obsessional scruples *7.* Reducing compulsive scruples *Part 3*—Practice and theory of changing scruples *8.* Getting help for scruples and OCD *9.* Technical asides: moral reasoning, scruples, and the psychology of religion *Appendix:* A step-by-step treatment for scrupulosity / *Appendix:* Obsessions and compulsions checklist

Why Are You Worrying? *Scruples and Obsessive-Compulsive Disorder,* Joseph W. Ciarrocchi

Paulist Press, 1995, $3.95, paper, 79 pp.

Description Encourages readers to realize the power of religious belief in reducing worry in their lives. Using the biblical tradition of wisdom, the book suggests the importance of spiritual perspective in helping people cope with ordinary or severe worries.

Author Joseph W. Ciarrocchi is associate professor of pastoral counseling at Loyola College in Maryland. He is also a clinical psychologist whose treatment and research interests are in the area of compulsive behaviors.

Contents *Introduction:* Worry and the soul *1.* Worry: definition and impact *2.* The worry cycle *3.* Stopping the worry spiral. An overview *4.* Know thyself: naming the fear *5.* Step One—lowering the volume *6.* Step Two—facing the fear *7.* Step Three—wisdom: doing and not doing *8.* A spiritual overview

Winning the Worry War Don Baker

Victor Books, 1989, $6.95, paper, 120 pp., for counselors

Description Written by a "classic worrier," this book suggests a solution to the problem of worry, a good dose of "thank-you therapy." Based on Phil. 4:6. Formerly published in cloth as *Thank You Therapy.*

Author Don Baker is minister-at-large for the Conservative Baptist Association of America.

Contents *1.* That's anxiety *2.* The transforming power of thankfulness *3.* The giant step of faith *4.* Accepting the circumstances *5.* Standing on the promises *6.* Trusting God for the unknown *7.* Anxiety about discipline *8.* Anxiety about God's provision *9.* Anxiety about God's timing *10.* Anxiety about prayer *11.* Anxiety about death *12.* Friendly anxiety

How to Win over Worry *A Practical Formula for Successful Living,* John Haggai

Harvest House Publishers, 1987, $6.99, paper, 199 pp., for counselees

Description For over 30 years people have turned to Dr. John Haggai's best-selling book *How to Win over Worry* for practical answers and solutions to the problems of worry. In this revised and expanded edition, you will see how thousands have stopped being victimized by worry and how you can learn to win over it. By accepting God's miraculous prescription for worry, you can escape its devastating effects and replace the worry in your life with the perfect peace of God.

Author Dr. John Haggai, internationally acclaimed author, lecturer, and "leader of leaders," has helped people around the world with his practical formula for worry.

Contents *Part 1:* Surveying the problem *1.* Meet public enemy number one *2.* Throw away your pop gun *3.* Worry is a sin *Part 2:* Praise *4.* The requirement to rejoice *5.* How to control your feelings *6.* Count your many blessings *7.* Anticipate apathy *8.* Master the art of altruism *Part 3:* Poise *9.* Our impelling motive *10.* Poise through thought control *11.* Poise through self-control *12.* Poise through enthusiasm *13.* Poise through relaxation *14.* Poise through scheduling *15.* Poise through sidelines *16.* Poise through seizing the day *17.* Poise through skill *18.* Poise through industry *19.* Poise through stewardship *20.* Poise through surrender *Part 4:* Prayer *21.* Why pray? *22.* How to pray *23.* When to pray *24.* For what to pray *Part 5:* Peace *25.* Perfect peace

Overcoming Worry and Fear Paul A. Hauck

Westminster/John Knox Press, 1975, $9.99, paper, 112 pp., for counselees

Description This book explains the cognitive-behavioral techniques which are most successful in reducing fears. Describes common fears, irrational ideas, fruits of fear, and methods for overcoming them.

Author Paul A. Hauck has been a full-time clinical psychologist in private practice in Rock Island, Ill., since 1968. He received his Ph.D. in 1953 from the University of Utah. In 1987 he was honored with the Distinguished Psychologist Award in Illinois. He travels widely, speaking and disseminating his views. He has over 30 articles published as well as 12 books. His writings have sold about 400,000 copies.

Contents *1.* A glance at our most common fears *2.* The psychology of fear *3.* The real cause of fear *4.* Neurotic characteristics of fear *5.* Overcoming fears *6.* Pitfalls to recovery *7.* Putting it all together

Tame Your Fears *Transform Them into Faith, Confidence, and Action,* Carol Kent

NavPress, 1994, $10.00, paper, 208 pp., for counselees

Description Kent examines the ten most common fears of women and suggests ways to use them

as stepping stones to deeper faith and renewed confidence.

Author Carol Kent is an author, speaker, and founder of Speak Up with Confidence seminars.

Contents *Part 1:* Hope . . . when life gets scary. *1.* If I'm such a great Christian, why do I have this problem? *2.* What happens inside my head when I get afraid? *Part 2:* Overcoming the fears of things that haven't happened . . . yet! *3.* Why do I let irrational panic immobilize me? *4.* Why does the fear of things that might happen consume my mental and spiritual energy? *Part 3:* Overcoming the fear of being vulnerable *5.* Why does everything I do have to be perfect? *6.* If I let you get close to me will you still like me? *Part 4:* Overcoming the fear of abandonment *7.* If I don't meet the expectations of others, what will happen to them and me? *8.* What if the people I've given my love to leave me or betray me? *Part 5:* Overcoming the fear of truth *9.* If I remember and reveal what happened to me, will the pain be insurmountable? *10.* How can I have these doubts about God and still call myself a Christian? *Part 6:* Overcoming the fear of making the wrong choices *11.* What if I never live up to my potential? *12.* What if reaching my goals isn't enough?

Lord of My Rocking Boat Carole Mayhall

NavPress, 1992, $5.00, paper, 157 pp., for counselees

Description Discover how the Lord's clear voice can quiet the waves and bring you inner peace and strength even in the midst of life's greatest storms.

Author Carole Mayhall (B.A., Wheaton College) is a popular conference speaker and author of numerous works.

Contents *Part 1:* What rocks my boat? *1.* Problems *2.* People *3.* Priorities *4.* Pain *5.* Worthless things *6.* Personalities *7.* Prisons *8.* The tidal wave *9.* Leaks *10.* Soaring *Part 2:* Who then is this? *11.* The God of details *12.* The God of sunshine *13.* The God of delights

Five Remedies for Worry D. F. Miller

Ligouri Publications, $.75, paper, 24 pp., for counselees

Description Clarifies three important facts about worry: Some worry is necessary, excessive worry is harmful, much of worry is useless. Helps those who worry keep anxieties working for them, not against them.

Coping with Anxiety Frank B. Minirth and Paul D. Meier

Christian Family Video, 1991, $19.95, video, for both counselors and counselees

Description Part of the Minirth-Meier Church Counseling Video Library. The series is designed to enhance the counseling process as clients take the videos home for viewing. This title focuses on controlling anxiety from a psychological, physical, and biblical standpoint.

Authors Doctors Minirth and Meier have gained national prominence for their successful blending of biblical principles with proven clinical and medical treatment. They are nationally recognized authors of over 60 biblically based books on common psychological issues with over three million copies in print.

Worry-Free Living Frank B. Minirth, Paul D. Meier, and Don Hawkins

Janet Thoma (a division of Thomas Nelson), 1989, $10.99, paper, 224 pp., for both counselors and counselees

Description The Minirth-Meier Clinic's proven methods for dealing with the causes, symptoms, and cures of anxiety are available in this unique self-help book.

Authors Psychiatrists Frank Minirth and Paul Meier are senior officers of the Minirth-Meier Clinic in Richardson, Tex. Don Hawkins established *The Minirth-Meier Clinic* radio program. He now produces a nationwide call-in program called *Life Perspectives* as well as the radio feature *The Rapha Answer.*

Contents *Part 1:* The age of anxiety *1.* What this book can and can't do for you *Part 2:* How to overcome anxiety *2.* The hidden emotion in the age of anxiety *3.* Eight myths: "you'll get over it" *4.* Who's apt to become anxious? *5.* Over the brink *6.* The cover-ups: defense mechanisms *7.* Self-help or professional care? *Part 3:* How to prevent anxiety from recurring *8.* Ten ways to prevent anxiety *9.* The balanced lifestyle *10.* Self-talk/self-concept *11.* Friends in need *12.* Worry-free living is a choice / *Appendix: 1.* Guidelines for fighting fair *2.* Defense mechanisms *3.* The complexity of anxiety *4.* Treatment approaches for anxiety *5.* Anxiety—a biblical and theological perspective.

Anxiety—The Nagging Emotion Clyde M. Narramore

Narramore Christian Foundation, $.50, paper, for counselees

Description One of the many booklets available from the Narramore Christian Foundation. Designed to be handed to a person beginning to come to grips with a problem in living.

Author Dr. Clyde M. Narramore is a licensed psychologist and the president and founder of the Narramore Christian Foundation—a charitable, nonprofit educational, training, and counseling organization ministering primarily to the Christian community. He is also the founder of the Rosemead School of Psychology and author of 29 books.

How to Handle Fear Clyde M. Narramore

Narramore Christian Foundation, $.35, paper, for counselees

Description One of the many booklets available from the Narramore Christian Foundation. Designed to be handed to a person beginning to come to grips with a problem in living.

Author Dr. Clyde M. Narramore is a licensed psychologist and the president and founder of the Narramore Christian Foundation—a charitable, nonprofit educational, training, and counseling organization ministering primarily to the Christian community. He is also the founder of the Rosemead School of Psychology and author of 29 books.

Anxiety, Phobias, and Panic *Taking Charge and Conquering Fear,* Reneau Z. Peurifoy

LifeSkills, 1992, $12.95, paper, 285 pp., for both counselors and counselees

Description Designed as a series of 15 easy-to-follow lessons, this book begins by answering the most commonly asked questions about anxiety. The lessons then describe how to use powerful cognitive and behavioral approaches to change the way you think, feel, and act. The book is full of practical exercises showing the reader how to apply the concepts and ideas it presents. Instructions for the exercises are given step-by-step in simple language. In use nationwide by therapists and treatment facilities. Though not distinctively religious, it is widely known as a very effective tool for counselors. Forty-two thousand copies in print. German and Spanish translations due next year.

Author Reneau Z. Peurifoy, M.A., M.F.C.C., has a private practice in Sacramento, Calif. He has specialized in anxiety-related problems since 1981. He also works with couples and problems with school-aged children.

Contents *1*. What, why, and how *2*. Reducing the symptoms of anxiety *3*. Identifying and reducing the sources of anxiety *4*. Eight common forms of distorted thinking *5*. Learning to enjoy being human *6*. Becoming a positive realist *7*. The excessive need for approval *8*. Eliminating the self-defeating behaviors commonly associated with anxiety *9*. The process of change *10*. Feeling good about yourself *11*. Making anger your ally *12*. Standing up for yourself *13*. Staying on track *14*. Continuing your growth

Conquering Fear *A Guide to Living Anxiety-Free in the Stress-Filled '90's,* Karen Randau

Rapha Resources, 1992, $9.99, paper, for counselees

Description Through actual case studies and God's healing power, *Conquering Fear* untangles the mysteries behind your emotional overload and teaches healthy ways to express your emotions. You can overcome the anxiety and fear that stifles creativity, thwarts relationships, and crushes self-esteem.

Learning More about Anxiety Attacks Karen Randau

Rapha Resources, $2.50, paper, for both counselors and counselees

Description A thoughtful approach that helps people understand the frightening mysteries of anxiety. This concise booklet helps anxiety-prone victims learn how to like themselves and how to express their emotions in a healthy manner.

Recovery from Fear Dale Ryan and Juanita Ryan

InterVarsity Press, 1992, $4.99, paper, 60 pp., for both counselors and counselees

Description This Bible study is part of a series of 16 volumes on various recovery themes. Each book contains studies on six biblical texts. Leader's notes are provided for group study.

Authors Dale Ryan is the executive director of the Recovery Partnership, the parent organization to the National Association for Christian Recovery. Juanita Ryan is a counselor in private practice in Hacienda Heights, Calif.

Contents *1*. Abram's fear and God's faithfulness *2*. Gideon's fear and God's encouragement *3*. Peter's fear and God's empowerment *4*. Esther's fear and God's people *5*. Moses' fear and God's provisions *6*. David's fear and God's protection / *Leader's notes*

Let Go of Fear *Tackling the Worst Enemy,* Carlos G. Valles

Ligouri Publications, 1993, $9.95, paper, for counselees

Description How to understand and confront the crippling fears that stifle our emotional and spiritual lives.

Tips for the Worry Wart Edward R. Walsh

Ligouri Publications, 1989, $.75, paper, 24 pp., for counselees

Description Presents practical, proven techniques to help readers control their worries, channel their anxieties, and gradually rid themselves of this disruptive habit.

Does God Really Love Me? *Turning God's Love Loose in Your Life,* Earl D. Wilson

InterVarsity Press, 1986, $4.99, paper, 96 pp., for both counselors and counselees

Description Helping readers overcome feelings of guilt, inferiority, and fear, Earl D. Wilson shows how to recognize and appreciate God's love.

Author Earl D. Wilson (Ph.D., University of Oregon) is associate professor of clinical and counseling psychology at Western Conservative Baptist Seminary and director of Lake Psychological and Counseling Services in Oregon.

Contents *1*. Why all this talk about love? *2*. God's extravagant love *3*. Savoring: the secret to feeling loved *4*. A sinner looks at love *5*. Understanding the source of love *6*. Love as a lifestyle *7*. Does love have a price tag? *8*. Why does God love us anyway?

Finding Freedom from Fear *A Contemporary Study from the Psalms,* David Wright

Zondervan Publishing House, 1990, $7.95, paper, 184 pp., for counselees

Description Answers the question: How can the Bible help me cope with my anxieties and fears? Presents the unique spiritual resources that Christians possess to face and conquer fear. Provides helpful explanations of what fear is, where it comes from, how it affects our lives, and how to cope with it successfully. David Wright uses the life of King David and selected Psalms as well as popular psychological material to illustrate and explore fear, stress, and faith.

Author Wright studied at Indiana Weslyan University and Western Evangelical Seminary. He has served various congregations as youth pastor and pastor and is currently director of Weslyan Bible Institute in England.

Contents *1.* The daily adventure of living with confidence *2.* Understanding our built-in alarm *3.* Taking the interactive approach *4.* Raising courage in the sanctuary of God's presence *5.* Building a stable life foundation *6.* Gaining perspective through praise *7.* Finding hope in personal history *8.* Finding comfort in a community of faith *9.* Creating a climate of confidence.

Afraid No More! H. Norman Wright

Tyndale House Publishers, 1989, $7.99, paper, 166 pp., for both counselors and counselees

Description An experienced counselor shows how to recognize fear, replace it with faith, and become the person God intended.

Author H. Norman Wright is the founder and director of Family Counseling and Enrichment and the seminar ministry Christian Marriage Enrichment in Tustin, Calif. A counselor and seminar speaker, he is also a prolific author.

Contents *1.* The key to freedom *2.* How to stop feeding your fears *3.* Understanding your need for control *4.* Taking the risk out of intimacy *5.* Moving beyond rejection *6.* Learning to love again *7.* Neutralizing failure *8.* Enjoying the success you deserve *9.* Worry—first cousin to fear *10.* Five steps for defeating fear *11.* Meeting your fears with faith

Coping with Anxiety

Abbey Press, 1994, $.50 each, paper, 8 pp., for counselees

Description Part of the New CareSteps series from Abbey Press. Each CareStep pamphlet (three-panel) is filled with insightful advice and quotes from respected leaders in the helping professions.

Very useful during the early stages of recovery. The underlying message in all CareSteps pamphlets is the emphasis on using all one's resources—emotional, physical, mental, social, and spiritual to cope with life's biggest challenges. This title emphasizes getting life in balance, realizing anxiety is the fear of discomfort, asking oneself if anxiety is really grieving, and getting professional help if necessary.

When Fear and Anxiety Seem to Take Control

Abbey Press, $.50 each, paper, 8 pp., for counselees

Description Part of the CareNotes series from Abbey Press. CareNotes are short booklets that help readers identify issues and begin the process of seeking resolution. Anecdotal and uplifting. Beautiful photographs grace the covers. Over 20 million CareNotes have been sold in just over five years. Can be used as an alternative to a greeting card or in conjunction with pastoral care visits.

Anxiety Disorders Association of America

Anxiety Disorders Association of America. An organization

Description The ADAA is a secular organization dedicated to promoting the welfare of individuals with anxiety disorders such as phobias, post-traumatic stress disorder, panic attacks, and other problems related to anxiety. They offer a national referral database for therapists who specialize in anxiety disorders and self-help support groups.

6. Burnout

Be Good to Yourself *Giving Yourself Permission to Enjoy Life,* Rich Buhler

Janet Thoma (a division of Thomas Nelson), 1994, $9.99, paper, 192 pp., for counselees

Description The seasoned counselor and popular radio host helps readers discover a healthy balance between meeting the needs of others and nurturing their own personal needs.

Author Rich Buhler is host of the nationally syndicated radio program *Table Talk.*

A Guide to Retreat *For All God's Shepherds,* Reuben P. Job

Abingdon Press, 1994, $14.95, paper, 200 pp., for both counselors and counselees

Description If leaders are to remain vital in their ministry, and if they are to become spiritually, emotionally, and physically healthy, pastors need time apart for sanctuary, nourishment, healing, and renewal. This project offers spiritual direction for the leader's time apart, providing flexible structure and content for times of personal reflection. Includes retreat patterns, an essay, excerpted readings, follow-up devotional exercises, an anthology of related readings, and more.

Author Reuben P. Job is a consultant in spiritual formation to the General Board of Discipleship, where he was formerly world editor of the Upper Room publishing program.

Contents When all I hear is silence / When others tell me who I am / In the midst of faults and failures / The tension between doing and being / Do I have a future in the church? / Who really calls and sends?

Before Burnout *Balanced Living for Busy People,* Frank B. Minirth, Paul D. Meier, et al.

Moody Press, 1990, $8.99, paper, 189 pp., for counselees

Description Hard-working people are often the most productive employees and workers in the church. But when overused, this strength can become a weakness and lead to burnout. In this book, you'll find practical ideas to help prevent burnout and relate to yourself, your loved ones, and God in more healthy, enjoyable ways.

Authors Frank Minirth, M.D., is president of the Minirth-Meier Clinic in Richardson, Tex. Don Hawkins, Th.M., is director of radio communications for Rapha, Inc. Paul Meier, M.D., is executive vice president of the Minirth-Meier Clinic in Richardson, Tex. Chris Thurman, M.D., is a licensed psychologist at the Minirth-Meier Clinic.

Contents *1.* The burnout prone personality *2.* Two kinds of perfectionists *3.* Road hazards of the obsessive-compulsive *4.* Is my thinking straight? *5.* Facing my feelings *6.* How did I get this way? *7.* Perfect or perfectionist? *8.* At the end of my rope *9.* Reaching balance or burnout *10.* Human ability and divine enablement *11.* Solving our relational problems *12.* Relating positively to others *13.* Handling the circumstances of life *14.* Beyond death—the last enemy

Burnout Frank B. Minirth and Paul D. Meier

Christian Family Video, 1991, $19.95, video, for both counselors and counselees

Description Part of the Minirth-Meier Church Counseling Video Library. The series is designed to enhance the counseling process as clients take the videos home for viewing. This title explores the symptoms and causes of burnout, with special emphasis on the road to recovery and how to counter the stresses that can cause burnout in your life.

Authors Doctors Minirth and Meier have gained national prominence for their successful blending of biblical principles with proven clinical and medical treatment. They are nationally recognized authors of over 60 biblically based books on common psychological issues with over three million copies in print.

How to Beat Burnout *Help for Men and Women,* Frank B. Minirth, Don Hawkins, et al.

Moody Press, 1986, $7.99, paper, 152 pp., for counselees

Description Defines the problem, discusses the symptoms and treatment, and describes permanent solutions. Over 106,000 copies in print.

Authors Frank Minirth, M.D., is president of the Minirth-Meier Clinic in Richardson, Tex. Don Hawkins, Th.M., is director of radio communications for Rapha, Inc. Paul Meier, M.D., is executive vice president of the Minirth-Meier Clinic in Richardson, Tex. Richard Flournoy, Ph.D., is a licensed psychologist in full-time private practice in the Dallas area.

Contents *1.* What is burnout and who gets it? *2.* Warning: downward spiral ahead *3.* Unfulfilled expectations: the burnout burden *4.* Bitterness: a hidden root *5.* The workaholic and his workplace *6.* Burning out for God *7.* Jesus treats 12 tired men *8.* Starting the upward spiral physically *9.* Starting the upward spiral emotionally *10.* Starting the upward spiral spiritually *11.* The rekindling of hope *12.* Recovery from burnout

Burnout! Clyde M. Narramore

Narramore Christian Foundation, $.50, paper, for both counselors and counselees

Description One of the many booklets available from the Narramore Christian Foundation. Designed to be handed to a person beginning to come to grips with a problem in living.

Author Dr. Clyde M. Narramore is a licensed psychologist and the president and founder of the Narramore Christian Foundation—a charitable, nonprofit educational, training, and counseling organization ministering primarily to the Christian community. He is also the founder of the Rosemead School of Psychology and author of 29 books.

Compassion Fatigue *Worn Out from Fatigue,* Randy Reynolds

Serendipity, 1990, $6.95, paper, 80 pp., for both counselors and counselees

Description A 7- or 14-week course utilizing Scripture and discussion questions. Designed to be used by anyone in a caregiving situation. This might be a professional, a volunteer, or one family member giving care to another.

Author Randy Reynolds is director of Renewal Counseling in Tuscon, Ariz., and served as a pastor for more than 15 years.

Contents *1.* Worn out from caring *2.* The gift of caring *3.* The causes of burnout *4.* Dependency *5.* Indispensable? *6.* Self-protection *7.* Recovery

Wounded Warriors *Surviving Seasons of Stress,* R. Loren Sandford

Victory House Publishing, 1987, $7.95, paper, 124 pp., for counselees

Description Pastor R. Loren Sandford openly shares his own struggles with pastoral burnout, stress, and depression and explores ways of recovery. His topics include three kinds of damage (onset, breakdown, and incapacity), personal survival, breaking destructive life patterns, and living with a wounded warrior.

Author R. Loren Sandford is a graduate of Fuller Theological Seminary and pastors in Colorado. He previously served as director of Elijah House where he worked as a full-time counselor.

Contents *1.* Three kinds of damage *2.* Stage 1—onset *3.* Stage 2—breakdown begins *4.* Stage 3—incapacity *5.* Personal survival—what the wounded one can do *6.* Breaking destructive life patterns *7.* Living with a wounded warrior *8.* Epilogue

Ministry Burnout John A. Sanford

Westminster/John Knox Press, 1992, $8.95, paper, 115 pp., for counselors

Description John Sanford deals concretely with the circumstances that give rise to spiritual exhaustion and identifies its underlying dynamics. He studies each problem in detail and provides approaches and practical suggestions for dealing with it. Reviews the psychology of the ministering person to show how an individual can mitigate such problems by being more realistic with himself or herself.

Author John A. Sanford is a Jungian analyst and pastoral counselor in private practice in San Diego. He is the author of numerous books.

Contents *1.* Ministry burnout: a special problem *2.* The problem of the endless task *3.* The airy work of the ministering person *4.* The revolving wheel *5.* Dealing with expectations *6.* Help through relationship *7.* Feeding the soul *8.* The problem of egocentricity *9.* The face we put on *10.* Elijah's problem *11.* The problem of the exhausted ego *12.* Finding energy again

Freedom from the Performance Trap *Letting Go of the Need to Achieve,* David A. Seamands

Victor Books, 1988, $9.99, paper, 204 pp., for counselees

Description No matter how hard performance-oriented Christians try, they never feel like they're accomplishing all they should. David Seamands shows how the grace of God can free believers from the performance trap.

Author David Seamands is professor emeritus of pastoral ministries and counselor in residence at Asbury Theological Seminary in Wilmore, Ky.

Contents *1.* The miracle of grace *2.* Barriers to grace *3.* Parental grace—or disgrace *4.* How it all began *5.* The bad news *6.* The consequences of disgrace *7.* The good news *8.* Grace and guilt *9.* Grace and emotions *10.* Grace and self-esteem *11.* Grace and negative emotions *12.* The panorama of God's grace

Burning Out for God *How to Be Used by God without Being Used Up,* Elizabeth Skoglund

InterVarsity Press, 1988, $2.99, paper, 32 pp., for counselors

Description It's better to burn out than rust out, or so the saying goes. But are these really the only two choices? Is anything less than burning out for God a sin? Elizabeth Skoglund, author and psychologist, shows that the real issue is not the amount of time and energy we put into Christian activity, but something much more fundamental.

7. Child Abuse

When Child Abuse Comes to Church
Recognizing Sexual Abuse, Knowing What to Do about It, Bill Anderson

Bethany House Publishers, 1992, $8.99, paper, 174 pp., for counselors

Description A practical guidebook, not only for those who have made the terrible discovery that child sexual abuse has occurred right in their own congregation—it is for all who want to make their church safer for their children. Includes how to deal with the growing number of "perpetrators" in dire need of help and how to guide, counsel, and comfort parents of young victims.

Author Bill Anderson has pastored churches in Ohio, Pennsylvania, and Michigan. He is a graduate of Bob Jones University and Faith Theological Seminary.

Contents Child sexual abuse—an unavoidable subject *1.* Crisis: a framework for making critical decisions *2.* Investigation: what to do when you suspect abuse *3.* Denial: the brick wall blocking progress *4.* Newsplash: how to deal with the media *5.* Healing: how to identify victims *6.* Roadblocks: frustrations that hinder healing *7.* Tensions: walking the tightrope when people disagree *8.* Ethical dilemmas: finding answers to tough questions *9.* Prevention: getting beyond "it can't happen here"

The Child's Song *The Religious Abuse of Children,* Donald Capps

Westminster/John Knox Press, 1995, $9.95, paper, 188 pp.

Description Theological ideas and biblical injunctions have frequently been employed to legitimate the physical abuse of children. Capps exposes some abuses that theology and the Bible have inflicted on vast numbers of children by well-intentioned adults. More than an exposé, the book is about reconciliation and the healing of the child self.

Author Donald Capps is professor of pastoral theology at Princeton Theological Seminary. He is author of *The Poet's Gift.*

Contents *Part 1:* The loss of innocence *1.* Alice Miller on "the mutilated soul" *2.* Augustine: the vicious cycle of child abuse *3.* Religious sources of childhood trauma *4.* Letter to the Hebrews: the lasting effects of childhood trauma *5.* Abraham and Isaac: the sacrificial impulse *6.* The child Jesus as endangered self *Part 2:* Reclaiming the garden *7.* A garden of childhood verses *8.* The soul made happy

Child Abuse—What You Can Do about It
Angela R. Carl

College Press, $5.95, paper, 128 pp., for counselors

Description A twofold approach for educating young children about the realities of child abuse. Instructional material takes the children through the material, and just as importantly the leader's guide teaches the teacher how to present this sensitive subject.

Cry Softly! *The Story of Child Abuse,* Margaret O. Hyde

Westminster/John Knox Press, 1986, $10.00, cloth, 212 pp., for counselees

Description In this best-selling book, the author discusses the various forms of abuse—physical, sexual, and emotional—and provides nonsensational examples of each. She traces the extensive history of child abuse, explores ways to prevent it, and includes suggestions for further reading.

Author Margaret O. Hyde is author of an outstanding list of books for young people. Hyde has written documentaries for NBC-TV and taught children, young adults, and adults.

Contents *1.* Cry softly, keep the secret, or leave the house *2.* Who are the child abusers? *3.* Who are the crying children? *4.* Children of very long ago *5.* Hurt children in yesterday's England *6.* Child abuse: American style *7.* Preventing child abuse *8.* Help for the child who cries softly / *Hotlines / Suggestions for further reading / National organizations concerned with child abuse*

Counseling for Family Violence and Abuse Grant L. Martin

Word Publishing, 1987, $13.99, cloth, 281 pp., for counselors

Description Part of the resources for Christian Counseling series from Word. Dr. Martin provides guidelines for working with the abuser as well as the abused.

Author Grant L. Martin is a licensed psychologist and marriage and family therapist in Seattle, Wash.

Contents *Part 1:* Spousal abuse *1.* The frequency and history of spousal abuse *2.* The nature of spousal abuse *3.* Crisis counseling in spousal abuse *4.* Treatment of battered women *5.* Treatment of men who batter *Part 2:* Child abuse *6.* Understanding physical and emotional child abuse *7.* Sexual abuse of children *8.* Evaluation and treatment of sexually abused children *9.* Treatment of the sexual offender *Part 3:* Elder abuse *10.* Abuse of the elderly / *Recommended resources*

Critical Problems in Children and Youth
Counseling Techniques for ADD, Sexual Abuse, Custody Battles & Related Issues, Grant L. Martin

Word Publishing, 1992, $13.99, cloth, 254 pp., for counselors

Description This book is written for Christian psychologists, counselors, pastors, and students who want to be an effective instrument to point hurting children and families to the source of hope and health.

Author Grant L. Martin (Ph.D., University of Washington), a licensed psychologist and marriage and family therapist, is counselor with CRISTA Counseling Service, where he has served for over 18 years. He is also an adjunct professor in the graduate counseling program at Seattle Pacific University. Widely published, he is vice president and executive board member for the Christian Association for Psychological Studies (CAPS).

Contents *1.* Initial interviews with children *2.* Attention-deficit hyperactivity disorder: assessment *3.* Attention-deficit hyperactivity disorder: treatment *4.* The sexually abused child: identification and treatment *5.* Childhood trauma, dissociative states, and ritual abuse *6.* Custody evaluations: initial considerations *7.* Custody evaluations: the assessment process

Journal of Child Sexual Abuse *Research, Treatment & Program Innovations for Victims, Survivors . . . ,* Robert Gerrner, ed.

The Haworth Press, Inc., 1995, $34.00/year, paper, 125 pp.

Description A new journal that seeks to assist those helping victims, survivors, and offenders.

Contents Representative articles— *1.* Focused play and non-directive play therapy: can they be integrated? *2.* Interpretation of facial expressions of emotions by sexually abused girls *3.* The treatment of male sexual offenders: countertransference reactions

Childhelp USA

Childhelp USA. An organization

Description Though not a Christian organization, Childhelp USA is the nation's largest nonprofit organization combating child abuse. Along with their hotline (1-800-4-A-CHILD), they provide programs in direct intervention and treatment of abused children, family services, research, and public education.

National Center for Missing and Exploited Children

National Center for Missing and Exploited Children. An organization

Description As America's resource center for child protection, the National Center for Missing and Exploited Children spearheads national efforts to locate and recover missing children and raises public awareness about ways to prevent child abduction, molestation, and sexual exploitation. A private, nonprofit organization established in 1984.

National Committee for the Prevention of Child Abuse

National Committee for the Prevention of Child Abuse. An organization

Description A volunteer-based organization dedicated to involving all concerned citizens in actions to prevent child abuse—defined as any or all of the following: physical abuse, emotional maltreatment, neglect, and sexual abuse. Provides education, research briefs, advocacy programs, and a catalog of outstanding booklets on child abuse topics. Though not a Christian organization, a resource packet for Christian religious leaders on child abuse prevention is also available.

8. Counseling Children

Teaching Your Children to Tell Themselves the Truth *Helping Children before Misbeliefs Become Deeply Entrenched,* William Backus and Candace Backus

Bethany House Publishers, 1992, $8.99, paper, 175 pp., for both counselors and counselees

Description A handbook for parents to help build their child's self-esteem, happiness, coping skills, and good behavior. It offers practical, easy-to-follow suggestions for enabling the child to utilize the truth for solving life's problems. The child will learn to understand his/her feelings and deal effectively with them. Families are shown how to develop effective communication with one another.

Authors William Backus is a licensed clinical psychologist and an ordained Lutheran clergyman. He is founder and director of the Center for Christian Psychological Services, St. Paul, Minn., and an associate pastor of a large Lutheran church. Candace Backus is a counselor and vice president of Minnesota Psychtests, Inc.

Contents *1.* Finding out what children tell themselves *2.* Eavesdropping on a child's self-talk *3.* Entering your child's world *4.* Who's to blame? *5.* The power of emotions *6.* Managing strong feelings *7.* When your child is depressed *8.* Practical help with a child's anxiety 9. "You make me angry!" *10.* Self-mastery *11.* The bottom line—solving problems with the truth *12.* "To tell you the truth . . ."—communicating honestly *13.* Eyes on the prize

Helping Kids Cope *A Parents' Guide to Stress Management,* Arnold Burron

Chariot Family Publishing, 1992, $7.99, paper, 160 pp., for both counselors and counselees

Description Parents will learn how to recognize signs and sources of stress in their children at home and at school. Parents will also be able to teach their children how to manage the stress of adversity, focusing on improved family communication for building stress-resistant relationships.

Author Dr. Arnold Burron is professor of education at Northern Colorado University.

Counseling and Children Walter Byrd and Paul Warren

Word Publishing, 1989, $15.99, cloth, 230 pp., for counselors

Description This volume addresses behavioral issues pertaining to children from birth through 11 years and contains the most up-to-date and insightful information to advise bewildered parents.

Authors Walter Byrd is medical director and staff psychiatrist with the Minirth-Meier-Byrd Clinic in Fairfax, Va. Paul Warren is the medical director of the Minirth-Meier Clinic Child/Adolescent Division in Richardson, Tex.

Contents *Part 1:* The young child *1.* Winning the child rearing contest *2.* Needs of the young *3.* Options of the young child *4.* Ways for change with the young child *5.* More ways for change with the young child *6.* Specific problems and disorders of the young child *7.* The child with emotional disorders *Part 2:* The grade school child *8.* Needs of the grade school child *9.* Options of the grade school child *10.* Ways for change with the grade school child *11.* Anger and sibling rivalry *12.* Childhood depression and the fearful, anxious child *13.* Codependency, child abuse, and the dysfunctional family *14.* Children with habit disorders, chronic illness, and handicaps *15.* The child with an attention deficit disorder *16.* Learning disabilities *17.* The spiritual training of the child

Today I Feel Shy William L. Coleman

Bethany House Publishers, 1993, $8.99, paper, 69 pp., for counselees

Description Delightful, practical reading to help small children overcome shyness. Photo illustrations.

Author Bill Coleman has written half a dozen best-selling devotional books for children in addition to his other books. His experience as a pastor, father, and writer help give him his special relationship with children.

How to Answer Big Questions from Little Children Dixie Ruth Crase

New Hope, 1990, $3.95, paper, 47 pp., for counselors

Description Child development professor Dixie Crase answers a wide range of children's queries in this release. In addition to valuable answers, Dr. Crase gives 17 guidelines for adults to follow in answering children's questions.

Author Dixie Ruth Crase earned a Ph.D. in child development and family relations from Ohio State University. Dr. Crase is a professor of child development at Memphis State University, where she has taught for almost 25 years.

Contents Guidelines for encouraging and/or responding to children's big questions about God, Jesus, Bible, church, self, family, others, natural world

The Hyperactive Child James Dobson

Focus on the Family, 1992, $.35, paper, 15 pp., for counselees

Description Defines hyperactivity and its symptoms. Explains causes, relationship of nutrition, changes in adolescence, and use of drugs to control hyperactivity.

Author James C. Dobson, Ph.D., is founder and president of Focus on the Family. A licensed psychologist, he has authored 12 best-selling books on the family, including *The Strong Willed Child, Love Must Be Tough, Parenting Isn't for Cowards,* and the *New Dare to Discipline.*

When a Hug Won't Fix the Hurt *Walking with Your Child through Crisis,* Karen Dockrey

Victor Books, 1993, $7.99, paper, 175 pp., for counselees

Description With the conviction that God walks alongside in crisis, this book provides skills and strategies for the challenge of parenting through crisis. Helpful features include insights into a child's feelings during the crisis, ideas to help family and friends, and suggestions for additional resources.

Author Karen Dockrey, a youth worker and curriculum writer, has two school-age daughters;

one had leukemia, the other a severe hearing loss.

Contents *1.* Respond to feelings *2.* Walk through crisis together *3.* Equip to participate fully in life *4.* Invite friends to help *5.* Walk on through anger *6.* Let your child be a child *7.* Work closely with the school *8.* Answer questions honestly *9.* Expect family pain *10.* Choose to live the joy

Helping Children Cope with Death Robert V. Dodd

Herald Press, 1984, $3.95, paper, 56 pp., for both counselors and counselees

Description Robert V. Dodd helps parents and other adults know how to assist children in dealing with their feelings about death—that of a friend or loved one, or their own anticipated death.

Author Robert V. Dodd (M.Div., Duke University) has served a number of churches and participated in studies in clinical pastoral education. He is the author of a number of other works.

Contents *1.* Children experience death too *2.* What not to tell them *3.* What we should tell them *4.* The parable of the butterfly *5.* What to do with them *6.* Should children attend funerals? *7.* When a child is dying *8.* More than we could have imagined

When Your Child . . . John Drescher, Kenneth Gibble, and Neta Jackson

Herald Press, 1986, $7.95, paper, 160 pp., for counselees

Description Winner of the 1987 Silver Angel Award from Religion in Media. Twenty-five essays deal with specific situations such as loss of a pet, stealing, college attendance, a learning disability, and teenage pregnancy. Though problem centered, *When Your Child* is not pessimistic. It shows how parents, aided by faith and Christian community, worked through various situations.

An Early Journey Home *Helping Dying Children and Grieving Families,* Mary Ann Froehlich

Baker Book House, 1992, $8.99, paper, 205 pp., for both counselors and counselees

Description Mary Ann Froehlich has helped several dying children and their grieving families face death. The insights and sensitivities she has gained from her experiences are reflected in this hopeful, helpful book. She offers genuine solace to parents and siblings who are facing the death of a dearly loved child. Christians are shown how to put away their fears so they might give significant support to the terminally ill and their families.

Author Dr. Froehlich is a registered music therapist (board certified) and a certified child life specialist. She is the author of two other books.

Contents *1.* An early journey home *2.* My own journey *Part 1:* The biblical journey: preparing the helper *3.* Helpers without answers *4.* Our biblical models: fellow sufferers in Scripture *5.* When suffering turns to gold *Part 2:* Taking the journey: helping the dying child *6.* Helping through the illness and hospitalization *7.* Helping patients and families through death *8.* Zain's journey: advice from the experts *Part 3:* The long journey after: helping the grieving family *9.* Helping after the death *10.* Surviving the unbearable: more advice from the experts *11.* Special situations: miscarriages, catastrophic accidents, losing adult children *12.* Helpers or judges?: murder, the killer AIDS *13.* A family portrait *14.* A final note to helpers *Part 4: Children's health care resources / Health care organizations / Illness and grief support organizations / Therapy techniques for hospitalized children / Books*

Learning More about Attention-Deficit Disorder Juan I. Garcia

Rapha Resources, $2.50, paper, for both counselors and counselees

Description This booklet presents the most up-to-date information available on ADD. Dr. Garcia encourages families in their struggles to establish a near-to-normal environment for the child afflicted with this disorder.

Precious in His Sight *A Guide to Child Advocacy,* Diana Garland

New Hope, 1993, $6.95, paper, 84 pp., for counselors

Description Child advocates act on behalf of preschoolers, children, and youth to do for them what they cannot do for themselves. Advocates also work alongside others to empower them in what they are trying to accomplish.

Author Diana Garland (Ph.D.) is the dean of the Carver School of Social Work at the Southern Baptist Theological Seminary in Louisville, Ky. She directs the Gheens Center for Christian Family Ministry and is the organizer of the Southern Baptist Child Advocacy Network.

Contents Through children's eyes / Welcoming children / Children whom no one minds / Children in poverty / Children without hope / Children in chaos / When ministry isn't enough

After the Adoption *Learning to Cope with Sibling Rivalry, Spiritual Values . . . ,* Elizabeth Hormann

Fleming H. Revell, $9.99, paper, for both counselors and counselees

Description A practical guide to bonding the adoptive family. Parents who have adopted or anticipate adopting need this experienced advice on bonding the new child into the family.

Is This Kid "Crazy"? *Understanding Unusual Behavior,* Margaret O. Hyde

Westminster/John Knox Press, 1983, $12.00, cloth, 212 pp., for both counselors and counselees

Description Most psychology books for this age group are either self-help books or textbooks. In an innovative departure from the mold, Margaret O. Hyde presents brief sketches that illustrate behavior termed "crazy" and deals with people's reactions to it.

Author Margaret O. Hyde is author of an outstanding list of books for young people. Hyde has written documentaries for NBC-TV and taught children, young adults, and adults.

Contents *1.* Would you know a crazy person if you met one? *2.* Betty, Jane, Timmy, and Maria *3.* What's wrong with this child? *4.* The world of autistic children *5.* Schizophrenia *6.* Depression *7.* Anorexia nervosa and other eating disorders *8.* Weird, but dangerous? / *Mental health terms / Suggestions for further reading / For further information / Adolescent clinics in the United States and Canada*

Learning Disabilities *Parenting the Misunderstood,* Nancy Jessen and Dan Jessen

Serendipity, 1991, $6.95, paper, 112 pp., for counselees

Description A 7- or 14-week course utilizing Scripture and discussion questions. Designed to be used by parents of children with a learning disability as well as for any interested relative, friend, or teacher of an LD child.

Contents *1.* The one-way kid *2.* An uncommon gift *3.* Can't anyone help us? *4.* The homework question *5.* Square peg in a round hole *6.* What's a parent to do? *7.* Dealing with LD teens

Understanding Your Child's Problems *Biblically Based, Medically Reliable,*

Psychologically Sound Counsel, Grace H. Ketterman

Fleming H. Revell, 1983, $12.99, paper, 383 pp., for counselees

Description Biblically and medically sound advice for Christian parents dealing with mental, physical, emotional, and behavioral problems in their children.

Author Grace H. Ketterman, M.D., is the medical director of the Crittenton Center for Children and Adolescents in Kansas City, Mo. She is the author of many other books on parenting issues.

Contents *Introduction:* Preparing to help your child *Part 1:* The root causes of childhood problems *1.* Training and discipline problems *2.* Communication problems *3.* Mental and physical problems *Part 2:* The critical need to understand your child *4.* The foundational make-up of children *5.* The emotional and mental needs of children *6.* The social development of children *7.* The spiritual nature of children *Part 3:* The most common childhood problems *8.* Behavioral problems *9.* Emotional problems *10.* Physical problems *11.* Psychological problems *12.* Social problems *Part 4:* The resource guide for troubled parents *13.* Warning signs—how to recognize them *14.* Self-esteem—how to build it *15.* Information—how to research the data *16.* Sudden crisis—how to respond *17.* Child abuse—how to understand and overcome it *18.* Family priorities—how to reorder them

Pastoral Care with Children in Crisis
Andrew D. Lester

Westminster/John Knox Press, 1985, $11.99, paper, 142 pp., for counselors

Description After discussing underlying principles, Lester gives concrete and creative suggestions that can be used to help 5–12-year-old children share their feelings. He describes techniques of play, art, storytelling, and writing that can be employed by ministers to develop sensitive, nurturing relationships with the children in their charge.

Author Andrew D. Lester is professor of religion, Southern Baptist Theological Seminary. He has published numerous articles and books.

Contents *Part 1:* The pastor and children *1.* The pastoral neglect of children *2.* Children are parishioners too! *3.* What children in crisis need from the pastor *4.* Some basic principles of pastoral care to children *Part 2:* Methods of pastoral care of children in crisis *5.* The use of play in pastoral conversation *6.* Pastoral care through art *7.* Storytelling and pastoral care *8.* Pastoral care through writing

When Children Suffer *A Sourcebook for Ministry with Children in Crisis,* Andrew D. Lester

Westminster/John Knox Press, 1987, $16.00, cloth, 256 pp., for counselors

Description Andrew Lester serves as editor as 21 contributors draw upon personal experience to discuss the nature of crises that devastate children and suggest ways in which ministers can respond.

Author Andrew D. Lester is professor of religion, Southern Baptist Theological Seminary. He has published numerous articles and books.

Contents *1.* Ministry with children in crisis *Part 1:* Understanding the school-age child *2.* A developmental understanding of the school-age child *3.* Faith development and the school-age child *4.* What children need from significant adults *5.* Understanding and caring for the child in crisis *Part 2:* Ministry with children in particular crises *6.* Children whose parents are divorcing *7.* The bereaved child *8.* The hospitalized child *9.* The terminally ill child *10.* The chronically ill child *11.* Abused children *12.* Disabled children *13.* Children with learning disabilities *14.* Children suffering from stress and anxiety *Part 3:* Resources for ministry with children in crisis *15.* Talking about faith with children *16.* Pastoral assessment of the child and the family *17.* The extended family *18.* Referral: when, where, how

Critical Problems in Children and Youth
Counseling Techniques for ADD, Sexual Abuse, Custody Battles & Related Issues, Grant L. Martin

Word Publishing, 1992, $13.99, cloth, 254 pp., for counselors

Description This book is written for those Christian psychologists, counselors, pastors, and students who want to be an effective instrument to point hurting children and families to the source of hope and health.

Author Grant L. Martin (Ph.D., University of Washington), a licensed psychologist and marriage and family therapist, is counselor with CRISTA Counseling Service, where he has served for over 18 years. He is also an adjunct professor in the graduate counseling program at Seattle Pacific University. Widely published, he is vice president and executive board member for the Christian Association for Psychological Studies (CAPS).

Contents *1.* Initial interviews with children *2.* Attention-deficit hyperactivity disorder: assessment *3.* Attention-deficit hyperactivity disorder: treatment 4. The sexually abused child: identification and treatment 5. Childhood trauma, dissociative states, and ritual abuse 6. Custody evaluations: initial considerations 7. Custody evaluations: the assessment process

The Hyperactive Child *What You Need to Know about ADD—Facts, Myths, and Treatment,* Grant L. Martin

Victor Books, 1992, $8.99, paper, 192 pp., for both counselors and counselees

Description This book will help the reader identify the symptoms and causes of ADHD and find caring professionals who can offer effective treatment. Shows how to evaluate the pros and cons of medication for ADHD, to improve the way a parent deals with a child at home, to devise appropriate educational strategies for home and school, and to discover sound spiritual guidance for the problem. Contains an outstanding appendix on a wide variety of further resources for ADHD.

Author Grant L. Martin (Ph.D., University of Washington), a licensed psychologist and marriage and family therapist, is counselor with CRISTA Counseling Service, where he has served for over 18 years. He is also an adjunct professor in the graduate counseling program at Seattle Pacific University. Widely published, he is vice president and executive board member for the Christian Association for Psychological Studies (CAPS).

Contents *Part 1:* Identification of ADHD *1.* Do I have a hyperactive child? *2.* Why is my child hyperactive? *3.* How do I find help? *Part 2:* Treatment of ADHD *4.* How can I help parents? *5.* How can my child change? *6.* How can the physician help? *7.* How can the school help? *8.* How can God help? *Part 3:* Resources for ADHD

The Parent's Guide to Solving School Problems Elaine K. McEwan

Harold Shaw Publishers, 1992, $9.99, paper, 323 pp., for counselees

Description This practical how-to guide for busy parents answers questions and provides advice on topics like reading, writing, math, learning problems, motivation, behavior and social problems, stress and anxiety, learning disabilities, and attention deficit disorder. A particularly helpful feature of the book is the list of resources and reading materials that accompany each chapter. The book is user-friendly and written without educational jargon. Parents will find helpful hints on how to make the formal school system (either public or private) work for them.

Author Elaine K. McEwan is an experienced teacher and administrator. She is currently Assistant Superintendent for Instruction in a Chicago suburb. She is the author of several parenting books, a fiction series for kids, and a contributing editor to *Christian Parenting Today* magazine. She speaks widely to parent groups and writes a regular advice column for parents in her local newspaper.

Contents *1.* What's the problem? *2.* It's all their fault *3.* Reading and writing *4.* Two plus two equals five *5.* He won't do it *6.* Maximizing your child's learning *7.* Nobody likes me *8.* She won't follow the rules *9.* Learning disabilities and attention deficit disorder *10.* The troubled student / *Conclusion*—The spiritual side to school problems / *Appendixes A–D / Resources*

Tough Kids *Help for Parenting Difficult Children,* David R. Miller

Chariot Family Publishing, 1993, $7.99, paper, 192 pp., for both counselors and counselees

Description Parents experiencing behavioral problems with their children can identify problems and move them toward resolution with help and encouragement from family counselor Dr. David Miller. *Tough Kids* gives biblical perspective to parenting difficult children, as well as many anecdotes from real families who were "at the end of their rope" over problem behavior.

Author David R. Miller, married for more than three decades and a father and grandfather, earned his doctorate in counseling psychology from the University of South Carolina in 1981. Dr. Miller is a licensed counselor in Va., has authored seven books, and is a frequent seminar leader for single and step parents. Dr. Miller is professor of counseling and psychology at Liberty University in Lynchburg, Va.

Your Child's Hidden Needs *Build Healthy Relationships through Preventive Parenting,* Bruce Narramore

Fleming H. Revell, 1980, $8.99, paper, 219 pp., for counselees

Description Six reasons why children misbehave. Includes effective exercises for resolving and preventing behavioral problems.

61

Author Dr. Bruce Narramore is the author of many books integrating biblical teaching and psychology. He is dean of Rosemead School of Psychology at Biola University in southern Calif.

Contents *Part 1:* Parenting can be positive *1.* An ounce of prevention is worth a pound of cure *2.* Your child is different *Part 2:* Your child's hidden needs *3.* Mommy, do you love me? *4.* Living in a world of giants *5.* Is your child "too good"? *6.* "I'm bored" *Part 3:* Why children misbehave *7.* When hidden needs aren't met *8.* Isn't anything normal? *9.* Your child and Adam *10.* Finding your child's hidden needs *Part 4:* Exercises for growing parents *11.* What do we do next?

Children Who Are Shy Clyde M. Narramore

Narramore Christian Foundation, $.35, paper, for counselees

Description One of the many booklets available from the Narramore Christian Foundation. Designed to be handed to a person beginning to come to grips with a problem in living.

Author Dr. Clyde M. Narramore is a licensed psychologist and the president and founder of the Narramore Christian Foundation—a charitable, nonprofit educational, training, and counseling organization ministering primarily to the Christian community. He is also the founder of the Rosemead School of Psychology and author of 29 books.

Children with Nervous and Emotional Problems Clyde M. Narramore

Narramore Christian Foundation, $.35, paper, for both counselors and counselees

Description One of the many booklets available from the Narramore Christian Foundation. Designed to be handed to a person beginning to come to grips with a problem in living.

Author Dr. Clyde M. Narramore is a licensed psychologist and the president and founder of the Narramore Christian Foundation—a charitable, nonprofit educational, training, and counseling organization ministering primarily to the Christian community. He is also the founder of the Rosemead School of Psychology and author of 29 books.

Danger Signals in Your Child's Behavior Clyde M. Narramore

Narramore Christian Foundation, $.50, paper, for counselees

Description One of the many booklets available from the Narramore Christian Foundation. Designed to be handed to a person beginning to come to grips with a problem in living.

Author Dr. Clyde M. Narramore is a licensed psychologist and the president and founder of the Narramore Christian Foundation—a charitable, nonprofit educational, training, and counseling organization ministering primarily to the Christian community. He is also the founder of the Rosemead School of Psychology and author of 29 books.

Ten Danger Signals in Your Child's Behavior Clyde M. Narramore

Narramore Christian Foundation, 1990, $19.99, video, for both counselors and counselees

Description Dr. Narramore and Mark McNear list ten danger signals that should not be overlooked. This video is especially valuable for parents and teachers.

Author Dr. Clyde M. Narramore is a licensed psychologist and the president and founder of the Narramore Christian Foundation—a charitable, nonprofit educational, training, and counseling organization ministering primarily to the Christian community. He is also the founder of the Rosemead School of Psychology and author of 29 books.

Three Cheers for Big Ears Mary Rose Pearson

Tyndale House Publishers, 1992, $2.99, paper, 48 pp., for counselees

Description Children will grasp important lessons about accepting themselves and others in *Three Cheers for Big Ears*. When the neighborhood children ridicule Joshua about his big ears, he begins to wonder why God made him that way. But Joshua soon discovers that God can use him just the way he is—it's what he is like on the inside that counts. With sensitivity and insight, this book helps children learn to be thankful for who they are, and it reminds us all that God wants us to be kind to everyone—even those who are unkind to us.

Author Mary Rose Pearson has taught children in church classes for over 56 years. She has authored 12 books for ministry to children.

Love Letters *Responding to Children in Pain,* Doris Sandford

Multnomah Books (Questar), $8.99, paper, 120 pp., for counselors

Description These love letters are warm answers to letters from children who have experienced major hurts. Each page is filled with actual letters and pictures written and drawn by kids, along with sympathetic and comforting responses by Sandford. Wonderful for hurting children and the adults who love them.

bivaD: For Parents of Learning Disabled Children Anne Sheppard

The Pilgrim Press, 1983, $1.75, paper, 24 pp., for counselees

Description (bivaD is the way a dyslexic boy named David occasionally spelled his name.) Part of the Looking Up series of booklets from the Pilgrim Press. For the cost of a greeting card, this booklet provides the reader with 24 pages of insight, wisdom, Scripture readings, meditation, direction, comfort, and prayer.

Identifying a Hyperactive Child John Taylor

Focus on the Family, 1992, free, 3 pp., for both counselors and counselees

Description A checklist developed by Dr. John Taylor to help parents know if their child is hyperactive. Rates 21 behaviors to determine degree of hyperactivity.

Things That Go Bump in the Night *How to Help Your Children Overcome Their Pain,* Paul Warren and Frank B. Minirth

Janet Thoma (a division of Thomas Nelson), 1993, $17.99, cloth, 288 pp., for counselees

Description Parents can help their children work through and resolve the natural fears of childhood. Discusses the fears common to each passage of childhood development and how to deal with those fears.

Authors Dr. Paul Warren is a behavioral pediatrician and adolescent specialist, as well as the medical director of the Minirth-Meier Clinic Child/Adolescent Division in Richardson, Tex. Dr. Frank Minirth is cofounder of the Minirth-Meier Clinic. He is the coauthor of more than 30 books.

Contents *Part 1:* The power of fear—understanding the deep-seated fears of childhood *1.* The monster in my closet is growing *Part 2:* Infant and toddler—the bottle and blanky set *2.* Rock-a-bye baby—the fears of infancy *3.* Fears of the toddler and early preschooler *Part 3:* Late preschooler—the sandbox set *4.* The cat that went bump in the night—the fear of power people *5.* Fears in the daily grind—practical guidelines for problem solving *6.* Tell me a story *Part 4:* Grade-schoolers—the skateboard set *7.* Avoiding entitlement *8.* What do you think of me? *9.* Helping the mind deal with fears *Part 5:* Teenagers—the mall and car-keys set *10.* I'm not me, but I'm not you—the terrors of the teen years *11.* What am I getting into?—a fear of life itself *12.* The shift to adulthood *Part 6:* The extended family and other situations *13.* Granny knows best? the grandparent's role *14.* Single parenting *15.* Fear strikes back—signs of growth

Kids Have Feelings, Too! *Helping Your Children Understand and Deal with Their Emotions,* H. Norman Wright and Gary Jackson Oliver

Victor Books, 1993, $14.99, cloth, 235 pp., for counselees

Description This book is designed to stress the important role emotions play in a child's development, give parents tools to nurture healthy emotional response in their child, deal with specific emotions that tend to be most problematic, and help parents deal with their own feelings and responses.

Authors H. Norman Wright is a best-selling author, licensed marriage, family, and child therapist, and director of Family Counseling and Enrichment. Gary J. Oliver is a psychologist at Southwest Counseling Associates and visiting professor at Denver Seminary.

Contents *1.* Understanding healthy emotional response *2.* Growing emotionally healthy children *3.* Parenting by design *4.* Dealing with depression *5.* Dealing with anger *6.* Dealing with grief and loss *7.* Dealing with fear and anxiety *8.* Dealing with guilt and shame *9.* Identifying stress in your child *10.* Helping your children handle stress *11.* Your child's self-esteem *12.* Dealing with your emotional responses to your children

Recognizing and Helping Hurting Children *A Training Video for Teachers and Parents,* H. Norman Wright

Gospel Light Video, 1995, $19.95, video, 1 hour

Description H. Norman Wright can help you reach out to children who are suffering or depressed. This one-hour video will help you recognize depression or the signs of abuse, find ways to help children, and know when to refer children for professional help.

Author H. Norman Wright is one of America's best-known Christian marriage and family counselors. He is the author of more than 55 books.

Contents 1. Recognize and deal with stress in children 2. Define abuse and recognize the signs 3. Explore the feelings and concerns of children of divorce 4. Know how to understand and reach children in pain 5. Recognize and help ADD/ADHD children 6. Know when and how to refer to professional counselors or social workers

Children With Attention Deficit Disorders

Children With Attention Deficit Disorders. An organization

Description Secular organization that helps parents who have ADD children. Assists in the establishment of self-help support groups.

9. Codependency

Confronting Toxic People *Taking Your Personal Power,* Susan Forward

> CompCare Publishers, 1989, $9.95, cassette(s), 40 minutes, for both counselors and counselees

Description A live 40-minute seminar wherein best-selling author Susan Forward outlines a four-step program to help ACAs and ACDFs clear up many adult conflicts by dealing with childhood issues and experiences. Moves listeners beyond denial.

Author Susan Forward, Ph.D., is a pioneer in the treatment of adult victims of child abuse and adult children of alcoholics. She maintains a private practice in California.

Day By Day Love Is a Choice *Daily Devotions for Codependents,* Richard Fowler, Jerilyn Fowler, Brian Newman, and Deborah Newman

> Janet Thoma (a division of Thomas Nelson), 1991, $7.99, paper, 396 pp., for counselees

Description Part of the Serenity Meditation series. Daily inspirational messages based on the ten-stage recovery process from the best-selling *Love Is a Choice.*

From Bondage to Bonding *Escaping Codependency—Embracing Biblical Love,* Nancy Groom

> NavPress, 1992, $15.00, paper, 206 pp., for both counselors and counselees

Description While most books on the subject of codependency focus on escaping from damaging relationships, few provide much insight into the flip side of the issue—enjoying true healing and experiencing genuine love. This work begins by examining the complex roots of codependency in the light of the Bible's teachings on relating to self, others, and God. Demonstrates how to replace the damaging influences in your life with healthy ones and showing how to make genuine biblical love a central part of your life. A thorough and nontechnical approach to assessment and recovery, this book will help you discover how the gospel can restore you to healthy biblical bonding with God and others. A workbook is also available for group study.

Author Nancy Groom, author of *Married without Masks,* is a freelance writer and teacher on the subject of relationships, recovery, and spiritual growth. She lives with her husband and son in Miami, Fla.

Contents *Part 1:* What does bondage look like? *1.* Codependency: a self-focused way of life *2.* Self-forfeiture: resigned to helplessness *3.* Self-contempt: inclined to feel worthless *4.* Self-aggrandizement: desperate to control *5.* Self-sufficiency: determined to stay safe *6.* Self-deception: committed to denial *Part 2:* Where does bondage come from? *7.* Fervent longings *8.* Painful losses *9.* Self-protective pretense *10.* Autonomous independence *Part 3:* What is the route to bonding? *11.* The healing grief *12.* The wonder of grace *13.* The freedom of surrender *Part 4:* What does bonding look like? *14.* Reciprocal grace: free to love and forgive *15.* Courageous vulnerability: free to abandon denial *16.* Mutual freedom: free to relinquish control *17.* Spiritual vitality: free to trust and obey *18.* Sacrificial love: free to risk and suffer

From Bondage to Bonding—Guidebook *A Working Guide to Recovery from Codependency & Other Injuries of the Heart,* Nancy Groom

> NavPress, 1992, $15.00, paper, 215 pp., for both counselors and counselees

Description Companion guide to the book of the same title. Twenty-four sessions for individual or group use. Includes helpful guidelines, instructions for leaders, and worksheets. Christ-centered and biblical.

Author Nancy Groom, author of *Married without Masks,* is a freelance writer and teacher on the subject of relationships, recovery, and spiritual growth. She lives with her husband and son in Miami, Fla.

Love Is a Choice *Recovery for Codependent Relationships,* Robert Hemfelt, Frank Minirth, and Paul Meier

Janet Thoma (a division of Thomas Nelson), 1989, $10.99, paper, 288 pp., for both counselors and counselees

Description Minirth-Meier's successful ten-step recovery process from codependency—a condition in which a person's happiness depends upon people, things, or behaviors.

Authors Dr. Robert Hemfelt is a psychologist who specializes in the treatment of chemical dependencies, codependency, and compulsive disorders. Doctors Minirth and Meier have gained national prominence for their successful blending of biblical principles with proven clinical and medical treatment. They are nationally recognized authors of over 60 biblically based books on common psychological issues with over three million copies in print.

Contents *Part 1:* What codependency is *1.* The thread that runs so true *2.* The way codependency works *Part 2:* The causes of codependency *3.* Unmet emotional needs *4.* Lost childhood *5.* The repletion compulsion *Part 3:* Factors that perpetuate codependency *6.* The snowball effect of addiction *7.* Denial *8.* Anger *Part 4:* Codependency in interpersonal relationships *9.* Codependent or healthy relationships *10.* Codependent or interdependent relationships *11.* Making relationships work *12.* The roles people play *Part 5:* The ten stages of recovery *13.* Exploring your relationships *14.* Breaking the addiction cycle *15.* Leaving home and saying goodbye *16.* Grieving your loss *17.* Seeing yourself in a new light *18.* New experiences in reparenting *19.* Accountability and maintenance

Love Is a Choice—Workbook *Recovery for Codependent Relationships,* Robert Hemfelt, Frank Minirth, Paul Meier, et al.

Janet Thoma (a division of Thomas Nelson), 1991, $10.99, paper, 288 pp., for counselees

Description The doctors counsel you directly in this unique workbook. Based on the codependency recovery principles in *Love Is a Choice.* Interactive, fill-in-the-blank format.

Authors Dr. Robert Hemfelt is a psychologist who specializes in the treatment of chemical dependencies, codependency, and compulsive disorders. Doctors Minirth and Meier have gained national prominence for their successful blending of biblical principles with proven clinical and medical treatment. They are nationally recog-

nized authors of over 60 biblically based books on common psychological issues with over three million copies in print.

Contents *Part 1:* The causes of codependency *1.* Getting started *2.* What is codependency? *3.* Running on empty *4.* The well-hidden truth *5.* When the lid comes off *6.* Little kid lost *7.* Bad pennies *Part 2:* The ten stages of recovery *8.* Exploration and discovery *9.* Relationship history/inventory 1 *10.* Relationship history/inventory 2 *11.* Addiction control *12.* Leaving home and saying goodbye *13.* Grieving your loss *14.* New self-perceptions *15.* New experiences *16.* Reparenting *17.* Relationship accountability *18.* Maintenance *Part 3:* Defining healthy relationships *19.* Codependent or healthy relationships *20.* Making relationships work

Naming the Family Secret *Addiction, Co-Dependency, and Recovery,* Kathleen Kircher

Ave Maria Press, 1990, $6.95, cassette(s), 65 minutes, for counselees

Description Offers listeners ways to get in touch with their own backgrounds and secrets. She explores multiple and complex aspects of co-dependence and addiction, as well as the miracles of transformation, conversion, and recovery that can take place.

Author Kathleen Kircher is the executive director of the North American Conference of Separated and Divorced Catholics. A respected authority on family transitions and addiction recovery, she is a member of the faculty of Colgate-Rochester Divinity School.

Codependency *PowerLoss, SoulLoss,* Dorothy May

Paulist Press, 1994, $14.95, paper, 320 pp., for counselees

Description There are many books on codependency on the market today, mainly dealing with theoretical and anecdotal material. But there is very little that people who are hurting can apply to the ordinary issues of their lives. Written in the form of 123 questions and answers, each followed by a space for personal reflections, this book is a finely tuned blend of theoretical and practical applications of work in the field.

Author Dorothy May, who holds a Ph.D. from Northwestern University, is a clinical psychologist and senior addictions counselor. She has worked in private practice for 15 years and has also taught at local colleges and universities.

Contents *1.* Loss of soul: disempowerment *2.* Psychological processes *3.* Addictions *4.* Sexual abuse *5.* Return of the soul: personal empowerment in recovery

Living on the Border of Disorder *How to Cope with an Addictive Person,* Dan O'Neill and Cherry Boone O'Neill

Bethany House Publishers, 1992, $7.99, paper, 205 pp., for counselees

Description Addresses how to avoid the emotional and relational traps of life when living with an addictive person—freeing the one who lives within the addictive cycle and offering the kind of support a loved one needs on the road to recovery.

Authors Dan and Cherry Boone O'Neill have multifaceted careers: Dan is president of Messenger Communications; Cherry, daughter of Pat and Shirley Boone, is an experienced entertainer and songwriter whose recovery from anorexia nervosa became a national story.

Contents *1.* Life on the border *2.* We're all in this together *3.* The healing trio: medical, cognitive, and rational theories *4.* Hanging from a cliff *5.* Denial, discernment, deceit, disclosure *6.* The quick fix *7.* Backlash *8.* Learning to forgive *9.* Bargaining *10.* The 911 approach *11.* The codependent and other roles that don't work *12.* Positive roles and personality types *13.* Giving up *14.* The tunnel that leads to the light

Co-Dependency *Breaking Free from Entangled Relationships,* Richard Peace

Serendipity, 1991, $6.95, paper, 112 pp., for both counselors and counselees

Description A 7- or 14-week course utilizing Scripture and discussion questions. Designed for anyone interested in learning about codependency and willing to approach the problem compassionately and with an open mind. The assumption is that the group will all probably have dependent inclinations (or suspect that they do).

Contents *1.* What is codependency? *2.* Letting others use us *3.* Letting others define who we are *4.* Letting my feelings go numb *5.* Getting in touch with my history *6.* Getting in touch with the present *7.* Getting in touch with God

Co-Dependency Confusion Randy Reynolds and David Lynn

Zondervan Publishing House, 1992, $4.99, paper, 96 pp., for both counselors and counselees

Description Part of the Recovery Discovery series of workbooks. Describes strategies that move Christians out of the confusion of codependency and toward a healthy relationship with God and others.

Authors Randy Reynolds is director of Renewal Counseling in Tuscon, Ariz., and served as a pastor for more than 15 years. David Lynn is a pastoral counselor and author.

Can Christians Love Too Much? *Breaking the Cycle of Codependency,* Margaret Josephson Rinck

Zondervan Publishing House, 1991, $9.95, paper, 221 pp., for both counselors and counselees

Description Some people confuse Christian nurturing with destructive enabling and caretaking behaviors. This work explains codependency, its characteristics and how to break its grip. This thought-provoking volume examines the impact of Christian beliefs and practices on the development of codependent behavior and on the process of recovery. It provides an integrated approach to identifying and treating codependency from a Christian perspective.

Author Dr. Margaret Josephson Rinck is a clinical psychologist in private practice in Cincinnati, Ohio. She periodically conducts psychotherapy groups for "Women Who Love Too Much." She has numerous courses and audio programs on skills training and interpersonal relationships.

Contents *1.* Loving too much *2.* Codependency and loving too much *3.* Codependents and their relationships *4.* The roots of codependency *5.* Codependency—an addiction *6.* The cycle of codependency *7.* Breaking the cycle of codependency *8.* Codependency and the church community *9.* One woman's story / *Appendixes A–E*

Recovery from Codependency Dale Ryan and Juanita Ryan

InterVarsity Press, 1992, $4.99, paper, 60 pp., for both counselors and counselees

Description This Bible study is part of a series of 16 volumes on various recovery themes. Each book contains studies on six biblical texts. Leader's notes are provided for group study.

Authors Dale Ryan is the executive director of the Recovery Partnership, the parent organization to the National Association for Christian Recovery. Juanita Ryan is a counselor in private practice in Hacienda Heights, Calif.

Contents *1.* Letting go of over-responsibility *2.* Letting God give us rest *3.* Letting go of denial *4.* Letting God help us tell the truth *5.* Letting go of blame *6.* Letting God take care of those we love / *Leader's notes*

Freedom from Codependency *A Christian Response,* Philip St. Romain

Ligouri Publications, 1991, $3.95, paper, 112 pp., for counselees

Description Explains the characteristics of codependency, whom it affects, and how it develops. Includes a practical plan for recovery based on the 12 steps of Alcoholics Anonymous.

Contents *1.* What is codependency? *2.* The shame game *3.* The first steps to recovery *4.* Living your own life *5.* Resolving emotional pain *6.* What is Christian love? *7.* Codependency and ministry / *Appendix 1:* Addictive behaviors checklist / *Appendix 2:* Caretaking versus caring for / *Appendix 3:* The 12 steps of Alcoholics Anonymous

Steps to Hope Joyce M. Shutt

Herald Press, 1990, $6.95, paper, 128 pp., for counselees

Description Families coping with dependency and failure will find hope through the Beatitudes and 12-step program uniquely combined in this work. Shutt offers families mired in the swamp of alcohol and drug addiction a path to higher ground. She speaks to any of us trapped in destructive habits and shows us how we can break our addictions.

Author Joyce M. Shutt graduated from Gettysburg Lutheran Seminary in 1980 and began pastoring her home church that same year. Since her ordination in 1980, she has pastored the Fairfield Mennonite Church.

Please Don't Say You Need Me *Biblical Answers for Codependency,* Jan Silvious

Zondervan Publishing House, 1989, $7.99, paper, 176 pp., for both counselors and counselees

Description Helps readers learn to identify and break the cycle of an unhealthy, codependent relationship in a loving, scriptural manner.

Author Jan Silvious served for 14 years as a counselor, administrator, writer, and teacher for Precept Ministries in Chattanooga, Tenn. She presently hosts her own radio program.

Contents Definition of terms *1.* What's wrong with me? *2.* What are the symptoms of codependency? *3.* Why do I act this way? *4.* Codependency in parent–child relationships *5.* Codependency in marriage *6.* Codependency in friendship *7.* Codependency in the workplace *8.* Help! I'm codependent *9.* Maintaining healthy relationships / *Appendixes*

Please Remind Me How Far I've Come *Reflections for Codependents,* Jan Silvious and Carolyn Capp

Zondervan Publishing House, 1990, $6.99, paper, 96 pp., for both counselors and counselees

Description Topical reflective devotions for recovering codependents with a journal/diary section for the reader to record personal and spiritual growth. Includes a Scripture devotional section.

Authors Jan Silvious is an author, speaker, and lay counselor in Chattanooga, Tenn. She is presently host for *Jan's Journal,* a radio ministry in Chattanooga. Carolyn Capp was an executive secretary and counselor with Precept Ministries in Chattanooga, Tenn., for eight years.

Toxic Love *The Illusion of Self-Worth,* Malcolm Smith

Pillar Books & Publishing Company, 1992, $3.95, paper, 64 pp., for counselees

Description Malcolm Smith explains the subtle trap of living your life to make others happy, showing the difference between loving to get approval and loving unconditionally.

Author Malcolm Smith is involved in a teaching ministry based in Texas.

Co-Dependency *Breaking Free from the Hurt and Manipulation of Dysfunctional Relationships,* Pat Springle

Word Publishing, 1992 (2d ed.; 9th printing), $10.99, paper, 299 pp., for counselors

Description This is an extensive treatment of the methods applied to heal a codependent person. The unique feature of this book is the extensive self-help workbook section at the end of each of the 21 chapters. Pat Springle gives a penetrating look into the causes, symptoms, and solutions for codependency, focusing on the biblical principles used to heal an individual.

Author Pat Springle is currently senior vice president, Church and Family Resources for Rapha, Inc. He served on the staff of Campus Crusade for Christ for 18 years. He is the author of several other recovery-oriented works.

Contents *Part 1:* The problem *1.* Glimpses *2.* The cause of codependency *3.* Lack of objectivity *4.* A warped sense of responsibility *5.* Controlled/controlling *6.* Hurt and anger *7.* Guilt *8.* Loneliness *9.* The codependent Christian *Part 2:* The solution *10.* Identity—a sense of worth *11.* Lordship: a sense of belonging *12.* Find a friend *13.* Three ingredients: #1: identity *14.* Three ingredients: #2: detach *15.* Three ingredients: #3: decide *Part 3:* The process *16.* Emerging *17.* Relating to the other person: lordship or love *18.* The reality of God *19.* Enjoying the Lord *20.* Three stages of growth *21.* Waiting on the Lord

Conquering Codependency *A Christ-Centered 12-Step Process,* Pat Springle

LifeWay, 1991, $9.95, paper, 186 pp., for both counselors and counselees

Description Part of the LifeWay Support Group Ministry commissioned by the Southern Baptist Convention. This title will help individuals acknowledge and define their compulsions, understand the role their parents have played, deal with painful guilt, and depend on God through Christ to restore them to spiritual and emotional health. Designed for both individual and discovery-group study. The book provides self-paced, interactive study and resources for the 12 weekly sessions. A leader's guide is also available ($4.95) that provides administrative guidance and suggested activities for the weekly discovery-group sessions.

Author Pat Springle is currently senior vice president, Church and Family Resources for Rapha, Inc. He served on the staff of Campus Crusade for Christ for 18 years. He is the author of several other recovery-oriented works.

Contents About the author / *Introduction/* What are the 12 steps? / The methodology of the 12 steps / Foundational concepts / Choose a schedule and plan / How to begin a 12-step group / Meeting formats / How to lead a 12-step group / How to be a sponsor / Group leadership models / Foundations for recovery: *Step 1:* The process begins *Step 2:* The changing cycle *Step 3:* Turning it over *Step 4:* Honesty at work *Step 5:* Out of the darkness *Step 6:* Willing to be willing *Step 7:* Ready for change *Step 8:* Choosing to forgive *Step 9:* Making amends *Step 10:* People of the extremes *Step 11:* A growing relationship *Step 12:* Practicing and sharing / Handout masters / Newcomer's pack / The 12 steps and 12 traditions of Alcoholics Anonymous

Learning More about Codependency Pat Springle

Rapha Resources, 1992, $2.50, paper, 65 pp., for both counselors and counselees

Description Takes the reader through the symptoms of behavior and characteristics of codependency, and its effects on others as you journey toward personal identity and emotional health.

Author Pat Springle is currently senior vice president, Church and Family Resources for Rapha, Inc. He served on the staff of Campus Crusade for Christ for 18 years. He is the author of several other recovery-oriented works.

Rapha's 12-Step Program for Overcoming Codependency Pat Springle

Rapha Resources, 1991, $11.99, paper, 196 pp., for counselors

Description Helps the codependent recognize painful problems and offers biblical strategies that give hope and promise healing. This brilliant, new, one-of-a-kind program goes beyond all others to lead codependents to acknowledge their compulsions, depend upon God through Christ to restore them to spiritual and emotional health, understand the part their parents may have had, and deal with painful guilt. Charts, self-tests, personal questionnaires, self-paced inventories all combine to make this "Workbook Process" a rewarding step on the road to recovery.

Author Pat Springle is currently senior vice president, Church and Family Resources for Rapha, Inc. He served on the staff of Campus Crusade for Christ for 18 years. He is the author of several other recovery-oriented works.

Untangling Relationships *A Christian Perspective on Codependency,* Pat Springle

LifeWay, 1993, $9.95, paper, 224 pp., for both counselors and counselees

Description Part of the LifeWay Support Group Ministry commissioned by the Southern Baptist Convention. This title helps those persons who are codependents or those who live and work with codependents to better understand the painful effects of codependency. Targets: Understanding what causes a person to become a compulsive "fixer"; learning why codependency creates tangled relationships, experiencing in a small group atmosphere love, trust, honesty; and learning biblical guidance that shows persons how, with God's help, they can break free of their destructive patterns of trying to help everyone and fix everything. Designed for both individual and discovery-group study. The book provides self-paced, interactive study, and resources for the 12 weekly sessions. A leader's guide is also available ($4.95) that provides administrative guidance and suggested activities for the weekly discovery-group sessions.

Author Pat Springle is currently senior vice president, Church and Family Resources for Rapha, Inc. He served on the staff of Campus Crusade for Christ for 18 years. He is the author of several other recovery-oriented works.

Contents About the author / *Introduction* / *Unit 1*—Understanding codependency *Unit 2*—Lack of objectivity *Unit 3*—A warped sense of responsibility *Unit 4*—Controlled—controlling *Unit 5*—Hurt and anger *Unit 6*—Guilt and shame *Unit 7*—Lonely and pressured *Unit 8*—Identity: a sense of worth *Unit 9*—Belonging *Unit 10*—Three-step process to a healthy life *Unit 11*—Learning to grieve *Unit 12*—New ways of relating

God, Where Is Love? *Break Free from the Pain of Codependency,* Claire W.

Zondervan Publishing House, 1993, $8.99, paper, 128 pp., for counselees

Description For singles or marrieds who struggle with the pain of codependency, here is a guide for improving relationship and communication skills. Part of the God, Help Me series from Zondervan. These self-help books are designed, not only to explain the recovery process, but to guide and support the reader throughout that process. Emotional and spiritual healing are promoted through Bible verses, questions for reflection, writing assignments, and the personal examples of the author and other people who have experienced recovery.

Author Claire W. draws on her Ph.D. training in clinical psychology and her work as a counselor as she writes for Christians in recovery.

Contents *Part 1:* How do I learn to love and be loved? *1.* The problem of codependency *2.* The work of recovery *3.* Understanding, healing, and growth *4.* Communication and intimacy *5.* Communication and problem solving *Part 2:* How can I tell if it's love? *6.* Intimacy *7.* Sex *8.* Expectations *9.* Commitment *10.* Lynn and Steve in recovery / *Guidelines for groups*

Co-Dependents Anonymous, Inc.

Co-Dependents Anonymous, Inc. An organization

Though not a Christian organization, CDA provides a variety of helpful services to those struggling with codependency. Call for a free information packet.

10. Crisis Counseling

Trusting God in a Family Crisis Jim Conway, Sally Conway, and Becky Conway Sanders

> InterVarsity Press, 1989, $9.99, paper, 224 pp., for counselees

> **Description** Three authors handle the crisis of Becky's leg amputation in three very different ways. The book helps the readers process any major crisis in life and to experience the emotional and spiritual growth that can result from any crisis.

> **Authors** Jim Conway holds five degrees in psychology and theology and is the author of many books. His wife, Sally Conway, holds an M.S. in human development. Together they own and operate Mid-Life Dimensions/Christian Living Resources, a nonprofit organization ministering to people at various stages of life through a variety of media formats. Becky Conway Sanders is a licensed recreation therapist and certified handicapped ski instructor.

Pastoral Care with Children in Crisis Andrew D. Lester

> Westminster/John Knox Press, 1985, $11.99, paper, 142 pp., for counselors

> **Description** After discussing underlying principles, Lester gives concrete and creative suggestions that can be used to help 5–12-year-old children share their feelings. He describes techniques of play, art, storytelling, and writing that can be employed by ministers to develop sensitive nurturing relationships with the children in their charge.

> **Author** Andrew D. Lester is professor of religion, Southern Baptist Theological Seminary. He has published numerous articles and books.

> **Contents** *Part 1:* The pastor and children *1.* The pastoral neglect of children *2.* Children are parishioners too! *3.* What children in crisis need from the pastor *4.* Some basic principles of pastoral care to children *Part 2:* Methods of pastoral care of children in crisis *5.* The use of play in pas-

toral conversation *6.* Pastoral care through art *7.* Storytelling and pastoral care *8.* Pastoral care through writing

Yet Will I Trust Him *Accepting the Sovereignty of God in Times of Need,* Peg Rankin

> Regal Books, 1987, $7.99, paper, 178 pp., for counselees

> **Description** It's easy to accept God's will when life is going well—but what about the hard times? Here is a compassionate guide for yielding to God's sovereignty and remembering his promise to never leave us or forsake us.

> **Author** Peg Rankin is a former English teacher, now Bible teacher, layperson ministering to laypeople. In demand nationally and internationally, she presents up to 250 lectures annually on a variety of topics. She is the author of two other books.

> **Contents** *Part 1:* Who is God? *1.* The God of Scripture *2.* The King of kings *3.* The first cause of actions *4.* A master of creativity *Part 2:* Where is God? *5.* A biblical view of crisis *6.* A personal crisis *7.* Universal crises *8.* Precious promises *Part 3:* Why must we have crises? *9.* Snakes and lions *10.* Wrestling with God *11.* The problem of suffering *12.* God's sovereignty in healing *13.* Claiming God's best *14.* Acknowledging His sovereignty *15.* From curse to blessing *Part 4:* What do crises accomplish? *16.* The glory of suffering *17.* Rooted in Christ *18.* Nothing but leaves *19.* The believer's choice *20.* The fruit of the Spirit *Part 5:* How can I have victory? *21.* Emotion or action *22.* A widow's victory *23.* Active passivity *24.* Stages of suffering *25.* The upward spiral *26.* Identification with Christ *27.* Personal thoughts

Pastoral Care with Adolescents in Crisis G. Wade Rowatt Jr.

> Westminster/John Knox Press, 1989, $13.99, paper, 168 pp., for counselors

> **Description** Drawing upon personal experience, clinical knowledge, social research, and interviews, Wade Rowatt outlines the pressures that today's young people experience and offers principles and methods for responding. He focuses on five major areas of adolescent crises:

71

family problems, sexual problems, substance abuse, school pressures, and depression and suicide.

Author G. Wade Rowatt Jr. is professor of psychology of religion and associate dean of the School of Theology, Southern Baptist Theological Seminary, Louisville, Ky. He is a coauthor of *The Two Career Marriage* and has written many other books and articles.

Contents *1.* Adolescents in crisis *2.* Developmental issues and crises *3.* Principles of caring *4.* Methods of pastoral care and counseling *5.* Family problems *6.* Sexual problems *7.* Peer and academic problems *8.* Depression and suicide *9.* Substance abuse *10.* The churches respond

Counseling in Times of Crisis Judson J. Swihart and Gerald C. Richardson

Word Publishing, 1987, $15.95, cloth, 210 pp., for counselors

Description This book presents the dynamics of crisis and an outstanding biblical view for understanding them. The book is unique in that it offers specific issues to be addressed in counseling different types of crisis. Five major categories of crisis are described with various counseling techniques. Lay leadership in the church, as a counseling resource, is also addressed.

Authors Judson Swihart holds a Ph.D. in human development and family studies from Kansas State University. He is a licensed clinical social worker with many years of experience in individual and family counseling. He has published professional and popular articles. He directs the International Family Center in Kansas and teaches at Kansas University. Gerald C. Richardson (deceased in Feb. 1993) held a D.Min. degree (California School of Theology) and was president of the Growing Edge Counseling Center in Acadia, Calif. He was a licensed child, marriage, and family counselor as well as a pastor for six years.

Contents *Part 1:* The foundation *1.* The dynamics of crisis *2.* A biblical view of crisis *Part 2:* The framework *3.* Health related crisis *4.* People crisis *5.* Life-cycle crisis *6.* Financial crisis *7.* Spiritual crisis *Part 3:* The techniques *8.* Counseling techniques for crisis intervention *9.* Prevention of crisis *10.* Lay leadership and crisis support / *Appendix:* Verses for encouragement

Pastoral Care Emergencies *Ministering to People in Crisis,* David K. Switzer

Paulist Press, 1989, $12.95, paper, 223 pp., for counselors

Description A handbook for ministering to those in crisis. Provides fresh insights into the dynamics of several common and critical situations that pastors/church leaders are called to respond to.

Author David K. Switzer is professor of pastoral care and counseling at the Perkins School of Theology, Southern Methodist University, Dallas, Tex. He received his Ph.D. in theology from Southern California School of Theology. He is widely published in journals and has contributed to many books on pastoral counseling.

Contents *1.* What is a pastoral emergency? *2.* The carer and the caring: who we are and how we go about it *3.* Responding to persons' needs in situational crises *4.* Visiting the physically ill *5.* Hospital emergencies *6.* Ministry to the dying *7.* Pastoral response to bereavement *8.* Responding to suicidal persons and their families *9.* Marriage and family life: family systems, counseling, divorce *10.* Marriage and family emergencies: family violence, homosexuality, psychiatric emergencies, alcoholism

Crisis Counseling *What to Do and Say during the First 72 Hours,* H. Norman Wright

Regal Books, 1993, $19.95, cloth, 336 pp., for counselors

Description Combines the best of professional resources, biblical advice, and practical experience to give pastors and counselors a well-balanced approach for those first critical hours in a crisis. Expanded and revised from the 1985 edition. Includes new material throughout as well as a new chapter on post-traumatic stress disorder.

Author Dr. H. Norman Wright is one of America's best known Christian marriage and family counselors at the Family Counseling and Enrichment Center in Tustin, Calif. He is author of more than 50 books. He has also served on the faculty of Talbot School of Theology and the Graduate School of Marriage Counseling of Biola University.

Contents *1.* What is a crisis? *2.* Crisis counseling from a biblical perspective *3.* Applications of biblical principles *4.* The process of crisis intervention *5.* The crisis of depression *6.* The crisis of suicide *7.* The crisis of death *8.* The crisis of divorce *9.* Ministering to children in crisis *10.* The crisis of adolescence *11.* Crisis in the transitions of life *12.* Stress and the type A personality: a potential crisis *13.* Trauma, aftershock, and post-traumatic stress disorder / *Conclusion:* Using Scripture and prayer, and making referrals

Christian Helplines International

Christian Helplines International. An organization

Description A national association of local Christian crisis helplines. Assists Christian groups in organizing their local ministries. CHI provides help in organizing, incorporating, training board members, obtaining tax exempt status, and recruiting and training volunteers. Provides a comprehensive training course in personal counseling and evangelism—print/video format.

11. Depression and Related Issues

Clinical Depression

What Do You Do When You Become Depressed? Jay E. Adams

P & R Publishing, 1975, $.25, paper, for counselees

Description Encourages reader to commit to Christ and obedience in spite of feelings. Nouthetic approach.

Author Dr. Adams is the author of numerous books on Christian counseling. He has served on a seminary faculty (Westminster Theological) and in the pastorate. He is founder of the Christian Counseling and Educational Foundation in Laverock, Pa., and visiting professor of practical theology at two seminaries.

Out of the Darkness *My Experience with Depression*, Virginia Conner

New Hope, 1988, $2.95, paper, 61 pp., for counselees

Description Each person who develops depression experiences it a little differently. *Out of the Darkness* is one woman's story of how she struggled with and overcame a severe depression. It is also the story of how family, friends, an understanding counselor, and the author's deep faith in God helped her regain a positive outlook on life. A section of general coping tips designed to help the depressed person and those seeking to help depressed loved ones is included in the back of the book.

When Life Seems Hopeless Mary M. Fenocketti

Ligouri Publications, 1989, $.75, paper, 24 pp., for counselees

Description This booklet outlines a series of gentle, practical steps aimed at helping readers to hope again. Includes a number of encouraging, inspirational Scripture quotations.

A Soul under Siege *Surviving Clergy Burnout,* C. Welton Gaddy

Westminster/John Knox Press, 1991, $12.95, paper, 174 pp., for counselors

Description Gaddy describes his experiences as a pastor who went from good to bad health (including a deep depression) and back to even better health. With sometimes painful confession but sound theology, the author takes a realistic look at those aspects of the ministry which can be destructive.

Author C. Welton Gaddy has a wide range of pastoral experience. Most recently he was pastor, Highland Hills Baptist Church, Macon, Ga. He earned his Ph.D. and Th.M. in Christian ethics from the Southern Baptist Theological Seminary, Louisville, Ky.

Contents *Introduction:* Bottoming up *1.* Exploding myths and facing facts 2. "Honest confession is good for the soul" *3.* Who's crazy here? *4.* When it is better to receive than to give *5.* Healing hurts *6.* Straight talk: lessons for living

Coping with Depression *In the Ministry and Other Helping Professions,* Archibald D. Hart

Word Publishing, 1984, $8.99, paper, 156 pp., for counselors

Description "Surviving the ministry is to a large extent surviving depression" believes the author. This book offers expert analysis of the problem and a sensitive guide for dealing with it.

Author Archibald D. Hart is dean of the Graduate School of Psychology and professor of psychology at Fuller Theological Seminary. A skilled psychotherapist and committed Christian, Dr. Hart brings to this book the same combination of professional knowledge and personal concern that has made his other works successful.

Contents *1.* Depression in the 20th century *2.* The emotional hazards of ministry *3.* Spiritual causes and consequences of psychological depression *4.* The many faces of depression 5. The purposeful news of depression 6. The concept of loss and the depression cycle 7. The phases of depression—onset 8. The phases of depression—middle stage 9. The phases of depression—recovery 10. The professional treatment of depression 11. Why ministers burn out 12. Building resistance to depression

Counseling the Depressed Archibald D. Hart

Word Publishing, 1987, $15.99, cloth, 275 pp., for counselors

Description Dr. Hart offers both theoretical and clinical explanations, describes therapeutic approaches at various life stages, and warns of specific pitfalls to avoid when counseling for depression.

Author Dr. Archibald D. Hart is dean of the Graduate School of Psychology at Fuller Theological Seminary.

Contents *Part 1:* Understanding depression *1.* Popular misconceptions about depression *2.* The problem of depression *3.* What is clinical depression? *4.* Diagnosing depression *5.* Understanding reactive depression *6.* Understanding biologically caused depression *Part 2:* Counseling a depressed person *7.* Preparing to counsel a depressed person *8.* The psychodynamics of depression *9.* Counseling reactive depression *Part 3:* Counseling age-related problems *10.* Depression in childhood *11.* Depression in adolescence *12.* Depression in the elderly *Part 4:* Counseling specific life problems *13.* Depression in women *14.* Depression in the mid-life *15.* Depression in bereavement *Part 5:* Pitfalls in counseling *16.* Counseling the suicidal person *17.* Avoiding legal problems *18.* Getting help when you need it

Dark Clouds, Silver Linings *Depression Can Be a Healing Emotion When You Learn to Cooperate with It,* Archibald D. Hart

Focus on the Family, 1993, $14.99, cloth, 185 pp., for counselees

Description Dr. Hart offers hope through heartening stories of well-known Christians who have fought back from despair. Offers practical advice for coaxing friends or loved ones out of the valley of depression.

Author Dr. Archibald D. Hart is professor of psychology and dean of the Graduate School of Psychology at Fuller Theological Seminary.

Contents *Section 1:* Questions and answers about depression *1.* Depression: its nature and symptoms *2.* What causes depression *3.* Women and depression *4.* Depression in children and adolescents *Section 2:* Healing your depression *5.* Coping with depression 1 *6.* Coping with depression 2 *7.* Self-management of depression *8.* Profes-

sional treatment of depression *9.* Caring, supportive relationships *Section 3:* Growth experiences through depression *10.* Joni Eareckson Tada *11.* Florence Littauer *12.* Ben Patterson

Overcoming Depression Paul A. Hauck

Westminster/John Knox Press, 1973, $9.99, paper, 141 pp., for counselees

Description This book focuses on three psychological causes of depression: self-blame, self-pity, and other-pity. Guilt and forgiveness are treated.

Author Paul A. Hauck has been a full-time clinical psychologist in private practice in Rock Island, Ill., since 1968. He received his Ph.D. in 1953 from the University of Utah. In 1987 he was honored with the Distinguished Psychologist Award in Illinois. He travels widely, speaking and disseminating his views. He has over 30 articles published as well as 12 books. His writings have sold about 400,000 copies.

Contents *1.* How may I help you? *2.* Bad me! *3.* Be kind to yourself *4.* Poor me! *5.* Poor you! *6.* Some final advice

What to Do If You Are Depressed Patrick Kaler

Ligouri Publications, 1978, $.75, paper, 24 pp., for counselees

Description Offering hope, understanding, and guidance, the author explains the different types of depression and suggests possible solutions.

What of the Night? *A Journey through Depression and Anxiety,* Jeffrey J. Knowles

Herald Press, 1993, $7.95, paper, 144 pp., for counselees

Description The painful tracking of a seven-month ordeal in the grip of depression and anxiety. Isaiah's troubled query about Israel's future reflects the author's wonderings about his own survival, and whether his formerly comfortable faith and neatly placed God are big enough for such monstrous enemies. Much of the book was written while the wounds were still open, before the questions were answered. Here is no well-rehearsed testimonial, polished with the passage of time, but rather a work which will convince the reader that at least one other human being has gone down this road before. The chapters form around the distorted concepts which reared up to monopolize the author's world for long periods. They wore names like pain, trust, time, and medicine. Bigger than, but common to, them all was faith. Knowles's journey toward that final chapter on faith is the living flesh behind the table of contents.

Author Jeffrey Knowles is the research chief for the Ohio Governor's Office of Criminal Justice Services with degrees from Milligan College and Georgia State University. He is married, the father of three, and an elder.

Contents *1.* Mornings of rudest awakenings *2.* Christians and medication—strangers in a strange land *3.* Pain—defined, redefined, redeemed *4.* Trust—the reach for God's left hand *5.* The crisis of self-image *6.* Time—the cruel joke *7.* Faith of mice and mustard seeds / *Epilogue*

How to Win over Depression Tim LaHaye

Zondervan Publishing House, 1974, $4.99, paper, 241 pp., for counselees

Description Of the four methods used to treat depression—psychotherapy, drug therapy, shock therapy, and spiritual therapy—Dr. LaHaye thinks the most effective is spiritual therapy. This book contains the biblical techniques he used in counseling over 1,000 depressed people. He deals with mental attitude, self-image, anger, and self-pity, and proposes remedies to problems people may have concerning these areas.

Author Dr. Tim LaHaye is president and founder of Family Life Seminars and is a Family Life leader. He has written many other books on counseling and family life issues.

Contents *1.* The problem of depression *2.* Struggles against depression *3.* The symptoms of depression *4.* The cycles of depression *5.* The causes of depression *6.* Is there a cure for depression? *7.* The place of anger in depression *8.* Self-pity and depression *9.* How to overcome depression *10.* Depression and your mind *11.* Depression and your self-image *12.* Depression and the occult *13.* Depression and music *14.* Ten steps to victory over depression *15.* How to help your children avoid depression *16.* How to help a depressed friend *17.* The miserable majority *18.* An eighty-five-year-old optimist

How to Understand and Overcome Depression Ernest Larsen

Ligouri Publications, 1977, $3.95, paper, 128 pp., for counselees

Description Hand in hand with the reader, Larsen walks up five steps to find acceptance of self, others, and God. He offers help in finding open doors in the walls of depression.

Contents *1.* Depression—cause and cure *2.* What prayer can do *3.* Five ways of praying / *Conclusion*

The Storm Within *Renewing Faith during the Fury of Pain and Depression,* Mark Littleton

Tyndale House Publishers, 1994, $7.99, paper, 200 pp., for counselees

Description Disappointment and suffering may be especially frustrating to Christians who have trusted God to meet their needs. Many are full of doubts and questions yet don't want to give up on God. Written out of the author's own struggle with depression and illness, *The Storm Within* takes an experiential rather than philosophical approach to the issues. Journal entries, poetry, arguments with God, and quotes from spiritual giants in despair all bring a new understanding of God's faithfulness to the mind of the suffering Christian.

Author Mark Littleton is the widely published author of 14 magazine articles and books.

Contents *Part 1:* Emotional obliteration! *1.* Descent into darkness *2.* What is a dark night of the soul? *3.* The dark night of the soul in today's world *4.* Depression and the dark night of the soul *5.* The fall and suffering *Part 2:* The journey *6.* The disappearance of God *7.* Lists, arguments, complaints, and glimmers of hope *8.* Disheartening revelations *9.* God's Word no longer works *Part 2:* Hope in the hell, and words for the way *10.* Suffering and the New Testament *11.* God does work all things for good *12.* What's God doing? *13.* God's sovereignty *14.* What is God trying to teach me? *15.* If you are in the middle of it / *Conclusion:* This too shall pass *16.* Out and free.

Happiness Is a Choice Frank B. Minirth and Paul D. Meier

Christian Family Video, 1991, $19.95, video, for both counselors and counselees

Description Part of the Minirth-Meier Church Counseling Video Library. The series is designed to enhance the counseling process as clients take the videos home for viewing. This title presents the symptoms, causes, and cures of depression from spiritual and medical perspectives.

Authors Doctors Minirth and Meier have gained national prominence for their successful blending of biblical principles with proven clinical and medical treatment. They are nationally recognized authors of over 60 biblically based books on common psychological issues with over three million copies in print.

Happiness Is a Choice—New Second Edition *A Manual on the Symptoms, Causes, and Cures of Depression,* Frank B. Minirth and Paul D. Meier

Baker Book House, 1978, $6.99, paper, 248 pp., for both counselors and counselees

Description Beyond descriptions of depression and its causes, symptoms, and treatments, the authors offer basic steps and guidelines for recovering and sustaining a happy and fulfilling life. Over 500,000 copies in print. The new second edition of this phenomenal best-seller includes updated treatments.

Authors Paul D. Meier and Frank Minirth are vice president and president, respectively, of the Minirth-Meier Psychiatric Clinic, Richardson, Tex.

Contents *Part 1:* What is depression? *1.* Who gets depressed? *2.* What are the symptoms of depression? *3.* Is suicide a sin? *4.* Are grief reactions the same as depression? *Part 2:* What causes depression? *5.* Is genetics a good excuse? *6.* How deep do the roots of depression run? *7.* What are the primary sources of emotional pain? *8.* Do "nice guys" finish last? *9.* Can depression be acted out? *10.* What precipitating stresses bring on depression? *11.* What are the personality dynamics that bring on depression? *Part 3:* How can one overcome depression? *12.* Are there some basic guidelines for a happy life? *13.* How do you handle anger? *14.* When are medication and hospitalization advantageous? *15.* How do you handle anxiety? *16.* How do you find lifelong happiness? / *Appendixes:* Classifications of depression—Case studies of depressed individuals—Drugs and the treatment of depression

Coming Apart, Coming Together *One Man's Journey out of Depression,* Andrew Paige

Ligouri Publications, 1993, $5.95, paper, 132 pp., for counselees

Description The author of this book is a priest who experienced a major depressive episode that lasted nearly a year. In a nonclinical style, the author reflects on his experience, what caused it, how it impacted him and his faith, and how he was able to recover.

Depression *You Can Learn from It,* Andrew Paige

Ligouri Publications, 1994, $1.00, paper, for counselees

Description Depression can strike anyone. The author, a priest who experienced depression, shares his experience and insight in overcoming this illness. Readers will discover how to learn from the pain of depression . . . and how to find the help they need. Dispels myths about depression.

Recovery from Depression Dale Ryan and Juanita Ryan

InterVarsity Press, 1992, $3.95, paper, 60 pp., for both counselors and counselees

Description This Bible study is part of a series of 16 volumes on various recovery themes. Each book contains studies on six biblical texts. Leader's notes are provided for group study.

Authors Dale Ryan is the executive director of the Recovery Partnership, the parent organization to the National Association for Christian Recovery. Juanita Ryan is a counselor in private practice in Hacienda Heights, Calif.

Contents *1.* Experiencing hopelessness *2.* Waiting for hope *3.* Making room for hope *4.* Receiving gifts of hope *5.* Growing toward hope *6.* Focusing on the source of hope / *Leader's notes*

It Won't Last Forever *A Child's Book about Living with a Depressed Parent,* Doris Sandford and Graci Evans

Gold 'n' Honey Books (Questar), 1993, $7.99, cloth, 24 pp., for counselees

Description Part of the Hurts of Childhood series from Gold 'n' Honey. The series was developed for children ages 5–11 who have experienced deep and tragic hurts. The books deal gently and compassionately with children's delicate feelings when they're forced to handle burdens far too big for them to carry.

To Run and Not Grow Tired Fran Sciacca

NavPress, 1991, $5.00, paper, 90 pp., for counselees

Description If you've sustained some inner wounds, and you're not sure how to heal them, take some time to restore your soul by looking at the lives of men and women who struggled to keep running when they were faced with adversity. A series of 12 inductive Bible studies.

Author Fran Sciacca holds an M.A. in systematic theology from Denver Theological Seminary. He and his wife are coauthors of the Lifelines series of Bible studies for young adults.

Contents *1.* Hannah—coping with criticism *2.* Peter—failing someone you love *3.* Sarah—misplaced hope *4.* Cain—self-pity: a doorway to destruction *5.* Jezebel—the appetite for control over others *6.* Paul—dealing with your past *7.* Martha—the threat of resentment *8.* King Saul—the desire for notoriety *9.* The ten spies—the corrosive power of negativism *10.* Joseph—victim or victor? *11.* Jesus—facing the death of someone you love *12.* The Holy Spirit—a misunderstood "counselor"?

To Walk and Not Grow Weary Fran Sciacca

NavPress, 1985, $5.00, paper, 81 pp., for counselees

Description Contains 12 inductive Bible studies that present cameos of God's people under pressure. Readers will learn how to identify human problems and welcome God's solutions.

Author Fran Sciacca holds an M.A. in systematic theology from Denver Theological Seminary. He and his wife are coauthors of the Lifelines series of Bible studies for young adults.

Contents *1.* Elijah—changing our schedule *2.* Moses—learning to let go *3.* Jonah—the regression of pride *4.* Job—when the lights go out *5.* David—dealing with guilt *6.* Solomon—the fruits of materialism *7.* Paul—depression as a tool in God's hand *8.* Asaph—looking to the world *9.* Jeremiah—searching for success *10.* Jesus—how to handle rejection *11.* Barnabas—encouraging others

Learning More about Depression Steven Spotts

Rapha Resources, $2.50, paper, 32 pp., for counselors

Description It is not a contradiction in terms to be a depressed Christian, especially with the pressures of the '90s. Dr. Spotts shows you how to work through depression before it advances beyond healthy limits.

Coping with Depression *The Common Cold of the Emotional Life,* Siang-Yang Tan and John Ortberg Jr.

Baker Book House, 1995, $8.99, paper, 118 pp.

Description Designed to be read by counselees during therapy. A guide to techniques for coping with depression and direction to determine whether outside help is needed. Written from a Christian perspective by a psychologist and pastor.

Authors Siang-Yang Tan is director of the doctor of psychology program in the Graduate School of Psychology at Fuller Theological Seminary. John Ortberg Jr. is a teaching pastor at Willow Creek Community Church in South Barrington, Ill.

Contents *1.* A snapshot of depression: the common cold of the emotional life *2.* Understanding depression *3.* Coping with depression: know your ABC's *4.* Affect: how are you feeling? *5.* Behavior: what are you doing? *6.* Cognition: how are you thinking? *7.* Beyond self-help: using other resources *8.* A case study

Understanding Depression *A Short-Term Structured Model,* Siang-Yang Tan and John Ortberg Jr.

Baker Book House, 1995, $17.99, cloth, 130 pp.

Description Equips pastoral counselors to provide a supportive environment for counselees who show signs of depression. Explains different types of depression, diagnostic questions, boundaries for short-term therapy, and warning signs the counselor should refer. Written for students or practicing pastoral counselors, each problem is adapted to the five-session Strategic Pastoral Counseling model developed by David G. Benner. A companion book of the Strategic Christian Living series, *Coping with Depression,* is available as a counselee handout or self-help resource.

Authors Siang-Yang Tan is director of the doctor of psychology program in the Graduate School of Psychology at Fuller Theological Seminary. John Ortberg Jr. is a teaching pastor at Willow Creek Community Church in South Barrington, Ill.

Contents *Series preface:* an introduction to Strategic Pastoral Counseling *1. Depression:* the common cold of emotional life *2.* Understanding depression *3.* The encounter stage *4.* The engagement stage: feelings *5.* The engagement stage: thinking *6.* The engagement stage: behavior *7.* The disengagement stage *8.* Strategic Pastoral Counseling: a case study

Climbing Up from Depression

Abbey Press, $.50 each, paper, 8 pp., for counselees

Description Part of the CareNotes series from Abbey Press. CareNotes are short booklets that help readers identify issues and begin the process of seeking resolution. Anecdotal and uplifting. Beautiful photographs grace the covers. Over 20 million CareNotes have been sold in just over five years. Can be used as an alternative to a greeting card or in conjunction with pastoral care visits.

Praying in Times of Depression

Abbey Press, $.50 each, paper, 8 pp., for counselees

Description Part of the CareNotes series from Abbey Press. CareNotes are short booklets that help readers identify issues and begin the process of seeking resolution. Anecdotal and uplifting. Beautiful photographs grace the covers. Over 20 million CareNotes have been sold in just over five years. Can be used as an alternative to a greeting card or in conjunction with pastoral care visits.

Depression After Delivery

Depression After Delivery. An organization

Description Though not a Christian organization, DAD will send a free information packet upon request with a variety of materials dealing with postpartum depression. Also distributes a number of information packets, each tailored for a different interest, such as professional therapists, attorneys, researchers, support groups, etc.

National Foundation for Depressive Illness

National Foundation for Depressive Illness. An organization

Description A recorded message provides diagnostic criteria for depression. Encourages consultation with medical professionals. Also provides a referral service, support organizations, and bibliographic resources. Nonprofit, secular organization.

Disappointment and Failure

Can Fallen Pastors Be Restored? *The Church's Response to Sexual Misconduct,* John Armstrong

Moody Press, 1995, $9.99, paper, 204 pp.

Description What should happen to ministers who fall to sexual sin? What is the best course of action for their good and the good of the church? This book is filled with compassionate, yet uncompromising advice.

Author Dr. John H. Armstrong is director of Reformation and Revival Ministries, Inc., and edi-

tor of *Reformation and Revival* journal. A pastor for more than 20 years, he serves as an itinerant minister based in Carol Stream, Ill.

Contents *1.* Scandal in the church *2.* Forgive and forget? *3.* All sins are not created equal *4.* Sexual sin: a biblical exegesis *5.* Is he qualified? *6.* Disqualified? *7.* And now, a word from the past *8.* The case for pastoral removal *9.* The heart of the matter *10.* How shall we restore the fallen man? *11.* Guarding against misconduct *12.* Six proposals and a plea for reformation

Growing through Failure David Batty

Turning Point Ministries, Inc., 1991, $5.00, spiral, for both counselors and counselees

Description Part of the Group Studies for new Christians support group materials from Turning Point Ministries. A leader's guide is also available.

When Your Marriage Disappoints You Janet Chester Bly

NavPress, 1991, $4.00, paper, 96 pp., for both counselors and counselees

Description Contemporary, nonthreatening, easy to use. Designed to offer women hope, comfort, and healing in their difficult marriage through application of Scripture and anecdotes. For new Christians or mature believers who have been stymied in marriage, the booklet can be used for personal study, in groups of all sizes, or in one-on-one relationships. Format includes a short article, added sections for self-evaluation, and extra helps resources.

Author Janet Chester Bly is a freelance writer, speaker, and cofounder with her husband, Stephen, of Welcome to the Family Seminars. She has published 13 books, including *How to Be a Good Mom* and *Be Your Mate's Best Friend.*

Contents *Introduction*—Do yourself a big favor / Crisis point—where did things go wrong? Evaluation—how imperfect is your marriage? *Bible Lessons: 1.* Toughing it out *2.* Forgiveness that makes a difference *3.* Old-fashioned problem solving *4.* Life beyond reality / *Extra help:* Nobody said it would be easy / A new attitude / Garbage advice / Tackling special problems / Caught in the middle / *Bibliography*

Despair—Sickness or Sin? *Hopelessness and Healing in the Christian Life,* Mary Louise Bringle

Abingdon Press, 1990, $14.95, paper, 224 pp., for counselors

Description Offers a profoundly original way to understand the despair in one's own life or in the lives of others. This volume blends perceptive insights from modern psychology with those of Christian tradition. Her discussion will be useful to those who find little value in "pop" psychology and "positive thinking" theology, yet who yearn to make some sense of human despair.

Things Fail, People Fall *Getting Up and Going On with Life after You've Fallen,* Deborah Brunt

New Hope, 1992, $1.95, paper, 129 pp., for counselees

Description After experiencing a devastating failure in a personal ministry, Deborah Brunt set out to discover how God views failure and what his Word says to people who have failed. Through her research, Brunt discovered that things fail, people fall. She sets forth clear biblical guidelines to follow for getting up and going on with God's help after you've failed.

Author Deborah Brunt is a writer and speaker living in Corinth, Miss. She has published numerous articles in Christian and regional magazines. She also writes Sunday school curriculum and church drama.

Contents *1.* Face downward: God's people can fail *2.* Face downward: I was tripped! *3.* Glance backward: the sin factor *4.* Glance backward: the support factor *5.* Glance backward: but I didn't fall *6.* Gaze upward: God never fails *7.* Gaze upward: invite intimacy *8.* Look inward: test yourself *9.* Look inward: accept yourself *10.* Turn outward: look past the hurts *11.* Turn outward: look to the healers *12.* Turn outward: tend to the hurting *13.* Go forward: take a new path *14. Go forward:* one step at a time

No Easy Answers *Finding Hope in Doubt, Failure, and Unanswered Prayer,* William Lane Craig

Moody Press, 1990, $7.99, paper, 116 pp., for counselees

Description A compassionate, biblical approach to the complex issues of doubt, failure, and unanswered prayer. No pat answers, just honest insights into some of the most difficult questions facing Christians.

Losing It All and Finding Yourself *How to Pick Up the Pieces and Start Anew,* Richard W. Dortch

New Leaf Press, 1992, $5.95, paper, 106 pp., for counselees

Description Dortch knows what it means to lose it all. Fired from his job, forced out of his home, dismissed from his denomination, and facing an eight-year prison term for his involvement at PTL, he hit rock bottom. Standing among the ruins of his life, Richard Dortch dusted himself off and began the journey back. Only someone who has been there can take you up on the mountains and into the valleys and point out the way.

Author Richard Dortch is currently president and founder of Life Challenge, Inc., an agency caring for professionals in crisis, located in Clearwater, Fla.

Restoring the Wounded Woman *Recovering from Disappointment and Discouragement,* Melinda Fish

Chosen Books, 1993, $9.99, paper, 246 pp., for both counselors and counselees

Description Written to the woman who after years of desperate prayer sees her heartfelt desire unfulfilled. Whether it's to see a husband or child saved, escape abuse, recover from divorce, or grieve the loss of a loved one, the emotional results of hope/disappointment leave her passive and despairing.

Author Melinda Fish is copastor of Church of the Risen Savior, Trafford, Pa., author of three books, pastor's wife, mother of two children. She holds a B.A. from the University of Texas at Austin and is a frequent speaker at churches, retreats, seminars, and women's groups across the United States and abroad.

Contents *1.* The casualties of war *2.* Thrill ride to despair *3.* The barrenness syndrome *4.* The warfare begins: the violation of women *5.* Christian marriage: its rights and boundaries *6.* Submission or self-sabotage? *7.* The secret of intimacy *8.* The woman who hates men *9.* A woman's wounds: setup to destruction *10.* Blessed are they that mourn *11.* The death of a dream *12.* Getting over anger with God *13.* Restoring fellowship with God *14.* Taking your place

When a Leader Falls *What Happens to Everyone Else?* Debra Frazier and Jan Winebrenner

Bethany House Publishers, 1993, $8.98, paper, 208 pp., for both counselors and counselees

Description A book to bring healing for the victims of a Christian leader's sexual sin. Defines the destructiveness of the sin of adultery and why it's so wounding. It speaks to the pastor's wife who is left with accusations of guilt and the loss of position, ministry, and friends. It speaks to the congregation who is left without their shepherd, often confused and polarized. They need to know that restoration is possible for all those who are hurt by a leader's sin.

Authors Debra Frazier is a freelance writer and an instructor in English/writing at Richland Community College. Jan Winebrenner is also a freelance writer and author of four books.

How to Overcome Discouragement
Armin Gesswein

Christian Publications, 1991, $1.50, paper, 20 pp., for counselees

Description A brief booklet that encourages readers to face, deal with, and get rid of discouragement. Specific and directive. Thirteen editions have been published. Essentially pastoral in tone.

Author Armin Gesswein is an ordained Lutheran. He served as prayer coordinator for Billy Graham and is noted for his leadership in the Minister's Prayer Fellowship.

Betrayal of Trust *Sexual Misconduct in the Pastorate,* Stanley Grenz and Roy D. Bell

InterVarsity Press, 1995, $10.95, paper, 188 pp.

Description One of the first comprehensive evangelical treatments of sexual misconduct. Outlines how sexual misconduct by clergy is a breach of both power and sexual trust. It helps churches know how to aid those who have been abused and, importantly, gives guidance on prevention of abuse by clergy.

Authors Stanley J. Grenz is professor of theology and ethics at Carey/Regent College in Vancouver, B.C. Roy D. Bell is Erb/Gullison Professor of Family Ministries at Carey/Regent College.

Contents *1.* The scope of the problem *2.* The pastor at risk *3.* Misconduct as betrayal of a sexual trust *4.* Misconduct as betrayal of power trust *5.* Ministering to victims of misconduct *6.* The pastor and prevention of misconduct *7.* The church's response to misconduct

When Your Dreams Die *Finding Strength and Hope through Life's Disappointments,* Marilyn Willett Heavilin

Here's Life Publishers (c/o Thomas Nelson), 1990, $8.99, paper, 143 pp., for counselees

Description The death of a dream doesn't have to be the end. Learn how to live again when life doesn't turn out exactly as you planned.

Author Marilyn Willett Heavilin is a frequent speaker at churches, retreats, and conferences. She is the author of three best-selling books.

Contents *Letting go 1.* Letting go of your grief *2.* Letting go of destroyed dreams *3.* Letting go of damaged emotions *4.* Letting go of unforgiveness *Launching out 5.* Launching out to God *6.* Launching out in trust *7.* Launching out in prayer *8.* Launching out emotionally *9.* Launching out in truth *10.* Launching out spiritually *11.* Launching out with compassion *Living again 12.* Living again with new dreams *13.* Living again with confidence

Goodbye Prince Charming—The Journey Back from Disenchantment *Creating the Marriage You've Always Wanted,* Eileen Silva Kindig

NavPress/Piñion Press, 1994, $10.00, paper, 181 pp., for counselees

Description Many couples enter marriage high on idealism and full of expectations. Then as years unfold, they find themselves mired in disappointment. By exploring the dangers of storybook thinking, the author guides women back from disenchantment and shows how to nurture trust and intimacy—the keys to a marriage worth staying committed to.

Author A woman who worked through disenchantment in her own marriage, Kindig is a freelance writer residing in Medina, Ohio. She and her husband have been married 23 years.

Contents *1.* Someday my prince will come *2.* Happily ever after? *3.* The princess stands alone *4.* Prince Charming in the sky *5.* Choosing trust, accepting risk *6.* Cycles of rage *7.* After the tears *8.* Goodbye, Prince Charming *9.* Ah, romance! *10.* Buried treasure

Aftershock: *What to Do When Leaders (and Others) Fail You,* Ted Kitchens

Multnomah Books (Questar), 1992, $9.99, paper, 246 pp., for both counselors and counselees

Description Describes the forces at work behind the moral failures of Christians in and out of formal ministry.

Author Ted Kitchens is a senior pastor of Christ Chapel Bible Church of Fort Worth, Tex., where he has served for over a decade. He holds two master's degrees and a doctor of theology from Dallas Theological Seminary.

Contents *Part 1:* Victims of a tremor *1.* The cracks of our times: living in the gimme generation *2.* The ripple effect: a principle of corporate solidarity *Part 2:* The church on bedrock *3.* Sealing the cracks of time *4.* Seven reasons why Christians don't dare to discipline *5.* Something for everyone: heaven's answer to earth's fault line *Part 3:* Administering first-aid to the offender *6.* Truthing it . . . step by step *7.* To judge or not to judge, isn't that the question? *Part 4:* Administering to and through the church *8.* Truthing it . . . steps 3 & 4: coming to grips with family affairs *9.* By what power and whose authority? *10.* What sins demand our attention? *Part 5:* Administering first-aid to the fallen leader *11.* Fault-proofing your shepherd: how to keep your shepherd from falling *12.* Confronting the fallen shepherd: what to do if yours fails *13.* Restoring the fallen shepherd

If Ministers Fail, Can They Be Restored?
Tim LaHaye

Pyranee Books/Zondervan, 1990, $9.95, cloth, 190 pp., for counselors

Description A remarkably objective look at ministerial infidelity.

Author Dr. Tim LaHaye is president and founder of Family Life Seminars and is a Family Life leader. He has written many other books on counseling and family life issues.

Contents *Part 1:* If ministers fall . . . *1.* What on earth is going on in the church? *2.* The high cost of ministerial infidelity *3.* Why ministers fall into sexual sin *4.* The real reason ministers fall *5.* How to avoid sexual temptation *Part 2:* . . . Can they be restored? *6.* What a church should do when its minister falls *7.* What the Bible says about restoration *8.* Bible characters to whom God gave a second chance *9.* What some Christian leaders say about restoration *10.* A personal perspective *11.* A model for restoring fallen ministers *12.* How one church restored its minister

Why Is God Silent When We Need Him the Most? *A Journey of Faith into the Articulate Silence of God,* James Long

Zondervan Publishing House, 1994, $11.95, cloth, 169 pp., for counselees

Description Invites readers to embark on a journey that every Christian must take if faith is to survive the challenges of life. Here is perceptive observation and guidance.

Author James Long is an award winning writer and director of development for *Campus Life* magazine. Jim has held staff ministry positions at the denominational and local church levels.

Contents *Part 1:* The silence of God *1.* Silence: the sound of infinity *2.* Distraction: when life outshouts God *3.* Contradiction: conflicting voices *4.* Mystery: a whisper of purpose *5.* Language: translating the transcendent *Part 2:* The voice of God *6.* Creation: a muffled voice *7.* Scripture: a sure and certain voice *8.* Christ: the word became flesh *9.* Spirit: inside interpreter *10.* Spiritual insight: the mind of Christ *11.* The church: speaking the truth in love *12.* Perspective: teaching the silence to talk *Part 3:* The mystery of God *13.* Partial answers *14.* God's government: an incongruous kingdom *15.* God's will: the paradox of power *16.* Faith: beyond the shadow of doubt *17.* Fear: ultimate test of trust *18.* Prayer: monologues with God? *19.* Quiet: the articulate silence of God

Failure, the Back Door to Success
Erwin W. Lutzer

Moody Press, 1975, $7.99, paper, 138 pp., for counselees

Description No matter what the circumstances, failure can bring you spiritual victory. This popular book continues to help readers understand the biblical perspective of failure. More than 104,000 in print.

The Power of Realistic Thinking *How to Cope When How-to Books Fail,* Donald W. McCullough

InterVarsity Press, 1993, $8.99, paper, 219 pp., for counselees

Description McCullough seeks to ease frustration, bind wounds, and offer comfort for our deepest sorrows. Avoids no-cost solutions and ten-minute cures.

Author Donald W. McCullough is pastor of Solana Beach Presbyterian Church near San Diego.

Contents *Dreaming 1.* When can-do can't *2.* Can-do culture *3.* Can-do faith *Awake 4.* Confessing the limits *5.* False gods: materialism, power, and religion *Loved 6.* The view from the sanctuary *7.* A refining fire *Friday 8.* The difference Friday makes *9.* Never alone *Saturday 10.* The good news of brokenness *11.* Disciplines for living with God *12.* Disciplines for living in a broken world *Sunday 13.* Beyond positive thinking

In This Very Hour *Loss of a Dream,* Robin Prince Monroe

Broadman and Holman, 1995, $1.95, saddleback, 40 pp.

Description Part of the new In This Very Hour series from Broadman and Holman Publishers, a series of daily devotions with first-person accounts of victory by faith over life's most tragic disappointments.

Author Robin Prince Monroe is a homemaker, writer, and contributor to *Exceptional Parent* magazine. She lost a six-year-old daughter to leukemia and her son was born with Down's syndrome.

Contents A series of thirty-one brief, yet very well-written daily devotionals (Scripture passage and anecdote).

Sexual Misconduct in Counseling and Ministry *Intervention, Healing, and Self-Protection,* Peter Mosgofian and George Ohlschlager

Word Publishing, 1995, $16.95, paper, 350 pp.

Description Sexual misconduct by ministers and other Christian professionals has reached epidemic proportions. One major church insurer has handled over 1,200 cases in the past eight years, many involving child sexual abuse, many with multiple victims. How should the church respond when Christian counselors cross sexual boundaries? What should be done when the healer wounds? What is the church's responsibility both to misbehaving professionals and to their victims? Combining their extensive counseling experience and legal expertise, the authors of this volume offer a well-written, practical book loaded with thorny issues of sexual exploitation by religious professionals.

Authors George Ohlschlager is associate director and cofounder of the Redwood Family Institute. He holds an M.A. in counseling psychology from Trinity Evangelical Divinity School and an M.S.W. from the graduate School of Social Work and J.D. from the College of Law of the University of Iowa. Peter Mosgofian is executive director and cofounder of the Redwood Family Institute. He is a graduate of Humbolt State University and holds an M.A. in theology and marriage and family therapy from Fuller Theological Seminary.

Contents *Part 1*—The sexual revolution and the church *1.* Challenging forbidden sex *2.* Love, sex, and power: the dangerous triangle *3.* Theological issues in preventing for-

bidden sex *Part 2*—Forbidden sex between adults *4.* The dynamics of sexual misconduct *5.* Helping adult victims of sexual misconduct *6.* Problem cases in sexual misconduct *Part 3*—Forbidden sex against children *7.* Child sexual abuse in society and the church *8.* Who will heal the little ones? (by Carol Carrell) *Part 4*—Policy and practice in the church *9.* Misconduct, policy, and practice in the Protestant church *10.* Priestly misconduct and the Catholic church crisis *11.* Coincident abuse and congregational healing *Part 5*—Law and ethics in sexual misconduct *12.* Ethical issues in forbidden sex prevention *13.* The law of sexual misconduct *Part 6*—Turning the tide against sexual misconduct *14.* Helping sexual violators *15.* Before the fall: prevention guidelines *16.* Waging war on sexual abuse

If Only God Would Answer *What to Do When You Ask, Seek, and Knock . . . and Nothing Happens,* Steven Mosley

NavPress, 1992, $9.00, paper, 192 pp., for counselees

Description Addresses some of the unanswered questions and personal dilemmas we've all faced in our prayer lives. Offering more than instructions on how to spend more time on your knees or muster up more faith, it shows how to become part of the process of answered prayer. Shows how to pray for what God can do rather than continually focusing on personal failure.

Author Steven Mosley is a writer for Christian television and the author of several books.

Discouragement Clyde M. Narramore

Narramore Christian Foundation, $.35, paper, for counselees

Description One of the many booklets available from the Narramore Christian Foundation. Designed to be handed to a person beginning to come to grips with a problem in living.

Author Dr. Clyde M. Narramore is a licensed psychologist and the president and founder of the Narramore Christian Foundation—a charitable, nonprofit educational, training, and counseling organization ministering primarily to the Christian community. He is also the founder of the Rosemead School of Psychology and author of 29 books.

Ten Best Things You Can Do When You Fail Clyde M. Narramore

Narramore Christian Foundation, $.50, paper, for counselees

Description One of the many booklets available from the Narramore Christian Foundation. Designed to be handed to a person beginning to come to grips with a problem in living.

Author Dr. Clyde M. Narramore is a licensed psychologist and the president and founder of the Narramore Christian Foundation—a charitable, nonprofit educational, training, and counseling organization ministering primarily to the Christian community. He is also the founder of the Rosemead School of Psychology and author of 29 books.

What to Do When Your Dreams Don't Come True *Starting Over after Life's Disappointments,* David Shibley

New Leaf Press, 1993, $7.95, paper, 176 pp., for counselees

Description When you are forced by circumstances or detours to wait a long time, you may think a dream will never come true. Here is healing and spiritual refreshment when hopes have been crushed. Discusses: How dreams must die so that destiny can live; major barriers to the realization of dreams; God's purposes for allowing failure or disappointment; how to find joy in the midst of pain and heartbreak.

Author David Shibley is president and founder of Global Advance, a missions ministry. He is the author of eight books and numerous articles.

Restoring the Fallen *Guidelines for Restoration,* Michael Smith

New Leaf Press, 1991, $7.95, paper, 160 pp., for counselors

Description Designed to answer many of the questions that have arisen in recent years by the fall of many prominent Christian leaders. Dr. Smith writes from a pastor's heart with a desire to be loving to the fallen individual and yet return the church to a disciplined, biblical foundation.

Author Dr. Michael Smith has attended Clemson University, Tabernacle Baptist Bible College, Faith Baptist College and Seminary, and Covington Theological Seminary. He is the pastor of Cover Creek Baptist Church in Pickens, S.C. He is also president of Faith Baptist College and Seminary, and executive director of Worldwide Tentmakers, Inc., both in Anderson, S.C.

Contents *1.* When a believer sins *2.* What is forgiveness? *3.* Restoration defined *4.* Attitudes in restoration *5.* Responsibilities in restoration *6.* David—example of biblical restoration *7.* When a pastor sins *8.* Integrity and accountability in the ministry *9.* Practical guidelines for restoration *10.* Fruits of restoration

Lord of the Valley *Hope for the Hurting,* James R. Spruce

Beacon Hill Press of Kansas City, 1993, $4.95, paper, 71 pp., for counselees

Description From a pastor's heart comes understanding and insight for those living in the valley of despair. James R. Spruce acknowledges the reality and intensity of our questions about suffering . . . and affirms the Christian's hope that there is a place of rest for those who hurt. A series of short readings on a variety of topics.

Author James R. Spruce (D.Min.) pastors the Flint, Mich., Central Church of the Nazarene. He has authored two other books.

So What If You've Failed? Penelope Stokes

NavPress, 1990, $3.95, paper, 91 pp., for counselees

Description This study guide will help you put failure in perspective—whether it's a minor foible, a well-intentioned mistake, or a sin. You'll also learn how to break the cycle of fear and guilt by admitting your fault, learning from your mistake, and allowing God to relieve you of the burden of failure.

Author Penelope J. Stokes, Ph.D., is a freelance writer and editor from Blue Earth, Minn. A former college professor, she is the author of five books.

Contents *Introduction:* Have you ever felt like a flop? *Crisis point:* But I tried so hard! *Evaluation:* Why do I feel like a failure? *Bible Lessons: 1.* You've got to do it right *2.* Big Uh-oh, little oops *3.* Looking good *4.* Repeat performance *5.* Growing on / *Questions:* The incomplete shalom workout / *Journal:* Writing for deeper insights / *Activity:* Take another look / *Bibliography:* Resources for recovery

Saying Goodbye to Disappointments *Finding Hope When Your Dreams Don't Come True,* Jan Stoop and David Stoop

Janet Thoma (a division of Thomas Nelson), 1993, $16.99, cloth, 224 pp., for both counselors and counselees

Description Helps women overcome the core issue interfering with their efforts to lead satisfying lives—stored hurt and anger. Offers positive means for facing these powerful emotions by treating the underlying causes of depression, hopelessness, poor relationships, and lack of motivation.

Authors Dr. David Stoop is a clinical psychologist in private practice in Newport Beach, Calif., and is program director for the Minirth-Meier Clinic West. Jan Stoop has led seminars and retreats focusing on marriage and family issues. A graduate of Fuller Theological Seminary, she is presently a doctoral candidate in clinical psychology.

Contents *Part 1:* From dream to disappointment *1.* Great expectations *2.* What do women want anyway? *3.* What else do women want? *4.* What are our dreams? *5.* Dreams: the story of our unmet needs *Part 2:* From disappointment to depression *6.* How could it all go so wrong? *7.* Trying harder only makes it worse *8.* The end of the chain: depression *Part 3:* From depression to a new hope: the joy of fulfillment *9.* Climbing out of the pit *10.* Canceling the debt *11.* Finding the courage to dream again

Encourage Me *Caring Words for Heavy Hearts,* Charles Swindoll

Zondervan Publishing House, 1982, paper, 87 pp., for counselors

Description Written to provide encouragement to those who are hurting. In his unique, Scripture-based style, Swindoll skillfully combines the Bible and anecdotes to provide help to the discouraged. A series of short, devotional readings.

Author Charles Swindoll is the president of Dallas Theological Seminary, hosts the radio program *Insight for Living,* and is a best-selling author.

Disappointment with God *Three Questions No One Asks Aloud,* Philip Yancey

Zondervan Publishing House, 1988, $9.99, paper, 260 pp., for counselees

Description This book won the ECPA Gold Medallion Award and was voted the Book of the Year by readers of *Christianity Today* in 1990. *Disappointment with God* deals with the issues that discourage or disillusion people in their personal relationship with God. It considers three questions—Is God silent? Is God unfair? and Is God hidden? The first part of the book presents a survey of the entire Bible, examining how God interacted with human history. The second part gets more personal, addressing the questions in an honest, struggling way. It faces the struggles Christians have in maintaining faith in the midst of adversity. Ideal for counselees who are struggling with doubt, self-image problems, unanswered prayer, personal and family disappointments.

Author Philip Yancey earned graduate degrees in communications and English from Wheaton College Graduate School and the University of Chicago. He joined the staff of *Campus Life* magazine in 1971 and worked there as editor for eight years. Since 1978 he has primarily concentrated on freelance writing. More than 600 of his articles have appeared in 80 different publications. Five of his 11 books have received Gold Medallion Awards from the Evangelical Christian Publishers Association.

Contents *Book 1*—God within the shadows *Part 1:* Hearing the silence *1.* A fatal error *2.* Up in smoke *3.* The questions no one asks aloud *4.* What if *5.* The source *Part 2:* Making contact: the Father *6.* Risky business *7.* The parent *8.* Unfiltered sunlight *9.* One shining moment *10.* Fire and the Word *11.* Wounded lover *12.* Too good to be true *Part 3:* Drawing closer: the Son *13.* The descent *14.* Great expectations *15.* Divine shyness *16.* The postponed miracle *17.* Progress *Part 4:* Turning it over: the Spirit *18.* The transfer *19.* Changes in the wind *20.* The culmination *Book 2*—Seeing in the dark *21.* Interrupted *22.* The only problem *23.* A role in the cosmos *24.* Is God unfair? *25.* Why God doesn't explain *26.* Is God silent? *27.* Why God doesn't intervene *28.* Is God hidden? *29.* Why Job died happy *30.* Two wagers, two parables

Staying Faithful When the Church Lets You Down

Abbey Press, $.50 each, paper, 8 pp., for counselees

Description Part of the CareNotes series from Abbey Press. CareNotes are short booklets that help readers identify issues and begin the process of seeking resolution. Anecdotal and uplifting. Beautiful photographs grace the covers. Over 20 million CareNotes have been sold in just over five years. Can be used as an alternative to a greeting card or in conjunction with pastoral care visits.

12. Disability

Journal of Religion in Disability & Rehabilitation *Innovations in Ministry for Independent Living,* William A. Blair

The Haworth Pastoral Press, quarterly, $18.00/year, a reference or academic work

Description A new journal that aims to inform religious professionals about developments in the field of disability and rehabilitation in order to facilitate greater contributions on the part of pastors, religious educators, and pastoral counselors. An interdisciplinary, interfaith, and multicultural forum, the journal also aims to focus the attention of the traditional academic disciplines within religion, such as ethics, sacred literature, theology, philosophy, and liturgies, on the phenomena of disability and rehabilitation. Representative articles: Ministry to Persons with Disabilities—Can We Do Better?; The Disability Triage—Denial, Marginalization, and Legislation; From Weakness to Strength—A Spiritual Response to Disability; Faith, Despair, and Disability; Two Suggestions for Total Participation in Worship.

Counseling Families of Children with Disabilities Rosemarie S. Cook-Hughes

Word Publishing, 1990, $15.95, cloth, 209 pp., for counselors

Description The professional or pastoral counselor who desires to effectively help families can find practical help in this concise and informative book. In addition to a solid theoretical framework in composing several perspectives of crisis counseling, the author uses a developmental approach to explain stages in the child's and family's life. In the appendix is a reproducible family annotation form, which helps the counselor assess the family's needs and form a plan to meet those needs.

Author Rosemarie Scott Cook-Hughes, Ph.D., is an associate professor at Regent University, School of Counseling and Family Services, Virginia Beach, Va. She is also a licensed professional counselor and author of *Parenting a Child with Special Needs.*

Contents *1.* An overview of disability *2.* The five-factor model of family stress *3.* Prenatal and postnatal diagnoses *4.* The toddler/preschool years *5.* The school years *6.* Transitioning: the school bus isn't coming anymore *7.* Providing for the future *8.* Effects on the marital couple and the siblings *9.* A faith perspective: spiritual growth *10.* The church's ministry to those with disabilities / *Annotated Family Appraisal Resources* / Trusts for those with disabilities / l'Arche Homes and Camphill Villages

Parenting a Child with Special Needs Rosemarie S. Cook-Hughes

Zondervan Publishing House, 1992, $8.99, paper, 224 pp., for counselees

Description Christian parents struggle with core faith issues when their child has special emotional, physical, or mental needs. Parents also need practical help and direction when facing the reality of providing for their child's spiritual needs. This book contains real, everyday experiences of parents of children with many types of disabilities. It also tells the author's own story and faith walk. You'll learn everything you wanted to know about parenting a child with special needs including: getting the news, how the news affects the rest of the family, caring for the infant, toddler, and adult, and how to tell others.

Author Rosemarie Scott Cook-Hughes, Ph.D., is an associate professor at Regent University, School of Counseling and Family Services, Virginia Beach, Va. She is also a licensed professional counselor.

Binding Up the Brokenhearted *A Handbook of Hope for the Chronically Ill and Disabled,* Cynthia Moench

College Press, 1991, $6.95, paper, 140 pp., for counselees

Description What if the doctor told you that you were not going to die, but would never get well? This book has been written by someone who has lived the roller coaster life of the chronically ill. This book is to help those who are sick and disabled come to grips with the pain, misunderstanding, and seeming hopelessness of the situation. It is to help them gain a clearer understanding of the need to restructure their lives, restructure their faith, and come to accept the reality of a divine plan for their lives. Examines changes wrought by illness and disability, human and spiritual ways of adapting, and restructuring life to accommodate illness.

Author Cynthia Moench lives in the San Francisco Bay area with her husband, Jim. She owned and operated a floral business until nine years ago when she contracted Chronic Fatigue Syndrome and was no longer able to work. However, she utilized her writing talents and produced two novels and articles for several periodicals. She speaks about living with chronic illness and disability to support groups and church groups alike.

Contents *1.* That dreaded word, incurable *2.* The mental and emotional battle *3.* And finally, acceptance *4.* The spiritual battle *5.* Choosing to cope *6.* Coping in relationships *7.* Practical daily applications *8.* Finishing well

Teaching Boys and Girls Who Learn Slowly Clyde M. Narramore

Narramore Christian Foundation, $.35, paper, for counselors

Description One of the many booklets available from the Narramore Christian Foundation. Designed to be handed to a person beginning to come to grips with a problem in living.

Author Dr. Clyde M. Narramore is a licensed psychologist and the president and founder of the Narramore Christian Foundation—a charitable, nonprofit educational, training, and counseling organization ministering primarily to the Christian community. He is also the founder of the Rosemead School of Psychology and author of 29 books.

Hope for Families *New Directions for Parents of Persons with Retardation & Other Disabilities,* Robert Perske

Abingdon Press, 1981, $11.95, paper, 96 pp., for both counselors and counselees

Description In 28 brief, optimistic chapters, Perske shows the many ways that parents and families can overcome their fears and inhibitions. Discussion questions are included in most chapters.

Author Robert Perske is a freelance writer, well known for his work in the field of mental retardation.

Contents *1.* The reason for this book *2.* Unrealized expectations *3.* Bewildering times *4.* Change *5.* Changing world views *6.* Understandable monkey wrenches *7.* People first *8.* Theology: bad to better *9.* Overwhelming the hordes *10.* The developmental principle *11.* Golden gains *12.* Human dignity *13.* Normalization *14.* Risk, courage, heroism *15.* Relative human experience *16.* The need to give *17.* Sexual development *18.* Increasing funds *19.* Peer group education *20.* Family systems *21.* Brothers and sisters *22.* Family games *23.* Healthy launching pads and proper landing fields *24.* Parental/professional relationships *25.* Candid consumers *26.* Pilot families *27.* Toward a better world *28.* Epilogue

Yes I Can *Challenging Cerebral Palsy,* Doris Sandford and Graci Evans

Heart to Heart, $9.99, cloth, 32 pp., for counselees

Description Designed for children ages 5–11. Stacy was born with a physical disability and she learns that sometimes others are handicapped in their attitudes. With a smile and good humor she sets out to correct the wrong beliefs others may have about being physically challenged.

Access to God Joni Eareckson Tada

Joni and Friends, $1.00, paper, 96 pp., for counselees

Description Do you know someone with a physical disability? *Access to God* offers spiritual comfort to those physically burdened. Joni intertwines the narrative and artwork with Scripture portions to knit a message of comfort, hope, and salvation.

I'll Love You Forever *Accepting Your Child When Expectations Are Unfulfilled,* H. Norman Wright and Joyce Wright

Focus on the Family, 1993, $15.99, cloth, 176 pp., for counselees

Description The touching story of Matthew, the Wrights' profoundly retarded child, and the growth and joy he brings to his parents. A moving parable for all parents who must deal with such issues as grieving, unfulfilled expectations, and the discovery of a child's greatest potential.

Authors Norman Wright is the director of Family Counseling and Enrichment and the seminar ministry, Christian Marriage Enrichment. He has taught family counseling and psychology at the graduate level for more than 25 years. His wife, Joyce Wright, is a career homemaker.

Contents *1.* Matthew's story *2.* The wandering child *3.* The homegoing *4.* Handling the news of loss *5.* When any child dies *6.* Special losses *7.* Your marriage and other children *8.* Families that make it *9.* Fathers and their grief *10.* What do I say to others *11.* Why me?

When a Disability Makes You Feel Left Out

Abbey Press, $.50 each, paper, 8 pp., for counselees

Description Part of the CareNotes series from Abbey Press. CareNotes are short booklets that help readers identify issues and begin the process of seeking resolution. Anecdotal and uplifting.

Beautiful photographs grace the covers. Over 20 million CareNotes have been sold in just over five years. Can be used as an alternative to a greeting card or in conjunction with pastoral care visits.

All God's Children

Joni and Friends, paper. An organization

Description You and your church can learn to help any person with a disability. This handbook is for pastors, elders, ministry leaders, and every concerned Christian who wants to reach out to persons with disabilities.

Joni and Friends

Joni and Friends. An organization

13. Divorce

Adult Recovery from Divorce

Recovery from Divorce *How to Become Whole Again after the Trauma of Divorce,* Bob Burns

Oliver Nelson (a division of Thomas Nelson), 1993, $9.99, paper, 212 pp., for counselees

Description Part of the Fresh Start series from Thomas Nelson. A compassionate look at the pain of divorce and the steps toward recovery. Christians touched by divorce will find biblically based guidance and comfort.

Author Bob Burns is founder and board chairman of Fresh Start Seminars, Inc., a recovery program for persons going through divorce.

Contents *1.* What am I going through? *2.* The mating game *3.* Till death do us part *4.* The ripping apart of one flesh *5.* Putting off until tomorrow what I don't want today *6.* The volcano within *7.* Microwave solutions to crockpot problems *8.* How low can I go? *9.* Redefining normal *10.* How does God feel about me?

Divorcing with Dignity *Mediation—The Sensible Alternative,* Tim Emerick-Cayton

Westminster/John Knox Press, 1993, $9.99, paper, 99 pp., for counselors

Description When divorce is inevitable, this practical guide provides an alternative to the standard methods of litigation used by divorcing couples. Based on the author's professional experience in law and as a minister who has mediated more than 500 couples, Tim Emerick-Cayton shows how mediation reduces costs, hostility, and confusion.

Author Tim Emerick-Cayton is senior partner and conflict/family mediator, Pacific Professionals, Inc., and executive director, conflict/family mediator, and pastoral counselor, Pacific Professional Consortium.

Contents *1.* What is divorce mediation? *2.* Is mediation right for me? *3.* How does mediation work? *4.* What about . . . ? Most frequently asked questions *5.* What about

the children? *6.* What happens if . . . ? *7.* What does the Spirit have to do with mediation? *8.* Where do we begin?

When Your Long-Term Marriage Ends *A Workbook for Women,* Elaine Evian

Resource Publications, Inc., 1994, $14.95, paper, for counselees

Developing a Divorce Recovery Ministry *A How-to-Manual,* Bill Flanagan

Thomas Nelson Publishers, 1991, $19.95, paper, 258 pp., for counselors

Description As one of the pioneers of Christian divorce recovery ministry, Dr. Flanagan shows you how to design the program, gather a leadership team, create a caring community, and reach out to the growing number of divorced persons in your community. Everything you need to start and build an effective ministry, regardless of the size of your church, is included in this valuable resource. There are helpful reproducible pages to distribute to your leadership team and staff.

Author Dr. Bill Flanagan (masters in theology, Princeton Theological Seminary; doctorate, Fuller Theological Seminary) is minister with single adults at St. Andrew's Presbyterian Church in Newport Beach, Calif. He coordinates a ministry that reaches hundreds of single people each week. Since 1977 he has conducted Divorce Recovery Workshops across the country reaching out a hand of hope and healing to over 10,000 persons.

Contents *Part 1:* Considering a divorce recovery ministry *1.* The divorce recovery ministry *2.* Questions you should ask before beginning a divorce recovery ministry *Part 2:* Preparing for the divorce recovery ministry *3.* A basic overview of the workshop *4.* Laying the foundation of your leadership team *5.* Job descriptions and responsibilities *6.* Leadership training *7.* Guidelines for leading a workshop discussion group *8.* Lecture outlines *Part 3:* Making the workshop happen *9.* Facilities *10.* The workshop budget *11.* Advertising and publicity *12.* Getting organized *13.* After the healing begins / *Appendix:* Workshop lectures

In This Very Hour *Loss of a Marriage,* B. J. Funk

Broadman and Holman, 1995, $1.95, saddleback, 44 pp.

Description Part of the new In This Very Hour series from Broadman and Holman Publishers, a series of daily devotions with first-person accounts of victory by faith over life's most tragic disappointments.

Author After ten years of marriage, Funk found herself married to an alcoholic spouse who wanted the "freedom" of being single again. She is in constant demand as a speaker and divorce support group leader.

Contents A series of thirty-one brief, yet very well-written daily devotionals (Scripture passage and anecdote).

Cementing the Torn Strands *Rebuilding Your Life after Divorce,* Jeenie Gordon

Fleming H. Revell, 1991, $8.99, paper, 191 pp., for counselees

Description Editor's Choice for Guideposts Book Club. "Getting through divorce is a gut-wrenching experience . . . ," writes Jeenie Gordon. "My goal is to teach coping skills, not only for separation/divorce, but also in order to face all of life as an emotionally healthy being." She achieves this goal by writing from a biblical perspective, a therapist's insight, and her own unique experiences both as a child of divorce and a divorcee. This unique approach to divorce recovery provides tremendous affirmation and insight to readers. It helps them deal with such feelings as anger, depression, and rejection while teaching healthy concepts that will lead them to full, contented lives.

Author Jeenie Gordon, M.S., M.A., M.F.C.C., is a marriage, family, and child therapist in private practice. She is also a high school counselor and has counseled over 8,000 teenagers. She is a popular seminar speaker.

Contents *1.* How can I survive? *2.* Letting go of the marriage *3.* Dealing with the former spouse *4.* Learning to be real *5.* Getting on with life *6.* Forgiveness, the path to freedom *7.* Single parenting, the job nobody wants *8.* Relax? You've got to be kidding! *9.* Risk a new relationship? Forget it! *10.* Learning by waiting *11.* This thing called trust *12.* A messenger from God

Nowhere to Turn Rhonda Graham

Pacific Press, 1993, $9.99, paper, 160 pp., for counselees

Description A deeply moving story about a Christian home split by divorce. Its lessons of starting over, trusting God for every need, and the results of judgmentalism are vital for every Christian.

When Divorce Happens *A Guide for Family and Friends,* James Greteman and Joseph Dunne

Ave Maria Press, 1990, $5.95, paper, 122 pp., for counselees

Description How can you help friends or loved ones who are sorting through the pain of divorce? There are no magic words or quick fixes, says Brother James Greteman and Joseph Dunne—but there are ways of being there, helping them get on with rebuilding their lives, discovering new friends, and leading them into non-threatening groups and activities that help broaden interests. Greteman offers practical advice on how divorce can be converted into a process of personal growth, both for those experiencing it and for those close to them.

Authors James Greteman, C.S.C., is a clinical marriage and family therapist with the Catholic Charities office in Salina, Kans. He holds a master's degree from the University of Notre Dame. Coauthor Joseph Dunne is a professional writer and editor. He holds a Ph.D. from the University of Notre Dame.

Contents *1.* The story *2.* The myth: "and they lived happily ever after" *3.* The tapestry of our lives *4.* Encouragement *5.* Encouraging the "sinner" *6.* The divorce process *7.* Overload *8.* Anger *9.* Dealing with anger *10.* Unfinished business *11.* Children *12.* Storytelling *13.* Action checklist

The Single Again Handbook *Finding Meaning and Fulfillment When You're Single Again,* Thomas Jones

Oliver Nelson (a division of Thomas Nelson), 1993, $12.99, paper, 304 pp., for counselees

Description Gives practical advice for those reentering the single life. Divided into three sections: regaining balance, finding fulfillment, and building healthy relationships.

Author Thomas Jones is the vice president of Fresh Start Seminars, Inc. Previously he has served as a Presbyterian minister and taught in several colleges and seminaries.

Splitting Up *When Your Friend Gets a Divorce,* Dandi Daley Knorr

Harold Shaw Publishers, 1988, $7.99, paper, 148 pp., for counselors

Description Designed to help caring friends and relatives understand what it is that they can and cannot do for someone who is going through a divorce. You've just heard that your friend's marriage has fallen apart. What do you say when you see her? How can you help? This book offers practical advice from the author and from the resources of hundreds of divorced men and women who explain how they felt their friends and churches sometimes helped and sometimes increased the hurt.

Author Knorr was on staff with Campus Crusade for Christ for nine years and served as a missionary in Poland for one year. She has published 11 adult Christian nonfiction books and 11 children's fiction books.

Contents *Part 1:* "Fire!": ten possible reactions to divorce *1.* Turn and run away *2.* Walk away, thankful *3.* Town crier *4.* "Have I gotta house for you!" *5.* My house burned too! *6.* The prophet of doom *7.* Fanning the flames *8.* Step aside! I'm a fireman! *9.* Forget about smoke damage *10.* Sit by the fire with a friend *Part 2:* Becoming a real friend *11.* Meeting needs *12.* A time to exhort—a time to exit *13.* Parents—a special case *14.* Stories of helpful people

Helps for the Separated and Divorced *Learning to Trust Again,* Medard Laz

Ligouri Publications, 1981, $2.50, paper, 64 pp., for counselees

Description Based on the actual experiences of those who have lived through a separation or divorce, this sympathetic book offers hope and guidance.

Contents *1.* Not a failure *2.* Losses and gains *3.* Working through grief *4.* What about the children? *5.* Learning to trust again *6.* Your need for caring love *7.* What to do about guilt feelings *8.* Close the door gently *9.* Resurrection to a new life.

Divorce Recovery *Life after Divorce,* Keith Madsen

Serendipity, 1991, $6.95, paper, 96 pp., for both counselors and counselees

Description A 7- or 14-week course utilizing Scripture and discussion questions. Designed to be used by those who are divorced or are in the process of becoming divorced.

Surviving Separation and Divorce *How to Keep Going When You Don't Really Want To,* Sharon G. Marshall

Baker Book House, 1988, $5.99, paper, 127 pp., for counselees

Description When in a state of shock, one cannot follow the theme of a book that must be read from cover to cover. For this reason, this book is written in "seed thought" (devotional/meditation) style. Its three sections take the person distraught over a broken heart through the pain, the healing, and the recovery. It makes a thoughtful gift at a time when helping seems futile. Already in its fifth printing, it is widely used in grief and divorce recovery groups. Forty brief readings with reflective questions, poetry, and Scripture passages. Part 1 describes the physical, emotional, and spiritual reactions to divorce. Part 2 offers keys for survival. Part 3 describes areas where growth can take place.

Author A frequent guest on radio and talk shows, Marshall is the author of two other books. She is a professional educator, speaker, and writer. She founded and directs SCORE for college, a program that has been named as a model for helping high risk students become eligible, upon high school graduation, for the college or university of their choice.

When a Friend Gets a Divorce *What Can You Do?* Sharon G. Marshall

Baker Book House, 1990, $6.99, paper, 128 pp., for counselors

Description Provides readers with practical advice on how to be a real friend to those mourning the end of a marriage—how to offer comfort, support, a listening ear, and when asked, helpful advice. Divided into three sections, it discusses the inner destruction brought on by divorce, common requests for help and their real meaning, and tools that work.

Author A frequent guest on radio and talk shows, Marshall is the author of two other books. She is a professional educator, speaker, and writer. She founded and directs SCORE for college, a program that has been named as a model for helping high risk students become eligible, upon high school graduation, for the college or university of their choice.

Contents *Part 1:* What's happening? The dynamics of loss *1.* Who is this new person? *2.* Don't they know they're God's kids? *3.* Why are reactions different? *4.* But nothing is wrong *5.* I'm a mass of confusion *6.* If only . . . if then . . . if not, then *7.* A big black cloud is chasing me *8.* I celebrate life *Part 2:* Please, please help me! Inner cries from your friends *9.* Don't stay away *10.* Listen, listen closer *11.* Don't take sides *12.* Don't criticize *13.* Show you care *14.* Share what used to be normal *15.* Be cautious about money *16.* Help me survive on Sundays *17.* Enlist others to help *18.* Don't speak for God *19.* Open heart, close mouth *20.* Time, time, time *Part 3:* What works—tools for helpers *21.* Prayer *22.* Love *23.* Communication *24.* Respect *25.* Laughter *26.* Journaling *27.* Expressing anger *28.* God's release *29.* Professional help—when and how to refer

Counseling Families After Divorce
Wholeness for the Broken Family, David Miller

Word Publishing, 1995, $15.99, cloth, 1,994 pp.

Description Designed to help counselors understand the changing family and ways to assist them in dealing with various difficulties associated with transition. Part of the new Contemporary Christian Counseling series from Word.

Author Dr. David R. Miller is the professor of counselor education at Liberty University in Lynchburg, Va. He is a licensed professional counselor who has published several other books.

Contents *1.* The rise of the nontraditional family *2.* The trauma of divorce: disturbing the nest *3.* Children of divorce: the broken bough *4.* Adolescents and parental divorce: a twisted chain *5.* The single parent: forever changed *6.* The remarriage family *7.* Counseling and the divorce process *8.* Counseling children of divorce *9.* Counseling adolescents and young adults *10.* Counseling single parents *11.* Counseling and remarriage *12.* Future family—what works!

What Happened? *My Experience with Divorce,* Dorothy Miller

New Hope, 1987, $2.95, paper, 61 pp., for counselees

Description Dorothy Miller hadn't planned on divorce, but it happened. This book is her courageous account of coping with divorce. Included at the end of the book are suggestions for dealing with divorce written by Thomas W. Newman, a pastor in Birmingham, Ala.

Author Dorothy Miller is a former church staff member and denominational employee. She attended Baylor University.

After the Divorce Clyde M. Narramore

Narramore Christian Foundation, $.50, paper, for counselees

Description One of the many booklets available from the Narramore Christian Foundation. Designed to be handed to a person beginning to come to grips with a problem in living.

Author Dr. Clyde M. Narramore is a licensed psychologist and the president and founder of the Narramore Christian Foundation—a charitable, nonprofit educational, training, and counseling organization ministering primarily to the Christian community. He is also the founder of the Rosemead School of Psychology and author of 29 books.

When Your Long-Term Marriage Ends *A Workbook for Divorced Women,* Elaine Newell

Resource Publications, Inc., 1994, $14.95, paper, 136 pp., for counselees

Description Focuses on recovery for women who "grew up with their husbands," raised a family together, then suddenly found themselves alone. The author shares how she faced and eventually overcame her fears. Each chapter includes exercises to help readers identify and "discuss"—journal style—their feelings around each phase of recovery.

Author Elaine Newell has her degree in journalism and is a student of metaphysics and psychology.

Contents *1.* Accepting responsibility *2.* Getting help *3.* Dealing with anger *4.* Taking charge *5.* Alone vs. lonely *6.* Love and hate—the two edged sword *7.* Being good to yourself, being good to him *8.* Dating, mating, relating *9.* Leaving with love *10.* The new you

Meditations for the Divorced Judy Osgood

Gilgal Publications, 1989, $6.95, paper, 72 pp., for counselees

Description No one wins in a divorce. Everyone loses, and that loss is particularly difficult when the divorcee feels estranged from God and the church. How do counselors reconcile their personal feelings about divorce and, when necessary, put them aside to help a client despite them? The faith-related experiences of those who have walked this road provide an eye-opening picture of what helps and what doesn't. The book shows how they felt God reaching out to them through friends and professionals throughout this painful process.

Author Judy Osgood serves as editor of this work and three others on bereavement. She became involved in the bereavement field after her teenaged son's death from chemotherapy complications. Her research revealed the need for books written on specific types of grief by those who had experienced it and led to the Gilgal Meditation series.

When Your Ex Won't Pay *Getting Your Kids the Financial Support They Deserve,* Nancy S. Palmer and Ana Tangel-Rodriguez

Piñon Press, 1995, $10.99, paper, 168 pp.

Description This book is for custodial parents facing the uphill battle of claiming financial support for their children. Helps them be aware of their options, be prepared to present their case, and be armed with facts before they visit an attorney or a social services office.

Authors Nancy S. Palmer is the chair of family law of the Florida Bar. Ana Tangel-Rodriguez has been a contract attorney with the state of Florida in child support since 1985.

Contents *1.* The way it is *2.* After the divorce *3.* Just what is child support? *4.* Walking through the process *5.* The emotional impact *6.* What if we were never married? *7.* Today's complex families *8.* Making changes in support amounts *9.* But a court order won't pay my bills *10.* Feeling good about yourself *11.* Where does the U.S. go from here? / *Appendixes:* Information resources / Sample worksheets / Family law enforcement in the fifty states

Life after Divorce Dorothy Payne

The Pilgrim Press, 1982, $1.75, paper, 24 pp., for counselees

Description Part of the Looking Up series of booklets from the Pilgrim Press. For the cost of a greeting card, this booklet provides the reader with 24 pages of insight, wisdom, Scripture readings, meditation, direction, comfort, and prayer.

Divorced: Surviving the Pain *Meditations on Divorce,* Alice Stolper Peppler

CPH Publishing, 1993, $6.99, paper, 96 pp., for counselees

Description These devotions help readers find comfort in the Lord and move toward a new beginning in him. An ideal inspiration companion for the difficult journey through divorce.

Catholics Experiencing Divorce William Rabior and Vicki Wells Bedard

Ligouri Publications, 1990, $2.50, paper, 79 pp., for counselees

Description Sensitive and easy to understand, this book offers practical advice and encouragement for starting over after divorce. It helps readers: make the transition from coupleness to singleness; learn to accept their loss; turn their pain into peace; find a new future; and more. It includes a resource section with continuing education, career guidance, housing assistance, and counseling information. The book was praised by the Catholic Press Association for its pastoral content.

Authors William Rabior is a Catholic priest and registered clinical social worker who has done extensive work with divorced persons. Vicki Bedard is a communications specialist who has also worked extensively with the divorced. This book is used as a text for a weekend retreat entitled "Healing the Wounds of Divorce."

Life after Divorce *Practical Biblical Steps from an Expert Who's Been There,* Bobbie Reed

CPH Publishing, 1993, $9.99, paper, 196 pp., for counselees

Description This how-to handbook offers practical steps on how to grow through the painful recovery from divorce. Readers learn to: identify ten destructive thought patterns and turn them into constructive ones; recognize, resolve, and redirect anger; protect children from fallout; laugh again; love again; handle sex and singleness; set goals and keep growing.

Author Divorced in 1973 with two young sons, Bobbie Reed, Ph.D., has turned a difficult journey through divorce into a dynamic ministry to single and single-again adults. She is a popular speaker for singles conferences across the United States.

Contents As you begin: divorce! What an ugly word! *1.* I don't want to be divorced! *2.* I feel so depressed *3.* I find I'm often angry *4.* I still have to deal with my ex *5.* I don't know how to let go *6.* I'm not ready to forgive *7.* I'm beginning to live again *8.* I am celebrating my new life *9.* I want to help my children cope *10.* I may someday love again *11.* I'm still a sexual being *12.* I need my friends / *Appendix:* Developing a divorce recovery support group

Divorce Recovery Randy Reynolds and David Lynn

Zondervan Publishing House, 1992, $4.99, paper, 96 pp., for both counselors and counselees

Description Part of the Recovery Discovery series of workbooks. This title walks the reader through a divorce recovery process that includes dealing with loneliness, sex, one's part in the divorce, and the new blended family.

When Your Children Divorce Elaine R. Seppa

InterVarsity Press, 1995, $9.95, paper, 165 pp.

Description When your children divorce, a whole range of complicated relationships emerges. How should you relate to your former son or daughter-in-law? What if someone new comes into your daughter's life? What about the grandchildren? Elaine Seppa writes with honesty about her own experiences as two sons divorced and remarried.

Author Elaine R. Seppa is a mother and homemaker who lives with her husband, Karl, in Seattle.

Contents *1.* The shocking news *2.* "I feel ashamed and guilty" *3.* "I'm angry, worried, and afraid" *4.* But it's time to move on *5.* "How can I help my hurting child?" *6.* What about the ex spouse, and the new one? *7.* New roles with your grandchildren *8.* When your child is an unfit parent *9.* Facing embarrassing and shameful truths *10.* Fathers speak out about their children's divorces *11.* The church's response *12.* Gaining perspective through small groups *13.* Refreshed and renewed *14.* Where are you now?

Healing the Wounds of Divorce *A Spiritual Guide to Recovery,* Barbara Leahy Shlemon

Ave Maria Press, 1992, $5.95, paper, 136 pp., for counselees

Description Shlemon shares her own healing process and offers 17 short chapters dealing not only with such issues as children, finances, and relatives, but also with spiritual concerns such as fear, guilt, and forgiveness. Each chapter concludes with a prayer that enables readers to place their experience, with all its pain and incompletion, before the Lord.

Author Barbara Leahy Shlemon has been involved in the healing ministry since 1965. A registered nurse, she has traveled nationally and internationally, directing retreats and workshops, addressing conferences and conventions.

Contents *1.* Denial *2.* Rejection *3.* Fear *4.* Grief *5.* Anger *6.* Shame *7.* Guilt *8.* Children *9.* Finances *10.* Relatives *11.* Loneliness *12.* Friendship *13.* Intimacy *14.* Dating *15.* Self-esteem *16.* Forgiveness *17.* Surrender / *Appendix:* Annulment

Single Again *Life after Divorce,* James Singleton

Serendipity, 1991, $6.95, paper, 96 pp., for both counselors and counselees

Description A 7- or 14-week course utilizing Scripture and discussion questions. Designed for anyone who is divorced and is ready and willing to embrace a new life of singleness.

Contents *1.* The death of a dream *2.* Unpacking the boxes *3.* Hide and blame *4.* The unwelcome anger *5.* The power of forgiveness *6.* Growing aloneness *7.* Renewing friendship

Learning More about Divorce Recovery David A. Smart

Rapha Resources, $2.50, paper, for both counselors and counselees

Description Grounded in biblical teaching, this booklet points the way to healing damaged emotions and destructive behaviors, and stimulates personal growth and self-worth.

A Time for Healing *Coming to Terms With Your Divorce,* Harold Ivan Smith

LifeWay, 1995, $11.95, paper, 200 pp.

Description Part of the LifeWay Support Group series from the Southern Baptist Convention. Designed to be used by individuals or groups to work through the various adjustments that follow divorce. An excellent facilitator's companion guide is also available from the publisher.

Author Harold Ivan Smith is an author and speaker on issues related to singles. He is the author of over 50 books.

Contents *Introduction* / Steps for starting a group / Goals for a support group / Foundational concepts for support groups / Actions basic to effective group leadership / Training potential group facilitators / Three ways to use

A Time for Healing / Additional leadership helps / Overview of group sessions *Group session 1:* Viewing your divorce as a process *Group session 2:* Relinquishing your attachments *Group session 3:* Revising your assumptive world *Group session 4:* Readjusting to new realities *Group session 5:* Resisting discount relationships *Group session 6:* Accepting resurrection *Group session 7:* Reviewing holiday traditions *Group session 8:* Understanding sexuality *Group session 9:* Some biblical dimensions / Feelings chart / Group covenant / Self-evaluation checklist

Growing through Divorce *Expanded Edition—With Working Guide,* Jim Smoke

Harvest House Publishers, 1985, $8.99, paper, 256 pp., for both counselors and counselees

Description Offers practical guidance for anyone facing divorce. Based on the author's firsthand experience of working with thousands of formerly married persons, this book can transform your life from an old ending to a new beginning!

Author Jim Smoke is nationally known for his ministry to single adults. He annually travels thousands of miles throughout North America conducting Growing through Divorce Seminars and speaking at singles conferences.

Contents *1.* Is this really happening to me? *2.* Letting go *3.* Getting the ex-spouse in focus *4.* Assuming responsibilities for myself *5.* Assuming responsibilities for my children *6.* Assuming responsibilities for my future *7.* Finding a family *8.* Finding and experiencing forgiveness *9.* 37 going on 17 *10.* Remarriage—yours, mine, and maybe our families *11.* How I've grown through my divorce *12.* How I've grown in my remarriage *13.* How to keep the scales of justice from tilting *14.* Growing through divorce—a summary

Living beyond Divorce *The Possibilities of Remarriage,* Jim Smoke

Harvest House Publishers, 1984, $6.99, paper, 159 pp., for counselees

Description Many men and women find themselves still single 5, 7, 10 years after losing a mate by divorce or death. What happens to them during those years? What challenges do they face? What triumphs do they experience? What if they never remarry? *Living beyond Divorce* explores and answers some of these questions. The author has spent ten years helping people through divorce and now probes the feelings, hopes, changes, and expectations of the many who have not sought instant remarriage as their answer to being single again.

Author Jim Smoke is nationally known for his ministry to single adults. He annually travels thousands of miles throughout North America conducting Growing through Divorce Seminars and speaking at singles conferences.

Contents The question of remarriage *1.* Is there life after divorce? *2.* Adjusting your focus *3.* The healing process *4.* The uncomfortable crown *5.* The myths of divorce *6.* Parenting beyond divorce *7.* The relational roller coaster *8.* Learning to wait *9.* Searching for new things *10.* Beyond divorce as a woman *11.* Beyond divorce as a man *12.* The good things in living alone *13.* Am I ready for marriage?

The Complete Divorce Recovery Handbook: *Grief, Stress, Guilt, Children, Co-dependence, Dating, Re-marriage,* John P. Splinter

Zondervan Publishing House, 1992, $9.99, paper, 288 pp., for counselors

Description Written by divorced people and field-tested with hundreds, this book covers many aspects of divorce recovery.

Author John Splinter (M.A.) is the director of Single Life Ministries, one of the largest ministries to single adults in the Midwest.

Contents *1.* Good grief *2.* Feelings: oh, woe, whoa, feelings! *3.* Stressed out! *4.* How did we get where we are? *5.* Walking through guilt *6.* Facing forgiveness *7.* Children of divorce *8.* But can we communicate? *9.* Getting your act together *10.* Biblical perspectives on divorce and remarriage *11.* Dating after divorce *12.* Creating healthy marriages / *Appendix:* Dealing with attorneys

Finding Your Place after Divorce *Help and Hope for Women Starting Again,* Carole Sanderson Streeter

Harold Shaw Publishers, 1992, $7.99, paper, 161 pp., for counselees

Description Writing as one who has gone through the trauma of divorce, Streeter does more than weep with those who weep. She gives comfort, advice, and practical suggestions for recovery and healing. Her outlines of the immediate, short-term, and long-term goals are extremely helpful. A great book for women wounded by divorce and those who minister to them.

Contents *1.* Life among the breakage *2.* Nobody but yourself *3.* You are forgivable *4.* At home in your home *5.* Your children's needs *6.* Never whimper at work *7.* No stranger to your feelings *8.* Small doses of significance / *Additional resources*

Life after Divorce *A Single Mother's Guide,* Jim Talley

NavPress, 1991, $8.00, paper, 179 pp., for counselees

Description Life after divorce is a shock. You face a host of decisions and critical responsibilities—often with no help and no idea of how to proceed. This book will help you face the realities of your situation, stabilize your life, and begin to move onto the road to recovery. Includes objective insights and a practical, step-by-step plan for progress.

Author Jim Talley has been the associate minister of single adults at the First Baptist Church in Modesto, Calif., since 1976. A popular international speaker and conference guest, Jim has a Ph.D. in counseling and is the author of six books.

Contents *1.* It's not easy being a single parent *2.* Understanding the agony *3.* Stabilizing life after divorce *4.* Resetting expectations *5.* Recognizing the special needs of your children *6.* Accepting the realities of parenting *7.* God understands the frustrated parent *8.* Building spiritual vitality in your kids *9.* Knowing when you're ready for another relationship *10.* The weekend war *11.* The "r" word can be the key to recovery *12.* Remarriage: ready, set . . . wait a minute! *13.* Blended and compounded families *14.* Am I succeeding as a single parent?

Counseling and Divorce David A. Thompson

Word Publishing, 1989, $15.99, cloth, 200 pp., for counselors

Description An experienced pastor examines the causes of divorce and demonstrates how pastors and congregations can minister to the divorced and the divorcing. The emphasis is care and compassion from a Christian perspective.

Author David A. Thompson is professor of practical theology and counseling at Bethany College of Missions in Bloomington, Minn. He has been a pastor, hospital chaplain, college teacher, and chaplain in the U.S. Navy during 18 years of ministry.

Contents *1.* The causes of divorce *2.* The crisis of divorce *3.* The criticisms of divorce *4.* Some pictures of divorce *5.* The process of divorce *6.* The person who intervenes *7.* The context of divorce *8.* The challenge of remarriage *9.* Divorce and the seasons of life *10.* Divorce and the ministry / *Appendix 1:* Helpful books / *Appendix 2:* Divorce recovery group program

Devotions for the Divorcing William E. Thompson

Westminster/John Knox Press, 1984, $8.99, paper, 98 pp., for counselees

Description Offers a glimmer of hope and reflective inspiration for people in the midst of divorce. For those who are lonely, guilty, depressed, frustrated, and unhappy, this collection of 40 Scripture readings with accompanying meditations and prayers provides relief from the daily pressures and traumas of marriage failure.

Author William E. Thompson is associate pastor of the Church of the Pilgrims, Washington, D.C. He has 20 years' experience in the parish and has been active as a staff planner for retreats for people without partners.

Dear God, I'm Divorced! Sara Arline Thrash

Baker Book House, 1991, $7.99, paper, 101 pp., for counselees

Description A unique format that combines anecdotes with excerpts from the author's prayer diary. Explains the recovery process in warm, empathetic terms.

Contents *Season 1:* devastation *Season 2:* deliverance

Starting Over *When Marriage Ends,* Joyce J. Tyra

Herald Press, 1992, $5.95, paper, 96 pp., for counselees

Description When marriage ends, and the fairy tale of living happily ever after crumbles, after a time we have to begin again. That's what this concise, deeply moving book is about: endings and beginnings. After the divorce papers are filed away, the past is over and starting over begins. If you are recently divorced, this book is for you. Tyra draws on experiences and stories of women whose dream marriages have been shattered by divorce.

Author When suddenly single at age 45, Joyce J. Tyra was thrust from her familiar role as housewife and mother into the role of single parent and head of the household. She earned a B.A. in journalism and an M.A. in English, which she teaches in Miami, Fla.

Flying Solo *Meditations for the Single Again,* Thomas Whiteman

Oliver Nelson (a division of Thomas Nelson), 1994, $8.99, paper, 192 pp., for counselees

Description Unique meditations designed for people coping with the pain of divorce that offer genuine hope and understanding. Excellent insight into the Word of God and how it applies to life.

Author Whiteman is president of Fresh Start Seminars and the director of Life Counseling Services in Pennsylvania.

When Your Son or Daughter is Going Through a Divorce *How to be a Positive Influence during a Difficult Experience,* Thomas Whiteman and Debbie Barr

Thomas Nelson Publishers, 1995, $9.99, paper, 192 pp.

Description Practical suggestions for parents on how and when to provide emotional support to your children and grandchildren.

Authors Thomas Whiteman, Ph.D., is a licensed psychologist in Paoli, Pa. Debbie Barr is a freelance writer who resides in Winston, N.C.

Healing the Wounds of Divorce

Abbey Press, $.50 each, paper, 8 pp., for counselees

Description Part of the CareNotes series from Abbey Press. CareNotes are short booklets that help readers identify issues and begin the process of seeking resolution. Anecdotal and uplifting. Beautiful photographs grace the covers. Over 20 million CareNotes have been sold in just over five years. Can be used as an alternative to a greeting card or in conjunction with pastoral care visits.

Helping Children Cope with Divorce

Children, Divorce, and the Church
Douglas E. Adams

Abingdon Press, 1992, $10.95, paper, 128 pp., for both counselors and counselees

Description A book aimed at the mutual support group for the child who is a victim of a traumatic divorce. Includes line art from children and an appendix on how to start such a recovery group.

Author Douglas E. Adams is senior minister of Southside Christian Church in Lima, Ohio.

Contents *1.* Children don't get divorced *2.* Divorce in a child's eyes *3.* Helping children through divorce *4.* Mistakes parents make *5.* Lingering side effects *6.* Helping children cope with divorce *7.* The divorce is never over *8.* Step families *9.* Divorce in the church

With My Mom, With My Dad Maribeth Boelts

Pacific Press, 1992, $5.95, paper, 32 pp., for counselees

Description A picture book for young children. When two parents in one home become two parents in two homes, a child's security can shatter. Although many things change with divorce, children need to be reassured again and again that a parent's love is forever the same.

Author Maribeth Boelts is the author of six books for children and is a former elementary and preschool teacher. She and her husband are the parents of two children.

Letters to Jess and Kate *A Unique and Innovative Approach to Helping a Child Understand Divorce,* James Cantelon

Oliver Nelson (a division of Thomas Nelson), 1994, $9.99, paper, 192 pp., for counselees

Description Specifically geared toward single parents challenged by the effects of divorce on their children. Uses a conversational approach to enlighten parents to the thoughts and feelings of their children in light of divorce.

Author James D. Cantelon has been a pastor for 20 years. He has been the host of *100 Huntly Street.*

What Children Need to Know When Parents Get Divorced *A Book to Read with Children Going through the Trauma of Divorce,* William L. Coleman

Bethany House Publishers, 1983, $5.99, paper, 128 pp., for counselees

Description This is a short, simple book to be read with children (ages 6–11) of divorced parents, to help them cope with this agonizing experience. Designed to help the child make the adjustment to life with only one parent. Illustrated with sensitive photographs.

Author Bill Coleman has written half a dozen bestselling devotional books for children in addition to his other books. His experience as a pastor, father, and writer help give him his special relationship with children.

If My Parents Are Getting Divorced, Why Am I the One Who Hurts? Jeenie Gordon

Zondervan Publishing House, 1993, $7.99, paper, 144 pp., for counselees

Description A book for teenagers whose parents are divorcing. As a high school guidance counselor of over 8,000 adolescents, a child of divorce, and a divorcee, Jeenie Gordon knows how to help hurting teenagers through the pain of divorce. This book teaches teenagers how to cope with their pain in healthy ways. It gives practical ways of dealing honestly with parents, others, and self. Thought-provoking questions at the end of every chapter help teens apply the insights in the chapter to their own situation. In addition, this section encourages teens to grapple with difficult issues and make positive changes.

Author Jeenie Gordon, M.S., M.A., M.F.C.C., is a marriage, family, and child therapist in private practice. She is also a high school counselor and has counseled over 8,000 teenagers. She is a popular seminar speaker.

Contents *1*. Introduction *2*. How can I survive? *3*. That old feeling *4*. Coping with this mess *5*. Stuff I tell myself *6*. Making a plan *7*. Where are my parents when I need them? *8*. Getting parents off your back *9*. Home sweet home *10*. Becoming real—cut the phony stuff *11*. The see-saw syndrome *12*. Home free *13*. I'll take love any way I can get it *14*. God 'n dad (are they different?) *15*. Growing beyond pain

Children and Divorce *What to Expect—How to Help,* Archibald D. Hart

Word Publishing, 1989, $8.99, paper, 179 pp., for counselors

Description As divorce becomes more common, Dr. Archibald Hart urges parents to face squarely the crushing impact divorce can have on children—against the often glib assumption that children "bounce back" easily after their parents break up. A practical book from a widely experienced family counselor.

Author Archibald D. Hart is dean of the Graduate School of Psychology and professor of psychology at Fuller Theological Seminary. A skilled psychotherapist and committed Christian, Dr. Hart brings to this book the same combination of professional knowledge and personal concern that has made his other works successful.

Contents *1*. Divorced at 12 *2*. The damaging effects of divorce *3*. Healing your resentment *4*. Common mistakes made by divorced persons *5*. Your child's feelings *6*. What children learn from divorce *7*. Anxiety and the divorced child *8*. Anger and the divorced child *9*. Improving the

self-esteem of your child *10*. Depression and the divorced child *11*. Your ex-spouse is still a parent *12*. The question of remarriage: stepparents and single parents *13*. Building a blended family

When Your Parents Pull Apart *A Teen's Guide to Surviving Divorce,* Angela Elwell Hunt

Tyndale House Publishers, 1995, $6.99, paper, 144 pp.

Description For teens whose parents are getting divorced. Each chapter begins with a fictional story that introduces a common problem to families in the midst of a divorce, then discusses the problem objectively and compassionately. Christ-centered.

Author Angela Elwell Hunt is a best-selling author. She and her husband have been in youth ministry for 16 years.

In the Middle *What to Do When Your Parents Divorce,* Mary Kehle

Harold Shaw Publishers, 1987, $5.99, paper, 88 pp., for counselees

Description This book is written for preteens whose parents are getting divorced. It deals with the child's feelings and suggests ways to deal with them. In addition, it addresses the issues of divorced parents dating, remarrying, and the blending of two families. Both spiritual and psychological principles are incorporated in helping the preteen deal with these most difficult emotions and experiences.

Author Mary Kehle holds a Ph.D. in counseling psychology and is a registered nurse and sex educator. She is in private practice as a psychologist where she does marital and individual therapy.

Contents *1*. Why do I feel so mad? *2*. Did I do something wrong? *3*. What if something terrible happens? *4*. What if I just feel like crying? *5*. What is happening in court? *6*. What if my parents start dating? *7*. What if my parent remarries? *8*. How can I get along with my stepfamily? *9*. What about all my other new relatives? *10*. Can I have a happy marriage someday?

Divorce Recovery for Teenagers *Help Your Kids Recover, Heal, and Grow When Their Families Are Ripped Apart,* Stephen Murray and Randy Smith

Zondervan Publishing House, 1990, $10.95, paper, 153 pp., for both counselors and counselees

Description Murray and Smith give you a complete, step-by-step divorce recovery workshop that you can put to use right now. It's got everything you'll need to hold your own workshops—complete outlines for every session; guidelines on recruiting, training, and keeping staff; tips on how to attract the kids you really want to come, even instructions on what snacks to have on hand!

Authors Stephen Murray is minister of youth at St. Andrew's Presbyterian Church in Newport Beach, Calif. Randy Smith is a licensed marriage, family, and child counselor who practices in Costa Mesa, Calif.

Contents *Section 1:* The impact of divorce on teenagers *1.* Ministering to families in divorce *2.* What teenagers go through when their parents divorce *3.* Teens' emotions in divorce—grieving the loss *4.* Caring means preparing: the competent youth worker *5.* Helping teens by counseling them *Section 2:* The divorce recovery workshop / *Appendix A:* Workshop forms and letters / *Appendix B:* One-day workshop / *Appendix C:* Friday night/Saturday workshop / *Appendix D:* Weekend retreat workshop / *Appendix E:* Bibliography

Please Come Home *A Child's Book about Divorce,* Doris Sandford and Graci Evans

Gold 'n' Honey Books (Questar), 1993, $7.99, cloth, 24 pp., for counselees

Description Part of the Hurts of Childhood series from Gold 'n' Honey. The series was developed for children ages 5–11 who have experienced deep and tragic hurts. The books deal gently and compassionately with children's delicate feelings when they're forced to handle burdens far too big for them to carry.

Kids Caught in the Middle—Children's Edition *An Interactive Workbook for Children,* Gary Sprague

Janet Thoma (a division of Thomas Nelson), 1993, $10.99, paper, 115 pp., for counselees

Description Designed to help children sort through the issues of divorce recovery. Anecdotal sketches, activities, illustrations, and shared experiences help the child sort through feelings of confusion, guilt, worry, and resentment. Can be used with a parent or other support person.

Author Gary Sprague is the executive director of KIDS HOPE, which runs seminars, retreats, and camps for children.

Contents *Section 1:* How it feels *1.* Feeling bad, sad, mad, and glad *2.* Shock fear and confusion too *3.* It isn't my fault *4.* I am not alone! *Section 2:* Things that change *5.* Mom and dad live in different places now *6.* There's never enough money *7.* New friends and new schools *8.* I visit them every other weekend *Section 3:* New family relationships *9.* Mom has a new boyfriend, Dad has a girl-friend too *10.* New parents, new siblings *Section 4:* Where is God when I hurt? *11.* Hurts band-aids can't cover *12.* What the Bible says about suffering *13.* What the Bible says about comfort *Section 5:* Dysfunctional family secrets *14.* What is adultery? *15.* What is abuse? *16.* What is addiction? *17.* Breaking the cycle

Kids Caught in the Middle—Teenager Edition *An Interactive Workbook for Teens,* Gary Sprague

Janet Thoma (a division of Thomas Nelson), 1993, $10.99, paper, 115 pp., for counselees

Description Designed to help teenagers sort through the issues of divorce recovery. Anecdotal sketches, self-tests, and fill-in-the blank questions help the teenager sort through feelings of confusion, guilt, worry, and resentment. Can be used on their own or with a support person.

Author Gary Sprague is the executive director of KIDS HOPE, which runs seminars, retreats, and camps for children.

Contents *Section 1:* How it feels *1.* Stages of grief recovery *2.* Other unpopular feelings *3.* It isn't my fault *4.* I am not alone! *Section 2:* Things that change *5.* We're a single parent family *6.* There's never enough money *7.* New friends and new schools *8.* I visit them every other weekend *Section 3:* New family relationships *9.* My parents are dating just like me *10.* New parents, new siblings *Section 4:* Where is God when I hurt? *11.* Hurts band-aids can't cover *12.* What the Bible says about suffering *13.* What the Bible says about comfort *Section 5:* Dysfunctional family secrets *14.* What is adultery? *15.* What is abuse? *16.* What is addiction? *17.* Breaking the cycle

My Parents Got a Divorce *Children Tell How They Went from Hurt to Hope,* Gary Sprague

Chariot Family Publishing, 1992, $7.99, paper, 125 pp., for counselees

Description A book by kids, primarily for kids. With frank honesty and heartfelt emotion, these boys and girls from divorced families tell how it felt when their parents got a divorce. Their common message—healing does happen. They tell how God eased their pain, and they help others from divorced families. Written in brief paragraph form. Each chapter covers a different part of the divorce experience. The material is arranged according to the building blocks of recovery, which are: the emotional issues, lifestyle adjustments, blended family concerns, and the spiritual questions.

Author Gary Sprague is the executive director of KIDS HOPE, which runs seminars, retreats, and camps for children.

Contents *1.* Introduction *2.* How I felt *3.* My new life *4.* My new family *5.* Where is God? *6.* My story *7.* Letters to God / *Epilogue:* My three dads

Healing the Hurt *For Teenagers Whose Parents Are Divorced,* Mildred Tickfer

Baker Book House, 1984, $4.99, paper, 94 pp., for counselees

Description This book is a call to courage—a call for teenagers to develop and grow gracefully through the difficult situation of divorce.

Author Mildred Tickfer, R.N., is a staff educator at Pine Rest Christian Hospital in Grand Rapids, Mich., and a seasoned church youth and children's worker.

Contents *1.* Confusion: I don't know what to do *2.* Betrayal: how could they . . . ? *3.* Doubt and fear: could they stop loving me? *4.* Anger: the two-edged sword *5.* Grief: mourning the loss *6.* In the middle: I feel like a ping pong ball *7.* Switching roles: I don't want to be the parent *8.* Jealousy: mom has a new boyfriend/dad has a new wife *9.* Living: let's get on with it

When Your Parents Call It Quits *Surviving Family Breakdown,* Dan Webster

NavPress, 1991, $2.00, paper, 18 pp., for counselees

Description Targets teenagers dealing with divorcing or divorced parents. Part of the student Survival series from NavPress. Largely anecdotal with several reflection questions.

Author Dan Webster is the director of student ministries at Willow Creek Community Church in South Barrington, Ill.

Innocent Victims *How to Help Your Children Overcome the Trauma of Divorce,* Thomas Whiteman

Janet Thoma (a division of Thomas Nelson), 1993, $9.99, paper, 252 pp., for both counselors and counselees

Description Part of the Fresh Start series of self-help titles from Thomas Nelson. An indispensable book for parents, relatives, mental health professionals, teachers, guardians, day-care workers, and other concerned adults. Practical, straightforward guidelines on how to help children cope with divorce. Utilizes real-life stories.

Author Thomas Whiteman (Ph.D., Bryn Mawr College), president of Fresh Start Seminars, is founder and director of Life Counseling Services in Pennsylvania.

Contents *Section 1:* Understanding your children *1.* Through the eyes of a child *2.* Why don't we think alike? *Section 2:* Your children's reaction *3.* Typical reactions *4.* The initial stage *5.* The secondary stage *6.* The acceptance stage *7.* Long-term effects *Section 3:* Helping your children *8.* Breaking the news *9.* Restructuring *10.* Parenting as a single

Divorce: When It's Tearing You Apart

Abbey Press, 1993, $.50 each, paper, 8 pp., for counselees

Description Part of the CareNotes for Teens series from Abbey Press. CareNotes are 5 x 7 booklets designed to offer strength and help to (young) people in crisis. Each CareNote gently introduces an issue, then encourages a person to take appropriate steps toward resolution. Over 20 million CareNotes have been sold.

Helping Your Child When Divorce Hits Home

Abbey Press, $.50 each, paper, 8 pp., for counselees

Description Part of the CareNotes series from Abbey Press. CareNotes are short booklets that help readers identify issues and begin the process of seeking resolution. Anecdotal and uplifting. Beautiful photographs grace the covers. Over 20 million CareNotes have been sold in just over five years. Can be used as an alternative to a greeting card or in conjunction with pastoral care visits.

14. Domestic Violence

Battered into Submission *The Tragedy of Wife Abuse in the Christian Home,* James Alsdurf and Phyllis Alsdurf

InterVarsity Press, 1990, $9.99, paper, 168 pp., for both counselors and counselees

Description Examines how and why wife abuse affects Christian marriages. Profiles abusers and victims, analyzes the influence of religious and cultural values, and discusses the church's role in intervention and reconciliation. Winner of a 1990 *Christianity Today* Critic's Choice Award.

Authors James Alsdurf (Ph.D.) is a clinical and forensic psychologist for the Bureau of Community Corrections in Hennepin County, Minn. Phyllis Alsdurf is a writer and the former editor of *Family Life Today* magazine.

Contents *1.* A nightmare in the Christian home *2.* Who is the battered woman and why does she stay? *3.* What kind of men abuse their wives? *4.* Evil: the heart of violence *5.* Blaming the victim *6.* Wife abuse and the submission of women *7.* The process of reconciliation *8.* Marriage, divorce, and wife abuse *9.* The church and reconciliation / *Conclusion:* Violence in the land / *Appendix:* The response of clergy to the problem of wife abuse

Victims into Victors *Beyond Family Violence,* Anne Amos

Morehouse Publishing, 1991, $6.95, paper, 63 pp., for counselees

Description This collection of essays and personal stories raises our awareness of domestic violence within Christian communities; calls Christians to examine what they value in family relationships; and helps concerned pastoral caregivers offer compassionate and practical support for victims. Anne Amos serves as editor of this collection.

Contents Women: prisoners in their own homes / The struggle to have domestic violence recognized as an issue within the church / The dark side of Bible bashing: ally of domestic violence / I am made in the image of God / "There is no going back" / Remember your wedding vows / "No marriage covenant is ever license to abuse" / "She made me do it" / You must forgive "seventy times seven"

/ Forgiveness is for the future / Family life is not always Christian / Walking down the Jericho road / *Conclusion*

Family Secrets *My Experience with Family Violence,* Anonymous

New Hope, 1988, $2.95, paper, 57 pp., for counselees

Description A first-person account of a child growing up with family violence. It is set apart from other books on the subject in that this account took place in what appeared to be a model home. But this book is not an act of revenge. No names are mentioned. It is the author's desire that as readers become aware of such secrets, more questions will be asked, more help given. The book concludes with suggestions for coping and a resource list for further reading.

Author The author wishes to remain anonymous.

Breaking Free from Domestic Violence Jerry Brinegar

CompCare Publishers, 1993, $11.95, paper, 158 pp., for both counselors and counselees

Description Unlike other books that simply deplore family violence or explain how violence repeats itself through successive generations, this book has an encouraging message: We can do something about it. Specific answers for what to do if you are being abused, your children are being abused, you are an adult survivor, you are an abused elder, or you are a perpetrator.

Author Jerry L. Brinegar, Ph.D., is an approved supervisor in the American Association of Marriage and Family Therapists, a licensed MFT, and a certified police stress and crisis intervention instructor.

Contents *Part 1:* The breakdown victims / Types of family violence / Waking up to the problem *Part 2:* The roots of family violence *Part 3:* Stopping the violence *Part 4:* The breakthrough / Making marriage work / Making parenting work / Empowerment for change / *Appendix:* National organizations that can help

Pastoral Care of Battered Women Rita-Lou Clarke

Westminster/John Knox Press, 1986, $7.95, paper, 122 pp., for counselors

Description The battering of women has reached epidemic proportions. This book fills the gap in the resources of the pastoral care field. Rita-Lou Clarke provides a thorough and clear discussion of the nature of battering and its cultural aspects, as well as the psychological and theological dimensions of the problem. She then gives practical guidance for care, considering such topics as couple counseling and help for the abusers.

Author Rita-Lou Clarke is associate pastor, First Presbyterian Church of Garden Grove, Calif. She is on the board of the Orange County Coalition against Domestic Violence and has worked with a shelter for battered women.

Contents *1.* The battered woman in the cultural context *2.* The psychological dimension of battering *3.* Theological issues related to battering *4.* The role of the pastor / *The Exodus / Journey / Bibliography / Resources*

Violence in the Family *A Workshop Curriculum for Clergy and Other Helpers,* Marie M. Fortune

The Pilgrim Press, 1991, $19.95, spiral, 278 pp., for counselors

Description Here is a resource for both individuals and groups working in violence in the family, particularly spouse and childhood sexual abuse. Placed squarely in the context of religious values and concerns, this manual provides a detailed methodology for effective training of clergy and other professional helpers. Sample outlines and detailed workshop models, with supplementary materials make possible a step-by-step, how-to-do-it approach to training.

Author Marie Marshall Fortune is an ordained minister of the United Church of Christ. She is founder and director of the Center for Prevention of Sexual and Domestic Violence.

Contents *Part 1:* Preparation *1.* Introduction *2.* Goals and objectives *3.* An approach to education and training *Part 2:* Application *4.* Workshop planning *5.* Tips for trainers *6.* Workshop models: the religious response to violence in the family *7.* Content material to supplement presentations *Part 3:* Resources *Part 4:* Appendix

Defiant Hope *Spirituality for Survivors of Family Violence,* James Leehan

Westminster/John Knox Press, 1993, $11.99, paper, 176 pp., for both counselors and counselees

Description Takes seriously the religious and spiritual dimensions of violence in families. The book recognizes the religious roots of abusive behavior and the spiritual conflicts it generates. The author acknowledges the anger, confusion, and frustration that haunt the lives of survivors. He affirms them as psychologically and spiritually healthy responses to violence and betrayal in one's family. The recovery community has long known how critical a strong spirituality is for overcoming the devastation associated with dysfunction. This book draws upon the spiritual traditions of the Jewish and Christian faiths. It explores the defiant nature of hope; the virtuous nature of anger that zealously asserts what is right; and the toughness of forgiveness that challenges abuse, while at the same time it refuses to let past pain control one's life. Prayer is also viewed as a form of spiritual defiance which challenges God and the world about the injustices of family violence.

Author James Leehan, M.A., M.S.S.A., L.P.C., L.S.W., M.F.T., an Episcopal priest, is the director of the University Christian Movement in Cleveland and an adjunct faculty member at Cleveland State University. He has been involved in the recovery movement since 1978.

Contents *1.* The spiritual epidemic of family violence *2.* Restoring spirituality—defiant hope *3.* Recovering crushed dreams *4.* Challenging lessons that betray *5.* Dreaming dreams to see visions *6.* Tough forgiveness *7.* Unmasking our illusions about God *8.* Integration through prayer / *Appendix A:* Religious messages that destroy spirituality / *Appendix B:* Guided meditations that destroy spirituality / *Appendix C:* Guided meditations for survivors

Pastoral Care of Survivors of Family Abuse *How to Recognize and Deal with the Long-term Effects of Physical and Emotional Abuse,* James Leehan

Westminster/John Knox Press, 1989, $12.99, paper, 151 pp., for counselors

Description Drawing upon 15 years of experience in the field, Leehan discusses distinguishing between victims and survivors, recognition of abuse, misuse of Scripture to justify family violence, and ways to address abuse. Ministers and congregations are seen as a source of support that no other sector of society can provide. This book will be an asset to anyone involved in helping a survivor of abuse. Also helps professionals and pastors become sensitive to survivor's needs when involved in public speaking and counseling.

Author James Leehan, M.A., M.S.S.A., L.P.C, L.S.W., M.F.T., an Episcopal priest, is the director of the University Christian Movement in Cleveland and an adjunct faculty member at Cleveland State University. He has been involved in the recovery movement since 1978.

Contents *1.* The crowd of survivors among us *2.* What happened to the survivors among us? (types of abuse) *3.* What have the survivors learned? (effects of abuse) *4.* Behaviors that try the patience of saints (dysfunctional behavior patterns) *5.* Family values and family violence (misuse of Scripture) *6.* Judge not: The pitfalls of a moral response *7.* Spirituality for survivors *8.* Being all things to all survivors *9.* Binding up the wounds

Counseling for Family Violence and Abuse Grant L. Martin

Word Publishing, 1987, $15.99, cloth, 281 pp., for counselors

Description Part of the Resources for Christian Counseling series from Word. Dr. Martin provides guidelines for working with the abuser as well as the abused.

Author Grant L. Martin is a licensed psychologist and marriage and family therapist in Seattle, Wash.

Contents *Part 1:* Spousal abuse *1.* The frequency and history of spousal abuse *2.* The nature of spousal abuse *3.* Crisis counseling in spousal abuse *4.* Treatment of battered women *5.* Treatment of men who batter *Part 2:* Child abuse *6.* Understanding physical and emotional child abuse *7.* Sexual abuse of children *8.* Evaluation and treatment of sexually abused children *9.* Treatment of the sexual offender *Part 3:* Elder abuse *10.* Abuse of the elderly / *Recommended resources*

Family Violence *The Compassionate Church Responds,* Melissa A. Miller

Herald Press, 1994, $8.95, paper, 184 pp., for both counselors and counselees

Description Miller guides readers through such issues as the survivor's healing, power dynamics in the family, congregational response to survivors and offenders, and hard faith questions.

Author Melissa A. Miller has been a counselor at Shalom Counseling Services in Ontario, Canada,

since 1985. She has extensive experience working with issues of family violence. She is a clinical member of the American Association of Marriage and Family Therapy.

Contents *1.* Setting the stage *2.* The abuse of physical power *3.* The abuse of sexual power *4.* The abuse of emotional power *5.* The healing path for survivors *6.* Offenders *7.* A challenge to the compassionate church *8.* Resolutions *9.* The church of counterculture *10.* The churches respond *11.* What to do when there's nothing to do *12.* Forgiveness and reconciliation *13.* Full circle: benefits of facing family power issues / How to use this book

Violence and Abuse in the Home
Clyde M. Narramore

Narramore Christian Foundation, $.50, paper, for both counselors and counselees

Description One of the many booklets available from the Narramore Christian Foundation. Designed to be handed to a person beginning to come to grips with a problem in living.

Author Dr. Clyde M. Narramore is a licensed psychologist and the president and founder of the Narramore Christian Foundation—a charitable, nonprofit educational, training, and counseling organization ministering primarily to the Christian community. He is also the founder of the Rosemead School of Psychology and author of 29 books.

When Anger Hits Home *Taking Care of Your Anger without Taking It Out on Your Family,* Gary Jackson Oliver and H. Norman Wright

Moody Press, 1992, $16.99, cloth, 249 pp., for counselees

Description Instead of a time bomb to be avoided, anger can be a valuable gift to use in accomplishing God's will. This helpful book clears up the myths about this least understood emotion and provides a step-by-step approach to constructively redirecting its power.

Authors Gary J. Oliver is a psychologist at Southwest Counseling Associates and visiting professor at Denver Seminary. Dr. H. Norman Wright is one of America's best known Christian marriage and family counselors at the Family Counseling and Enrichment Center in Tustin, Calif. He is author of more than 50 books. He has also served on the faculty of Talbot School of Theology and the Graduate School of Marriage Counseling of Biola University.

Shattered and Broken *Wife Abuse in the Christian Community: Guidelines for Helping and Healing,* S. Rutherford and Linda McDill

Fleming H. Revell, $8.99, paper, for counselors

Description Written to provide help, hope, and healing for abused women, this timely book also instructs pastors and counselors in how to deal with the victims of abuse.

Help for the Battered Woman *One Woman's True Story Plus Resource Sections on Getting Help,* Lydia Savina

Bridge Publishing, $9.95, paper, for counselees

Description Deals openly with patterns and examples of spouse and child abuse, the pathology of the abusers, and responses of the battered. Included are listings of support groups, shelters, and special helps on dealing with police, courts, and friends. The last section deals with the proper Christian response to battering.

Breaking the Cycle of Abuse *A Biblical Approach to Recognizing and Responding to Domestic Violence,* Catherine Scott

Chariot Family Publishing, 1992, $7.99, paper, 176 pp., for both counselors and counselees

Description Practical help and biblical advice for those living in an abusive situation or struggling with an abusive past. Readers will identify the destructive cycle and scars that mark abusive relationships, then discover God's protective provisions for healing. Information on how to build adequate support networks, reconcile the past, and prepare for the future.

Author Catherine Scott writes from her years of experience and crisis intervention training.

In the Name of Submission Kay Marshall Strom

Multnomah Books (Questar), 1991, $6.99, paper, 139 pp., for counselees

Description Here's advice and hope for victims, friends, and churches to work to stop the cycle of domestic violence. Organizations to turn to for help are included.

When There's Hitting and Hurting at Home

Abbey Press, $.50 each, paper, 8 pp., for counselees

Description Part of the CareNotes series from Abbey Press. CareNotes are short booklets that help readers identify issues and begin the process of seeking resolution. Anecdotal and uplifting. Beautiful photographs grace the covers. Over 20 million CareNotes have been sold in just over five years. Can be used as an alternative to a greeting card or in conjunction with pastoral care visits.

15. Eating Disorders

Eating Disorders James Alsdurf and Phyllis Alsdurf

> InterVarsity Press, 1993, $.99, paper, 32 pp., for counselees

> **Description** Writing for concerned friends and family, Phyllis and James Alsdurf offer insight into the causes of eating disorders, steps for recovery, a list of resources, and a chart of "red flags" that may signal an eating disorder.

Chaotic Eating *A Guide to Recovery,* Kaye V. Cook and Helen Bray-Garretson

> Zondervan Publishing House, 1992, $7.99, paper, 128 pp., for both counselors and counselees

> **Description** This book blends clinical experience, biblical principles, and research findings into a comprehensive theory of eating that addresses personal, societal, and spiritual realities. Focuses on practical strategies for change.

> **Authors** Helen Bray-Garretson and Kaye V. Cook are practicing clinicians with expertise in the theory and treatment of eating disorders. Bray-Garretson is a psychologist for both Housatonic Center for Mental Health in Lakeville, Conn., and the Hillcrest Educational Center in Lenox, Mass. Cook is a professor of psychology at Gordon College in Wenham, Mass.

> **Contents** *1.* Every woman's obsession *2.* Can fat hurt you? *3.* Bulimia: the secret millions share *4.* Anorexia nervosa: dieting to death *5.* Transforming our eating habits *6.* Filling our empty spaces *7.* Confronting our false beliefs *8.* God cares how you eat *9.* Eating our way through life *10.* You can change how you eat!

Escaping Anorexia and Bulimia *What You Need to Know about Eating Disorders and How to Avoid Them,* Donald Durham and Paul Hanson

> Focus on the Family, 1992, $.35, paper, 15 pp., for counselees

> **Description** A nicely done booklet that describes the symptoms and dangers of eating disorders. Uses anecdotes and basic information. Encourages the reader to seek professional help.

> **Authors** Dr. Don Durham is a psychologist and the clinical director at Remuda Ranch—a treatment center for women with eating disorders. Dr. Paul Hanson is a medical consultant at the same facility.

Hope, Help, and Healing for Eating Disorders *A New Approach to Treating Anorexia, Bulimia, and Overeating,* Gregory L. Jantz

> Harold Shaw Publishers, 1995, $11.99, paper, 180 pp.

> **Description** Eating disorders affect the whole person. Yet treatments often focus on emotional issues alone. Sensing the incompleteness of most methods, Dr. Jantz set out to develop a plan that treats the emotional, physical, and spiritual aspects of eating problems. His practical and promising approach can be used by those with food disorders and by their families and friends. Each chapter contains questions and activities to lead readers through progressive steps to healing.

> **Author** Gregory Jantz, Ph.D., is executive director of THE CENTER for Counseling and Health Resources, Inc., with locations in Seattle and the Puget Sound region.

> **Contents** *1.* The ticking time bomb *2.* Control or controlled? *3.* Family ties *4.* The hidden shadow of abuse *5.* The addiction of choice *6.* Denial's detour *7.* The faulty pattern of pride *8.* Present health complications *9.* Future considerations *10.* The power of nutrition *11.* Acknowledging anger *12.* Facing fear and guilt *13.* The healing journey *14.* Finding the way to forgiveness *15.* The perfect Father *16.* Learning to live *17.* How others can help you *18.* General questions on eating disorders *19.* General questions about bulimia *20.* General questions about anorexia *21.* The whole-person approach

Surrendering Hunger *365 Devotions for Christians Recovering from Eating Disorders,* Jan Johnson

Harper and Row, 1993, $12.00, paper, 400 pp., for counselees

Description Features a Scripture passage, a thought for the day, a question for the day, and a brief prayer in each meditation. This supporting volume to *When Food Is Your Best Friend* is a collection of daily devotionals for Christians recovering from overeating, anorexia, and bulimia.

Author Jan Johnson, coauthor of *Creating a Safe Place,* is a Christian writer in recovery from overeating. She has led many successful church groups based on principles of Overeaters Anonymous and has been a contributor to *Christianity Today, Moody* magazine, and *Today's Christian Woman.*

When Food Is Your Best Friend *And Worst Enemy,* Jan Johnson

Harper and Row, 1993, $10.00, paper, 176 pp., for both counselors and counselees

Description Deals with food compulsions from a Christian 12-step perspective. Illustrated with histories, this work takes the reader through a three-part journey that defines the issues, points to recovery, and details how to maintain recovery. Also explores the ways eating may eclipse the search for spiritual life.

Author Jan Johnson, coauthor of *Creating a Safe Place,* is a Christian writer in recovery from overeating. She has led many successful church groups based on principles of Overeaters Anonymous and has been a contributor to *Christianity Today, Moody* magazine, and *Today's Christian Woman.*

Feast of Famine *A Physician's Personal Struggle to Overcome Anorexia Nervosa,* Joan M. Johnston

Recovery Publications, Inc., 1992, $13.95, paper, 368 pp., for both counselors and counselees

Description For the millions who suffer from anorexia nervosa, *Feast of Famine* offers the compelling story of one woman's 14-year struggle with this disease.

Author Joan M. Johnson is a family practice physician working in Alberta, Canada.

Contents *1.* In the beginning *2.* Descent into darkness *3.* Reprieve *4.* The second fall *5.* Resurrection *6.* Finding recovery *7.* Transformation: when famine becomes feast / *A final word:* Anger, forgiveness, and healing / *Appendix:* Uncharted territory: bulimia and compulsive eating disorders.

Courage to Go On, The *Life after Addiction,* Cynthia Rowland McClure

Baker Book House, 1990, $8.99, paper, 201 pp., for counselees

Description In this sequel to *The Monster Within,* McClure tells about the years since she had bulimia. She faced a new monster: breast cancer. She fell in love and married. To those who question whether God is working in their lives, McClure answers a resounding "Yes!" and challenges them to go on even when the answers are not clear.

Author McClure has personally worked through the issues of overcoming an eating disorder. She now leads workshops aimed at helping others understand and overcome them as well. She is the author of two other books on eating disorders.

Food for the Hungry Heart *Daily Devotions for Overeaters,* Cynthia Rowland McClure

Janet Thoma (a division of Thomas Nelson), 1991, $7.99, paper, 372 pp., for counselees

Description Part of the Serenity Meditation series. The perfect companion for anyone involved in a 12-step recovery program from food addiction. Format: a brief Scripture passage, followed by several encouraging paragraphs, concluding with a prayer or application.

Author McClure has personally worked through the issues of overcoming an eating disorder. She now leads workshops aimed at helping others understand and overcome them as well. She is the author of two other books on eating disorders.

Conquering Eating Disorders *A Christ-Centered 12-Step Process,* Robert S. McGee and William Drew Mountcastle

LifeWay, 1994, $9.95, paper, 210 pp., for both counselors and counselees

Description Part of the LifeWay Support Group Ministry commissioned by the Southern Baptist Convention. This title is an effective, proven program for anyone who uses food as a relief agent from emotional pain. For those who suffer from anorexia, bulimia, or compulsive overeating and their compulsive-addictive patterns. Designed for both individual and discovery-group study. The book provides self-paced, interactive study, and resources for the 12 weekly sessions. A leader's guide is also available ($4.95) that provides administrative guidance and suggested activities for the weekly discovery-group sessions.

Authors Robert McGee is founder and president of Rapha, a health care organization that provides in-hospital and outpatient care, with a Christ-centered perspective, for adults and adolescents suffering from psychiatric and substance abuse problems. William Drew Mountcastle is a counselor who specializes in eating disorders.

Rapha's 12-Step Program for Overcoming Eating Disorders Robert S. McGee and William Drew Mountcastle

Rapha Resources, $11.99, paper, for counselors

Description Here is an effective, proven program for anyone who has experienced the devastating effects of anorexia, bulimia, or compulsive overeating. The book tackles the compulsive-addictive patterns in which a person uses food in an emotionally or physically abusive way, and it presents an ongoing process for effective and permanent change.

Authors Robert McGee is founder and president of Rapha, a health care organization that provides in-hospital and outpatient care, with a Christ-centered perspective, for adults and adolescents suffering from psychiatric and substance abuse problems. William Drew Mountcastle is a counselor who specializes in eating disorders.

Eating Disorders Frank B. Minirth and Paul D. Meier

Christian Family Video, 1991, $19.95, video, for both counselors and counselees

Description Part of the Minirth-Meier Church Counseling Video Library. The series is designed to enhance the counseling process as clients take the videos home for viewing. This title presents the causes, symptoms, and treatment of eating disorders from a clinical and biblical standpoint.

Authors Doctors Minirth and Meier have gained national prominence for their successful blending of biblical principles with proven clinical and medical treatment. They are nationally recognized authors of over 60 biblically based books on common psychological issues with over three million copies in print.

Food Chains Video William Drew Mountcastle

Rapha Resources, $25.00, video, 1 hour, for both counselors and counselees

Description This insightful one hour video explains the causes, effects, and therapeutic processes of eating disorders.

Author William Drew Mountcastle is a counselor who specializes in eating disorders.

Dying to Be Thin *Help and Hope for Anorexics, Bulimics and Compulsive Eaters,* Elizabeth Round

Lion Publishing, 1992, $2.99, paper, 48 pp., for both counselors and counselees

Description Part of Lion's Pocketbook series. A former eating disorder client discusses reasons no one needs to be a victim of eating disorders.

Contents *1.* Hooked on dieting *2.* The eating disorders *3.* Anorexia nervosa *4.* Bulimia nervosa *5.* Looking for a way out *6.* The first step to recovery *7.* Sharing your feelings *8.* Putting an end to anorexia *9.* Curing compulsive eating *10.* Short-term triggers *11.* Long-term causes *12.* Finding hope *13.* Towards recovery *14.* Life can be good

The Monster Within *Overcoming Bulimia,* Cynthia Joy Rowland

Baker Book House, 1984, $5.99, paper, 189 pp., for counselees

Description This is the true story of Cynthia Rowland, a former television news reporter, who for many years had her secret personal "monster" bulimia. When Rowland checked into the Minirth-Meier Clinic in Dallas, Tex., a Christian psychiatric center, she found an expert team of therapists who helped her battle and overcome the monster.

Author McClure has personally worked through the issues of overcoming an eating disorder. She

107

now leads workshops aimed at helping others understand and overcome them as well. She is the author of two other books on eating disorders.

The Love Hunger Action Plan Sharon Sneed

Janet Thoma (a division of Thomas Nelson), 1993, $12.99, paper, 288 pp., for counselees

Description More than just a diet book, this action plan will help anyone needing weight control. Offers practical guidance for losing and maintaining weight, and understanding of the inner emotional and spiritual needs that trigger weight gain.

Author Dr. Sharon Sneed is a registered dietitian and practicing nutritional consultant. She is widely published.

Contents *Action step 1*—Fight fat *Action step 2*—Follow the new love hunger in action food management plan *Action step 3*—Develop new eating strategies *Action step 4*—Instead of that, try this *Action step 5*—Set your mind upon change *Action step 6*—Adopt winning behaviors and guidelines for permanent weight loss *Action step 7* Enjoy fitness as part of your new lifestyle *Action step 8*—Weight loss Q & A *Action step 9*—150 Action tips for permanent weight loss *Action step 10*—Be prepared for maintenance and relapse / *Appendixes*

Learning More about Eating Disorders Steven W. Spotts

Rapha Resources, $2.50, paper, for counselees

Description Dr. Spotts explains what eating disorders are, their consequences, and how to effectively deal with emotions and feelings in order to recover.

Counseling Those with Eating Disorders Raymond E. Vath

Word Publishing, 1986, $15.99, cloth, 236 pp., for counselors

Description Dr. Vath offers practical guidelines for dealing with this emotional/physical ailment which preys especially upon women.

Author Raymond Vath is a psychiatrist in private practice in Bellevue, Wash. He is also assistant professor of psychiatry at the University of Washington.

Contents *Part 1:* The nature, causes, and consequences of anorexia nervosa and bulimia *1.* The story of eating disorders *2.* Eating is a complex activity *3.* Diagnostic criteria *4.* What eating disorders do to the body *5.* Appetite control: are all created equal? *6.* The effects of starvation *7.* Social perception versus reality *Part 2:* The treatment of anorexia and bulimia *8.* Helping the helper *9.* The best little girl in the world—perfectionism *10.* The worst little girl in the world—self-esteem *11.* What is a woman?—sexual identity *12.* To be or not to be?—depression *13.* To tell the truth—deception *14.* The power struggle—control *15.* Miss Peter Pan—dependency *16.* Healthy living *17.* Free at last *18.* If it's someone you know

The Thin Disguise *Understanding and Overcoming Anorexia and Bulimia,* Pam W. Vredevelt, Deborah Newman, et al.

Janet Thoma (a division of Thomas Nelson), 1992, $14.99, cloth, 288 pp., for both counselors and counselees

Description The most complete, comprehensive, and authoritative book on how to overcome these disorders in women. A balanced, Scripture-based recovery program written by the Minirth-Meier Clinic doctors and counselors.

Authors Pam Vredevelt, M.S., is a licensed professional counselor and director of Christian Counseling Services in Portland, Oreg. Deborah Newman, D.Phil., is a psychotherapist specializing in eating disorders with the Minirth-Meier Clinic. Harry Richards is the clinical director of the inpatient eating disorder program of the Minirth-Meier Clinic in McKinney, Tex. Frank Minirth, M.D., is cofounder of the Minirth-Meier Clinic, one of the largest psychiatric clinics in the United States.

Contents *Part 1:* Beginning the search for answers *1.* What is an eating disorder? *2.* What are the symptoms? *3.* What happens to my body? *4.* What keeps the cycle going? *Part 2:* The pathway to recovery *5.* Breaking the cycle of secrecy *6.* A family affair *7.* Unveiling the masks *8.* The pain of perfectionism *9.* Feeling free *10.* Sexuality and shame *11.* Saying goodbye to losses *12.* Establishing healthy eating patterns *13.* I like the way I look *14.* Setting up a support system *15.* Healthy eating for life *16.* A word to loved ones *17.* One final word

Beyond Chaotic Eating *A Way Out of Anorexia, Bulimia, and Compulsive Eating,* Helena Wilkinson

HarperCollins, 1993, $9.00, paper, 187 pp., for counselees

Description Writing from her experience as an ex-anorexic and counselor, Helena Wilkinson explores the underlying contributory factors including family background, sexuality struggles, and emotional hunger. Provides guidelines for full recovery from chaotic eating. She outlines the various types of help available, including counseling, family and group therapy, friendship, and self-help.

Author Helena Wilkinson is editor of *Carer and Counselor* and the author of two autobiographical books on eating disorders and a consultant to Anorexia and Bulimia Care.

Contents *Part 1:* A cry from the heart *1.* Untangling the web *2.* Running from life *3.* Hiding a monster *4.* Easing the pain *Part 2:* The unfathomed depths *5.* Background: family and effects *6.* Sexuality: healthy and unhealthy *7.* Hunger: inside and out *Part 3:* The journey through *8.* Decision to change *9.* Options for help *10.* Body and nutrition *11.* Facing tough feelings *12.* Making wide choices *13.* Playing new messages *14.* Pursuing true life

Battling an Eating Disorder

Abbey Press, $.50 each, paper, 8 pp., for counselees

Description Part of the CareNotes series from Abbey Press. CareNotes are short booklets that help readers identify issues and begin the process of seeking resolution. Anecdotal and uplifting. Beautiful photographs grace the covers. Over 20 million CareNotes have been sold in just over five years. Can be used as an alternative to a greeting card or in conjunction with pastoral care visits.

American Anorexia/Bulimia Association

American Anorexia/Bulimia Association. An organization

Description Though not a Christian organization, this group functions as a clearinghouse for information on eating disorders.

16. Employment and Career

Take This Job and Love It Stanley C. Baldwin

> InterVarsity Press, 1991, $8.99, paper, 144 pp., for counselees
>
> **Description** Helps readers solve job problems and make their work count for God.
>
> **Author** Stanley Baldwin is the author of many books.
>
> **Contents** *1.* Serving God in the workplace *2.* Can I best glorify God in full-time Christian work? *3.* How can I glorify God in secular work? *4.* When your job involves moral compromise *5.* Getting along with your boss *6.* Overcoming unfair treatment *7.* Loving a difficult coworker *8.* Making a boring job interesting *9.* When your job is hazardous to your health *10.* Overcoming work-related stress *11.* Are you a workaholic? *12.* Changing careers

Finding the Work That You Love *A Woman's Career Guide,* Astrid Berg

> Resource Publications, Inc., 1994, $15.95, paper, 203 pp., for both counselors and counselees
>
> **Description** [Secular] resource for women evaluating career options. If you are exploring work options, use this manual to pinpoint your unique skills and work style so that you can pursue the occupational field best suited to you. The new companion audio tape will lead you through the visualization exercises found in the book.
>
> **Author** Astrid Berg teaches college-level courses in career planning and counseling. She holds a master's degree in counseling.
>
> **Contents** How this guide will help you find the work you love *Part 1:* Background *1.* Changing world, changing work, changing women *2.* Career development for women *Part 2:* Self-assessment *3.* Personality: discover your inner self *4.* Interests: discover what you love to do *5.* Skills: inventory your experiences *6.* Needs, values, roles: understanding what motivates you *7.* Creating your life path *Part 3:* Taking action *8.* Researching career opportunities *9.* Researching education opportunities *10.* Making a choice by fulfilling your dreams.

How to Love the Job You Hate Jane Boucher

> Thomas Nelson Publishers, 1994, $9.99, paper, 228 pp., for counselees
>
> **Description** Practical advice on how to increase job satisfaction by taking charge of a bad situation with positive new attitudes and behaviors. For those who feel like they have to drag themselves out of bed and force themselves to go to work.
>
> **Author** Jane Boucher is a business consultant, professional speaker, and the founder of Boucher Consultants, a nationally recognized firm specializing in effectiveness.

How to Find a Job *Your 30 Day Action Plan to Success,* Robin Casey

> Oliver Nelson (a division of Thomas Nelson), 1993, $8.99, paper, 144 pp., for counselees
>
> **Description** A simple, yet highly effective 30-day program that helps readers learn to market their services and skills to find a job.
>
> **Author** Robin Casey has been a successful job placement counselor in California and a corporate resources manager.
>
> **Contents** *1.* Start with a positive attitude *2.* Join a support network *3.* Commit yourself to a strategic plan *4.* Assess your valuable qualities *5.* Interview yourself thoroughly *6.* Create your personal benefit statement *7.* Get your facts and figures straight *8.* Reexamine your career/life goals *9.* Identify what is negotiable *10.* Consider all your options *11.* Tailor your resumé *12.* Research possible job sources *13.* Go prospecting by phone *14.* Create a network of informational interviews *15.* Thoroughly research each company *16.* Understand and prepare to meet the employer's needs *17.* Visit three agencies *18.* Prepare to get great references *19.* Prepare your positive image *20.* Polish your communication skills *21.* Review and organize all materials *22.* Inspire a clear vision of performance *23.* Focus on opportunities one at a time *24.* Practice your presentation *25.* Overcome hesitations and objections *26.* Follow up each interview and get feedback *27.* Make necessary adjustments in strategy *28.* Make realistic choices and commitments *29.* Negotiating, accepting, or declining an offer *30.* Keeping the job you find

Choosing Your Career *The Christian's Decision Manual,* Martin E. Clark

P & R Publishing, 1989, $5.95, paper, 120 pp., for counselees

Description A practical resource for Christians making career decisions. It has been used frequently in Christian high schools and colleges, as well as by adults facing career transitions. It offers a thorough treatment of a Christian view of work, a decisions model, practical exercises, and answers to the questions most frequently frustrating to believers as they try to "find God's will." It has been used extensively by Christian counselors because its precepts are tied to theistic presuppositions and specific Scripture passages.

Author Martin Clark holds B.A. and M.A. degrees in Bible and the Ed.D. in counseling. He is a licensed professional counselor in Ohio and is certified by the National Board for Certified Counselors. His private counseling and consulting practice has focused on adult career development and related management issues. He served as a pastor and then as director of counseling services at Cedarville College for ten years.

Contents *1.* Foundation principles *2.* The Christian value of work and career elements of the Lord's will *3.* The person God has made *4.* Decision making *5.* Spiritual gifts and career choice circumstances *6.* The call *7.* Being a whole person

Career Exploration Kit Lee Ellis

Christian Financial Concepts, 1992, $15.00, for counselees

Description For persons in grades 8–10 who want to investigate career choices. Contains a 20-page career guidance manual, an audio cassette explaining the career development process, and a career interest inventory consisting of a 12-page survey and 8-page interpretive guide.

Author Lee Ellis is the director of Career Pathways, associated with Christian Financial Concepts.

Career Pathways Full Assessment Package Lee Ellis

Christian Financial Concepts, 1990, $95–115.00, for counselees

Description This mail-order assessment is an important first step in the process of finding direction for your career search. The assessment is suitable for adults and older teens. Upon submission of the completed instruments, the client will receive a comprehensive report covering four areas: personality, interests, skills, and work priorities.

Author Lee Ellis is the director of Career Pathways, a division of Christian Financial Concepts.

PathFinder *A Guide to Career Decision Making,* Lee Ellis

Christian Financial Concepts, 1992, paper, 164 pp., for counselees

Description This is an excellent reference for individuals and families who are making career decisions. Begins by focusing on a biblical perspective on work, provides a wealth of information for making career and life decisions, provides practical steps for choosing the right career field, gives instructions for getting a job, and presents biblical principles for Christian living.

Author Lee Ellis is the director of Career Pathways, associated with Christian Financial Concepts.

Contents *1.* Looking at your work from a biblical perspective *2.* Understanding your pattern *3.* Defining your purpose *4.* Making career decisions *5.* Making educational and training decisions *6.* Career planning resources *7.* Establishing a budget *8.* Writing a resumé *9.* Searching for a job *10.* Starting a business *11.* Facing tough times *12.* Applying biblical principles

Your Career in Changing Times Lee Ellis and Larry Burkett

Moody Press, 1993, $16.99, cloth, 336 pp., for counselees

Description Find a God-honoring vocation that fits your abilities and temperament. A Christian's complete guide to biblically based career planning, from selecting the right college to setting prudent retirement goals.

Authors Since 1976, Larry Burkett has directed Christian Financial Concepts, a nationwide, nonprofit organization dedicated to teaching biblical principles of handling money. He has published over 20 books on finances with a total distribution of over two million. He is heard daily on two radio broadcasts carried by over 1,000 outlets worldwide. Christian Financial Concepts also publishes a free newsletter that focuses on current economic issues. Lee Ellis is the director of Career Pathways, associated with Christian Financial Concepts.

The Crazy-Making Workplace
Archibald D. Hart

111

Servant Publications/Vine Books, 1993, $10.99, paper, 280 pp., for counselees

Description Takes a long overdue look at the dynamics that contribute to stress, conflict, boredom, and burnout. Our jobs can be places where we serve God and experience great personal satisfaction. But all too often they become breeding grounds for defensiveness, denial, anxiety, gossip, and marital infidelity. Hart provides help for Christians who want to be responsible and capable workers, and who want their work environment to be more healthy and rewarding places for everyone to enjoy.

Author Dr. Archibald Hart is the dean of the Graduate School of Psychology and professor of psychology at Fuller Theological Seminary in Pasadena, Calif.

Contents *1.* Can a workplace be toxic? *2.* What makes a workplace dysfunctional? *3.* How to keep work from killing you *4.* Are you poisoning your workplace? *5.* Toxic bosses *6.* Dealing with the crazy-makers *7.* Your job, the pressure cooker, and occupational stress *8.* Burnout on the job *9.* Women at risk *10.* Sex, power, and the workplace *11.* Changing your job *12.* Crazy-making work and your family

Suddenly Unemployed *How to Survive Unemployment and Land a Better Job,* Helen K. Hosier

Here's Life Publishers (c/o Thomas Nelson), 1992, $10.99, paper, 277 pp., for counselees

Description Here's the encouragement, advice, and practical know-how needed to survive unemployment. Valuable insight and information from someone who's been there.

Author During her unemployment, Helen K. Hosier worked as a freelance writer. She is the author and/or ghostwriter for more than 50 books.

Contents *Part 1:* Where you are today *1.* When the unthinkable happens to you *2.* The first things to do *3.* Private victories precede public victories *4.* Be a master, not a victim, of your situation *5.* Where do you go from here? *6.* Chasing the pink slip blues *7.* The age factor *Part 2:* Where you can be tomorrow *8.* Turning the corner *9.* The market-driven approach *10.* Resumania *11.* Writing to influence *12.* The job interview *13.* The job offer *14.* When you don't get the job offer *15.* Final considerations / *Appendix A:* Questions and answers / *Appendix B:* Recommended reading / *Appendix C:* A guide to library research / *Appendix D:* Would you like to know God personally?

Starting Over, but Not from Scratch *Mental and Spiritual Health between Jobs,* Richard Kew

Abingdon Press, 1994, $8.95, paper, 144 pp., for both counselors and counselees

Description Includes case studies, prayers, and devotional pieces. Gives special attention to career switchers, provides spiritual assistance for persons in transition, guidance in journaling, and practical suggestions and advice for the family.

Author Richard Kew is the executive director of the Society for Promoting Christian Knowledge USA. He is ordained and has served as parish priest in the Church of England and the Episcopal Church since 1986.

Contents *1.* New beginnings *2.* From the white house to your house *3.* Crisis as opportunity *4.* Change, change, change *5.* Churches, clergy, and your job hunt *6.* There's nothing wrong with foxhole religion *7.* The journal of your job hunt *8.* A disciplined life *9.* Handling disappointment *10.* Job hunting is a spiritual journey *11.* So your spouse is job hunting? *12.* Happily ever after

Patching Your Parachute *How You Can Beat Unemployment,* Dale Larsen and Sandy Larsen

InterVarsity Press, 1993, $6.99, paper, 144 pp., for counselees

Description Covers the basics of identifying interests and work patterns, setting and meeting goals, using "forced free-time" effectively, making ends meet without sacrificing fun, and considering alternatives like retraining or self-employment. The authors also go beyond the basics in covering spiritual hurts, emotional stress, and strained relationships. Brimming with comfort, hope, and practical ideas.

Authors Dale and Sandy Larsen have written more than 30 Bible study guides in addition to articles for *Christianity Today, Moody* magazine, and the *Christian Herald.*

Contents *1.* Not just a victim *2.* Getting unstuck: reclaiming control *3.* Buying time *4.* Doing more on less or living high on the hog on a pig-hock budget *5.* What do you really want? *6.* Beyond the end of your rope: a guide to other resources *7.* Making the best of underemployment *8.* Making your own way *9.* Helping each other

You're Not Alone *Daily Encouragement for Those Looking for a New Job,* Richard Malone

Thomas Nelson Publishers, 1992, $8.99, paper, 228 pp., for counselees

Description Provides an uplifting counterpoint to the depression that accompanies job loss, uncertainty, and change. An excellent book for mental health counselors, career counselors, and spouses of job seekers. Format: a Scripture passage, several encouraging paragraphs, followed by a brief prayer/meditation.

Author Richard Malone is a graduate of Trinity Evangelical Divinity School. He is an executive in the publishing industry.

The Survivor's Guide to Unemployment
Tom Morton

NavPress/Piñion Press, 1992, $10.00, paper, 224 pp., for counselees

Description An outstanding resource that will help the reader move beyond resumés and interviews. It will help the reader cope emotionally and think clearly. Although not written from a distinctively Christian perspective, the book is an excellent source of practical help for anyone facing unemployment.

Author Tom Morton was unemployed for 17 months before starting work at the Casper, Wyo., *Star-Tribune.* He is an award-wining reporter with ten years of experience in religious, investigative, and environmental journalism.

Contents *Part 1:* "I've never felt so scared"—coping with immediate concerns *1.* I thought I was somebody, then I lost my job *2.* There's no guarantees anymore—anticipating job loss *3.* When you get the word *4.* What to tell your family *5.* Assessing your financial situation *6.* Filing for unemployment benefits *7.* Hunkering down for the long haul *Part 2:* "How am I going to make it?"—surviving day-by-day *8.* Renewing your self-esteem *9.* Take good care of yourself *10.* Take good care of your family *11.* Resourcefulness—seeking out charity *12.* Guard your soul—temptations *13.* Watch your back—employment scams *14.* Part-time work, temporary work, self-employment *15.* When you're at the end of your rope *Part 3:* "Where do I go from here?"—the road back to employment *16.* Developing a focus *17.* Crafting a resumé *18.* The art of networking *19.* The art of interviewing *20.* When you are employed again

The Career Counselor *Guidance for Planning Careers and Managing Career Crises,* Leslie Parrott and Les Parrott

Word Publishing, 1995, $14.95, paper, 329 pp.

Description If you are searching for a job or just surviving in the one you've got, this book may open up new Christian-based insights that could make a difference for you. This timely book is a survival guide for men and women caught in career crisis. Counselors will also find it to be a valuable resource as they help clients struggling with tough career decisions.

Authors Dr. Leslie Parrott is a marriage and family therapist who served as vocational counselor at Seattle Pacific University. She is also adjunct professor of vocational counseling at SPU. Dr. Les Parrott is associate professor of clinical psychology at SPU. Together, they codirect the Center for Relationship Development at Seattle Pacific University.

Contents *Part 1*—The big picture *1.* The world of work *2.* God's will, calling, and the career journey *3.* The power of family in career development *4.* Applying biblical insights in to career counseling *Part 2*—Specific struggles *5.* Teenagers and career exploration *6.* Young adults and career decision making *7.* Midcareer change *8.* Postretirement adjustment *9.* Surviving a career crisis *10.* Women and career development *11.* Special populations and career development *Part 3*—Special issues *12.* Assessing personality, interests, aptitudes, and abilities *13.* Equipping for the job search *14.* Developing a career resource center *15.* Keys to a successful career

In This Very Hour *Loss of a Job,* Marty Schoenleber

Broadman and Holman, 1995, $1.95, saddleback, 44 pp.

Description Part of the new In This Very Hour series from Broadman and Holman Publishers, a series of daily devotions with first-person accounts of victory by faith over life's most tragic disappointments.

Author Marty Schoenleber is a church planter, teaching pastor, and published poet.

Contents A series of thirty-one brief, yet very well-written daily devotionals (Scripture passage and anecdote).

How to Keep Your Head Up When Your Job's Got You Down Doug Sherman

NavPress, 1993, $2.00, paper, for counselees

Career Development Survey Bob Tippie

Maret Software International, $99.99, software, for both counselors and counselees

Description A comprehensive tool designed to help anyone assess their career direction. Useful to anyone involved with adolescents.

Author Bob Tippie is an ordained Baptist minister with an active counseling and consulting practice. He holds a bachelor's degree in psychology and a master's in pastoral counseling.

Between Jobs: Keeping Faith and Hope Alive Daniel J. Welte

Ligouri Publications, 1991, $.75, paper, 24 pp., for counselees

Description The author shares practical tips and personal reflections gathered during his job-searching process. They form a basic spirituality for people who are "between jobs."

Unemployed/Unfulfilled *Down but Not Out,* David Williams

Serendipity, 1990, $6.95, paper, 80 pp., for both counselors and counselees

Description A 7- or 14-week course utilizing scripture and discussion questions. Designed for anyone who is unemployed, underemployed, dissatisfied with their work, or would like to be a part of a support group with others dealing with common issues of employment.

Contents *1.* The toughest job *2.* Emotion control *3.* Discovering the real you *4.* The meaning of work *5.* The hunt begins *6.* Coming up empty *7.* Keeping hope alive

Pulling Together When You're Out of Work

Abbey Press, $.50 each, paper, 8 pp., for counselees

Description Part of the CareNotes series from Abbey Press. CareNotes are short booklets that help readers identify issues and begin the process of seeking resolution. Anecdotal and uplifting. Beautiful photographs grace the covers. Over 20 million CareNotes have been sold in just over five years. Can be used as an alternative to a greeting card or in conjunction with pastoral care visits.

INTERCHRISTO Christian Placement Network

INTERCHRISTO Christian Placement Network. An organization

Description An international employment locating service for Christian organizations. Clients fill out a form which is then fed into the INTERCHRISTO computer, and potential matches are sent to the client. Fee based.

17. Family Therapy

General Works on Family Therapy

The Family *A Christian Perspective on the Contemporary Home,* Jack O. Balswick and Judith K. Balswick

Baker Book House, 1990, $12.99, paper, 325 pp., a reference or academic work

Description A contemporary, readable study on family issues and theory. Combines social science research, clinical insight, and biblical truth.

Authors Jack and Judith K. Balswick are colleagues on the faculty of Fuller Theological Seminary. Jack Balswick teaches sociology and family development and directs research for marriage and family ministries. Judith Balswick teaches marriage and family ministries and is the director of clinical training.

Contents *Part 1:* Theological and social perspectives on family life *1.* A theological basis for family relationships *2.* The family as a developing system *Part 2:* Marriage: the foundation of family life *3.* Mate selection *4.* Establishing a strong marriage *5.* Christian marriage: a model for modern society *Part 3:* Parenting: the expansion of family life *6.* The goal of parenting *7.* Child development *8.* Adolescence and midlife *Part 4:* Sexuality: identity in family life *9.* Changing gender roles: the effect on family life *10.* Authentic sexuality *Part 5:* Communication: the heart of family life *11.* Expressing love—achieving intimacy *12.* Expressing anger—dealing with conflict *Part 6:* The social dynamics of family life *13.* Family power and empowering *14.* Family stress *15.* Divorce and remarriage *Part 7:* Family life in modern society *16.* The family and issues of modernity *17.* Creating a positive environment for family life

Shaking the Family Tree *Using Your Family's Past to Strengthen Your Family's Future,* William Berman, Dale Doty, and Jean Huff Graham

Victor Books, 1991, $8.99, paper, 191 pp., for both counselors and counselees

Description Provides a blueprint for resolving leftover family issues and conflicts, establishing healthy relationships with parents and in-laws, and developing intimacy in marriage as a foun-

dation for effective parenting. Offers specific advice for dealing with such timely issues as schoolwork, childhood depression, adolescence, sexuality, adoption, hyperactivity, codependency, addictions, and single parenting. By combining biblical insights with the principles and techniques of family therapy (including genograms and circumplexes), *Shaking the Family Tree* offers exciting and practical tools for constructing an emotionally healthy future for ourselves and our children.

Authors Christian Family Institute of Tulsa, Okla., has provided professional counseling and counselor training since 1977. Dale R. Doty, Ph.D., is the institute's founder and director of training; William B. Berman, Ph.D., is the director of clinical services. Jean Huff Graham is a freelance writer and has completed advanced training at Christian Family Institute.

Contents *1.* Leftovers, flip-flops, and family trees *2.* Echoes from the past *3.* Measuring the family cycle *4.* First things first *5.* Rx for change *6.* Remedial parenting 101 *7.* Problems in the system *8.* Putting it all together *9.* The absent parent *10.* Recasting the mold *11.* School daze *12.* Avoiding the big talk *13.* Hearing aids *14.* Teenage tactics *15.* The disturbed child *16.* Chosen children

Religion and the Family *When God Helps,* Laurel Arthur Burton

The Haworth Pastoral Press, 1994, $26.95, paper, 215 pp., for counselors

Description This fascinating book guides family therapists in recognizing the importance of their client's spirituality, or religion, to therapy. Explores how such spirituality can be used as a resource in understanding and healing family problems.

Author Laurel Arthur Burton, Th.D., is Bishop Anderson of Religion and Medicine and chair of the Department of Religion, Health, and Human Values at Rush University in Chicago, Ill.

Contents *1.* Does God enter the system? *2.* A hermeneutical approach to religion and family therapy *3.* Foundation for a spiritually based psychotherapy *4.* Therapeutic change in religious families: working with the God construct *5.* Spirituality and systems therapy: partners in clinical practice *6.* Mixing oil and water religiously: counseling interfaith families *7.* Family therapy with the faithful: Christians as clients *8.* Assessing the role of religion in family functioning *9.* Religion in family therapy journals—a review and analysis

Family Love *What We Need, What We Seek, What We Must Create,* Alfred H. Ells

Thomas Nelson Publishers, 1995, $12.99, paper, 256 pp.

Description Teaches how to break painful family patterns and create healthier ways to give and receive love. Offers seven specific steps to help readers free themselves from painful legacies.

Author Alfred Ells is a marriage and family counselor, seminar speaker, and author of several best-selling books.

Contents *Part 1:* From generation to generation *1.* The truth about family *2.* Passing on healthy love patterns *Part 2:* Healthy family closeness *3.* The ties that bind or bless *4.* We were never close *Part 3:* Making marriage work *5.* Come close . . . stay away *6.* The paradox of romantic attraction *7.* Negotiating closeness *Part 4:* Fashioning our children's legacy *8.* Partner or parent? *9.* How to parent without partnering *10.* The equation family *Part 5:* Re-created families *11.* The family dream *12.* Stepping back in order to go forward *13.* The re-created family

The Church's Ministry with Families *A Practical Guide,* Diana S. Richmond Garland and Diane L. Pancoast

Word Publishing, 1992, $14.99, paper, 258 pp., for counselors

Description Sixteen professionals in church and social work develop the theory and practice of ministering to families. This is a comprehensive sourcebook for pastors and family life ministers, Christian colleges and seminaries, church educators, Christian social and family ministry volunteer workers.

Authors Diana S. Richmond Garland is associate professor of social work at the Carver School of Social Work, Southern Baptist Theological Seminary in Louisville, Ky. Coauthor Diane L. Pancoast, formerly a research associate and assistant professor of social work at Portland State University, is now a consultant and trainer for welfare agencies.

Contents *Part 1:* A theoretical and theological overview *1.* The church's ministry with families: an overview *2.* A

biblical foundation for ministry *3.* Understanding how families develop *4.* A network focus for family ministry *5.* The church as a context for professional practice *Part 2:* Application in churches and agencies *6.* Developing and empowering parent networks *7.* Using church and family ritual *8.* Providing professional services to widows and the bereaved *9.* Serving children and families through agency consultation *10.* Building multigenerational support networks *11.* Serving the older person: the church's role *12.* Delivering service in black churches *13.* Helping natural helpers *14.* Living with contradictions? Training natural helpers *15.* Issues for the future

All My Feelings Are OK *An Innovative Program to Help Families Identify and Express Their Feelings,* Linda Kondracki

Fleming H. Revell, 1993, $7.99, paper, 132 pp., for both counselors and counselees

Description Encourages parents and children to express feelings. Includes lessons just for parents as well as read-along family pages and fun activities.

Author Linda Kondracki is founder and national program director of Confident Kids, a Christian support-group program for elementary-aged children and parents.

Contents *1.* I need every feeling *2.* No stuffing, please *3.* Keep out! *4.* I'm all shook up! *5.* The family that feels together, grows together

I Always, Always Have Choices *Guides for Growing a Healthy Family,* Linda Kondracki

Fleming H. Revell, 1992, $7.99, paper, 142 pp., for both counselors and counselees

Description An innovative six-step program for helping every member of the family make wise decisions. Includes teaching material for the parents, a learning section for the family, and activity sections for practicing decision making.

Author Linda Kondracki is founder and national program director of Confident Kids, a Christian support-group program for elementary-aged children and parents.

Contents *1.* Choices, choices everywhere! *2.* C = claim the problem *3.* H = how many choices can I find? *4.* O = own God's Word O = one choice to try *5.* S = see it through *6.* E = evaluate the results

Let's Talk . . . and Listen Too! *An Innovative Program . . . to Help Families*

Learn Communication Skills, Linda Kondracki

> Fleming H. Revell, 1993, $11.99, paper, 128 pp., for both counselors and counselees

> **Description** Helps parents and children improve the quality of their communication by: saying what they are feeling, listening attentively, making themselves perfectly clear, fighting fair, saying it without words, checking for intended meaning. Cartoons, Bible studies, craft ideas, and games are among methods families can use to enjoy new levels of communication.

> **Author** Linda Kondracki is founder and national program director of Confident Kids, a Christian support-group program for elementary-aged children and parents.

Counseling Families George A. Rekers

> Word Publishing, 1988, $15.99, cloth, 211 pp., for counselors

> **Description** Dr. Rekers treats an array of family counseling issues—from becoming new parents to the "empty nest syndrome," from disruptions such as a runaway or divorce to preventive and enrichment possibilities for family living.

> **Author** Dr. Rekers is a professor of neuropsychiatry and behavioral science at the University of South Carolina School of Medicine in Columbia.

> **Contents** *1.* The need for family counseling *2.* Detecting the underlying problems *3.* Biblical perspectives for goal setting *4.* Goals of family counseling *5.* Wellness and family counseling *6.* Approaches to family counseling *7.* Methods of family counseling *8.* Challenges in family counseling / *Appendixes 1.* Models of family counseling *2.* Selected references on family counseling methods *3.* Selected references on family relationships and prevention

Lisa's Parents Fight Doris Sandford and Graci Evans

> Gold 'n' Honey Books (Questar), 1993, $6.99, cloth, 28 pp., for counselees

> **Description** Part of the In Our Neighborhood series from Gold 'n' Honey. The series was developed for children ages 5–11 who have difficult issues to cope with. The books deal gently and compassionately with children's delicate feelings when they're forced to handle situations that are hard to understand.

The Family Script *An Instructional Guide on How To Portray a Dysfunctional Family,* Sonlight Publishing

> Sonlight Publishing, 1992, $4.00, spiral, 23 pp., for counselors

> **Description** Provides directions for a spontaneous impromptu skit or informal play which portrays a dysfunctional family. The roles included are the narrator, addict, chief enabler, hero, scapegoat, lost child, mascot, and professional enabler. Props are listed, costumes described, and brief instructions provided for each character. Sample script is included. Procession questions are also listed.

> **Author** Sonlight Publishing, Inc., was established in 1991 for the purpose of preparing and bringing Christian recovery materials to the marketplace.

GenoGraph Bob Tippie

> Maret Software International, $99.99, software, for both counselors and counselees

> **Description** A genealogy program for counselors. On-screen graphics makes interpretation easy.

> **Author** Bob Tippie is an ordained Baptist minister with an active counseling and consulting practice. He holds a bachelor's degree in psychology and a master's degree in pastoral counseling.

Family Therapy *Christian Perspectives,* Hendrika VandeKemp, ed.

> Baker Book House, 1991, $12.99, paper, 224 pp., a reference or academic work

> **Description** A print symposium of six chapters by family therapists who add to the insights of intergenerational family therapy the richness of a multidenominational Christian tradition. Denominational traditions represented by the authors include Mennonite, Moravian, Church of Christ, Baptist, Presbyterian, Christian Reformed, Lutheran, Catholic, and Judeo-Christian. The focus on religion as a major dynamic variable in families fills a serious gap in the family therapy literature. Yost summarizes the contributions of Christian Midelfort, an early Lutheran family therapist who stressed religion and ethnicity. VandeKemp describes her Christian family life in the context of the Kantor & Lehr systems theory. Schreck addresses himself to the relational life

117

tasks of identity, intimacy, industry, and integrity. Hibbs brings the contextual family therapy dimensions of facts, individual psychology transactional patterns, and relational ethics to bear on congregational life. Kasner and Joyce explore the interpersonal, transgenerational nature of being itself, using the contextual model. Dueck examines the models, metaphors, paradigms, and stories that permeate the ethics of family life.

Editor Hendrika VandeKemp, who is professor of psychology at Fuller Theological Seminary, was educated at Hope College (B.A.) and the University of Massachusetts/Amherst (M.S., Ph.D.). She is the author of *Psychology and Theology in Christian Thought, 1672–1965* and numerous articles on the integration of psychology and theology on family therapy.

Coping with the Traumas of Family Life
Various contributors

Beacon Hill Press of Kansas City, 1989, $3.95, paper, 120 pp., for both counselors and counselees

Description Part of the Dialog series from Beacon Hill Press. Offers 13 sessions dealing with sexually active teens, working spouses, disciplining children, affairs, miscarriage, stepfamilies, rebellious children, and outcast parents.

Contents *1.* The working couple with children *2.* Bills, budget, and bank loans *3.* Untangling the triangle *4.* My dad drinks too much *5.* A father's reflections on a miscarriage *6.* When your child has a learning disability *7.* When it's time to discipline the kid *8.* The rebel of the clan *9.* Helping the outcast parent *10.* When teens start doing more than just thinking about sex *11.* Suicide: the most tragic death of all *12.* Stepfamilies, keeping in step *13.* When Jenny comes marching home (again)

Edge TV—Family Relationships

NavPress, 1992, $24.95, video with leader's guide, for both counselors and counselees

Description For youth workers who want to steer their group away from "church appropriate" discussions and get them talking about what's really going on in their lives. *Edge TV* (a video magazine for church youth groups) is the place to start. Created in partnership with Youth Specialties and IMS Productions, each episode of *Edge TV* is packed with high energy visuals, no-holds-barred drama, startling interviews, Christian music videos, captivating humor—and an honest approach to Jesus Christ that will get kids asking some very interesting questions.

Blended and Stepfamilies

Yours, Mine, and Ours *Facing the Challenge of Blended Families,* Emil J. Authelet

Thomas Nelson Publishers, 1994, $10.99, paper, 288 pp., for both counselors and counselees

Description This insightful book guides parents of blended families to achieve the healthy, satisfying relationships that God desires for them and their children. A wonderful resource for counselors, psychologists, and church leaders who work with blended families.

Author Dr. Emil J. Authelet is a family counselor who writes from his 20 years of experience in a blended family.

Blended Families *Yours, Mine, Ours,* William Cutler and Richard Peace

Serendipity, 1990, $6.95, paper, 80 pp., for both counselors and counselees

Description This 7- or 14-week course is designed for support groups that are wanting to learn about becoming better stepparents. Designed for anyone parenting a blended family who is willing to be open about the joys and trials of such a family. Intelligent use of Scripture and dialogue throughout.

Contents *1.* The phenomenon called blended families *2.* Stepfamilies vs. first families *3.* The children *4.* The "ex" factor *5.* The stretching, straining family ties *6.* Nurturing the marriage *7.* Finding inner strength

Willing to Try Again *Steps toward Blending a Family,* Dick Dunn

Judson Press, 1993, $10.00, paper, 106 pp., for counselees

Description Whether a person is preparing to remarry, already trying to build a stepfamily, or seeking to advise families, *Willing to Try Again* is an invaluable tool. With more than 1,300 stepfamilies created in the United States every day, these people are not alone in the struggle to understand and help nurture stepfamilies. More than half of this book is dedicated to real-life situations to illustrate the successes and failures of stepfamilies. In addition, the book includes a supplement for persons preparing for remarriage.

Author Dick Dunn has been a United Methodist minister for over 30 years, the last ten as minister of singles and stepfamilies at the Roswell United Methodist Church in Roswell, Ga. He has been remarried the past 11 years and leads a large stepfamily program at his church.

Contents *1.* Children and stepfamilies *2.* Challenges of stepparenting *3.* Being a biological parent in a stepfamily *4.* Outside relationships that affect stepfamilies *5.* Helpful stepfamily tools *6.* A matter of faith / Supplement for persons preparing for remarriage *7.* When is a person ready for remarriage? *8.* Critical issues to discuss *9.* Prenuptial agreements and wills *10.* The wedding

Blended Family, The Tom Frydenger and Adrienne Frydenger

Chosen Books, 1984, $8.99, paper, 181 pp., for counselees

Description A couple learning to live with their own blended family share practical insights for making it work.

Authors Tom and Adrienne Frydenger are professional family counselors.

Contents *1.* Looking back down the aisle *2.* Laying the foundation *3.* A vision of unity *4.* Children reacting *5.* Stepping in as a stepparent *6.* Bonding *7.* Discipline *8.* Working with the other household *9.* A richer blend: family bonding *10.* Let grace abound

Resolving Conflict in the Blended Family Tom Frydenger and Adrienne Frydenger

Chosen Books, 1991, $8.99, paper, 188 pp., for counselees

Description Counsel for handling the different types of conflict in blended families, with vivid anecdotes from the authors' experiences and those of other blended families.

Authors Tom and Adrienne Frydenger are professional family counselors.

Contents *1.* Straight talk *2.* Why can't we work together? *3.* Biological parents' resentments *4.* Stepparents' resentments *5.* Children's resentments *6.* First steps *7.* We are a family *8.* Conflicting loyalties *9.* Resolving conflict *10.* Coparenting *11.* Survivors

Remarried with Children *A Blended Couple's Journey to Harmony,* Don Houck and LaDean Houck

Here's Life Publishers (c/o Thomas Nelson), 1991, $9.99, paper, 216 pp., for counselees

Description With personal transparency, humor, and a no-holds-barred approach, the Houcks share their insights on life as a remarried couple with children.

Authors Don and LaDean Houck are the founders of Blended Blessings, a speaking and teaching ministry to remarried couples and their families.

Contents *1.* Miracle in the making *2.* Potholes and deep ruts *3.* Mr. Perfect *4.* The big "c" word *5.* The common thread—bonding *6.* One nail at a time *7.* The real you *8.* Expressing your true self *9.* Two-sided coin *10.* Manning the battleship *11.* Wise battle plans *12.* The money crunch *13.* Removing locked doorknobs *14.* Power parenting *15.* Woman to woman: the closets of your heart *16.* Man to man: the marriage that sizzles

Growing in Step *Your Guide to Successful Stepparenting,* Dan Houmes and Paul D. Meier

Baker Book House, 1985, $5.99, paper, 169 pp., for counselees

Description A loving and sensitive guide to help stepparents and stepchildren adjust to each other in the most spiritually and emotionally healthy ways possible.

Authors Dan Houmes is a licensed marriage and family therapist at Christian Counseling Services, Inc., in Ft. Lauderdale, Fla. Paul Meier is vice president of the Minirth-Meier Psychiatric Clinic and author or coauthor of many books on Christian psychiatry and counseling.

Contents *1.* Step by step *2.* The storm after the calm—previewing stepfamily problems *3.* It's not really the same—understanding the differences between intact families and stepfamilies *4.* If I had to do it over—determining the healthy reasons for remarrying *5.* Telling them about him/her—sharing the news of a prospective stepparent *6.* Yours, mine, and ours—blending three families into one *7.* The third parent in our family—coping with the other natural parent *8.* Outside looking in—reaching back into the family by the non-custodial parent *9.* The shake-and-bake family—solidifying ready-made families *10.* The summit meeting—turning crisis into compatibility *11.* Happy painful days—surviving the unexpected disappointments of shared custody *12.* The bond that isn't there—overcoming the absence of the natural parent bond *13.* Engrave them in stone—summarizing guidelines for blending families

Remarriage in Midlife *Plan It First, Make It Last,* Helen Hunter

Baker Book House, 1991, $9.99, paper, 206 pp., for counselors

Description One of the few books directed at people who remarry when they are over 40 years of age. Armed with study data, her own and others' experiences, and interviews with professionals, Hunter stresses that couples should take into account financial realities, adult children's feelings, aging parents, and family traditions. Chapters on how to deal with rejection from family members, bonding, money issues, and illness and death. This book can spare people problems and, in fact, lead them to a more fulfilled remarriage. Hunter shares her faith and credits God with the success of her marriage.

Author Helen Hunter is a professional freelance writer, doing newsletters, publicity, and training manuals for a number of companies. Hunter studied writing and journalism at the University of Iowa and Coe College in Cedar Rapids.

Contents *1.* Changes and challenges in midlife *2.* Help from the top *3.* From wreckage to renewal *4.* An ounce of prevention is still worth a pound of cure *5.* Marrying the multitudes: secondary relationships *6.* Step relationships: adult to adult *7.* Expect problems *8.* Bonding to primary relationships *9.* Handling hurts *10.* Holidays: rest or ruin? *11.* For richer or poorer *12.* In sickness and in health *13.* Parenting our parents *14.* Dream a new dream

Living in a Step Family Without Getting Stepped On *Helping Your Children Survive the Birth Order Blender,* Kevin Leman

Thomas Nelson Publishers, 1995, cloth, 288 pp.

Description Offers stepfamilies a practical strategy for resolving the tension from the original birth order being disrupted.

Author Dr. Kevin Leman is the author of 13 books on family and marriage, a psychologist, and host of the syndicated radio program *Parent Talk.*

I Only See My Dad on Weekends *Kids Tell Their Stories About Divorce and Blended Families,* Beth Matthews with Karen Dockrey

Chariot Books, 1995, $4.95, paper, 42 pp.

Description Written for children 8–12, this book gives a voice to four children living in blended families. Each child explains how God can give security in a new and different family environment.

Author Karen Dockrey is a youth minister and writer.

Contents *1.* Memories and feelings *2.* Sad times *3.* Happy times *4.* God then, now, and in my future *5.* Our advice to you *6.* Other friends who can help

Stepparent Is Not a Bad Word *Advice and Perspectives for Parenting Your Stepchildren,* David Z. Nowell

Janet Thoma (a division of Thomas Nelson), 1994, $9.99, paper, 228 pp., for both counselors and counselees

Description A valuable and timely resource that covers every potential problem from discipline to disagreement over foundational beliefs.

Author David Z. Nowell, Ph.D., works in the division of external affairs at Baylor University. His Ph.D. is in religion.

Help for Remarried Couples and Families Richard P. Olsen

Judson Press, $7.95, paper, for both counselors and counselees

Description Help for the remarried couple as they seek to create a loving relationship. Includes guidance for parents and children adjusting to a new family.

Merging Families *A Step-by Step Guide for Blended Families,* Bobbie Reed

CPH Publishing, 1992, $7.95, paper, 192 pp., for counselees

Description Offers practical advice for strengthening family relationships, helping children adjust, and preventing conflicts in second marriages.

Author Bobbie Reed speaks from experience. Having spent ten years as a single mother raising two sons, Dr. Reed has turned her journey into a dynamic ministry to single and single-again adults. She is now happily remarried.

Contents As you begin—Blended families: stages of development *Stage 1*—Prepare for the marriage *1.* Know what to expect *2.* Decide with past losses *3.* Decide where to live *4.* Develop a budget *5.* Tell the family *6.* Plan the ceremony *Stage 2*—Create the new family *7.* Understand the configuration *8.* Agree on house rules and discipline *9.* Develop family interactions *10.* Prevent inappropriate sexual involvement *Stage 3*—Develop the relationships *11.* Accept the children *12.* Understand the stepparent-parent challenges *13.* Form a parenting coalition *14.* Involve the extended family *Stage 4*—Accept and deal with losses and realities *15.* Let go of fantasies *16.* Acknowledge tough realities *17.* Release the children *18*. Reach for each other / *Blended families*—they can be successful

My Real Family *A Child's Book about Living in a Step-family,* Doris Sandford and Graci Evans

Gold 'n' Honey Books (Questar), 1993, $7.99, cloth, 24 pp., for counselees

Description Part of the Hurts of Childhood series from Gold 'n' Honey. The series was developed for children ages 5–11 who have experienced deep and tragic hurts. The books deal gently and compassionately with children's delicate feelings when they're forced to handle burdens far too big for them to carry.

Remarriage and Blended Families
Stephen R. Treat

The Pilgrim Press, 1986, $1.75, paper, 24 pp., for both counselors and counselees

Description Part of the Looking Up series of booklets from the Pilgrim Press. For the cost of a greeting card, this booklet provides the reader with 24 pages of insight, wisdom, Scripture readings, meditation, direction, comfort, and prayer.

There's a New Family in My House!
Blending Stepfamilies Together, Laura Sherman Walters

Harold Shaw Publishers, 1993, $8.99, paper, 209 pp., for both counselors and counselees

Description As various combinations of stepparents, stepchildren, and stepsiblings come together into a new place called "home," guidance and support can help you become a family that is able to meet each person's needs. This book encourages families to participate together in building their new home.

Author Laura Sherman Walters specializes in child and adult therapy through her private practice in the Chicago area. In addition to her credentials in psychotherapy, she is a consultant to various counseling and child-care agencies and has taught courses in marriage and family issues.

Contents *1*. What should we call ourselves?—definitions and tools for family building *2*. What's the problem, anyway?—the 11 most common issues in the blended family *3*. My bags are packed—emotional baggage and the new family *4*. Who can I feel close to? Achieving family intimacy *5*. What does it mean to grieve? Separation and loss *6*. What are the children going through? Under-

standing children and their feelings *7*. "Where is my other Mom or Dad?" Parents without custody *8*. A new family order—establishing and enjoying a new family *9*. Spiritual journeys—how blended families can forgive and come together / *Exercises for families*

Facing the Challenge of Living in a Stepfamily

Abbey Press, $.50 each, paper, 8 pp., for counselees

Description Part of the CareNotes series from Abbey Press. CareNotes are short booklets that help readers identify issues and begin the process of seeking resolution. Anecdotal and uplifting. Beautiful photographs grace the covers. Over 20 million CareNotes have been sold in just over five years. Can be used as an alternative to a greeting card or in conjunction with pastoral care visits.

Parenting Skills

Common Sense Discipline *What to Say and Do When Kids Need Help,* Roger Allen and Ron Rose

Chariot Family Publishing, 1993, $8.99, paper, 240 pp., for counselees

Description Here is an authoritative, comprehensive, and user-friendly guide to sensible and effective discipline written with the Christian parent in mind. Dr. Roger Allen, a psychologist and counselor in Tyler, Tex., and Ron Rose, director of Faith in Families, share their perspectives on this vital topic and offer suggestions for parents and those who deal with children between the ages of birth and 18 years.

Different Children—Different Needs *The Art of Adjustable Parenting,* Charles F. Boyd

Questar Publishing, 1995, $10.99, paper, 219 pp.

Description Applies the popular DISC model of personality temperament to parent–child relationships. Equips parents to adjust their personal parenting styles to meet the needs of each individual child, making each child feel esteemed and valued. Biblical content throughout.

Author Charles F. Boyd is a teaching pastor at Grace Community Church in Little Rock, Ark. He received his master of theology degree from Dallas Seminary with high honors and has pastored for 14 years.

Contents *Part 1*—"Train up a child . . ." *1.* Parent pollution *2.* The epitaph of the unaccepted *Part 2*—Understanding *3.* Why you are who you are *4.* The "D" style: Directive parents, determined children *5.* The "I" style: Interactive parents, influencing children *6.* The "S" style: Supportive parents, soft-hearted children *7.* The "C" style: Corrective parents, conscientious children *8.* Becoming a student of your child *Part 3*—Building *9.* Family fit *10.* Mirror, mirror *11.* Mirroring your child's strengths and weaknesses *12.* Mirroring your child's emotions *13.* Keep those loving cups full *14.* Dealing with conflict *15.* Parents are also partners

Empowering Parents *How to Raise Obedient Children—It's Possible It's Right,* William Backus and Candace Backus

Bethany House Publishers, 1992, $7.99, paper, 171 pp., for both counselors and counselees

Description Parents today are often afraid to take charge of their children, seemingly convinced they must put up with outrageous behavior. Could it be they feel guilty about taking authority over their children? *Empowering Parents* is built upon the biblical foundation that it is a parent's God-given duty and right to control their children, not to be controlled by them. It is written to encourage parents in the "right" of using their authority to control, discipline, and train their children, and to show parents how to do these things. A simple manual that can be followed by any parent. It presents child-training methods that have been demonstrated effective. Basis: truthful parental communication of expected behavior, positive and potent reinforcement for right behavior and attitudes, consistent and appropriate discipline for wrong behavior and attitudes.

Authors William Backus is a licensed clinical psychologist and an ordained Lutheran clergyman. He is founder and director of the Center for Christian Psychological Services, St. Paul, Minn., and an associate pastor of a large Lutheran church. Candace Backus is a counselor and vice president of Minnesota Psychtests, Inc.

Contents *Part 1:* Parenting principles *1.* Feeling powerless *2.* Guilt *3.* "Shaping" children *Part 2:* Parenting techniques *4.* Do I really have power? *5.* Reinforcement made clear *6.* "Reinforcement didn't work" *7.* Change yourself first *8.* "I'd do anything for you dear" *9.* Unintentional reinforcement *10.* Using punishment effectively *11.* Physical punishment: yes or no? *12.* Ten common mistakes *13.* Starting a point system *Part 3:* Dealing with common problems *14.* Bedtime *15.* No more tantrums *16.* Lying *17.* Stealing *18.* How and when to talk

Teaching Your Children to Tell Themselves the Truth *Helping Children before Misbeliefs Become Deeply Entrenched,* William Backus and Candace Backus

Bethany House Publishers, 1992, $8.99, paper, 175 pp., for both counselors and counselees

Description A handbook for parents to help build their child's self-esteem, happiness, coping skills, and good behavior. It will offer practical, easy-to-follow suggestions for enabling the child to utilize the truth for solving life's problems. The child will learn to understand his/her feelings and deal effectively with them. Families will be shown how to develop effective communication with one another.

Authors William Backus is a licensed clinical psychologist and an ordained Lutheran clergyman. He is founder and director of the Center for Christian Psychological Services, St. Paul, Minn., and an associate pastor of a large Lutheran church. Candace Backus is a counselor and vice president of Minnesota Psychtests, Inc.

Contents *1.* Finding out what children tell themselves *2.* Eavesdropping on a child's self-talk *3.* Entering your child's world *4.* Who's to blame? *5.* The power of emotions *6.* Managing strong feelings *7.* When your child is depressed *8.* Practical help with a child's anxiety *9.* "You make me angry!" *10.* Self-mastery *11.* The bottom line—solving problems with the truth *12.* "To tell you the truth . . ."—communicating honestly *13.* Eyes on the prize

Single Parenting *A Practical Guide to Help,* Robert G. Barnes

Tyndale House Publishers, 1989, $7.99, paper, 176 pp., for counselees

Description In-depth answers to important questions single parents have. With biblical insight, Barnes points the way to personal and family healing.

Author Dr. Robert G. Barnes has been involved in family ministry since 1974. He is executive director of Sheridan House, a residential treatment center for teenage boys and girls, a marriage and family counseling center, and a social services center.

Contents *Part 1:* The first wilderness journey—finding yourself *1.* Who am I? *2.* I'm all alone *3.* Why me? *4.* I deserve it *5.* Out of the wilderness *Part 2:* The second wilderness journey—leading your children *6.* Train up a child *7.* The four E's of training *8.* The philosophy of life

9. Self-esteem *10.* Communication *11.* Making it special *12.* Sex education *13.* Sibling rivalry *14.* Discipline *15.* Chores and responsibilities *16.* Handling money *17.* Visitation *18.* Blending two families *19.* The unresponsive child *20.* No longer a parent

If My Kids Drive Me Crazy, Am I a Bad Mom? Janet Chester Bly

NavPress, 1991, $4.00, paper, 87 pp., for counselees

Description Designed to be shared with non-Christian women. Explores practical and spiritual answers to this relevant question. Focuses on felt needs, uses real-life scenarios and narrative. Presents scriptural truth in sensitive, unassuming ways. Includes five sessions and a Bible study that requires no Bible background. Additional tips and resources included.

Author Janet Chester Bly is a freelance writer and speaker, and cofounder with her husband, Stephen, of Welcome to the Family Seminars. She has published 13 books, including *How to Be a Good Mom.*

Contents *Introduction*—What mother never told you about kids *Question*—How can I survive the mothering years? *Time out*—A choice for quality mothering *Lesson one*—Who are you, mom? *Lesson two*—What does mothering mean? *Lesson three*—Who is this stranger in the crib? *Lesson four*—Love and all that good stuff *Lesson five*—Hanging in for the long haul / *Extras:* How to be a good mom / Tips for frazzled days / Goals for great mothering / Coming to grips with your faith / Resources for mothers

Meditations for the New Mother Helen Good Brenneman

Herald Press, 1985 (revised), $12.95, cloth, 78 pp., for counselees

Description Created to meet the need for a sustaining faith and a quiet confidence in God when a new baby arrives. Daily meditations for the first 30 days strengthen and inspire for the lifelong task of motherhood.

Family Cycles *How Understanding the Way You Were Raised Will Make You a Better Parent,* William Lee Carter

NavPress, 1993, $12.00, paper, 231 pp., for both counselors and counselees

Description Written by a Rapha consultant and contributing editor to *Christian Parenting Today,* this book examines the generational patterns that cause you to adopt many of the same par-

enting traits and techniques that characterized your parents. If you are determined not to repeat the mistakes your parents made, *Family Cycles* will help make sense of the past—so you can give your kids the best possible shot at the future.

Author As a professional child psychologist, Dr. William Lee Carter works extensively with children, adolescents, and their families. He is also a speaker and consultant for Rapha seminars and conferences.

Contents *Part 1:* Now that I'm a parent, why do I feel and act the way I do? *1.* Can I break the chains from my past? *2.* Why can't I control my emotions? *3.* Why do I feel so isolated and alone? *4.* Why do I worry so much? *5.* Why am I sad when I want to be happy? *6.* Why am I so self-centered? *7.* Why do I feel so lousy about me? *Part 2:* Ways the parent protects himself from the pain of the past *8.* Understanding why I can't stand conflict *9.* Understanding why I can't express my emotions *10.* Understanding why I fear negative emotions *11.* Understanding why I overpower my child *12.* Understanding why I can't face reality *Part 3:* Parenting the way you wish you'd been parented *13.* Exchanging trust for mistrust *14.* Exchanging unhappiness for satisfaction *15.* Exchanging frustration for gratitude *16.* Exchanging withdrawal for relationship *17.* Exchanging security for independence *18.* Exchanging control for boundaries *19.* Exchanging conflict for choices, consequences *Part 4:* Leaving the past behind—qualities of the maturing parent *20.* Listening *21.* Examining *22.* Influencing *23.* Warning *24.* Separating *25.* Relating

Raising Your Child, Not Your Voice Duane Cuthbertson

Victor Books, 1994, $9.95, paper, 196 pp., for counselees

Description How can you change a child's strong will without breaking his spirit? If you want to establish sound discipline strategies, this book will help you teach your child without straining your vocal cords.

Parenting Adolescents *Easing the Way to Adulthood,* William Cutler and Richard Peace

Serendipity, 1990, $6.95, paper, 80 pp., for counselees

Description A 7- or 14-week course for parents of adolescents. Focuses on understanding adolescence and parenting skills. Strong use of Scripture and dialogue.

Contents *1.* The pressures of being a teenager. *2.* The challenge of parenting teens *3.* The changes a teen goes through 4. Communicating love 5. Nurturing self-worth 6. Dealing with crises 7. Passing on faith

Breaking through to Your Teen Kass Perry Dotterweich

Ligouri Publications, 1992, $.75, paper, 24 pp., for counselees

Description A mother of four teenagers offers six ways to help parents adapt their parenting style to meet the unique challenges of raising a teenager.

When You Work Outside the Home 6 Studies on Creative Parenting for Working Moms, Judy Hamlin

Victor Books, 1993, $4.99, paper, 64 pp., for counselees

Description Part of the Searching for Answers series from Victor. These six short sessions on creative parenting look at the importance and impact of mothering from a child's viewpoint. Shows how to make the most of those last 15 minutes before parting for the day, how to maximize family mealtimes, how to pray with your child, how to involve dad in the process, and how to remove guilt and find forgiveness for past mistakes in parenting.

Author Dr. Judy Hamlin (Ph.D. in adult education, University of Southern Mississippi) is an authority on small groups and women's ministry.

When You Feel Like Screaming! Help for Frustrated Mothers, Pat Holt and Grace Ketterman

Harold Shaw Publishers, 1988, $6.99, paper, 84 pp., for counselees

Description If you've ever felt like you want to scream, like you're losing control, or guilty because you've yelled at your kids in the past, *When You Feel Like Screaming* is for you! The authors provide helpful information and realistic instructions to transform your parenting patterns. They'll help you understand why you respond the way you do, how your children respond, and how you can achieve the strength that comes with gentleness.

Authors Pat Holt is an author, a mother, and the administrator of a Christian school. Dr. Grace Ketterman, also a mom, is a pediatrician, a psy-

chiatrist, and the medical director of a psychiatric hospital for children and adolescents.

Contents 1. When you lose control 2. For reasonable reasons 3. But it's affecting your children 4. After the storm 5. Mission impossible? 6. How to get control of yourself 7. Corralling your kids 8. The key to healing

Complete Book of Baby and Child Care, The Revised and Expanded, Grace H. Ketterman

Fleming H. Revell, 1982, $12.99, paper, 560 pp., for counselees

Description Revised and updated. A comprehensive and specific discussion of every aspect of parenting from prenatal considerations to parenting through age 12 and beyond.

Author Grace H. Ketterman, M.D., is the medical director of the Crittenton Center for Children and Adolescents in Kansas City, Mo. She is the author of many other books on parenting issues.

Contents Part 1: Preparing to have a child 1. Having a child—are you ready? 2. Getting pregnant—what you need to know 3. Carrying a baby—a word for expectant mothers 4. Sharing responsibility—a word for expectant fathers 5. Giving birth—an experience to treasure Part 2: Nurturing a newborn child 6. Getting acquainted—the first thirty days 7. Establishing relationships—the next two years of life 8. Winning the eating game—the nutrition factor Part 3: Treating your sick child 9. General medical information you need to know 10. Your problem solver for injuries and illnesses Part 4: Rearing a confident child 11. The components of personality development 12. The necessity of spiritual training 13. The importance of loving correction 14. The fun side of family living 15. The seesaw world of the adolescent Part 5: Helping a troubled child 16. Handling difficulties and suffering 17. Solving their behavioral problems 18. Learning from school experiences 19. Rearing special children.

Mothering The Complete Guide for Mothers of All Ages, Grace H. Ketterman

Chariot Family Publishing, 1994, $12.99, paper, 508 pp., for counselees

Description Whether you're just thinking about having a baby, or you're a grandmother, you'll find everything you need to know about mothering in this comprehensive guide from pediatrician and child psychologist (and mother of three) Grace Ketterman. Filled with valuable advice and insights for every phase of mothering, this easy-to-use handbook will equip readers to be the best mothers they can be.

Author Grace H. Ketterman, M.D., is the medical director of the Crittenton Center for Children and Adolescents in Kansas City, Mo. She is the author of many other books on parenting issues.

Parenting Preschoolers *From Car Seats to Kindergarten,* Rachel Kiepe

Serendipity, 1992, $6.95, paper, 80 pp., for both counselors and counselees

Description A 7- or 14-week course utilizing Scripture and discussion questions. Deals with the stresses of being parents of preschoolers. Designed to be used by anyone with young children, or who is about to have children, and is willing to be open about the joys and trials of being a parent.

Contents *1.* This isn't what I ordered *2.* Stress and conflict *3.* Where's my owner's manual? *4.* New time priorities *5.* Home, work, and guilt *6.* When the kids drive you crazy *7.* A parent's guiding light

A Hug, a Kiss, and a Kick in the Pants Kay Kuzma

Chariot Family Publishing, 1994, $7.99, paper, 200 pp., for both counselors and counselees

Description Parent tested strategies for discipline that work. Here are alternatives to corporal punishment that help parents prevent misbehavior as they steer children onto the road to obedience.

Parenting without Pressure *How to Turn Family Battles into Family Bonding,* Teresa A. Langston

NavPress, 1993, $12.00, paper, 180 pp., for counselees

Description Recommended by judges, therapists, social workers, ministers, and public school counselors, *Parenting without Pressure* is a whole-family workbook designed to help replace daily battles with communication, respect, and unconditional love. By taking a step-by-step approach to parenting, author Teresa Langston supplies parents with the tools necessary to bring peace and harmony into their homes. Whether their kids are completely out of control, or are simply exhibiting run-of-the-mill teenage behavior, parents will find *Parenting without Pressure* techniques simple and easy to use.

Author Nationally respected for her innovative parenting approach, Teresa Langston is a popular radio and TV guest and has been featured in numerous print articles throughout the country. A university lecturer and national conference presenter, she is on the Central Florida Parents Anonymous Advisory Council and affiliated with other community service organizations.

Discipline with Love *A Practical Guide for Establishing Systematic Discipline in Your Home,* Robert S. McGee

Rapha Resources, $6.99, paper, for both counselors and counselees

Description Based on the way our heavenly Father corrects us, this book helps parents form a plan that encourages love, self-control, response to authority, and obedience to God.

Author Robert McGee is founder and president of Rapha, a health care organization that provides in-hospital and outpatient care, with a Christ-centered perspective, for adults and adolescents suffering from psychiatric and substance abuse problems.

Child-Rearing and Personality Development *Second Edition,* Paul D. Meier, Donald Ratcliff, and Frederick Rowe

Baker Book House, 1993 (2d edition), $12.99, cloth, 256 pp., a reference or academic work

Description The authors offer two purposes for writing: First, to help Christians develop biblically sound parenting skills; second, to outline some aspects of child development that will encourage a better understanding of children. This revised edition includes easy-to-understand text, facts and guidance to assist the emotional and spiritual development of children, guidelines for establishing when a child's problems require therapy, and discussion of development from birth to adolescence.

Authors Paul D. Meier is vice president of the Minirth-Meier Psychiatric Clinic, Donald E. Ratcliff is assistant professor of psychology and sociology at Toccoa Falls College. Frederick L. Rowe directs the Minirth-Meier Clinic in San Diego, Calif.

Contents *1.* Preparing to parent *2.* A new life begins *3.* Babies and toddlers *4.* Preschoolers *5.* The school years

6. Adolescence *7.* When good parenting is not enough *8.* A final challenge

Help! I'm A Parent! *How to Handle Temper Tantrums, Sibling Fights, . . . and more,* Bruce Narramore

Zondervan Publishing House, 1995, $5.99, paper, 189 pp.

Description First written in 1972, over 150,000 copies have been sold. Now Dr. Narramore has revised and expanded his bestseller to include new material dealing with contemporary problems such as the challenges faced by single parents and working mothers. An exceptional companion workbook is also available. Suitable for group study.

Author Dr. Bruce Narramore is a licensed psychologist. He is professor of psychology at Rosemead School of Psychology, Biola University.

Contents *1.* Help! I'm a parent! *2.* Children misbehave when their needs aren't met *3.* Kids will be kids *4.* Discipline or punishment *5.* Three tools for toddler taming and child training *6.* Let nature discipline your child *7.* Logical consequence: You can teach your children to obey *8.* To spank or not to spank? *9.* Creating a plan and making it work *10.* Keeping your cool while your children are losing theirs *11.* Building your child's self-image *12.* How not to talk to your children about sex *13.* Working mothers: women in two worlds *14.* Questions parents ask *15.* Keeping ahead of your children

Sometimes I Don't Like My Kids Candice Schap

Pacific Press, 1991, $7.95, paper, 124 pp., for counselees

Description An honest look at the frustrations of mothering, written for anyone who has ever assumed, "I thought I was the only one who ever felt that way!" From experience as mother of four, the author shares down-to-earth suggestions for identifying and dealing with the anger you face in mothering. More than a book of parental woes, this is a manual of recovery—the recovery of joy in the Lord and in your family.

Author Homemaker and mother of four. Speaker for women's groups and retreats of all denominations, Bible study and workshop leader, approved speaker for the Christian Women's Clubs evangelistic outreach of Stonecroft Ministries.

Contents *1.* Birthing is the easy part *2.* The hard stuff *3.* Dealing with hopelessness *4.* Dealing with resentment

5. Dealing with anger *6.* Dealing with disappointment *7.* Identifying the hot spots *8.* Consider it all joy

Shame-Free Parenting Sandra D. Wilson

InterVarsity Press, 1992, $9.95, paper, 216 pp., for both counselors and counselees

Description Even though we may have had impaired parents, we can give our children repaired parents. This book helps parents get healthier themselves so they can raise healthier children.

Author Dr. Sandra Wilson, a therapist and a nationally sought conference speaker, is a visiting professor/instructor at Asbury and Denver Seminaries and Trinity Evangelical Divinity School.

Contents *1.* Shame-bound parenting: roots and fruits *2.* Choosing life: recovering *3.* Choosing truth: re-viewing *4.* Choosing grace: releasing *5.* We can learn what we don't know *6.* We can learn and teach about God *7.* We can learn to really love our children *8.* We can learn to have realistic expectations *9.* We can learn to communicate with talk and touch *10.* We can learn to feel good about feelings *11.* We can learn to like limits *12.* We can learn to have fun *13.* We can learn to give wings—not strings *14.* Life-giving legacies

Kids Have Feelings, Too! *Helping Your Children Understand and Deal with Their Emotions,* H. Norman Wright and Gary Jackson Oliver

Victor Books, 1993, $15.99, cloth, 235 pp., for counselees

Description This book is designed to stress the important role emotions play in a child's development, to give parents tools to nurture healthy emotional response in their child, to deal with specific emotions that tend to be most problematic, and to help parents deal with their own feelings and responses.

Authors H. Norman Wright is a best-selling author, licensed marriage, family, and child therapist, and director of Family Counseling and Enrichment. Gary J. Oliver is a psychologist at Southwest Counseling Associates and visiting professor at Denver Seminary.

Contents *1.* Understanding healthy emotional response *2.* Growing emotionally healthy children *3.* Parenting by design *4.* Dealing with depression *5.* Dealing with anger *6.* Dealing with grief and loss *7.* Dealing with fear and anxiety *8.* Dealing with guilt and shame *9.* Identifying stress in your child *10.* Helping your children handle stress *11.* Your child's self-esteem *12.* Dealing with your emotional responses to your children

Raising Emotionally Healthy Kids
H. Norman Wright and Gary J. Oliver

Victor Books, 1995, $9.99, paper, 240 pp.

Description Two seasoned family counselors share what they've learned in their 50 years of experience counseling Christian families.

Authors H. Norman Wright is a best-selling author and a licensed marriage, family, and child therapist. Gary Jackson Oliver is a psychologist at Southwest Counseling Associates near Denver.

Daily Meditations for Parenting Our Kids
Thomas Wright

Recovery Publications, Inc., 1993, $8.95, paper, 384 pp., for counselees

Description Written primarily for parents in recovery, this book includes 366 meditations and affirmations full of wisdom, insight, and comfort—poignant reflections for every parent facing the day-to-day challenges of raising kids.

Coping with the Stresses of a New Baby

Abbey Press, $.50 each, paper, 8 pp., for counselees

Description Part of the CareNotes series from Abbey Press. CareNotes are short booklets that help readers identify issues and begin the process of seeking resolution. Anecdotal and uplifting. Beautiful photographs grace the covers. Over 20 million CareNotes have been sold in just over five years. Can be used as an alternative to a greeting card or in conjunction with pastoral care visits.

Single Parenting

From One Single Mother to Another
Advice and Encouragement from Someone Who's Been There, Sandra P. Aldrich

Regal Books, 1992, $9.99, paper, 192 pp., for counselees

Description This is a book for every woman who finds herself raising children alone and wondering if she can do it. Sandra Aldrich was left with a ten-year-old son and an eight-year-old daughter when her young husband died from brain cancer in 1982. But with healthy measures of faith and humor, she got through the tough

years. Now, her message to struggling moms is "if I can do it, then by God's grace, so can you!" Her writing style is fast-paced and both instructs and encourages. Told with transparent honesty, this account is filled with practical advice, including dealing with stress, finances, discipline, and loneliness. It also lists resource groups and a bibliography of helpful books.

Author Sandra P. Aldrich is senior editor of *Focus on the Family* magazine. A former Kentuckian, she's known for her zany sense of humor and family stories that make her a popular speaker at singles' groups and women's retreats. She is also a frequent guest on radio and TV. She holds a B.A. and M.A. from Eastern Michigan University and has authored one other book.

Contents *1.* If I can do it, you can, too *2.* So, how do we handle loneliness? *3.* Guilt, who needs it? *4.* Keep 'em talking and keep listening *5.* Guiding our teens through sexual waters *6.* Battling the bills and winning the war *7.* Any houseboats for sale or rent? *8.* And we're to do all that without yelling? *9.* We love our kin, but we'll raise our kids *10.* When the kids fight *11.* Help! When I tied my son's tie, he turned blue *12.* Counting wrinkles, celebrating joys, anticipating life *13.* New adventures are ours to grab let's be ready for them / *Support groups for families*

Huddle Up *Creating Family Unity As a Single Parent,* Gloria Chisholm

Fleming H. Revell, 1993, $8.99, paper, for counselees
Description For the 7,000,000 single mothers in the United States today, here's hope and help for creating family unity. Written with honesty and humor by a single mother who's been there.

Single Parents *Flying Solo,* William Cutler

Serendipity, 1991, $6.95, paper, 96 pp., for counselees

Description A 7- or 14-week course utilizing Scripture and discussion questions. Designed for people wanting to become a part of a support group while discussing issues related to our needs as single parents. These issues will be discussed from both a "how-to-cope-well" perspective and a biblical perspective.

Contents *1.* Suddenly single *2.* The single parent and work *3.* Single parents and social life *4.* The other parent *5.* Making it work *6.* Embracing singleness *7.* Finding inner strength

Empowering Single Parents *Ten Ways to Increase Your Effectiveness,* Greg Cynaumon and Dana Cynaumon

Moody Press, 1994, $9.99, paper, 240 pp., for counselees

Description Minirth-Meier counselor and talk show host Greg Cynaumon explains how to develop a balanced parenting style and build structure and discipline into family life. Not just another set of pat answers.

Authors Greg Cynaumon hosts a radio talk show on family and parenting and is a counselor at the Minirth-Meier Clinic West in Newport Beach, Calif. Dana Cynaumon is a much published copywriter and has served as a national press relations coordinator and as an editor for three national automotive magazines. He is now an account executive writer and photographer with an advertising agency.

Contents *1.* Understand your child's secret thoughts about the divorce *2.* Develop a well-balanced single-parenting style *3.* Develop boundaries and limits, the antidote to chaos *4.* Cultivate the fine art of single-parent communication *5.* Make the most of quality time *6.* Skillfully maneuver through postdivorce issues *7.* Take care of your own emotional needs *8.* Understand risks and spot warning signals *9.* Appreciate the importance of role models and resources *10.* Understand that you're not damaged goods

Just One of Me *Confessions of a Less-Than-Perfect-Single Parent,* Dandi Daley Knorr

Harold Shaw Publishers, 1989, $7.99, paper, 196 pp., for counselees

Description Helps single parents realize they are not alone. The author has experienced the constant struggle of trying to be both father and mother, playmate and authority, bottle washer and financial provider. With a strong dose of humor, she supplies encouragement and concrete biblical help, examining "Superparent Syndrome" and "Child-sized" greatness. Begins with a humorous quiz that exposes "Superparent Syndrome." Part 1 helps the reader accept herself and seek God as the ideal partner in raising kids. Part 2 focuses on accepting the children with all their weaknesses. In Part 3, scores of single parents express their views on the hottest topics: how much truth to tell, priorities, remarriage, etc. Part 4 contains practical advice and information on child support, visitation, and other

concerns. Each chapter is followed by study questions suitable for individual or group study.

Author Dandi Knorr was on staff with Campus Crusade for Christ for nine years and served as a missionary in Poland for one year. She has published 11 adult Christian nonfiction books and 11 children's fiction books.

Single with Children Caryl Waller Krueger

Abingdon Press, 1993, $7.95, paper, 173 pp., for counselees

Description Offers helpful "how-to" suggestions for coping with the many adjustments and responsibilities of being "single with children."

Author Caryl Waller Krueger is a child development specialist, columnist, and nationwide lecturer. She is the author of numerous books on parenting.

Contents *1.* Heart to heart *2.* I was divorced and devastated *3.* He died and left me alone *4.* They didn't think a man could do it *5.* My biological clock was running out *6.* Look at me, up and off welfare! *7.* Suddenly, I knew this child needed me *8.* Could I survive alone with three teenage daughters? *9.* Survival *10.* Tattle-tales *11.* Looking back and looking ahead *12.* Help—resources for single parents

Single Moms/Single Dads *Help and Hope for the One Parent Family,* David R. Miller

Chariot Family Publishing, 1990, $7.95, paper, 175 pp., for both counselors and counselees

Description Though marriages end, parenting does not, and becoming a single parent plunges a Christian into a labyrinth of pain, confusion, and concern. Many books deal with the theological and emotional aspects of divorce or death. This book is different. It reaches into the everyday life of a single parent and offers practical, biblical, common-sense insight, and support for the most important job we have.

Author David R. Miller, married for more than three decades and a father and grandfather, earned his doctorate in counseling psychology from the University of South Carolina in 1981. Dr. Miller is a licensed counselor in Virginia, has authored seven books, and is a frequent seminar leader for single and stepparents. Dr. Miller is professor of counseling and psychology at Liberty University in Lynchburg, Va.

Contents *1.* Accepting the challenge *2.* A "D" day approaches *3.* The challenge *4.* Infants and young children

5. The school-aged child 6. The "tween-ager" 7. Single parenting the adolescent 8. Discipline and the single parent 9. Detours, pitfalls, and stumbling blocks 10. Long-term adjustment 11. Preparing for remarriage 12. Step family readjustment 13. Future family 14. Just for dads

Rest Stops for Single Mothers *Devotions to Encourage You on Your Journey,* Susan Titus Osborn and Lucille Moses

Broadman and Holman Publishers, 1995, $10.95, paper, 227 pp.

Description Written by two single mothers, this collection of devotions invites you to experience the refreshment of Jesus' help and rest as you work to raise a family alone. Each brief yet intensely personal entry is accompanied by Scripture, a prayer, and suggestions for journaling.

Authors Susan Titus Osborn, a single mother for six years, is editor of *The Christian Communicator.* Lucille Moses, assistant editor of the above and contributor to three devotional books, has been a single mother for more than 20 years.

Contents 1. New beginnings 2. Looking at ourselves 3. Coping with windy days 4. Life after death 5. Joy blooming 6. Picking flowers or weeds 7. The price of freedom 8. Harvest time 9. Essential planning 10. Setting boundaries 11. Growing in strength 12. Celebration of love

Parenting Alone *A Network Discussion Guide,* Jane Porter

Harold Shaw Publishers, 1992, $3.99, paper, 48 pp., for both counselors and counselees

Description This fill-in-the-blank format discussion guide combines questions and Scripture passages to study eight topics related to single parenting.

Author Jane Porter is coordinator of Parenting Together, a program of Christian Service Brigade for single parents. Widowed when her three children were teenagers, Porter leads discussions for single parent groups. She graduated from Taylor University with a major in elementary education and holds an M.A. in education from Indiana University.

Contents 1. Alone—does it have to mean aloneness? Mark 14, et al. 2. Help—is there any available? Ps. 16, et al. 3. Worry—will we make it? Matt. 6:25–34 4. Opportunity—what do you see? Num. 13:1–7, 17–33 5. Victim—look what's happened to me! Gen. 37:1–28 6. Forgiveness—who will benefit? Matt. 18:15–35 7. Bad choices—can I overcome them? Lk. 15, et al. 8. Hope—can life ever be better? Ps. 69, et al.

Handbook for Single Parents William Rabior and Vicki Wells Bedard

Liguori Publications, 1991, $2.95, paper, 79 pp., for counselees

Description This practical handbook is a godsend to single parents. It offers much-needed advice for coping with common pitfalls and situations like depression, standard-of-living decrease, the absent parent, loneliness, dating, and many others. It also explains the importance of discipline and offers suggestions for adapting to or improving the single parent/child relationship.

Authors William Rabior is a Catholic priest and registered clinical social worker who has done extensive work with divorced persons. Vicki Bedard is a communications specialist as well as a single parent herself and has given workshops on single parenting.

I Didn't Plan to Be a Single Parent Bobbie Reed

CPH Publishing, 1981, $7.95, paper, 158 pp., for counselees

Description A realistic, understanding book that helps one meet the pressures, responsibilities, and opportunities that accompany single parenthood.

Author Bobbie Reed speaks from experience. Having spent ten years as a single mother raising two sons, Dr. Reed has turned her journey into a dynamic ministry to single and single-again adults. She is now happily remarried.

Contents 1. Single parenting: the task 2. Single parenting with custody 3. Single parenting without custody 4. Sharing custody 5. Evaluating expectations 6. Redefining roles, rules, and responsibilities 7. Developing a supportive network 8. Dating, the second time around 9. Exploring your resources 10. Resolving legal issues 11. Letting the children go 12. That's my kid! 13. Thanks, mom! Thanks, dad!

Never a Day Off *Surviving Single Parenthood,* Elizabeth Hilbun Rigdon

Beacon Hill Press of Kansas City, 1990, $1.95, paper, 60 pp., for counselees

Description A brief booklet that uses personal stories and Scripture to encourage single parents.

One-Parent Families *Healing the Hurts,* Harold Ivan Smith

129

Beacon Hill Press of Kansas City, 1981, $4.95, paper, 104 pp., for both counselors and counselees

Description Offers suggestions for churches in helping single parents.

Author Harold Ivan Smith is well known for his combined ministries of writing, speaking, and counseling, especially in the area of singles ministries in the church.

Contents *1.* Where do we begin? *2.* How can we learn to care? *3.* Your church can make a difference *4.* How do we help the children? *5.* Where will they go to Sunday school? *6.* How can we win them?

The Fresh Start Single Parenting Workbook Thomas Whiteman

Thomas Nelson Publishers, 1993, $14.99, paper, 304 pp., for counselees

Description This interactive workbook helps single parents minimize the negative aspects of single parenting. Provides an eight-step, easy-to-follow plan for working through the harmful effects of losing a partner, picking up the pieces, creating a healthy new lifestyle for you and your children. Part of the Fresh Start series of self-help titles from Thomas Nelson.

Author Thomas Whiteman (Ph.D., Bryn Mawr College), president of Fresh Start Seminars, is founder and director of Life Counseling Services in Pennsylvania.

Contents *1.* The plight of the single parent *2.* Looking back *3.* Are we a dysfunctional family? *4.* Breaking the cycle *5.* The overburdened parent *6.* The overburdened child *7.* Just for dads *8.* From dating to remarriage *9.* Remarried . . . with children

Doing Your Best As a Single Parent

Abbey Press, $.50 each, paper, 8 pp., for counselees

Description Part of the CareNotes series from Abbey Press. CareNotes are short booklets that help readers identify issues and begin the process of seeking resolution. Anecdotal and uplifting. Beautiful photographs grace the covers. Over 20 million CareNotes have been sold in just over five years. Can be used as an alternative to a greeting card or in conjunction with pastoral care visits.

Coping with Difficult, Rebellious, or Runaway Children

What Did I Do Wrong? What Can I Do Now? *Practical Help for Parents Who Think It's Too Late,* William Backus and Candace Backus

Bethany House Publishers, 1990, $7.99, paper, 172 pp., for both counselors and counselees

Description This is a book for parents who think it's too late as they relate to their teen and adult children. Both from a professional and a personal level, the authors convey the encouragement, practical suggestions, and truth-renewal that hurting parents need. It is a resource of God's grace for troubled people. Section 1 deals with what went wrong—the types of problems parents face, theories of who's responsible, and what is really known about behavior causes. Section 2 covers how to cope—dealing with guilt, feelings, forgiveness, misbeliefs in relationships, talking with the child, and when confession and making amends is appropriate. Section 3 is on what to do if all else fails—dealing with sorrow, depression, and discovering the power of hope and prayer.

Authors William Backus is a licensed clinical psychologist and an ordained Lutheran clergyman. He is founder and director of the Center for Christian Psychological Services, St. Paul, Minn., and an associate pastor of a large Lutheran church. Candace Backus is a counselor and vice president of Minnesota Psychtests, Inc.

Contents *1.* The downward spiral *2.* Fear *3.* Guilt *4.* Remorse *5.* Forbidden feelings *6.* Denial: walking in darkness *7.* The miracle of vulnerability *8.* Letting yourself go *9.* Freeing your child *10.* Tuning in *11.* Hope *12.* The invitation to rest *13.* Love never fails *14.* Joyful endings *15.* Big dilemmas *16.* A final word: the truth about psychology's "answers"

Getting Out of Your Kids' Faces and Into Their Hearts *A Simple Way to Stop Nagging and Start Nurturing,* Valerie Bell

Zondervan Publishing House, 1995, $10.99, paper, 177 pp.

Description Offers a simple, flexible, practical, and sometimes humorous relational system for raising kids. Too many parents try to manage their children rather than develop a relationship to them, which steals emotional energy needed for relating. Encourages parents to improve their own behavior as adults.

Author Valerie Bell is a popular conference speaker and Christian broadcaster.

Contents *Part 1*—Getting out of your kids' faces . . . *1.* When something is missing *2.* How do I know if I'm a good parent? *3.* The problem with being an "in your face parent" *4.* How to keep displaced passions from destroying your family life *Part 2*—. . . And into their hearts *5.* You are the memory *6.* Dancing with a limp *7.* Huckleberry days *8.* "Everybody's weird in their own special way" *9.* Heat's on! *10.* Not perfect but present *11.* The healing power of touch *12.* Encouragement for the organizationally challenged *13.* When going back to Egypt seems appealing

Kid Think *Revolutionary Insights into the Six Most Common Behavioral Problems,* William Lee Carter

Rapha Resources, 1992, $11.99, paper, 224 pp., for counselors

Description Enables parents to understand the ways children think and reason, then shows how to use this knowledge to apply a skills-oriented parenting technique. Includes a leader's guide for group study.

Learning More about Teenage Rebellion William Lee Carter

Rapha Resources, 1991, $2.50, paper, 56 pp., for counselees

Description For parents wrestling with their teenagers over the issue of control, this booklet will help them understand the emotions at work and the approaches they can take.

Raising Your Child, Not Your Voice Duane Cuthbertson

Victor Books, for counselees

Description How can you change a child's strong will without breaking his spirit? If you want to establish sound discipline strategies, this book will help you teach your child without straining your vocal cords.

The Strong Willed Child James Dobson

Tyndale House Publishers, 1989, $14.99, cloth, 240 pp., for both counselors and counselees

Description Practical ways to discipline a child without breaking his spirit.

Author James C. Dobson, Ph.D., is founder and president of Focus on the Family. A licensed psychologist, he has authored 12 best-selling books

on the family, including *The Strong Willed Child, Love Must Be Tough, Parenting Isn't for Cowards,* and the *New Dare to Discipline.*

The Wounded Parent *Hope for Discouraged Parents,* Guy Greenfield

Baker Book House, (2d ed.), $9.99, paper, 150 pp., for counselees

Description For parents of wayward children. Guy Greenfield offers comfort, hope, and advice on rebuilding parent–child relationships.

Author Guy Greenfield is professor of Christian ethics at Southwestern Baptist Theological Seminary, Fort Worth, Tex.

Contents *1.* When your child goes astray *2.* A parent's shattered dreams *3.* The pain of rejection *4.* Managing your emotions *5.* When other people's children turn out well *6.* Looking back—what went wrong? and what if? *7.* Overcoming discouragement *8.* Building new relationships *9.* Building a new self image *10.* Wounded parents supporting each other *11.* A theology for wounded parents *12.* Postscript: redemption and prevention

Bringing Your Teen Back to God Robert Laurent

Chariot Family Publishing, 1990, $7.99, paper, 176 pp., for counselees

Description Gives parents tools to both help prevent serious problems and address specific existing problems. Should be of value to any parent of a teenager or preteenager.

Spanking—Why? When? How? Roy Lessin

Bethany House Publishers, 1993, $4.99, paper, 186 pp., for counselees

Description Must reading for every parent confused about society's permissiveness and unsure about the Bible's teaching on discipline.

The Hurting Parent *Help for Parents of Prodigal Sons and Daughters,* Margie Lewis and Greg Lewis

Zondervan Publishing House, 1994, $9.99, paper, 210 pp., for counselees

Description Written for those parents who feel they have failed their divinely appointed task of Christian parenthood. Includes discussion questions for groups.

Authors Margie Lewis is a graduate of Asbury College and Asbury Theological Seminary. Greg

Lewis is a professional writer and coauthor of numerous articles and books.

Six Things You Should Know about Rebellious Children Clyde M. Narramore

Narramore Christian Foundation, $.50, paper, for both counselors and counselees

Description One of the many booklets available from the Narramore Christian Foundation. Designed to be handed to a person beginning to come to grips with a problem in living.

Author Dr. Clyde M. Narramore is a licensed psychologist and the president and founder of the Narramore Christian Foundation—a charitable, nonprofit educational, training, and counseling organization ministering primarily to the Christian community. He is also the founder of the Rosemead School of Psychology and author of 29 books.

Adolescents in Turmoil, Parents under Stress *A Pastoral Ministry Primer,* Richard D. Parsons

Paulist Press, 1987, $7.95, paper, 145 pp., for counselors

Description A Christian, value-based approach to the understanding of and caring for the adolescent in turmoil and parents under stress.

Author Dr. Richard D. Parsons is professor of psychology in the Graduate Department of Pastoral Counseling at Neumann College, Aston, Pa. He maintains a private practice and is recognized as an expert in the field of problems of adolescents.

Contents *1.* Working with the adolescent—a special challenge *2.* Adolescence: storm and stress *3.* Communications *4.* Moving toward independence and the art of letting go *5.* Sex and the adolescent: an issue broader than the birds and the bees *6.* Drugs: use and abuse *7.* Nurturing the adolescent through school and other inconveniences *8.* Loneliness and alienation: adolescent without connection *9.* Suicide: the darkest of all moments

The Good News About Your Strong-Willed Child *Understanding and Raising the Child Who Opposes You,* Randy Reynolds and Paul Moede

Zondervan Publishing House, 1995, $9.99, paper, 200 pp.

Description When parents have a "difficult" child, they may be part of the problem. So, treating the

family as a system rather than breaking it down into individual "problems" is a first, important step to successful parenting.

Authors Randy Reynolds is director of Renewal Counseling in Tuscon, Ariz., and served as a pastor for more than 15 years. Paul Moede is on the staff of The International Bible Society and a freelance writer.

Contents *1.* My child versus the good child *2.* Caught in the conflict *3.* Building parental authority *4.* Creating a positive family atmosphere *5.* Finding the balance *6.* Moving your children toward maturity *7.* Gaining respect *8.* Achieving emotional stability *9.* Developing responsive loops *10.* A firm foundation

Relief for Hurting Parents *What to Do and How to Think When You're Having Trouble with Your Kids,* Buddy Scott

Rapha Resources, 1992, $9.95, paper, 196 pp., for counselees

Description Lets readers know they are not failures, God has not forsaken them, and they are definitely not alone. Scott, a specialist in teen counseling, has written a guide that is sincere, honest, and hardhitting. Detailed and exhaustive. Also available in group study and video formats.

Parents in Pain *Overcoming the Hurt and Frustration of Problem Children,* John White

InterVarsity Press, 1979, $10.99, paper, 245 pp., for counselees

Description White offers comfort and counsel to the parents of children with severe problems like rebellion, alcoholism, drug abuse, homosexuality, and suicide. Whether parent, potential parent, or friend, this book will help you. It describes what you can and can't do. Recognizing the limits of your responsibility will save you from unnecessary anguish and self-blame.

Author White studied medicine at the University of Manchester, England, served as a missionary, and later studied psychiatry at the University of Manitoba, Canada. Dr. White enjoys an international ministry. His books have sold over one million copies.

Contents *1.* The age of uncertainty *2.* Whose fault? *3.* False comfort *4.* Erosion of trust: the pain begins *5.* Storms and peace *6.* The threat to the marriage *7.* Professional help *8.* In trouble with the law *9.* Relinquishment *10.* From utopia to Galilee *11.* Toward human dignity *12.* The model parent *13.* Dialog with divinity *14.* Epilogue

Help and Hope for Troubled Teens

Ave Maria Press, 1992, $24.95, video, 28 minutes, for counselees

Description Why do so many teens and their families seem so troubled? What are the danger signs of inappropriate behavior? Here's a detailed analysis of various helps—from group therapy to tough love type groups—and a discussion of some key ingredients for successful child rearing.

Child Find of America, Inc.

Child Find of America, Inc. An organization

Description Though not a Christian organization, assists in locating children taken in custody disputes, runaway children, and abducted children.

Children of the Night

Children of the Night. An organization

Description A (secular) national hotline for runaway and abused children. The hotline is designed to serve children who are "on the streets" and need emergency shelter. The children call, and someone comes to pick them up and take them to a shelter. Maintains a national listing of runaway shelters. Located in Los Angeles.

Covenant House *(Runaway Children)*

Covenant House. An organization

Description Provides phone counseling and help to runaway children.

Missing Children Help Center

Missing Children Help Center. An organization

Description Though not a Christian organization, assists in the process of locating runaway children and those abducted by parents or criminals by placing the child's photograph in various media formats (magazines, TV, etc.). No fee involved.

National Center for Missing and Exploited Children

National Center for Missing and Exploited Children. An organization

Description As America's resource center for child protection, the National Center for Missing and Exploited Children spearheads national efforts to locate and recover missing children and raises public awareness about ways to prevent child abduction, molestation, and sexual exploitation. A private, nonprofit organization established in 1984.

National Network of Runaway and Youth Services

National Network of Runaway and Youth Services. An organization

Description Helps parents and police locate missing and runaway children.

National Runaway Switchboard

National Runaway Switchboard. An organization

Description National organization that networks groups dedicated to locating runaway children.

Operation Lookout National Center for Missing Youth

Operation Lookout National Center for Missing Youth. An organization

Description Focuses on locating missing children (runaways, stranger abductions, custodial interference, and unexplained disappearances) under the age of 18 in the northwestern United States. They have an excellent case resolve rate of 82 percent. Though not a Christian organization, services include search and crisis intervention, poster design, photo and poster distribution, national networking, systems walk-through, toll-free helpline, and more.

Society for Young Victims

Society for Young Victims. An organization

Description Though not a Christian organization, provides information about missing children, conducts school education workshops.

Tough Love

Tough Love. An organization

Description A support organization that provides support group materials and guidance designed to empower parents dealing with difficult adolescents.

18. Financial Counseling

God's Managers *A Budget Guide and Daily Financial Record Book for Christians,* Ray Bair and Lillian Bair

> Herald Press, 1985 (revised), $4.75, paper, 48 pp., for counselees

> **Description** A popular family budget guide and daily record book to show families where their money goes and how they can manage their spending, saving, and giving in a healthier way.

> **Authors** Ray and Lillian Bair have held God's Managers Seminars in congregations since 1981. They are involved in the Belmont Mennonite Congregation in Elkhart, Ind.

> **Contents** *Introduction* "Give an account of your management" How to begin *Part 1:* Discovering where all the money goes *Part 2:* Creating a monthly budget *Part 3:* Keeping accurate records *Part 4:* Annual evaluation of the past year and planning for the next / Defining what it is you manage / Illustrations of the kind of items that can go under each category / Overflow

The 15 Minute Money Manager Bob Barnes and Emilie Barnes

> Harvest House Publishers, 1993, $8.99, paper, 273 pp., for counselees

> **Description** At last a money management book for busy people! Watch your finances come into focus as you apply the author's proven 15-minute principle: invest a small amount of time and make a big difference. Sixty-two short, quick-reading chapters have hundreds of ready-to-use ideas that will help you in various areas of financial planning.

> **Authors** Bob and Emilie Barnes are the founders of More Hours in My Day Time Management Seminars. They work full-time together in this special ministry to men and women across the country.

A Woman's Guide to Financial Peace of Mind Ron Blue and Judy Blue

> Focus on the Family, 1991, $8.99, paper, 235 pp., for counselees

> **Description** Financial expert Ron Blue and his wife, Judy, have found that women's financial concerns are largely determined by the season of life in which they find themselves. A young single, a mother of small children, and an empty-nester, for example, have very different questions and needs. This book is organized accordingly, with separate chapters describing the particular concerns of each season and how to meet them with biblical and practical wisdom.

> **Authors** Ron Blue is managing partner of Ronald Blue & Co., a financial advisory firm with offices in Atlanta, Orlando, and Indianapolis. Judy Blue is a homemaker and mother of five with a master's in counseling and guidance from Indiana University.

> **Contents** *Part 1:* The keys to successful money management *1.* Making ends meet *2.* Cornerstones of success *3.* Reading the signs *Part 2:* The financial seasons of a woman's life *4.* Getting started: young single *5.* Bridging the coping gap: young married *6.* Two incomes or one: young children *7.* Another coping gap: teen and college-age children *8.* The empty nest *9.* Retirement: work's end or second wind? *10.* Single again: widowhood *11.* Going it alone: single parent *12.* Career single *Part 3:* Common concerns *13.* When and where to get professional advice *14.* Life insurance do's and don'ts *15.* Health insurance do's and don'ts *16.* Getting ahead step-by-step

Avoiding Common Financial Mistakes Ron Blue

> NavPress, 1990, $1.99, paper, 23 pp., for counselees

> **Description** This booklet is designed to help you develop financial habits that will work to your advantage in the long run, rather than limit your potential. Among other things, you'll learn to: set realistic financial goals, stay out of debt, spend less than you earn, base your financial plans on biblical principles rather than cultural ones, and develop a workable budget over a two-year period.

Mastering Money in Your Marriage Ron Blue

Regal Books, 1993, $9.99/$11.99, spiral, 148 pp., for counselees

Description Part of the HomeBuilders Couples series from Gospel Light. This title helps couples learn biblical principles about money and ways to resolve conflict regarding it.

Author Ron Blue is the founder of Ronald Blue & Co., a professional firm offering counsel in handling personal finances from a biblical perspective.

Contents *Introduction* / HomeBuilder's principles / A word about finances *1.* Managing your money wisely *2.* Stewardship *3.* Financial priorities *4.* Setting financial goals *5.* Credit, borrowing, and debt *6.* Giving *7.* Training others to manage money / *Conclusion:* One final project

Answers to Your Family's Financial Questions Larry Burkett

Tyndale House Publishers, 1994, $5.99, paper, 236 pp., for both counselors and counselees

Description Questions about credit, saving and investing, taxes, insurance, and much more are covered in this easy-to-read handbook that shows how the Bible can guide our financial lives.

Author Since 1976, Larry Burkett has directed Christian Financial Concepts, a nationwide, nonprofit organization dedicated to teaching biblical principles of handling money. He has published over 20 books on finances with a total distribution of over two million. He is heard daily on two radio broadcasts carried by over 1,000 outlets worldwide. Christian Financial Concepts also publishes a free newsletter that focuses on current economic issues.

Contents *1.* Attitudes *2.* Husband's and wife's responsibilities *3.* Budgeting *4.* Money and children *5.* Lending *6.* Borrowing and debt *7.* Giving *8.* Inheritance and wills *9.* Investment and savings *10.* Buying and selling *11.* Vocational decisions *12.* Single's finances *13.* Retirement

Complete Financial Guide for Single Parents, The *Sound Money Strategies for Mothers and Fathers on Their Own,* Larry Burkett

Victor Books, 1991, $8.99, paper, 228 pp., for counselees

Description Sound, biblically based advice on a variety of topics.

Author Since 1976, Larry Burkett has directed Christian Financial Concepts, a nationwide, nonprofit organization dedicated to teaching biblical principles of handling money. He has published over 20 books on finances with a total distribution of over two million. He is heard daily on two radio broadcasts carried by over 1,000 outlets worldwide. Christian Financial Concepts also publishes a free newsletter that focuses on current economic issues.

Contents *Section 1:* Divorcees *1.* The plight of divorcees *2.* The unexpected divorce *3.* Facing the job market *4.* The financial struggles of a single parent *5.* Housing, cars, and kids *6.* Alimony, child support, and lawsuits *7.* A practical budget *Section 2:* Widows *8.* A warning for widows *9.* Widows without an inheritance *10.* What every widow needs to know about wills, trusts, insurance, social security, and taxes *11.* Remarriage decisions / *Appendixes* a. Steps to making a budget b. Wills and trusts c. Social security benefits d. Veteran's benefits e. Insurance benefits f. Buying a car g. Housing h. Federal estate taxes i. State death taxes j. Checklist of important documents

Complete Financial Guide for Young Couples, The *A Lifetime Approach to Spending, Saving, and Investing,* Larry Burkett

Victor Books, 1989, $10.99, cloth, 228 pp., for counselees

Description Get off on the right foot financially in your marriage and be good stewards of all God has given you. This book shows you how to establish a workable budget, choose the right kind of insurance, and much more.

Author Since 1976, Larry Burkett has directed Christian Financial Concepts, a nationwide, nonprofit organization dedicated to teaching biblical principles of handling money. He has published over 20 books on finances with a total distribution of over two million. He is heard daily on two radio broadcasts carried by over 1,000 outlets worldwide. Christian Financial Concepts also publishes a free newsletter that focuses on current economic issues.

Contents *Part 1:* Developing a short-range plan *1.* God's wisdom *2.* Money, an outside indicator *3.* Combatants or companions *4.* God's minimum standards *5.* How God uses money in a marriage *6.* Credit cards *7.* Early marriage symptoms *8.* Correcting problems *9.* A workable budget *10.* A workable plan *11.* Establishing a budget *12.* The guideline budget *13.* The money barometer: economic danger signs *14.* Questions and answers on family finance *Part 2:* Critical family issues *15.* Long-range goals *16.* Insurance *17.* Inheritance *18.* Retirement *Part*

3: Children's finances *19.* Declining Christianity *20.* Training children ages 1–10 *21.* Training children ages 11–16 *22.* Training children ages 17–20 *Part 4:* Ten keys to successful investing

Counselor Self-Study Course Larry Burkett

Christian Financial Concepts, 1992, $59.95, three-ring, 600 pp., for counselors

Description This course provides in-depth training for individuals who desire to become volunteer debt and budget counselors. The syllabus contains valuable material, including case studies, counseling procedures and tips, credit information, resource material on a variety of topics, detailed glossary of financial terms, and review questions. Required supplements are Larry Burkett's *How to Manage Your Money* and *The Financial Planning Workbook*—both sold separately.

Author Since 1976, Larry Burkett has directed Christian Financial Concepts, a nationwide, nonprofit organization dedicated to teaching biblical principles of handling money. He has published over 20 books on finances with a total distribution of over two million. He is heard daily on two radio broadcasts carried by over 1,000 outlets worldwide. Christian Financial Concepts also publishes a free newsletter that focuses on current economic issues.

Contents How to use this course / Suggested study schedules *Assignment 1:* How to manage your money *Assignment 2:* The financial planning workbook *Assignment 3:* Counseling procedures *Assignment 4:* Your credit rights *Assignment 5:* Selected readings / *Resources* / Glossary / Answers to review questions / Referral / Counselor program

Debt Free Living *How to Get Out of Debt and Stay Out,* Larry Burkett

Moody Press, 1989, $12.50, paper, 249 pp., for counselees

Description Follow the true-to-life experiences of several marriages on the brink of economic ruin. As each couple goes through financial counseling, biblical principles for getting out of debt emerge. Covers bankruptcy alternatives and other useful information.

Author Since 1976, Larry Burkett has directed Christian Financial Concepts, a nationwide, nonprofit organization dedicated to teaching biblical principles of handling money. He has published over 20 books on finances with a total

distribution of over two million. He is heard daily on two radio broadcasts carried by over 1,000 outlets worldwide. Christian Financial Concepts also publishes a free newsletter that focuses on current economic issues.

Contents *Part 1:* Three couples slide into debt *1.* A national policy of growth through debt *2.* Sliding toward a crisis *3.* It didn't begin yesterday *4.* Things come to a head *5.* If I don't talk about it, it'll go away *6.* If only the baby had been well *7.* Three personal traits that lead to debt *Part 2:* Three couples and a fourth, climb out of debt *8.* The Bible speaks on debt and borrowing *9.* Learn to face reality *10.* Develop and carry out a plan for paying off debts *11.* Don't use borrowed money for speculative ventures *12.* Commit to faithfully repay creditors *13.* Two common errors that lead to debt *14.* Learn to live within a financial plan *15.* Accept responsibility for your life *16.* Three major expenses that lead to debt *Part 3:* Overview of credit, debt, and borrowing *17.* Understanding credit *18.* Bill consolidation loans *19.* Dealing with creditors *20.* Living with bankruptcy *21.* Where to find help / *Appendixes*

Family Budget Workbook, The *Gaining Control of Your Personal Finances,* Larry Burkett

Moody Press/Northfield, 1993, $11.99, paper, 100 pp., for counselees

Description Financial expert Larry Burkett introduces the ultimate family money management workbook. His sensible, realistic plan for getting and keeping your finances under control includes easy-to-use worksheets that make following the plan as easy as possible.

Author Since 1976, Larry Burkett has directed Christian Financial Concepts, a nationwide, nonprofit organization dedicated to teaching biblical principles of handling money. He has published over 20 books on finances with a total distribution of over two million. He is heard daily on two radio broadcasts carried by over 1,000 outlets worldwide. Christian Financial Concepts also publishes a free newsletter that focuses on current economic issues.

Contents *1.* Getting started *2.* Where are we? *3.* Short-range planning *4.* Budget problems *5.* The guideline budget *6.* Budget analysis *7.* The control system *8.* Begin now (forms)

Financial Counselor's Manual Larry Burkett

Christian Financial Concepts, 1991, three-ring, 73 pp., for counselors

Description CFC prepared this manual as a guide for those who provide financial counseling and planning. Designed for those already familiar with basic counseling techniques.

Author Since 1976, Larry Burkett has directed Christian Financial Concepts, a nationwide, non-profit organization dedicated to teaching biblical principles of handling money. He has published over 20 books on finances with a total distribution of over two million. He is heard daily on two radio broadcasts carried by over 1,000 outlets worldwide. Christian Financial Concepts also publishes a free newsletter that focuses on current economic issues.

Contents *Introduction* / Counseling prerequisites / *Resources* / Counselor requirements *1.* Counseling location *2.* When to counsel *3.* Who to counsel *4.* Counseling files *5.* Pre-counseling technique *6.* Counseling technique *7.* First counseling visit *8.* Second counseling visit *9.* Third counseling visit *10.* Fourth and subsequent counseling visits / *Appendixes*

Financial Freedom Library Volume 1
Larry Burkett

Moody Press, 1991, $14.95, paper, 6 with 75+ pp., for both counselors and counselees

Description A series of booklets that covers a variety of financial topics. Volume 1 contains: Financial freedom; Giving and tithing; Personal finances; Major purchases; Insurance plans; Sound investments.

Author Since 1976, Larry Burkett has directed Christian Financial Concepts, a nationwide, non-profit organization dedicated to teaching biblical principles of handling money. He has published over 20 books on finances with a total distribution of over two million. He is heard daily on two radio broadcasts carried by over 1,000 outlets worldwide. Christian Financial Concepts also publishes a free newsletter that focuses on current economic issues.

Financial Freedom Library Volume 2
Larry Burkett

Moody Press, 1991, $14.95, paper, 6 with 75+ pp., for both counselors and counselees

Description A series of booklets that covers a variety of financial issues. Volume 2 includes: Surviving the '90s economy; Sound business decisions; Sound business principles; Wills and trusts; Your financial future; Financial sampler.

Author Since 1976, Larry Burkett has directed Christian Financial Concepts, a nationwide, non-profit organization dedicated to teaching biblical principles of handling money. He has published over 20 books on finances with a total distribution of over two million. He is heard daily on two radio broadcasts carried by over 1,000 outlets worldwide. Christian Financial Concepts also publishes a free newsletter that focuses on current economic issues.

Financial Planning Organizer, The
Software for Personal Finances, Larry Burkett and Bill Wise

Moody Press, 1992, $49.95, software, for counselees

Description This software helps you get in the control seat of budget analysis then progress toward the goal of debt-free living. On-line help from Burkett will encourage you to wisely manage your money. PC/DOS 2.0 or higher.

Author Since 1976, Larry Burkett has directed Christian Financial Concepts, a nationwide, non-profit organization dedicated to teaching biblical principles of handling money. He has published over 20 books on finances with a total distribution of over two million. He is heard daily on two radio broadcasts carried by over 1,000 outlets worldwide. Christian Financial Concepts also publishes a free newsletter that focuses on current economic issues.

Financial Planning Workbook Instructor's Manual, The Larry Burkett

Christian Financial Concepts, 1991, $6.50, paper, 72 pp., for counselors

Description Provides overviews and helpful hints for teaching the workshop.

Author Since 1976, Larry Burkett has directed Christian Financial Concepts, a nationwide, non-profit organization dedicated to teaching biblical principles of handling money. He has published over 20 books on finances with a total distribution of over two million. He is heard daily on two radio broadcasts carried by over 1,000 outlets worldwide. Christian Financial Concepts also publishes a free newsletter that focuses on current economic issues.

Contents Introduction / Teaching the workshop / Instructor's prerequisites / Instructor's hints / Workshop introduction / Getting started / Where are we? Short-range planning for variable expenses / Budget problems / The guidelines budget / The budget analysis / The control system / Long-range planning / Visuals / Optional forms

Financial Planning Workshop, Video Series, The *A Family Budgeting Seminar,* Larry Burkett

Christian Financial Concepts, 1991, $99.95, video, for both counselors and counselees

Description A four-hour presentation on developing a budget for home money management. Includes a copy of *The Financial Planning Workbook Instructor's Manual* at no extra charge.

Author Since 1976, Larry Burkett has directed Christian Financial Concepts, a nationwide, non-profit organization dedicated to teaching biblical principles of handling money. He has published over 20 books on finances with a total distribution of over two million. He is heard daily on two radio broadcasts carried by over 1,000 outlets worldwide. Christian Financial Concepts also publishes a free newsletter that focuses on current economic issues.

Contents *1.* Getting started *2.* Where are we? *3.* Short-range planning *4.* Budget problems *5.* The guideline budget *6.* Budget analysis *7.* The control system (1) *8.* The control system (2) *9.* Summary/Q/A

How to Manage Your Money Audio Series *An In-Depth Bible Study on Personal Finances,* Larry Burkett

Christian Financial Concepts, 1990, $30.00, cassette(s), for counselees

Description A Bible study that helps Christians weed out the religious "folklore" about money and discover God's "true" will in finances. The audio format of this series has been updated and now includes testimonies. It consists of 12 sessions in 30-minute segments. An instructor's manual is also available for this series from CFC.

Author Since 1976, Larry Burkett has directed Christian Financial Concepts, a nationwide, non-profit organization dedicated to teaching biblical principles of handling money. He has published over 20 books on finances with a total distribution of over two million. He is heard daily on two radio broadcasts carried by over 1,000 outlets worldwide. Christian Financial Concepts also publishes a free newsletter that focuses on current economic issues.

Contents *1.* What is wealth? *2.* God's will in finances *3.* The perils of money *4.* Release from servitude *5.* Financial planning—God's way 1 *6.* Financial planning—God's way 2 *7.* Motives for accumulating wealth *8.* How much is enough? *9.* Sharing by God's plan *10.* Who deserves help? *11.* God's principles of financial decisions *12.* The challenge

How to Manage Your Money Instructor's Manual Larry Burkett

Christian Financial Concepts, 1991, $6.50, paper, 68 pp., for counselees

Description The updated *How to Manage Your Money Instructor's Manual* presents an overview and helpful hints for each lesson in the Bible study.

Author Since 1976, Larry Burkett has directed Christian Financial Concepts, a nationwide, non-profit organization dedicated to teaching biblical principles of handling money. He has published over 20 books on finances with a total distribution of over two million. He is heard daily on two radio broadcasts carried by over 1,000 outlets worldwide. Christian Financial Concepts also publishes a free newsletter that focuses on current economic issues.

Contents *1.* What is wealth? *2.* God's will in finances *3.* The perils of money *4.* Release from servitude *5.* Financial planning—God's way 1 *6.* Financial planning—God's way 2 *7.* Motives for accumulating wealth *8.* How much is enough? *9.* Sharing by God's plan *10.* Who deserves help? *11.* God's principles of financial decisions *12.* The challenge

How to Manage Your Money Video Series *An In-Depth Bible Study on Personal Finances,* Larry Burkett

Christian Financial Concepts, 1990, $99.95, video, for both counselors and counselees

Description A Bible study that helps Christians weed out the religious "folklore" about money and discover God's "true" will in finances. The video format of this series has been updated and now includes testimonies. It consists of 12 sessions in 30-minute segments and comes with a copy of the *How to Manage Your Money Instructor's Manual* at no extra charge.

Author Since 1976, Larry Burkett has directed Christian Financial Concepts, a nationwide, non-profit organization dedicated to teaching biblical principles of handling money. He has published over 20 books on finances with a total distribution of over two million. He is heard daily on two radio broadcasts carried by over 1,000 outlets worldwide. Christian Financial Concepts also publishes a free newsletter that focuses on current economic issues.

Contents *1.* What is wealth? *2.* God's will in finances *3.* The perils of money *4.* Release from servitude *5.* Financial planning—God's way 1 *6.* Financial planning—God's way 2 *7.* Motives for accumulating wealth *8.* How much is enough? *9.* Sharing by God's plan *10.* Who deserves help? *11.* God's principles of financial decisions *12.* The challenge

Investing for the Future Larry Burkett

Victor Books, 1992, $15.95, cloth, 260 pp., for counselees

Description Includes: Why invest? the six best investments, seven investments to steer clear of, where to go for specific and reliable investment advice, the "seasons of investing," and more. Contains an excellent resource directory of investment information.

Author Since 1976, Larry Burkett has directed Christian Financial Concepts, a nationwide, non-profit organization dedicated to teaching biblical principles of handling money. He has published over 20 books on finances with a total distribution of over two million. He is heard daily on two radio broadcasts carried by over 1,000 outlets worldwide. Christian Financial Concepts also publishes a free newsletter that focuses on current economic issues.

Contents *1.* The economy *2.* Three important principles *3.* Why invest? *4.* Risk and return *5.* The investment hall of horrors *6.* The best investments *7.* Strategy for investing *8.* Critical factors *9.* Where to go for advice *10.* Following Solomon's advice *11.* The financial seasons of life, ages 20–40 *12.* The financial seasons of life, ages 40–60 *13.* The financial seasons of life, ages 60 and up *14.* Evaluating investments: the five-tier system *15.* Evaluating cash investments *16.* Evaluating bond investments *17.* Evaluating stocks and stock funds *18.* Investing in real estate *19.* Evaluating collectibles and precious metals *20.* Evaluating insurance *21.* Social security and estate planning

Personal Finances *Includes Budgeting and Debt Reduction,* Larry Burkett

Christian Financial Concepts, 1994, $19.99, video, for both counselors and counselees

Description Part of the new Financial Freedom Video Library from Christian Financial Concepts. Financial freedom comes as a direct result of

careful planning and wise spending decisions. Although sacrifice is involved, Burkett maintains that you can reduce expenditures substantially without a significant reduction in your standard of living. Surprised? Don't be. Thirty minutes with Larry Burkett may be just what you need to see how it's done and to start on the road to financial freedom.

Author Since 1976, Larry Burkett has directed Christian Financial Concepts, a nationwide, non-profit organization dedicated to teaching biblical principles of handling money. He has published over 20 books on finances with a total distribution of over two million. He is heard daily on two radio broadcasts carried by over 1,000 outlets worldwide. Christian Financial Concepts also publishes a free newsletter that focuses on current economic issues.

Two Masters Larry Burkett

Christian Financial Concepts, 1982, $14.95, video, for counselees

Description This drama of two families' financial struggles and the hard-hitting discussions with Larry Burkett create an awareness of the importance of keeping finances under God's control. The 52-minute video will introduce freedom from financial pressure to your Bible study group, Sunday school class, or congregation. It examines the roots of financial problems common to most families today and proposes the solution in an easy-to-understand format.

Author Since 1976, Larry Burkett has directed Christian Financial Concepts, a nationwide, non-profit organization dedicated to teaching biblical principles of handling money. He has published over 20 books on finances with a total distribution of over two million. He is heard daily on two radio broadcasts carried by over 1,000 outlets worldwide. Christian Financial Concepts also publishes a free newsletter that focuses on current economic issues.

Victory over Debt *Rediscovering Financial Freedom,* Larry Burkett

Moody Press/Northfield, 1992, $8.99, paper, 214 pp., for counselees

Description The respected financial consultant and best-selling author outlines timeless principles for becoming free from the bondage of debt.

He teaches everything from creating and adhering to a budget, to when it's better to rent than buy a home, to what it means to file for bankruptcy.

Author Since 1976, Larry Burkett has directed Christian Financial Concepts, a nationwide, nonprofit organization dedicated to teaching biblical principles of handling money. He has published over 20 books on finances with a total distribution of over two million. He is heard daily on two radio broadcasts carried by over 1,000 outlets worldwide. Christian Financial Concepts also publishes a free newsletter that focuses on current economic issues.

Contents *Part 1:* Three couples slide into debt *1.* A national policy of growth through debt *2.* Sliding toward a crisis *3.* It didn't begin yesterday *4.* Things come to a head *5.* If I don't talk about it, it'll go away *6.* If only the baby had been well *7.* Three personal traits that lead to debt *Part 2:* Three couples and a fourth, climb out of debt *8.* The Bible speaks on debt and borrowing *9.* Learn to face reality *10.* Develop and carry out a plan for paying off debts *11.* Don't use borrowed money for speculative ventures *12.* Commit to faithfully repay creditors *13.* Two common errors that lead to debt *14.* Learn to live within a financial plan *15.* Accept responsibility for your life *16.* Three major expenses that lead to debt *Part 3:* Overview of credit, debt, and borrowing *17.* Understanding credit *18.* Bill consolidation loans *19.* Dealing with creditors *20.* Living with bankruptcy *21.* Where to find help / *Appendixes*

Your Finances in Changing Times (Audio Version) *A Seminar on Biblical Principles of Finances,* Larry Burkett

Christian Financial Concepts, 1990, $30.00, 5 cassettes, for counselees

Description Larry Burkett shows families how to respond to today's financial crises. The cassette format is useful during activities that make reading impossible. One study guide is provided with the cassettes. A 25-page syllabus containing an outline of the Bible verses covered in the seminar is also available ($2.00). This allows the user to easily take notes.

Author Since 1976, Larry Burkett has directed Christian Financial Concepts, a nationwide, nonprofit organization dedicated to teaching biblical principles of handling money. He has published over 20 books on finances with a total distribution of over two million. He is heard daily on two radio broadcasts carried by over 1,000 outlets worldwide. Christian Financial Concepts

also publishes a free newsletter that focuses on current economic issues.

Contents *1.* Identifying attitudes about money *2.* Setting goals to financial freedom *3.* Living God's way with His money *4.* Money management for kids *5.* Singles, inheritance, and retirement

Your Finances in Changing Times Video Seminar *A Seminar on Biblical Principles of Finances,* Larry Burkett

Christian Financial Concepts, 1990, $99.95, video, for counselees

Description Larry Burkett shows families how to respond to today's financial crises. The 5 1/2-hour video format is excellent for two-day churchwide showings or community meetings. One study guide is provided with the video cassettes.

Author Since 1976, Larry Burkett has directed Christian Financial Concepts, a nationwide, nonprofit organization dedicated to teaching biblical principles of handling money. He has published over 20 books on finances with a total distribution of over two million. He is heard daily on two radio broadcasts carried by over 1,000 outlets worldwide. Christian Financial Concepts also publishes a free newsletter that focuses on current economic issues.

Contents *1.* Identifying attitudes about money *2.* Setting goals to financial freedom *3.* Living God's way with His money *4.* Money management for kids, singles, inheritance, and retirement

Managing Your Money Richard A. Fish

Beacon Hill Press of Kansas City, $1.95, paper, 24 pp., for counselees

Description Part of the Christian Living series from Beacon Hill. Describes various aspects of responsible financial stewardship.

The Financially Challenged *A Survival Guide for Getting Through the Week, the Month . . . ,* Wilson J. Humber

Moody Press, 1995, $8.99, paper, 233 pp.

Description Providing one eye-opening principle after another, this "survival guide" shows you how to manage your money wisely. It will help you see beyond your current financial situation to a more secure financial future.

Author Jody Humber (Ph.D., Arizona State University) is a certified financial planner, registered investment advisor, and general securities principal. He is in private practice as an investment, tax, and estate counselor.

Contents *1.* Attitude is paramount *2.* Your income *3.* Giving *4.* Your reserves: savings and insurance *5.* Spending your reserves: unemployment and underemployment *6.* Your home *7.* Your car *8.* Debt—the black hole *9.* Spending plans *10.* Your personal plan

Saving the Best for Last *Planning a Secure Future for Your Family,* Wilson J. Humber

Moody Press, 1994, $11.99, paper, 168 pp., for counselees

Description Common sense and sound biblical principles. Apply both and avoid becoming one of the 19 of 20 Americans who needlessly suffer financial setbacks. This practical guide helps you increase your income, reduce expenses, and take care of your family's financial needs through a well-planned living trust.

Author Jody Humber (Ph.D., Arizona State University) is a certified financial planner, registered investment advisor, and general securities principal. He is in private practice as an investment, tax, and estate counselor.

Contents *Introduction:* Redefining the road to success *1.* Detours: anticipating and preventing problems *2.* Bad maps: discarding obsolete information *3.* Good maps: getting the right information *4.* Road hazards: preparing for inevitable obstacles *5.* Your individual map: selecting the plan that's right for you *6.* Caution: passing zone: passing your inheritance *7.* Your travel itinerary: tending to details *8.* Taking the best route: which trust is best for you? *9.* Special vehicles-special trusts: increasing gifts, endowments, and bequests *10.* Financial decisions: what to do once you get there

The Christian's Guide to Wise Investing
Gary D. Moore

Zondervan Publishing House, 1994, $14.99, paper, 336 pp., for counselees

Description Provides readers with a wealth of practical information on how to invest money with social, ethical, and stewardship principles in mind. Among the topics included are: developing a lifelong plan, getting the right advice, becoming bond wise, gift and estate planning, understanding seven key investment principles, pitfalls and strategies for stocks, positive real estate investing, how to read financial forms.

Author Gary D. Moore is former senior vice president for Paine Webber in Tampa, Fla.

How to Handle Severe Financial Loss
Clyde M. Narramore

Narramore Christian Foundation, $19.99, video, for counselees

Description When you suffer a loss, large or small, there are four things you are likely to do. But they don't help. Dr. Clyde Narramore gives seven workable principles.

Author Dr. Clyde M. Narramore is a licensed psychologist and the president and founder of the Narramore Christian Foundation—a charitable, nonprofit educational, training, and counseling organization ministering primarily to the Christian community. He is also the founder of the Rosemead School of Psychology and author of 29 books.

Lost in the Money Maze? *How to Find Your Way Through,* Patricia H. Rushford

Aglow Publications, 1992, $8.95, paper, 181 pp., for counselees

Description Money. Whether you love it or hate it, have a little or a lot, one fact is inescapable. You need it. Whether you consider yourself a financial failure or a financial genius, or fit somewhere in between, this book has something for you. This work blends solid money management tools with practical advice on how to: identify the "money-eaters" that devour your income; find a bookkeeping system that works for you; make wise decisions about buying on credit; include the entire family in financial planning; earn extra money from your time, trash, talent, and treasures; and how to trust God through it all.

Author Patricia H. Rushford, R.N., M.A. in counseling, has written numerous articles and 14 books. She is a contributing editor to *Christian Parenting Today* and adjunct professor at Western Evangelical Seminary.

Contents *Part 1:* The money maze *1.* Confession of a financial failure *2.* Financial geniuses and the rest of us *Part 2:* Confronting the monsters in your maze *3.* Foiling the money-eaters *4.* Charging your way through the money maze *5.* Bypassing the bargain bunnies *6.* Earn your way over the top *Part 3:* Putting your finances in order *7.* Building a budget *8.* Budgeting—a family affair *9.* Climbing paper mountains *10.* Finding financial freedom / *Appendix:* Support groups—places of growth and healing

The Money Trap *My Experience with Financial Difficulties,* Lynne Stamm-Rex

New Hope, 1989, $2.95, paper, 57 pp., for counselees

Description Easy credit and a craving for the good life lured Lynne Stamm-Rex and her husband into the trap called debt. When her husband, Mark, lost his job, the trap swung shut on them. In this painfully honest account Lynne shares how financial counseling and entrusting every aspect of their lives to God's guidance finally enabled them to escape the money trap. A financial counselor has provided insight into ways you can avoid being trapped by finances; his advice is found at the end of the book.

Author Lynne Stamm-Rex holds a degree in Christian education. She is a youth leader in her church and also performs musically throughout the East Coast.

Christian Financial Concepts

Christian Financial Concepts, founded 1976. An organization

Description Since 1976, Larry Burkett has directed Christian Financial Concepts, a nationwide, nonprofit organization dedicated to teaching biblical principles of handling money. He has published over 20 books on finances with a total distribution of over two million. He is heard daily on two radio broadcasts carried by over 1,000 outlets worldwide. Christian Financial Concepts also publishes a free newsletter that focuses on current economic issues.

19. Forgiveness

Caring Enough to Forgive/Caring Enough Not to Forgive *True Forgiveness and False Forgiveness,* David W. Augsburger

Herald Press, 1981, $6.95, paper, 176 pp., for both counselors and counselees

Description Explores true and false forgiveness. The author points out how important forgiveness is—it draws people together, comes to terms with the past, and then allows it to truly be past. It sets us free to meet genuinely with one another. Editors Choice 1981 Book of the Year—Campus Life.

Author David Augsburger (Ph.D., School of Theology at Clairmont, Calif.) is professor of pastoral care at the Associated Mennonite Biblical Seminaries in Elkhart, Ind. He has authored many books (including *Conflict Mediation across Cultures: Pathways and Patterns* and numerous books on recovery-oriented topics) and has had hundreds of articles published in magazines.

Contents *Book One 1.* Forgive—by realizing wrongdoing *2.* Forgive—by reaffirming love *3.* Forgive—by releasing the past *4.* Forgive—by renewing repentance *5.* Forgive—by rediscovering the community *6.* On the other hand . . . *Book Two 1.* Don't forgive—when forgiveness puts you one up *2.* Don't forgive—when forgiveness is one way *3.* Don't forgive—when forgiveness distorts feelings *4.* Don't forgive—when forgiveness denies anger *5.* Don't forgive—when forgiveness ends open relationship *6.* On the other hand . . .

Secret Wounds and Silent Cries Dewey Bertolini

Victor Books, 1993, $7.99, paper, 156 pp., for counselees

Description Is there any release from the prison of bitterness? Once himself a captive of bitterness, this author proclaims "Yes." He recounts his 17-year struggle with the man who broke his emotional backbone, his father. The author tells how, through God's intervention, that relationship was significantly restored. This book provides a biblically based approach to winning a personal battle with bitterness, discussing such issues as: how bitterness starts, forgiving others, forgiving yourself, living with situations that can't be changed, and breaking the cycle of bitterness in the next generation.

Author Dewey Bertolini is a speaker and consultant for Scripture Press. He also serves as assistant to the president at Western Baptist College.

Contents *1.* The legacy of a loser *2.* Slow but certain suicide *3.* Forgive and forget? *4.* The moment of truth *5.* It ain't over 'til it's over *6.* A permanent ending *7.* Breaking the chains *8.* I'm glad you asked

What the Bible Says about Forgiveness Marilyn Gustin

Ligouri Publications, 1994, $1.00, paper, 32 pp., for counselees

Description Perfect for Scripture study groups or individuals. Cites appropriate Scripture passages related to a very specific area of life.

Blessing Your Enemies, Forgiving Your Friends *A Scriptural Journey into Personal Peace,* Kirsten Johnson Ingram

Ligouri Publications, 1993, $5.95, paper, 128 pp., for counselees

Description The author shares personal experience and rich insights from Scripture to guide readers through the journey of blessing and toward the grace of forgiving. Each chapter contains a Scripture reference, a prayer, and a theme to help readers embrace their own neediness. Also contains workbook material, stories, self-examination questions, spiritual exercises, and journaling pages.

Author Kirsten Johnson Ingram is the author of nine books, including the best-seller *Being a Christian Friend.* She is a spiritual director and licensed Eucharistic minister.

Contents *1.* Lord, who is my enemy? *2.* Whom should I pray for? *3.* How to bless when forgiving is hard *4.* Painkiller emotions *5.* What forgiving is and isn't *6.* Words

143

that make you sick 7. Rush to judgment 8. The sword and the cross 9. Blessed are the peacemakers 10. Your gift at the altar 11. Continuing toward inner peace

Forgiveness *No Guilt, No Grudges,* Dale Larsen and Sandy Larsen

Harold Shaw Publishers, 1984, $3.99/$4.99 (student/teacher), paper, 74 pp., for both counselors and counselees

Description Designed for teenagers. Fill-in-the-blank format. What do you do when somebody hurts you, really hurts you, and it won't go away? Plan revenge? Keep it all inside while you turn bitter? Go and smash a wall? Hate yourself? Or how about when you hurt someone else? How do you get rid of the guilt you feel? God has an answer to both of those problems. It's called forgiveness. This study guide will help you dig into the Bible and discover how God's forgiveness can turn your life right-side-up. Teacher's guide contains entire text and facilitator's notes.

Authors Dale and Sandy Larsen have written more than 30 Bible study guides in addition to articles for *Christianity Today, Moody* magazine, and the *Christian Herald.*

Contents 1. Forgiveness—who needs it? Psalm 51 2. How perfect is perfect? Ex. 20:1–17 3. But isn't God all-loving? 2 Pet. 3:1–10 4. So what can a failure do? Matt. 9:9–13 et al. 5. What does Jesus have to do with forgiveness? Mark 2:1–12; Jn. 1:5–22 6. How far does forgiveness go? Luke 15:20–32, Eph. 2:1–9 7. What makes grace work for us? Eph. 2:8–9 8. If I'm forgiven, why do I still feel guilty? 1 Jn. 1:8–2:2 et. al. 9. I'm forgiven—so what? Luke 7:36–50 10. Why should I forgive anybody? Matt. 18: 21–35 11. How can I forgive somebody who doesn't deserve it? Eph. 4:31–32 et al. 12. What if I don't forgive? Gen. 45:1–8 et al. 13. Forgiveness—who needs it? I do! Psalm 51

How to Say I Forgive You *A Workshop,* Judy Logue

Ligouri Publications, 1994, $14.95, cassette(s), for counselees

Description This workshop on cassette addresses the psychological and spiritual aspects of forgiveness. Although especially attuned to women, male listeners can also learn much about the nature of forgiveness and alienation from this tape.

Learning How to Forgive Mary Francis Luthy

Ligouri Publications, 1989, $3.75, paper, 24 pp., for counselees

Description This booklet clears up common misconceptions about the nature of forgiveness, explains a five-phase process for healing, and reveals that forgiveness is at the heart of our faith.

Forgive and Love Again *Healing Wounded Relationships,* John W. Nieder and Thomas M. Thompson

Harvest House Publishers, 1991, $7.99, paper, 202 pp., for counselees

Description Shows readers how to overcome obstacles to forgiveness, tenderly confront the ones you love, and know if reconciliation is possible.

Authors John Nieder is the host of the daily broadcast *The Art of Family Living* that airs on over 100 stations. Dr. Thomas M. Thompson is director of pastoral ministries for *The Art of Family Living.* Both are graduates of Dallas Theological Seminary.

Contents 1. Hope for the wounded heart *Part 1:* Choosing to forgive 2. When your heart screams no 3. Accept no substitutes 4. The dangers of unforgiveness 5. The model of true forgiveness 6. The essentials of true forgiveness 7. Where do you go to forgive? 8. Let yourself off the hook 9. Do you need to forgive God? *Part 2:* Learning to love again 10. Maintaining a forgiving heart 11. Healing emotionally 12. When does love confront? 13. How love confronts 14. The realities of reconciliation 15. Unique demands of marriage

Forgiveness Therapy David W. Schell

Abbey Press, 1993, $3.95, paper, 80 pp., for counselees

Description The 35 liberating lessons contained in *Forgiveness Therapy* can help you put yourself back in control, transcend the most hurtful circumstances, and make the healing choice of wellness over bitterness. Format: a series of about 30 short sayings, proverbs, and admonitions accompanied by whimsical cartoons on every page.

Getting Bitter or Getting Better *Choosing Forgiveness for Your Own Good,* David W. Schell

Abbey Press, 1990, $5.95, paper, 156 pp., for counselees

Description In a comprehensive and congenial style, the author maps a journey that challenges and encourages the reader at each progressive stage.

Author David W. Schell, Ed.D., is a fellow and diplomate of the American Board of Medical Psychotherapists. He is a frequent conference speaker on the subject of psychotherapeutic forgiveness.

Contents *1.* Introduction *2.* Resistance to therapeutic forgiveness *3.* Recognizing the need to forgive *4.* Beginning with self-forgiveness *5.* Becoming a forgiving person *6.* Forgiving, healing, and growing *7.* Conclusion

If Only . . . *Leaving Behind Patterns of Blame That Keep Us From Growing in Faith,* David A. Seamands

Victor Books, 1995, $8.99, paper, 156 pp.

Description Combats the increasing trend toward the evasion of responsibility in dealing with the regrets and disappointments in life.

Author David A. Seamands is professor emeritus of pastoral ministries at Asbury Seminary and is the author of numerous books.

Forgive and Forget *Healing the Hurts We Don't Deserve,* Lewis B. Smedes

Harper and Row, 1993, $17.00, paper, 171 pp., for both counselors and counselees

Description Smedes' best-selling book on what forgiveness includes and what it does not include.

Author Lewis B. Smedes is professor of integrative studies in the Graduate School of Psychology at Fuller Theological Seminary and the award-winning author of ten books.

Forgiveness Malcolm Smith

Pillar Books & Publishing Company, 1992, $3.95, paper, 64 pp., for counselees

Description Deals with false ideas about forgiveness. Uses vivid images from the Bible to reveal what true forgiveness is. Smith directs readers through several practical steps proven to help them put away bitterness and experience heavenly release.

Author Malcolm Smith is involved in a teaching ministry based in Texas.

Forgiving Our Parents, Forgiving Ourselves *Healing Adult Children of Dysfunctional Families,* David Stoop and James Masteller

Servant Publications/Vine Books, 1991, $12.99, paper, 336 pp., for counselees

Description Begins by exploring the family patterns that perpetuate dysfunction. Step-by-step you will begin to learn to construct a psychological family tree that will help you uncover family secrets and family habits that have profoundly shaped your adult identity. As you develop greater understanding of your family of origin, you will be able to take the essential step of forgiveness. When this happens, you will find yourself moving into a place of profound spiritual healing which will change your life forever.

Authors David Stoop, Ph.D., is the clinical director of the Minirth-Meier-Stoop Clinics in southern Calif. James Masteller, D.Min., is a marriage and family therapist with the Minirth-Meier Clinic in southern Calif.

Contents *Part 1:* Unpacking family baggage *1.* Family: who needs it? *2.* The family system *3.* My family and me *4.* The sins of the fathers *5.* Three-way relationships *Part 2:* The freedom of forgiveness *6.* Releasing others, releasing ourselves *7.* Forgiving, forgetting, denying, accepting *8.* Superficial forgiveness *9.* What's anger got to do with it? *10.* The blame game *11.* Confrontation, retaliation, reconciliation

How to Forgive Yourself and Others *Steps to Reconciliation,* Eamon Tobin

Ligouri Publications, 1993, $3.95, paper, 62 pp., for counselees

Description Since the first edition of *How to Forgive Yourself and Others* was published in 1983, Father Tobin has received many letters from people sharing their experiences of forgiveness and reconciliation. When it came time to revise and expand his best-selling booklet, Father Tobin consulted those letters for help and suggestions. What results is an even more complete guide to forgiveness. Although the booklet still contains all the helpful, original material, it now deals with other important issues of reconciliation. It offers new guidelines for forgiving a deceased person—thought to be a crucial part of the grieving process. New sections on forgiving God and the church have been added. Father Tobin has expanded his section on forgiveness of self, which, he says, can be the biggest challenge of all.

Contents *Part 1:* Forgiveness: what it's all about *Part 2:* Forgiveness: how to go about it—Forgiving others—The living—The deceased—The self—God—Church—Forgiving a continuing hurt / *Conclusion*

Finding a Way to Forgive

Abbey Press, $.50 each, paper, 8 pp., for counselees

Description Part of the CareNotes series from Abbey Press. CareNotes are short booklets that help readers identify issues and begin the process of seeking resolution. Anecdotal and uplifting. Beautiful photographs grace the covers. Over 20 million CareNotes have been sold in just over five years. Can be used as an alternative to a greeting card or in conjunction with pastoral care visits.

20. Grief and Loss

General Works on Grief

Grief's Slow Work Harold Bauman

Herald Press, 1960, $1.95, paper, 16 pp., for counselees

Description Harold Bauman explains the process of grief and the experiences one normally goes through during the bereavement.

Everyday Comfort *Readings for the First Month of Grief,* Randy Becton

Baker Book House, 1993, $5.99, paper, 96 pp., for counselees

Description Randy Becton, himself a cancer survivor, has written a deeply empathetic and useful resource for those in grief. Uniquely arranged in reader-friendly, devotional form, *Everyday Comfort* is like having a daily talk with a friend who knows what to say. Becton avoids pie-in-the-sky platitudes.

Author Randy Becton is a counseling minister for and producer of *Herald of Truth* television program and is founder and executive director of Caring Cancer Ministry in Abilene, Tex.

Don't Waste Your Sorrows *New Insight into God's Eternal Purpose in the Midst of Adversity,* Paul E. Billheimer

Bethany House Publishers, 1977, $6.99, paper, 130 pp., for counselees

Description Covers a wide range of issues associated with suffering and grief. Encourages confidence in God's master design in spite of life's difficulties. Strong scriptural content.

Contents *1.* What price glory? *2.* The chief sufferer of the universe *3.* A moral universe *4.* Legal deliverance *5.* The mystery of suffering *6.* Faith greater than achieving faith *7–8.* The great business of life—learning agape love *9.* Learning agape love through family relationships *10.* Learning agape love through wrongful suffering *11.* Learning agape love through life's failures *12.* Learning agape love through aging

Mourning after Suicide Lois A. Bloom

The Pilgrim Press, 1986, $1.75, paper, 24 pp., for counselees

Description Part of the Looking Up series of booklets from the Pilgrim Press. For the cost of a greeting card, this booklet provides the reader with 24 pages of insight, wisdom, Scripture readings, meditation, direction, comfort, and prayer.

When You Walk through a Storm Jeris Bragan

Pacific Press, 1993, $7.95, paper, 128 pp., for counselees

Description Pain, disappointment, and grief are real, and they hurt. This is a brilliant and sensitive survival guide for believers who are hurting and struggling to face another day.

Author Jeris Bragan is currently serving a 99-year prison term for a murder he insists he did not commit. Prior to his incarceration in 1977, he was president of the Searcher Corp., a private investigative consulting firm. His gift for writing is evidenced by his numerous published articles and two books.

Hearts in Motion—Minds at Rest *Living through the Loss of a Loved One,* Mary Brite

Barbour and Company, 1993, $7.95, paper, 113 pp., for counselees

Description An invaluable handbook for survivors. Important topics are discussed in a candid manner. Three easy-to-use checklists simplify the many tasks facing survivors and provide organization and efficiency at a time when chaos is more likely to rule. Spiritual and emotional issues relating to death are ably presented, including three penetrating questions frequently asked by survivors. Helpful Scripture and books for all types of survivors are provided.

Contents *1.* When death comes *2.* When you first hear the news *3.* What you must know about organ donations

4. Choosing the type of service 5. Through the services 6. The first month 7. Normal emotions 8. Three questions we often face 9. Support for survivors 10. Helpful books and scriptures 11. Caring and sharing within God's family / *Appendix A:* Checklist of things requiring immediate attention / *Appendix B:* Checklist to take you through the services / *Appendix C:* For advance preparation

Dealing with Grief and Loss *Hope in the Midst of Pain,* William Cutler and Richard Peace

Serendipity, 1990, $6.95, paper, 80 pp., for both counselors and counselees

Description A 7- or 14-week course utilizing Scripture and discussion questions. Designed for anyone who is facing a situation of loss or would like to have the support of others.

Contents *1.* When it all collapses *2.* Denial *3.* Anger *4.* Bargaining *5.* Depression *6.* Acceptance *7.* Hope

Will I Ever Feel Good Again? *A Guided Journal,* Karen Dockrey

Fleming H. Revell, 1993, $7.99, paper, 160 pp., for counselees

Description A guided journal that helps teens walk through guilt and grief to a place of healing. Helps teens explore sad, guilty, angry, and confused feelings. Includes a leader's guide. Assures teens that with help from God and trusted loved ones, they will indeed find the hope and healing needed to enjoy life.

Author Karen Dockrey, a former youth minister, is the author of several books for youth and youth workers.

In Grief's Lone Hour John M. Drescher

Herald Press, 1986 (revised), $1.95, paper, 16 pp., for counselees

Description A series of two-page devotionals that gradually describes the grief process. Shares insights on normal responses to grief and points the way to hope and comfort.

Author Drescher has written over 30 books and more than 100 journal and magazine articles. He has served as pastor, bishop, editor, and seminary teacher.

Not by Accident *Comfort in Times of Loss,* Isabel Fleece

Moody Press, 1964, $3.50, paper, 28 pp., for counselees

Description A story of the great love God showers upon believers as they face tragedy and the peace he gives in the midst of despair.

Grief Therapy Karen Katafiasz

Abbey Press, 1993, $3.95, paper, 80 pp., for counselees

Description Demonstrates how the grieving process takes time and deserves attention. With succinct, meaningful guidelines and hope-filled illustrations, it reassures those who grieve that out of their pain can come profound, transformed healing. Format: a series of about 30 short sayings, proverbs, and admonitions accompanied by whimsical cartoons on every page.

When Will I Stop Hurting? June Cerza Kolf

Baker Book House, 1992, $3.99, paper, 57 pp., for counselees

Description This book provides helpful advice for those who are grieving—and it is given in a manner which is both professional and practical. Creative ways of easing pain and depression are offered. Sympathetic suggestions are given for handling holidays and dealing with insomnia, anger, guilt, and forgiveness. The book closes with a discussion of letting go of grief and finding out how healing occurs.

Author June Cerza Kolf has spent many years working with the terminally ill and grieving. Presently she directs volunteers for a home health care agency in California and leads support groups and workshops on grief. She is a member of the Elisabeth Kübler-Ross Center, and the National Hospice Organization and serves on the board of the High Desert Unit of the American Cancer Society. Her work can be seen in trade journals and inspiration publications including *Guideposts* and the *Christian Reader.*

Contents *1.* The wound / The symptoms of grief / Guilt / Forgiveness / The duration of grief / Dealing with memories / Holidays / The sense of loss *2.* The flood / Shock / Sighing / Crying / Anger / Depression / Insomnia / Appetite / Antidepressants / Facing the pain / Making decisions / Laughter / Support *3.* The rainbow / The healing process / Letting go / Piles of paper / Asking for help / The final stage / Growth returns / Reaching out / The pot of gold

Dancing in the Dark *A Sister Grieves,* Elsie K. Neufeld

Herald Press, 1990, $7.95, paper, 200 pp., for counselees

Description The journey through grief is always difficult. For a Christian, in some ways it is easier—in others, it is not. When your brother is killed in a car accident by a drunk driver, it is hard to follow Jesus' call to forgive. Neufeld goes beyond her grief and seeks to understand how to forgive and understand the one who caused her sorrow. Through sharing her participation in a grief recovery program, she provides her readers with tools and direction in their own journeys of grief and loss.

Losses and Changes Randy Reynolds and David Lynn

Zondervan Publishing House, 1992, $4.99, paper, 96 pp., for both counselors and counselees

Description Part of the Recovery Discovery series of workbooks. Helps Christians work through the feelings and doubts that arise from life's changes and losses.

How to Deal with Grief George Rice

Beacon Hill Press of Kansas City, 1988, $1.95, paper, 39 pp., for counselees

Contents *1.* The nature of grief *2.* Letting God and his church help us *3.* Some short-range helps

Praying Our Goodbyes Joyce Rupp

Ave Maria Press, 1988, $6.95, paper, 183 pp., for counselees

Description About the experience of leaving behind and moving on—the stories of union and separation that are written in all of our hearts. It focuses on the spirituality of change. It is a book for anyone who has experienced loss, whether it be a job change, end of a friendship, death of a loved one, financial struggle, midlife crisis, or an extended illness. It is designed to help in the healing process. Each chapter concludes with probing questions. The book ends with 24 prayer experiences incorporating images, symbols, and rituals as sources of strength and stepping stones toward healing.

Author Joyce Rupp (O.S.M.) holds a master's degree in religious education, is a trained spiritual

director, and has given retreats for 20 years. Along with writing, speaking at conferences, and giving retreats, she currently is engaged in graduate studies in transpersonal psychology.

Recovery from Loss Dale Ryan and Juanita Ryan

InterVarsity Press, 1992, $4.99, paper, 60 pp., for both counselors and counselees

Description This Bible study is part of a series of 16 volumes on various recovery themes. Each book contains studies on six biblical texts. Leader's notes are provided for group study.

Authors Dale Ryan is the executive director of the Recovery Partnership, the parent organization to the National Association for Christian Recovery. Juanita Ryan is a counselor in private practice in Hacienda Heights, Calif.

Contents *1.* The God who grieves *2.* The God who sees our losses *3.* The God who hears us when we are depressed *4.* The God who loves us when we feel afraid *5.* The God who is with us when we feel alone *6.* The God who offers healing / *Leader's notes*

The Comforter *A Journey through Grief,* Doris Sandford and Graci Evans

Heart to Heart, 1992, $4.99, paper, 32 pp., for counselees

Description This story of hope details emotional transitions common to all grief recovery—yet emphasizes that every woman's journey is unique. Appropriate as a gift to the bereaved woman.

Turn Again to Life *Growing through Grief,* Abraham Schmitt

Herald Press, 1987, $8.95, paper, 136 pp., for counselees

Description When someone close to us loses a loved one through death, we are often unsure of what to say or do. In this book Schmitt uses stories drawn from his counseling files to help us better understand the grief process and learn ways to be supportive during this time. It is also appropriate to give to those experiencing grief themselves. Positive, productive ways to cope with sorrow are suggested.

Author Abraham Schmitt (master's and doctor's degrees in social work from the University of Pennsylvania) has been a professor and holds a certificate in marriage and family counseling. He is currently in private practice as an individual and marriage and family therapist. He is the author of seven books.

Contents *1.* How do you mend a broken heart *2.* A tenacious journey back *3.* The emotional phases of grief *4.* Choosing to live again *5.* Preparing for death and loss *6.* Helping children express grief *7.* Unhealthy dying and unhealthy grieving *8.* A battered heart finds courage *9.* A model for healthy grieving *10.* Let God do the mending *11.* A lengthy process *12.* Turn again to life.

Goodbyes Are Not Forever Joy Swift

Pacific Press, 1987, $1.99, paper, 96 pp., for counselees

Description The real authorities on grief recovery are those who have sustained the loss of someone very near and dear and survived intact. In this respect the author of this book qualifies with the highest credentials, having lost all five of her children in a very short space of time. This book is for anyone who has lost a loved one, especially a child. But it is also for anyone who would like to know how to help those bereaved.

Author Ten years ago, four of Joy Swift's children were murdered, and a fifth child died 18 days later of cancer.

Contents *1.* When tragedy strikes *2.* Stages of grief *3.* Getting through the funeral *4.* Family ties *5.* Someone to talk to *6.* Search for strength *7.* So many questions *8.* Forgiving our trespasses *9.* Learning to adjust *10.* Advice to friends

In This Very Hour *Loss of a Relationship,* Jill Marie Taylor and Laura Rodriguez

Broadman and Holman, 1995, $1.95, saddleback, 46 pp.

Description Part of the new In This Very Hour series from Broadman and Holman Publishers, a series of daily devotions with first-person accounts of victory by faith over life's most tragic disappointments.

Authors Taylor's husband left her for her best friend; Rodriguez's family partially disintegrated after the loss of her father.

Contents A series of thirty-one brief, yet very well-written daily devotionals (Scripture passage and anecdote).

Grief for a Season Mildred Tengbom

Bethany House Publishers, 1989, $6.99, paper, 155 pp., for counselees

Description Attractively designed, this is a book that anyone—pastors, physicians, nurses, friends, and family members—will want to share with those working through grief. A manual that guides those who are grieving, at their own pace, through the various stages of grief.

Author Mildred Tengbom has written 20 books and has served as a missionary for 17 years.

Contents *1.* Bearing grief or baring grief *2.* Presence *3.* The season *4.* Questions and doubts *5.* Small steps toward recovery *6.* Death is not natural! *7.* The odd things I do *8.* Weariness *9.* Loss of a home *10.* Irritable days *11.* Emotions and faith *12.* Nothing we can do *13.* I wish I had *14.* Storytelling *15.* Facing death *16.* After death *17.* The pain of separation *18.* Acceptance *19.* Finding meaning in life again *20.* Does grieving go on forever? *21.* Life after death

Grief: How It Can Help You Edward R. Walsh

Ligouri Publications, 1988, $.75, paper, 24 pp., for counselees

Description Explains how mourning brings healing and peace and warns that failing to grieve can cause serious and lasting personal problems. Offers practical advice about how to help those in mourning.

Can Anything Good Come Out of Losing? *Coping with Loss,* Dan Webster

NavPress, 1991, $2.00, paper, 18 pp., for counselees

Description Targets teenagers dealing with loss. Part of the student Survival series from NavPress. Mostly anecdotal with several reflection questions.

Author Dan Webster is the director of student ministries at Willow Creek Community Church in South Barrington, Ill.

7 Ways to Handle Grief Florence Wedge

Ligouri Publications, 1981, $.75, paper, 24 pp., for counselees

Description This booklet offers the reader seven time-tested tips to help the bereaved move from the darkness of loneliness and pain to the light of hope and recovery.

The Toughest Days of Grief Meg Woodson

Zondervan Publishing House, 1994, $9.99, paper, 192 pp., for both counselors and counselees

Description Highlights the special issues surrounding the grieving process during particularly difficult days such as anniversaries and holidays. Also covers the stages of grief, shows how different personality types grieve, and explains why springtime worsens normal depression.

Author Meg Woodson is an award-winning writer and grief counselor. She holds advanced degrees in theology and psychology.

Recovering from the Losses of Life
H. Norman Wright

Fleming H. Revell, $14.99, paper, for counselees

Description In this tenderly encouraging book, Wright helps readers identify and face a variety of losses and guides them through the grieving process.

Author Dr. H. Norman Wright is one of America's best known Christian marriage and family counselors at the Family Counseling and Enrichment Center in Tustin, Calif. He is author of more than 50 books. He has also served on the faculty of Talbot School of Theology and the Graduate School of Marriage Counseling of Biola University.

Death Is Only a Horizon *Thought in Time of Bereavement*

Ligouri Publications, $1.95, paper, 16 pp., for counselees

Description This full-color booklet comforts those in mourning through soothing Scripture verses, reflections, and quotations. Written from a Catholic perspective. Includes addresses of organizations that offer support.

Getting through Annual Reminders of Your Loss

Abbey Press, $.50 each, paper, 8 pp., for counselees

Description Part of the CareNotes series from Abbey Press. CareNotes are short booklets that help readers identify issues and begin the process of seeking resolution. Anecdotal and uplifting. Beautiful photographs grace the covers. Over 20 million CareNotes have been sold in just over five years. Can be used as an alternative to a greeting card or in conjunction with pastoral care visits.

Sharing Your Grief, Easing Your Loss

Abbey Press, $.50 each, paper, 8 pp., for counselees

Description Part of the CareNotes series from Abbey Press. CareNotes are short booklets that help readers identify issues and begin the process of seeking resolution. Anecdotal and uplifting. Beautiful photographs grace the covers. Over 20 million CareNotes have been sold in just over five years. Can be used as an alternative to a greeting card or in conjunction with pastoral care visits.

Taking the Time You Need to Grieve Your Loss

Abbey Press, $.50, paper, 8 pp., for counselees

Description Part of the CareNotes series from Abbey Press. CareNotes are short booklets that help readers identify issues and begin the process of seeking resolution. Anecdotal and uplifting. Beautiful photographs grace the covers. Over 20 million CareNotes have been sold in just over five years. Can be used as an alternative to a greeting card or in conjunction with pastoral care visits.

When Grief Won't Go Away

Abbey Press, $.50 each, paper, 8 pp., for counselees

Description Part of the CareNotes series from Abbey Press. CareNotes are short booklets that help readers identify issues and begin the process of seeking resolution. Anecdotal and uplifting. Beautiful photographs grace the covers. Over 20 million CareNotes have been sold in just over five years. Can be used as an alternative to a greeting card or in conjunction with pastoral care visits.

Rainbows for All God's Children

Rainbows for All God's Children, Inc. An organization

Description An ecumenical, not-for-profit, international organization that offers training and curriculum for establishing peer support groups in churches, synagogues, schools, or social agencies. These programs are available for children and adults of all ages and religious denominations who are grieving a death, divorce, or any other painful transition in their family. Four distinct age-directed programs are developed. To date, more than 350,000 children and adolescents have participated throughout 47 states and 9 foreign countries.

Helping a Grieving Adult

Grief Liam J. Atchinson and Precious Atchinson

NavPress, 1993, $5.00, paper, 72 pp., for counselees

Description Whether the loss comes from death, divorce, or other circumstances, this discussion guide will help you gain the courage to face tragedy as bad, not natural. Rather than forcing you into one more situation where you feel more "Christian" by shrugging off the loss as "all for the best," this guide helps steer you away from denial and into a healthy grieving and healing process.

Authors Liam J. Atchinson is director of instruction for the master of arts in biblical counseling program and associate professor of biblical studies at Colorado Christian University. Precious Atchinson is a wife, mother, and grief counselor in private practice in Lakewood, Colo. She is a conference speaker and leads grief therapy groups.

Contents *Session 1*—The courage to travel to the moral frontier *Session 2*—The courage to face loss *Session 3*—The courage to hope *Session 4*—The courage to love and give *Session 5*—The courage to comfort *Session 6*—The courage to meet the suffering God / *Help for leaders*

It's Not Fair! *Through Grief to Healing,* Karen Dockrey

New Hope, 1992, $1.95, paper, 22 pp., for counselees

Description Targets teenagers. When grief comes to your friend, what will you say? Your first instinct may be to run because you don't know what to say or because you fear saying the wrong thing. Don't! Your friend needs you. It's better to make a mistake than to do nothing at all. *It's Not Fair! Through Grief to Healing* can equip you not only to be there for your friend but to genuinely help her.

Author Karen Dockrey works with youth at Bluegrass Baptist Church in Hendersonville, Tenn.

How Can I Help? *Reaching Out to Someone Who Is Grieving,* June Cerza Kolf

Baker Book House, 1991, $6.99, paper, 144 pp., for counselors

Description This book offers step-by-step directives for helping those who are grieving. It suggests appropriate actions and explains how to listen and help a bereaved person. The book begins with the initial shock and goes through the entire first year with such topics as filling the void, new routines, trouble spots, understanding grief symptoms, planning ahead, and new starts in living.

Author June Cerza Kolf has spent many years working with the terminally ill and grieving. Presently she directs volunteers for a home health care agency in California and leads support groups and workshops on grief. She is a member of the Elisabeth Kübler-Ross Center and the National Hospice Organization and serves on the board of the High Desert Unit of the American Cancer Society. Her work can be seen in trade journals and inspiration publications including *Guideposts* and the *Christian Reader.*

Contents *Part 1:* The initial contact *1.* Responding to the news *2.* Offering condolences *3.* Clichés *4.* Assistance in practical matters *5.* Other responses *6.* Anticipatory grief *7.* The shock factor *8.* The forgotten griever *9.* Unconditional support *Part 2:* The week after the funeral *10.* The importance of support *11.* Employers and employees *12.* Sharing of memories *13.* Decision making *14.* The beginning of the grief process *15.* The symptoms of grief *16.* Physical problems *17.* Guilt *Part 3:* The first six months *18.* Offering support *19.* Listening skills *20.* The death of a parent *21.* Disposing of belongings *22.* Loneliness *23.* Forgiveness *24.* Holidays *25.* Tough love *26.* Bereavement support groups *Part 4:* The one-year anniversary *27.* A new lifestyle *28.* Change in residence *29.* Other changes *30.* Reaching out *31.* Delayed or displaced grief *32.* Listening to our hearts *33.* Long-distance help *34.* Self-care *35.* Providing respect

Helping People through Grief *A Sensitive Guide to Help You Know How and When to Share Your Concern,* Delores A. Kuenning

Bethany House Publishers, 1987, $8.99, paper, 272 pp., for counselors

Description A practical and sensitive handbook intended to be of use when there is a special need to have information about a particular kind of grief. The range of subjects includes miscarriage, children with cancer, releasing a child for adoption, the emotional aftermath of abortion, and the devastation of Alzheimer's disease. Other crises covered are divorce, rape, abduction and murder of a child, and suicide. This book is currently being used as a continuing education course for nurses and in college and seminary death education courses. Also used as a resource for various support groups. Anecdotes, vivid/empathetic emotional descriptions, additional resources, and do's and don'ts for caregivers are also listed.

Author Delores A. Kuenning is the wife of a United Church of Christ clergyman and has been a freelance writer for more than 25 years and has written extensively on social, medical, and spiritual issues. Her most recent book is *Life after Vietnam*—on post-traumatic stress disorder.

Contents How to use this book *1.* My introduction to grief *2.* Does God cause tragedies? What does God promise? *3.* The birth of an impaired or handicapped baby *4.* Loss of a baby through miscarriage, stillbirth, or early infant death *5.* Death of an infant from Sudden Infant Death Syndrome *6.* Abduction and murder of a child *7.* Loss of a child through kidnapping, fate unknown *8.* Children with cancer *9.* Some do's and don'ts *10.* Releasing a child for adoption *11.* The emotional aftermath of an abortion *12.* The emotional aftermath of rape *13.* The pain of divorce *14.* Mastectomy, disfigurement, or disability *15.* Death by suicide *16.* Sudden catastrophic death *17.* Life-threatening or terminal illness *18.* The death of a spouse *19.* Alzheimer's disease *20.* Nursing home placement, death as release, life's full cycle *21.* Our hopes and God's promises

Caring for People in Grief Phyllis J. Le Peau

InterVarsity Press, 1993, $4.99, paper, 64 pp., for counselors

Description Part of the seven-title Caring People Bible Studies from InterVarsity Press. Seven study guides and an introductory handbook cover all the basics of caregiving, from developing the character traits of caring to dealing with tough needs like depression, grief, and illness. Perfect for churches starting a caregiving program, groups ministering in hospitals and to shut-ins, or laypeople helping a friend through crisis.

Author Phyllis J. Le Peau is a registered nurse and a former Nurses Christian Fellowship staff member. Currently, she is assistant program director for Wellness, Inc.

Contents *1.* Facing your own death (Ps. 90) *2.* Overcoming the fear of death (Heb. 2:9–18) *3.* Offering comfort (Jn. 11:17–44) *4.* Offering peace (Jn. 14:1–7) *5.* Offering hope (Rev. 14:1–7) *6.* Offering grace (2 Cor. 4:7–5:8) *7.* Saying goodbye to an elderly friend (Gen. 48:1–12; 49:22–50:14) *8.* Dealing with a child's death (2 Sam. 12:15–23) *9.* The gift of good grief (1 Thess. 4:13–18)

How to Comfort the Grieving: *A Dozen Ways to Say "I Care,"* Victor M. Parachin

Ligouri Publications, 1991, $.75, paper, 24 pp., for counselees

Description Presents 12 practical and sensitive ways to console friends or relatives mourning the loss of a loved one.

Getting through Grief *Caregiving by Congregations,* Ronald H. Sunderland

Abingdon Press, 1993, $10.95, paper, 144 pp., for counselors

Description Provides a foundation for congregational-based ministry to persons who are grieving. Contending that grief work is the responsibility of the congregation, the author shows congregations how to set up teams who go through grief education and then carry out their mission in their congregation. He gives special attention to grief work with children and teenagers and stresses the importance of ongoing grief support groups.

Author Ronald H. Sunderland, Ed.D., is associate director and senior research fellow at Foundation for Interfaith Research and Ministry.

For Those Who Hurt Charles Swindoll

Zondervan Publishing House, 1977, $1.95, paper, 46 pp., for counselees

Description Designed to be given to someone who has just experienced a significant loss. Beautiful photographs and tender words and Scripture encourage the grieving to work through the process with their faith as an anchor. Very nicely done booklet.

Author Charles Swindoll is president of Dallas Theological Seminary, hosts the radio program *Insight for Living,* and is a best-selling author.

The Courage to Care *Helping the Aging, Grieving and Dying,* Jeffrey A. Watson

Baker Book House, 1992, $10.99, paper, 186 pp., for counselors

Description *Courage to Care* integrates the biblical theology of aging, grief, and death with the significant findings from the behavioral sciences on the respective topics. *Courage to Care* includes powerful case studies, statistics, charts,

153

graphs, discussion questions, endnotes, bibliography, and subject index. The author of *Courage to Care* is an accomplished pastoral practitioner with 14 years of experience in parish counseling, hospice, hospital/nursing home chaplaincy, and the training of clinical/pastoral caregivers. He holds theological degrees from both Protestant and Roman Catholic graduate schools as well as behavioral science credentials from a secular university. The Scripture is eloquent in its trilogy of metaphors: "The grass withers . . . the flower fades . . . but the Word of God stands forever." Dying mankind, like a withering meadow, is described through a historical/theological model in Part 1. Dying individuals, like fragile flowers, are described through a pastoral/psychological model in Part 2. But the ever enlivening Word of God, woven throughout the fabric of the whole book, points to true hope and life in Jesus Christ.

Author Senior minister of Grace Bible Church in Seabrook, Md., professor of gerontology at Washington Bible College, consultant in bioethics and chaplaincy. Former pastoral care at Prince George's Hospital and at the Joseph Richey Hospice. Graduate of Capital Bible Seminary, Catholic University, and Dallas Theological Seminary. Engaging seminar speaker.

Contents *Part 1:* Biblical caregiving *1.* Why should we face aging, grief, and death *2.* How the Old Testament helps us face aging, grief, and death *3.* How the New Testament helps us face aging, grief, and death *Part 2:* Personal caregiving *4.* The fear of death *5.* The grief of loss *6.* The pain of suicide *7.* The challenge of aging *8.* The mentoring of children *9.* The care of sufferers / *For further reading*

Grief Ministry *Helping Others Mourn,* Donna Reilly Williams and JoAnn Sturzl

Resource Publications, Inc., 1992, $14.95, paper, 217 pp., for counselors

Description A comprehensive text on developing a grief ministry. A facilitator's (teaching) guide is also available from the publisher.

Authors With an advanced degree in pastoral studies, Donna Reilly Williams specializes in grief and transition therapy in her private practice in Woodinville, Wash. JoAnn Sturzl is a pastoral minister at St. Mary's Parish in Sioux Falls, S. Dak.. She is a licensed personality and human relations educator.

Contents *1.* Gifted, called, and sent *2.* Death in our society *3.* The question of control *4.* The dynamics of grief *5.* Symptoms and duration of grief *6.* Person-to-person skills *7.* Death and the journey within *8.* Prayer and ministry *9.* Children and death *10.* The death of a baby *11.* Job related grief experiences *12.* Divorce as a grief experience *13.* Grief in the AIDS community *14.* Suicide *15.* Funerals

Helping a Grieving Child

Helping Children Cope with Death
Robert V. Dodd

Herald Press, 1984, $3.95, paper, 56 pp., for both counselors and counselees

Description Robert V. Dodd helps parents and other adults to know how to assist children in dealing with their feelings about death—that of a friend, or loved one, or their own anticipated death.

Author Robert V. Dodd (M.Div., Duke University) has served a number of churches and participated in studies in clinical pastoral education. He is the author of a number of other works.

When Someone You Love Dies *An Explanation of Death to Children,* Robert V. Dodd

Abingdon Press, 1986, $1.95, paper, 16 pp., for counselors

Description An exceptionally well-written book. Designed to be read to children by a caring adult.

Author Robert V. Dodd (M.Div., Duke University) has served a number of churches and participated in studies in clinical pastoral education. He is the author of a number of other works.

Contents *1.* A note to parents *2.* Introduction for children *3.* Why does it hurt so much? *4.* Why do people act so strange? *5.* What happens when you die? *6.* What about heaven? *7.* Why did it have to happen? *8.* What happens at the funeral? *9.* Where can we find help? *10.* Will it ever stop hurting?

Dad! Why'd You Leave Me? Dorothy R. Frost

Herald Press, 1992, $4.95, paper, 96 pp., for counselees

Description Aimed at helping preadolescent children deal with grief. When ten-year-old Ronnie's father dies, Ronnie is angry, confused, and lonely. His friends seem afraid to talk to him. Uncle Rod asks him how he likes being the head of the house. Nothing is normal. Some adults, like George, the cop, and Mrs. Hayes, the school principal, are more helpful. As Ronnie and his family grieve, they learn they are still a family. With each other's help, they can make it through the bad times.

Author Dorothy R. Frost completed the Ed.D. at the University of the Pacific. She is an experienced high school teacher and middle school guidance counselor. She is active in a United Congregational church in Rhode Island.

Morgan's Baby Sister *A Read-Aloud Book for Families Who Have Experienced the Death of a Newborn,* Patricia Polin Johnson and Donna R. Williams

Resource Publications, Inc., 1993, $10.95, paper, 55 pp., for counselees

Description Part of the Helping Children Hurt series which was created to assist parents or other adult caregivers with the difficult and often painful task of helping children understand their feelings about tragedies they experience. Professional and pastoral counselors may give *Morgan's Baby Sister* to families who are grieving the death of a newborn, miscarriage, sudden infant death syndrome, or stillborn. A special section at the back of the book offers guidance to parents and caregivers along with discussion questions.

Authors Patricia Polin Johnson teaches religious education to preschool, primary, and high school students. Donna Reilly Williams specializes in grief and transition therapy in her private practice in Woodinville, Wash.

Teenagers Talk about Grief June Cerza Kolf

Baker Book House, 1991, $4.99, paper, 59 pp., for counselees

Description This is one of the only books on the market written specifically for teenagers who are grieving. It is written in an easy-to-understand format with many quotes and examples. Teenagers are often forgotten grievers. Like adults, however, they encounter the anger, guilt, mood swings, and other emotions associated with deep personal loss. This book offers solid,

compassionate help to teens, yet is brief enough to be meaningfully digested by young people.

Author June Cerza Kolf has spent many years working with the terminally ill and grieving. Presently she directs volunteers for a home health care agency in California and leads support groups and workshops on grief. She is a member of the Elisabeth Kübler-Ross Center and the National Hospice Organization and serves on the board of the High Desert Unit of the American Cancer Society. Her work can be seen in trade journals and inspiration publications including *Guideposts* and the *Christian Reader.*

Contents *1.* Acknowledgment *2.* Adjustment *3.* Acceptance

Explaining Death to a Child Clyde M. Narramore

Narramore Christian Foundation, $.35, paper, 6 pp., for counselors

Description One of the many booklets available from the Narramore Christian Foundation. Designed to be handed to a person beginning to come to grips with a problem in living.

Author Dr. Clyde M. Narramore is a licensed psychologist and the president and founder of the Narramore Christian Foundation—a charitable, nonprofit educational, training, and counseling organization ministering primarily to the Christian community. He is also the founder of the Rosemead School of Psychology and author of 29 books.

When a Child Grieves Ralph Ranieri

Ligouri Publications, 1994, $1.00, paper, 241 pp., for counselees

Description How does a child grieve? Most of the myths adults have about childhood and grief only add to the confusion. Ralph Ranieri, an experienced family counselor who also works with dying people and their families in a hospice setting, helps to dispel some of the myths. Offers advice on talking to children about death, spirituality, and the reality of heaven. Includes guidance on taking children to funerals and going through the recovery process.

It Must Hurt a Lot *A Child's Book about Death,* Doris Sandford and Graci Evans

155

Gold 'n' Honey Books (Questar), 1993, $7.99, cloth, 24 pp., for counselees

Description Part of the Hurts of Childhood series from Gold 'n' Honey. The series was developed for children ages 5–11 who have experienced deep and tragic hurts. The books deal gently and compassionately with children's delicate feelings when they're forced to handle burdens far too big for them to carry.

Grieving *When You Lose Someone Close*

Abbey Press, 1993, $.50 each, paper, 8 pp., for counselees

Description Part of the CareNotes for Teens series from Abbey Press. CareNotes are 5 x 7 booklets designed to offer strength and help to (young) people in crisis. Each CareNote gently introduces an issue, then encourages a person to take appropriate steps toward resolution. Over 20 million CareNotes have been sold.

Helping a Child Grieve and Grow

Abbey Press, $.50 each, paper, 8 pp., for counselees

Description Part of the CareNotes series from Abbey Press. CareNotes are short booklets that help readers identify issues and begin the process of seeking resolution. Anecdotal and uplifting. Beautiful photographs grace the covers. Over 20 million CareNotes have been sold in just over five years. Can be used as an alternative to a greeting card or in conjunction with pastoral care visits.

Coping with the Loss of a Child

In This Very Hour *Loss of an Unborn Child,* Cathy Butler

Broadman and Holman Publishers, 1995, $1.95, saddleback, 38 pp.

Description Part of the new In This Very Hour series from Broadman and Holman Publishers, a series of daily devotions with first-person accounts of victory by faith over life's most tragic disappointments.

Author Cathy Butler, M.Div., is former products editor for the Women's Missionary Union of the SBC.

Contents A series of thirty-one brief, yet very well-written daily devotionals (Scripture passage and anecdote).

Song for Sarah *A Young Mother's Journey From Grief to Beyond,* Paula D'Arcy

Harold Shaw Publishers, 1994, $10.99, paper, 124 pp.

Description Excerpts from the author's journal detail a time and a life that was suddenly and unkindly ended. The pain and outrage of death eventually brought the author such insight and growth that these words for her daughter became not a cry but a song.

Author Paula D'Arcy is a counselor in private practice in Massachusetts specializing in issues of grief, relationships, and spirituality.

Contents A series of excerpts from the author's journal.

At the Death of a Child *Words of Comfort and Hope,* Donald L. Deffner

CPH Publishing, 1993, $2.75, paper, 32 pp., for both counselors and counselees

Description An important booklet to keep on hand for the unexpected death of a child. Pastors and Christian caregivers appreciate this practical handout that helps them comfort and counsel bereaved parents. It offers insights on how to address the emotional, physical, and spiritual anguish, pointing both the caregiver and the bereaved to the hope of the gospel. Also addresses baptism and includes prayers.

An Early Journey Home *Helping Dying Children and Grieving Families,* Mary Ann Froehlich

Baker Book House, 1992, $8.99, paper, 205 pp., for both counselors and counselees

Description Mary Ann Froehlich has helped several dying children and their grieving families face death. The insights and sensitivities she has gained from her experiences are reflected in this hopeful, helpful book. She offers genuine solace to parents and siblings who are facing the death of a dearly loved child. Christians are shown how to put away their fears so they might give significant support to the terminally ill and their families.

Author Dr. Froehlich is a registered music therapist (board certified) and a certified child life specialist. She is the author of two other books.

Contents *1.* An early journey home *2.* My own journey *Part 1:* The biblical journey: preparing the helper *3.* Helpers without answers *4.* Our biblical models: fellow sufferers in Scripture *5*. When suffering turns to gold *Part 2:* Taking the journey: helping the dying child *6*. Helping through the illness and hospitalization *7*. Helping patients and families through death *8*. Zain's journey: advice from the experts *Part 3:* The long journey after: helping the grieving family *9*. Helping after the death *10*. Surviving the unbearable: more advice from the experts *11*. Special situations: miscarriages, catastrophic accidents, losing adult children *12*. Helpers of judges?: murder, the killer AIDS *13*. A family portrait *14*. A final note to helpers *Part 4:* Children's health care resources / Health care organizations / Illness and grief support organizations / Therapy techniques for hospitalized children / *Books*

I'll Hold You in Heaven *Healing and Hope for the Parent Who Has Lost a Child,* Jack Hayford

Regal Books, 1990, $4.99, paper, 124 pp., for counselees

Description Parents who have lost a child through miscarriage, stillbirth, abortion, or early infant death have a special kind of grief. Pastor Jack Hayford offers his warm, encouraging, hopeful message to parents.

Author Dr. Jack W. Hayford is senior pastor of the Church on the Way in Van Nuys, Calif. His ministry reaches around the world through television, radio, and the books and music he has written.

Contents *1*. The gift of lives *2*. When does significance begin? *3*. Life to what degree? *4*. Destiny in the afterworld *5*. In heaven as a person *6*. Instruments of healing *7*. The heartbeat of love *8*. Three steps to loving

Roses in December *Finding Strength within Grief,* Marilyn Willett Heavilin

Thomas Nelson Publishers, 1991 (6th printing), $8.99, paper, 130 pp., for counselees

Description Written by a mother who lost three sons, this best-selling book offers practical, sensitive advice for those who are grieving.

Author Marilyn Willett Heavilin is a frequent speaker at churches, retreats, and conferences. She is the author of three best-selling books.

Contents The rose of preparation / The rose of sorrow / The rose of comfort / The rose of forgiveness / The rose of remembrance / The rose of friendship / The rose of understanding / The rose of innocence / The rose of tenderness / The rose of uniqueness / The rose of love / The rose of victory

I Will Not Leave You Desolate *Some Thoughts for Grieving Parents,* Martha Whitmore Hickman

Abingdon Press, 1994, $5.95, paper, 64 pp., for counselees

Description Focusing specifically on dealing with the trauma and pain of the death of a child, this book provides help for parents and others who are bereaved. Simple and appropriate, the book contains short sections that are easy to read and understand.

Author Martha Whitmore Hickman is the well-known author of more than 20 books. She is widely recognized for her work in the area of bereavement.

Contents *1*. I had a child who died *2*. A preliminary word about grief and the Christian faith *3*. Believing it—I can't believe it happened *4*. Who's to blame? *5*. Living with the unfinished business *6*. Being able to let go *7*. The long view—looking ahead to loss *8*. The short view *9*. Letting go of the grief event *10*. Letting go of the things *11*. The rest of the family *12*. Where can we go for help? *13*. Keeping the energy of grief moving *14*. Some balancing acts *15*. When we start to feel better *16*. The rest of our life *17*. A new heaven and a new earth / *Organizations and books*

Grandma's Tears *Comfort for Grieving Grandparents,* June Cerza Kolf

Baker Book House, 1995, $5.99, paper, 85 pp.

Description Grandparents are often overlooked when a grandchild dies, yet they often carry a double burden: the loss of the grandchild and the sorrow of their own grieving children. Kolf offers support and hope in a way that does not overwhelm the bereaved. Practical strategies for surviving the stages of grief are offered as Kolf empathizes with grandparents who grieve.

Author June Cerza Kolf has spent many years working with the terminally ill and grieving. Presently she directs volunteers for a home health care agency in California and leads support groups and workshops on grief. She is a member of the Elisabeth Kübler-Ross Center and the National Hospice Organization and serves on the board of the High Desert Unit of the American Cancer Society. Her work can be seen in trade journals and inspiration publications including *Guideposts* and the *Christian Reader.*

Contents *1*. The needs *2*. The grief process *3*. The future

That Nothing Be Wasted *My Experience with the Suicide of My Son,* Mary Langford

New Hope, 1988, $2.95, paper, 56 pp., for counselees

Description Mary Langford's world shattered when she learned that her son James had committed suicide. In simple, yet moving language, she recounts her family's journey through grief and into healing in the days and months following his death. Through all the pain and questioning, their faith in God enabled them not only to survive, but to bring good out of tragedy. John Hewett, author of *After Suicide,* has provided suggestions on how to cope with a loved one's suicide; they are found at the back of the book.

Author Mary Langford earned her master's degree in marriage and family counseling from Southwestern Baptist Theological Seminary in Fort Worth, Tex.

Justin, Heaven's Baby Sharon Marshall

Beacon Hill Press of Kansas City, 1983, $5.95, paper, 119 pp., for counselees

Description Describes the loss of a child and ensuing recovery of the mother. Justin's story cannot be read with dry eyes. Justin was only supposed to live a few days, but he fought for his right to life, astounding doctors and claiming the hearts of onlookers in the process. Those who wonder how good can come from hopelessness will want to read Justin's story. Helps readers find strength to trust God through the trials of their own lives, however difficult their journey may be.

Author A frequent guest on radio and talk shows, Marshall is the author of two other books. She is a professional educator, speaker, and writer. She founded and directs SCORE for college, a program that has been named a model for helping high risk students become eligible, upon high school graduation, for the college or university of their choice.

Meditations for Bereaved Parents Judy Osgood

Gilgal Publications, 1983, $6.95, paper, 72 pp., for counselees

Description While all grief shares some common elements, no one understands exactly how a bereaved parent feels unless they have had a child die. This title provides a window into that pain

through the stories of 35 mothers and fathers who share their grief-related experiences. They ask hard "Why God" questions and share faith-related insights they gained in searching for answers. A valuable resource for counselors because of the insights it provides to the agony of losing a child as well as the suggestions it offers for providing help.

Author Judy Osgood serves as editor of this work and three others on bereavement. She became involved in the bereavement field after her teenaged son's death from chemotherapy complications. Her research revealed the need for books written on specific types of grief by those who had experienced it and led to the Gilgal Meditation series.

Coping with Sudden Infant Death Syndrome Mary Peninger

Liguori Publications, 1991, $.75, paper, 24 pp., for counselees

Description Explains SIDS, suggests ways to cope with the loss of a child, and helps friends offer comfort and support. Includes helpful Scripture readings, prayers, and information on SIDS support groups.

When a Child Dies Carol Pregent

Ave Maria Press, 1992, $6.95, paper, 120 pp., for counselees

Description The story of the author's 17-year-old daughter's illness and subsequent death. Gently encourages the movement through the grief process, the eventual adoption of a routine, and the significance of the healing presence of God.

Author Carol Pregent, a mother and homemaker living in Sidney, Ohio, is a sensitive and encouraging companion for those struggling to rise from the ashes of death to a new wholeness.

Contents *1.* Death *2.* People *3.* Funeral *4.* Grief *5.* God *6.* Memories *7.* Life *8.* Pieces *9.* Faith *10.* Hope *11.* Love *12.* Prayer *13.* Help *14.* Suggestions

Free to Grieve—Healing and Encouragement *For Those Who Have Experienced Miscarriage and Stillbirth,* Maureen Rank

Bethany House Publishers, 1985, $7.99, paper, 176 pp., for counselees

Description The author offers the most comprehensive explanation available concerning the factors that make miscarriage and stillbirth so difficult to face. Guidance to the grieving and help in looking toward the future is woven around in-depth stories of mothers who have borne these losses.

Author Maureen Rank, herself the survivor of four miscarriages, is a writer and seminar speaker with a degree in home economics and family relations from Iowa State University.

Contents *Section 1:* Learning to grieve *1.* A peculiar kind of grief *2.* Does everyone need to mourn? *3.* A grief in process *Section 2:* Finding out why *4.* Questions only you can answer *5.* Questions that tests will help you answer *6.* Now for your questions *Section 3:* Restoring relationships *7.* If your doctor let you down *8.* Protecting your marriage *9.* How to help your friends support you *10.* Working through your children's grief *Section 4:* Exploring alternatives *11.* Another pregnancy? *12.* The adoption option *13.* Fulfillment is not just a child away

Cries from the Heart *Prayers for Bereaved Parents,* Margaret B. Spiess

Baker Book House, 1991, $5.99, paper, 58 pp., for counselees

Description "They said, 'God only sends these trials to those who are strong.' Then if I were weak, would my son still be alive?" That cry from the heart came soon after the author's son died in an accident. Sometimes bewildered, occasionally angry, often insightful, the thoughts in these 50 short prayer poems ask hard questions of God and search for his meaning in tragedy.

Author Margaret B. Spiess is a graduate of Centenary College with a major in English literature. Her other published works are *Gather Me Together, Lord* and *Hold Me Steady, Lord.*

Losing a Child Elaine Storkey

Lion Publishing, 1992, $2.99, paper, 48 pp., for both counselors and counselees

Description Part of Lion's Pocketbook series. A professional counselor helps readers face the pain of a child's death and points to hope for the future.

Goodbyes Are Not Forever Joy Swift

Pacific Press, 1987, $1.99, paper, 96 pp., for counselees

Description The real authorities on grief recovery are those who have sustained the loss of someone very near and dear and survived intact. In this respect the author of this book qualifies with the highest credentials, having lost all five of her children in a very short space of time. This book is for anyone who has lost a loved one, especially a child. But it is also for anyone who would like to know how to help those bereaved.

Author Ten years ago, four of Joy Swift's children were murdered, and a fifth child died 18 days later of cancer.

Contents *1.* When tragedy strikes *2.* Stages of grief *3.* Getting through the funeral *4.* Family ties *5.* Someone to talk to *6.* Search for strength *7.* So many questions *8.* Forgiving our trespasses *9.* Learning to adjust *10.* Advice to friends *11.* Personal reflections

Help for Bereaved Parents Mildred Tengbom

CPH Publishing, 1981, $3.95, paper, 55 pp., for counselees

Description Based on research, the experiences of others, and the author's own experience, this book sensitively offers concern, help, and suggestions for recovery from grief to husbands and wives as they support each other in the bereavement. The book also includes a list of Bible readings for a time of loss and a list of verses that declare God's forgiveness and absolution.

Author Mildred Tengbom has written 20 books and has served as a missionary for 17 years.

Contents *1.* The unique grief of parents *2.* General characteristics of grief *3.* It's hard to support another when you yourself are hardly surviving *4.* Rebuilding and strengthening the marriage relationship *5.* Hope

Empty Arms *Support for Those Who Have Suffered Miscarriage or Stillbirth,* Pam W. Vredevelt

Multnomah Books (Questar), 1984, $7.99, paper, 126 pp., for both counselors and counselees

Description This book is the outcome of Vredevelt's search for understanding and encouragement. With the empathy personal experience brings, she is able to gently offer comfort to the woman who has just experienced miscarriage or stillbirth and insight to friends and family who want to help and encourage effectively.

Author Pam Vredevelt is a pastor's wife and professional counselor at Christian Counseling Services, Gresham, Oreg. She graduated from Multnomah School of the Bible in Portland, Oreg., and earned her master's degree in communication from Portland State University.

Contents *1.* The shocking news *2.* Our next step—delivery *3.* Grief . . . the road to healing *4.* Managing anger *5.* Untying guilt's knot *6.* Spiritual battles and emotions *7.* Responding to the reactions of others *8.* Husbands hurt too *9.* Helping children to understand *10.* Please . . . someone give me some answers *11.* After a stillbirth *12.* The challenge of a postpartum body *13.* Eating for health *14.* Mood swings and exercise *15.* New beginnings *16.* The Bible offers hope and comfort

Of Wheels and Wings *Thoughts on the Death of a Son,* John Wesley White

Thomas Nelson Publishers, 1993, $9.99, paper, 85 pp., for counselees

Description A touching story of the pain and grief, hope and healing involved in dealing with death. The story of one man's loss of his 36-year-old son and the anger, questions, despair, and comfort he experienced while struggling to let his son go.

Author John Wesley White has been one of Billy Graham's associate evangelists for the last 30 of his 50 years preaching the gospel.

Gone but Not Lost *Grieving the Death of a Child,* David W. Wiersbe

Baker Book House, 1992, $5.99, paper, 116 pp., for counselees

Description A thoughtful gift for a family—Christian or non-Christian—that has experienced the death of a child. Each brief chapter helps parents face one's element of sorrow, anger, and guilt.

Author David W. Wiersbe considers ministry to the grieving an important part of his pastorate in Roscoe, Ill. He is a chaplain of fire and rescue units and works with local support groups for the grieving.

Contents *1.* The wounded parent *2.* A place called heaven: questions parents ask *3.* Out of the depths *4.* Part of you is gone *5.* The grieving process *6.* Grief is not rational *7.* The tears of God *8.* Styles of grieving *9.* Facts and feelings *10.* The mourner's creed *11.* The marital strain *12.* Needing to know *13.* Guilt *14.* Mad at God *15.* Going through *16.* Questions *17.* The rope of hope *18.* Mary, the mother of Jesus *19.* Preserving the memories *20.* Re-

sistance and acceptance *21.* Circle of love, circle of grief *22.* A ready response *23.* A new beginning

Making Peace with God after Losing a Child

Abbey Press, $.50 each, paper, 8 pp., for counselees

Description Part of the CareNotes series from Abbey Press. CareNotes are short booklets that help readers identify issues and begin the process of seeking resolution. Anecdotal and uplifting. Beautiful photographs grace the covers. Over 20 million CareNotes have been sold in just over five years. Can be used as an alternative to a greeting card or in conjunction with pastoral care visits.

When a Child Dies

Abbey Press, $.50 each, paper, 8 pp., for counselees

Description Part of the CareNotes series from Abbey Press. CareNotes are short booklets that help readers identify issues and begin the process of seeking resolution. Anecdotal and uplifting. Beautiful photographs grace the covers. Over 20 million CareNotes have been sold in just over five years. Can be used as an alternative to a greeting card or in conjunction with pastoral care visits.

Children's Hospice International

Children's Hospice International. An organization

Description Secular program that seeks to coordinate support systems and a referral network for seriously ill children and their families as well as for those who have encountered the sudden loss of a child through accident or violence. Operates a clearinghouse so that information on research, programs, support groups, and education and training programs can be more readily assimilated and disseminated.

Compassionate Friends, The

The Compassionate Friends. An organization

Description A self-help organization that helps when there has been the death of a child. Provides referrals to over 650 existing chapters throughout the United States.

H.A.N.D. of Santa Clara County *(Helping after Neonatal Death)*

H.A.N.D. of Santa Clara County. An organization

Description A secular organization that assists in the establishment of support groups, offers phone counseling, a booklist, and medical information for professionals.

SHARE: Pregnancy and Infant Loss Support, Inc.

SHARE: Pregnancy and Infant Loss Support, Inc. An organization

Description Provides a bimonthly newsletter and networks over 250 chapters of support groups for bereaved parents.

SIDS Alliance

SIDS Alliance. An organization

Description Organization that assists those dealing with sudden infant death syndrome.

Sudden Infant Death Syndrome Alliance

Sudden Infant Death Syndrome Alliance. An organization

Description This infoline provides telephone counseling, written resources, and support group information.

Coping with the Loss of a Loved One

Living through the Loss of Someone You Love *One Woman's Story of Loss, Grief and New Found Hope,* Sandra P. Aldrich

Regal Books, 1992, $8.99, paper, 234 pp., for counselees

Description For those who have lost someone they love, or for those who minister comfort. Also for professionals, pastors, and family counselors, to assist them in their ministry to help the hurting. The first half of the book shares the personal struggles as the author accompanies her young husband through his losing battle with cancer. The second half offers practical advice for facing the problems and challenges that are inevitable when such a loss occurs. Encouragement and faith are throughout.

Author Sandra P. Aldrich is the senior editor of *Focus on the Family* magazine. As community service representative for a large Michigan funeral home chain in 1985–86, Aldrich conducted numerous grief seminars for service clubs, schools, hospitals, and churches. She was also one of the experts called in by schools after the *Challenger* space shuttle disaster in 1986. She holds a B.A. and M.A. from Eastern Michigan University and has also authored *From One Single Mother to Another.*

Contents *Book One*—Living with my clown *1.* Tangled threads *2.* Everything's normal? *3.* Don't you care, God? *4.* Prayer at midnight *5.* Donnie, you're free! *6.* Since then *Book Two*—Legacy of my clown *1.* Turning grief to good *2.* Moving through grief *3.* Handling money *4.* How to help *5.* Abnormal grief *6.* Talking to children about grief *7.* Coping with normal depression *8.* Surviving the loss

Young Widow *Learning to Live Again,* Kate Convissor

Zondervan Publishing House, 1992, $8.99, paper, 176 pp., for counselees

Description Going beyond a diary format and the tired "stages of grief" approach, this author/journalist clearly addresses the unique and rocky transitions younger widows experience.

Author Kate Convissor is a freelance writer. She is remarried and lives in Grand Rapids, Mich., with her husband and six children.

When Your Parent Dies *A Concise and Practical Source of Help and Advice for Grieving Adults,* Cathleen L. Curry

Ave Maria Press, 1993, $6.95, paper, 152 pp., for counselees

Description Provides accessible, easy-to-handle advice drawn from experience and study. Discusses the feelings we experience in saying goodbye, preparing for a parent's death, the stages of grief, the beginning of healing, helping the surviving parent, and helping our own children with grief. Also deals with breaking unhealthy generational cycles of behavior.

Author Cathleen Curry is active in Catholic Family Services programs of the Sioux Falls Diocese. She is a graduate of Briar Cliff College.

Contents *1.* Saying goodbye *2.* Beginning the healing *3.* Grief and mourning *4.* Breaking the cycle *5.* Prayer and spirituality *6.* The surviving parent *7.* Helping children with grief *8.* Now and at the hour of our death *9.* Go with God

When Your Spouse Dies *A Concise and Practical Source of Help and Advice,* Cathleen L. Curry

Ave Maria Press, 1990, $5.95, paper, 128 pp., for counselees

Description When the author's own husband died at age 47 leaving her with nine children, she experienced physical, psychological, and spiritual shock. Eighteen years later she wrote this book. Deals with widowhood and establishes eight practical guideposts for getting through the first year. The stages of grief are covered, as well as expressions of mourning, loneliness, sexuality, support networks, financial priorities, good health practices, and the importance of spiritual growth.

Author Cathleen Curry is active in Catholic Family Services programs of the Sioux Falls Diocese. She is a graduate of Briar Cliff College.

Contents *1.* Widowhood is . . . *2.* First steps *3.* Mourning *4.* Being single and lonely *5.* Prayer *6.* Tender loving care *7.* Financial headaches *8.* Children and death *9.* Closing the door gently

Coping with Life after Your Mate Dies
Donald Cushenbery and Rita Cushenbery

Baker Book House, 1991, $6.99, paper, 90 pp., for counselees

Description Written to be read quickly and easily at a stressful time. The authors have interviewed others and relived their own sorrow. They share principles for victorious living at a day-to-day level.

Authors Both retired teachers, the Cushenberys now conduct surviving mate workshops.

Contents *1.* Living with grief *2.* Handling your finances *3.* Caring for your physical and emotional needs *4.* Making living arrangements *5.* Moving ahead with your new life *6.* Contemplating remarriage *7.* An overview

The Grief Adjustment Guide Charlotte Greeson and Mary Hollingsworth

Multnomah Books (Questar), 1992, $15.99, paper, 255 pp., for counselees

Description This guide/journal sensitively offers help through the difficult time following a loved one's death. It gives detailed legal, financial, emotional, relational, and household assistance.

Who Will Wind The Clock? *Lessons on Loss,* Margaret Jensen

Thomas Nelson Publishers, 1993, $9.99, paper, 160 pp., for counselees

Description The author's struggle to overcome the grief and heartache of suddenly losing her husband. Grippingly honest, Jensen reveals the frustrations she endured in working to defeat the anguish inside her.

Author Margaret Jensen is a popular storyteller and best-selling author.

Helps for the Widowed Medard Laz

Ligouri Publications, 1983, $2.50, paper, 64 pp., for counselees

Description Helps readers become capable of handling issues that must be faced after the loss of a life partner.

Contents *1.* Life is changed—not ended *2.* Working through your grief *3.* What about the children? *4.* What to do about guilt feelings *5.* Handling special days *6.* Finding God in your life *7.* New horizons.

A Grief Observed C. S. Lewis

Zondervan Publishing House, 1995 (this ed.), $10.00, paper, 160 pp.

Description Written in moments of sadness, longing, and tenuous faith after his wife's death, C. S. Lewis bared his soul and probed the fundamental issues of life, death, faith, and hope in the midst of loss.

Author C. S. Lewis (1898–1963) was known to students at Cambridge and Oxford Universities as a brilliant scholar and tutor, and to the world as a Christian author of unusual distinction.

Grieving the Loss of Someone You Love
Daily Meditations to Help You through the Grieving Process, Raymond R. Mitsch

Servant Publications/Vine Books, 1993, $7.99, paper, 200 pp., for counselees

Description A series of thoughtful daily devotions that shares wisdom, insight, and comfort that will help hurting people through and beyond grief.

Author Raymond R. Mitsch, Ph.D., is founder and director of Cornerstone Counseling Center. He has authored three daily devotionals.

Contents A series of 70 two-page readings.

In This Very Hour *Loss of a Loved One,*
Robin Prince Monroe

Broadman and Holman, 1995, $1.95, saddleback, 40 pp.

Description Part of the new In This Very Hour series from Broadman and Holman Publishers, a series of daily devotions with first-person accounts of victory by faith over life's most tragic disappointments.

Author Robin Prince Monroe is a homemaker, writer, and a contributor to *Exceptional Parent* magazine. She lost a six-year-old daughter to leukemia and her son was born with Down's syndrome.

Contents A series of thirty-one brief, yet very well-written daily devotionals (Scripture passage and anecdote).

It Hurts to Lose a Special Person Amy Ross Mumford

Chariot Family Publishing, $4.99, paper, 24 pp., for counselees

Description The combination of words and photographs makes this an ideal gift to unfold God's grace and love for the person suffering from the loss of a loved one.

Meditations for the Widowed Judy Osgood

Gilgal Publications, 1985, $6.95, paper, 72 pp., for counselees

Description Written by 33 men and women who shared their pain in a series of short articles. In addition, they share what enabled them to heal and build new lives for themselves. A valuable resource for counselors because of the insights it provides into the agony of losing a mate as well as the suggestions it offers for providing help.

Author Judy Osgood serves as editor of this work and three others on bereavement. She became involved in the bereavement field after her teenaged son's death from chemotherapy complications. Her research revealed the need for books written on specific types of grief by those who had experienced it and led to the Gilgal Meditation series.

Until Death Do Us Part Joyce J. Tyra

Randall House Publications, 1989, $5.00, paper, 98 pp., for counselees

Description If you are recently widowed, this book is especially for you. It provides practical suggestions, understanding, and comfort. But above all, it offers a glimmer of hope to help you until you realize you are not alone, and that someday your grief will slowly subside. Eventually, with God's help, you will reconstruct your shattered life and enjoy the world again. To help eliminate emotional and financial confusion for those we love, personal fill-in-the-blank inventory pages are included at the end of the text.

Author When suddenly single at age 45, Joyce J. Tyra was thrust from her familiar role as housewife and mother into the role of single parent and head of the household. She earned a B.A. in Journalism and a M.A. in English, which she teaches in Miami, Fla.

When Loved Ones Are Called Home Herbert H. Wernecke

Baker Book House, 1972, $2.99, paper, 64 pp.

Description A simple collection of stories, poems, and Scripture readings to help the grieving understand and work through the grief process. Over 350,000 copies in print.

Spring Follows Winter *My Experience with the Death of My Husband,* Lynn Yarbrough

New Hope, 1987, $2.95, paper, 60 pp., for counselees

Description A first-person account of one woman's struggle with the death of her husband. Included at the end of the book are suggestions from a professional on coping with the death of a spouse.

Author Lynn Yarbrough directed a publications work in Birmingham, Ala., and is now a missionary to China.

Finding Meaning in Life after the Loss of a Loved One

Abbey Press, 1994, $.50 each, paper, 8 pp., for counselees

Description Part of the New CareSteps series from Abbey Press. Each CareStep pamphlet (three-panel) is filled with insightful advice and quotes from respected leaders in the helping professions. Very useful during the early stages of recovery. The underlying message in all CareSteps pamphlets is the emphasis on using all one's resources—emotional, physical, mental, social, and spiritual to cope with life's biggest challenges. This title emphasizes setting aside time to grieve, creating a new relationship with the loved one, being patient while trying to cope, taking a closer look at one's beliefs, and looking for a turning point.

Finding Your Way after the Death of a Spouse

Abbey Press, $.50 each, paper, 8 pp., for counselees

Description Part of the CareNotes series from Abbey Press. CareNotes are short booklets that help readers identify issues and begin the process of seeking resolution. Anecdotal and uplifting. Beautiful photographs grace the covers. Over 20 million CareNotes have been sold in just over five years. Can be used as an alternative to a greeting card or in conjunction with pastoral care visits.

Grieving the Loss of Your Parent

Abbey Press, $.50 each, paper, 8 pp., for counselees

Description Part of the CareNotes series from Abbey Press. CareNotes are short booklets that help readers identify issues and begin the process of seeking resolution. Anecdotal and uplifting. Beautiful photographs grace the covers. Over 20 million CareNotes have been sold in just over five years. Can be used as an alternative to a greeting card or in conjunction with pastoral care visits.

When Death Comes Unexpectedly to Someone You Love

Abbey Press, $.50 each, paper, 8 pp., for counselees

Description Part of the CareNotes series from Abbey Press. CareNotes are short booklets that help readers identify issues and begin the process of seeking resolution. Anecdotal and uplifting. Beautiful photographs grace the covers. Over 20 million CareNotes have been sold in just over five years. Can be used as an alternative to a greeting card or in conjunction with pastoral care visits.

AARP Widowed Persons Service

AARP Widowed Persons Service. An organization

Description An outreach program in which trained widowed volunteers offer support to newly widowed persons in over 220 communities nationwide. WPS identifies community leadership and resources that help newly widowed persons recovering from the trauma of a spouse's death, and then rebuild their lives. Cooperates with local religious organizations, social service and mental health agencies.

21. Guilt and Shame

Helps for the Scrupulous Russell M. Abata

Ligouri Publications, 1993, $4.95, paper, 97 pp., for counselees

Description Guidance and practical advice for those who worry compulsively about sin and its threatened punishment of hell.

If I'm Forgiven, Why Do I Still Feel Guilty? Bernard Bangley

Harold Shaw Publishers, 1992, $7.99, paper, 129 pp., for counselees

Description Written in a popular style for anyone thinking through questions of guilt, God's forgiveness, and the complexity of life. Anecdotes illustrate every point. Strong reliance upon Scripture. Includes an eight-step plan for resolving guilt. Workbook pages included.

Author Bernard Bangley holds an M.Div. from Union Theological Seminary in Richmond, Va. An ordained Presbyterian pastor since 1962, he has held a variety of pastorates. He is a widely known conference speaker and lecturer on psychology and has authored six books.

Contents *Part 1:* Our human tendencies *1.* Denial is not confession *2.* Good for the soul *Part 2:* The nature of God *3.* God as friend *4.* The forgiving nature of God *Part 3:* Roadblocks to guilt-free living *5.* The problem is how you feel (not what you think) *6.* Inherited guilt *Part 4:* Ways to reconciliation *7.* It's between you and others *8.* Forgiving yourself *Part 5:* Preparing for the rest of your life *9.* Spiritual preparation for next time *10.* Emotional preparation for next time

The Doubting Disease *Help for Scrupulosity and Religious Compulsions,* Joseph W. Ciarrocchi

Paulist Press, 1995, $14.95, paper, 181 pp.

Description Brings together the most current information available today on religion and scruples, scrupulosity and obsessive-compulsive disorders.

Author Joseph W. Ciarrocchi is associate professor of pastoral counseling at Loyola College in Maryland. He is also a clinical psychologist whose treatment and research interests are in the area of compulsive behaviors.

Contents *Part 1*—Scruples: an orientation and overview *1.* Scrupulosity: an overview *2.* Scruples and obsessive-compulsive disorder *3.* Scruples: common and uncommon *4.* Scruples in the history of pastoral care *Part 2*—Changing scruples *5.* Targeting scruples and developing motivation *6.* Reducing obsessional scruples *7.* Reducing compulsive scruples *Part 3*—Practice and theory of changing scruples *8.* Getting help for scruples and OCD *9.* Technical asides: moral reasoning, scruples, and the psychology of religion / *Appendix:* A step-by-step treatment for scrupulosity / *Appendix:* Obsessions and compulsions checklist

Why Do I Feel Guilty When I've Done Nothing Wrong? Ty C. Colbert

Thomas Nelson Publishers, 1993, $6.99, paper, 144 pp., for counselees

Description Helps to distinguish between good and bad guilt, shows how to gain control over guilt and shame, identifies the four types of guilt and shame and explains how each affects mental health and behavior. Moves beyond "feel, forgive, and forget" type books and therapies.

Author Ty C. Colbert, Ph.D., is a clinical psychologist. He specializes in issues pertaining to anger and guilt, ACOA, codependency, depression, and sexual addiction.

Contents *1.* What is guilt? *2.* Where does guilt come from? *3.* How to eliminate false guilt *4.* Identifying destructive shame *5.* Healing destructive shame *6.* The complex nature of guilt *7.* Searching for your true self

Getting a Grip on Guilt Judith Couchman

NavPress, 1990, $3.99, paper, 96 pp., for counselees

Description In this compelling Bible study guide, Judith Couchman helps you tackle guilt—and sets you on the road to experiencing real forgiveness from God. You'll learn to discern real guilt from false guilt and how to live a genuinely forgiven life.

Author Judith Couchman is director of communications for the Navigators and a freelance writer from Colorado Springs, Colo. She is the former editor of *Sunday Digest* and *Christian Life.*

Contents *Introduction:* When guilt won't go away / Crisis point—Am I really forgiven? *Evaluation:* An inside look *1.* Getting a grip on guilt *2.* When the guilt's for real *3.* Grabbing at grace *4.* Dumping it out / *More study:* Why the offense? *Activity:* A purging point to call your own / *Discussion:* Getting together about guilt / *Bibliography:* Toward guilt free living

Guilt Brent Curtis

NavPress, 1992, $5.00, paper, 70 pp., for both counselors and counselees

Description If you're tired of false guilt that robs you of joy, here is a guide that will give you an understanding of the roots of false guilt and the freedom that is offered to the believer through Christ's atoning work and resurrection. This small group discussion guide explores the roots and function of false guilt, distinguishes false and true guilt, explores how guilt is related to shame that affects our perceptions, and discusses repentance from independence as the road to freedom from guilt. Six self- or leader-guided sessions. Includes leader's guide.

Author Brent Curtis is formerly a teacher and Young Life staff member. He presently is a counselor in private practice in Colorado Springs. He has an M.A. in biblical counseling and a Ph.D. in religion and society.

Contents *Session 1:* Two kinds of guilt *Session 2:* Shame—the beginning of false guilt *Session 3:* From shame to false guilt *Session 4:* The shame-based home *Session 5:* Compulsions, addictions, and anxiety *Session 6:* True guilt: gateway to freedom / *Conclusion* / Help for leaders

Encountering Shame and Guilt *A Short-Term Structured Model,* Daniel Green and Mel Lawrence

Baker Book House, 1994, $17.99, cloth, 174 pp., for counselors

Description Part of the new Strategic Pastoral Counseling resources from Baker Book House. Designed to help pastoral counselors accomplish more in fewer sessions. Unique in several respects—each title has a separate parallel book the counselee reads during the week for added

support and reinforcement. Includes a clear, step-by-step approach for the counselor, a structured holistic and spiritual focus, and an explicitly Christian foundation. This title gives counselors strategic insight for uncovering and biblically resolving guilt and shame. The authors differentiate between objective guilt and subjective feelings of shame that may or may not be based on guiltiness before God and others. The companion book is *Why Do I Feel Like Hiding?*

Authors Daniel Green is clinical director of New Life Resources, Inc., in Wauwatosa, Wis. Mel Lawrence is senior associate pastor of Elmbrook Church, Waukesha, Wis.

Contents *1.* Defining guilt and shame *2.* Shame in three forms *3.* Guilt and shame in Christian belief *4.* Shame's impact *5.* Counseling shame-filled people *6. Session 1:* The encounter stage *7. Sessions 2, 3, and 4:* The engagement stage *8. Session 5:* The disengagement stage

Why Do I Feel Like Hiding? *How to Overcome Shame and Guilt,* Daniel Green and Mel Lawrence

Baker Book House, 1994, $7.99, paper, 123 pp., for counselees

Description Part of the new Strategic Christian Living resources from Baker Book House. Designed to help counselees make quick progress during therapy sessions. Corresponds to a separate parallel book the counselor uses as a basis for the counseling. This title shows how powerful emotions subtly manifest themselves in a number of ways. Through the use of illustrative case studies and Bible-based counsel, the authors guide readers toward understanding why they suffer from shame and guilt. The companion book is *Encountering Shame and Guilt.*

Authors Daniel Green is clinical director of New Life Resources, Inc., in Wauwatosa, Wis. Mel Lawrence is senior associate pastor of Elmbrook Church, Waukesha, Wis.

Contents *1.* Why do I feel like hiding? *2.* So what's the verdict on me? *3.* Thoughts and feelings *4.* The tutor: moral shame *5.* The deceiver: imposed shame *6.* Resolving imposed shame *7.* Clay vessels and natural shame *8.* A story / *Epilogue*—The cross of Christ, focus of shame

Guilt: How to Deal with It John Hamrogue and Joseph Krastel

Ligouri Publications, 1993, $1.95, paper, 97 pp., for counselees

Description Explores societal guilt, personal situations, and good and evil to help readers better cope with guilt in their own lives. Q & A format.

Guilt-Free Living *How to Know When You've Done Enough,* Robert Jeffress

Tyndale House Publishers, 1995, $15.99, cloth, 256 pp.

Description The line between legitimate guilt caused by sin and false guilt caused by improper expectations can blur at times. Jeffress identifies the sources and effects of counterfeit guilt. Covers feeling guilty in work, marriage, parenting, friendships, money, relaxation, and more.

Author Dr. Robert Jeffress is senior pastor of the First Baptist Church in Wichita Falls, Tex.

Free to Love Again *Coming to Terms with Sexual Regret,* Dick Purnell

Here's Life Publishers (c/o Thomas Nelson), 1989, $8.99, paper, for counselees

Description A discussion on how to experience restoration and forgiveness from God after a sexually promiscuous past.

Author Dick Purnell holds a master's degree in counseling from Indiana University and a master of divinity degree from Trinity Evangelical Divinity School. He is the national director of Single Life Resources.

Contents *Part 1:* Sexual regrets *1.* A treasure chest of hope *2.* Closing Pandora's box *3.* The emotional tug of war *4.* The ____ made me do it *5.* On the road to restoration *6.* The way of restoration *Part 2:* Steps to freedom *1.* Accept God's forgiveness *2.* Forgive yourself *3.* Expect powerful changes *4.* Guard your mind *5.* Dissolve immoral relationships *6.* Purify your passions *7.* Focus on your future / *Epilogue:* You can do it!

Learning More about Shame Russ Rainey

Rapha Resources, $2.50, paper, for both counselors and counselees

Description Sheds light on shame and true guilt and will help readers tell the difference between them.

Recovery from Guilt Dale Ryan and Juanita Ryan

InterVarsity Press, 1992, $4.99, paper, 60 pp., for both counselors and counselees

Description This Bible study is part of a series of 16 volumes on various recovery themes. Each book contains studies on six biblical texts. Leader's notes are provided for group study.

Authors Dale Ryan is the executive director of the Recovery Partnership, the parent organization to the National Association for Christian Recovery. Juanita Ryan is a counselor in private practice in Hacienda Heights, Calif.

Recovery from Shame Dale Ryan and Juanita Ryan

InterVarsity Press, 1992, $4.99, paper, 60 pp., for both counselors and counselees

Description This Bible study is part of a series of 16 volumes on various recovery themes. Each book contains studies on six biblical texts. Leader's notes are provided for group study.

Authors Dale Ryan is the executive director of the Recovery Partnership, the parent organization to the National Association for Christian Recovery. Juanita Ryan is a counselor in private practice in Hacienda Heights, Calif.

Contents *1.* The experience of shame *2.* The shame of public exposure *3.* The shame of being devalued *4.* The shame of rejection *5.* Internalized shame *6.* God's love for those in shame / *Leader's notes*

Shame and Grace *Healing the Hurts We Don't Deserve,* Lewis B. Smedes

Harper and Row, 1993, $10.00, paper, 177 pp., for both counselors and counselees

Description Shame is defined as the vague, undefined heaviness that presses on our spirit and dampens our gratitude for life, and diminishes our joy. The good news is shame can be healed. With warmth and wit, Smedes examines why and how we feel shame and presents a profound spiritual plan for healing. Step-by-step, Smedes outlines the road to well-being and the peace that comes from knowing we are accepted by "the grace of One whose acceptance of us matters most."

Author Lewis B. Smedes is professor of integrative studies in the Graduate School of Psychology at Fuller Theological Seminary and the award-winning author of ten books.

Contents *Part 1:* The heaviness of shame *1.* A very heavy feeling *2.* Shame's close relations *3.* Leading candidates for shame *Part 2:* The varieties of shame *4.* Healthy shame:

a voice from our true self *5.* Unhealthy shame: a voice from our false self *6.* Spiritual shame: the price we pay to see God? *7.* Social shame: the pain of rejection *8.* Our sense of shame: keeper of our mysteries *Part 3:* The sources of shame *9.* How parents can shame us *10.* How the church fed my shame *11.* How we shame ourselves *12.* Escapes from shame *Part 4:* Grace and the healing of our shame *13.* The beginning of our healing *14.* With our shadows *15.* Singing "Amazing Grace" without feeling like a wretch *16.* Places to find traces of grace *Part 5:* The lightness of grace *17.* Coming to terms with our shamers *18.* Accepting ourselves *19.* Living life lightly *20.* The return of joy / *Postscript:* a faith for the lighter life

Counseling and Guilt Earl D. Wilson

Word Publishing, 1987, $15.99, cloth, 212 pp., for counselors

Description Dr. Wilson exposes the shallowness of extreme measures that attempt to deal with guilt by stamping out the conscience or by using guilt as the motivation for acceptable behavior.

Author Earl Wilson is professor of clinical and counseling psychology at Western Conservative Baptist Seminary in Portland, Oreg.

Contents *Part 1:* Understanding guilt *1.* The challenge of counseling for guilt *2.* Biblical perspectives on guilt *3.* Psychological perspectives on guilt *4.* The need for an integrative approach on guilt *5.* Earned and unearned guilt *6.* The problem of motivation by guilt *7.* Love and guilt *8.* Relationships and guilt *Part 2:* Counseling and guilt *9.* Cognitive approaches to guilt *10.* Self-discovery approaches to guilt *11.* Dynamic approaches to guilt *12.* Behavioral and problem-solving approaches to guilt *Part 3:* Preventing guilt *13.* Practical ways to prevent guilt *14.* Avoiding counselor guilt

Does God Really Love Me? *Turning God's Love Loose in Your Life,* Earl D. Wilson

InterVarsity Press, 1986, $4.99, paper, 96 pp., for both counselors and counselees

Description Helping readers overcome feelings of guilt, inferiority, and fear, Earl D. Wilson shows how to recognize and appreciate God's love.

Author Earl D. Wilson (Ph.D., University of Oregon) is associate professor of clinical and counseling psychology at Western Conservative Baptist Seminary and director of Lake Psychological and Counseling Services in Oregon.

Contents *1.* Why all this talk about love? *2.* God's extravagant love *3.* Savoring: the secret to feeling loved *4.* A sinner looks at love *5.* Understanding the source of love *6.* Love as a lifestyle *7.* Does love have a price tag? *8.* Why does God love us anyway?

Released from Shame *Recovery for Adult Children of Dysfunctional Homes,* Sandra D. Wilson

InterVarsity Press, 1990, $8.99, paper, 175 pp., for both counselors and counselees

Description Explains the patterns of thinking and feeling common to adult children of dysfunctional homes and helps readers start on their own journey toward recovery.

Author Dr. Sandra D. Wilson is counseling coordinator for Faith Evangelical Free Church in Milford, Ohio, and visiting professor at Trinity Evangelical Divinity School.

Contents *1.* My story—"half a loaf" *2.* Understanding shame and stumbling *3.* Shame in dysfunctional families *4.* Rules in dysfunctional families *5.* Abuse and shaming in dysfunctional families *6.* Abuse and shaming in Christian families *7.* Understanding consequences and change *8.* Released from shaming our flaws *9.* Released from shaming our feelings *10.* Released from shame-based dependency *11.* Released from shame-bound concepts of God and religion *12.* Released to forgive the shamers *13.* Released for potential and purpose

Making Peace with Your Past H. Norman Wright

Fleming H. Revell, 1985, $8.99, paper, 190 pp., for counselees

Description Biblical guidance for overcoming the negative effects of past experiences.

Author H. Norman Wright is the founder and director of Family Counseling and Enrichment, and the seminar ministry Christian Marriage Enrichment in Tustin, Calif. A counselor and seminar speaker, he is also a prolific author.

Contents *1.* Excess baggage—where can you put it? *2.* How did you collect all that baggage? *3.* "Me, change? impossible"—or is it? *4.* Imaging to heal the past *5.* Relinquishing your resentments *6.* Coping with rejection *7.* Breaking away from perfectionism *8.* Resisting overcoercion *9.* Overcoming overindulgence *10.* Healing emotional paralysis *11.* Treating your wounds

Learning How to Forgive Yourself

Abbey Press, $.50 each, paper, 8 pp., for counselees

Description Part of the CareNotes series from Abbey Press. CareNotes are short booklets that help readers identify issues and begin the process of seeking resolution. Anecdotal and uplifting. Beautiful photographs grace the covers. Over 20 million CareNotes have been sold in just over five years. Can be used as an alternative to a greeting card or in conjunction with pastoral care visits.

Overcoming Guilt with Faith and Love

Abbey Press, $.50 each, paper, 8 pp., for counselees

Description Part of the CareNotes series from Abbey Press. CareNotes are short booklets that help readers identify issues and begin the process of seeking resolution. Anecdotal and uplifting. Beautiful photographs grace the covers. Over 20 million CareNotes have been sold in just over five years. Can be used as an alternative to a greeting card or in conjunction with pastoral care visits.

Scrupulous Anonymous *A Self Help Organization for the Scrupulous*

Ligouri Publications, 1994, $1.00, paper, 97 pp., for counselees

Description Puts readers in touch with the self-help organization that has helped thousands find peace of mind. SA works by correspondence and provides mutual help for victims of scrupulosity (intense fretting over salvation and forgiveness).

22. Illness

AIDS

Counseling and AIDS Gregg R. Albers

Word Publishing, 1990, $15.99, cloth, 223 pp., for counselors

Description Deals with the human issues, emotional fallout, common questions, and the ways to help victims and their loved ones.

Author Gregg Albers is the director of health services at Liberty University in Lynchburg, Va., and is the author of several other books.

Contents *Part 1:* Understanding AIDS victims and the disease *1.* AIDS: the victims *2.* AIDS : the disease *3.* AIDS: the effects *4.* AIDS: addiction *5.* AIDS: ethics *Part 2:* Counseling AIDS patients *6.* Counseling those who need testing *7.* Counseling when the test is positive *8.* Counseling those who are ill *9.* Counseling the terminally ill *10.* Counseling families of AIDS patients *Part 3:* Ministering to those in need *11.* The church's role in AIDS

AIDS: What Every Teen Should Know Jim Auer

Ligouri Publications, 1991, $.75, paper, 24 pp., for counselees

Description Auer doesn't alienate by preaching or by using scare tactics. Instead, he offers candid information about how AIDS is and is not transmitted, discusses whether or not "safe sex" has a place in Christian education, and explains why abstinence is the only 100% effective way to protect oneself from AIDS.

The Samaritan's Imperative, Ministry to People with AIDS Michael J. Christensen

Abingdon Press, 1991, $9.95, paper, 205 pp., for counselors

Description Written in a lively, readable style with easy-to-understand steps and engaging real-life stories gleaned from the daily landscape of America's most feared disease. Christensen deals with the moral and theological implications of AIDS and offers readers powerful principles and ex-

emplary illustrations of how to withhold judgments and be a good neighbor to someone living with the HIV virus. The second part of the book explains how clergy and laity alike can become effective chaplains and caregivers.

Author Michael Christensen is an AIDS chaplain at San Francisco General Hospital and director of the United Methodist AIDS Project. A graduate of Yale Divinity School, he is the author of two other books. Representative chapters: What to do when you don't know what to do. How to bring healing and hope. Pastoral care as death draws near.

Touched by AIDS Margaret Ann Cummings

New Hope, 1992, $1.95, paper, 19 pp., for counselees

Description A brief booklet that helps young people understand the issues associated with AIDS. Discusses how to help an infected friend.

Author Margaret Ann Cummings is active in an Interfaith AIDS Council and is a volunteer with AIDS patients and their families in crisis.

Mommy, What's AIDS? *A Read-Together Story for Families,* Joyce Dodge

Tyndale House Publishers, 1989, $3.95, paper, 48 pp., for counselees

Description This resource is designed for parents and teachers to read aloud with children. It gives a sensitive, biblical response to the questions kids are asking about AIDS. This book can be used as a tool to discuss the critical subject of AIDS in a nonthreatening, loving way, and it gives children important information and practical suggestions for responding to something that is affecting more and more of our world every day.

Author Joyce Dodge is a minister's wife, schoolteacher, and speaker. She has developed seminars on the biblical approach to sexuality.

AIDS: Ministry in the Midst of an Epidemic *A Medical/Theological Perspective,* Wendell W. Hoffman and Stanley J. Grenz

Baker Book House, 1990, $12.99, paper, 304 pp., for counselors

Description A physician and ethicist examine the history and facts of the AIDS epidemic and take away Christians' excuses for not becoming involved in ministry to those touched by this crisis.

Authors Wendell W. Hoffman is a consultant in infectious diseases at the Central Plains Clinic, Sioux Falls, S.Dak., where he maintains an active practice in the treatment of AIDS. Stanley Grenz is professor of systematic theology and Christian ethics at North American Baptist Seminary.

Contents *Introduction:* Identifying the barriers to an AIDS ministry *Part 1:* Medical perspectives and context *1.* The history of AIDS *2.* The cause of AIDS *3.* The epidemiology of AIDS *4.* The clinical manifestations of AIDS *5.* The treatment of AIDS *6.* The prevention and control of AIDS *Part 2:* Theological perspectives and context *7.* Overcoming barriers: the background for an AIDS ministry *8.* Crossing barriers through compassion *9.* Other motivations for an AIDS ministry *10.* Care giving in the AIDS ministry *11.* Ministering to sideline victims of the AIDS crisis *12.* Broader concerns of an AIDS ministry / *Epilogue:* Toward an interventionalist ethic

A Time to Love *When AIDS Takes a Son, a Friend,* Helen M. Hostetler

Herald Press, 1989, $9.95, paper, 232 pp., for counselees

Description In this book, a mother tells a candid story of agony and anguish as AIDS took her son. Persons with AIDS are often treated as social outcasts. The author challenges the church to reflect on its ministry to them, to be redemptive, to walk with those in pain, offering care, friendship, trust, and hope.

Author Helen Hostetler (R.N.) worked on the staff of a hospital as staff nurse and coordinator of education for 30 years. She teaches an adult Sunday school class and is active in prayer and Bible study groups.

HIV Positive Debra Jarvis

Lion Publishing, 1992, $2.99, paper, 48 pp., for both counselors and counselees

Description Part of Lion's Pocketbook series. Focuses on living with AIDS rather than dying with the disease. Comfort and hope for those who are HIV positive.

Author Debra Jarvis leads AIDS support groups with a focus on spirituality, under the auspices of the Seattle AIDS Support Group. She is a former hospital chaplain of the UC San Francisco Medical Center.

Contents *1.* Denial *2.* Anger *3.* Blame *4.* Forgiveness *5.* Support *6.* Peace *7.* Balance *8.* Relationships *9.* Love *10.* Healing *11.* Death *12.* Pain *13.* Grief *14.* Hope

The Journey through AIDS *A Guide for Loved Ones and Caregivers,* Debra Jarvis

Lion Publishing, 1992, $10.95, paper, 272 pp., for both counselors and counselees

Description Jarvis, a hospital chaplain and author of *HIV Positive,* offers the results of years of counseling and speaking experience—along with practical advice and caregiver resources in this compassionate guide.

Author Debra Jarvis leads AIDS support groups with a focus on spirituality, under the auspices of the Seattle AIDS Support Group. She is a former hospital chaplain of the UC San Francisco Medical Center.

Contents *1.* Should you take this trip? *2.* Knowing the terrain *3.* On the road *4.* Food for the journey *5.* Friends along the way *6.* Are we there yet? *7.* Arrivals and dangers *8.* Walking through the valley *9.* Souvenirs from the journey *10.* Afterword *11.* Guided meditations

AIDS—Sharing the Pain *A Guide for Caregivers,* Bill Kirkpatrick

The Pilgrim Press, 1990, $9.95, paper, 146 pp., for counselors

Description An indispensable handbook for all involved in the care and counseling of people suffering from HIV. Its approach is positive, practical, compassionate, pastorally sensitive, and Christian.

Author Bill Kirkpatrick, an Anglican priest, is co-founder of Reaching Out, a caring and listening center in London, where he works with HIV sufferers.

Contents *1.* Introduction: healing wounds mutually shared *2.* The disease of disease *3.* AFRAIDS *4.* In the pain *5.* Sharing the pain *6.* Death and bereavement *7.* Rites of passage *8.* Living our dyings *9.* Ministers and other caregivers *10.* Ethical and moral perspectives *11.* The church's involvement a litany of reconciliation / Prayer / Glossary / Resources and services

Deadly Secrets Karen Scalf Linamen and Keith Wall

NavPress, 1990, $9.00, paper, 230 pp., for counselees

Description An anecdotal story of one man's dealing with AIDS. The true life story, based on the journals of one young man who lived a harrowing journey from darkness to light, from loneliness to love, from secrecy to sharing.

Authors Karen Scalf Linamen is a freelance writer and author or coauthor of four books. Keith A. Wall is a magazine editor for *Focus on the Family.*

When Someone You Know Is Dealing with AIDS Victor M. Parachin

Ligouri Publications, 1992, $.75, paper, 23 pp., for counselees

Description Helps readers understand what the gospel response to AIDS must be. The author then offers seven caring ways to reach out to friends and loved ones dealing with AIDS-related illnesses or deaths.

David Has AIDS Doris Sandford and Graci Evans

Gold 'n' Honey Books (Questar), 1993, $6.99, cloth, 28 pp., for counselees

Description Part of the In Our Neighborhood series from Gold 'n' Honey. The series was developed for children ages 5–11 who have difficult issues to cope with. The books deal gently and compassionately with children's delicate feelings when they're forced to handle situations that are hard to understand.

Annotated Bibliography Series Brad Sargent

The Barnabas Center, 1994, paper, 300 pp., a reference or academic work

Description Brad Sargent, director of the Barnabas Center for Emerging Issues, is creating a series of resource materials for HIV/AIDS ministry. Soon to be available are the first in his Annotated Bibliography series for HIV/AIDS Ministry: A nearly 300-page bibliography including list-

ings, brief descriptions, and or/full review of over 400 Christian and secular books. This will categorize books especially for: pastors and church leaders; the general Christian audience; parents, Sunday school teachers, and other educators; people living with HIV/AIDS, their family, and friends; those developing an HIV ministry. No doubt, this will become the premier resource for anyone serious about involvement in the HIV/AIDS crisis.

AIDS: A Manual for Pastoral Care
Ronald S. Sunderland and Earl E. Shelp

Westminster/John Knox Press, 1988, $6.99, paper, 76 pp., for counselors

Description This brief manual is designed to help pastors, chaplains, and other caregivers who are called upon to engage in a special ministry of compassion to the victims of AIDS and their families and friends.

Authors Ronald H. Sunderland is research fellow at the Institute of Religion, Houston, Tex. He is coauthor with Dr. Shelp of *AIDS and the Church: The Second Decade* and *A Biblical Basis for Ministry.* Earl E. Shelp is assistant professor of medical ethics at Baylor College of Medicine and also a research fellow at the Institute of Religion.

Contents *1.* AIDS—the medical facts *2.* Confronting the reality of AIDS *3.* Grief recognition and response *4.* Pastoral care of people with AIDS *5.* Ethical issues *6.* Three cases

When Someone You Know Has AIDS

Abbey Press, $.50 each, paper, 8 pp., for counselees

Description Part of the CareNotes series from Abbey Press. CareNotes are short booklets that help readers identify issues and begin the process of seeking resolution. Anecdotal and uplifting. Beautiful photographs grace the covers. Over 20 million CareNotes have been sold in just over five years. Can be used as an alternative to a greeting card or in conjunction with pastoral care visits.

AIDS Information Ministries

AIDS Information Ministries. An organization

Description A Christian HIV/AIDS education organization. Their focus is on AIDS education for churches, youth, and communities.

AIDS Resource Ministry

AIDS Resource Ministry. An organization

Description ARM's ministry is focused on providing spiritual/emotional support. This is offered through support groups for HIV-infected individuals, and family/friends; a buddy program to persons with AIDS; and individual "soaking prayer" ministry to persons with AIDS. Also equips churches for AIDS ministry via two-day training.

Americans for a Sound AIDS/HIV Policy

Americans for a Sound AIDS/HIV Policy. An organization

Description Founded in 1987, ASAP promotes traditional values in political policy making on HIV/AIDS issues. Provides the following materials: a set of sample HIV/AIDS policies adopted by local congregations; data on condom effectiveness related to HIV transmission; HIV and the religious community; HIV/AIDS counseling issues and more.

Beyond Rejection Ministries

Beyond Rejection Ministries, Inc. An organization

Description (Ecumenical) Catholic organization that provides HIV counseling, referrals, education, outreach, hospice networking for those infected with HIV and their families and loved ones.

Christian AIDS Services Alliance (CASA)

Christian AIDS Services Alliance. An organization

Description With roots going back to 1988, the Christian AIDS Services Alliance (CASA) is a nationwide referral, resource, and support network. It consists of Christian HIV/AIDS ministries, local churches from both denominational and nondenominational affiliations, Christian social service agencies, and individuals deeply concerned about the HIV epidemic. Each CASA affiliate offers a unique local ministry providing a combination of services in one or more of the following areas: spiritual support and referrals, personal support, involvement, and counseling, health-related services, material/financial assistance, technical support and referrals, education/training and resources. Maintains one of the best state-by-state referral lists/networks.

Love and Action

Love and Action. An organization

Description An interdenominational Christian ministry extending the compassion of Jesus Christ to individuals who are HIV positive or have AIDS, their families, friends, and churches. Love & Action volunteers serve through hospital visitation, outpatient care, support groups, and through church community AIDS education. Assists in the formation of AIDS support groups.

MAP International

MAP International. An organization

Description An independent Christian organization having ministry to persons with HIV/AIDS, their family, and friends. A special focus is on educating church leaders and congregations as well as health workers in Africa and Latin America.

National AIDS Hotline

National AIDS Hotline. An organization

Description Provides a wide variety of services including: information about AIDS/HIV; referral services (testing, legal counsel, housing, etc.). Spanish service: 1-800-344-7432.

National AIDS Information Clearinghouse

National AIDS Information Clearinghouse. An organization

Description Though not a Christian organization, this information networking service can provide you with important information.

Foundation for Children with AIDS, The

The Foundation for Children with AIDS. An organization

Description Though not a Christian organization, this center provides compassionate help for those dealing with the difficulties associated with AIDS and children.

Cancer

Everyday Strength *A Cancer Patient's Guide to Spiritual Survival,* Randy Becton

Baker Book House, 1989, $6.99, paper, 157 pp., for counselees

Description A counselor who has personally battled with cancer offers help for spiritual and emotional health in the midst of debilitating illness. A series of daily devotional readings incorporates Scripture, poetry, and anecdotes.

Author Randy Becton is a counseling minister for and producer of *Herald of Truth* television and is founder and executive director of Caring Cancer Ministry in Abilene, Tex.

Cancer *A Christian's Guide to Coping and Caring,* Christine Blazer Bigley

Beacon Hill Press of Kansas City, 1994, $6.96, paper, 88 pp., for both counselees and counselors

Description Here is a guide for coping and caring that brings together the resources of the Christian faith and practical knowledge about living with cancer. Written for both individuals and churches that desire to effectively understand and minister to people with cancer and their families.

Within the Shadow *A Biblical Look at Suffering, Death and the Process of Grieving,* Shelley Chapin

Victor Books, 1991, $7.99, paper, 179 pp., for counselees

Description Shelley Chapin was 28 years old when she first contracted cancer. Those were difficult days of fear, anxiety, and thoughts of death. Chapin writes to share with us how God works his good even in suffering. She gently leads us through her own experiences of cancer and chronic pain to a deeper knowledge of our heavenly Father. Chapin also provides us with practical insights into how to minister to those who hurt. A "must read" book for those who suffer, for families, for ministers, for physicians, and for caregivers of all kinds.

Author Shelley Chapin is a family counselor, author, musician, teacher, and conference speaker. She holds a master's degree from Dallas Theological Seminary and is enjoying doctoral studies in the field of counseling.

Dying to Live Georgia Comfort

Tyndale House Publishers, 1992, $8.99, paper, 131 pp., for counselees

Description The inspiring story of one woman's courageous fight against breast cancer. Going beyond clinical facts, Georgia Comfort presents the human side of coping with a disease that could be called a national epidemic. From the initial diagnosis to the trauma of a bone marrow transplant, *Dying to Live* testifies to the author's faith and the prayers of others who gave her strength and determination to live.

Author Georgia Comfort lives with her husband, Philip, and their three sons in Carol Stream, Ill. She is an accomplished pianist.

Contents *1.* "You have cancer" *2.* The disease spreads *3.* The disease spreads even further *4.* My three sons *5.* My friend Barb *6.* Struggling with mortality *7.* A bleak prognosis *8.* Preparing for bone marrow transplant *9.* The big blast *10.* Life out of death *11.* After death comes resurrection *12.* My last week in the hospital *13.* Going home *14.* An alien in my own world *15.* Trying to make a comeback *16.* Determined to live *17.* Overcoming despair *18.* I believe the true report

You'll Never Believe What They Told Me *Trusting God Through Cancer,* Emily Dockrey and Karen Dockrey

Chariot Books, 1995, $4.95, paper, 42 pp., for kids

Description Part of the Kids Helping Kids series from Chariot. Young Emily Dockrey learns she has leukemia. In dialogue format, she explains to other children how the support of family, friends, and God helped each step of the way to recovery.

Authors At the time of writing, Emily Dockrey is a 7th grade student. Karen Dockrey is a youth minister and writer.

Contents *1.* How long did you say this illness lasts? *2.* It's easier to read about it *3.* The hardest part of the fight *4.* A typical clinic week *5.* The good God pokes in *6.* Finding life in the midst of pain *7.* Other friends who can help

Living with Cancer Episcopal Radio-TV Foundation, The

Morehouse Publishing, $12.95, cassette(s), 70 minutes, for counselees

Description Addresses the emotional and spiritual challenges illness presents. Offers information, personal sharing, spiritual witness, and encouragement for those struggling with cancer or for those who minister to cancer patients. Includes discussion guide. A Good Neighbor Project, distributed by Morehouse Publishing.

A Cancer Battle Plan *Six Strategies for Beating Cancer from a Recovered "Hopeless Case,"* Anne E. Frahm and David J. Frahm

NavPress/Piñion Press, 1992, $12.00, paper, 167 pp., for counselees

Description The author shares the strategies she used to beat terminal cancer in just five weeks. Backed by the research of more than 30 doctors, nutritionists, and cancer scientists, *A Cancer Battle Plan* explains: how to give your immune system the tools it needs to fight disease, how detoxification and a nutrition-based rebuilding process can help you win your battle, and how to help someone fighting cancer.

Authors Anne E. Frahm heads her own nonprofit organization called HealthQuarters. Her vision through this organization is to meet the information, education, and encouragement needs of fellow cancer warriors. David J. Frahm is a writer, photographer, and career consultant.

Contents *1.* A war story *2.* Principle one—know your enemy *3.* Principle two—cut off enemy supply lines *4.* Principle three—rebuild your natural defense system *5.* Principle four—bring in reinforcements *6.* Principle five—maintain morale *7.* Principle six—carefully select your professional help *8.* Coming alongside in the battle

When Your Friend Gets Cancer *How You Can Help,* Amy Harwell

Harold Shaw Publishers, 1987, $6.99, paper, 112 pp., for counselors

Description Drawing upon her own experience with cancer and on extensive research, Amy Harwell gives practical guidelines for being a true, helping friend.

Author Amy Harwell is an energetic businesswoman whose consulting services have been widely used in the industry. An active volunteer in the American Cancer Society's CanSurmount program, she also speaks widely on the experience of crisis illness.

Contents *1.* Checking your attitudes about cancer and about friendship *2.* Reaching out immediately and boldly *3.* Getting prepped on cancer facts, figures, and feelings *4.* Offering your helping hands *5.* Sharing your healing hurt *6.* Helping your friend make death and dying decisions (if asked) *7.* Being there for your friend / *Information centers*

Cancer in the Young *A Sense of Hope,* Margaret O. Hyde and Lawrence E. Hyde

Westminster/John Knox Press, 1985, $10.00, cloth, 212 pp., for counselees

Description With straightforward information about cancer in young people, the authors attempt to demystify the disease, which is often regarded with intense fear. Includes a long and detailed glossary.

Author Margaret O. Hyde is author of an outstanding list of books for young people. Hyde has written documentaries for NBC-TV and taught children, young adults, and adults.

Contents *1.* Cancer in the young *2.* From cancer phobia to facts *3.* What is cancer? *4.* Leukemia *5.* Other kinds of cancer in the young *6.* Tests and treatments *7.* Young cancer patients speak out *8.* Camps and other fun for young cancer patients *9.* Looking toward tomorrow / Glossary / Suggested reading / Further information / Camps for children with cancer and their siblings

Conquering Cancer *An Invitation to Hope,* Paul Johnson

Zondervan Publishing House, 1991, $9.99, paper, 256 pp., for counselees

Description This book tells the cancer patient just what to expect at each stage of the diagnosis and treatment and explores medical discoveries that give people hope of recovery from cancer. Includes excerpts from Dr. Paul Johnson's cancer diary and selected readings on a dozen topics designed to build the cancer patient's confidence.

Author Paul Johnson, M.D., retired after 40 years of practice, has a weekly medical radio program and is public relations officer for the King County Medical Association.

Contents A word from a cancer sufferer *Part 1:* You and your cancer *1.* Modern miracles *2.* You and your doctor *3.* What to expect from surgery *4.* What to expect from radiation therapy *5.* What to expect from chemotherapy *6.* Taking charge *7.* On the road to recovery *Part 2:* The promise of tomorrow *8.* Understanding cancer cells *9.* The body's defenses *10.* Developments to watch *Part 3:* A cancer diary / *Where to find help*

When Cancer Comes *Mobilizing Physical, Emotional and Spiritual Resources . . . ,* Dan Koppersmith, Ginger Koppersmith, and Don Hawkins

Moody Press, 1993, $16.95, cloth, 284 pp., for both counselors and counselees

Description Readers learn how to transform their fear into hope and discover how the right attitude, proper care, and a strong faith can put them on the road to recovery and spiritual victory.

Authors Don Hawkins (Th.M., Dallas Theological Seminary) is host of the popular national radio talk show *Life Perspectives* and the author of numerous books on counseling. Daniel L. Koppersmith (M.D.) is a board certified pathologist and psychiatrist with Rapha Treatment Centers in Houston. Ginger Koppersmith (R.N., B.S.N.) is a psychiatric nurse with experience as a researcher at M.D. Anderson Cancer Center in Houston.

Contents *1.* A war story *2.* What is cancer? *3.* A perspective on physical illness *4.* How do you get cancer? *5.* Cancer and the physical *6.* Cancer and the emotional *7.* Cancer and the spiritual *8.* Treating cancer *9.* Encouraging the cancer patient's family *10.* Living with cancer, dying of cancer *11.* Preventing cancer *12.* Research toward eliminating cancer

Living with Cancer Mary Beth Moster

Tyndale House Publishers, 1989, $8.99, paper, 192 pp., for counselees

Description Sensitive, scriptural, complete. This book will help readers cope with the fears and facts of cancer, including self-esteem, treatment, side effects, emotional pain, and spiritual questioning.

Contents *1.* A very special nurse *2.* Cells gone berserk *3.* Self-esteem and the cancer patient *4.* Special problems *5.* Family in turmoil *6.* If cancer strikes a child *7.* Is God always good? *8.* The ultimate hope *9.* Our human emotions *10.* Living above the circumstance *11.* Facing difficult situations *12.* Why me, God? *13.* Lord, teach us to pray *14.* What about miracles? *15.* If I should die?

Coping with Cancer *12 Creative Choices,* John E. Packo

Christian Publications, 1991, $7.95, paper, 234 pp., for counselees

Description John E. Packo offers practical advice on handling the pressure, emotions, and harrowing experience of cancer. He knows firsthand what it feels like to hear the doctor announce a diagnosis of cancer. He knows that the treatments are nauseating and frightening, and that the path to recovery is strewn with uncertainty. But he also knows that you can fight back and show how to focus on God's will and care for you—perhaps for miraculous healing, perhaps

for strength to face the ordeal. *Coping with Cancer* can help you or someone you love make creative choices if faced with cancer.

Author Packo earned his master and doctor of ministry degrees from Luther Rice Seminary in Jacksonville, Fla. He currently pastors Trinity Alliance Church in Miamisburg, Ohio.

No Longer Afraid *Living with Cancer,* Doris Sandford and Graci Evans

Heart to Heart, 1992, $9.99, cloth, 32 pp., for counselees

Description Designed for children ages 5–11. This title is the story of Jamie, who when she is told she has cancer wonders if she will live. She had always dreamed of owning a special horse. She learns that some wishes do come true.

Confronting the Big C *A Family Faces Cancer,* Henry D. Weaver

Herald Press, 1984, $5.95, paper, 80 pp., for counselees

Description Describes the reactions of the author and his family to the diagnosis of cancer. He shows how hope, support of friends, prayer, and good medical care worked together to heal. Winner of the 1985 Silver Angel Award from Religion in Media.

Author Weaver holds a doctorate in physical chemistry from the University of Delaware. He is the deputy director of the Education Abroad Program of the University of California.

In God's Hand *One Woman's Experience with Breast Cancer,* Becky Lynn Wecksler and Michael Wecksler

Herald Press, 1989, $5.95, paper, 104 pp., for counselees

Description This is the story of a young woman with breast cancer. Overnight she realizes how precious her God-given life is as she and her family struggle to cope with the disease. She thought she had faith. But when she knows she cannot control her destiny, only then does she truly grasp the meaning of trusting the Lord.

Author Becky Lynn Wecksler continues her nursing career working part-time in the recovery room for a rural trauma center.

Facing Cancer As a Family

Abbey Press, $.50 each, paper, 8 pp., for counselees

Description Part of the CareNotes series from Abbey Press. CareNotes are short booklets that help readers identify issues and begin the process of seeking resolution. Anecdotal and uplifting. Beautiful photographs grace the covers. Over 20 million CareNotes have been sold in just over five years. Can be used as an alternative to a greeting card or in conjunction with pastoral care visits.

Recovering after a Mastectomy

Abbey Press, $.50 each, paper, 8 pp., for counselees

Description Part of the CareNotes series from Abbey Press. CareNotes are short booklets that help readers identify issues and begin the process of seeking resolution. Anecdotal and uplifting. Beautiful photographs grace the covers. Over 20 million CareNotes have been sold in just over five years. Can be used as an alternative to a greeting card or in conjunction with pastoral care visits.

When Someone You Love Has Cancer

Abbey Press, 1994, $.50 each, paper, 8 pp., for counselees

Description Part of the New CareSteps series from Abbey Press. Each CareStep pamphlet (three-panel) is filled with insightful advice and quotes from respected leaders in the helping professions. Very useful during the early stages of recovery. The underlying message in all CareSteps pamphlets is the emphasis on using all one's resources—emotional, physical, mental, social, and spiritual—to cope with life's biggest challenges. This title emphasizes arming oneself with information, expressing one's feelings, maintaining as normal a lifestyle as possible, letting the spirit sustain, letting go—if or when it's time.

When You First Learn It's Cancer

Abbey Press, $.50 each, paper, 8 pp., for counselees

Description Part of the CareNotes series from Abbey Press. CareNotes are short booklets that help readers identify issues and begin the process of seeking resolution. Anecdotal and uplifting. Beautiful photographs grace the covers. Over 20

million CareNotes have been sold in just over five years. Can be used as an alternative to a greeting card or in conjunction with pastoral care visits.

American Cancer Society Infoline

American Cancer Society. An organization

Description The ACS is a large organization that networks resources for dealing with cancer.

Cancer Information Hotline

Cancer Information Hotline. An organization

Description Though not a Christian organization, provides information and telephone counseling.

Candlelighters Childhood Cancer Foundation

Candlelighters Childhood Cancer Foundation. An organization

Description Though not a Christian organization, this group offers compassionate assistance to families dealing with children and cancer.

Chronic Illness

Caring at Home for Someone Ill or Disabled Martha O. Adams

Abbey Press, 1992, $.50 each, paper, 8 pp., for counselees

Author Martha O. Adams has worked as a public schoolteacher and religious educator for churches of many denominations. As the daughter of an AD-afflicted mother, she speaks and writes as an advocate for caregivers. She has published articles and poems in various magazines and journals and has authored two Abbey Press CareNotes.

Counseling the Sick and Terminally Ill Gregg R. Albers

Word Publishing, 1989, $15.99, cloth, 212 pp., for counselors

Description This volume helps Christian counselors learn more about the health care system today, understand patient and family responses to illness, give appropriate counsel for special medical situations, and encourage churches in establishing health care ministries.

Author Gregg Albers is the director of health services at Liberty University in Lynchburg, Va., and is the author of several other books.

Contents *Part 1:* Caring in times of sickness *1.* The response to illness *2.* Understanding illness *3.* Health care and illness *Part 2:* Counseling in times of sickness *4.* Counseling and illness *5.* Counseling the acutely and critically ill *6.* Counseling the chronically ill *7.* Counseling the psychiatrically ill *8.* Counseling the terminally ill *Part 3:* Ministry in times of sickness *9.* Special medical situations *10.* Spiritual fruit from illness / *Appendix:* Emotional support care plan

A Way with Pain Mary Batchelor

Lion Publishing, 1992, $2.99, paper, 48 pp., for both counselors and counselees

Description Part of Lion's Pocketbook series. Offers positive, practical help—showing a way to live successfully in spite of chronic pain.

Contents *1.* For people in pain *2.* Different kinds of pain *3.* Why?—and Why me? *4.* What is pain? *5.* Is the pain real? *6.* Can I find healing? *7.* Whose life is it anyway? *8.* Challenging the limits *9.* Practical hints *10.* It's not just the pain *11.* Distracting the pain *12.* The power of positive thinking *13.* Relating to others *14.* Common purposes *15.* A purpose in pain

Fight the Good Fight *A Family Faces and Survives Crisis,* Philip Bedsworth and Joyce Bedsworth

Herald Press, 1991, $6.95, paper, 128 pp., for counselees

Description Leukemia, lung cancer, and kidney failure. These diseases are common. For all three to strike the same person is not. Surviving them demands a fight which nearly wrenches a family apart. This book tells the story of Philip Bedsworth, who repeatedly nears death, confronts the terror and fatigue that accompany unending sickness, and faces the complex decisions made possible and inevitable by modern technology. It tells the story of his wife, Joyce, who struggles to survive as job demands and responsibilities as wife and mother begin to tear her apart. And the story of Sara and Steven, who know Daddy may die anytime. *Fight the Good Fight* ultimately tells the story of anyone who has been forced to wrestle with chronic illness—wondering what lies on the other side if death comes and what lies on this side if pain-filled life continues.

Authors Philip Bedsworth (died March 1993) was a graduate of Goshen College and Associated

Mennonite Biblical Seminary. He taught and pastored in Puerto Rico, Iowa, Indiana, and Kansas. Joyce Bedsworth received her nursing education at Goshen College and has earned master's degrees from the University of Iowa and Wichita State University. She is presently director of nursing at Schowalter Villa, a 320-resident retirement community in Hesston, Kans.

Contents *1.* White blood *2.* In the beginning *3.* I know who holds tomorrow *4.* Can dem dry bones live again? *5.* Off to see the wizards *6.* Bear ye one another's burdens *7.* God be with you till we meet again *8.* Life in the cocoon *9.* Coming home *10.* Starting over *11.* Two steps forward, one step backward *12.* The dark night of the soul *13.* Dying to live *14.* Each one's life is but a breath *15.* When you pass through the waters

Strength for Today *Daily Devotions for the Chronically Ill,* Sharon Broyles

Harper and Row, 1993, $12.00, paper, 400 pp., for counselees

Description This collection provides hope and encouragement to those whose every day requires acts of spiritual strength and courage. Featuring 365 carefully selected scriptural texts, devotional thoughts, and prayers, *Strength for Today* is for those who may appear healthy, but wrestle with fear and loss continually.

Author Sharon Broyles is a writer suffering from chronic illness.

You Gotta Keep Dancin' Tim Hansel

Chariot Family Publishing, $8.99, paper, 150 pp., for counselees

Description Tim Hansel shares from his own personal experience of chronic pain in his best-selling book. Hansel's message of choosing joy in the midst of pain can give hope to others who suffer physically and emotionally.

Life Is a Gift *My Experience with the Serious Illness of My Child,* Jo Lacy

New Hope, 1987, $2.95, paper, 60 pp., for counselees

Description This book is the unforgettable, poignant story of how Jo Lacy faced the serious illness of her child and reached the conclusion that life is a gift. At the end of the book are specific suggestions for coping from Norma Steven, professor at Belmont College, Nashville, Tenn.

Author Jo Lacy is an instructor of children's literature courses at the University of Texas at Arlington. She holds degrees in elementary education and administration/supervision from North Texas State University.

Waiting for a Miracle *Devotions for the Physically Weak,* Jan Markell

Baker Book House, 1993, $5.99, paper, 155 pp., for counselees

Description Devotions by one who has been there speak to those in chronic pain and with long-term illness. Poems, musings, and Scripture address spiritual and emotional needs.

Binding Up the Brokenhearted *A Handbook of Hope for the Chronically Ill and Disabled,* Cynthia Moench

College Press, 1991, $6.95, paper, 140 pp., for counselees

Description What if the doctor told you that you were not going to die, but would never get well? This book has been written by someone who has lived the roller coaster life of the chronically ill. This book is to help those who are sick and disabled come to grips with the pain, misunderstanding, and seeming hopelessness of the situation. It is to help them gain a clearer understanding of the need to restructure their lives, restructure their faith, and come to accept the reality of a divine plan for their lives. Examines changes wrought by illness and disability, human and spiritual ways of adapting, and restructuring life to accommodate illness.

Author Cynthia Moench lives in the San Francisco Bay area with her husband, Jim. She owned and operated a floral business until nine years ago when she contracted Chronic Fatigue Syndrome and was no longer able to work. However, she utilized her writing talents and produced two novels and articles for several periodicals. She speaks about living with chronic illness and disability to support groups and church groups alike.

Contents *1.* That dreaded word, incurable *2.* The mental and emotional battle *3.* And finally, acceptance *4.* The spiritual battle *5.* Choosing to cope *6.* Coping in relationships *7.* Practical daily applications *8.* Finishing well

From Grim to Green Pastures *Meditations for the Sick and Their Caregivers,* Richard L. Morgan

Abingdon Press/Upper Room Books, 1994, $8.95, paper, for counselees

Description Eighty brief, daily meditations clearly focused on issues of sick persons and their caregivers. Contains a strong emphasis on Scripture.

Author Richard L. Morgan is an ordained Presbyterian minister and hospital chaplain.

When Someone You Love Is Critically Ill
Victor M. Parachin

Ligouri Publications, 1991, $.75, paper, 24 pp., for counselees

Description Helps readers to be good friends in a bad time with ten caring suggestions. A special section of prayers will help readers pray for and with their loved one. Written from a Catholic perspective.

Living Well with Chronic Illness Marcia Van't Land

Harold Shaw Publishers, 1995, $9.99, paper, 280 pp.

Description Walks alongside the "chronic situationer," through the painful and sometimes lengthy process of finding the right doctor, the crucial matters of helping children understand, coping with chronic pain, deciding on courses of treatment, and facing the potential of early death. Included are many time-tested tips and up-to-date resources.

Author Marcia Van't Land, mother of three preschoolers, was diagnosed with Acute Intermittent Porphyria. Through thirteen years of relapses, surgeries, and hospitalizations, she, husband Tom, and their children have learned countless lessons about grace and perseverance. Marcia leads workshops and teaches adult education.

Contents *Part 1*—Coming to terms with chronic illness *1.* The chronic condition *2.* What is wrong with me? *3.* This is how I feel *Part 2*—Dealing with the world of medicine *4.* Doctor who? *5.* You and your hospital *6.* Chronic pain *7.* Emotional health *Part 3*—A lifestyle of coping *8.* Becoming overcomers *9.* Coping as a family *10.* Especially for caregivers *11.* Maintaining friendships *Part 4*—Realities of a terminal condition *12.* Important decisions *13.* Death and dying

Strength for the Day *Living Well with Chronic Illness,* Marcia Van't Land

Harold Shaw Publishers, 1994, $7.99, paper, 180 pp., for counselees

Description Author Marcia Van't Land knows personally the common discouragements, changed priorities, and daily challenges of living with chronic illness. With candor, encouragement, and real faith, the author speaks to the many needs—spiritual, practical, and physical—of the "chronic situationer" and family. A beneficial resource for friends, family, and those facing illness themselves.

Where Is God When It Hurts? Philip Yancey

Zondervan Publishing House, 1990, $8.99, paper, 285 pp., for counselees

Description Centers on the problem of physical pain. If God is love, why does he allow his children to suffer? This book shows how even the deepest pain can be filled with spiritual promise. A best-seller (500,000 copies) since its publication in 1976, the book was extensively revised and expanded in 1990 with more than 100 pages added. *Where Is God When It Hurts?* should speak to anyone for whom life just doesn't make sense. It is written for the person in pain as well as the one who wants to reach out and help, but just doesn't know how. Won the ECPA Gold Medallion Award as best inspirational book the year it was published.

Author Philip Yancey earned graduate degrees in communications and English from Wheaton College Graduate School and the University of Chicago. He joined the staff of *Campus Life* magazine in 1971 and worked there as editor for eight years. Since 1978 he has primarily concentrated on freelance writing. More than 600 of his articles have appeared in 80 different publications. Five of his 11 books have received Gold Medallion Awards from the Evangelical Christian Publishers Association.

Contents *1.* The problem that won't go away *Part 1:* Why is there such a big deal as pain? *2.* The gift nobody wants *3.* Painless hell *4.* Agony and ecstasy *Part 2:* Is pain a message from God? *5.* The groaning planet *6.* What is God trying to tell us? *7.* Why are we here? *8.* Arms too short to box with God *Part 3:* How people respond to suffering *9.* After the fall *10.* On my feet dancing *11.* Other witnesses *12.* Extreme cases *Part 4:* How can we cope with pain? *13.* Frontiers for recovery *14.* Fear *15.* Helplessness *16.* Meaning *17.* Hope *Part 5:* How does faith help? *18.* Seeing for yourself *19.* The rest of the body *20.* A Whole new world outside / *Discussion guide*

Feeling the Loneliness of Illness

Abbey Press, $.50 each, paper, 8 pp., for counselees

Description Part of the CareNotes series from Abbey Press. CareNotes are short booklets that help readers identify issues and begin the process of seeking resolution. Anecdotal and uplifting. Beautiful photographs grace the covers. Over 20 million CareNotes have been sold in just over five years. Can be used as an alternative to a greeting card or in conjunction with pastoral care visits.

Living Creatively with Chronic Illness

Abbey Press, $.50 each, paper, 8 pp., for counselees

Description Part of the CareNotes series from Abbey Press. CareNotes are short booklets that help readers identify issues and begin the process of seeking resolution. Anecdotal and uplifting. Beautiful photographs grace the covers. Over 20 million CareNotes have been sold in just over five years. Can be used as an alternative to a greeting card or in conjunction with pastoral care visits.

Living with Chronic Illness

Abbey Press, 1994, $.50 each, paper, 8 pp., for counselees

Description Part of the New CareSteps series from Abbey Press. Each CareStep pamphlet (three-panel) is filled with insightful advice and quotes from respected leaders in the helping professions. Very useful during the early stages of recovery. The underlying message in all CareSteps pamphlets is the emphasis on using all one's resources—emotional, physical, mental, social, and spiritual—to cope with life's biggest challenges. This title emphasizes dealing creatively with pain and frustration, restructuring one's physical and emotional lifestyle, giving oneself tender care, affirming the spirit, learning from the pain, and turning to others for support.

Terminal Illness

Counseling the Sick and Terminally Ill Gregg R. Albers

Word Publishing, 1989, $15.99, cloth, 212 pp., for counselors

Description This volume helps Christian counselors learn more of today's health care system, understand patient and family response to illness, give appropriate care for special situations, and encourage churches in establishing health care ministries.

Author Gregg Albers is the director of health services at Liberty University in Lynchburg, Va., and is the author of several other books.

Contents *Part 1:* Caring in times of sickness *1.* The response to illness *2.* Understanding illness *3.* Health care and illness *Part 2:* Counseling in times of sickness *4.* Counseling and illness *5.* Counseling the acutely and critically ill *6.* Counseling the chronically ill *7.* Counseling the psychiatrically ill *8.* Counseling the terminally ill *Part 3:* Ministry in times of sickness *9.* Special medical situations *10.* Spiritual fruit from illness / *Appendix:* Emotional support care plan

The Last Thing We Talk About *Help and Hope for Those Who Grieve,* Joseph Bayly

Chariot Family Publishing, 1989, $5.99, paper, 128 pp., for counselees

Description Offers help and hope for the terminally ill and dying. An excellent resource for pastors and those who work with the terminally ill.

Almost Home *Living with Suffering and Dying,* Sr. Thea Bowman

Ligouri Publications, $39.95, video, 30 minutes, for counselees

Description Sr. Thea Bowman, F.S.P.A., offers an intensely personal, truly inspiring message to those who are seriously ill, to their loved ones, and to those who minister to the sick.

Author A Redemptorist Pastoral Communications project.

How to Comfort the Dying Judith A. Caron

Ligouri Publications, 1989, $.75, paper, 24 pp., for counselees

Description Explains how to offer support and compassion to the dying as they face four images—life, God, loss, and death, that recur in the daily struggle with terminal illness.

Withdrawing Life-Support Systems *Help for Making Decisions,* Judith A. Caron

Ligouri Publications, 1989, $.75, paper, 23 pp., for counselees

Description A Catholic hospital chaplain helps readers understand the church's position on withdrawing life support systems. She explains both how life is to be treasured and preserved, and how it is permissible in certain cases to stop life support efforts and allow the person to die in peace.

Pastoral Care under the Cross *God in the Midst of Suffering,* Richard C. Eyer

CPH Publishing, 1995, $12.99, paper, 160 pp., for counselors

Description Identifies the counseling needs of the suffering, sick, dying, grieving, AIDS patients, and their families, the depressed, and those with mental disorders. Has a section on medical ethics.

An Early Journey Home *Helping Dying Children and Grieving Families,* Mary Ann Froehlich

Baker Book House, 1992, $8.99, paper, 205 pp., for both counselors and counselees

Description Mary Ann Froehlich has helped several dying children and their grieving families face death. The insights and sensitivities she has gained from her experiences are reflected in this hopeful, helpful book. She offers genuine solace to parents and siblings who are facing the death of a dearly loved child. Christians are shown how to put away their fears so they might give significant support to the terminally ill and their families.

Author Dr. Froehlich is a registered music therapist (board certified) and a certified child life specialist. She is the author of two other books.

Contents *1.* An early journey home *2.* My own journey *Part 1:* The biblical journey: preparing the helper *3.* Helpers without answers *4.* Our biblical models: fellow sufferers in Scripture *5.* When suffering turns to gold *Part 2:* Taking the journey: helping the dying child *6.* Helping through the illness and hospitalization *7.* Helping patients and families through death *8.* Zain's journey: advice from the experts *Part 3:* The long journey after: helping the grieving family *9.* Helping after the death *10.* Surviving the unbearable: more advice from the experts *11.* Special situations: miscarriages, catastrophic accidents, losing adult children *12.* Helpers of judges?: murder, the killer AIDS *13.* A family portrait *14.* A final note to helpers *Part 4:* Children's health care resources / Health care organizations / Illness and grief support organizations / Therapy techniques for hospitalized children / Books

Ready to Live, Prepared to Die *A Provocative Guide to the Rest of Your Life,* Amy Harwell

Harold Shaw Publishers, 1995, $9.99, paper, 155 pp.

Description Harwell takes readers on this soul-searching journey through the realization of our dreams, and the mundane but important tasks of handling hospitalization, wills, organ donation, guardianship, funeral plans, and saying good-bye to those we love. Included are thoughtful questions and a helpful checklist.

Author Amy Harwell is an energetic business woman whose consulting services have been widely used in the industry. An active volunteer in the American Cancer Society's CanSurmount program, she also speaks widely on the experience of crisis illness.

Contents *Introduction:* Called to take the final journey *1.* When my journey began *2.* Pick your destination *3.* Heroic efforts and the suicide question *4.* Advance directives (living will, durable power of attorney for health care, durable power of attorney for property) *5.* Instructions (organ donation, guardianship, estate planning, wills, important papers) *6.* Strains and tensions *7.* Good-byes, forgiveness, and blessings *8.* Final moments *9.* Funerals *10.* Thoughts on afterlife *11. Trip* delayed *12.* Prepared to die, ready to live! / *Ready to live checklist*

Holding on . . . While Letting Go *Reflections in Times of Grave Illness,* Joan E. Hemmenway

The Pilgrim Press, 1985, $1.75, paper, 24 pp., for counselees

Description Part of the Looking Up series of booklets from the Pilgrim Press. For the cost of a greeting card, this booklet provides the reader with 24 pages of insight, wisdom, Scripture readings, meditation, direction, comfort, and prayer.

Comfort and Care for the Critically Ill June Cerza Kolf

Baker Book House, 1993, $8.99, paper, 193 pp., for counselors

Description This book is intended for those who can no longer be medically cured. It provides hope and suggestions for comfort and measures that will keep the patient and family well cared for physically, emotionally, and spiritually in whatever time remains. An encouraging book for patients, pastors, counselors, doctors, nurses, hospice workers, and caregivers. Packed full of encouraging advice with lists of options and choices to allow for the greatest quality of life for each day remaining. Includes everything from using a bag of frozen peas for comfort to directions on making funeral arrangements.

Author June Cerza Kolf has spent many years working with the terminally ill and grieving. Presently she directs volunteers for a home health care agency in California and leads support groups and workshops on grief. She is a member of the Elisabeth Kübler-Ross Center, and the National Hospice Organization and serves on the board of the High Desert Unit of the American Cancer Society. Her work can be seen in trade journals and inspiration publications including *Guideposts* and the *Christian Reader.*

Contents *Part 1:* The patient *1.* The physical aspect *2.* The emotional adjustment *3.* The spiritual approach *Part 2:* The caregiver *4.* Caring for yourself *5.* Caring for the patient *6.* Making final arrangements *7.* Understanding death

My Friend Is Dying *Prayers and Reflections,* Mary E. Latela

Ligouri Publications, 1993, $3.95, paper, 64 pp., for counselees

Description A particularly well-done prayer guide for those with a Christian loved one dying. Thirty meditations contain Scripture and Psalm readings, prayers, and reflections on themes such as: we have nothing to fear, God keeps us safe, we can and must trust in the Lord, and God helps us prepare to say our goodbyes.

Toward My Father's House *Hope-Filled Meditations for the Terminally Ill,* Mary Jane Mason

Ligouri Publications, 1993, $3.95, paper, 53 pp., for counselees

Description Brief meditations designed for the terminally ill. A Scripture passage and several paragraphs of prose encourage the terminally ill to hope in God throughout their struggle. Thirty meditations dealing with topics such as bitterness, grief, courage, acceptance, darkness, longing, peace, trust, and grace.

Meditations for the Terminally Ill and Their Families Judy Osgood

Gilgal Publications, 1989, $6.95, paper, 72 pp., for counselees

Description Opens the doors on a taboo subject in a gentle, loving way that encourages discussion when loved ones want to talk about everything and can't find the words to say anything. It is a book filled with ideas for living the end of one's life without regrets, a book that counselors can use to help patients face reality, a book to help those new to the field understand what dying people and their loved ones need, and a book to help the dying relate to God before it's too late.

Author Judy Osgood serves as editor of this work and three others on bereavement. She became involved in the bereavement field after her teenaged son's death from chemotherapy complications. Her research revealed the need for books written on specific types of grief by those who had experienced it and led to the Gilgal Meditation series.

Into Thy Hands Robert W. Rae

Herald Press, 1988, $1.95, paper, 16 pp., for counselees

Description Prepares one for dying. It is divided into three areas: Practical preparation for dying; completion of cherished relationships; and spiritual preparation for heaven. *Into Thy Hands* urges readers to affirm Jesus' question "Do you believe that God can give you deathless life through me?" It offers a prayer of faith suitable for the reader's response.

Author Robert W. Rae is a retired Presbyterian minister, a graduate of McCormick Theological Seminary, Chicago, Ill. He has served Presbyterian churches in Minnesota and Iowa. He has had several works published by Herald Press.

Help for Families of the Terminally Ill
Mildred Tengbom

CPH Publishing, 1983, $3.95, paper, 48 pp., for counselees

Description This sensitive, loving work offers families of terminally ill patients practical means of coping and triumphing over this potentially devastating ordeal. Tengbom outlines choices people have in a clear, concise, and understanding manner. She offers common sense advice about coun-

seling opportunities, self-help methods, and assistance from social service agencies. It also serves as a biblical reference center, pinpointing the spiritual hope and encouragement Christian families need to face in this demanding situation.

Author Mildred Tengbom has written 20 books and has served as a missionary for 17 years.

Contents *1.* "I can't believe it" *2.* You always have a choice *3.* Shall we tell our loved one? *4.* "Doctor, my question is . . ." *5.* Taking care of unfinished business *6.* Caught on an emotional roller coaster *7.* Living while dying: setting new goals *8.* Relationships *9.* Exploring every possible cure *10.* How can I help my loved one? *11.* Children's special needs *12.* Help for you *13.* Home or hospital? *14.* New problems *15.* Finally / Bible readings that assure us of God's comfort and help / Bible readings that assure us of life after death

Fear No Evil *One Man Deals with Terminal Illness,* David Watson

Harold Shaw Publishers, 1992, $7.99, paper, 178 pp., for counselees

Description Watson shares his pain, fear, and uncertainty with his own battle with terminal illness while maintaining courage, faith, and overflowing love for God.

The Courage to Care *Helping the Aging, Grieving, and Dying,* Jeffrey A. Watson

Baker Book House, 1992, $10.99, paper, 186 pp., for counselors

Description *Courage to Care* integrates the biblical theology of aging, grief, and death with the significant findings from the behavioral sciences on the respective topics. *Courage to Care* includes powerful case studies, statistics, charts, graphs, discussion questions, endnotes, bibliography, and subject index. The author of *Courage to Care* is an accomplished pastoral practitioner with 14 years of experience in parish counseling, hospice, hospital/nursing home chaplaincy, and the training of clinical/pastoral caregivers. He holds theological degrees from both Protestant and Roman Catholic graduate schools as well as behavioral science credentials from a secular university. The Scripture is eloquent in its trilogy of metaphors: "The grass withers . . . the flower fades . . . but the Word of God stands forever." Dying mankind, like a withering meadow, is described through a historical/theological model in Part 1. Dying individuals, like fragile flowers, are described through a pastoral/psychological model in Part 2. But the ever en-livening Word of God, woven throughout the fabric of the whole book, points to true hope and life in Jesus Christ.

Author Senior minister of Grace Bible Church in Seabrook, Md., professor of gerontology at Washington Bible College, consultant in bioethics & chaplaincy. Former pastoral care at Prince George's Hospital and at the Joseph Richey Hospice. Graduate of Capital Bible Seminary, Catholic University, and Dallas Theological Seminary. Engaging seminar speaker.

Contents *Part 1:* Biblical caregiving *1.* Why should we face aging, grief, and death *2.* How the Old Testament helps us face aging, grief, and death *3.* How the New Testament helps us face aging, grief, and death *Part 2:* Personal caregiving *4.* The fear of death *5.* The grief of loss *6.* The pain of suicide *7.* The challenge of aging *8.* The mentoring of children *9.* The care of sufferers / *For further reading*

Happily Ever After *Coping with Terminal Illness,* Richard Youkey and Eunice Youkey

College Press, 1993, $3.95, paper, 56 pp., for counselees

Description The story of how one Christian prepared to spend an eternity with God. When Richard Youkey discovered that he was dying of cancer, he treated his approaching death as a weekend trip. How to face the reality of imminent death to the praise and glory of God.

Living Fully with a Life-Threatening Illness

Abbey Press, $.50 each, paper, 8 pp., for counselees

Description Part of the CareNotes series from Abbey Press. CareNotes are short booklets that help readers identify issues and begin the process of seeking resolution. Anecdotal and uplifting. Beautiful photographs grace the covers. Over 20 million CareNotes have been sold in just over five years. Can be used as an alternative to a greeting card or in conjunction with pastoral care visits.

Making a Loving Life-Support Decision

Abbey Press, $.50 each, paper, 8 pp., for counselees

Description Part of the CareNotes series from Abbey Press. CareNotes are short booklets that help readers identify issues and begin the process of seeking resolution. Anecdotal and uplifting. Beautiful photographs grace the covers. Over 20 million CareNotes have been sold in just over five years. Can be used as an alternative to a greeting card or in conjunction with pastoral care visits.

Using Hospice Care When a Loved One Is Dying

Abbey Press, $.50 each, paper, 8 pp., for counselees

Description Part of the CareNotes series from Abbey Press. CareNotes are short booklets that help readers identify issues and begin the process of seeking resolution. Anecdotal and uplifting. Beautiful photographs grace the covers. Over 20 million CareNotes have been sold in just over five years. Can be used as an alternative to a greeting card or in conjunction with pastoral care visits.

Children's Hospice International

Children's Hospice International. An organization

Description (Secular) Seeks to coordinate support systems and a referral network for seriously ill children and their families and for those who have encountered the sudden loss of a child through accident or violence. Operates a clearinghouse so that information on research, programs, support groups, and education and training programs can be more readily assimilated and disseminated.

HOSPICELINK

Hospice Education Institute. An organization

Description Networking organization (secular) that supports a national hospice directory and various counseling services.

National Hospice Organization

National Hospice Organization. An organization

Description Networking organization for hospice providers and information about hospice.

23. Lay Counseling

Ready to Restore *The Layman's Guide to Christian Counseling,* Jay E. Adams

P & R Publishing, 1981, $6.95, paper, 120 pp., for counselors

Description Here at last is a guide to Christian counseling written specifically for laymen. Although this work is simple and easy to use as a beginning textbook, unlike many other books it is neither simplistic nor superficial. Its contents are the fruit of the author's arduous Bible study as well as his long and successful ministry of the Word in counseling.

Author Dr. Adams is the author of numerous books on Christian counseling. He has served on a seminary faculty (Westminster Theological) and in the pastorate. He is founder of Christian Counseling and Educational Foundation in Laverock, Pa., and visiting professor of practical theology at two seminaries.

Contents *1.* Who should counsel? *2.* Goals, attitudes, and dangers *3.* What is counseling? *4.* Ready to restore *5.* What about unbelievers? *6.* The counseling process *7.* 25 basic principles *8.* Discipline: a two-edged sword *9.* Help on data gathering *10.* A biblical analysis of the problem *11.* Finding the biblical solution *12.* Implementing a biblical plan *13.* Follow through: working the plan *14.* Using homework *15.* Problems frequently faced *16.* How to grow as a counselor

Telling the Truth to Troubled People *A Manual for Christian Counselors,* William Backus

Bethany House Publishers, 1985, $9.99, paper, 256 pp., for counselors

Description A manual for Christian counselors providing background information, counseling techniques, terminology, and a scriptural basis for bringing counseling back into the church. Integrates biblical and psychological (cognitive) facts. Includes case histories, dialogue exchanges, and review questions at the end of each chap-

ter. Intended for use as a text for a lay counseling class. Encourages supervised training.

Author William Backus is a licensed clinical psychologist and an ordained Lutheran clergyman. He is founder and director of the Center for Christian Psychological Services, St. Paul, Minn., and an associate pastor of a large Lutheran church.

Contents *Part 1:* Counseling and the Christian church *1.* So you want to be a counselor! *2.* Counseling belongs in the church *Part 2:* Discernment, diagnosis, and change *3.* Looking under the skin *4.* Planning treatment in advance *5.* What you should know about tests *6.* The limits of counseling *7.* What do we mean by abnormal? *8.* Truth, the fiery core of counseling *9.* Get a new mind *10.* "In the beginning—God": the first interview *11.* What do you do for a whole hour? *12.* Terminating with a future and a hope *Part 3:* Counseling for common disorders *13.* Anxiety disorders *14.* Depression *15.* Anger *16.* "My doctor says it's psychological" *17.* Obsessive-compulsive disorders *18.* Schizophrenia *19.* Bipolar (manic-depressive) disorders *20.* The antisocial personality *21.* Sexual deviation

How to Help a Heartbroken Friend *What to Do and What to Say When a Friend Is Going Through Tough Times,* David B. Biebel

Thomas Nelson Publishers, 1993, $8.99, paper, 180 pp., for counselors

Description A down-to-earth guide for comforting those who hurt. This book teaches people to be true soul mates. Appropriate for individual or group study, with thought-provoking questions for reflection and discussion.

Author David B. Biebel (M.T.S./D.Min., Gordon Conwell Theological Seminary) is ordained in the Evangelical Free Church of America. He has served in a variety of pastoral and para-church roles including Focus on the Family, where he edited the *Physician* magazine. He has written or collaborated on seven books.

Contents *1.* What to say when you don't know what to say *2.* A loneliness that must be shared *3.* An emptiness that must be filled *4.* Healing the wounds on their own terms *5.* Becoming your friend's soulmate *6.* Life goes on *7.* What to do when you don't know what to do *8.* Somebody to hold me *9.* To tell the truth *10.* Moving with the pain *11.* Beauty for ashes *12.* Seven habits of highly effective comforters

You Can Make a Difference *Changing Situations That Hurt Others,* Betty Bock

New Hope, 1993, $6.95, paper, 116 pp., for counselors

Description Provides guidelines for advocacy in regard to people such as the aging, persons with disabilities, persons with AIDS, divorced individuals, abuse and rape survivors, the homeless, and persons in poverty.

What You Can Say When You Don't Know What to Say *Reaching Out to Those Who Hurt,* Lauren Littauer Briggs

Harvest House Publishers, 1985, $5.99, paper, 169 pp., for counselors

Description Your invitation to share the forgiving, healing love of Jesus Christ. This book will provide positive solutions to difficult situations and help you know how and when to share your concern and God's understanding.

Author Lauren Littauer Briggs sparkles with vibrant love for people. She is a frequent speaker at Christian leaders and speakers seminars where she shares her sensitivity and insights into the hurts of others.

Contents *1.* I don't know what to say *2.* Tears that taught me how to comfort *3.* Understanding the hurting *4.* Becoming comforters *5.* Difficult decisions *6.* The first two steps in comforting *7.* The third step *8.* Practical ways to help *9.* Help with the funeral *10.* Picking out a card *11.* Long-term help *12.* The loss of a child *13.* The loss of a home *14.* The loss of two fathers *15.* The loss of a mother *16.* The loss of a brother *17.* The forgotten griever *18.* Be there! / *Appendix:* How to form a support group

Counselors, Comforters and Friends *Establishing a Caregiving Ministry in Your Church,* Shelley Chapin

Victor Books, 1992, $9.99, paper, 168 pp., for counselors

Description This book explores both the biblical foundations and practical concerns of establishing a caregiving ministry in your church, and it does so with someone who has experienced the need firsthand. Shelley Chapin has lived with cancer since 1982 and has worked to help many churches build a caring community. Among the

topics discussed are Jesus' ministry of comfort, qualifications of caregiving, creating and maintaining a caregiving program, and building support groups. This book also features a complete appendix, listing supportive ministries in the community, important phone numbers, helpful books, and other resources for the caregiver.

Author Shelley Chapin is a family counselor, author, musician, teacher, and conference speaker. She holds a master's degree from Dallas Theological Seminary and is enjoying doctoral studies in the field of counseling.

Contents *Section 1:* Exploring the need for comfort *1.* The reality of suffering, grief, and death *2.* The basic needs of those who suffer *3.* The need for comfort within the church *Section 2:* Exploring the ministry of comfort *4.* The comfort we have received *5.* Jesus' ministry of comfort *6.* The many faces of comfort *Section 3:* Dealing with grief and depression *7.* The colorful world of emotions *8.* A closer look at grief *9.* A closer look at depression *10.* Comforting those who suffer *Section 4:* Establishing a ministry of care within the church *11.* A willing heart and a desire to serve *12.* Recruiting the volunteers *13.* A sample training program *14.* Details and maintenance of the program *15.* The ongoing role of the minister *16.* Support groups and the church *Section 5:* A storehouse of information / *A:* Supportive ministries in the community at large/ *B:* Books and other resources

How to Be a People Helper—Revised and Updated *Insights That will Help You Help Your Friends, Family and Co-workers,* Gary R. Collins

Tyndale House Publishers, 1995, $8.99, paper, 208 pp.

Description Over 200,000 copies sold. This classic best-seller is now revised and updated for a new generation. Enables readers to be more sensitive to the needs of others. Supplemented with an index for easy reference.

Author Gary R. Collins, Ph.D., is a clinical psychologist and president of the American Association of Christian Counselors, the largest organization for religious therapists in the country.

Encouragement *The Key to Caring,* Larry Crabb and Dan B. Allender

Zondervan Publishing House, 1990, $8.99, paper, 144 pp., for counselors

Description "Encourage one another" says the book of Hebrews. But encouragement is much more than a pat on the back. Encouragement is the most basic form of counseling—a skill that can be mastered by laypeople as well as counselors. This book shows you how to be an encourager. Includes such practical "how to's" as: developing a careful selection of words, cultivating active listening skills, using biblical fellowship to break through the surface community of self-satisfied smiles and shallow greetings, recognizing opportunities for encouragement.

Authors Dr. Crabb is director of biblical counseling and chairman of the Department of Biblical Counseling at Colorado Christian University in Morrison, Colo. He earned his Ph.D. in clinical psychology from the University of Illinois in 1970. He is the author of numerous books on self-understanding and counseling technique. Dan Allender is an associate with the Institute of Biblical Counseling and professor of counseling at Colorado Christian College. He is the author of *Bold Love.*

Contents *1.* Introduction *2.* The power of a well-timed word *3.* Surface community: the obstacle to encouragement *4.* Total openness—the wrong solution *5.* Total commitment—the right solution *6.* The character of an encourager *7.* When do we tell somebody else how we feel? *8.* How encouragement works *9.* Encouragement—the context for change *10.* Opportunities for encouragement *11.* Responding to opportunities *12.* Techniques for encouragement *1 13.* Techniques for encouragement *2 14.* The local church—a restoring community

Wise Counsel *Skills for Lay Counseling,* John W. Drakeford and Claude V. King

LifeWay, 1988, $9.95, paper, 213 pp., for counselors

Description Practical training in 13 sessions for lay leaders to learn basic counseling skills for use in daily situations. A basic ten-step counseling model helps participants learn to counsel families, singles, youth, seniors, and those in crisis. A leader's guide is also available ($4.95) as is a video ($99.95).

Contents *Introduction:* Group covenant about the authors *Unit 1:* The lay counseling ministry *Unit 2:* Identify the problem *Unit 3:* Determine an action plan *Unit 4:* A fundamental skill—listening *Unit 5:* Building relationships *Unit 6:* Expectations and boundaries *Unit 7:* Counseling sick and grieving persons *Unit 8:* Marriage and family counseling *Unit 9:* Providing guidance for behavior change *Unit 10:* Counseling youth *Unit 11:* Resentment, guilt, and suicide *Unit 12:* Counseling through group experiences

The Counsel of a Friend *Your Personal Counseling Handbook for Reaching Those in Need,* Lynda D. Elliott

Janet Thoma (a division of Thomas Nelson), 1993, $12.99, paper, 352 pp., for counselors

Description A definitive handbook on counseling a friend as well as specific advice on how to handle depression, anger, fear, or illness. Offers instruction on how to give support to friends without giving too much or fostering dependency. Includes what to say, how to listen, how to provide a climate for change, what to do if there is no change, and how to keep from overidentifying.

Author Lynda D. Elliott has a B.S. in psychology from the University of Alaska and is a licensed social worker.

Contents *Part 1:* The willing heart *1.* But I don't know what to say! *2.* Won't someone listen to me? *3.* What if they won't change? *4.* More what if's . . . ? *Part 2:* The helping heart *5.* Depression *6.* Anger *7.* Fear and worry *8.* Grief *9.* Betrayal *10.* Abuse *11.* Bitterness *12.* Guilt *13.* Self-esteem *14.* Illness *15.* Temptation *Part 3:* The steadfast heart *16.* How to persevere through the problem *17.* The dimension of spiritual warfare *18.* The importance of celebration

The Handbook of Christian Counseling *A Practical Guide,* Timothy D. Foster

Thomas Nelson Publishers, 1995, $14.99, paper, 288 pp.

Description Extremely practical no-nonsense guide for those who counsel. By giving strategies for comforting, confronting, and bringing about positive change, Foster gives readers everything they need to counsel others in this revised and updated version of *Called to Counsel.*

Author Timothy Foster, Ph.D., is senior psychologist for the Department of Labor and Employment Security for the state of Florida. He has a private practice in Tampa and Clearwater, Fla.

Contents *1.* Getting started *2.* The counselor *3.* The counseling process *4.* Counseling do's and don'ts *5.* How emotions work *6.* The limitations of counseling *7.* A positive mental attitude *8.* The most common marriage problems *9.* Marriage counseling issues *10.* Dealing with grief *11.* Counseling spiritual problems *12.* Counseling family problems *13.* Closing words to pastors *14.* Closing words to pastors' wives *15.* Closing words to lay counselors

The Christian Counselor's Pocket Guide
Selwyn Hughes

Bethany House Publishers, 1985, $3.99, paper, 96 pp., for counselors

Description Almost 50,000 copies of this handy pocket guide have been sold. This new edition includes further insights and additional Scripture references to help the Christian in responding to questions that are most often asked about the Christian life and personal problems.

Author Selwyn Hughes is the founder/director of Crusade for World Revival. A minister for over 25 years, he has given a great deal of time and research to the subject of personal counseling. He is responsible for the counselor training program at Waverly Abbey House in England.

Contents *Section 1:* Difficulties of the unconverted *Section 2:* Christian problems (emotional difficulties) *Section 3:* Intellectual excuses

How Can I Help? *A Christian's Guide to Personal Counseling,* W. H. Skip Hunt

Janet Thoma (a division of Thomas Nelson), 1994, $14.99, paper, 288 pp., for counselors

Description A complete training workbook with interactive materials to prepare volunteers for hospital or home visitation, support group counseling, and church supported helplines or crisis centers. Integrates spiritual counseling, evangelism, and biblical counseling techniques.

Author W. H. Skip Hunt is founder and board chairman of Christian Helplines, a network of 40 telephone helpline crisis centers.

Contents *Part 1:* Personal counseling *1.* How can I help? *2.* Integrated counseling model *3.* Reach out with ARMS I *4.* Reach out with ARMS II *5.* HELP solve the problem I *6.* HELP solve the problem II *7.* Put the counseling responses in practice *Part 2:* Personal evangelism *8.* LOVE them to Christ: Part 1, the home run presentation *9.* LOVE them to Christ: Part 2, the power of personal testimony *10.* LOVE them to Christ: Part 3, the two triangle presentation *11.* Know what you believe *12.* CARE to confront *13.* Follow Christ: volunteer and serve him *Part 3:* Appendixes: course syllabus, Christian Helplines, Inc., Christian telephone counseling

Caring for Emotional Needs Phyllis J. Le Peau

InterVarsity Press, 1993, $4.99, paper, 64 pp., for counselors

Description Part of the seven-title Caring People Bible Studies from InterVarsity Press. Seven study guides and an introductory handbook cover all the basics of caregiving—from developing the character traits of caring to dealing with tough needs like depression, grief, and illness. Perfect for churches starting a caregiving program, groups ministering in hospitals and to shut-ins, or laypeople helping a friend through a crisis.

Author Phyllis J. Le Peau is a registered nurse and a former Nurses Christian Fellowship staff member. Currently, she is assistant program director for Wellness, Inc.

Contents *1.* Caring for the whole person (1 Ki. 19:1–18) *2.* Caring for those who worry (Phil. 4:4–9) *3.* Caring for those who are fearful (Matt. 14:22–33) *4.* Caring for those who are lonely (2 Tim. 4:6–22) *5.* Caring for those who are angry (Eph. 4:1–3, 25–32) *6.* Caring for those who are bitter (1 Sam. 18) *7.* Caring for those who are depressed (Ps. 42) *8.* Caring for those who have low self-esteem (Mark 9:33–35) *9.* Finding emotional wholeness (Gal. 5:16–25)

Caring for People in Conflict Phyllis J. Le Peau

InterVarsity Press, 1993, $4.99, paper, 64 pp., for counselors

Description Part of the seven-title Caring People Bible Studies from InterVarsity Press. Seven study guides and an introductory handbook cover all the basics of caregiving—from developing the character traits of caring to dealing with tough needs like depression, grief, and illness. Perfect for churches starting a caregiving program, groups ministering in hospitals and to shut-ins, or laypeople helping a friend through a crisis.

Author Phyllis J. Le Peau is a registered nurse and a former Nurses Christian Fellowship staff member. Currently, she is assistant program director for Wellness, Inc.

Contents *1.* Causes of conflict (Jas. 4:1–12) *2.* The healing community (Acts 6:1–7) *3.* Humbling yourself (Gen. 13) *4.* Confronting others (Matt. 18:15–20) *5.* Admitting wrong (Ps. 51) *6.* Forgiving ourselves (Acts 7:54–8:3; 9:1–31) *7.* Forgiving others (Gen. 37 & 45) *8.* Waiting for forgiveness (Acts 15:36–41) *9.* Moving on (Matt. 26:31–35)

Caring for People in Grief Phyllis J. Le Peau

InterVarsity Press, 1993, $4.99, paper, 64 pp., for counselors

Description Part of the seven-title Caring People Bible Studies from InterVarsity Press. Seven study guides and an introductory handbook cover all the basics of caregiving—from developing the character traits of caring to dealing with tough needs like depression, grief, and illness. Perfect for churches starting a caregiving program, groups ministering in hospitals and to shut-ins, or laypeople helping a friend through a crisis.

Author Phyllis J. Le Peau is a registered nurse and a former Nurses Christian Fellowship staff member. Currently, she is assistant program director for Wellness, Inc.

Contents *1.* Facing your own death (Ps. 90) *2.* Overcoming the fear of death (Heb. 2:9–18) *3.* Offering comfort (Jn. 11:17–44) *4.* Offering peace (Jn. 14:1–7) *5.* Offering hope (Rev. 14:1–7) *6.* Offering grace (2 Cor. 4:7–5:8) *7.* Saying goodbye to an elderly friend (Gen. 48:1–12; 49:22–50:14) *8.* Dealing with a child's death (2 Sam 12:15–23) *9.* The gift of good grief (1 Thess. 4:13–18)

Caring for Physical Needs Phyllis J. Le Peau

InterVarsity Press, 1993, $4.99, paper, 62 pp., for counselors

Description Part of the seven-title Caring People Bible Studies from InterVarsity Press. Seven study guides and an introductory handbook cover all the basics of caregiving—from developing the character traits of caring to dealing with tough needs like depression, grief, and illness. Perfect for churches starting a caregiving program, groups ministering in hospitals and to shut-ins, or laypeople helping a friend through a crisis.

Author Phyllis J. Le Peau is a registered nurse and a former Nurses Christian Fellowship staff member. Currently, she is assistant program director for Wellness, Inc.

Contents *Part 1:* Understanding physical needs *1.* God cares for physical needs (Matt. 6:25–34) *2.* Caring for the whole person (Ps. 32) *3.* Praying for healing (Jas. 5:13–20) *4.* Why suffering? (Gen. 3:1–21) *Part 2:* Meeting physical needs *5.* The paralytic (Mark 2:1–12) *6.* Naaman, the leper (2 Ki. 5:1–15) *7.* Mephibosheth (2 Sam 9:1–13) *8.* A hungry crowd (Matt 14:13–21)

Caring for Spiritual Needs Phyllis J. Le Peau

InterVarsity Press, 1993, $4.99, paper, 62 pp., for counselors

Description Part of the seven-title Caring People Bible Studies from InterVarsity Press. Seven study guides and an introductory handbook cover all the basics of caregiving—from developing the character traits of caring to dealing with tough needs like depression, grief, and illness. Perfect

for churches starting a caregiving program, groups ministering in hospitals and to shut-ins, or laypeople helping a friend through a crisis.

Author Phyllis J. Le Peau is a registered nurse and a former Nurses Christian Fellowship staff member. Currently, she is assistant program director for Wellness, Inc.

Contents *1.* What are spiritual needs? (Ps. 38) *2.* Recognizing spiritual needs (Matt. 9:1–13) *3.* The need for a relationship with God (Rom. 5:1–11) *4.* The need for meaning and purpose (1 Pet. 1:1–16) *5.* The need to be loved and belong (1 Jn. 4:7–21) *6.* The need for assurance (Rom. 8:18–39) *7.* The need to persevere (Jas. 1:2–18) *8.* Caring for those who doubt (Luke 7:18–30) *9.* Caring for those in spiritual warfare (Eph. 6:10–20)

Character of Caring People, The Phyllis J. Le Peau

InterVarsity Press, 1993, $4.99, paper, 58 pp., for counselors

Description Part of the seven-title Caring People Bible Studies from InterVarsity Press. Seven study guides and an introductory handbook cover all the basics of caregiving—from developing the character traits of caring to dealing with tough needs like depression, grief, and illness. Perfect for churches starting a caregiving program, groups ministering in hospitals and to shut-ins, or laypeople helping a friend through a crisis.

Author Phyllis J. Le Peau is a registered nurse and a former Nurses Christian Fellowship staff member. Currently, she is assistant program director for Wellness, Inc.

Contents *1.* Called to care (Isa. 61:1–3) *2.* Faith (Gen. 22:1–19) *3.* Hope (Col. 1:15–29) *4.* Love (Luke 10:25–42) *5.* Generosity (2 Cor. 9: 6–15) *6.* Encouragement (Heb. 10:19–25) *7.* Hospitality (1 Pet. 4:7–11) *8.* Accepting our limits (Ex. 18:13–24)

Handbook for Caring People Phyllis J. Le Peau

InterVarsity Press, 1993, $4.99, paper, 62 pp., for counselors

Description Part of the seven-title Caring People Bible Studies from InterVarsity Press. Seven study guides and an introductory handbook cover all the basics of caregiving—from developing the character traits of caring to dealing with tough needs like depression, grief, and illness. Perfect for churches starting a caregiving program, groups ministering in hospitals and to shut-ins, or laypeople helping a friend through a crisis.

Author Phyllis J. Le Peau is a registered nurse and a former Nurses Christian Fellowship staff member. Currently, she is assistant program director for Wellness, Inc. Bonnie J. Miller is a staff member with Nurses Christian Fellowship and the creator of Love That Heals Seminars.

Contents *1.* Love that heals *2.* The person God uses *3.* Caring through forgiveness *4.* Communicating to people in need *5.* Caring for spiritual needs *6.* Caring for people who suffer *7.* Caring for people in crisis *8.* Caring for people in grief *9.* Letting God care for us *10.* Starting a support group / *Resource 1:* Record keeping / *Resource 2:* When professional help is needed

Resources for Caring People Phyllis J. Le Peau

InterVarsity Press, 1993, $4.99, paper, 58 pp., for counselors

Description Part of the seven-title Caring People Bible Studies from InterVarsity Press. Seven study guides and an introductory handbook cover all the basics of caregiving—from developing the character traits of caring to dealing with tough needs like depression, grief, and illness. Perfect for churches starting a caregiving program, groups ministering in hospitals and to shut-ins, or laypeople helping a friend through a crisis.

Author Phyllis J. Le Peau is a registered nurse and a former Nurses Christian Fellowship staff member. Currently, she is assistant program director for Wellness, Inc.

Contents *1.* Past experiences (2 Cor. 1:1–11) *2.* Healthy self-image (Jn. 13:1–17) *3.* Listening (Isa. 50) *4.* Obedience (Luke 22:39–53) *5.* Scripture (Ps. 19) *6.* Prayer (Luke 11:1–13) *7.* God's Spirit (Rom. 8:1–27) *8.* Christian community (Acts 4:23–37)

Counsel Yourself and Others from the Bible *The First Place to Turn for Tough Issues,* Bob Moorehead

Multnomah Books (Questar), 1994, $16.99, cloth, 284 pp., for both counselors and counselees

Description Focuses on the 33 most common questions and problems for which Christians seek counsel, including depression, marriage problems, bitterness, anger, and anxiety. Includes the most relevant Bible passages as part of the book text, as well as additional scriptural references.

Author Dr. Bob Moorehead is senior pastor of Overlake Christian Church in Kirkland, Wash., one of the largest churches in the Pacific Northwest.

He holds the Ph.D. from the California Graduate School of Theology.

When Someone You Know Is Hurting *What You Can Do to Help,* M. Gregory Richards

Harper Collins, 1994, paper, 239 pp., for counselors

Description Though not written from a distinctively Christian perspective, Richards offers this complete and compassionate guide to caring for others. He shows us what to do, what to say, and most of all, how to stand by our hurting friends in their times of crisis.

Author M. Gregory Richards is an Episcopal pastor living in Beverly Hills, Calif., with his wife and two sons. For 15 years he served a congregation that included many of Hollywood's notables.

Contents *Part 1:* Becoming more responsive to those you care about *1.* Be aware of your own feelings *2.* Act *3.* Be *Part 2:* Developing the tools of caring *4.* Become an effective listener *5.* Understand the emotions of grief *6.* Know available resources *Part 3:* Responding to crisis and loss *7.* At a time of death *8.* At the death of a child *9.* With the terminally ill *10.* At the hospital *11.* In crises of aging *12.* In financial crisis and unemployment *13.* With families facing breakup or abuse *14.* When dealing with chemical dependency and eating disorders *15.* When you are over your head

Introduction to Biblical Counseling George C. Scipione

Christian Counseling and Education Foundation, $195.55, 9 videos, 18 hours, for counselors

Description Filmed in a classroom setting, this video series will encourage and direct you and your congregation to become proficient in biblically addressing the difficulties faced daily by your members.

Author The Christian Counseling and Educational Foundation is associated with the nouthetic counseling movement.

To Love Mercy *Becoming a Person of Compassion, Acceptance, and Forgiveness,* C. Samuel Storms

NavPress, 1991, $10.00, paper, 189 pp., for counselors

Description Perhaps the biggest reason many of us are reluctant to minister to one another is that we simply don't know how. We don't understand what it means to "love mercy." On one level, this book is a "how-to" book. It contains the tools you'll need to care for the brokenhearted, encourage the downcast, and advise the ill-informed. Yet it's also a liberating book. As Dr. Storms explores the possibilities of extending care to others, he introduces the wonderful promise of experiencing it yourself.

Author Dr. C. Samuel Storms is an author, conference speaker, and the pastor of Christ Community Church in Ardmore, Okla. He holds a Th.M. from Dallas Theological Seminary and a Ph.D. from the University of Texas at Dallas.

Contents *1.* A pastor's confession *2.* Barriers to burden bearing *3.* God made us hungry *4.* But it sounds so selfish *5.* Do we blame it all on sin? *6.* The beginnings of mercy *7.* Is Jesus really enough? *8.* An ordinary man and his extraordinary love *9.* Where never is heard a discouraging word *10.* Meekness, rebounds, and licorice seeds *11.* God's second greatest gift *12.* The arithmetic of forgiveness *13.* Mercy in practice *14.* "Blessed are the merciful"

Family, Friends and Strangers Lowell D. Streiker

Abingdon Press, 1989, $9.95, paper, 220 pp., for counselors

Description A guide that shows the layperson how to offer good advice and effective care to others. Includes some rules for giving advice, a list of "don'ts" so you know what your limits are, and ways to deal with anger and depression, as well as methods for counseling your spouse, a neighbor, or a family member.

Peer Counseling Training Course, The
Revised by Joan Sturkie and Maggie Phillips

Resource Publications, Inc., 1991, $49.95, three-ring, 204 pp., for counselors

Description Divided into two sections. Section one of *The Peer Counseling Training Course* is designed to help students develop basic peer counseling skills. Section two helps students develop ways to put them to practice in the school setting.

Contents *Part 1:* Developing peer counseling skills *1.* Developing social ease *2.* An introduction to active listening *3.* Using active listening *4.* Sending effective messages *5.* Developing self-awareness *6.* Helping skills *7.* Values clarification *8.* Decision making *9.* Starting and ending a helping relationship *Part 2:* Using peer counseling skills *10.* Helping with school-related problems *11.* Counseling

students with attendance problems *12.* Peer relationships in school *13.* Dealing with family issues *14.* Peer counselors and drugs *15.* Death, loss and suicide *16.* Sexuality *17.* AIDS *18.* Codependency *19.* Eating disorders

Peer Helper's Pocketbook Joan Sturkie and Valerie Gibson

Resource Publications, Inc., 1992, $7.95, paper, 104 pp., for counselors

Description Fills a need for a quick, easy-to-read peer helping reference. Use this on-the-spot guide to look up information or review what to do in certain situations.

Authors Joan Sturkie is a nationally recognized author and peer counseling consultant. She is a popular motivational speaker. Valerie Gibson has a degree in urban studies. She has extensive experience in working with today's young people.

Contents *Introduction* / *1.* Tips: rules for helping peers / Meeting a stranger *2.* Skills: developing active listening skills / Responding to helpees / Sending effective messages / Practicing values clarification / Problem solving and decision making / Intervening in a crisis *3.* The helper–helpee relationship: initiating contact / Defining your role / Establishing trust / Being aware of boundaries *4.* Self-awareness: how to check your self-awareness / Questions to ask yourself *5.* Referrals: when to refer / Where to refer / Steps in referring / Mandatory reporting to authorities *6.* Covering the issues: suicide / Self-esteem / Child abuse / Family problems / Death and dying / Eating disorders / School problems / Peer pressure / Substance abuse / Teenage pregnancy *7.* Motivation

Lay Counseling *Equipping Christians for a Helping Ministry,* Siang-Yang Tan

Zondervan Publishing House, 1990, $12.99, paper, 256 pp., for counselors

Description A handbook on lay counseling including both overviews and how-to information for leaders and lay counselors themselves. Foreword by Gary Collins.

Author Siang-Yang Tan is director of the doctor of psychology and associate professor in the Graduate School of Psychology at Fuller Theological Seminary in Pasadena, Calif. He is a licensed psychologist with a Ph.D. in clinical psychology from McGill University.

Contents *1.* The need for lay counseling ministries *2.* Biblical basis for lay counseling *3.* A biblical model for effective lay counseling *4.* The literature of lay counseling *5.* Building a ministry of lay counseling *6.* Selection of lay counselors *7.* Training of lay counselors *8.* Supervision of lay counselors *9.* Evaluation of lay counselors *10* The local church and lay counseling *11.* Potential pitfalls in lay counseling *12.* Conclusions about lay counseling / *Appendixes:* postcounseling questionnaire—client / Postcounseling questionnaire—counselor / Some local churches with lay counseling ministries / Ethical standards for Christian counselors / Christian Association for Psychological Studies / Proposed code of ethics / Sample forms

How to Help the Hurting *When Friends Face Problems with Self-Esteem, Self-Control, Fear, Depression,* Everett L. Worthington Jr.

InterVarsity Press, 1985, $8.99, paper, 168 pp., for counselors

Description A follow-up book to *When Someone Asks for Help* (IVP 1982). Both books use a five-step approach to helping. Whereas the first book dealt with basic listening skills, this one deals with how to rethink and plan changes in five types of problems. The book is written in an engaging style and contains tables and flow charts that makes lay counseling or friendship helping easy. Abstract. Self-esteem, self-control, fear, depression, loneliness each receive two chapters. Conceptualizing for change and effecting change are treated accordingly.

Author Everett Worthington holds a Ph.D. in counseling from the University of Missouri-Columbia and has worked at Virginia Commonwealth University since 1978. As a licensed clinical psychologist, he has directed a community counseling agency, supervised others, and maintained a part-time private practice.

Contents *1.* Who me? Help others? *2.* I'm just a toad *3.* Improving self-image *4.* Wanted: self-control *5.* Winning the battle for self-control *6.* The tyranny of fear *7.* Calming the fearful *8.* Depression: a downward spiral *9.* Helping the depressed *10.* The pain of loneliness *11.* Defeating loneliness *12.* Helping others in crisis *13.* Thine is the power

When Someone Asks for Help *A Practical Guide for Counseling,* Everett L. Worthington Jr.

InterVarsity Press, 1982, $12.99, paper, 239 pp., for counselors

Description This book has sold over 40,000 copies. It has been used primarily by friends helping their friends with problems, but it has also been used in a variety of lay counseling courses. The book describes a five-stage format for helping and gives practical suggestions about how to act

at each stage. A sample dialogue is used throughout to illustrate.

Author Everett Worthington holds a Ph.D. in counseling from the University of Missouri-Columbia and has worked at Virginia Commonwealth University since 1978. As a licensed clinical psychologist, he has directed a community counseling agency, supervised others, and maintained a part-time private practice.

Contents *1.* Me, a helper? *2.* What is Christian helping? *3.* What are people like and what causes problems? *4.* Solving problems *5.* Communication problems *6.* Understanding emotions *7.* Messages that don't help *8.* Understanding your friend's problem *9.* Showing you understand *10.* Rethinking the problem *11.* Planning for change *12.* When the plan goes into effect *13.* The adventure of helping

Training Christians to Counsel H. Norman Wright

Harvest House Publishers, 1977, $16.99, paper, 225 pp., for counselors

Description A full course designed to be used for training lay counselors in the local church.

Author Dr. H. Norman Wright is one of America's best known Christian marriage and family counselors at the Family Counseling and Enrichment Center in Tustin, Calif. He is author of more than 50 books. He has also served on the faculty of Talbot School of Theology and the Graduate School of Marriage Counseling of Biola University.

Contents *Part 1:* Training manual *1.* Introduction to counseling *2.* Answers, observations, and goals of counseling *3.* The biblical framework for counseling *4.* A model for counseling I *5.* A model for counseling II *6.* A model for counseling III *7.* Ministering to the depressed person I *8.* Ministering to the depressed person II *9.* Helping the suicidal person I *10.* Helping the suicidal person II *11.* Counseling married couples I *12.* Counseling married couples II *13.* Ministering to the divorced person I *14.* Ministering to the divorced person II *15.* Ministering to the dying and bereaved person I *16.* Ministering to the dying and bereaved person II / Alternate session—Ministering to the sick—Hospital calling / Theological teaching in counseling / Bible study in counseling / Bibliography for counseling *Part 2:* Articles on counseling / Hazards to effective pastoral counseling I & II / Jesus' style of relating / Effective counseling and psychotherapy: an integrative view of research / Rapid treatment for a troubled marriage / Marriage therapy / The marriage conference / The growth model in marital therapy / Group procedures for increasing positive feedback / Counseling the homosexual

Call to Comfort *A Counseling Manual for Every Christian,* Tom Yarbrough

Resource Publications, Inc., 1988, $9.95, paper, 131 pp., for counselors

Description In *Call to Comfort,* you'll find the means to assist your fellow Christians when they are struggling. To be a lay counselor, you don't have to be a professional, but it is a serious call and you must know what you're doing. Yarbrough provides examples, technical information, and biblical support so that you can help troubled people.

Author Tom Yarbrough taught for 11 years at Oklahoma Baptist University and practiced private counseling for seven years in Arizona. He holds a doctor of counseling degree and has done many workshops in his field.

Contents *1.* Unexpected comfort/counseling *2.* Distress signals *3.* Signs of cover-up *4.* Troubled people *5.* Christian personality versus secular *6.* Quality comfort/counseling *7.* Dynamics of comforting *8.* Awesome objective *9.* Steps for specific comfort/counseling *10.* Manual of extra helps

Christian Counselor's Handbook, The

Tyndale House Publishers, 1991, $14.99, paper, 240 pp., for counselors

Description Whether used personally or in counseling others, this easy-to-use handbook provides scriptural answers to personal problems. Offers relevant Scriptures, summary of the problem, biblical perspectives, brief counseling ideas, and encouragements for prayer. Listed are more than 70 topics including divorce, faith, abortion, and prayer.

Stephen Ministries

Stephen Ministries. An organization

Description Since 1975, Stephen Ministries has set the pace in the area of lay caring ministry. Kenneth C. Hauck, an ordained Lutheran minister and a clinical psychologist, is the founder and executive director of Stephen Ministries. The Stephen series is a complete system of training and organizing laypersons for caring ministry in and around their congregations. The Stephen series serves over 4,000 congregations in over 60 different denominations. The ministry system is designed to be used by and to benefit laypeople regardless of their occupational, educational, or cultural experience.

24. Marital Crisis

Solving Marriage Problems *Biblical Solutions for Christian Counselors,* Jay E. Adams

> Zondervan Publishing House, 1986, $8.99, paper, 144 pp., for counselors

> **Description** A basic guide to addressing the many issues pastors and counselors come across in counseling couples. Nouthetic approach.

> **Author** Dr. Adams is the author of numerous books on Christian counseling. He has served on a seminary faculty (Westminster Theological) and in the pastorate. He is founder of Christian Counseling and Educational Foundation in Laverock, Pa., and visiting professor of practical theology at two seminaries.

> **Contents** *1.* Why marriage counseling is so important *2.* The counselor's own marriage *3.* What causes marriage problems? *4.* Unbiblical concepts of marriage: central errors *5.* Unbiblical concepts of marriage: related errors *6.* Sinful living patterns in general *7.* Particular sinful living patterns 1 *8.* Particular sinful living patterns 2 *9.* The importance of relationships with others *10.* Particular problem relationships 1 *11.* Particular problem relationships 2 *12.* General influences in society *13.* How to discover marriage problems *14.* Illusions and false solutions *15.* Basic aims in marriage *16.* Problems particular to sex roles 1—wives *17.* Problems particular to sex roles 2—husbands

The Fight-Free Marriage *The Conflict Without Casualty Strategy to a Satisfying Marriage,* Tom Anastasi

> Thomas Nelson Publishers, 1995, $12.99, paper, 256 pp.

> **Description** Teaches couples how understanding each other's personality types and using conflict resolution skills can help build satisfying and lasting relationships.

> **Author** Tom Anastasi is a psychologist, author, and professor in the department of organizational behavior at Boston University. He is also a practicing family therapist in New Hampshire.

The Ultimate Marriage Builder *A Do-It-Yourself Encounter Weekend for You and Your Mate,* Dave Arp and Claudia Arp

> Janet Thoma (a division of Thomas Nelson), 1994, $14.99, paper, 288 pp., for counselees

> **Description** A marriage renewal book for couples who would prefer not to attend a formal marriage retreat but still want the intimacy and openness the retreats offer. Includes sections on remembering, teamship, communicating, playing together, setting goals, and returning home.

> **Authors** Claudia Arp is a columnist for *Christian Parenting Today* magazine and cofounder with her husband of Marriage Alive International. Claudia and Dave Arp have written many popular books on marriage and the family.

> **Contents** *Part 1:* Before the getaway *1.* Saying yes to your marriage *2.* Setting the stage *Part 2:* The getaway *3.* Friday evening: rekindling the spark *4.* Saturday morning: vive la différence *5.* Saturday afternoon: fun and fresh air *6.* Saturday evening: romancing your mate *7.* Sunday: room to grow *Part 3:* Getaway enhancers *8.* The ultimate mini marriage builder menu *Part 4:* After the getaway *9.* Looking back and looking forward

When Caring Is Not Enough *Resolving Conflicts through Fair Fighting,* David W. Augsburger

> Herald Press, 1983, $6.95, paper, 196 pp., for counselees

> **Description** Provides clearly defined skills for fair fighting. Through the book readers will grow in their understanding of a just, fair, and trustworthy relationship. Explores 30 ways of working toward mutuality and equality.

> **Author** David Augsburger (Ph.D., School of Theology at Clairmont, Calif.) is professor of pastoral care at the Associated Mennonite Biblical Seminaries in Elkhart, Ind. He has authored many books (including *Conflict Mediation across Cultures: Pathways and Patterns* and numerous

books on recovery-oriented topics) and has had hundreds of articles published in magazines.

Newly Married *How to Have a Great First Year,* David Brown

Serendipity, 1990, $6.95, paper, 95 pp., for counselees

Description This is a 7- or 14-week course designed for those wanting to become a support group that discusses issues that arise for couples during their first year of marriage. Enables couples to get off to a great start in their life together. Strong use of Scripture and creative learning strategies.

Contents *1.* Setting up house *2.* Respectfully yours *3.* We can work it out *4.* Communicating heart-to-heart *5.* Sexual intimacy *6.* Enjoying life together *7.* Serving together

Torn Asunder *Recovering from Extramarital Affairs,* Dave Carder and Duncan Jaenicke

Moody Press, 1992, $16.99, cloth, 250 pp., for both counselors and counselees

Description Evangelical Christian or not, there's a 50-50 chance you or your spouse will have an extramarital affair by the time you're 40. This timely book helps the infidel and the spouse sort out the causes, get in touch with the hurts, vent the angers, and proceed with rebuilding trust and restructuring intimacy.

Authors Dave Carder (M.A., Calvary Bible College; M.A., Wayne State University) serves as assistant pastor for counseling ministries at the First Evangelical Free Church of Fullerton, Calif. With his wife he conducts marriage and family seminars. Duncan Jaenicke (B.A., University of Illinois) is acquisitions editor at Moody Press. He has done postgraduate work in psychology and counseling and frequently writes in these areas.

Contents *Section 1:* Understanding extramarital affairs *1.* "What God hath joined together": in pursuit of healing for shattered marriages *2.* Sorting out the chaos: the one-night stand and sexual addiction *3.* Sorting out the chaos: the entangled affair *4.* Causes: environments that encourage affairs to flourish *5.* Other factors contributing to infidelity *Section 2:* Healing from affairs *6.* Understanding the recovery: the infidel's process *7.* Understanding the recovery: the spouse's process *8.* Why? Deciphering the message of the affair *9.* Anger in affairs: getting good out of getting mad *10.* Can I trust you again? Rebuilding trust *11.* "And they shall be as one"—restructuring intimacy / *Epilogue:* To tell or not to tell? The secret affair / *Appendix A:* What to tell the kids / *Appendix B:* Materials for use with a couples' support group / *Appendix C:* Selected bibliography

Will the Defense Please Rest? *A Guide to Marital Harmony,* Les Carter

Baker Book House, 1986, $7.99, paper, 224 pp., for both counselors and counselees

Description The author draws from his wide experience as a marriage counselor to offer solid help. He goes beyond the ordinary suggestions for satisfying solutions to the problem of defensiveness.

Author Les Carter is a Christian psychotherapist who maintains an active counseling practice at the Minirth-Meier Clinic.

Contents *Part 1:* Identifying defensiveness *1.* Defensiveness is a choice *2.* Examine yourself *3.* The wide world of defensiveness *4.* Defensiveness becomes a habit *Part 2:* The causes of defensiveness *5.* Fragile ego—handle with care *6.* Good is never enough *7.* But I insist *8.* Anger: the troublesome emotion *9.* Marital myths *Part 3:* The pursuit of harmony *10.* The First Peter principle *11.* Let freedom ring *12.* Following the original game plan *13.* Keeping pride in check *Part 4:* The how to's of harmonious living *14.* A formula for harmonious communications *15.* Taking the initiative

Hope for the Separated *Wounded Marriages Can Be Healed,* Gary Chapman

Moody Press, 1992 (18th printing), $7.99, paper, 119 pp., for both counselors and counselees

Description A realistic and compassionate look at the problems and perspectives of separated couples, challenging them to explore reconciliation.

Author Gary Chapman (M.R.E., Ed.D., Southwestern Baptist Theological Seminary) has been the director of adult ministries at Calvary Baptist Church in Winston-Salem, N.C., since 1971. He is also the director of Marriage and Family Life Consultants, Inc. He is the author of several other works.

Contents *1.* What happened to our dream? *2.* Taking constructive action *3.* Self-development during separation *4.* Developing your relationship with God *5.* Developing your relationship with your mate *6.* Long distance love *7.* How will I handle the loneliness? *8.* What about my bitterness? *9.* If your spouse returns *10.* If your spouse demands a divorce *11.* Facing the future

Moving on After He Moves Out Jim Conway and Sally Conway

InterVarsity Press, 1995, $11.95, paper, 225 pp.

195

Description Jim and Sally Conway offer help to the abandoned woman and those around her—family members, therapists, friends—who want to help.

Authors Jim and Sally Conway have been teaching, pastoring, and counseling for over 30 years. They are cofounders of Mid-Life Dimensions and popular speakers.

Contents *Part 1:* The disintegration *1.* All dressed up—but nowhere to go *2.* The river of destruction *3.* The roses are dead, but the thorns are still out *Part 2:* The disposable woman *4.* When a woman becomes disposable *5.* The many faces of abandonment *6.* Why a woman becomes disposable *Part 3:* The recovery process *7.* Shock. *8.* Restore the relationship if possible *9.* From pain to acceptance *Part 4:* Rebuilding your life *10.* Legal issues *11.* Money and work *12.* Children *13.* Selfhood *14.* Dating and sex *Part 5:* Preventing abandonment *15.* Stop history from repeating itself / *Epilogue:* Whatever happened to Ann?

Traits of a Lasting Marriage *What Strong Marriages Have in Common,* Jim Conway and Sally Conway

InterVarsity Press, 1991, $9.99, paper, 262 pp., for both counselors and counselees

Description A book built upon research of 186 married couples to discover the factors that enabled the couples to experience long-term marriages. Ten traits are identified, and specific instruction is given so that couples or groups can develop these traits.

Authors Jim Conway holds five degrees in psychology and theology and is the author of many books. His wife, Sally Conway, holds an M.S. in human development. Together they own and operate Mid-Life Dimensions/Christian Living Resources, a nonprofit organization ministering to people at various stages of life through a variety of media formats.

Contents *Part 1:* A familiar pattern *1.* Stages of marriage *2.* Potential pitfalls *Part 2:* Ten traits of an intimate marriage *3.* A lifelong commitment *4.* Mutually satisfying communication *5.* Spiritual vitality *6.* Effective conflict resolution *7.* Energy from friends *8.* Sexual intimacy *9.* Time to laugh and play *10.* Realistic expectations *11.* Serving each other *12.* Alive and growing *Part 3:* Strengthening and rebuilding marriage *13.* Facing major problems *14.* Making your marriage better *15.* Rebuilding a crumbling marriage

When a Mate Wants Out *Secrets for Saving a Marriage,* Sally Conway and Jim Conway

Zondervan Publishing House, 1992, $15.95, cloth, 217 pp., for both counselors and counselees

Description A book built upon the 15 years of work the Conways have done with thousands of couples who are wanting to get divorced. Although well-researched and documented, the book focuses on the layperson who wants to save the marriage or as a help to the counselor who is working with severely dysfunctional marriages.

Authors Jim Conway holds five degrees in psychology and theology and is the author of many books. His wife, Sally Conway, holds an M.S. in human development. Together they own and operate Mid-Life Dimensions/Christian Living Resources, a nonprofit organization ministering to people at various stages of life through a variety of media formats.

Contents *Part 1:* At first . . . *1.* Don't panic *2.* Have hope *3.* Understand why this happened *4.* Listen and look selectively *5.* Vow to work hard *6.* Handle your mate's affair wisely *Part 2:* Meet your mate's needs *7.* Walk in your spouse's shoes *8.* Listen attentively to your spouse *9.* Deal with emotional clatter *10.* Consider the career pressure *11.* Build your mate's self-esteem *12.* Maintain "externals" *13.* Confront sparingly and practice patience *14.* Flex, change, and grow *Part 3:* Meet your needs *15.* Know your boundaries *16.* Esteem yourself *17.* Put yourself in God's hand *Part 4:* Together again at last *18.* Rebuild carefully *19.* Encourage hurts to heal *20.* Invest for a lifetime *Part 5:* To pastors and counselors *21.* Work toward restoration, not divorce

What to Do When You Find Out Your Wife Was Sexually Abused John Courtright and Sid Rogers

Zondervan Publishing House, 1994, $10.99, paper, 160 pp., for counselees

Description This book is written for the husbands of sexual abuse victims—men who are trying to cope with the fear, pain, confusion, and anger in living with a woman who is recovering from past sexual abuse.

Authors John Courtright is a sales director for Anderson Consulting. Dr. Sid Rogers is pastor of Grace Evangelical Free Church and adjunct professor at Talbot School of Theology. Both have dealt with past sexual abuse in their own marriages and now lead seminars for husbands of sexual abuse victims.

Contents *1.* When the past crashes into the present *2.* Early warning signs *3.* Ripples of chaos in a life of calm *4.* When her crisis becomes your crisis *5.* Have I become the enemy? *6.* Finding the emerald city *7.* A friend for all seasons *8.* Understanding the recovery process *9.* "You are the man" *10.* Playing your position *11.* Communicating terms of peace *12.* Doing what comes naturally

Marriage Builder, The *A Blueprint for Couples and Counselors,* Larry Crabb

Zondervan Publishing House, 1992, $8.99, paper, 192 pp., for both counselors and counselees

Description Dr. Crabb cuts to the heart of the biblical view of marriage: the "one-flesh" relationship. He argues convincingly that the deepest needs of human personality—security and significance—ultimately cannot be satisfied by a marriage partner. We need to turn to the Lord, rather than to a spouse, to satisfy our needs. This frees both partners for "soul-oneness," a commitment to minister to our spouses' needs rather than manipulating them to meet our own needs. With soul oneness comes renewed "body-oneness" where couples enjoy sexual pleasure as an expression and outgrowth of a personal relationship. Discussion questions have been added to aid couples who want to come to a deeper understanding of marriage.

Author Dr. Crabb is director of biblical counseling and chairman of the Department of Biblical Counseling at Colorado Christian University in Morrison, Colo. He earned his Ph.D. in clinical psychology from the University of Illinois in 1970. He is the author of numerous books on self-understanding and counseling technique.

Contents *Part 1:* The goal of marriage *1.* Oneness: what it is and why it is important *2.* Spirit oneness: who meets my needs? *3.* Soul oneness—manipulation or ministry? *4.* Soul oneness—communication, or what do I do when I'm angry? *5.* Body oneness—physical pleasure with personal meaning *Part 2:* Building the foundation *6.* Building block 1: grace *7.* Building block 2: commitment *8.* Building block 3: acceptance *Part 3:* Discussion guides for individual chapters

Men and Women *Enjoying the Difference,* Larry Crabb

Zondervan Publishing House, 1991, $15.99, paper, 224 pp., for both counselors and counselees

Description Men and women share a deadly problem that kills good relating. The problem is this: We are committed, first of all, to ourselves. Each of us holds fast to an overriding concern for our own well-being. Giving numerous examples from his counseling and speaking ministry, Crabb explores how we can turn away from ourselves

and toward each other, how we can become what he calls "other-centered." Dr. Crabb maintains that we are different in important ways that, if understood and honored, can lead to a deep enjoyment of one another, an enjoyment that can last forever.

Author Dr. Crabb is director of biblical counseling and chairman of the Department of Biblical Counseling at Colorado Christian University in Morrison, Colo. He earned his Ph.D. in clinical psychology from the University of Illinois in 1970. He is the author of numerous books on self-understanding and counseling technique.

Contents *Part 1:* Why relationships don't work: the problem men and women share *1.* What's wrong with our marriage? *2.* Facing ourselves honestly *3.* The real problem *4.* Surely I'm not that bad! *5.* Change is possible *6.* Celebrating forgiveness *Part 2:* How relationships do work: the difference men and women can enjoy *7.* A tough question *8.* Is there really a difference? *9.* Masculinity and femininity *10.* Unique ways to freely love *11.* Relating as men and women *12.* Enjoying the difference

Be-Good-to-Your-Marriage Therapy Kass Perry Dotterweich

Abbey Press, 1991, $3.95, paper, 68 pp., for counselees

Description A warm-hearted guide for couples who know the rules of love and romance but need occasional encouragement to rekindle the sparkle and joy of their love. Contains 30 simple, beautiful, and wonderfully illustrated "rules" to love and give and live by.

When You Don't Agree *A Guide to Resolving Marriage and Family Conflicts,* James G.T. Fairfield

Herald Press, 1988 (6th ed.), $6.95, paper, 240 pp., for counselees

Description An easy-to-read self-study book that helps readers understand the nature and causes of interpersonal conflict and leads step-by-step to a working understanding of Christ-centered conflict management. Unique in that each segment has self-study questions designed to give readers experience in the procedures and lead to more positive Christian living. Many practical stories. Counselors can hand this book to clients who are experiencing conflict in the family, on the job, or in the community. Widely used by Sunday school classes and small groups.

Author James Fairfield is known for his work in positive response generation, a term he developed for his clients in church and social agencies. A graduate of Eastern Mennonite Seminary, Fairfield is a consultant in communications.

Contents *Part 1:* Common conflict styles *1.* The presence of conflict *2.* Defining conflict *3.* Five conflict styles *4.* The long view of conflict *5.* Which style is more valuable? *6.* Analyze your progress *7.* In hope of change *Part 2:* Improving communication skills *8.* Some problems in speaking *9.* Meanings are inside *10.* Sending and perceiving a message *11.* Improving your sending skills *12.* The art of listening *13.* Analyze your progress *Part 3:* A larger love *14.* The different kinds of love *15.* The strength of self-giving love *16–19.* Skills of self-giving love *Part 4:* Confronting your problem *20.* Knowing your feelings *21.* The problem of anger *22.* "I" and "You" messages *23.* Helping the other person *Part 5:* Setting new conflict patterns *24.* Desiring to change *25.* Seven characteristics of creative conflict *26.* Some additional destructive conflict traits *27.* Plan for constructive conflict *28.* Improve on your conflict *Part 6:* Putting it together *29.* Where you have been *30.* Six equal rights *31.* Skills and integrity, a personal view

Courage to Love *When Your Marriage Hurts,* Gerald Foley

Ave Maria Press, 1992, $6.95, paper, 160 pp., for counselees

Description Focusing on relationship building, Foley invites couples to reconciliation, to rebuild trust, to learn the new skills necessary for healthy communication, and to grow spiritually through the lived reality of married life. He emphasizes ways to counter cultural trends that are detrimental to permanent marriage and a strong family life. Covers such crucial topics as self-awareness, conflict resolution, forgiveness, the stages of a relationship, and intimacy. Each chapter concludes with a reflection and questions that encourage dialogue and discussion between spouses.

Author Ordained a Roman Catholic priest in 1961 (M.A., St. Paul's Seminary; M.S.W., University of Minnesota). Served as director of Catholic charities agency, parish pastor, and marriage ministries including Catholic Engaged Encounter and Retrouvaille.

Contents *Part 1:* Resources for troubled marriages *1.* Sources of hope *2.* Who supports this couple in marriage? *Part 2:* Self-awareness and communication *3.* Will the real me please appear? *4.* I never knew you felt that way! *5.* He never talks to me! *6.* What did you just say? *Part 3:* Relationships *7.* Why all this misery? *8.* Who is the dirtiest fighter? *9.* Can I ever trust you again? *10.* Will you forgive me? *11.* How often should a couple make love?

Part 4: Spirituality *12.* Isn't it possible God could have made a mistake? *13.* Perfect love can make sacrifice a joy *14.* This is my body, given for you . . . *15.* What is most important in my life? *16.* Even roses have thorns

When Victims Marry *Building a Stronger Marriage by Breaking Destructive Cycles,* Don Frank and Jan Frank

Thomas Nelson Publishers, 1990, $9.99, paper, 208 pp., for counselees

Description Help and hope for couples struggling in their marriages due to victimization in their past. Specific steps to rebuild the marriage foundation and enhance intimacy.

Authors Jan Frank holds a master's degree in marriage, family, and child counseling and is the author of the best-selling *A Door of Hope.* Don Frank, her husband, is a high school teacher and gifted communicator.

Contents *1.a.* Faulty foundations—Jan *1.b.* Faulty foundations—Don *2.* Preparing the soil *3.* Who needs an architect? Or blueprints? *4.* Periodic inspections *5.* Plumbing check *6.* Repairing the foundation *7.* Framing the house *8.* Walls of support/walls of division *9.* Insulation vs. isolation *10.* Is the roof leaking? *11.* Homeowner's insurance *12.* Stumbling blocks to unity *13.* Dwelling in unity

Counseling and Marriage Ruby M. Friesen and DeLoss D. Friesen

Word Publishing, 1989, $15.99, cloth, 247 pp., for counselors

Description In this helpful and informative volume, the authors discuss intimacy, conflict management and prevention, confidentiality, spouse abuse, when to refer, separation, and divorce, and how to handle the termination of counseling. Part of the Resources for Christian Counselors series from Word.

Authors Ruby M. Friesen, Ph.D., is in private counseling practice with her husband, DeLoss D. Friesen, in Portland, Oreg.

Contents *1.* Beginning with the counselor *2.* Beginning with the counselee *3.* Individual approach vs. systems approach *4.* Setting the structure for hope *5.* What next? Decision strategies for the counselor *6.* The marital pyramid and the place of communication *7.* Conflict management: "Don't let the sun go down on your wrath" *8.* Helping your clients tell themselves the truth *9.* Intimacy: leaving and cleaving *10.* Intimacy: the emotional-physical connection *11.* Confidentiality in marriage counseling *12.* When to refer *13.* An ounce of prevention *14.* "To everything there is a season" *15.* Spouse abuse *16.* Separation and divorce *17.* Termination of counseling *18.* Premarriage counseling

The Dynamics of a Successful Marriage *A Do-It-Yourself Marriage Enrichment Course,* Gene Getz and Elaine Getz

Regal Books, 1988, video/book, 262 pp., for both counselors and counselees

Description Whether you are just beginning or are well along on your journey together as a married couple, this video seminar and accompanying book will help you discover the dynamics of a successful marriage. Couples can use this video seminar and book at home together or in a home study group with friends. Pastors can use this package in church as a married couples class or as a counseling tool.

Authors Dr. Gene Getz is senior pastor at Fellowship Bible Church—North, in Plano, Tex. He is director of the Center for Church Renewal in Dallas, Tex., and is also adjunct professor at Dallas Theological Seminary. Elaine Getz has served with her husband in full-time Christian ministry since 1956.

Contents *1.* Becoming one *2.* Breaking family ties *3.* Loving as Christ loved *4.* Submitting to each other *5.* Learning to love *6.* Understanding each other *7.* Meeting one another's sexual needs

Reclaiming the Dream Brian W. Grant

Abingdon Press, $9.95, paper, 176 pp., for counselors

Description A great resource for those who may be called into marriage counseling but are not professional counselors. The book helps you handle the different stages of the counseling relationship—the initial request for help, identifying the problem, referrals to professional care, and closure.

On the Brink of Divorce *6 Studies of Hope & Encouragement for Women Facing the Possibility of Separation,* Judy Hamlin

Victor Books, 1992, $4.99, paper, 64 pp., for both counselors and counselees

Description Part of the Searching for Answers series from Victor. Takes a look at removing painful scars, helping children in the middle of struggling marriages, and identifying causes for marriage on the brink. Offers reasons to hope for a lasting, fulfilled marriage. Utilizes an interactive format.

Author Dr. Judy Hamlin (Ph.D. in adult education/University of Southern Mississippi) is an authority on small groups and women's ministry.

Contents *1.* Removing the scars—forgiveness (I) *2.* Removing the scars—forgiveness (II) *3.* God has a plan for your life—patience! *4.* First things first—children *5.* Ground rules for a good marriage *6.* Light at the end of the tunnel—hope / *Leader's notes*

A Change of Heart *Restoring Hope in Marriage,* Donald R. Harvey

Baker Book House, 1993, $16.99, cloth, 224 pp., for counselors

Description Hope in a marriage rejuvenates commitment and replenishes love. It is rooted in the spiritual hope which enables Christians to persevere to the end. Without this life-giving ingredient, love and faithfulness will wither and die. Husbands and wives on the edge of throwing it all away can follow the godly principles set forth in this book. The happy result can be a change of heart and a marriage restored.

Author Donald R. Harvey, Ph.D., is currently a member of the graduate faculty at Trevecca College and maintains a counseling practice in Nashville, Tenn.

Contents *Introduction / Part 1:* The loss of hope *1.* Terri's story *2.* Not all the same story *3.* A progressive problem *4.* Giving up *5.* On the subject of hope *Part 2:* Restoring hope *6.* It can't be the way it was *7.* "I'm wrong" *8.* "I'm sorry" *9.* "I'm changed" *10.* "I'm committed" *Part 3:* Living the hope *11.* Facing forgiveness *12.* Extending trust *13.* A sow's ear *14.* A change of hearts

The Drifting Marriage *The Most Common Causes of Marital Failure among Christians,* Donald R. Harvey

Fleming H. Revell, 1988, $14.99, paper, 255 pp., for counselors

Description How to recognize and prevent the most common forms of marital failure among Christians. An important book for Christians who desire to enjoy a healthy marriage according to God's plan. Dr. Harvey gives you a clear picture of what marital failure is, provides an opportunity to prevent or change the "drifting" process in your marriage, and offers guidelines for fulfilling your Christian marital responsibilities.

Author Donald R. Harvey, Ph.D., is currently a member of the graduate faculty at Trevecca College and maintains a counseling practice in Nashville, Tenn.

Contents *Part 1:* The problem of drifting *1.* Drifting: the danger *2.* Profile of a failing marriage *3.* The nature of drifting *Part 2:* Contributions to drifting *4.* Avoiding sensitive issues *5.* Sensitivity and insensitivity *6.* The cares of this life *7.* Dealing with anger *8.* Pushed to extremes *Part 3:* How to prevent a drifting marriage *9.* Christian responsibilities *10.* Loving your mate *11.* Esteeming your mate *12.* Counseling: why, when, and who? / *Conclusions:* The future of Christian marriage

Surviving Betrayal: Counseling an Adulterous Marriage *A Clear Action Plan for Restoration,* Donald R. Harvey

Baker Book House, 1995, cloth

Description Offers help and guidance to those counseling couples affected by infidelity.

Author Donald R. Harvey, Ph.D., is currently a member of the graduate faculty at Trevecca College and maintains a counseling practice in Nashville, Tenn.

When the One You Love Wants to Leave *Guidance and Comfort for Those Facing Marital Crisis,* Donald R. Harvey

Baker Book House, 1993, $9.99, paper, 223 pp., for both counselors and counselees

Description Common sense, Bible-based principles that deal with extreme marital crisis. In this new edition, workbook pages are added to help individuals work through feelings. Advice for healing the badly bruised relationship.

Author Donald R. Harvey, Ph.D., is currently a member of the graduate faculty at Trevecca College and maintains a counseling practice in Nashville, Tenn.

Strengthening Marital Intimacy Ronald E. Hawkins

Baker Book House, 1991, $8.99, paper, 140 pp., for counselors

Description Shows couples how to grow together by applying biblical teachings on God's intentions for an intimate relationship. Questions for both husband and wife to answer are included to encourage an assessment of the current level of intimacy and its further development.

Author Ronald E. Hawkins, associate provost at Liberty University, is a former professor of counseling and pastor.

Contents *1.* God's design—the intimate marriage *2.* Intimacy: a goal for marriage *3.* Commitment: the foundation for marriage *4.* Commitment to wisdom's directions *5.* Commitment to reality *6.* Commitment to God's sovereignty *7.* Commitment to the other person *8.* Commitment to the control and enjoyment of sexuality *9.* Commitment to communication *10.* Commitment to companionship

Resolving Conflict in Your Marriage Bob Horner and Jan Horner

Regal Books, 1993, $9.99/$11.99, spiral, 138/124 pp., for both counselors and counselees

Description Part of the New HomeBuilders Couples series from Regal Books. A ready-to-use series that can be led by Christian couples in churches, in homes, and on retreats—without any training. This title helps couples turn conflict into love and understanding.

Authors Bob and Jan Horner are staff members of Campus Crusade for Christ and speakers at Family Life Conferences.

Contents *Introduction* / HomeBuilders principles / A word about resolving conflict *1.* Recognizing conflict *2.* Transparency *3.* Listening *4.* Confronting *5.* Forgiving *6.* A blessing for an insult / Where do you go from here?

Let's Have It Out *The Bare Bones Manual of Fair Fighting,* Arthur S. Hough

CompCare Publishers, 1991, $7.95, paper, 109 pp., for both counselors and counselees

Description Shows how to fight fair and clean with spouses, friends, family members, and co-workers. Describes a four-step process of fair fighting: 1. Approaching your partner; 2. Starting a fair chair fight; 3. Negotiation; 4. Ending the fight. Also defined are the foul plays of a dirty fight and how to deal with unfair partners.

Author Arthur S. Hough, Ph.D., is a widely recognized professor of communication at San Francisco State University and a dynamic workshop leader.

Contents *1.* What happens when we fight? *2.* The basic premise: a fair and caring partner *3.* How not to fight at all *4.* Before you fight *5.* Stage 1 *6.* Stage 2 *7.* Stage 3 *8.* Stage 4 *9.* A good, short-fair-chair fight *10.* The dirty fight *11.* Black belt fighting *12.* The anatomy of anger *13.* What to do if someone comes at you angry *14.* Feelings *15.* If this is fair-chair fighting, where are we now?

Goodbye Prince Charming—The Journey Back from Disenchantment *Creating the Marriage You've Always Wanted,* Eileen Silva Kindig

NavPress/Piñon Press, 1994, $10.00, paper, 212 pp., for counselees

Description Many couples enter marriage high on idealism and full of expectations. Then as years unfold, they find themselves mired in disappointment. By exploring the dangers of storybook thinking, the author guides women back from disenchantment and shows how to nurture trust and intimacy—the keys to a marriage worth staying committed to.

Author A woman who worked through disenchantment in her own marriage, Kindig is a freelance writer residing in Medina, Ohio. She and her husband have been married 23 years.

Contents *1.* Someday my prince will come *2.* Happily ever after? *3.* The princess stands alone *4.* Prince Charming in the sky *5.* Choosing trust, accepting risk *6.* Cycles of rage *7.* After the tears *8.* Goodbye, Prince Charming *9.* Ah, romance! *10.* Buried treasure

When You Disagree *Resolving Marital Conflicts,* Jack Mayhall and Carole Mayhall

NavPress, 1992, $2.00, paper, 22 pp., for both counselors and counselees

Description It is possible to have a good disagreement. In this booklet, you'll discover five ways to have a creative conflict, and you'll learn how to use disagreements to help you become better friends.

Authors Carole Mayhall (B.A., Wheaton College) is a popular conference speaker and author of numerous works. Jack Mayhall is on staff with the Navigators.

Love, Infidelity and Sexual Addiction *A Codependent's Perspective,* Christine A. McKenna

Abbey Press, 1992, $6.95, paper, 148 pp., for counselees

Description For persons with partners who are struggling with sexual addiction, this book offers hope and healing by dispelling the denial surrounding this disease and provides a practical 12-step system of spiritual and emotional self-

help. The author's spiritual approach is particularly fresh and inspirational.

Author Christine A. McKenna is the pen name for an established author in the area of addiction recovery with over 20 years' experience as a teacher and counselor.

Contents *1.* Introduction *2.* Sexual addiction *3.* Sexual coaddiction *4.* The shame-based family; the spiritually centered family *5.* Denial *6.* Signs of obsession *7.* Compulsive behavior *8.* Finding help: the solution *9.* A healthy relationship *10.* Forgiveness

Marriage Savers *Helping Your Friends and Family Avoid Divorce,* Michael J. McManus

Zondervan Publishing House, 1995, $14.99, paper, 352 pp.

Description Written to help churches learn creative ways to assist couples in establishing marital stability, saving struggling marriages, and building strong families.

Author Michael McManus is a syndicated newspaper columnist writing on issues of ethics and religion, a radio commentator on family-related news and a former *Time* magazine correspondent.

Contents *1.* America's churches: part of America's divorce problem *2.* The splintered American family *3.* The church: missing in action *4.* Helping keep your teenagers chaste *5.* Getting serious—help for the seriously dating couple *6.* A crucial need: weigh your relationship's strengths and weaknesses *7.* Marriage prep—help for the engaged couple *8.* Newlyweds: the honeymoon is over *9.* Marriage encounter: the best marriage saver *10.* Saving troubled marriages: marriage ministry, Retrouvaille, solution-oriented therapy *11.* Helping the separated, the divorced, and step families *12.* The need to reform divorce law and marriage law *13.* Community marriage policy: how to cut your town's divorce rate

Separated and Waiting *How to Find Direction and Comfort in the Midst of Marital Separation,* Jan Northington

Oliver Nelson (a division of Thomas Nelson), 1994, $9.99, paper, 192 pp., for both counselors and counselees

Description Uniquely designed to encourage men and women who are physically separated from their spouse and are waiting either for their marriage to be reconciled or to see their marriage end.

Author Jan Northington is a freelance writer and conference speaker.

Contents *1.* Choose to wait with a new attitude *2.* Choose to learn *3.* Choose to grieve *4.* Choose to look at your value 5. Choose to stop worrying 6. Choose to get serious with God 7. Choose to balance your life 8. Choose to stay in touch with God 9. Choose to thrive

The Myth of the Greener Grass J. Allan Petersen

Tyndale House Publishers, 1989, $8.99, paper, 222 pp., for both counselors and counselees

Description A family counselor speaks frankly about extramarital affairs and offers both preventative and healing measures.

Author Dr. J. Allen Petersen is a well-known family counselor and seminar speaker, and founder and president of Family Concern, Inc.

Contents 1. Is anyone faithful anymore? 2. Rooftop romance 3. Why do partners cheat? 4. Marriage myths and legends 5. Lead us not into temptation 6. It happened—now what? 7. Untangling the triangle 8. Anatomy of an affair 9. Affair-proof your marriage 10. A road to recovery

Healing the Hurt of Infidelity William Rabior

Ligouri Publications, 1991, $.75, paper, 23 pp., for counselees

Description This booklet succinctly offers suggestions to heal the harsh wounds associated with infidelity. It shows how those hurt by infidelity in marriage can replace anger and mistrust with love and understanding. It contains eight proven "Techniques for Survival" which have saved many marriages. The booklet offers the information needed to start rebuilding a marital relationship following the experience of infidelity and offers ways to save a damaged marriage.

Author William Rabior is a Catholic priest and registered clinical social worker who has done extensive marriage and family counseling.

Marriage Makers—Marriage Breakers
Counseling for a Stronger Relationship, William Rabior and Jack Leipert

Ligouri Publications, 1992, $4.95, paper, 111 pp., for counselors

Description In this book, two pastors who are also clinical social workers, Rev. Bill Rabior and Rev. Jack Leipert, combine nearly 30 years of marriage counseling experience to offer this treasure chest of practical advice, ideas, and insights. Part 1 alerts readers to the marriage breakers which can eat away at their sacred bond. Using exam-

ples from the lives of the couples they have counseled, the authors offer practical suggestions to help spouses work together to minimize threats like unresolved anger, poor communication skills, and lack of shared spiritual values. In Part 2, marriage makers, the authors offer workable approaches that enhance the making of a good marriage. Readers will discover how good fighting strategies, humor, and play can keep marriage vibrant and exciting.

Authors Both authors are Catholic pastors and clinical social workers with extensive background in marriage and family counseling. They have spoken across the United States on marriage and family enrichment and the healing of troubled relationships.

Contents *Part 1:* Marriage breakers / Anger / Poor communication skills / Lack of quality time together / Stinkin' thinkin' / Lack of shared spiritual values *Part 2:* Marriage makers / Exceptions and miracles / Good ways to fight / Humor, play, and ritual / Marriage and the Ten Commandments / Marriage and the Beatitudes

Your Marriage—Making It Work *Ten Consumer-Tested Principles for a Lasting Marriage,* Peg Rankin and Lee Rankin

Lion Publishing, 1986, $6.99, paper, 144 pp., for counselees

Description Down-to-earth help for every couple that wants a lasting and loving relationship. Every chapter finishes with a "How do you rate?" self-quiz that gives you a chance to decide how you want to put this information to use. Anecdotal and illustrated.

Authors Team Bible teachers conducting seminars in victorious living, laypeople ministering to laypeople. Lee Rankin is a full-time corporate executive joining his wife on weekends for seminar engagements. Peg Rankin is a Christian speaker in demand nationally and internationally, presenting up to 250 lectures annually on a variety of topics.

Contents 1. How do you choose? 2. Getting down to business—living out your vows 3. Learning to communicate 4. Learning to forgive 5. The insult of infidelity 6. Establishing roles and responsibilities 7. Building a successful partnership 8. The spice of life—those little things 9. Total commitment

Pastor, Our Marriage Is in Trouble *A Guide to Short-Term Counseling,* Charles L. Rassieur

The Haworth Pastoral Press, 1992, $19.95, paper, 129 pp., for counselors

Description An experienced counselor outlines a step-by-step approach that takes the pastor from beginning to end in a process of short-term intervention and counseling.

Author Charles L. Rassieur is a minister and licensed consulting psychologist who serves as counselor for seminarians and church professionals in the Minneapolis/St. Paul area.

Contents *1.* Introduction to pastoral marriage counseling *2.* Initiating short-term marriage counseling *3.* Individual sessions with each spouse *4.* Concluding joint sessions *5.* Special concerns in marriage counseling / *Pastoral marriage counseling questionnaire*

Marriage Crises Randy Reynolds and David Lynn

Zondervan Publishing House, 1992, $4.99, paper, 96 pp., for both counselors and counselees

Description Part of the Recovery Discovery series of workbooks. This title covers some of the basic patterns in which couples get stuck, offering help and hope to troubled marriages.

Ounce of Prevention *Divorce Proofing Your Marriage,* Gary Richmond and Lisa Bode

Vine Books, 1995, $9.95, paper, 273 pp.

Description Marriage and family experts identify deadly patterns of relating that can destroy a marriage. Describes 30 "red flags" that may signal trouble ahead.

Authors Gary Richmond is a pastor at First Evangelical Free Church in Fullerton, Calif. Lisa Bode is a licensed marriage, family, and child counselor practicing in Anaheim, Calif.

Contents *1.* Great expectations, no expectations *2.* He made them male and female *3.* A person of substance: commitment and integrity *4.* Making marriage a priority *5.* Building trust *6.* Staying inside the lines: establishing boundaries *7.* A journey into deepening friendship: developing intimacy *8.* Keeping romance alive *9.* Growing together: managing differences *10.* Arguing for fun and profit: conflict resolution *11.* I'm in charge here! *12.* Keeping in-laws in line *13.* Unwanted surprises: sexual dysfunction and sexual deception *14.* Echos from Eden: family of origin issues *15.* The seventh commandment: concerning adultery *16.* Breaking the cycle: verbal, physical, and sexual abuse / *Appendixes*

Christian Men Who Hate Women *Healing Hurting Relationships,* Margaret Josephson Rinck

Zondervan Publishing House, 1990, $8.95, paper, 208 pp., for both counselors and counselees

Description Dr. Rinck examines in detail how misogynistic (men who hate women) relationships begin, what happens in these relationships, and how both parties contribute to the dysfunction. Defines misogyny and misogynistic relationships, provides therapeutic treatment suggestions, explains the church's role in misogynistic relationships.

Author Dr. Margaret Josephson Rinck is a clinical psychologist in private practice in Cincinnati, Ohio. She periodically conducts psychotherapy groups for "Women Who Love Too Much." She has numerous courses and audio programs on skills training and interpersonal relationships.

Contents *1.* The dilemma of submission and abuse *2.* The misogynist *3.* Women who marry misogynists *4.* Issues in the Christian marriage *5.* Root problem: shame and fear of abandonment *6.* A word to the man/a word to the woman *7.* The woman in therapy and treatment *8.* The misogynist in therapy and treatment *9.* The steps to recovery *10.* What can the Christian community do? / *Appendixes A–E*

Why Some Christians Commit Adultery *Causes and Cures,* John Sandford

Victory House Publishing, 1990, $9.95, paper, 205 pp., for counselors

Description Endeavors to show helping professionals how to avoid pitfalls and traps that can lead to spiritual and physical adultery. Topics covered: spiritual adultery, idolatry, defilement, attachments, transference, and unhealed inner hurts and fractures that can lead to adultery. Provides help and hope for the believer who wants to stand in the face of overwhelming sexual compulsions. It opens the door to forgiveness and wisdom for one who has been hurt by leaders who have fallen.

Author John Sandford is a veteran counselor with over 35 years' experience. He is author/coauthor of more than seven best-selling titles that relate to recovery and inner healing.

Contents *Section 1:* Personal causes and cures for sexual sins *1.* Spiritual adultery, affairs, and physical adultery *2.* Defilement, affairs, and adultery *3.* Attachments, transferences, affairs, and adultery *4.* Fornication, affairs, and

203

adultery 5. Pornography, voyeurism, fantasy, and masturbation *Section 2:* Historical, theological, and cultural causes 6. Historical causes for sexual sins 7. Theological and cultural causes for sexual sins 8. Contemporary theological imbalances that cause sexual sins and other sins

Communicating in Marriage Judson J. Swihart

InterVarsity Press, 1981, $.99, paper, 31 pp., for counselees

Description Discusses basic communication skills and offers a series of exercises for building them.

Marriage Inventory Bob Tippie

Maret Software International, $99.99, software, for both counselors and counselees

Description Designed for marriage counseling. Covers areas in the premarital inventory with the addition of a "resentment category."

Author Bob Tippie is an ordained Baptist minister with an active counseling and consulting practice. He holds a bachelor's degree in psychology and a master's in pastoral counseling.

Contents Communication / Sexual issues / Financial issues / Roles and authority / Views toward divorce / Home of origin / Emotional stability / Interpersonal relationships / Abuse/dysfunction indicators / Resentment indicators

Broken Promises *Understanding, Healing, and Preventing Affairs in Christian Marriages,* Henry A. Virkler

Word Publishing, 1992, $15.99, cloth, 306 pp., for counselors

Description Part 1 tries to answer the question, "How do people, including even deeply committed Christians, become involved in affairs?" Integrating the ideas from a large group of writers, the author develops a model that lists ten major ways and reasons people become involved in adultery. Part 2 gives practical advice on counseling a couple during and after an affair has occurred. This section may also be helpful to Christians who discover their spouse has been or continues to be involved in an affair. Part 3 gives suggestions for couples and pastors on strengthening and affair-proofing marriages.

Author For 15 years, Virkler was involved in Christian counseling in the Atlanta area. During the same period he taught at the Psychological Studies Institute, a Christian counselor training program. He presently teaches in the psychology and counseling programs at Liberty University.

Love Life for Every Married Couple *How to Fall in Love, Stay in Love, Rekindle Your Love,* Ed Wheat and Gloria Oakes

Zondervan Publishing House, 1980, $8.99, paper, 246 pp., for counselees

Description This book tells couples how they can fall in love, build love, or rekindle lost love. Dr. Wheat discusses such subjects as the thrill of romantic love, how to become best friends, how to sexually love your partner, how to stay in love, and the prescription for a superb marriage. He also directs a chapter to those persons who, without help from their partner, want to save their marriage at all costs.

Author Ed Wheat, M.D., a family physician, now retired and disabled, from 1952–1988. He completed his medical degree at the University of Arkansas in 1951. He has authored six books and directed Scriptural Counsel, Inc.—a life and marriage counseling service.

Contents *1.* A love affair—it can happen to you *2.* Discoveries—the false and the true *3.* Does the plan still work? *4.* Love—solving the mystery *5.* The five ways of loving *6.* How to love your partner sexually *7.* Romantic love—the thrill factor *8.* The gift of belonging *9.* Becoming best friends *10.* The agape way *11.* The secret of staying in love *12.* A pattern for lovers *13.* Prescription for a superb marriage *14.* Removing the barriers *15.* How to save your marriage alone *16.* Resources for change

When It's Hard to Trust Steve Wilke, Dave Jackson, and Neta Jackson

Tyndale House Publishers, 1991, $3.99, paper, 144 pp., for both counselors and counselees

Description Based on the Recovery of Hope Counseling Program, this book recounts the experiences of those who rebuilt their marriages after a devastating affair.

Authors Dr. Steve Wilke is a licensed clinical psychologist and the founder of the Recovery of Hope Counseling Program, which operates nine counseling centers in the United States. Dave and Neta Jackson are freelance writers and editors.

Contents *1.* Change her? Change him? No, change me *2.* Seeds of destruction, seeds of hope *3.* But is he trustworthy? *4.* Can you ever trust again? *5.* What is recovery of hope?

When We Can't Talk Anymore Steve Wilke, Dave Jackson, and Neta Jackson

Tyndale House Publishers, 1991, $3.99, paper, 144 pp., for both counselors and counselees

Description Couples facing disillusionment will find strength from these inspiring true stories of forgiveness and hope following years of conflict.

Authors Dr. Steve Wilke is a licensed clinical psychologist and the founder of the Recovery of Hope Counseling Program, which operates nine counseling centers in the United States. Dave and Neta Jackson are freelance writers and editors.

Contents *1.* What's the matter? Have a bad day? *2.* Married singles *3.* Intimate strangers *4.* Talking that works *5.* What is recovery of hope?

Hope for Troubled Marriages *Overcoming Common Problems and Major Differences,* Everett L. Worthington Jr.

InterVarsity Press, 1993, $9.99, paper, 175 pp., for both counselors and counselees

Description This book has over 500 practical suggestions for improving one's marriage. The book opens by helping couples develop a positive vision for their marriage. It then involves a self-assessment of the marriage and encourages readers to skip the sections of the book where they feel they do not need improvement and focus on the areas where they do. It demonstrates how to fix fractured communication patterns, find healthy ways to negotiate conflict, grow beyond blaming one another, confess and forgive, rediscover intimacy, discover a new level of commitment, and find restoration after infidelity.

Author Everett Worthington holds a Ph.D. in counseling from the University of Missouri-Columbia and has worked at Virginia Commonwealth University since 1978. As a licensed clinical psychologist, he has directed a community counseling agency, supervised others, and maintained a part-time private practice.

Contents *1.* A positive vision of marriage *2.* The blurred vision—what causes marital breakdown? *3.* A vision of healing *4.* Bringing the vision into focus *5.* Preparing to change *6.* Confession and forgiveness *7.* Closeness *8.* Communication *9.* Resolving conflict *10.* Assigning and accepting responsibility *11.* Commitment

I Care about Your Marriage *Helping Friends and Families with Marital Problems,* Everett L. Worthington Jr.

Moody Press, 1994, $8.99, paper, 293 pp., for counselors

Description Written by a professional psychologist, this training manual teaches you how to provide practical, biblical help.

Author Everett L. Worthington Jr. (Ph.D., University of Missouri) is married and has four children. An experienced marriage counselor, he is the author of numerous other books on marriage counseling.

Contents *Part 1:* Understanding the need for marital helping *1.* Help, I have marriage problems *Part 2:* Understanding marriage *2.* The cause of marriage problems *3.* Where problems surface *4.* Helping after marriage *5.* Helping prevent divorce or deal with divorce and remarriage *Part 3:* Understanding yourself as a marriage helper *6.* Evaluate yourself *7.* Mistakes helpers make *8.* Become a people helper *Part 4:* Understanding how to start helping with marriage problems *9.* Bird's eye view of helping *10.* Have a positive attitude *11.* Use your own marriage as a positive model *12.* Stay cool in marital crises *13.* Stick with long-term problems *Part 5:* Understanding how to help improve marriage *14.* Help strengthen the Christian core *15.* Help build closeness *16.* Help promote communication *17.* Help resolve conflicts *18.* Help change negative thinking *19.* Help cope with complicating problems *20.* Help partners forgive *21.* Help strengthen commitment *Part 6:* Understanding the necessity of hope *22.* Hope—even for the most troubled marriages

Marriage Conflicts *A Short-Term Structured Model,* Everett L. Worthington Jr. and Douglas McMurry

Baker Book House, 1994, $17.99, cloth, 178 pp., for counselors

Description Part of the new Strategic Pastoral Counseling Resources from Baker Book House. Designed to help pastoral counselors accomplish more in fewer sessions. Unique in several respects—each title has a separate parallel book the counselee reads during the week for added support and reinforcement. Includes a clear, step-by-step approach for the counselor, a structured holistic and spiritual focus, and an explicitly Christian foundation. This title compels husband and wife to stop and rethink their entire way of looking at one another. They discuss how to assess the problem, promote confession and forgiveness, attain a new vision for the marriage, and motivate constructive attitudes. The companion book is *Value Your Mate.*

Authors Everett L. Worthington Jr. holds a Ph.D. in psychology from the University of Missouri and is professor of psychology at Virginia Commonwealth University. Douglas McMurry is pastor of Christ Presbyterian Church, Richmond, Va. He formerly worked as a psychiatric social worker in Scotland.

Contents *Part 1:* Overview of strategic pastoral counseling for marriage conflict *1.* The need for strategic pastoral marital counseling *2.* The strategy and the model *Part 2:* Three stages of strategic pastoral counseling for marriage conflicts *3.* Encounter stage: promoting a healing relationship *4.* Engagement stage: assessing problems *5.* Engagement stage: history and healing *6.* Engagement stage: the Christian core *7.* Engagement stage: four essential elements *8.* Engagement stage: covenant and commitment *9.* Disengagement stage: moving back to pastoral care *Part 3:* Application *10.* A suggested five-session plan *11.* Case examples

Marriage Counseling *A Christian Approach to Counseling Couples,* Everett L. Worthington Jr.

InterVarsity Press, 1989, $17.99, paper, 382 pp., for counselors

Description This book integrates theory and practice of marriage counseling with Christians. It tells counselors what to do, how to do it, and why. It suggests and gives examples of practical techniques. The book has been used by many training programs, seminaries, Christian universities, and professional schools, including some secular graduate programs. A 1990 finalist for the Christian Book Publisher's Gold Medallion Award in the text reference category. The final appendix summarizes secular theories of marital counseling from a Christian perspective. Combines cognitive-behavioral and family systems theory into a practical manual for counseling. Problems are conceptualized in terms of the major need people have (for meaning) and two derived needs (intimacy and control). A Christian framework for marriage is presented. Assessment, joining, directives, initiating change, promoting forgiveness, commitment, and counseling termination are covered.

Author Everett Worthington holds a Ph.D. in counseling from the University of Missouri–Columbia and has worked at Virginia Commonwealth University since 1978. As a licensed clinical psychologist, he has directed a community counseling agency, supervised others, and maintained a part-time private practice.

Contents *Part 1:* Introduction *1.* The need for marriage counseling by and for Christians *Part 2:* Understanding marriage *2.* Individuals and their coupling *3.* Principles of marriage within the family *4.* The marriage throughout the family life cycle *Part 3:* Early phase of counseling troubled marriages *5.* Overview of counseling, assessment, intervention, and termination *6.* Joining the couple *7.* Assessing the marriage *8.* Setting goals *9.* Conducting assessment and feedback sessions *Part 4:* Changing troubled marriages *10.* Promoting change through counseling *11.* Changing intimacy *12.* Changing communication *13.* Changing conflict *14.* Changing hurt, blame, and sin *Part 5:* Promoting commitment *15.* Consolidating changes *16.* Termination *17.* Commitment of the counselor / *Appendix:* Current theories of marriage counseling

Value Your Mate *How to Strengthen Your Marriage,* Everett L. Worthington Jr. and Douglas McMurry

Baker Book House, 1994, $7.99, paper, 123 pp., for counselees

Description Part of the new Strategic Christian Living Resources from Baker Book House. Designed to help counselees make quick progress during therapy sessions. Corresponds to a separate parallel book the counselor uses as a basis for the counseling. This title compels husband and wife to stop and rethink their entire way of looking at one another and think through the eight dimensions of successful marriages. The companion book is *Marriage Conflicts.*

Authors Everett L. Worthington Jr. holds a Ph.D. in psychology from the University of Missouri and is professor of psychology at Virginia Commonwealth University. Douglas McMurry is pastor of Christ Presbyterian Church, Richmond, Va. He formerly worked as a psychiatric social worker in Scotland.

Contents *1.* The valley of trouble *2.* The pattern *3.* Value *4.* Faith in Jesus *5.* Christianity *6.* Core vision of marriage *7.* Confession and forgiveness *8.* Closeness *9.* Communication *10.* Conflict management *11.* Cognition *12.* Covenant and commitment

After You Say "I Do" *A Marriage Manual for Couples,* H. Norman Wright, Wes Roberts, and Judy Roberts

Harvest House Publishers, 1979, $7.99, paper, 80 pp., for both counselors and counselees

Description This study manual has been designed to assist you in making your marriage a fulfilling and growing relationship. Material was drawn from various national marriage enrichment seminars.

Authors Dr. H. Norman Wright is one of America's best known Christian marriage and family counselors at the Family Counseling and Enrichment Center in Tustin, Calif. He is author of more than 50 books. He has also served on the faculty of Talbot School of Theology and the Graduate School of Marriage Counseling of Biola University. Wes Roberts is president of Life Enrichment in Denver, Colo. He has served as director of the counseling ministry of a church. His wife, Judy, is a registered nurse and has led numerous seminars on home management and marriage enrichment.

Contents *1.* What is marriage? *2.* Uniqueness and acceptance in marriage *3.* Love as a basis for marriage *4.* What did you expect from marriage? *5.* Goals in marriage *6.* Fulfilling needs in marriage *7.* Roles, responsibilities, and decision making *8.* In-laws or out-laws—it's your choice *9.* Communication *10.* Conflict or "sound the battle cry" *11.* Sex in marriage

Communication: *Key to Your Marriage,* H. Norman Wright

Regal Books, 1974, $9.95, paper, 194 pp., for both counselors and counselees

Description His ideas are ready to help you not just talk about communication but to do it. If you're married you will learn to communicate at new and deeper levels and to understand your mate better. If you're planning marriage, you will learn to avoid lots of typical pitfalls trapping thousands of couples today. A leader's guide is also available.

Author H. Norman Wright has taught at Biola University and has been on the faculty of Talbot Theological Seminary. He is founder and director of Christian Marriage Enrichment and Family Counseling Enrichment in Tustin, Calif.

Contents *1.* What is a "Christian" marriage? *2.* Who's in charge here? *3.* How do you make it work? *4.* What was that I never heard you say? *5.* Why can't we talk about it? *6.* Is anger always a no-no? *7.* How to handle anger *8.* The high cost of anxiety *9.* How to cope with conflict *10.* Communicate to build self-esteem

How to Change Your Spouse *Without Ruining Your Marriage,* H. Norman Wright and Gary Jackson Oliver

Servant Publications/Vine Books, 1994, $16.99, cloth, 250 pp., for both counselors and counselees

Description This book will help readers learn to tell the difference between manipulating and bringing out the best in their spouse, learn to ask instead of complain, understand how gender differences affect a relationship and what to do about it, master a step-by-step approach to making peace and resolving conflict, and discover how the MBTI can be an excellent tool for getting along with a spouse.

Authors Dr. H. Norman Wright has been counseling couples for more than 30 years. Gary J. Oliver, Ph.D., is clinical director of Southwest Counseling Associates.

Contents *1.* Can you change your spouse? *2.* Roadblocks to change *3.* Creating the climate for change *4. & 5.* We are different, aren't we? *6.* It takes all types *7.* How'd you reach that conclusion? *8.* You're either and "in-y" or an "out-y" *9.* Learning to speak your partner's language *10.* Conflict: the pathway to intimacy *11.* If you married a perfectionist or controller *12.* How to change your spouse *13.* How'd they do that?

Marriage Counseling *A Practical Guide for Pastors and Counselors,* H. Norman Wright

Gospel Light Publishing, 1995, $19.99, cloth

Description H. Norman Wright's classic book has been updated to provide the latest information to counselors and pastors. Here are solid, practical, biblical steps that will help you develop a highly effective, focused approach to marriage counseling.

Author Dr. H. Norman Wright is one of America's best known Christian marriage and family counselors at the Family Counseling and Enrichment Center in Tustin, Calif. He is author of more than 50 books. He has also served on the faculty of Talbot School of Theology and the Graduate School of Marriage Counseling of Biola University.

Marriage Counseling *How to Support the Couples in Your Church,* H. Norman Wright

Gospel Light Video, $49.95, video, 2 hours, for counselors

Description A must see for pastors and leaders who want to brush up or learn some effective tools for helping couples stay together. A two-tape set. Part of the Counselor Training Video series.

He Wins, She Wins *Turn the Battle for Control in Your Marriage into a Win-Win Partnership,* Glenn P. Zaepfel

Oliver Nelson (a division of Thomas Nelson), 1994, $16.99, cloth, 256 pp., for both counselors and counselees

Description Deals with power games and leadership/submission issues in the marital relationship.

Focuses on ways spiritual truth can be distorted to manipulate a marriage partner and how to heal hurts caused by destructive power struggles.

Author Dr. Glenn P. Zaepfel is founder and president of Columbia Counseling Center in Columbia, S.C. He is a licensed counseling psychologist and licensed professional counselor.

WESCOM, Inc.

WESCOM, Inc. An organization

Description Assists in the establishment of support groups that focus on marital infidelity.

25. Midlife Crisis

Baby Boomer Blues *Understanding and Counseling Baby Boomers and Their Families,* Gary R. Collins and Timothy Clinton

Word Publishing, 1992, $15.99, cloth, 272 pp., for counselors

Description Part of the new Contemporary Christian Counseling series from Word. Provides an analysis of the baby-boomer phenomenon. Addresses the timeless Christian values that challenge every population segment while indicating how boomers can adjust their dreams to reality and move into midlife with the axis of biblical principles of growth.

Authors Dr. Gary Collins, a licensed psychologist, is editor both for this series and for Resources for Christian Counseling. Former professor of psychology at Trinity Evangelical Divinity School, he is also executive director of the American Association of Christian Counselors. Dr. Timothy Clinton is associate dean at Liberty University.

Contents *Part 1:* Understanding baby boomers *1.* Who are the baby boomers? *2.* Baby boomer careers *3.* Baby boomer values *4.* Baby boomer families *5.* Baby boomer religion *6.* Baby boomer followers: the baby busters *Part 2:* Counseling baby boomers *7.* Connecting with baby boomers *8.* Counseling approaches with baby boomers *9.* Marriage counseling with baby boomers *10.* Personal counseling with baby boomers *11.* Spiritual counseling with baby boomers *Part 3:* Reaching the baby boomers *12.* Helping baby busters and the children of baby boomers *13.* Helping parents of baby boomers *14.* The future of baby boomers

Men in Mid-Life Crisis Jim Conway and Sally Conway

Chariot Family Publishing, 1992, $8.95, paper, 316 pp., for counselees

Description A well-researched and documented book intended to help people understand the mid-life development era and how to help clients and counselees work through this time. The book is also useful as a self-help tool for the in-

dividual in crisis. Over 500,000 copies in print in six languages.

Authors Jim Conway holds five degrees in psychology and theology and is the author of many books. His wife, Sally Conway, holds an M.S. in human development. Together they own and operate Mid-Life Dimensions/Christian Living Resources, a nonprofit organization ministering to people at various stages of life through a variety of media formats.

Contents *Part 1:* It's for real *1.* The crisis *2.* Expert opinions *3.* Believe me, it really happens *Part 2:* Inside the man *4.* The cultural squeeze *5.* Second adolescence *6.* The enemy horde *Part 3:* Dead end roads *7.* Depression *8.* A new self *9.* Early retirement *10.* The affair *11.* Escaping the affair *12.* A new God *Part 4:* Life is progressive *13.* Adults keep developing *14.* This crisis came to pass *Part 5:* The wife's crisis *15.* Bewildered at 35 *16.* Barren at 50 *Part 6:* Unavoidable concerns *17.* The marriage knot *18.* In love again *19.* A sexy marriage *20.* Work that's fun *21.* Aging with finesse *22.* Children in transition *23.* Parenting in parents *24.* Creative retirement *25.* Sooner or later *Part 7:* Help is on the way *26.* We can help *27.* A man helps himself

Women in Mid-Life Crisis Jim Conway and Sally Conway

Tyndale House Publishers, 1988, $10.99, paper, 394 pp., for counselees

Description A book that resulted from the research in Jim Conway's Ph.D. and Sally Conway's M.S. at the University of Illinois. Although well documented and researched, the book is also intended for lay readers. The developmental evaluation of the woman in her late 30s or early 40s is not to be confused with her menopausal passage that will occur in her late 40s or early 50s. The late 30s crisis is very similar to a man in midlife crisis. Over 150,000 copies in print in two languages.

Authors Jim Conway holds five degrees in psychology and theology and is the author of many books. His wife, Sally Conway, holds an M.S. in human development. Together they own and operate Mid-Life Dimensions/Christian Living Resources, a nonprofit organization ministering to people at various stages of life through a variety of media formats.

Contents *Part 1:* Surprised by mid-life crisis *1.* Collision of expectations and reality *Part 2:* Trapped by roles *2.* The homemaker runs dry *3.* The professional shifts dreams *4.* Wonder woman tries it all *Part 3:* Squeezed from the outside *5.* Culture's creation *6.* A stale marriage *7.* Her husband's own crisis *8.* The pain of parenting *9.* Too much too fast *10.* The marks of time *Part 4:* Discouraged on the inside *11.* Defeated by a sagging self-esteem *12.* Trapped by depression *13.* Tempted to escape *Part 5:* Excited about succeeding *14.* Keeping up with life's clocks *15.* Answering life's questions *16.* Preventing a crisis *17.* Helping a woman in crisis *18.* Blooming at mid-life

Your Husband's Mid-Life Crisis *What a Woman Can Do When Her Husband Comes "Unglued" in Mid-Life,* Sally Conway

Chariot Family Publishing, 1990, $8.95, paper, 276 pp., for counselees

Description A book intended for a counselor who is trying to help a woman whose husband is in mid-life crisis or for the woman herself as a self-help book. It is built upon research of the common issues that wives of mid-life men need to process. Over 250,000 copies in print in three languages. Includes a section containing 13 Bible studies.

Author Sally Conway holds an M.S. in human development. Together with her husband, Jim, they own and operate Mid-Life Dimensions/Christian Living Resources, a nonprofit organization ministering to people at various stages of life through a variety of media formats.

Contents *Part 1:* Your husband's mid-life crisis *1.* Coming unglued *2.* They never warned me! *3.* Why so much at one time? *4.* But who cares about me? *Part 2:* Your dilemma *5.* Life of a mid-life wife *6.* Life with a mid-life man *7.* Life in a triangle *8.* Life without him *9.* Life with the children *Part 3:* Help for you *10.* Peace that empowers *11.* Strength, stability, and sanity *12.* The friendship connection *13.* Older, but better *Part 4:* Helping your husband *14.* Winning attitudes *15.* Success in understanding his needs *16.* Helping him win *17.* Aiding his reentry *18.* More than conquerors *Part 5:* Bible studies—13 studies from the Bible

Men at Mid-Life *Steering through The Detours,* James A Harnish

Abingdon Press, 1993, $9.00, paper, for counselees

Description Inspirational and practical ideas for handling a man's concerns such as personal identity, fear, forgiveness, sex and sensuality, spiri-

tuality, friendship, and more. Excellent resource for a husband and wife.

Midlife *The Crisis That Brings Renewal,* Pete Menconi

Serendipity, 1990, $6.95, paper, 80 pp., for both counselors and counselees

Description A 7- or 14-week course designed for a support group while exploring the problems and potential of midlife. This course is designed for anyone who is approaching, involved in, or just finished with midlife.

Contents *1.* Midlife, an overview *2.* Midlife transition *3.* The midlife crisis *4.* Midlife reevaluation *5.* Midlife rediscovery *6.* Midlife reaffirmation *7.* Midlife redirection

Growing through Mid-Life Crisis *Thoughts from Solomon and Others,* John Sterner

CPH Publishing, 1985, $9.99, cloth, 144 pp., for counselees

Description Through enlightening anecdotes, personal experiences, and large doses of Solomon's wisdom, Dr. Sterner teaches many important lessons in life, mid-life, and otherwise.

Author John Sterner of Trenton, Mich., is a Presbyterian minister, psychotherapist, and author.

Contents *Part 1:* The problem *1.* What's it all about? *2.* Healthy, wealthy, and wise . . . and depressed *3.* The big four zero *4.* The big four zero, continued *Part 2:* Some easy solutions (which usually fail) *5.* Trying harder *6.* Founding the clan *7.* Religious and respectable *8.* Getting smart *9.* Turning on *10.* Dropping out *Part 3:* The difficult solutions (which usually work) *11.* Relating to a "new" God *12.* Relating to a new "me" *13.* Relating to a new (?) world *14.* Relating to the same old principle *Part 4:* The conclusion of the matter

Menopause and Midlife Robert G. Wells and Mary C. Wells

Tyndale House Publishers, 1993, $14.99, paper, 162 pp., for both counselors and counselees

Description This book is a fresh, medically up-to-date, balanced look at the subject of menopause in the setting of midlife stresses. The authors clearly show how the one affects the other and offers the reader ways to successfully cope during these middle years. The book focuses on many aspects of menopause such as its symptoms, how it is medically diagnosed, and how it can be treated. It deals with the subject of hormone replacement—benefits, side effects, and risks. The goal of *Menopause and Midlife* is to permit women to make an informed decision about how they would like their menopause to be managed and how they can work with their doctors and counselors toward that end. Practical coping strategies, sexual changes, what a mate can expect to do, and help when a wife is going through "the change." Question and answer section.

Authors Robert G. Wells, M.D., is an obstetrician and gynecologist with a thriving practice in southern Calif. A fellow of the American College of Obstetricians and Gynecologists, he is an expert in the field of menopause and its management. He has written extensively for medical journals and is the author of *Prescription for Living* and *Miracle of Life*. Coauthor Mary Wells is both patient coordinator and lay counselor at the Menopause Center of Long Beach which she and Dr. Wells founded in 1987.

Contents *1.* Taking control of your menopause and midlife *2.* Menopause, emotions, and midlife stresses *3.* Understanding menopause *4.* Hormone replacement therapy *5.* A matter of choice *6.* Estrogen and the cardiovascular system *7.* Estrogen and osteoporosis *8.* Surviving menopause—Mary's story *9.* Sexuality in midlife *10.* Maximizing your health in midlife *11.* Making the most of midlife *12.* A word to husbands *13.* Answers to your questions about menopause and midlife

Counseling and the Search for Meaning
Paul R. Welter

Word Publishing, 1987, $15.99, cloth, 269 pp., for counselors

Description Dr. Welter addresses the question of meaning from a Christian perspective and discusses specific avenues of treatment, including creativity, humor, service to others, raising self-esteem, accepting responsibility, and prevention of meaninglessness.

Author Paul R. Welter, a counseling psychologist, is professor in the Department of Counseling and School of Psychology at Kearney State College, Kearney, Neb.

Contents *Part 1:* Recognizing and understanding the problem *1.* Chasing the wind *2.* The nature of meaninglessness *3.* The causes and dynamics of meaninglessness *Part 2:* Specific counseling approaches and methods *4.* Love and meaning *5.* Counseling as releasing *6.* The existential approach to counseling *7.* The contributions of Victor Frankl *8.* The logotherapy approach *9.* Socratic questioning *10.* Paradoxical intention *11.* Dereflection *12.* Loss, grief, and emptiness *13.* Intervention with cancer patients

14. Counseling the depressed person for meaning *15.* Violence and meaning *16.* Addiction and meaning *17.* Guilt, grace, and meaning *18.* Suffering—pain or mercy? *19.* Counseling children for meaning *20.* Meaning as a resource in marriage counseling *21.* Counseling youth for meaning *22.* Finding meaning in the workplace *23.* Counseling the retired and elderly for meaning *24.* Self-esteem and meaning *25.* Helping clients become responsible *26.* Evil as a cause of meaninglessness *27.* Finding meaning through creating *28.* Humor *29.* The meaning of the moment *30.* Introducing clients to intergenerational resources *31.* The meaning of truth *32.* Terminating counseling *Part 3:* The counselor's use of self *33.* Receiving from clients *34.* The pastor's 2 families *35.* Joining your client *36.* The wind from heaven preventing meaninglessness *37.* Meaning, justice, and service *38.* Meaning and health *39.* Training listener-responders in churches / *Useful resources for counseling for meaning*

The Search for Meaning Workbook
William Willimon, Thomas H. Naylor, and Magdalena Naylor

Abingdon Press, 1994, $8.95, paper, 96 pp., for both counselors and counselees

Description Companion guide to the book of the same title (also available from Abingdon). An economist, pastor, and psychiatrist join forces to encourage readers to examine their lives and themselves intellectually, emotionally, and spiritually, and to examine systematically the why of our existence.

Authors Thomas Naylor is a writer, philosopher, and professor of economics at Duke University. William Willimon is dean of the chapel and professor of Christian ministry at Duke University. Magdalena Naylor is a psychiatrist specializing in the treatment of women and adolescents.

Contents *1.* A search process *2.* Meaninglessness *3.* Separation *4.* Having *5.* Being *6.* The personal search *7.* The longing for community *8.* The search for meaning in the workplace *9.* Tools for the search *10.* Soul crafting

Encountering Mid-Life, Emerging Renewed

Abbey Press, $.50 each, paper, 8 pp., for counselees

Description Part of the CareNotes series from Abbey Press. CareNotes are short booklets that help readers identify issues and begin the process of seeking resolution. Anecdotal and uplifting. Beautiful photographs grace the covers. Over 20 million CareNotes have been sold in just over five years. Can be used as an alternative to a greeting card or in conjunction with pastoral care visits.

26. Multiple Personality Disorder

More Than One *An Inside Look at Multiple Personality Disorder,* Terri A. Clark

Oliver Nelson (a division of Thomas Nelson), 1993, $17.99, cloth, 320 pp., for counselors

Description A resource that is both clinically sound and biblically based for therapists, counselors, medical professionals, and others interested in MPD. Helps patients, their families, and others understand this complex disorder. Defines MPD, lists symptoms, causes, and treatments. This title contains one of the best resource sections (appendix) on MPD and related disorders.

Author Terri A Clark, M.D., is a psychiatrist who has been in private practice since 1985. Dr. Clark is also the medical director of the New Life Program and chief of staff at Glenbrook Hospital.

Contents *Section 1:* Uncovering *1.* Beginnings *2.* Clinical origins and history of multiple personality disorder (MPD) *3.* Defining and describing the disorder *4.* Marie Elena's story *5.* Features and characteristics *6.* The alters *7.* A peek inside the mind *Section 2:* Roots *8.* Child abuse and MPD *9.* The process of forgetting *10.* Possession or pretending? *11.* Uncovering MPD *Section 3:* Spirituality *12.* Patricia remembers *13.* Satanic ritual abuse *14.* Successful therapy *Section 4:* Healing *15.* Goals of therapy *16.* Healing for individuals *17.* Key issues for working with multiples *18.* Of God and evil

More Than Survivors *Conversations with Multiple Personality Clients,* James G. Friesen

Here's Life Publishers (c/o Thomas Nelson), 1992, $10.99, paper, 224 pp., for both counselors and counselees

Description The author of *Uncovering the Mystery of MPD* reveals the stories of multiple-personality clients from across the nation. Inspiring and encouraging stories from survivors of MPD.

Author James G. Friesen, Ph.D., is the director of a counseling center in southern Calif. His discoveries in the area of MPD have made him a much sought-after speaker at national conferences of his peers. Friesen also serves as adjunct professor at Fuller Graduate School of Psychology. He is a licensed psychologist and licensed minister with graduate degrees in both areas.

Contents *1.* Waking up *2.* Crystal: receiving cleansing *3.* Newheart: the key is love *4.* Willie Marie: dolls, bears, and poetry *5.* Willie Marie: poems tell the story *6.* Questions and answers *7.* Crystal: God's mercy *8.* Christina: SRA uncovered *9.* Paula: intensive therapy *10.* Rick Hammond: spiritual warfare, Part 1 demonic engagement and release *11.* Rick Hammond: spiritual warfare, Part 2 about exorcism *12.* Elizabeth Power: each day is for living *13.* Meribeth: turning the corner *14.* Keltie: trampling the serpent *15.* Splendid people

Uncovering the Mystery of MPD *Its Shocking Origins, Its Surprising Cure,* James G. Friesen

Here's Life Publishers (c/o Thomas Nelson), 1991, $12.99, paper, 300 pp., for counselors

Description In a language everyone can understand, this ground-breaking book reveals the latest research on the problem of MPD and why its roots are often in satanic ritual abuse.

Author James G. Friesen, Ph.D., is the director of a counseling center in southern Calif. His discoveries in the area of MPD have made him a much sought-after speaker at national conferences of his peers. Friesen also serves as adjunct professor at Fuller Graduate School of Psychology. He is a licensed psychologist and licensed minister with graduate degrees in both areas.

Contents *Part 1:* Understanding *1.* Spiritual warfare: three levels *2.* Multiple personality disorder (MPD) *3.* Satanic ritual abuse (SRA) *Part 2:* Psychological restoration *4.* Diagnosing MPD *5.* Treatment for dissociation 1 *6.* Treatment for dissociation 2 *Part 3:* Spiritual restoration *7.* God's perspective *8.* Spiritual warfare in MPD therapy *9.* Exorcism *10.* Restoration that endures

Managing Ourselves—Building a Community of Caring Elizabeth Power

E. Power Associates, 1992, $17.95, spiral, 116 pp., for counselors

Description A "must-buy" for persons with MPD or dissociative disorders and those who work with them. This workbook concentrates on self-management that develops collaboration among alters. Created to help reduce the time, trauma, and expense of healing. Empowerment occurs through the focus on making choices and acting as one's own agent. The contents are nonjudgmental. Language and graphics have been carefully chosen to minimize risks of switching, and each segment is usually only one page to accommodate frequent switching of selves.

Author Elizabeth Power is a sought-after conference speaker, consultant, and trainer. Her work as a role model, program developer, and educator to clients, churches, and clinicians in the area of multiple personalities reaches around the world.

Contents Fifty-eight short, interactive chapters lead the reader through issues such as dissociation and society, self-image and selves, travel issues, safety, managing triggers, going public, multiple personalities, multiple spiritualities, memories, and more.

Managing Ourselves—God in Our Midst
Elizabeth Power

E. Power Associates, 1992, $12.95, spiral, 63 pp., for counselors

Description A companion workbook to *Building a Community of Caring* presents information, attitudes, and skills to help in the healing process and increases the reader's ability to respond to other selves and other people as Christ would. Explores reconciliation, the role of praise in healing, concepts of multiplicity in Scripture, and other important faith issues and questions.

Author Elizabeth Power is a sought-after conference speaker, consultant, and trainer. Her work as a role model, program developer, and educator to clients, churches, and clinicians in the area of multiple personalities reaches around the world. Her experiences in the church as a multiple struggling to maintain her faith led her to this workbook.

Contents Thirty-two short, interactive chapters deal with important subjects such as denominations, dogma and God, one body—many parts, Paul's experience, horror and healing, God's anger, many into one, reclaiming Christian symbols, and more.

DD-Anon Group One

DD-Anon Group One. An organization

Description DD-Anon stands for Dissociative Disorders Anonymous. A fellowship of men and women who share their experience, strength, and hope as they seek to remain supportive of loved ones who are being treated with dissociative disorders (usually MPD). Utilizes a 12-step format.

International Society for the Study of Multiple Personality & Dissociation

International Society for the Study of MPD. An organization

Description An international professional organization dedicated to the study of MPD.

27. Pastoral Counseling

Helps for Counselors Jay E. Adams

Baker Book House, 1980, $3.99, paper, 63 pp., for counselors

Description A collection of helpful hints and how to's, covering all aspects of counseling, what to look for, and how to proceed. A Scripture reference guide is included.

Author Dr. Adams is the author of numerous books on Christian counseling. He has served on a seminary faculty (Westminster Theological) and in the pastorate. He is founder of Christian Counseling and Educational Foundation in Laverock, Pa., and visiting professor of practical theology at two seminaries.

Shepherding God's Flock *A Handbook on Pastoral Ministry, Counseling, and Leadership,* Jay E. Adams

Zondervan Publishing House, 1986, $18.99, paper, 544 pp., for counselors

Description A textbook for students of pastoral ministry and a handbook for pastors.

Author Dr. Adams is the author of numerous books on Christian counseling. He has served on a seminary faculty (Westminster Theological) and in the pastorate. He is founder of Christian Counseling and Educational Foundation in Laverock, Pa., and visiting professor of practical theology at two seminaries.

Contents *Part 1:* Pastoral life *1.* Theology and pastoral work *2.* Pastoral theology *Section 1:* The shepherd life *3.* Counting the cost *4.* Areas of adequacy *5.* Five vital factors *6.* Family and social life *7.* Repossessing time *8.* Other factors to consider *Section 2:* The shepherd's call *9.* Candidating *10.* Going to and fro *Section 3:* The shepherd's care of the flock *11.* The shepherd visits *12.* House calling *13.* Specific congregational ministry *14.* Personal ministry: counseling *15.* Visiting the sick *16.* The hospital call *17.* Visiting in special situations *Part 2:* Pastoral counseling *1.* Pastoral counseling *2.* Mutual ministry in counseling *3.* Conducting a congregational counseling program *4.* Counseling members of other congregations *5.* Evaluation and upgrading pastoral counseling *6.* How to take

pastoral initiative *7.* Premarital counseling *8.* Care in counseling women *9.* Counseling older persons *10.* Educational counseling *11.* Instruction in counseling *12.* Counseling disabled persons *13.* A final note on pastoral counseling *14.* The shepherd's equipment *Part 3:* Pastoral leadership *1.* Shepherds lead *2.* Leadership in the church *3.* Leadership means equipping others *4.* Delegation and sharing *5.* Working with the eldership *6.* Working with another pastor *7.* Congregational meetings *8.* Communication in the body *9.* Communication links *10.* Enlisting and training *11.* Setting up a program *12.* Organizations in the congregation *13.* A church school for adults *14.* Leading children and youth *15.* Making the church library work *16.* Church buildings *17.* Finances in the local church *18.* Publicity *19.* Conclusion

Turning Points in Pastoral Care *The Legacy of Anton Boisen and Seward Hiltner,* LeRoy Aden and J. Harold Ellens

Baker Book House, 1990, $14.99, paper, 265 pp., a reference or academic work

Description Boisen and Hiltner sought to enhance the work of ministry by insisting on the high place pastoral care should occupy in pastoral work. They sought to improve ministerial competence and to broaden understanding. They introduced ministers to ideas, books, persons, and points of view, thereby enlarging their grasp of human distress and engendering hope for human wholeness. The book shows in heuristic detail how the form of contemporary pastoral care and counseling has been largely shaped by the pioneering work of Boisen and Hiltner. This book delineates their important contributions and offers significant proposals for building on their legacy. Comprised of 14 essays.

Authors LeRoy Aden is professor of pastoral care, Lutheran Theological Seminary in Philadelphia. He has edited three other books in Baker's Psychology and Christianity series. J. Harold Ellens is executive director emeritus of Christian Association for Psychological Studies and is a psychotherapist in private practice. He has edited one other book in Baker's Psychology and Chris-

214

tianity series and has published many other articles about pastoral care and counseling.

Contents *1.* An experiential theology *2.* A dynamic approach to theology *3.* A perspectival pastoral theology *4.* Conscience and Christian perfection *5.* The ethic of sincerity and the sincerity of ethics *6.* A psychology of religious experience *7.* A paradoxical understanding of religious experience *8.* A ministry of reconciliation *9.* Physicians of the soul *10.* Shepherds of the needy *11.* Pastoral care and the church *12.* Caring for society *13.* Boisen as autobiographer *14.* Hiltner's contributions to pastoral care and counseling

Mastering Pastoral Care Paul Anderson, Bruce Larson, and Doug Self

Multnomah Books (Questar), 1990, $13.99, cloth, 144 pp., for counselors

Description Addresses pastoral care in contemporary culture. The authors offer fresh models of pastoral care that spring from the daily challenges of pastoral life.

Authors Bruce Larson, a popular speaker and author, is a pastor at the Crystal Cathedral in Garden Grove, Calif. Paul Anderson is pastor of Trinity Lutheran Church in San Pedro, Calif., where he has served since 1970. Doug Self has been the pastor of the Church at Redstone in Redstone, Colo., for 12 years. He has also edited the *Pastoral Care Newsletter.*

Contents *Part 1:* The range of pastoral care *1.* Home visitation in an age of teleconferencing *2.* Letting the laity pastor *3.* Worship as pastoral care *4.* Ministering in the marketplace *Part 2:* Special concerns *5.* Caring for key leaders *6.* Strategies for ministering to inactives *7.* Nurturing the revitalized *Part 3:* Practicing care *8.* The art of pastoral listening *9.* Risking lay ministry *10.* Using the disciplines to care *11.* Helping people care for one another *12.* Balancing service and solace

Pastoral Responses to Sexual Issues
William V. Arnold

Westminster/John Knox Press, 1993, $12.99, paper, 176 pp., for counselors

Description Arnold goes right into the pastor's study, stands at the shoulder of the pastor, and offers both theological and psychological insight into sexual dysfunction in marriage, extramarital affairs, sexual abuse, adolescent sexuality, and homosexuality. Arnold stresses self-awareness as the key to dealing with sexual issues and advises the pastor not to rely strictly on intellectual information.

Author William V. Arnold is Marthina DeFriece professor of pastoral care and counseling and dean of the faculty, Union Theological Seminary, Richmond, Va.

Contents *Part 1:* The pastor's responsibility for self-awareness *1.* Caring for others means owning up to who we are *2.* Gender and self *3.* Climate, conduct, and referral *Part 2:* Sexual issues and pastoral care *4.* Sexual dysfunction in marriage *5.* Extramarital affairs *6.* Sexual discrimination and abuse *7.* Adolescence and sexuality *8.* Homosexuality

New Dictionary of Christian Ethics and Pastoral Theology David J. Atkinson, David F. Field, Arthur Holmes, and Oliver O'Donovan

InterVarsity Press, 1994, $39.99, cloth, 944 pp., for counselors

Description NDCEPT is organized in two parts. In the first part, 18 extended articles, arranged in theological order, introduce readers to the main themes of Christian ethics and pastoral theology. In the second part, over 700 articles, arranged alphabetically, flow like tributaries from those main themes. An easy-to-use reference system enables quick transition from the first to the second part and back again. Encompasses a wide range of subjects. It includes articles on traditional subjects like atonement, the kingdom of God, suffering, death and dying, and heaven and hell. Includes articles on timely issues like reproductive technology, transplant surgery, health and health care, economic and social justice, prison and prison reform, psychotherapy, family therapy, and more.

Editors David J. Atkinson is chancellor of Southwark Cathedral in London, England. He was formerly fellow and chaplain of Corpus Christi College, Oxford University. Editor David F. Field is director of professional ministry with the Church Pastoral Aid Society in Warwick, England. He was formerly vice principal of Oak Hill College in London, England. Consulting editor Arthur Holmes is professor of philosophy at Wheaton College in Wheaton, Ill. Consulting editor Oliver O'Donovan is regius professor of moral and pastoral theology at Oxford University.

Pastoral Counseling across Cultures
David W. Augsburger

Westminster/John Knox Press, 1986, $25.00, cloth, 405 pp., for counselors

Description A book that can help liberate readers from narrow provincialism. Offers Americans new ways of understanding themselves and their culture by helping them better understand their newly arrived neighbors.

Author David Augsburger (Ph.D., School of Theology at Clairmont, Calif.) is professor of pastoral care at the Associated Mennonite Biblical Seminaries in Elkhart, Ind. He has authored many books (including *Conflict Mediation across Cultures: Pathways and Patterns* and numerous books on recovery-oriented topics) and has had hundreds of articles published in magazines.

Contents *1.* The cross cultural counselor: a theology of presence *2.* The universal, the cultural, the unique: a theology of culture *3.* Individualism, individualness, and solidarity: a theology of humanness *4.* Inner control, outer controls, balanced control: a theology of grace *5.* Values, worldviews, and pastoral counseling: a theology of value *6.* Family, family theory, and therapy across cultures: a theology of the family *7.* Women and men in cross cultural therapy: a theology of liberation *8.* Ethical and moral issues in counseling across cultures *9.* Possession, shamanism, and healing across cultures: a theology of demonism *10.* Mental health and mental distress across cultures: a theology of human frailty *11.* Pastoral psychotherapy across cultures: models of pastoral counseling and theology

Strategic Pastoral Counseling *A Short-Term Structured Model,* David G. Benner

Baker Book House, 1992, $9.99, paper, 160 pp., for counselors

Description The book describes a short-term structured approach to counseling designed specifically for pastors and others working within a Christian context. The model is built around the master goal of facilitating spiritual growth. The book describes how pastoral counselors can respond to the problems presented to them in a maximum of five sessions. After providing a historical context for the development of contemporary pastoral counseling, the author goes on to present his strategic, highly focused plan for five-session counseling. It revolves around three stages: encounter, engagement, and disengagement. The book presents goals and strategies of counseling associated with each of these stages. A detailed case study illustrates the implementation of the principles described.

Author Dr. David G. Benner is a clinical psychologist currently serving as professor and chair of the Department of Psychology at Redeemer College and adjunct professor of psychology and Christianity at the University of Toronto (St. Michael's College). He has written and edited nine books and remains active in clinical work, specializing in the treatment of dissociative disorders.

Contents *1.* The context of pastoral counseling *2.* The uniqueness of pastoral counseling *3.* The strategic pastoral counseling model *4.* The stages and tasks of strategic pastoral counseling *5.* A case study of strategic pastoral counseling

Called into Crisis *The Nine Greatest Challenges of Pastoral Care,* James D. Berkley

Word Publishing, 1989, $11.95, cloth, 204 pp., for counselors

Description *Called into Crisis* offers helpers the crisis counsel they need to help those in crisis. Resourced by those who have been there, this book promises to help pastors transform people's major crises into opportunities to grow, to reorient life, to find the One who is life itself. The nine crises covered in the book were chosen through a survey of pastors' most difficult cases. A helpful feature is "Quickscan"—a brief synopsis of the chapter that can be quickly reviewed prior to responding to a call for help.

Author James D. Berkley, editor of *Your Church* magazine and general editor of the *Leadership Handbooks of Practical Theology,* is an ordained Presbyterian pastor with two decades of experience in parish positions. He holds a D.Min. degree from Fuller Theological Seminary and a B.S. in psychology from the University of Washington.

Contents *1.* Crisis *2.* Handling a crisis *3.* Marital conflict and divorce *4.* Sexual misconduct *5.* Domestic violence and abuse *6.* Homosexuality *7.* Major illnesses and injuries *8.* Death of a child *9.* Death of a spouse *10.* Suicide *11.* Alcohol and drug problems *12.* Beyond crisis

Measuring Up *The Need to Succeed and the Fear of Failure,* Stuart Briscoe, Knute Larson, and Larry Osborne

Questar Publishing, 1995, $11.95, cloth, 235 pp.

Description Aims at helping pastors struggling with the desire to please others.

Authors Stuart Briscoe has been pastor of Elmbrook Church in Waukesha, Wis., for over 20 years. Knute Larson is pastor of The Chapel, a downtown church in Akron, Ohio. Larry W. Osborne is pastor of North Coast Church in Oceanside, Calif.

Contents *Part 1*—The pressures *1.* The burden of potential *2.* In need of a good reputation *3.* Ministry from a cramped position *4.* What is successful preaching? *5.* Taking risks *Part 2*—Relationships *6.* Making the right moves *7.* Between ministry and family *8.* The price of progress *Part 3*—The ups and downs *9.* Defeat and disappointment *10.* Making the most of mistakes *11.* When things are going well *12.* Measuring success

Pastor and Church Finances *Biblical Guidelines for Churches and Pastors,* Larry Burkett

Christian Financial Concepts, 1990, $25.00, cassette(s), for counselors

Description An audio series full of practical financial information that pastors don't generally have the opportunity to learn in seminary. Includes procedural guidelines for the day-to-day operations of the church.

Author Since 1976, Larry Burkett has directed Christian Financial Concepts, a nationwide, non-profit organization dedicated to teaching biblical principles of handling money. He has published over 20 books on finances with a total distribution of over two million. He is heard daily on two radio broadcasts carried by over 1,000 outlets worldwide. Christian Financial Concepts also publishes a free newsletter that focuses on current economic issues.

Contents *1.* Overview—the pastor's role in finances *2.* Financial planning 1—the church's role in finances, how God uses money *3.* Financial planning 2—obstacles, short-range planning, budget percentage guidelines, long range goals *4.* Pastor's personal finances 1 *5.* Pastor's personal finances 2 *6.* Pastor's personal finances 3 *7.* Church administration 1 *8.* Church administration 2 *9.* Financial ministry in the church 1 *10.* Financial ministry in the church 2

The Poet's Gift *Toward the Renewal of Pastoral Care,* Donald Capps

Westminster/John Knox Press, 1993, $15.99, paper, 176 pp., for counselors

Description Donald Capps draws upon the poetry of William Stafford and Adrienne Rich to show how poetry can be beneficial to the field of pastoral care. He claims that poetry focuses on the immediate experience and attends to life itself, whereas theology and ethics focus on abstract discourse, seeking to achieve a more panoramic view of life.

Author Donald Capps is William Harte Felmeth professor of pastoral theology, Princeton Theological Seminary, Princeton, N.J. He has written several books on pastoral counseling and care.

Contents *1.* The self we bring to our vocation *2.* Pastoral conversation as embodied language *3.* Inviting the grieving back to life *4.* Learning to heed the unheard voices *5.* Pastoral care and the yearning for freedom

Why Do Christians Shoot Their Wounded? *Helping (Not Hurting) Those with Emotional Difficulties,* Dwight L. Carlson

InterVarsity Press, 1994, $10.99, paper, 180 pp., for both counselors and counselees

Description Physician Dwight L. Carlson marshals recent clinical evidence to demonstrate that many emotional hurts are just as biologically based as diabetes, cancer, and heart disease. For those who hurt, here is powerful liberation from guilt. For counselors and caregivers, here is vivid proof that people in pain deserve compassion, not condemnation.

Author Dr. Dwight Carlson, M.D., is a specialist in both internal medicine and psychiatry. He has an active psychiatry practice and is assistant clinical professor at UCLA.

Contents *Part 1:* How and why we shoot the wounded *1.* Don't shoot! I'm already wounded! *2.* Why we wound *3.* Can a Spirit-filled Christian have emotional wounds? *Part 2:* What causes emotional illness? *4.* It's not necessarily all in your mind *5.* It's not necessarily all in your mind continued *6.* How childhood experiences and stress cause emotional illness *7.* What about personal choice? *8.* Putting it all together *Part 3:* How shall the wounded be mended? *9.* The church business, school or hospital? *10.* How the strong can help—not shoot—the wounded *11.* What the wounded can do while the bullets are flying / *Appendix:* Are drugs of the devil or tools for healing?

Essentials for Chaplains Sharon E. Cheston and Robert Wicks

Paulist Press, 1993, $9.95, paper, 144 pp., for counselors

Description Cheston and Wicks serve as editors as ten of today's most pressing issues are discussed by an expert in the field. Within each topic are ten practical pastoral suggestions to keep chaplains focused and effective as they work with the many people involved in each issue. Topics treated are: sexual abuse of children, anger, grief, guilt and shame, confrontation, the elderly, anxiety, crisis intervention, women's issues, and professional burnout.

Authors Sharon Cheston, Ed.D., is associate professor and associate chair of the pastoral counseling department, Loyola College in Maryland. Robert J. Wicks, Psy.D., is professor and director of program development for pastoral counseling at Loyola College in Maryland.

Short-Term Pastoral Counseling Brian Childs

Abingdon Press, 1990, $10.95, paper, 144 pp., for counselors

Description Shows how problems such as poor job performance, minor depressions, grief, and some forms of obsession can be effectively resolved through short-term pastoral counseling.

Basic Types of Pastoral Care and Counseling Howard Clinebell

Abingdon Press, $19.95, cloth, a reference or academic work

The Biblical Basis of Christian Counseling for People Helpers *Relating the Basic Doctrines of the Bible to People's Problems,* Gary R. Collins

NavPress, 1993, $20.00, paper, 294 pp., for counselors

Description Dr. Gary Collins presents an accessible, user-friendly approach to counseling. Beginning from the standpoint of "what makes counseling Christian," this book touches on the relevance of theology to counseling and offers readers the theological tools they'll need to help people spiritually as well as psychologically.

Author Dr. Gary Collins is a respected presence in the counseling field, trusted for his professional expertise as well as his biblical soundness. He has written numerous successful counseling books, has recently headed up the American Association of Christian Counselors, and is the publisher of *Christian Counseling Today.* A teacher at Trinity Seminary for over 20 years, Dr. Collins

is a regular speaker at counseling conferences and symposiums around the world.

Contents *1.* Introduction: what makes counseling Christian? *2.* The Bible and counseling—revelation *3.* The Bible and counseling—hermeneutics *4.* God and counseling *5.* Human nature and counseling *6.* Sin and counseling *7.* Guilt and forgiveness in counseling *8.* Spiritual development and counseling *9.* The Christian counselor and counseling *10.* Spiritual dryness and counseling *11.* Suffering and counseling *12.* The church and counseling *13.* Miraculous interventions and counseling *14.* Supernatural agents and counseling *15.* Apologetics and counseling *16.* The impact of the future on counseling *17.* Diversity in Christian counseling

Encouragement *The Key to Caring,* Larry Crabb and Dan B. Allender

Zondervan Publishing House, 1990, $8.99, paper, 144 pp., for counselors

Description "Encourage one another," says the book of Hebrews. But encouragement is much more than a pat on the back. Encouragement is the most basic form of counseling—a skill that can be mastered by laypeople as well as counselors. This book shows you how to be an encourager. Includes such practical "how to's" as: developing a careful selection of words, cultivating active listening skills, using biblical fellowship to break through the surface community of self-satisfied smiles and shallow greetings, and recognizing opportunities for encourgement.

Authors Dr. Crabb is director of biblical counseling and chairman of the Department of Biblical Counseling at Colorado Christian University in Morrison, Colo. He earned his Ph.D. in clinical psychology from the University of Illinois in 1970. He is the author of numerous books on self-understanding and counseling technique. Dan Allender is an associate with the Institute of Biblical Counseling and professor of counseling at Colorado Christian College. He is the author of *Bold Love* and *The Wounded Heart.*

Contents *1.* Introduction *2.* The power of a well timed word *3.* Surface community: the obstacle to encouragement *4.* Total openness—the wrong solution *5.* Total commitment—the right solution *6.* The character of an encourager *7.* When do we tell somebody else how we feel? *8.* How encouragement works *9.* Encouragement—the context for change *10.* Opportunities for encouragement *11.* Responding to opportunities *12.* Techniques for encouragement *1 13.* Techniques for encouragement *2 14.* The local church—a restoring community.

Understanding People *Deep Longings for Relationship,* Larry Crabb

Zondervan Publishing House, 1987, $16.99, cloth, 224 pp., for both counselors and counselees

Description Dr. Crabb examines one of the most crucial problems in Christian counseling today: the use and abuse of the Bible. He illustrates two common weaknesses of biblical counselors: They often "spiritualize" problems and limit questions to those for which they can find a prooftext, or they regard the Bible as more or less irrelevant when grappling with the hard questions people ask. It is with these unsatisfactory alternatives in mind that Dr. Crabb develops a model for biblical counseling that is grounded on the authority and sufficiency of the Scriptures. The aim is to help readers at all levels answer the question: "How do I use Scripture in helping others?"

Author Dr. Crabb is director of biblical counseling and chairman of the Department of Biblical Counseling at Colorado Christian University in Morrison, Colo. He earned his Ph.D. in clinical psychology from the University of Illinois in 1970. He is the author of numerous books on self-understanding and counseling technique.

Contents *Part 1:* A sufficient Bible—finding answers in Scripture *1.* How do we know what to believe? *2.* The Bible warrants our confidence *3.* Does the Bible speak meaningfully to every problem? *4.* The Bible is a sufficient guide for relational living *Part 2:* Understanding people—a tarnished image and broken relationships *5.* How can people truly change? *6.* People bear the image of God *7.* Dependent beings—people are personal *8.* Foolish thinkers: people are rational *9.* The beginning of change—repentance *10.* Free to choose: people are volitional *11.* Feeling the impact of life: people are emotional *Part 3:* Growing toward maturity *12.* The evidence of maturity: love *13.* The essence of maturity: realized dependency

Short-Term Counseling *Utilizing Short-Term Therapy in Your Counseling Ministry,* David Dillon

Word Publishing, 1992, $15.99, cloth, 216 pp., for counselors

Description Discusses the use of short-term therapy in the context of pastoral ministry. Combines discussions of theory and practice in this relatively new field that are readily adaptable to pastoral settings.

Author Dr. David Dillon is an assistant professor of counseling psychology as well as chairman of the Department of Pastoral Counseling and Psychology at Trinity Evangelical Divinity School.

Contents *Part 1:* The basics *1.* Short-term counseling and the pastor *2.* The components of change *3.* Reality making *4.* Basics of successful counseling *5.* Social stage *Part 2:* The method *6.* Problem definition *7.* Attempted solutions *8.* Goal setting: adjusting the solution *Part 3:* The change *9.* Facilitating change: liberating the client *10.* Reframing *11.* Paradox in counseling

The Art of Clinical Supervision *A Pastoral Counseling Perspective,* Barry Estadt, John Compton, and Melvin C. Blanchette

Paulist Press, 1987, $12.95, paper, 309 pp., for counselors

Description An innovative understanding of the process of supervision along with the shared wisdom of experienced clinical supervisors. A series of 19 essays from a number of professionals.

Editors Rev. Barry Estadt (O.F.M., Ph.D.) is director and chairman of pastoral counseling programs at Loyola College of Maryland. Rev. John R. Compton (D.Min.) is an ordained minister of the American Lutheran Church and member of the graduate school faculty of Loyola College of Baltimore. Melvin C. Blanchette (S.S., Ph.D.) is an associate professor in the Department of Pastoral Counseling at Loyola College of Baltimore.

Contents *Part 1:* Overview of the supervisory alliance *1.* Toward professional integration *2.* The core process of supervision *Part 2:* The supervisory process *3.* The supervisory learning contract *4.* Supervisory formats and evaluation procedures *5.* Interpretation and resistance *6.* Transference and countertransference *7.* Termination *Part 3:* Supervision and the variety of helping modalities *8.* Short term counseling *9.* Supervisions in long term therapy *10.* Counseling with couples *11.* Group counseling: a model for teaching and supervision *12.* Crisis intervention: critical issues in supervision *13.* Family counseling *14.* Addiction counseling *15.* Spiritual direction: a model for group supervision *Part 4:* Special issues in supervision *16.* Religious issues *17.* Ethical issues in supervision *18.* Social justice issues in supervision *19.* Theological and pastoral integration

Søren Kierkegaard's Christian Psychology *Insights for Counseling and Pastoral Care,* Stephen C. Evans

Zondervan Publishing House, 1990, $8.95, paper, 135 pp., a reference or academic work

Description Views Kierkegaard as providing a model for Christian psychology. His thought is interpreted as a distinctively Christian depth psychology, in which the unconscious is heavily influenced by our need to find God and our need to flee from God. Humans are fundamentally spiritual creatures, and the implications of this for understanding human relationships and psychological development are profound. The book concludes with some reflections on the implications of such a view for applied psychology, including therapy.

Author Stephen C. Evans is professor of philosophy and curator of the Hong Kierkegaard Library at St. Olaf College in Minnesota. Evans received his B.A. at Wheaton College and his Ph.D. from Yale University. He is the author of nine books.

Contents *1.* Kierkegaard as a Christian *2.* Kierkegaard as a psychologist *3.* Human beings as spiritual creatures *4.* Kierkegaard's depth psychology I: sin, anxiety, and despair *5.* Kierkegaard's depth psychology II: the analysis of despair *6.* Kierkegaard's depth psychology III: sin, self deception, and the unconscious *7.* Kierkegaard as developmental psychologist *8.* Kierkegaard as therapist: applying psychology

Dangers, Toils and Snares *Resisting the Hidden Temptations of Ministry,* Richard Exley, Mark Galli and John Ortberg

Questar Publishing, 1995, $11.95, cloth, 172 pp.

Description Most pastors find themselves faced with moral temptation of some kind. They are party to intimate details of other people's sexual lives. They find themselves in positions of power and authority. Even as they work to help others, the voices of lust, pride, and ambition whisper. Now, three experienced pastors explain how temptation can be met and defeated.

Authors Richard Exley is senior pastor of The Christian Chapel in Tulsa, Okla. Mark Galli is associate editor of *Christian History* magazine. John Ortberg is senior pastor of Horizons Community Church in Diamond Bar, Calif.

Contents *Part 1*—The dangers of pastoral toil *1.* The perils of professional holiness *2.* Breaking the approval addiction *3.* Taming ambition *4.* Confessions of a lazy pastor *5.* Confronting the fear of controversy *6.* Pastoral anger: murder in the cathedral *7.* When you can't hold on *8.* A cure for seriousness *Part 2*—Sexual snares *9.* Handling sexual temptation *10.* An overlooked casualty of a "victimless sin" *11.* After the fall *Part 3*—The long view *12.* When sin won't let go

The Social Context of Pastoral Care *Defining the Life Situation,* George Furniss

Westminster/John Knox Press, 1994, $19.99, paper, 212 pp., for counselors

Description Because their field focuses primarily on the fields of theology and psychology, pastoral caregivers have often neglected to take into account the social forces that affect both the care seeker and caregiver. In this groundbreaking book, sociologist and chaplain George Furniss introduces them to a new "third" discipline, sociology, to draw upon their work.

The Holy Spirit and Counseling *Theology and Theory, Volume 1,* Marvin G. Gilbert and Raymond T. Brock

Hendrickson Publishers, 1985, $14.95, paper, 310 pp., a reference or academic work

Description Written with the pastor in mind. Examines the foundations of the Holy Spirit's role as "Comforter" in counseling, the role of the Spirit-filled counselor, and a brief survey of the prominent counseling theories. Encourages increasing reliance on and sensitivity for the Holy Spirit. Written from a charismatic/pentecostal perspective. Encourages inclusion of the Holy Spirit in the counseling process. Includes brief discussions of various popular schools of psychology.

Authors Marvin Gilbert, Ph.D. from Texas Tech.; former associate professor of psychology at Evangel College, Springfield, Mo.; currently academic dean, East Africa School of Theology, Nairobi, Kenya, East Africa. Raymond T. Brock, Ed.D. from the University of Tulsa, Okla.; former professor of psychology and chairman of the department of behavioral sciences, Evangel College; then associate professor of behavioral medicine in the Department of Psychiatry and Behavioral Medicine, Oral Roberts University School of Medicine, Tulsa, Okla.; retired as professor emeritus from Evangel College.

Contents *Section 1:* Theology *1.* The role of the Holy Spirit in interpersonal relations *2.* The Holy Spirit as paraclete *3.* The gifts of the Holy Spirit *Section 2:* Counseling *4.* The devotional life of the counselor *5.* Personal and spiritual growth *6.* Avoiding burnout through spiritual renewal *7.* Lay counseling in the local church *Section 3:* Theory *8.* Psychoanalytic theory *9.* Client-centered therapy *10.* Behavioral therapy *11.* Reality therapy *12.* Cognitive therapy *13.* Individual psychology: the theory and psychotherapy of Alfred Adler *14.* Systems theory *15.* Integrity therapy *16.* Actualizing therapy *17.* The Holy Spirit in relationship to counseling: reflections in the integration of theology and counseling

The Holy Spirit and Counseling *Principles and Practice—Volume 2,* Marvin G. Gilbert and Raymond T. Brock

Hendrickson Publishers, 1988, $14.95, paper, 269 pp., a reference or academic work

Description Building upon the theology and theory of volume 1, this volume deals with selected problems faced regularly by pastors and Christian counselors. How the presence of the Holy Spirit can enhance the psychotherapeutic interaction is examined in a variety of problem areas. The emphasis is that God himself, in the person of the Holy Spirit, still heals the broken hearted and guides both the counselor and the counselee into new and creative expressions of Spirit-empowered healing encounters.

Authors Marvin Gilbert, Ph.D. from Texas Tech.; former associate professor of psychology at Evangel College, Springfield, Mo.; currently academic dean, East Africa School of Theology, Nairobi, Kenya, East Africa. Raymond T. Brock, Ed.D. from the University of Tulsa, Okla.; former professor of psychology and chairman of the department of behavioral sciences, Evangel College; then associate professor of behavioral medicine in the Department of Psychiatry and Behavioral Medicine, Oral Roberts University School of Medicine, Tulsa, Okla.; retired as professor emeritus from Evangel College.

Contents *1.* Establishing and maintaining a counseling ministry *2.* Making referrals *3.* Marriage counseling *4.* Marriage enrichment *5.* Family therapy *6.* Counseling the parents of the handicapped child *7.* Ministering to the aging *8.* The role of psychology in physical rehabilitation *9.* Death, dying, and bereavement *10.* Group therapy *11.* Counseling with college students *12.* Cross-cultural counseling *13.* Guided imagery and inner healing.

Mastering Pastoral Counseling
Archibald D. Hart, Gary Gulbranson, and Jim Smith

Multnomah Books (Questar), 1992, $13.99, cloth, 172 pp., for counselors

Description Not a theory book, but a problem solver that takes practical issues straight on. Looks at counseling problems from the perspective of a pastor, not from the professional pastor's view.

Authors Archibald D. Hart is dean of the Graduate School of Psychology, Fuller Theological Seminary. Gary L. Gulbranson is pastor of Glen Ellyn

Bible Church, Glen Ellyn, Ill. Jim Smith is pastoral counselor at Highland Park Presbyterian Church in Dallas, Tex.

Contents *Part 1:* The pastor as counselor *1.* Using our spiritual resources *2.* Giving care ethically *3.* The preaching ingredient *4.* Regeneration, deliverance, or therapy *Part 2:* Counseling situations *5.* Crisis situations *6.* Short-term care *7.* Long-term care *8.* Counseling men, counseling women *9.* All in the family *Part 3:* Problems counseling brings *10.* Fitting it in *11.* Transference, loosening the tie that binds *12.* Maintaining your psychological balance

Counseling Cross-Culturally *An Introduction to Theory and Practice for Christians,* David J. Hesselgrave

Baker Book House, 1984, $14.95, paper, 436 pp., for counselors

Description Based on counseling experience in home and foreign cultures and on extensive research and intercultural counseling theories, both secular and Christian. This book addresses four distinct needs of contemporary Christian counselors ministering in multicultural and/or foreign contexts. The first section lays the theological foundation. The second section compares Christian and secular theory and practice in western and non-western worlds. The third section presents a well-rounded theory of Christian counseling that takes into account human universals, cultural differences, and individual uniqueness. Case studies are included.

Author David J. Hesselgrave (Ph.D.) has pastoral experience in rural and urban America, was a missionary in Japan for 12 years, and for 25 years has been a professor in the area of missions and intercultural studies at Trinity Evangelical Divinity School. He has authored or coauthored nine books.

Contents *Part 1:* Introductory considerations *1.* The Christian conscience and cross-cultural ministries *2.* Cross-cultural psychology and counseling—a timely birth *3.* Where do we go from here? *Part 2:* Counseling in the western and non-western worlds *4.* Secular approaches to individual counseling and therapy in the west *5.* Secular approaches to group counseling and therapy in the west *6.* Approaches to Christian counseling in the western world *7.* Christian approaches in the non-western world *Part 3:* A theory of Christian cross cultural counseling *8.* Like all other men—a search for human universals *9.* Like some other men—an inquiry into cultural differences *10.* Like no other men—understanding uniqueness *Part 4:* Counseling individuals and groups cross culturally *11.* Solving problems and producing change *12.* Counseling concerning the well-being of people *13.* Counseling concerning Christian conversion *14.* Counseling concerning growth and the development of the Christian lifestyle *15.* Counseling concerning Christian service

A Guide to Retreat *For All God's Shepherds,* Reuben P. Job

Abingdon Press, 1994, $14.95, paper, 200 pp., for both counselors and counselees

Description If leaders are to remain vital in their ministry, and if they are to become spiritually, emotionally, and physically healthy, pastors need time apart for sanctuary, nourishment, healing, and renewal. This project offers spiritual direction for the leader's time apart, providing flexible structure and content for times of personal reflection. Includes retreat patterns, an essay, excerpted readings, follow-up devotional exercises, an anthology of related readings, and more.

Author Reuben P. Job is a consultant in spiritual formation to the General Board of Discipleship, where he was formerly world editor of the Upper Room publishing program.

Contents When all I hear is silence / When others tell me who I am / In the midst of faults and failures / The tension between doing and being / Do I have a future in the church? / Who really calls and sends?

ReEntry *Making the Transitions from Missions to Life at Home,* Peter Jordan

Youth with a Mission Publishing, 1993, $6.99, paper, 112 pp., for counselees

Description "I'm really excited about this book and thank God for its vital message. It is 30 years overdue! Short-term missions without this emphasis and teaching can easily end up as a tragedy instead of a triumph"—George Verwer.

Counseling and Confession *The Role of Confession and Absolution in Pastoral Counseling,* Walter J. Koehler

CPH Publishing, 1992, $7.95, paper, 91 pp., for counselors

Description Offers pastors a balanced understanding of the relationships among modern psychology, pastoral counseling, and absolution.

Author Walter Koehler is a professor at the Lutheran Theological Seminary, Saskatoon, Canada.

Contents *1.* Accents and tensions in pastoral counseling *2.* Individual confession and absolution in Lutheran

theology and practice *3.* Contributions of individual confession and absolution to the pastoral counselor

Sex in the Parish Karen Lebacqz and Ronald G. Barton

Westminster/John Knox Press, 1991, $9.95, paper, 280 pp., for counselors

Description The authors examine the gift of sexuality in relation to the parish and the dynamics of sexual desire and temptation. Editor's note: This title affirms homosexual orientation.

Authors Karen Lebacqz is professor of Christian ethics, Pacific School of Religion, Berkeley, Calif. Ronald G. Barton is associate conference minister, Northern California Conference, United Church of Christ.

Contents *1.* The joy of sex—in the parish? *2.* Dynamics of desire *3.* The failure of limits *4.* Pastoral power *5.* An ethical framework *6.* Women in ministry: sex and sexism *7.* God and eros *8.* Single and sexual *9.* In the closet and out: gay and lesbian pastors *10.* The bishop's dilemma *11.* Conclusion

Hope in Pastoral Care and Counseling Andrew D. Lester

Westminster/John Knox Press, 1995, $16.99, paper, 176 pp.

Description Lester demonstrates that pastoral theology (as well as social and behavioral sciences) has neglected to address effectively the predominant cause of human suffering: a lack of hope, a sense of futurelessness. He also offers a starting point for the development of addressing these important dimensions of human life. He provides clinical theories and methods for pastoral assessment and of intervention with those who despair.

Author Andrew D. Lester is professor of pastoral theology and pastoral counseling at Brite Divinity School, Texas Christian University. He has published numerous articles and books.

When Children Suffer *A Sourcebook for Ministry with Children in Crisis,* Andrew D. Lester

Westminster/John Knox Press, 1987, $16.00, cloth, 209 pp., for counselors

Description Andrew Lester serves as editor as 21 contributors draw upon personal experience to discuss the nature of crises that devastate children and suggest ways in which ministers can respond.

Author Andrew D. Lester is professor of religion, Southern Baptist Theological Seminary. He has published numerous articles and books.

Contents *1*. Ministry with children in crisis *Part 1:* Understanding the school-age child *2*. A developmental understanding of the school-age child *3*. Faith development and the school-age child *4*. What children need from significant adults *5*. Understanding and caring for the child in crisis *Part 2:* Ministry with children in particular crises *6*. Children whose parents are divorcing *7*. The bereaved child *8*. The hospitalized child *9*. The terminally ill child *10*. The chronically ill child *11*. Abused children *12*. Disabled children *13*. Children with learning disabilities *14*. Children suffering from stress and anxiety *Part 3:* Resources for ministry with children in crisis *15*. Talking about faith with children *16*. Pastoral assessment of the child and the family *17*. The extended family *18*. Referral: when, where, how

Married to a Pastor's Wife *Strengthening Marriage Partnerships in Ministry Families,* H. B. London and Neil Wiseman

Victor Books, 1995, $15.99, cloth, 240 pp.

Description In a book designed to be read together, the authors explode 13 myths that plague pastors and their spouses. Some of these include: the church causes most family stress, the congregation determines our standard of living, children suffer when father is a pastor, the church expects too much, churches look for cookie-cutter pastors' wives, ministry makes marriage dull.

Authors H. B. London is assistant to the president at Focus on the Family. He has served for 32 years in the pastorate. Neil Wiseman is vice president of academics at Nazarene Bible College

Surviving in Ministry *Managing the Pitfalls,* Robert R. Lutz and Bruce T. Taylor

Paulist Press, 1990, $11.95, paper, 204 pp., for counselors

Description A holistic approach to surviving life in ministry through selected essays on the person in ministry, those around the person in ministry, and the opportunities for growth.

Editors Robert R. Lutz is a pastoral counselor on the treatment staff of the Isaac Taylor Institute of Psychiatry and Religion at Taylor Manor Hospital, Ellicott City, Md. He holds the doctorate in pastoral counseling from Loyola College. Coeditor Bruce T. Taylor, M.D., is the associate med-

ical director and director of admissions, Taylor Manor Hospital, and president of the board of directors of Changing Point, Inc.

Contents *1*. Surviving in ministry: a theological dilemma *2*. The spiritual life of the minister *3*. And at the center: integrity *4*. Anger and guilt *5*. Personality disorders in the religion professional *6*. Thou shalt not play *7*. Addicted . . . Who me? *8*. Approval and achievement: blessings or false gods? *9*. Surviving ministry from a woman's perspective: celebrating the joys and avoiding the pitfalls *10*. Building support *11*. Burnout: a spiritual pilgrimage *12*. When the bridge comes tumbling down, bearing the weight and tension of the task of ministry *13*. Clergy families: the struggle to be free *14*. The millstone around their necks, children of religious professionals *15*. Surviving in ministry: stresses, strategies, and successes from the clergy wife's perspective *16*. The spouses of religious professionals *17*. When the "Mrs." is a reverend *18*. Clergy couples *19*. The congregation: a family system

Homework Manual for Biblical Living— Volume 1 *Personal and Interpersonal Problems,* Wayne A. Mack

P & R Publishing, 1979, $5.95, paper, 233 pp., for counselors

Description Counselors needing specific assignments to give counselees, or individuals seeking practical helps for their own struggles will welcome Wayne Mack's homework manuals. This first volume deals with personal and interpersonal problems in over 30 categories such as anger, blame shifting, communication, dating, finances, obesity, pride, sex problems, sleep, suffering, thought patterns, and work. Dr. Mack presents a wealth of scriptural information for solving problems in each area covered.

Author Wayne A. Mack is a graduate of Wheaton College. He earned his D.Min. from Westminster Theological Seminary. A frequent lecturer on biblical counseling, he is chairman of Biblical Counseling Studies at Master's College and adjunct lecturer in biblical counseling/pastoral theology at Master's Seminary.

Homework Manual for Biblical Living— Volume 2 *Family and Marital Problems,* Wayne A. Mack

P & R Publishing, 1980, $4.95, paper, 98 pp., for counselors

Description Here is the second of Wayne Mack's homework manuals designed for counselors needing specific assignments to give counselees, or for individuals seeking practical helps in their own struggles. In this volume, Dr. Mack sheds biblical light on family and marital problems with joint and individual assignments on topics such as communication, developing common interests, marriage evaluation, child rearing, and family religion.

Author Wayne A. Mack is a graduate of Wheaton College. He earned his D.Min. from Westminster Theological Seminary. A frequent lecturer on biblical counseling, he is chairman of Biblical Counseling Studies at Master's College and adjunct lecturer in biblical counseling/pastoral theology at Master's Seminary.

The Psychology of Clergy H. Newton Malony and Richard A. Hunt

Morehouse Publishing, 1991, $18.95, paper, 164 pp., a reference or academic work

Description A probing analysis into the psychological issues and stresses of life in the ministry. Dr. Malony and Dr. Hunt examine effective ways that clergy handle the often overwhelming demands on their time. Offers methods of attaining balance and dealing with stress, marital relationships, and dual careers.

Authors H. Newton Malony and Richard A. Hunt are both professors of psychology at the Graduate School of Psychology, Fuller Theological Seminary.

Contents *1.* Ministry: a unique position *2.* Why people enter ministry *3.* What clergy do with their time *4.* The hazards of ministry *5.* Women in ministry *6.* The minister's love life *7.* Spouse and parish *8.* Dual careers in clergy life *9.* Staff relationships in ministry *10.* Ministerial effectiveness *11.* The life cycle of ministry *12.* Surviving and surmounting ministry

Bedside Manners *A Practical Guide to Visiting the Ill,* Katie Maxwell

Baker Book House, 1992, $5.99, paper, 112 pp., for counselors

Description A book filled with practical information to help readers through the visiting process. Covers visiting in hospitals and nursing homes, along with the do's and don'ts of visiting children and the terminally ill. Also included is a chapter on how to aid the primary caregiver. Cuts through the theory and gets right to the "how to."

Author Maxwell is a trained hospital counselor who has made over 6,000 visits to nursing home patients. She is a professional speaker and writer in the field of death and dying and author of several related books.

Contents *1.* The BE attitudes of visiting *2.* Visiting in hospitals *3.* Visiting shut-ins *4.* Visiting in nursing homes *5.* Visiting children *6.* Visiting the terminally ill *7.* Helping the primary caregiver *8.* The church's role in the visiting ministry

Counseling Christian Workers Louis McBurney

Word Publishing, 1986, $15.99, cloth, 296 pp., for counselors

Description This volume probes perfectionism, predictable crises for ministers, and therapeutic possibilities.

Author Louis McBurney (M.D.) counsels clergy at Marble Retreat in Colorado.

Contents *Part 1:* Understanding the hurting Christian *1.* Problems and pressures of the ministry *2.* Role-specific pressures *3.* Resistance to counseling *Part 2:* Common diagnostic considerations and counseling approaches *4.* Marital maladjustment *5.* Depressive illness *6.* Dysfunctional personality *Part 3:* Therapeutic techniques *7.* Basic principles of counseling *8.* Spiritual aspects of counseling Christian workers

Christian Counseling for Pastors and Laymen Frank B. Minirth and Paul D. Meier

Christian Family Video, 1992, $19.95, video, for counselors

Description Part of the Minirth-Meier Church Counseling Video Library. This title contains two hours of important principles of basic counseling and leadership skills to help staff and lay leaders minister to others. Includes topical discussions on awareness techniques, defense mechanisms, behavior modification, and when and how to refer for further help. A great way to refine and polish the skills of not only the staff of the church, but also all of those involved in education, training, outreach, and other areas of church ministry.

Authors Doctors Minirth and Meier have gained national prominence for their successful blending of biblical principles with proven clinical and medical treatment. They are nationally recognized authors of over 60 biblically based books on common psychological issues with over three million in copies in print.

Sins of the Body *Ministry in a Sexual Society,* Terry C. Muck

Word Publishing, 1989, $12.95, cloth, 212 pp., for counselors

Description This book addresses the twin challenges of ministry: maintaining personal purity while maintaining close human contact; and offering a compassionate, healing touch to those who struggle because sex had been misused. A series of hard-hitting articles dealing with a variety of critical issues associated with sexuality and the ministry.

Author Editor Terry Muck is executive editor of *Christianity Today* magazine and a former editor of *Leadership Journal.* He has earned the M.Div. from Bethel Theological Seminary in St. Paul, Minn., and the Ph.D. degree from Northwestern University in Evanston, Ill.

Contents *Part 1:* The personal peril *1.* The war within *2.* Perils of the professionally holy *3.* The war within continues *4.* After the affair: a wife's story *Part 2:* Pastoral precautions *5.* Transference: loosening the tie that binds *6.* Avoiding the scarlet letter *7.* Strategies to keep from falling *Part 3:* Pastoral responses *8.* Counseling sexual addicts *9.* Counseling the rape victim *10.* Helping the sexually abused *11.* Counseling the seductive female *12.* Lovingly leveling with live-ins *Part 4:* The way to recovery *13.* Treatment for infidelity fallout *14.* After the fiasco: restoring fallen Christians

Pastoral Care in Context *An Introduction to Pastoral Care,* John Patton

Westminster/John Knox Press, 1993, $20.00, cloth, 288 pp., a reference or academic work

Description Patton identifies and compares three paradigms of pastoral care: the classical, the clinical pastoral, and the communal contextual. This third paradigm emphasizes the caring community and the various contexts for care rather than focusing on pastoral care as the work of the ordained pastor. He also addresses four major problem areas to which pastoral care is directed.

Author John Patton is professor of pastoral theology, Columbia Theological Seminary, Decatur, Ga., and adjunct professor of pastoral care, Candler School of Theology, Emory University, Atlanta. He is the author of many pastoral care books and served as associate editor of *The Dictionary of Pastoral Care and Counseling.*

Contents *Part 1:* The communal and the contextual *1.* The communal: care as remembering *2.* The contextual: care as remembering *Part 2:* The carer as person, learner, and teacher *3.* Characteristics of the carer *4.* Care through consultation on caring *Part 3:* Human problems as contexts for care *5.* Limit and loss—the risks of care *6.*

Patience and patienthood—the need for care *7.* Abuse of self and others—the failure to care *8.* Special relationships *Part 4:* The pastor as counselor and theologian *9.* Pastoral counseling: a ministry of availability and introduction *10.* Theological reflection on pastoral caring

Confidentiality and Clergy *Churches, Ethics and the Law,* William W. Rankin

Morehouse Publishing, 1990, $8.95, paper, 144 pp., for counselors

Description Written out of the author's personal experience and research, this work is a focused resource on the ethics and law of confidentiality for the clergy.

Author William W. Rankin writes and lectures widely on the subject of ethics and on global issues. He is currently rector of St. Stephen's Episcopal Church, Belvedere, Calif.

Contents *1.* The ethos of the church and the ethics of its clergy *2.* The confession: its characteristics and development through the Church of England *3.* Confession in the Episcopal church *4.* Pastoral counseling: confidentiality versus the duty to divulge, the duty to care, and others *5.* Ethics and the limits of confidentiality *6.* Professional ethics and the law *7.* Managing yourself and parish under the impact of litigation

The Pastor and the Patient *A Practical Guidebook for Hospital Visitation,* Kent D. Richmond and David L. Middleton

Abingdon Press, 1992, $11.95, paper, 144 pp., for counselors

Description The authors provide a theological foundation for pastoral visitation, then invite the reader to understand the revolutionary changes that have taken place in the health care industry. Chapters deal with gaining entry and acquiring information. Offers help regarding patient needs, spiritual resources, and pastoral aftercare.

Authors Kent D. Richmond and David Middleton are chaplains in the Department of Pastoral Care, Lutheran General Hospital, Park Ridge, Ill.

Emotional Freedom *Theotherapy—God's Healing,* Mario E. Rivera

New Leaf Press, 1992, $5.95, paper, 128 pp., for counselors

Description An introduction to "theotherapy" that helps you identify and understand deep hurts. Shows you how to apply the Bible to them so that you can be truly free to be yourself and love others as Jesus commanded.

Author Dr. Mario Rivera is a trained psychologist and pastor who has personally counseled thousands and witnessed the healing power of the Holy Spirit in restoring broken lives to fulfillment and happiness.

Contents *1.* Fundamentals of theotherapy *2.* Seven emotional plagues *3.* Six truths that will change your life *4.* Doing first things first *5.* How to be happy all the time *6.* Living a quality life *7.* Psychological defenses *8.* Healing deep wounds *9.* Daring to live in intimacy *10.* You can start again

Facing Unresolved Conflicts Mario E. Rivera

New Leaf Press, 1992, $6.95, paper, 224 pp., for counselors

Description Discusses a variety of contributing factors of unresolved conflicts.

Author Dr. Mario Rivera is a trained psychologist and pastor who has personally counseled thousands and witnessed the healing power of the Holy Spirit in restoring broken lives to fulfillment and happiness.

Contents *1.* Meeting life's demands *2.* God is not finished with you yet *3.* Depression—no longer a mystery *4.* Ready to explode *5.* Canceling out fear with faith *6.* Whom do you trust? *7.* Rejection: its beginning and end *8.* What is troubling you? *9.* Unfinished business *10.* The "X" factor *11.* Changing your way of living *12.* Forgiveness—God's antidote *13.* Saying/hearing/listening *14.* The authentic you *15.* Reaching your full potential *16.* Finding your place in life *17.* How to be happy all the time *18.* Identifying the real culprits *19.* The cycle of healing

The Art and Vocation of Caring for People in Pain Karl A. Schultz

Paulist Press, 1994, $7.95, paper, 110 pp., for counselors

Description Explores practical insights into the problems, questions, and stages individuals experience when suffering or ministering to others who suffer or undergo great stress.

Author Karl A. Schultz is director of Genesis Personal Developmental Center in Glenshaw, Pa., and the developer of the "Job therapy" program for caregivers and sufferers in pastoral care.

Contents *1.* Wherever we go, we bring ourselves *2.* The therapeutic power of personal meaning and the human spirit *3.* Models of care-giving *4.* The language of suffering and care-giving *5.* Trust and integrity: essential caregiver dispositions *6.* The healing possibilities of humor *7.* Therapeutic applications of Job

The Guilt-Free Book for Pastors' Wives Ruth Senter

Victor Books, paper, for counselees

Description A warm and personal account from one who understands and walks the way of a pastor's wife with all of its challenges, struggles, and joys.

Sins of the Body *Ministry in a Sexual Society,* Marshall Shelly

Word Publishing, 1992, $11.99, cloth, 215 pp., for counselors

Description Addresses the twin challenges of ministry: maintaining personal purity and offering a compassionate, healing touch to those who struggle because the sexual gift has been misused.

The Pastor As Counselor Earl E. Shelp and Ronald H. Sunderland

The Pilgrim Press, 1991, $9.95, paper, 152 pp., for counselors

Description What makes counseling pastoral counseling? Virtually all clergy are called upon to provide counseling as a part of the church's general pastoral ministry. But what are the differences between pastors and lay specialists in the fundamentals and techniques of counseling? What gives pastoral counseling its special niche in the field of mental health therapies? Six experts seek to offer answers.

Editor Earl Shelp, Ph.D., is executive director of Foundation of Interfaith Research and Ministry in Houston, Tex. Coeditor Ronald H. Sunderland, Ed.D., is associate director and senior research fellow at Foundation for Interfaith Research and Ministry.

Contents *1.* Counseling in ministry *2.* Sermons and instruments of care and counseling *3.* The moral context of counseling *4.* Giving care through counseling *5.* Intimacy and relationships in counseling *6.* Healing in a theological perspective

Pastoral Care for Single Parents Harold Ivan Smith

Beacon Hill Press of Kansas City, 1982, $7.95, paper, 158 pp., for counselors

Description Attacks the tough question of how to truly meet the needs of one-parent families in the church.

Author Harold Ivan Smith is well known for his combined ministries of writing, speaking, and counseling, especially in the area of singles ministries in the church.

Contents *1.* Where can we begin? *2.* A biblical agenda: the Old Testament *3.* A biblical agenda: the New Testament *4.* Risks *5.* The pastor and the single family *6.* Barriers *7.* Guidelines for pastoral care *8.* Premarital counseling: a preventative tool *9.* Preventing the problem *10.* Remarriage *11.* Classification of second marriage *12.* Motivations for second marriage *13.* Reaching single parents for Christ *14.* What am I going to do about it?

Handbook for Basic Types of Pastoral Care and Counseling Howard W. Stone and William M. Clements

Abingdon Press, 1991, $21.95, cloth, 368 pp., a reference or academic work

Description A companion volume to Howard Clinebell's classic *Basic Types of Pastoral Care.* Clinebell's methodology is updated and reinterpreted by several authorities in the field.

Facing Death Together *The Pastor and the Family,* Kenneth E. Sullivan

Beacon Hill Press of Kansas City, 1989, $4.95, paper, 95 pp., for counselors

Description A practical treatment of the subject of the pastor's role when death has come. It is based on the author's pastoral experience and research.

Author Kenneth E. Sullivan is an ordained elder and grief counselor and is involved in crisis intervention ministry.

Contents *1.* The problem: grief and fear of death *2.* The personal *3.* The person in pain *4.* The pastor in perplexity / *Conclusion* / *Epilogue* / Prayers for pastoral ministry and personal meditation

Pastoral Care Emergencies *Ministering to People in Crisis,* David K. Switzer

Paulist Press, 1989, $12.95, paper, 223 pp., for counselors

Description A handbook for ministering to those in crisis. Provides fresh insights into the dynamics of several common and critical situations that pastors/church leaders are called to respond to.

Author David K. Switzer is professor of pastoral care and counseling at the Perkins School of Theology, Southern Methodist University, Dallas, Tex. He received his Ph.D. in theology from Southern California School of Theology. He is widely published in journals and has contributed to many books on pastoral counseling.

Contents *1.* What is a pastoral emergency? *2.* The carer and the caring: who we are and how we go about it *3.* Responding to person's needs in situational crises *4.* Visiting the physically ill *5.* Hospital emergencies *6.* Ministry to the dying *7.* Pastoral response to bereavement *8.* Responding to suicidal persons and their families *9.* Marriage and family life: family systems, counseling, divorce *10.* Marriage and family emergencies: family violence, homosexuality, psychiatric emergencies, alcoholism *11.* When and how to refer

Basic Skills for Christian Counselors *An Introduction for Pastoral Ministers,* Richard P. Vaughn

Paulist Press, $8.95, paper, for counselors

Description A "how-to" book with numerous case histories and examples whose aim is to teach church personnel how to be effective in pastoral ministry. Provides excellent help for those already engaged in counseling without any formal training.

Caring and Curing *A Proven Process for Health and Healing,* John Kie Vining

Institute for Pastoral Care, 1992, $8.00, paper, 104 pp., for counselors

Description Covers issues associated with pastoral counseling in the pentecostal tradition.

Author John Kie Vining holds a doctor of ministry degree from Columbia Theological Seminary. He is a licensed professional counselor in Georgia and Tennessee.

Contents *1.* This issue of pastoral counseling in the Pentecostal movement *2.* Health and healing in the Wesleyan movement *3.* Health and healing in the Holiness movement *4.* Health and healing in the Pentecostal movement *5.* Health and healing and pastoral counseling in the Pentecostal movement *6.* Conclusion: pastoral counseling—a new ministry in the Pentecostal movement

Pastoral Care and Counseling Never Involves Sex John Kie Vining

Institute for Pastoral Care, 1992, $4.00, paper, 36 pp., for counselors

Description This highly readable, soon-to-be formally published paper is an outstanding introduction to sexual ethics for pastoral counselors.

Author John Kie Vining holds a doctor of ministry degree from Columbia Theological Seminary. He is a licensed professional counselor in Georgia and Tennessee.

Contents Includes discussion on definitions, codes of ethics in the professional community, boundaries, ministerial neediness, pitfalls to avoid, the impact of ministerial sexual misconduct, transference and non-therapeutic counter-transference, referrals, and more.

Clinical Handbook of Pastoral Counseling *Volume 1,* R. J. Wicks, R. D. Parsons, and D. E. Capps

Paulist Press, 1985, $25.00, cloth, 707 pp., for counselors

Description A comprehensive ecumenical work that brings together leading Christian professionals who incorporate basic theory and practice with the use of illustrated examples. This newly revised edition contains additional information on supervision, family systems, ethics, research, and spiritual direction.

Editors—Robert J. Wicks is professor and director of program development of the graduate programs in pastoral counseling at Loyola College in Maryland. Richard D. Parsons is associate professor of counselor education, West Chester University, Pa. Donald Capps is William Harte Felmeth professor of pastoral theology at Princeton Theological Seminary.

Contents *1.* Introduction to pastoral counseling *2.* A prolegomenon to a history of pastoral counseling *3.* Directions in pastoral counseling *4.* Spirituality and personal maturity *5.* Christotherapy: an approach to facilitating psychospiritual healing and growth *6.* Countertransference and burnout in pastoral counseling *7.* The counseling relationship *8.* Assessment in pastoral care *9.* Crisis intervention and problem solving *10.* Consultation, collaboration, and referral *11.* Childhood and adolescence—a faith development perspective *12.* Pastoral counseling for middle adults: a Levinsonian perspective *13.* Pastoral care and counseling of the aging *14.* Marital and family therapy skills for pastoral therapists *15.* Women *16.* Minorities *17.* The handicapped *18.* Pastoral counseling in the parish setting *19.* Pastoral counseling in the hospital setting *20.* Prison *21.* Pastoral counseling in an industrial and corporate setting *22.* Pastoral counseling and the university *23.* The role of the pastoral counselor in the primary and secondary school *24.* Community service setting *25.* Military *26.* Anxiety and stress *27.* Loneliness: depression, grief, and alienation *28.* Anger and aggression *29.* Alcohol and other drug dependencies *30.* Sexual dysfunction *31.* Loss and bereavement *32.* Supervising pastoral care *33.* Essential elements of family systems approaches to pastoral counseling *34.* A philosophical foundation for professional and ethical issues in pastoral counseling *35.* Research in pastoral counseling, definitions, methods, and research training *36.* Spiritual direction

Clinical Handbook of Pastoral Counseling *Volume 2,* R. J. Wicks and R. D. Parsons

Paulist Press, 1993, $25.00, cloth, 741 pp., for counselors

Description Building on the groundbreaking original work with the same title, these articles focus on current issues, such as certain life stages, special populations, the devalued and abused, the addicted, and special issues of the 1990s. Like volume one, a comprehensive ecumenical work that brings together leading Christian professionals who incorporate basic theory and practice with the use of illustrated examples.

Editors—Robert J. Wicks is professor and director of program development of the graduate programs in pastoral counseling at Loyola College in Maryland. Richard D. Parsons is associate professor of counselor education, West Chester University, Pa.

Contents *Part 1:* The expanded challenges and opportunities of pastoral counseling *1.* Reaching to the unknown: religion and the psyche *2.* Lay Christian counseling *3.* Revisioning pastoral diagnosis *4.* The contributions of short-term dynamic psychotherapy to pastoral psychotherapy *Part 2:* The challenges and opportunities of special populations *5.* Cross-cultural pastoral psychotherapy *6.* Pastoral counseling with families at risk *7.* A feminist perspective on pastoral counseling with women *8.* Mental health treatment of religion professionals *9.* Counseling lesbians: a feminist perspective *10.* Pastoral counseling of the gay male [Editor's note: the previous two chapters propose an affirming view of homosexuality] *Part 3:* The challenges and opportunities of life stages *11.* Midlife transitions in men and women *12.* Marital conflict and marital spirituality *13.* Single parents in need of pastoral support *Part 4:* The challenges and opportunities of the de-valued and abused *14.* Pastoral care and counseling and issues of self-esteem *15.* Guilt *16.* Depression *17.* Counseling adult survivors of childhood sexual abuse *18.* Calling to accountability: the church's response to abusers *19.* Words can never hurt me? The psychological/emotional abuse of children *Part 5:* Problems, challenges, and opportunities of the addicted *20.* Bulimia and anorexia: signs of the times *21.* Pastoral counseling and psychoactive substance abuse disorders *22.* Adult children of alcoholics *23.* Pathological gambling and pastoral counseling *Part 6:* Special challenges and opportunities for the 1990s *24.* Posttraumatic stress disorder *25.* Suicide survivors: intervention—prevention—postvention *26.* Pastoral care of the unemployed *27.* Embracing pastoral ministry in the age of AIDS

African American Pastoral Care Edward P. Wimberly

Abingdon Press, 1992, $9.95, paper, 111 pp., for counselors

Description Suggests several narrative counseling techniques and relates these techniques to narrative aspects of preaching and worship in the black church. By linking personal stories and the pastors' stories to the heart of the Bible stories, counselors can use God's unfolding drama of salvation to bring healing and reconciliation to human lives.

Author Professor of pastoral care and counseling—Interdenominational Theological Center, Atlanta, Ga. Previous teaching posts at Oral Roberts School of Theology and Garrett-Evangelical Theological Seminary. Holds a Ph.D. in pastoral psychology and counseling from Boston University. Ordained minister in the United Methodist Church. Member of American Association of Pastoral Counselors and the American Association of Marriage and Family Therapists.

Contents *1.* Pastoral care and worship—caring and addiction *2.* Pastoral care and support systems—illness and bereavement *3.* Pastoral care and life crises *4.* A narrative approach to premarriage, marriage, and family counseling *5.* Personal resources for developing a narrative approach *6.* Indigenous pastoral care—facing the 21st century

Prayer in Pastoral Counseling *Suffering, Healing, and Discernment,* Edward P. Wimberly

Westminster/John Knox Press, 1990, $12.99, paper, 127 pp., for counselors

Description Makes a significant contribution to understanding the role of prayer in counseling. With ample case material and clear practical guidelines, the book demonstrates how spiritual direction and pastoral counseling can successfully be brought into the counseling process in ways that foster healing and stimulate growth. Several case studies are used to illustrate the use of a discernment model of prayer in pastoral and Christian counseling.

Author Professor of pastoral care and counseling—Interdenominational Theological Center, Atlanta, Ga. Previous teaching posts at Oral Roberts School of Theology and Garrett-Evangelical Theological Seminary. Holds a Ph.D. in pastoral psychology and counseling from Boston University. Ordained minister in the United Methodist Church. Member of American Association of Pastoral Counselors and the American Association of Marriage and Family Therapists.

Contents *1.* Healing prayers in pastoral counseling *2.* Early stages of counseling *3.* Framing the counseling problem *4.* Setting goals in marriage and family counseling *5.* Action stages of individual counseling *6.* Overcoming a tragic vision *7.* Action stages in marriage counseling

FIND *A Ministry Locating Service*

FIND, a reference or academic work

Description An outstanding service for anyone in helping professions or ministries. FIND is a database of over 1,500 national and regional organizations across the United States that assist families in all areas of need and development including those pertaining to illness and disability. Guidepost Outreach Ministries has contacted these agencies and received a detailed description of programs and services available to the public. Once you request and fill out a simple form, the staff at FIND compile and return to you a list of potential service agencies that can help.

Helping Someone Who Doesn't Want Help

Abbey Press, $.50 each, paper, 8 pp., for counselees

Description Part of the CareNotes series from Abbey Press. CareNotes are short booklets that help readers identify issues and begin the process of seeking resolution. Anecdotal and uplifting. Beautiful photographs grace the covers. Over 20 million CareNotes have been sold in just over five years. Can be used as an alternative to a greeting card or in conjunction with pastoral care visits.

The Minister's Hotline for Counseling Assistance

Rapha Resources, for counselors

28. Perfectionism

The Performance Illusion *Why Do We Try So Hard to Be Liked?* Chap Clark

NavPress, 1993, $10.00, paper, 180 pp., for counselees

Description In *The Performance Illusion,* Chap Clark takes us not through a book but on an adventure. First he brings us face-to-face with our most common terror—the terror of feeling we are not performing well enough for our parents, our wives or husbands, our children, our work, and sadly, even our God. In doing so, he exposes the tyranny of expectation that debilitates so many of us. As a result, we spend our lives exhausted by our dizzying activity, paralyzed by our fear of a poor performance. Then, just as we have lost hope, Clark shatters this "illusion of performance" by bringing us face-to-face with God's staggering love—a love that transcends our expectations and frees us from everyone else's.

Author Chap Clark is chairman of the Youth Ministries Department at Denver Seminary, an associate staff of Youth Specialties, and on the Young Life staff in the training department. He is the author of six books.

Contents *Part 1:* What's gone wrong? *1.* "I've been had!" *2.* In the name of love *3.* "If they could see me now!" *4.* Trust and obey *5.* The "blaming" syndrome—"It's not my fault!" *6.* "I did it my way!": the deity of loneliness *7.* What's gone wrong? *Part 2:* What must I do to be saved? *8.* Amazing grace *9.* What does grace look like? *10.* What must I do to be saved? *Part 3:* Performing for God versus responding to God's love *11.* What do I believe? *12.* Responding to God's love in my faith *13.* Responding to God's love in my family *14.* Responding to God's love in my friendships *15.* Responding to God's love in the tasks of life *16.* Carrying on the fight of freedom

How to Stop Living for the Applause *Help for Women Who Need to Be Perfect,* Holly G. Miller and Dennis Hensley

Servant Publications/Vine Books, 1992, $8.99, paper, 170 pp., for counselees

Perfectionism—Its Causes and Cures
Clyde M. Narramore

Narramore Christian Foundation, $.50, paper, 12 pp., for both counselors and counselees

Description One of the many booklets available from the Narramore Christian Foundation. Designed to be handed to a person beginning to come to grips with a problem in living.

Author Dr. Clyde M. Narramore is a licensed psychologist and the president and founder of the Narramore Christian Foundation—a charitable, nonprofit educational, training, and counseling organization ministering primarily to the Christian community. He is also the founder of the Rosemead School of Psychology and author of 29 books.

Perfect Every Time *When Doing It All Leaves You with Nothing . . . ,* Paula Rinehart

NavPress, 1992, $10.00, paper, 200 pp., for counselees

Description Explores the internal dynamics of the performance cycle. Rinehart shares honestly from her own life and from the lives of other women who try too hard and do too much. With compassion and clarity, she'll help you listen more to the God-given desires within and less to the dictates of our culture, your past, or other people. Ultimately, you'll discover a restored enjoyment of womanhood, giving you the ability to receive from God and others and to relax in a strength that's not your own.

Author Paula Rinehart is the author of the Starting Strong Bible study series for preteens and coauthored the award-winning best-seller *Choices: Finding God's Way in Dating, Sex, Singleness, and Marriage.* She lives with her husband and two children in Raleigh, N.C.

Contents *Part 1:* Profiles of women who do too much *1.* A journey I never intended to make: an unnerving invitation to sanity *2.* Standing on our mothers' shoulders—

reaching to the stars *3.* The push-ahead woman—when enough is never enough *4.* The indispensable woman: when you give until it hurts *5.* Ecstasy and agony: as the pendulum swings *Part 2:* The emotional roots of doing too much *6.* Mothers and daughters, shared identities, common quests *7.* A nightingale in a gilded cage: the hero and her dilemma *8.* The little girl in the cellar: why we hide *9.* Our greatest need: to discover an unreasonable love *Part 3:* The way change looks and feels *10.* Longings: making those important inner connections *11.* Relationships: enjoying intimate moments *12.* Embracing the journey: cultivating a spirit of adventure

Freedom from the Performance Trap
Letting Go of the Need to Achieve, David A. Seamands

Victor Books, 1988, $9.99, paper, 204 pp., for counselees

Description No matter how hard performance-oriented Christians try, they never feel like they're accomplishing all they should. David Seamands shows how the grace of God can free believers from the performance trap.

Author David Seamands is professor emeritus of pastoral ministries and counselor in residence at Asbury Theological Seminary in Wilmore, Ky.

Contents *1.* The miracle of grace *2.* Barriers to grace *3.* Parental grace—or disgrace *4.* How it all began *5.* The bad news *6.* The consequences of disgrace *7.* The good news *8.* Grace and guilt *9.* Grace and emotions *10.* Grace and self-esteem *11.* Grace and negative emotions *12.* The panorama of God's grace

The Control Trap *A Woman's Guide to Freedom from the Need to Manage People and Circumstances,* Barbara Sullivan

Bethany House Publishers, 1989, $8.99, paper, for counselees

Description A woman's guide to finding freedom from the need to control and manage people and circumstances through trusting God's sovereign grace.

Meditations for Christians Who Try to Be Perfect Joan C. Webb

Harper and Row, 1993, $10.00, paper, 400 pp., for counselees

Description Webb provides suggested Bible readings, key scriptural phrases, anecdotes, and other encouraging thoughts that will help Christians achieve balance, leave perfectionism behind, and learn to live by grace.

Author Joan C. Webb is a successful business-woman, speaker, and teacher.

29. Pregnancy and Related Issues

Adoption Resources

How to Adopt a Child *A Comprehensive Guide for Prospective Parents,* Connie Crain and Janice Duffy

Thomas Nelson Publishers, 1994, $12.99, paper, 304 pp., for both counselors and counselees

Description Written in a question and answer format, this complete resource book offers specific advice on how to adopt a child. User-friendly, this book addresses every kind of adoption (private, open, foreign, and state) plus laws prospective parents need to know.

Authors Connie Crain is an adoptive parent who has treated and cared for women who were giving up their children for adoption. Janice Duffy is an adoptive parent and is active in local adoption circles.

Contents *1.* The big question *2.* Some adoption terms *3.* Agency adoptions *4.* Private adoption *5.* International adoption *6.* Single-parent adoption *7.* State and special-needs adoption *8.* Common medical considerations *9.* International medical considerations *10.* Adoption / Resources

After the Adoption *Learning to Cope with Sibling Rivalry, Spiritual Values . . . ,* Elizabeth Hormann

Fleming H. Revell, $9.99, paper, for both counselors and counselees

Description A practical guide to bonding the adoptive family. Parents who have adopted or anticipate adopting need this experienced advice on bonding the new child into the family.

Meditations for Adoptive Parents Vernell Klassen Miller

Herald Press, 1992, $6.95, paper, 88 pp., for counselees

Description The perfect gift for adoptive parents in the style of the best-selling *Meditations for the New Mother.* Using her family experiences, Vernell Klassen Miller weaves many threads into the fabric of these meditations on adoption. She includes theories about bonding to infants and older children, the stages of relinquishment and adoption, the process of entitlement, and the advantages of the adoption process.

Author Vernell Klassen Miller is a full-time homemaker by choice. She also enjoys teaching Spanish to several home educating families and free-lance writing.

Brian Was Adopted Doris Sandford and Graci Evans

Gold 'n' Honey Books (Questar), 1993, $6.99, cloth, 28 pp., for counselees

Description Part of the In Our Neighborhood series from Gold 'n' Honey. The series was developed for children ages 5–11 who have difficult issues to cope with. The books deal gently and compassionately with children's delicate feelings when they're forced to handle situations that are hard to understand.

The Whole Life Adoption Book *Realistic Advice for Building a Healthy Adoptive Family,* Jayne E. Schooler

NavPress/Piñion Press, 1993, $12.00, paper, 217 pp., for both counselors and counselees

Description Adoptive families deal with a special dynamic that affects parents, birth children, and adopted children. Creating a nurturing family environment and being prepared for typical crisis points are essential. With encouragement and practical information from infancy to adulthood, *The Whole Life Adoption Book* discusses: what to consider before you adopt, how to tell a child he or she is adopted, how to help your child deal with memories of the past, how to understand the issues and behaviors that can surface in adolescence, how to respond when a child wants to search for his biological parents. This book offers hope and direction to those considering adoption and those desiring to improve the adoptive family relationships at any stage.

Author Jayne E. Schooler is the adoption coordinator for Warren County Children Services in Lebanon, Ohio. She and her husband have a birth daughter and an adopted son.

The Complete Adoption Handbook Kay Marshall Strom and Douglas R. Donnelly

Zondervan Publishing House, 1992, $8.99, paper, 224 pp., for counselees

Description Authors Kay Marshall Strom and adoption attorney Douglas Donnelly guide readers through the considerations and legalities that surround adoption and on to the final question: Is adoption for you? Contains a series of outstanding appendixes that include legal details state-by-state, additional resources, and reading.

Contents *1.* Is there a child for you? *2.* Adoption: whose choice? *3.* The classic story *4.* Yes, but . . . a realistic picture *5.* Love comes in many colors *6.* God's special children *7.* No longer babies *8.* Sometimes parents *9.* My brother's keeper *10.* A parent alone *11.* Growing together *12.* Help! *13.* No longer my child *14.* The children speak / *Appendixes*

The Fifteen Most Asked Questions about Adoption Laura L. Valenti

Herald Press, 1985, $8.95, paper, 224 pp., for counselees

Description An adoptive parent answers key questions facing those who want to adopt a child.

Author Laura Valenti is the mother of an adopted child from Central America. She lives with her family in rural Missouri.

Contents *1.* Who are the children in need of adoption and why? *2.* Where have all the babies gone? *3.* Who can adopt? *4.* What is a homestudy? *5.* What is foreign adoption? *6.* How long does it take to adopt? *7.* What is an adoption support group? *8.* How much does it cost to adopt? *9.* What about friends and relatives who are against adoption? *10.* Should we try foster parenting first? *11.* Why are there so many different kinds of adoptions? *12.* How will we know the right child for us? *13.* How much should we tell our adopted child? *14.* Open records—should we or shouldn't we? *15.* What if we need more help later?

How to Adopt a Child from Another Country Eileen M. Wirth and Joan Worden

Abingdon Press, 1994, $10.95, paper, 144 pp., for both counselors and counselees

Description A book of hope for people who wonder if the child they long for can ever be theirs. It is written by two women who have traveled the long road to a successful conclusion and have stayed around to help others on the journey. The book includes: introduction to foreign adoption, adoption quiz, tips for exploring adoption, differences between foreign and domestic adoptions, creative ways to finance the venture, a successful case study, suggestions for adjusting to the child, listings of foreign agencies by state, and what to expect realistically regarding cost.

Authors Eileen M. Wirth (M.A., University of Nebraska, M.A., University of Minnesota) is assistant professor of journalism at Creighton University in Omaha, Nebr. She is the mother of two foreign adopted children. Joan Worden (M.S.W., University of Nebraska) is an internationally recognized expert in the area of foreign adoption. She is the executive director of KESIL Adoption Agency in Nebraska. She is the mother of two foreign adopted children and three biological children.

Holt International Children's Services

For counselees

Description A Christian international adoption agency. Produces a magazine for adoptive parents.

Bethany Christian Services

Bethany Christian Services. An organization

Description Handles a variety of adoption services, including networking, legal assistance, support materials.

Liberty Godparent Home

Liberty Godparent Home. An organization

Description Maintains a 24-hour crisis pregnancy help line, operates a state licensed maternity home and a state licensed adoption agency, and provides information on beginning a crisis pregnancy helpline.

Crisis Pregnancy

No Easy Choices *The Dilemma of Crisis Pregnancy,* Sylvia Boothe

New Hope, 1990, $3.95, paper, 76 pp., for counselees

Description There are no easy choices for the young unwed mother. But there are ways to help her as she makes one of the most important decisions of her life. This book helps provide guidance and help for the concerned Christian who wants to minister to a woman with a crisis pregnancy. Whether you wish to be a part of an ongoing ministry, or want to help one young woman, *No Easy Choices* can help you. Discusses single parenting, marriage, and adoption.

Author Sylvia DeHart Boothe is coordinator for Alternatives to Abortion Ministries with the Home Mission Board in Atlanta, Ga. She earned her M.A. from the University of Texas.

Contents *1.* The crisis *2.* The minister *3.* Single parents *4.* Marriage *5.* Adoption *6.* Help *7.* Forgiveness

Not an Easy Time *Help While You Are Pregnant,* Sylvia Boothe

New Hope, 1990, $1.25, paper, 20 pp., for counselees

Description An easy-to-read book about what to do if you are young, single, and having a baby. It tells you what to eat, how to find a doctor, how you can finish school, and where you can go for help if you need money to pay for your baby's birth. Also helps with decisions about marriage, single parenting, and adoption. It also has an important message about God's love and forgiveness.

Author Sylvia DeHart Boothe is coordinator for Alternatives to Abortion Ministries with the Home Mission Board in Atlanta, Ga. She earned her M.A. from the University of Texas.

Caring Enough to Help *Counseling at a Crisis Pregnancy Center,* Ellen Curro

Baker Book House, 1991, $8.99, paper, 146 pp., for counselors

Description The tension, joys, heartaches, and frustrations experienced at a crisis pregnancy center come alive through the stories of frontline warfare in this battle for life. One can witness compassionate and confident help to those who face such questions as: What is an abortion? What are my options if I don't want an abortion? What do I do when my teenager says "I'm pregnant!"? Why didn't they tell me the pain from the abortion wouldn't go away? The resource list at the close is a must for counselors

of every level. The content of this book is presented as a series of letters from one woman to another.

Author Ellen Curro, M.Ed., P.A.-C., received her masters of education in counseling/guidance from Xavier University and her physician assistant training at George Washington University. She is a former counselor, teacher, physician assistant, and director of a crisis pregnancy center. Currently, she is president of Linking Education and Medicine. She has authored two additional books.

Contents *Part 1:* [Extra] ordinary days *1.* I can see *2.* Mom's solution *3.* Prayer *4.* Married couples *5.* Laughter *6.* Discouragement *7.* Adoption *8.* Almost aborted *Part 2:* The pro-life/abortion arena *9.* Sick *10.* Sharing *11.* Deception *12.* Repentance *13.* Birth control *14.* Pointing fingers *15.* Prevention *16.* A temple *Part 3:* Mourning: a baby dies *17.* Miscarriage *18.* Grief *19.* Post abortion *20.* For dads *21.* For grandparents *22.* For doctors and nurses *23.* For counselors, teachers, and friends *24.* For ministers *Part 4:* On a mission *25.* Ambassadors *26.* Rest and balance *27.* Holidays *28.* Cracked pots *29.* The Father's heart *30.* Singleness *31.* Hope / *Suggested resources*

A Question of Worth: A Special Presentation *To Encourage Church Involvement with Crisis Pregnancy Centers,* James Dobson

Word Publishing, 1988, $15.00, video, for counselees

Description More than 2,300 CPCs have opened their doors to befriend and counsel confused and often desperate mothers-to-be who would otherwise choose abortion. Dr. Dobson urges churches to lend assistance to these women by supporting their local crisis pregnancy centers. The video includes an excerpt from the "Turn Your Hearts toward Home" film series in which Dr. Dobson discusses the sanctity of life and the horror of abortion.

Author James C. Dobson, Ph.D., is founder and president of Focus on the Family. A licensed psychologist, he has authored 12 best-selling books on the family, including *The Strong Willed Child, Love Must Be Tough, Parenting Isn't for Cowards,* and the *New Dare to Discipline.*

The Pro-Life Corporate and Legal Handbook Thomas Glessner

Care Net, $5.00, paper, a reference or academic work

Description Up-to date information for all pro-life organizations. Includes details for incorporation, tax exempt status, and legal liability. Also contains copies of necessary legal forms.

No Other Choice *A Story about Making the Choice for Life,* Lissa Halls Johnson

Fleming H. Revell, 1986, $6.99, paper, 191 pp., for counselees

Description Fiction. This award-winning book (Campus Life, Book of the Year, 1987) is meant to present the differing views of abortion. Intended for women who need to forgive themselves and start the healing process after having an abortion.

Author Lissa Halls Johnson is the author of the bestselling, award-winning book *Just Like Ice Cream,* as well as other books for teens. She has written radio scripts, short stories, and articles for various publications including *Reader's Digest.*

Giving Women Real Choices *A New Approach Offering Help and Hope Instead of Abortion,* Frederica Mathewes-Green

Multnomah Books (Questar), 1994, $8.99, paper, 182 pp., for counselors

Description Examines some of the questions that surround abortion and the reasons why many women choose abortion. Identifies the problems that make an unplanned pregnancy appear an unbearable burden. Examines the resources available to alleviate those problems and how those resources can be improved. Based on the research, experience, and wisdom of those who serve pregnant women daily in pregnancy care centers.

Author Frederica Mathewes-Green is the director for Real Choices, a research project by the National Women's Coalition for Life, aimed at reducing the demand for abortion.

Help and Hope for Teenage Mothers Our Times Video

Ave Maria Press, 1992, $24.95, video, 28 minutes, for counselees

Description This video explores ways to help young mothers, focusing on such issues as health care, education, bonding between parent and child, surrogate families, peer support, and negotiating adult versus adolescent issues.

Pregnant and Single *Help for the Tough Choices,* Carolyn Owens and Linda Roggow

Zondervan Publishing House, 1992, $7.95, paper, 144 pp., for counselees

Description A sensitively written book presenting practical advice for the single woman who finds herself pregnant outside of marriage. It is a handbook and a guide for those facing pregnancy.

Authors Carolyn Owens is author of ten children's activity books and has published articles in *Freeway, Pentecostal Evangel, Home Life,* and others. In 1981, her book *A Promise of Sanity* won the Sherwood E. Wirt Award for excellence in Christian writing. Linda Roggow earned her M.S.W. from the University of Hawaii. She is a supervisor of social services for the New Horizons Adoption Agency in Minnesota and Iowa.

Contents *1.* Don't panic *2.* What's happening to me? *3.* Healthy mother and baby *4.* Who can I turn to? *5.* What are my options? *6.* How do I make a good decision? *7.* Am I ready for motherhood? *8.* Money matters *9.* Checking my motives *10.* Will I say "I do"? *11.* Making plans for adoption *12.* What about him? *13.* Grandparents have feelings too *14.* Faith helps

Daddy, I'm Pregnant Bill Putman

Multnomah Books (Questar), 1987, $7.99, paper, 114 pp., for counselees

Description Taken from a minister's journal, this book is about love and forgiveness . . . joy and sorrow. It's about a father's love in a time of crisis. It's about a family who weathered a disaster and experienced God's unspeakable grace and healing in the midst of it. Through all the questions and heartache, Putnam affirms God's unfailing presence. He speaks about choices that can bring healing and comfort, or bitterness and resentment.

The Search for a Past *The Adopted Adult's Unique Process of Finding Identity,* Jayne Schooler

Piñion Press, 1995, $10.99, paper, 200 pp.

Description Written for adults considering searching for their birth family. Will help prepare them emotionally and psychologically both for the search and what they'll find. Also an essential resource for adoptive parents, spouses of adoptees, adoption counselors and agencies, ministers, and care-group leaders.

Author Jayne E. Schooler is the adoption coordinator for Warren County Children Services in Lebanon, Ohio. She and her husband have a birth daughter and an adopted son.

Contents *Section 1*—Adoption—from the other side of childhood *1.* Growing up adopted—the unique struggles *2.* To search or not to search *3.* How to communicate the decision to search with your adopted parents *Section 2*—Starting the journey back *4.* Preparing emotionally for the search *5.* Initiating the search and first contact *6.* Facing a history of abuse and neglect *Section 3*—Dealing with special issues within the search *7.* A walk into the wilderness: learning of your adoption as an adult *8.* When the pieces don't fit: finding dead ends or death *9.* Revisiting an old wound: encountering denial or rejection *10.* Searching in mid-life: what are the implications? *11.* Searching as a teenager: what are the concerns? *Section 4*—Life will never be the same *12.* Incorporating birth family members into your life: concerns, challenges, rewards

How Could This Happen? *Dealing with Crisis Pregnancy,* Laurie Taylor

New Hope, 1992, $1.95, paper, 19 pp., for counselees

Description This book is written so that teenagers can understand the difficult decisions that their friend must face in dealing with crisis pregnancy and how they can help. This booklet is part of the Between Friends series.

Author Laurie Taylor is minister of childhood education at Hunter's Glen Baptist Church, Plano, Tex.

Pregnant and Alone *How You Can Help An Unwed Friend,* Henrietta VanDerMolen

Harold Shaw Publishers, 1989, $6.99, paper, 127 pp., for counselors

Description Here is a book that explores the difficult situation of crisis pregnancy and equips the birth mother, her family, and her circle of friends to make important decisions.

Author Henrietta VanDerMolen is involved in a ministry that provides encouragement and a loving home for young women with crisis pregnancies. A busy mother, businesswoman, and grandmother, she also serves on the board of directors for Wheaton Youth Outreach in Wheaton, Ill.

Contents *1.* Getting started *2.* Telling parents (and other significant people) *3.* The unwed father *4.* Life or death? *5.* Facts about abortion: how it's done *6.* To parent or not to parent *7.* All about adoption *8.* Choosing adoption *9.* Great expectations—and real life! *10.* A better way *11.* Where do you go from here?

Counseling for Unplanned Pregnancy and Infertility Everett L. Worthington Jr.

Word Publishing, 1987, $15.99, cloth, 285 pp., for counselors

Description Part of the Resources for Christian Counseling series, this book surveys all sorts of problem pregnancies, including adolescent pregnancies, twins, children close together, and later life pregnancies. It also discusses infertility. Gives practical guidance, based upon current research, on how to counsel family members with unplanned pregnancy or infertility. The book is ideal for counselors in crisis pregnancy centers, nurses, and social workers. The book is informative and contains substantial humor.

Author Everett Worthington holds a Ph.D. in counseling from the University of Missouri–Columbia and has worked at Virginia Commonwealth University since 1978. As a licensed clinical psychologist, he has directed a community counseling agency, supervised others, and maintained a part-time private practice.

Should I Keep My Baby? *Warm, Practical Help for Teenagers Facing Pregnancy Alone,* Martha Zimmerman

Bethany House Publishers, 1983, $4.99, paper, 112 pp., for counselees

Description A book especially written to teenage girls who are facing a pregnancy alone. Readers will receive advice and encouragement for dealing appropriately with a sense of guilt, new feelings, physical condition, boyfriend, coming baby, and future. A short, convincing presentation concerning abortion will gently but firmly lead readers away from this option.

Author Martha Zimmerman spent more than a year in careful research and writing of this book for young women.

Contents *1.* "What should I do?" *2.* "Whom should I tell?" *3.* Before saying "I do" *4.* "Should I parent my baby?" *5.* Growing in the soil of God's love *6.* How to care for you *7.* Help for the future

Abortion: Providing Alternatives

Care Net, $16/100, paper, for both counselors and counselees

Description How Christians can minister to women with crisis pregnancies.

Facing a Teen's Pregnancy Together

Abbey Press, $.50 each, paper, 8 pp., for counselees

Description Part of the CareNotes series from Abbey Press. CareNotes are short booklets that help readers identify issues and begin the process of seeking resolution. Anecdotal and uplifting. Beautiful photographs grace the covers. Over 20 million CareNotes have been sold in just over five years. Can be used as an alternative to a greeting card or in conjunction with pastoral care visits.

How to Start a CPC

Care Net, $9.50, paper, a reference or academic work

Description Thoroughly covers the seven steps of development. This manual is essential for developing centers as well as for existing centers.

Care Net

Care Net. An organization

Description A daughter ministry of the Christian Action Council. Launched in 1993 to be the most accessible and effective abortion alternative ministry ever known in the history of the pro-life movement. Trains pregnancy care centers, churches, and individuals to be involved in many aspects of providing practical care to women in crisis. Produces educational materials, provides training, and publishes numerous publications suitable for church education. Sponsors an annual conference, publishes *Sanctity of Human Life Update,* and a national newsletter.

The Nurturing Network

The Nurturing Network. An organization

Description An outstanding resource for anyone who comes in contact with a crisis pregnancy. A nationwide, nonprofit organization whose primary concern is the woman experiencing an unplanned, and possibly unwanted, pregnancy. Provides all the practical life-supporting resources a woman needs during this difficult time. Members of the organization include doctors, nurses, employers, educators, counselors, and friends. Provides many kinds of free assistance aimed at helping the woman experience a real, positive alternative to abortion. Among their services: guidance and counseling, nurturing homes for women where housing is a need, medical assistance, financial assistance, educational programs to allow women to continue their post-secondary education during pregnancy, employment opportunities to allow pregnant women permanent or temporary work, adoption counseling, preparation for parenthood.

Infertility

A Hope Deferred *A Couple's Guide to Coping with Infertility,* Jill Baughn

Multnomah Books (Questar), 1989, $7.99, paper, 182 pp., for counselees

Description Whether an infertile couple eventually has a child or not takes second place to the agony of waiting, to the pressure of coping with a daily grief that affects every area of a couple's life—from career decisions, to the marriage relationship, to faith in God's wisdom. How a couple faces this crisis can mean the difference between times of destruction and bitterness or times of emotional maturity and spiritual growth. A Christian couple's guide to coping positively with the wait.

Author Jill Baughn is a freelance writer and English instructor at Virginia Commonwealth University.

Contents *Part 1:* In the beginning *1.* Misunderstandings *2.* So what's the matter? *Part 2:* In the middle *3.* Helplessness *4.* Anger *5.* Self-pity *6.* Grief *7.* Low self-esteem *8.* Guilt *9.* "I can't give you anything but love baby" *Part 3:* Is there an end? *10.* Decisions, decisions *11.* God, have you forgotten us?

The Ache for a Child Debra Bridwell

Victor Books, 1992, $11.95, paper, 298 pp., for counselees

Description For anyone living with the daily ache of infertility, here is an encouraging and informative resource. Written by an author who knows the sorrow of pregnancy loss. Ethical, medical, and spiritual questions related to infertility are addressed.

Author Debra Bridwell is a technical writer who has written articles for *American Baby* magazine and for the *Stepping Stones* and *Resolve* newsletters. She helped establish the WE CARE support group for Christian women dealing with infertility, miscarriage, and stillbirth.

Contents *Part 1:* We might be infertile *1.* From naive excitement to anxious uncertainty *2.* The desire for a family *Part 2:* What can a doctor do? *3.* When is it time to see a doctor? *4.* The doctor's investigation *5.* Examining assisted reproduction techniques *6.* Finding help for making ethical decisions *7.* When ethical decisions become personal *Part 3:* God, why do we ache so much? *8.* Feeling broken *9.* Where are you God? *Part 4:* Is there anyone who understands? *10.* Learning to cope *11.* Husband and wife, supporting each other *12.* Support from family, friends, and the church *13.* Starting or joining a support group *Part 5:* Will we ever be parents? *14.* The hoped for pregnancy—a nervous joy *15.* The empty cradle: miscarriage and stillbirth *16.* Adoption *17.* Parenting after infertility or pregnancy loss *18.* Secondary infertility—living in-between *Part 6:* Is there life beyond infertility? *19.* Using infertility to benefit our lives *20.* Two as a family—choosing to lay down the burden

When a Husband Is Infertile *Options for the Christian Couple,* Byron C. Calhoun

Baker Book House, 1993, $6.99, paper, 115 pp., for counselees

Description An ob/gyn who is himself infertile discusses the medical facts, possibilities, and personal problems associated with male infertility from a Christian perspective.

Contents *1.* Discovering the problem *2.* Coping with the responses of others *3.* Am I still a man? *4.* Emotional consequences of being infertile *5.* Maintaining a strong marriage while coping with infertility *6.* Normal male reproductive functioning *7.* Problems leading to infertility *8.* Intervention *9.* Infertility and God's covenants *10.* Infertility and church leadership *11.* Infertility and Christian ethics *12.* Adoption *13.* Epilogue

Childless Is Not Less Vicky Love

Bethany House Publishers, 1984, $7.99, paper, 216 pp., for counselees

Description A guide to spiritual and emotional health for those who do not have, or have lost, children and may feel disappointed with themselves, with their mates, or even with God. The author, herself unable to have children, takes the reader on an inner pilgrimage through the childless life. Unique features include a theology of childlessness; the single non-parent; the couple's process through infertility, the grief, crisis, and restoration; and a final section exploring four valid resolution possibilities. Also available in Spanish, German, and Braille.

Author Vicky Love graduated summa cum laude from Eastern Oregon College in 1965 earning a B.S. in elementary education. She and her husband, missionaries for 20 years, are involved in church planting in Mexico.

Contents *Section 1:* Process *1.* When the quiver is empty *2.* Frustration with infertility *3.* Coping with hoping *4.* Good grief *Section 2:* People *5.* The single non-parent *6.* Partnership in process *7.* Couples in crisis *8.* Affirming families *Section 3:* Pointers and problem-solving *9.* Happy mother's day! *10.* The church and the childless *11.* Pointers for pastors and professionals *Section 4:* Possibilities *12.* Adoption as an option *13.* The Priscilla-Aquilla approach *14.* Me . . . a minister? *15.* A child-blessing ministry

Without Child *A Compassionate Look at Infertility,* Martha Stout

Harold Shaw Publishers, 1990, $7.99, paper, 146 pp., for counselees

Description With compassionate candor, the author describes her own experience of childlessness and explores all the dimensions of this life crisis.

Author Martha Stout has served as the director of public relations at Gordon College. She is studying to become a licensed counselor.

Contents *1.* The winter of my infertility *2.* Infertility: the emotional and psychological impact *3.* When grief fails *4.* The infertility investigation *5.* The pain of miscarriage *6.* Living without children: "child free or childless"? *7.* Adoption: chosen children *8.* Desert flowers

Infertility *Coping with the Pain of Childlessness,* Sue VanderBook and Rachel Kiepe

Serendipity, 1991, $6.95, paper, 96 pp., for both counselors and counselees

Description A 7- or 14-week course utilizing Scripture and discussion questions. Designed for anyone who is experiencing problems with infertility or would like to be part of a support group with others who are dealing with common issues of being infertile.

Contents *1.* The childless couple *2.* Why me? *3.* Surviving mother's day and father's day *4.* The medical solution *5.* Love renewed *6.* The adoption option *7.* The future

Dear God, Why Can't We Have a Baby? *A Guide for the Infertile Couple,* John VanRegenmorter, Sylvia VanRegenmorter, and Dr. Joe S. McIlhaney Jr.

Baker Book House, 1990 (5th ed.), $6.99, paper, 166 pp., for counselees

Description After struggling eight years with doubts, dashed hopes, loneliness, and well-meaning but ignorant advice, John and Sylvia VanRegenmorter have written about the insights gained, and often painful lessons learned, while they tried to cope with their infertility. Dr. Joe S. McIlhaney Jr., an infertility specialist, adds clear, nontechnical medical information on the diagnosis and treatment of infertility. The unique feature of the book is the combinations of perspectives on infertility: husband, wife, physician, pastor, and counselor. The result is a sensitive, comprehensive discussion, one that will prove significantly helpful to all who are affected by infertility and those who help them. Discusses emotional, medical, and moral aspects of infertility and should prove to be satisfying and beneficial in its completeness.

Authors The VanRegenmorters are both graduates of Calvin College. John VanRegenmorter holds the D.Min. from North American Baptist Seminary and serves as pastor of the First Christian Reformed Church. They have both been published in *Moody* and *Christianity Today* magazines. Coauthor Joe S. McIlhaney Jr., a Christian obstetrician-gynecologist, has an extensive infertility practice in Austin, Tex. He is also a medical examiner for Dr. Dobson's Focus on the Family board.

Contents *1.* The laughter of little children *2.* Avoiding the early pitfalls *3.* What constitutes a complete infertility workup? *4.* The infertility struggle *5.* Husband vs. wife or husband and wife? *6.* Beginning to cope with infertility *7.* Family friends and fellow Christians *8.* Infertility and the Christian faith *9.* What's right—what's wrong *10.* When is enough enough? *11.* Adoption as an option *12.* Learning to live with infertility

Counseling for Unplanned Pregnancy and Infertility Everett L. Worthington Jr.

Word Publishing, 1987, $15.99, cloth, 285 pp., for counselors

Description Part of the Resources for Christian Counseling series, this book surveys all sorts of problem pregnancies, including adolescent pregnancies, twins, children close together, and later-life pregnancies. It also discusses infertility. Gives practical guidance, based upon current research, on how to counsel family members with unplanned pregnancy or infertility. The book is ideal for counselors in crisis pregnancy centers, nurses, and social workers. The book is informative and contains substantial humor.

Author Everett Worthington holds a Ph.D. in counseling from the University of Missouri–Columbia and has worked at Virginia Commonwealth

University since 1978. As a licensed clinical psychologist, he has directed a community counseling agency, supervised others, and maintained a part-time private practice.

Longing to Have a Baby

Abbey Press, $.50 each, paper, 8 pp., for counselees

Description Part of the CareNotes series from Abbey Press. CareNotes are short booklets that help readers identify issues and begin the process of seeking resolution. Anecdotal and uplifting. Beautiful photographs grace the covers. Over 20 million CareNotes have been sold in just over five years. Can be used as an alternative to a greeting card or in conjunction with pastoral care visits.

American Fertility Society

American Fertility Society. An organization

Description Though not a Christian organization, the American Fertility Society is a private, nonprofit, professional medical organization devoted to advancing knowledge and expertise in all phases of reproductive medicine and biology. In addition to medical information, the AFS produces a wide range of patient information/education brochures.

American Fertility Society, The

The American Fertility Society. An organization

Description A (secular) private, nonprofit, professional medical organization devoted to advancing knowledge and expertise in all phases of reproductive medicine and biology. Provides patient education brochures, a monthly medical journal, ethical guidelines covering reproductive technologies. Also maintains a national referral service for infertility specialists of over 11,400.

RESOLVE

RESOLVE. An organization

Description A large (secular) organization that networks local groups that lend support and information on miscarriage, infertility, and adoption. Sponsors a newsletter, conference, book list, and more.

Stepping Stones

Stepping Stones. An organization

239

Description A free infertility newsletter written from a Christian perspective. Assists in the establishment of Christ-centered support groups.

Miscarriage

I'll Hold You in Heaven *Healing and Hope for the Parent Who Has Lost a Child,* Jack Hayford

Regal Books, 1990, $4.99, paper, 124 pp., for counselees

Description Parents who have lost a child through miscarriage, stillbirth, abortion, or early infant death have a special kind of grief. Pastor Jack Hayford offers his warm, encouraging, hopeful message to parents.

Author Dr. Jack W. Hayford is senior pastor of the Church on the Way in Van Nuys, Calif. His ministry reaches around the world through television, radio, and the books and music he has written.

Contents *1.* The gift of lives *2.* When does significance begin? *3.* Life to what degree? *4.* Destiny in the afterworld *5.* In heaven as a person *6.* Instruments of healing *7.* The heartbeat of love *8.* Three steps to loving

Morgan's Baby Sister *A Read-Aloud Book for Families Who Have Experienced the Death of a Newborn,* Patricia Polin Johnson and Donna R. Williams

Resource Publications, Inc., 1993, $10.95, paper, 55 pp., for counselees

Description Part of the Helping Children Hurt series which was created to assist parents or other adult caregivers with the difficult and often painful task of helping children understand their feelings about tragedies they experience. Professional and pastoral counselors may give *Morgan's Baby Sister* to families who are grieving the death of a child through miscarriage, stillbirth, or sudden infant death syndrome. A special section at the back of the book offers guidance to parents and caregivers along with discussion questions.

Authors Patricia Polin Johnson teaches religious education to preschool, primary, and high school students. Donna Reilly Williams specializes in grief and transition therapy in her private practice in Woodinville, Wash.

Miscarriage *A Quiet Grief,* Nelson Kraybill and Ellen Kraybill

Herald Press, 1990, $1.95, paper, 16 pp., for counselees

Description The loss of a baby through miscarriage can leave a couple filled with doubt, anger, and many questions. Nelson and Ellen Kraybill share the struggle they experienced in dealing with this pain.

Looking at Loss *My Experience with Miscarriage,* Claudia Swain

New Hope, 1988, $2.95, paper, 57 pp., for counselees

Description Claudia Swain and her husband eagerly awaited the birth of their child. This story tells of her miscarriage and how she coped with that loss. Specific suggestions on how to deal with miscarriage and a resource list for further reading are included at the end of the book.

Author Claudia Swain (Ph.D., North Texas University) works as a teacher, writer, and conference leader in the area of childhood education.

Empty Arms *Support for Those Who Have Suffered Miscarriage or Stillbirth,* Pam W. Vredevelt

Multnomah Books (Questar), 1984, $7.99, paper, 126 pp., for both counselors and counselees

Description This book is the outcome of Vredevelt's search for understanding and encouragement. With the empathy personal experience brings, she is able to gently offer comfort to the woman who has just experienced miscarriage or stillbirth and insight to her friends and family who want to help and encourage effectively.

Author Pam Vredevelt is a pastor's wife and professional counselor at Christian Counseling Services, Gresham, Oreg. She graduated from Multnomah School of the Bible in Portland, Oreg., and earned her master's degree in communication from Portland State University.

Contents *1.* The shocking news *2.* Our next step—delivery *3.* Grief . . . the road to healing *4.* Managing anger *5.* Untying guilt's knot *6.* Spiritual battles and emotions *7.* Responding to the reactions of others *8.* Husbands hurt too *9.* Helping children to understand *10.* Please . . . someone give me some answers *11.* After a stillbirth *12.* The challenge of a postpartum body *13.* Eating for health

14. Mood swings and exercise *15.* New beginnings *16.* The Bible offers hope and comfort

Mourning a Miscarriage

Abbey Press, $.50 each, paper, 8 pp., for counselees

Description Part of the CareNotes series from Abbey Press. CareNotes are short booklets that help readers identify issues and begin the process of seeking resolution. Anecdotal and uplifting. Beautiful photographs grace the covers. Over 20 million CareNotes have been sold in just over five years. Can be used as an alternative to a greeting card or in conjunction with pastoral care visits.

SHARE: Pregnancy and Infant Loss Support, Inc.

SHARE: Pregnancy and Infant Loss Support, Inc. An organization

Description Provides a bimonthly newsletter and networks over 250 chapters of support groups for bereaved parents.

Postabortion Syndrome

When Someone You Know Has Had an Abortion Linda Allison-Lewis

Ligouri Publications, 1992, $.75, paper, 23 pp., for counselees

Description This booklet will show you how to help the woman: deal with her pain, reclaim a sense of self-worth, trust in Christ's unconditional forgiveness. Also included is a list of resources that would be helpful for anyone dealing with abortion.

Women in Ramah *A Post Abortion Bible Study,* Linda Cochrane

Care Net, $9.50, paper, for both counselors and counselees

Description An extensive Bible study that allows the user to work through the feelings and experiences associated with the trauma that often follows abortion. Designed to be used either in group or one-or-one settings.

How to Help after an Abortion Ellen Curro

National Office of Post-abortion Reconciliation & Healing, 1991, $100.00, video, 3 hours, for counselors

Description This video series of four talks provides practical assistance for those wanting to help clients or friends who have been hurt by abortion. The seminar explores: recognizing postabortion; six areas of reconciliation in the spiritual healing process; helping the woman who says "I've had no problem with my abortion"; when, where, and how to refer. These talks were delivered to an audience of crisis pregnancy counselors, heads of postabortion ministries, pro-life leaders, clergy, health care professionals, and persons who have suffered from abortions. Provides introduction to postabortion stress and healing relationships with God, self, and others. Client issues such as denial, unresolved grief, anger, bonding with baby, siblings, and other relationships are covered. Recognizing problems and several models of treatment are presented. Helping extended family, knowing limits, referral resources, and several other topics are addressed.

Author Ellen Curro, M.Ed., P.A.-C., received her master's of education in counseling/guidance from Xavier University and her physician assistant training at George Washington University. She is a former counselor, teacher, physician assistant, and director of a crisis pregnancy center. Currently, she is president of Linking Education and Medicine. She has authored two additional books.

A Season to Heal *Help and Hope for Those Working through Post-Abortion Stress,* Luci Freed and Penny Yvonne Salazar

Thomas Nelson Publishers, 1993, $9.99, paper, 192 pp., for both counselors and counselees

Description Written by two therapists who help women through postabortion stress, this compassionate book assures readers that their pain is a valid, natural response to a very difficult time. As they name and grieve their losses, healing begins. Contains hands-on tests, inventories, and lists to help women assess the extent of their pain and pinpoint where healing needs to start. Then readers can find healing from the guilt, shame, anger, depression, and sadness that plague them.

Authors Luci Freed is the executive director of Crisis Pregnancy Support Center in Nashville, Tenn. Penny Yvonne Salazar is the executive director of Alternative Pregnancy Center.

Contents *Part 1:* The dilemma and the damage *1.* What is post-abortion stress? *2.* You are not alone *3.* Broken threads *Part 2:* The road to wholeness *4.* The healing process *5.* Step out of the dark *6.* Recognize real feelings and real losses *7.* Cancel empty debts *8.* Unlock the trap-door of guilt and shame *9.* Take off the lid *10.* Do not surrender to depression *11.* Find freedom in forgiveness *12.* Become reconciled *Part 3:* Hope for the journey *13.* Where do I go from here? / *Appendixes*

I'll Hold You in Heaven *Healing and Hope for the Parent Who Has Lost a Child,* Jack Hayford

Regal Books, 1990, $4.99, paper, 124 pp., for counselees

Description Parents who have lost a child through miscarriage, stillbirth, abortion, or early infant death have a special kind of grief. Pastor Jack Hayford offers his warm, encouraging, hopeful message to parents.

Author Dr. Jack W. Hayford is senior pastor of the Church on the Way in Van Nuys, Calif. His ministry reaches around the world through television, radio, and the books and music he has written.

Contents *1.* The gift of lives *2.* When does significance begin? *3.* Life to what degree? *4.* Destiny in the afterworld *5.* In heaven as a person *6.* Instruments of healing *7.* The heartbeat of love *8.* Three steps to loving

Abortion's Second Victim *Forgiveness and Emotional Healing for Post-abortion Women,* Pam Koerbel

AMG Publishers, 1991, $8.95, paper, 268 pp., for counselees

Description Since nearly one-fourth of America's women have had one or more abortions, you probably know one of abortion's second victims. This book is an anecdotal account of one woman's experience with abortion and the devastating aftereffects. She writes of her healing through Christ. A practical, biblically sound examination of abortion's spiritual and emotional aftermath. The first post-abortion woman to write a book from the perspective that abortion is wrong. Koerbel chronicles her personal journey through abortion in the book's first section. Next, medical, legal, and theological aspects of abortion are explained to women who suffer from post-abortion trauma. Included is a survey of 101 post-abortion women.

Author Pam Koerbel is the director of Post-Abortion Ministries (PAM) and author of numerous books, booklets, and brochures dealing with post-abortion syndrome. Koerbel and her husband travel throughout the United States teaching others how to deal biblically with abortion's spiritual and emotional aftermath. She is studying for a master's degree in biblical counseling at Trinity Theological Seminary. She is the mother of four living children. She can be contacted at: PAM, P.O. Box 3092, Landover Hills, MD. 20784-0092.

Contents *Part 1:* Anatomy of an abortion *1.* Freedom to choose *2.* Taking the cure *3.* Free at last *Part 2:* Understanding abortion *4.* Abortion American style *5.* Acquiescently aborted *6.* Actions analyzed *7.* Accountability *Part 3:* Resolving the aftermath *8.* Acquittal available *9.* Applying atonement *10.* Alone and anonymous *11.* Aching associates *12.* Achieving abundant life / Post-abortion support groups / Additional reading / Post-abortion workbooks

Helping Women Recover from Abortion *How to Deal with the Guilt, Emotional Pain, and the Emptiness,* Nancy Michels

Bethany House Publishers, 1988, $7.99, paper, 224 pp., for counselors

Description Provides biblical help both to those who have had abortions and to their counselors in restoring wholeness. Chapters deal with: effects of abortion; grief, shame, and confusion in the aftermath; working through anger; message of God's forgiveness; dealing with fear; forgiving self and others; and living with a forgiven abortion.

Author Nancy Michels is involved with Lutherans for Life.

Contents *1.* Why women have abortions *2.* The emotional effects of abortion *3.* Grief *4.* Denial *5.* Guilt and anger *6.* Bargaining, depression, isolation, and fear *7.* Forgiveness *8.* Forgiving herself *9.* Living with a forgiven abortion *10.* Abortion affects fathers, children / *Appendix A:* Scripture / *Appendix B:* Nine steps for personal growth / *Appendix C:* Post abortion support groups / *Appendix D:* Additional reading

Help for the Post Abortion Woman Teri Reisser and Paul Reisser

Care Net, $5.95, paper, for counselors

Description Written for women who think they may be suffering in the wake of an abortion. Also for loving family and friends, or those who desire to understand, help, or counsel women with post abortion syndrome.

Authors Paul Reisser, M.D., a family physician in southern Calif., serves on the Physician's Advisory Council for Focus on the Family. Teri Reisser, M.S., is presently director of services for the Right to Life League of southern Calif.

Identifying and Overcoming Post-Abortion Syndrome Teri Reisser and Paul Reisser

Care Net, $.35, paper, 24 pp., for counselees

Description This 24-page brochure gives explicit examples of post abortion syndrome and its symptoms. It aids the reader in determining if one needs counseling.

Authors Paul Reisser, M.D., a family physician in southern Calif., serves on the Physician's Advisory Council for Focus on the Family. Teri Reisser, M.S., is presently director of services for the Right to Life League of southern Calif.

The Mourning After *Help for the Postabortion Syndrome,* Terry L. Selby

Baker Book House, 1990, $7.99, cloth, 147 pp., for both counselors and counselees

Description The counselor who first identified postabortion syndrome explains its complexity, why it can be devastating, and how sufferers can come to grips with the need to feel grief.

Author Terry L. Selby, who earned his M.S.W. from the University of Minnesota, speaks frequently on PAS and its treatment at national conferences and on television and radio talk shows. He maintains a private practice in Bemidji, Minn.

Contents *1.* Introduction to postabortion syndrome *2.* My first encounters with PAS *3.* The mechanics of denial *4.* The stages of grief *5.* Victimization *6.* Breaking denial *7.* Guiding the grieving process *8.* The importance of faith / *Appendixes A.* Symptoms of post-traumatic stress *B.* Diagnostic criteria for postabortion syndrome *C.* Common abortion procedures *D.* Questions and answers about PAS *E.* Forms

Post-Abortion Trauma *9 Steps to Recovery,* Jeanette Vought

Zondervan Publishing House, 1991, $9.99, paper, 256 pp., for counselors

Description The book cogently describes the history of abortion and the physical, emotional, and spiritual effects of abortion and spells out a nine-step process for recovery.

Author Jeanne Vought (Ph.D., psychology) is the executive director of New Life Family Services and the author of *Helping Victims of Sexual Abuse.*

Contents *Part 1:* Understanding the problem *1.* How did we get into this mess? *2.* Where has the church been? *3.* Where have all the children gone? *4.* Why do women have abortions? *Part 2:* The effects of abortion *5.* Who has been affected by abortion? *6.* Physical effects of abortion *7.* Emotional effects of abortion *8.* Spiritual effects of abortion *Part 3:* Conquerors post-abortion support program *9.* What is the conquerors program? *10.* Men in the conquerors program *Part 4:* Nine steps to recovery *11.* Recognizing my powerlessness *12.* Identifying my feelings *13.* Dealing with guilt and shame *14.* Working through my grieving process *15.* Taking responsibility for the loss of my child *16.* Evaluating my relationships *17.* Forgiving myself *18.* Improving my self-image *19.* Continuing my healing process

How Abortion Affects Men—They Cry Alone Regis Walling

Ligouri Publications, 1987, $.75, paper, 23 pp., for counselees

Description This booklet takes a compassionate look at the forgotten victim. It shows that along with the unborn and women, men are also victims of abortion. It provides real help for men who are suffering—help to cope, help to accept their responsibilities in the matter, help to face the truth that "once a father, always a father," and help to find forgiveness.

Caught in the Crossfire *How Can I Forgive Her for Having an Abortion?*

Open Arms, 1991, $.15 each, for counselees

Description Addresses the sense of anger and betrayal some men experience toward loved ones who have had an abortion. Gently encourages forgiveness and reconciliation. Uses Scripture wisely.

Counselor Training Manual *A Biblical Approach to Post-Abortion Ministry*

Open Arms, 1989, $10.00, spiral, 120 pp., for counselors

Description A comprehensive guide designed to train lay counselors to be effective in this delicate area.

243

Contents *1.* An introduction to open arms *2.* Defining the problem *3.* Foundations for counseling *4.* The open arms ministry flow *5.* The gospel message *6.* Ministering to the Christian *7.* Coming to grips with the baby *8.* Is guided imagery valid? *9.* Hard case scenarios *10.* Reaching out with open arms counseling resources

Dear Children . . . *A Story of Post-abortion Healing*

Ligouri Publications, $39.95, video, 30 minutes, for counselees

Description A woman shares the compelling story of her own journey from the shame and guilt of abortion to God's loving forgiveness. Includes interviews with men and married couples. Won a Gabriel Award.

Author A Redemptorist Pastoral Communications project.

Have You Been Told . . . *Everything You Need to Know about Abortion?*

Open Arms, 1991, $.15 each, for counselees

Description Brief quotations from women who have suffered the negative emotional and physical effects of abortion. Refers to Open Arms support ministry.

Hope for Today *Healing after Abortion*

Open Arms, 1988, $.15 each, for counselees

Description Pamphlet that gently uses facts and Scripture to frame various issues associated with postabortion syndrome.

In His Image *A Post-Abortion Bible Study*

Open Arms, 1989, $7.00/$10.00 leader's guide, spiral, 60/60 pp., for both counselors and counselees

Description A Bible study based on the character of God designed to move the postabortion woman toward restoration. "Fill-in-the-blanks" format. Teacher's edition includes all answers and facilitator notes.

Contents Introduction / Bible study guidelines / The goodness of God / The patience of God / The holiness of God / The mercy of God / The love of God / The humility of God / The faithfulness of God

PACE Program (Postabortion Counseling and Education)

Christian Action Council, for counselors

Description The PACE program is a comprehensive counseling resource for dealing with postabortion syndrome. Call the CAC for a full information packet.

Seeking Peace and Healing after Abortion

Abbey Press, $.50 each, paper, 8 pp., for counselees

Description Part of the CareNotes series from Abbey Press. CareNotes are short booklets that help readers identify issues and begin the process of seeking resolution. Anecdotal and uplifting. Beautiful photographs grace the covers. Over 20 million CareNotes have been sold in just over five years. Can be used as an alternative to a greeting card or in conjunction with pastoral care visits.

Support Group Topics *Instructions and Outlines for Conducting a Post-abortion Support Group*

Open Arms, 1989, $5.00, spiral, 50 pp., for counselors

Description An immensely helpful book that provides instructions and outlines for leading a support group of this nature. Four central issues are addressed.

Contents *Part 1:* Introduction—open support groups / How to use this booklet / Conducting a support group *Part 2:* Topics *1.* Hurt, anger, and bitterness *2.* Dealing with depression *3.* Dealing with guilt *4.* Dealing with grief

American Victims of Abortion

American Victims of Abortion. An organization

Description Provides information about postabortion syndrome, research briefs, and resources and networks support organizations for victims.

National Office of Post-abortion Reconciliation & Healing, The

Project Rachel. An organization

Description An outreach of the internationally-respected Project Rachel. An outstanding source of information, ministry tools, and other resources for anyone involved in issues associated with post-abortion complications and/or syndrome. Produces a resources list with too many ministry and clinical tools to be listed here, but following you'll find a sample:—International post-abortion support services directory—Project

Rachel information packet—Bibliography of major articles and books concerning the detrimental effects of abortion—Psycho-spiritual healing after abortion—Mental health and abortion: review and analysis—and a large selection of audio tapes.

Open Arms

Open Arms. An organization

Description An international Christian postabortion ministry. Help and resources are provided for both men and women suffering from the guilt and anguish that often follows abortion. Assistance and training are provided for individuals and groups desiring to help the postaborted in their communities.

Post Abortion Ministries

Post Abortion Ministries. An organization

Description A Christian organization providing materials and teaching to train, educate, and motivate Christians to be involved in post abortion ministry. Provides a variety of printed resource materials.

Women Exploited by Abortion

WEBA. An organization

Description A Christ-centered organization consisting entirely of women who have undergone the trauma of abortion and are now courageously working to keep others from making the same tragic mistake. Produces and distributes a wide variety of pamphlets and books on postabortion syndrome such as:—Before you make the decision—Help for the victims of abortion—Testimony of an aborted woman . . . set free—Help for the postabortion woman.

Prenatal/Preparenting Issues

Teenage Mothers *Their Experience, Strength, and Hope,* Andre Beauchamp

Resource Publications, Inc., 1990, $8.95, paper, 77 pp., for counselees

Description A series of stories, poems, Scripture, and photographs that depicts the experiences of teenage pregnancy and motherhood. Affirms the value of making pro-life choices when faced with teenage pregnancy.

Author Andre Beauchamp is a priest, teacher, and researcher. He was the coordinator of Adult Religious Education for the province of Quebec.

Contents *1.* Rejection *2.* Being a mother *3.* Making a new life *4.* Meeting God *5.* The child *6.* "Thank You"

Meditations for the Expectant Mother Helen Good Brenneman

Herald Press, 1968, $12.95, cloth, 80 pp., for counselees

Description Thirty devotional meditations that discuss the things a woman thinks about from the time she knows she is pregnant to the birth of her child.

To the New Mother Helen Good Brenneman

Herald Press, 1969, $1.95, paper, 16 pp., for counselees

Description Five brief devotional/meditations for new mothers to encourage them in their faith and new role.

Getting Ready for Our New Baby *Warm Helpful Readings to Prepare Small Children for a New Baby,* William L. Coleman

Bethany House Publishers, 1984, $5.99, paper, 128 pp., for counselees

Description Devotional readings addressed to young siblings to help forestall problems and bring issues that youngsters may not be able to verbalize out in the open. Free verse style with warm photographs.

Author Bill Coleman has written half a dozen best-selling devotional books for this age group (3–7) in addition to his other books. His experience as a pastor, father, and writer help give him his special relationship with children.

Contents Where is the baby now? What is a hospital? What will our baby look like? Will Daddy still play with me? Who will stay with me when Mom goes to the hospital? Where will the baby sleep?

I'm Having a Baby *Help Me Lord!* Cathy Hickling

Creation House, 1988, $8.99, paper, 240 pp., for counselees

Description You can prepare for the wonderful little person who's growing inside you. Cathy

245

Hickling's Scripture selections, personal reflections, and prayer starters will help you prepare a little every day.

Author Cathy Hickling is a mother of four children. She and her husband publish a Christian newspaper in Pittsburgh, Pa.

Contents Be fruitful and multiply/Month 1: Days 1–29 knit together by God/Month 2: Days 30–59 early will I seek thee/Month 3: Days 60–89 I'm not fat—I'm pregnant!/Month 4: Days 90–119 created in his image/Month 5: Days 120–149 thy wife—a fruitful vine?/Month 6: Days 150–179 today my toes disappeared/Month 7: Days 180–209 come . . . all who labor/Month 8: Days 210–239 labor means work . . . not pain/Month 9: Days 240–266

The Complete Book of Baby and Child Care *Revised and Updated,* Grace H. Ketterman

Fleming H. Revell, 1982, $12.99, paper, 560 pp., for counselees

Description Revised and updated. A comprehensive and specific discussion of every aspect of parenting from prenatal considerations to parenting through age 12 and beyond.

Author Grace H. Ketterman, M.D., is the medical director of the Crittenton Center for Children and Adolescents in Kansas City, Mo. She is the author of many other books on parenting issues.

Contents *Part 1:* Preparing to have a child *1.* Having a child—are you ready? *2.* Getting pregnant—what you need to know *3.* Carrying a baby—a word for expectant mothers *4.* Sharing responsibility—a word for expectant fathers *5.* Giving birth—an experience to treasure *Part 2:* Nurturing a newborn child *6.* Getting acquainted—the first thirty days *7.* Establishing relationships—the next two years of life *8.* Winning the eating game—the nutrition factor *Part 3:* Treating your sick child *9.* General medical information you need to know *10.* Your problem solver for injuries and illnesses *Part 4:* Rearing a confident child *11.* The components of personality development *12.* The necessity of spiritual training *13.* The importance of loving correction *14.* The fun side of family living *15.* The seesaw world of the adolescent *Part 5:* Helping a troubled child *16.* Handling difficulties and suffering *17.* Solving their behavioral problems *18.* Learning from school experiences *19.* Rearing special children.

Meditations for Adoptive Parents Vernell Klassen Miller

Herald Press, 1992, $6.95, paper, 88 pp., for counselees

Description The perfect gift for adoptive parents in the style of the best-selling *Meditations for*

the New Mother. Using her family experiences, Vernell Klassen Miller weaves many threads into the fabric of these meditations on adoption. She includes theories about bonding to infants and older children, the stages of relinquishment and adoption, the process of entitlement, and the advantages of the adoption process.

Author Vernell Klassen Miller is a full-time homemaker by choice. She also enjoys teaching Spanish to several home educating families and freelance writing.

Loving Your Preborn Baby Carol VanKlompenburg and Elizabeth Siitari

Harold Shaw Publishers, 1990, $13.99, cloth, 166 pp., for counselees

Description This illustrated gift book combines accurate medical information and joyful awe to help parents appreciate the miracle of their preborn baby's life. Brief stories, quotations, and Scripture passages help the expectant mother with all the feelings, fears, and joys associated with pregnancy.

Authors Carol VanKlompenburg is an award-winning writer and mother of three. Coauthor Elizabeth Siitari is a board-certified family practitioner and mother of five.

Miracle of Life *Devotions for Expecting Mothers,* Robert G. Wells, Mary C. Wells, Ken Gire, and Judy Gire

Zondervan Publishing House, 1993, $14.99, cloth, 144 pp., for counselees

Description A weekly devotional for expectant mothers, complete with meditations, Bible readings, pages to keep a journal, and award-winning photographs by Lenart Nilsson.

Facing the Fears Pregnancy Brings

Abbey Press, $.50 each, paper, 8 pp., for counselees

Description Part of the CareNotes series from Abbey Press. CareNotes are short booklets that help readers identify issues and begin the process of seeking resolution. Anecdotal and uplifting. Beautiful photographs grace the covers. Over 20 million CareNotes have been sold in just over five years. Can be used as an alternative to a greeting card or in conjunction with pastoral care visits.

30. Premarital Counseling

Becoming Married Herbert Anderson and Robert Cotton Fite

Westminster/John Knox Press, 1993, paper, 170 pp., for counselors

Description Examines the issues surrounding the forming of the marriage bond, such as courtship, the early years of marriage, and specifically, the events that must take place for successful bonding to occur. Designed for couples planning to marry, parents of children planning to marry, and clergy who work with couples planning to marry.

Authors Herbert Anderson is a Lutheran pastor and professor of pastoral theology at Catholic Theological Union in Chicago. Robert Cotton Fite is an Episcopal priest and director of the pastoral counseling center at Lutheran General Hospital in Park Ridge, Ill.

Contents *1.* Leaving comes before cleaving *2.* A wedding of stories *3.* Planning a meaningful wedding *4.* When the ordinary is complicated *5.* Getting married changes things *6.* A covenant for abiding seriousness / *Appendixes: A.* Symbols for genograms *B.* Scripture texts for weddings

Engagement *Are You Fit to Be Tied?* David Brown

Serendipity, 1992, $6.95, paper, 96 pp., for counselees

Description A 7- or 14-week course utilizing Scripture and discussion questions. Designed for couples who are engaged or are thinking about becoming engaged.

Contents *1.* High hurdles *2.* Love is . . . *3.* Communication *4.* How close can we get? *5.* Resolving conflict *6.* Money: servant or master *7.* Sexual intimacy

Before the Wedding *Look before You Leap,* Michael E. Cavanaugh

Westminster/John Knox Press, 1994, $14.99, paper, 202 pp., for both counselors and counselees

Description Points out important areas of study in preparing for marriage. He begins with the phrase "look before you leap," which he then analyzes, giving to each word an important distinct meaning related to the partners, their relationship, and the institution of marriage.

Author Michael E. Cavanaugh is an education and pastoral consultant in Tiburon, Calif.

Contents *1.* Motive for getting married *2.* Correct and faulty thinking *3.* Growing as an individual *4.* Growing as a couple *5.* Parents and friends *6.* Communication *7.* Sexuality *8.* Parenthood *9.* Cautions *10.* Problems / Working with your minister / How ministers can help couples

Day by Day *Reflection Guide for the Engaged and Newly Married,* John J. Colligan and Kathleen A. Colligan

Paulist Press, 1994, $8.95, paper, 103 pp., for counselees

Description A practical guide to help couples work through the possible problems in a relationship and to grow in love and understanding of one another. In addition to wise advice, the authors offer questions and written exercises to help the couple discover more and more about themselves.

Authors The Colligans are the directors of Family Life Education for the Roman Catholic Diocese of Syracuse, southern region. They are also the directors of the JOHN 17 CENTER, an international effort devoted to strengthening family life and renewing spirituality in local churches.

Contents *1.* When you want to communicate *2.* When you want to go deeper in relationship *3.* When you're disappointed in each other *4.* When you're having an argument *5.* When the hurt lingers on *6.* When you want to talk about sex/sexuality / What did I learn about sex from mom and dad? Who makes the rules in our house? Why do we make love? *7.* When you question the roles of men and women *8.* When you're discussing money *9.* When you're worried about your in-laws *10.* When you're not feeling well *11.* When you want to talk about God *12.* When we're living the covenant / *Appendix:* When should we go for counseling?

Once More with Love *A Guide to Marrying Again,* Bobbi Coyle-Hennessey

Ave Maria Press, 1993, $8.95, paper, 192 pp., for counselees

Description Offers useful strategies for coping with the problems and issues of remarriage. Focuses on communication, conflict resolution skills, and presents resources to deepen and enrich relationships. Worksheets at the end of each chapter encourage in-depth individual reflections and honest sharing between partners.

Author Bobbi Coyle-Hennessey is a nationally recognized leader in divorce recovery work and a trailblazer with her breakthrough program for those considering remarriage after divorce or the death of a spouse.

Contents *1.* Preparation, feelings, and values *2.* Forgiveness, previous marital history, creative problem solving *3.* Creating a stepfamily *4.* Finances, houses, roles, step pets *5.* Intimacy *6.* Religious issues

For Better, for Worse *A Premarital Checklist,* John M. Drescher

Beacon Hill Press of Kansas City, 1990, $1.95, paper, 32 pp., for counselors

Description Designed to assist persons seriously contemplating marriage to think through key areas of concern that have much to do with happiness following marriage. This instrument can be used by the individual or couple or with a counselor to think through many important aspects of the marriage relationship. Structured around 61 discussion questions.

Author Drescher has written over 30 books and more than 100 journal and magazine articles. He has served as pastor, bishop, editor, and seminary teacher.

New Beginnings *Preparing Families for Remarriage in the Church,* Gordon E. Ellis

The Pilgrim Press, 1991, $14.95, paper, 132 pp., for counselors

Description Here is a straightforward, practical approach, both for adults and children, to the problems of remarriage after divorce. Both innovative and basic, the four-session process deals with feelings about divorce and living in a stepfamily. The counseling culminates with the family working together to create a unique marriage ceremony in which all may participate. Included are resources for marriage ceremonies, case studies, and a workbook for use in counseling children.

Contents *1.* Remarriage in the church following divorce? *2.* Is it faithful to the gospel? *3.* Preparing families for remarriage in the church: a model process *4.* Session 1—building a foundation *5.* Session 2—looking at yesterday and today with the couple *6.* Session 3—looking ahead with the couple *7.* The counseling process with the children *8.* Session 4—creating the remarriage ceremony *9.* Conclusion / *Appendix:* My parent is getting married: a workbook to help children prepare for the remarriage of a parent

Three to Get Ready *Premarital Counseling Manual,* Howard A. Eyrich

Baker Book House, 1992, $12.99, paper, 227 pp., for counselors

Description The bride, the groom, and the counselor—it does take three to set solid footings under a marriage. A leading guide for laying that foundation has now been updated and enlarged. The first edition of *Three to Get Ready* placed in the hands of seminarians and pastors is their first thorough manual on what is needed in premarriage counseling. This second edition has amassed even more help. Features include—a biblical overview of the task of preparing two people for marriage; worksheets, wedding planning guide, and consultant's handbook; Bible studies and psychological inventory questions.

Author Howard A. Eyrich is executive director of the Center for Biblical Counseling and Education in St. Louis, Mo. He is assistant professor of practical theology at Covenant Theological Seminary. He and his wife, Pamela, speak at family life and marriage enrichment seminars.

Contents *Part 1:* Preparation for premarital counseling *1.* Overview of the program *2.* The pastor-counselor and premarital counseling *3.* The Christian concept of an equal yoke *4.* Exposition of the marriage ceremony *Part 2:* Program for premarital counseling *5.* Eligibility, TJTA, trait factor, sex awareness inventory *6.* Interpret TJTA, God-designed marriage *7.* Communication, roles, love *8.* Budgeting, insurance and investments, children, *9.* Sex, birth control, family and social concerns *10.* Family worship, ceremony, reception *11.* Agenda, postmarital session *Part 3:* Practical helps for premarital counselors *12.* Selecting family traits *13.* Many weddings, much work *14.* A wedding manual for the church *15.* A wedding consultant program

248

A Handbook for Engaged Couples Alice Fryling and Bob Fryling

InterVarsity Press, 1989, $5.99, paper, 72 pp., for both counselors and counselees

Description The authors help engaged couples work through practical issues such as handling money and time, making decisions, dealing with parents, and more. Fill-in-the-blank workbook format.

Authors Alice Fryling is a homemaker, speaker, and writer who lives in Madison, Wis. She and her husband, Bob, have counseled many who are seeking God's best for their lives.

Contents *1.* The foundation *2.* Communication in marriage *3.* Problem solving I *4.* Living and working *5.* Family relationships *6.* Money *7.* Time *8.* Spiritual growth in marriage *9.* Moods and emotions *10.* The physical relationship during engagement *11.* The wedding *12.* The honeymoon *13.* Problem solving II. *14.* Sex in marriage *15.* Finding forgiveness in marriage

Saving Your Marriage Before It Starts
Seven Questions to Ask Before (And After) You Marry, Les Parrott III and Leslie Parrott

Zondervan Publishing House, 1995, $15.99, cloth, 158 pp.

Description The authors ask insightful questions that help couples identify and deal in advance with potential marriage problems. To bring learning home, workbooks for both the man and woman are also available.

Authors Les Parrott is professor of clinical psychology at Pacific Seattle University and a fellow at the University of Washington School of Medicine. Leslie Parrott is a counselor at Seattle Pacific University and instructor in the Graduate School of Counseling and Family Therapy.

Contents Before you begin *Question 1:* Have you faced the myth of marriage with honesty? *Question 2:* Can you identify your love style? *Question 3:* Have you developed the habit of happiness? *Question 4:* Can you say what you mean and understand what you hear? *Question 5:* Have you bridged the gender gap? *Question 6:* Do you know how to fight a good fight? *Question 7:* Are you and your partner soul mates?

How Can I Be Sure? *A Premarriage Inventory,* Bob Phillips

Harvest House Publishers, 1978, $5.99, paper, 155 pp., for both counselors and counselees

Description Fill-in-the-blank format. Fifteen areas related to marriage and family life are questioned. For use by pastor, counselors, or even couples themselves. Includes instructions for use.

Author Bob Phillips is associate pastor of counseling ministries at Northwest Church in Fresno, Calif. Holds a master in counseling from California State University and is a licensed marriage, family, and child counselor. His books have sold over 500,000 copies.

Contents Ways to use this book *1.* Family background *2.* Previous marital history *3.* Status of present relationship *4.* Religious background *5.* Children *6.* Finances *7.* Communication *8.* Sexual inventory *9.* Sample wedding ceremony *10.* Wedding checklist—additional resources *11.* Danger signs *12.* Discerning genuine love *13.* Descriptive characteristics *14.* Insight questions *15.* Decisions in marriage

Called Together *A Marriage Preparation Workbook,* Steve Prokopchak and Mary Prokopchak

Janet Thoma (a division of Thomas Nelson), 1994, $12.99, paper, 192 pp., for both counselors and counselees

Description Presents a clear, biblical approach to premarital counseling. Each chapter is loaded with self-revealing exercises to help partners reach inside themselves and talk about important issues.

Authors Steve Prokopchak is a Christian counselor who earned a master of human services degree from Lincoln University. He serves on the pastoral staff at Dove Christian Fellowship in Ephrata, Pa. Mary Prokopchak is a registered nurse who works with her husband in premarital and marital counseling.

Are We Compatible? *A Premarriage Guide,* C. E. Rollins

Thomas Nelson Publishers, 1995, $9.99, paper, 192 pp.

Description Examines characteristics of successful marriages and the warning signs of those ending in divorce and identifies key issues couples should consider but often overlook when considering marriage.

Author C. E. Rollins researched factors associated with compatible/incompatible married couples in a series of field studies. She is the author of several other books.

Remarriage and God's Renewing Grace *A Positive Biblical Ethic for Divorced Christians,* Dwight H. Small

Baker Book House, 1986, $8.99, paper, 232 pp., for counselors

Description Remarriage is approached from an analysis of biblical data uniquely placed within a New Testament theology of grace. God ministers to divorced people, not through inflexible law, but through forgiving, renewing grace. The aim of the book is reassurance for those who believe God is leading them to remarriage and restored family normalcy. Redemptive realism supersedes prohibition, stigma, and church strictures. While remarriage is neither God's intention nor "a right," it is the concession of God's restorative grace to imperfect couples who fail in marriage. Theologically, marriage is defined as a covenant of unity and fidelity, divorce as covenant breaking. Mosaic law provided for both divorce and remarriage. In the New Testament divorce as willful intention is rejected, but for human failure restorative grace is transcendent. The teaching of Jesus and Paul are interpreted and controversial views weighed. The presumption in Corinthians is affirmed in favor of conditional remarriage. Remarriage brings healing and family unit restoration.

Author Dwight Harvey Small is professor emeritus of sociology at Westmont College, Santa Barbara, Calif. He retired in 1982 after serving 12 years as teacher and counselor and previous to that 27 years as a pastor. An author of numerous books on marriage, ethics, theology, and devotional life.

Contents *Part 1:* The broader biblical understanding of marriage, divorce, and remarriage *1.* New wind blowing *2.* Covenant of unity and fidelity *3.* Grace transcendent, grace triumphant *Part 2:* The specific biblical teachings on divorce and remarriage *4.* Old Testament provision *5.* Jesus and the Pharisees *6.* Paul and the Corinthians *Part 3:* The ruling New Testament ethic of grace applied to divorce and remarriage *7.* Ethics for fragile saints *8.* Living in the interim

More Than "I Do" *A Pastor's Resource Book for Premarital Counseling,* Harold Ivan Smith

Beacon Hill Press of Kansas City, 1983, $6.95, paper, 88 pp., for counselors

Description Covers a wide range of issues pastors need to know about prior to and during premarital counseling. Background material, couple's inventory quizzes, and duplication of all materials found in the engaged couples book is included.

Author Harold Ivan Smith is well known for his combined ministries of writing, speaking and counseling, especially in the area of singles ministries in the church.

Contents *1.* Engagement and marriage—a biblical perspective *2.* A historical perspective on premarital counseling *3.* Goals of premarital counseling *4.* The congregation and premarital counseling *5.* The pastor and premarital counseling *6.* Premarital counseling *7.* Dangers in premarital counseling *8.* Developing a church policy *9.* Excuses *10.* Why the church insists on premarital counseling *11.* Premarital counseling: those special cases *12.* Premarital counseling for student marriages

Should I Get Married? M. Blaine Smith

InterVarsity Press, 1990, $9.99, paper, 307 pp., for both counselors and counselees

Description Debunks many common myths about marriage and provides answers to questions about dating, sexuality, compatibility, and commitment. Winner of a 1990 Book of the Year Award from Campus Life.

Author M. Blaine Smith, a Presbyterian resource pastor, is director of Nehemiah Ministries. He is author of several books. He holds the doctor of ministry degree from Fuller Theological Seminary.

Contents *Part 1:* Setting your sights *1.* The search for perspective *2.* Does God want me to be married or single? *Part 2:* God's guidance and the marriage decision *3.* Is God a matchmaker? *4.* How can I know God's will? *5.* Can I be certain? *Part 3:* Choosing a spouse *6.* Do you feel deep compassion for the person? *7.* Are you good friends? *8.* Are you both ready for marriage? *9.* Are you physically compatible? *10.* Are you intellectually compatible? *11.* Are you spiritually compatible? *13.* Are your expectations compatible? *14.* Finally deciding *Part 4:* Finding a spouse *15.* What will attract someone to you? *16.* Praying for a partner *17.* Taking initiative *18.* Should a woman initiate? *19.* Dealing with rejection *Part 5:* Confronting the fear of commitment *20.* Understanding the fear of commitment *21.* When the problem is your partner's *22.* When the problem is your own

Growing in Remarriage *Working through the Unique Problems of Remarriage,* Jim Smoke

Fleming H. Revell, 1990, $13.99, cloth, 188 pp., for counselees

Description Realistic, sensitive counsel. A test to determine marital readiness and answers to common questions.

Author Jim Smoke is the author of two other books on singleness. He is adjunct professor at Fuller Theological Seminary and director for the Center for Divorce Recovery in Tempe, Ariz.

Contents *1.* Preparing for remarriage: an overview *2.* Closing doors *3.* Remarriage: the question *4.* Relationships or rescue attempt *5.* The principles of preparation: a yardstick *6.* Living in remarriage *7.* Expectations versus realities *8.* When it all goes into the blender *9.* Adding branches to the family tree *10.* The seasons of remarriage *11.* Second marriages in trouble *12.* Children living in step *13.* Watching for the warning signs / Questions and suggestions / The "am I ready for marriage?" test / A second-marriage ceremony / Postscript and resources

Getting Ready for a Great Marriage *For Those Who Want Their Love to Last,* R. Paul Stevens

NavPress, 1990, $6.00, paper, 109 pp., for both counselors and counselees

Description In a day when divorce steadily stares down the best intentions and the strongest commitments, it's important to plan for a marriage that will last "until death do us part." Focusing on the often neglected notion of the marriage covenant—a lifelong partnership that is indwelt by God—this work is made up of short, wisdom-packed chapters that will help you build strong foundations for a lasting marriage.

Author R. Paul Stevens (D.Min., Fuller Theological Seminary) is the academic dean of Regent College in Vancouver, British Columbia. He is the author of several books and writes extensively on the subject of marriage.

Contents *1.* Why not marry for good? *2.* The divorce-less covenant *3.* The myth of marriage for love *4.* The right reasons for marrying *5.* The divine matchmaker *6.* When the infatuation wears off *7.* The lost art of courting *8.* Covenant readiness *9.* Ready to leave home *10.* Companionship marriage *11.* Right for each other *12.* True to each other *13.* Going all the way *14.* The celebration of sex *15.* Sexual readiness *16.* Sexual hurt *17.* Power and partnership *18.* Headship within equity *19.* A permanent wedding gift *20.* An army of two *21.* Why Jesus goes to weddings

A Premarital Guide for Couples and Their Counselors David A. Thompson

Bethany House Publishers, $5.99, paper, 64 pp., for both counselors and counselees

Description A unique set of six questionnaires for couples to complete. These can be given to their pastor or counselor so that they can realistically zero in on problem areas during actual sessions.

Author David A. Thompson, now a Navy chaplain, has had extensive training in counseling and the pastoral ministry.

Pre-Marriage Inventory Bob Tippie

Maret Software International, $99.99, software, for counselors

Description The *Pre-Marriage Inventory* is designed for use in every premarital counseling situation. Includes the ability to generate four sets of questions for use in counseling sessions. The questions assist in the structuring of the counseling sessions.

Author Bob Tippie is an ordained Baptist minister with an active counseling and consulting practice. He holds a bachelor's degree in psychology and a master's in pastoral counseling.

Contents Communication / Sexual issues / Financial issues / Roles and authority / Views toward divorce / Home of origin / Emotional stability / Interpersonal relationships / Abuse/dysfunction indicators

Counseling before Marriage Everett L. Worthington Jr.

Word Publishing, 1990, $15.99, cloth, 217 pp., for counselors

Description Part of the Resources for Christian Counseling series—this book takes a different look at premarital counseling for a number of reasons: First, it has major sections on the theology and psychology of divorce and of remarriage. Second, it has a large number of practical suggestions about interventions that prepare people for marriage, not just in sessions, but also from the pulpit, in groups, in educational settings, and with special programs. Third, the book is based on up-to-date research on marriage, divorce, and remarriage. Does not read like a research book.

Author Everett Worthington holds a Ph.D. in counseling from the University of Missouri–Columbia and has worked at Virginia Commonwealth University since 1978. As a licensed clinical psychologist, he has directed a community counseling agency, supervised others, and maintained a part-time private practice.

Contents The social, political, and philosophical pressures on modern marriage are summarized. Reviews literature on the effectiveness of marital preparation programs. Chapters describe the theological positions on divorce and remarriage and the latest research about the psychology of divorce and remarriage. Programs are suggested for educating the entire congregation on marriage, divorce, and remarriage.

Before You Remarry *A Guide to Successful Remarriage,* H. Norman Wright

Harvest House Publishers, 1988, $7.99, paper, 81 pp., for counselees

Description Drawing from the latest findings on adjustments in second marriages, well-known marriage and family counselor H. Norman Wright helps couples attain a much more realistic perception of themselves and the marriage they are about to enter. It will help couples plan for their happiness rather than leave it to chance.

Author Dr. H. Norman Wright is one of America's best known Christian marriage and family counselors at the Family Counseling and Enrichment Center in Tustin, Calif. He is author of more than 50 books. He has also served on the faculty of Talbot School of Theology and the Graduate School of Marriage Counseling of Biola University.

Contents *1.* What is marriage? *2.* Remarriage—are you ready? *3.* Uniqueness and acceptance in marriage *4.* Love as a basis for marriage *5.* What do you expect from marriage? *6.* Goals in remarriage *7.* Fulfilling needs in marriage *8.* Roles, responsibilities, and decision making *9.* In-laws or outlaws—it's your choice *10.* Communication *11.* Conflict (or "sound the battle cry") *12.* Finances *13.* Sex in marriage / *Your wedding ceremony* / *Evaluation*

Before You Say "I Do" *A Marriage Preparation Manual for Couples,* H. Norman Wright and Wes Roberts

Harvest House Publishers, 1978, $7.99, paper, 80 pp., for both counselors and counselees

Description This study manual has been designed to assist you in making your marriage a fulfilling and growing relationship. Material was drawn from various national marriage enrichment seminars.

Authors Dr. H. Norman Wright is one of America's best known Christian marriage and family counselors at the Family Counseling and Enrichment Center in Tustin, Calif. He is author of more than 50 books. He has also served on the faculty of Talbot School of Theology and the Graduate School of Marriage Counseling of Biola University. Wes Roberts is president of Life Enrichment in Denver, Colo. He has served as director of the counseling ministry of a church.

Contents *1.* What is marriage? *2.* Uniqueness and acceptance in marriage *3.* Love as a basis for marriage *4.* What did you expect from marriage? *5.* Goals in marriage *6.* Fulfilling needs in marriage *7.* Roles, responsibilities, and decision making *8.* In-laws or outlaws—it's your choice *9.* Communication *10.* Conflict (or "sound the battle cry") *11.* Sex in marriage

The Premarital Counseling Handbook
H. Norman Wright

Moody Press, 1992, $18.99, cloth, 271 pp., for counselors

Description Considered by many to be the standard in the field. Writing with a Bible in hand, Wright introduces theory, then gets right down to the business of how counseling sessions should be run. In this revised edition, he has added new material to cover such perplexing issues as interracial marriages and couples where one or both have come from dysfunctional families.

Author Dr. H. Norman Wright is one of America's best known Christian marriage and family counselors at the Family Counseling and Enrichment Center in Tustin, Calif. He is author of more than 50 books. He has also served on the faculty of Talbot School of Theology and the Graduate School of Marriage Counseling of Biola University.

31. Professional Issues

Journals and Periodicals

Biblical Counselor, The

The National Association of Nouthetic Counselors, bimonthly, free/donation, a reference or academic work

Description *The Biblical Counselor* is published to accomplish three purposes. First, articles are written to provide pastors and counselors with practical answers to specific counseling problems. Second, the newsletter contains polemical articles to articulate the difference between biblical counseling and other methods. Third, information on regional and national training conferences is included as a service to the biblical counseling community.

Christian Counseling Today

The American Association of Christian Counselors, quarterly, $35.00/year, free to AACC members, paper, approx. 50 pp., for both counselors and counselees

Description An attractive quarterly counseling magazine that focuses on issues facing today's Christian counselors. Thought provoking, practical, academically sound, psychologically accurate, and biblically solid, the magazine features interviews with Christian counseling leaders and articles on relevant topics such as: family counseling; abuse; legal issues in counseling; lay helping; building healthy families; sexual conflicts; the church as a healing community; and much more. Representative articles: What Makes a Family Healthy? Gary R. Collins; Family Counseling: An Approach That Works, Everett Worthington; Can Professional Counseling Be at Home in the Church? Allan McKechnie; Counseling Today's Teens, Les Parrott III. Forum—Inpatient Christian Counseling: Three Perspectives with McGee, Arterburn, and Minirth.

Cura Animarum *(Translated: The Cure of Souls)*

Association of Mental Health Clergy, for counselors

Description The official journal of the Association of Mental Health Clergy. Ecumenical in scope.

Focus on the Family

Focus on the Family, monthly, free, for counselees

Description Magazine format. Monthly publication that seeks to affirm and support the home. Magazine also deals with some recovery and life stage issues.

Journal of Biblical Counseling

Christian Counseling and Education Foundation, three times per year, $18.00, a reference or academic work

Description Journal that details the practice of nouthetic counseling in clinical and pastoral settings. Representative articles: Homework and Biblical Counseling; Helping Anorexics; Critiquing Modern Integrationists; How to Write for Publication.

Journal of Christian Healing, The

Association of Christian Therapists, quarterly, for counselors

Description The JCH seeks to enable health care providers to integrate the presence of the Holy Spirit into their practice.

Journal of Ministry in Addiction and Recovery

The Haworth Pastoral Press, biannually, $20.00, a reference or academic work

Description A new journal that seeks to provide a forum for networking, sharing ideas about addiction and recovery, providing a multidisciplinary approach to ministry, and offering pastoral caregivers and others in the addiction field innovative approaches to treating a variety of addictive behaviors. Representative articles: Addiction and Dualistic Spirituality: Shared Visions of God, Self, and Creation; The 12-Step Program and Christian Spirituality; Spirituality in Treatment Programs for Addicts; Grief Issues in Alcoholism and Addiction; Do Clergy Encourage Codependency?; Let God Be God: A Theological Justification for the Anonymity of God in the 12-Step Program.

Journal of Pastoral Care

Journal of Pastoral Care Publications, Inc., quarterly, $20.00, a reference or academic work

Description Published by a consortium of professional organizations in the fields of pastoral care, pastoral counseling, clinical pastoral education, and ministries in specialized settings such as hospitals, business and industrial contexts, and correctional chaplaincies. Includes articles that reflect the cutting edges of clinical pastoral education and other pastoral counseling movements.

Journal of Psychology and Christianity, The

The Christian Association for Psychological Studies, quarterly, $35, free to CAPS members, a reference or academic work

Description The *JPC* is an official publication of CAPS, designed to provide scholarly interchange among Christian professionals in the psychological and pastoral professions. Articles about clinical practice are included on a regular basis. The *JPC* is comprised of manuscripts that have been evaluated and selected by a board of referees, using a blind review system. While some manuscripts are solicited, none of the authors of published articles is paid for his or her efforts. Articles include theoretical and research material focusing on issues in psychology, theology, sociology, marital and family studies, social work, and related fields which can be useful to academic and applied communities in those disciplines. Articles bearing on the relationships between Christianity and psychology are particularly welcome. Applied articles treating current issues in clinical practice, pastoral counseling, family and community services, and similar matters are also included in the *JPC* as well as book reviews. CAPS also publishes *EnCAPSulate* a newsletter that covers information about conventions, members, fellowship, and personal news. Representative articles: Assessment Procedures for Attention Deficit Disorders in Children, Grant L.

Martin; A Call for Emphasis on Scholarship on Christian Marriage and Marriage Counseling, Everett L. Worthington Jr.; System Malfunction: Role Conflict and the Minister, Jennifer L. Kunst; Clarifying the Interplay of Developmental and Contextual Issues in Counseling Missionaries, Janice K. Ritchey and Christopher H. Rosik; Childhood Stress: A Review, Les Parrott III; Asian-American Christian Attitudes towards Counseling, Diane M. Misumi.

Journal of Psychology and Theology An Evangelical Forum for the Integration of Psychology and Theology

Rosemead School of Psychology, quarterly, $38.00, a reference or academic work

Description Communicates recent scholarly thinking on the interrelationships of psychological and theological concepts and considers applications of these concepts to a variety of professional settings. Representative articles: Investigating Life Stories: Personal Narratives in Pastoral Psychology; The Effects of God Language on Perceived Attributes of God; Relationship Between Religious Orientation and Love Styles, Sexual Attitudes, and Sexual Behaviors; Outcome Research and Religious Psychotherapies: Where Are We and Where Are We Going?

Journal of Religion in Psychotherapy

The Haworth Pastoral Press, quarterly, $24.00, a reference or academic work

Description The one resource needed by therapists and researchers who are interested in the role and dynamic of religion in the healing process of psychotherapy. Pastoral counselors, psychologists, marriage and family therapists, and social workers will be challenged by the exciting mix of theoretical, clinical, and research topics presented in each volume.

Psychology for Living

Narramore Christian Foundation, bimonthly, $18.00, paper, for counselees

Description Popular level magazine format that features concise, helpful articles, easy reading, practical answers, no outside advertising, a Bible devotional, questions and answers—Dr. Clyde Narramore comments and commentaries—a lively summary of recent news and developments that influence human behavior and have spiritual significance. Representative articles: Ten Secrets to Building Closer Relationships; Disciplining Adolescents; Narcissism: When Self Is the Center of a Person's World; Self-Tolerance and Spiritual Fitness.

Social Work and Christianity

National Association of Christians in Social Work, biannually, $10.00, a reference or academic work

Description An international journal that seeks to contribute to the growth of social workers in the Christian faith. Representative articles: Single-Parent Families, Dan Quayle, and Murphy Brown: What's a Christian Social Worker to Do?; Homosexual No More: Ministry and Therapy for the Recovering Homosexual; Professional Standards, Social Workers, and Missionary Organizations: Some Basic Recommendations; Bearing One Another's Burdens: Supporting Families of Dementia Sufferers.

STEPS The Magazine of Hope and Healing for Christians in Recovery

National Association for Christians in Recovery, quarterly, $20.00, for both counselors and counselees

Description A quarterly magazine format that focuses on recovery issues from a distinctively Christian perspective. Designed for the lay, pastoral, and professional Christian counselor. Representative articles: Beyond Victim Recovery: New Age or New Testament?; Crossing Out "Cross Talk"; Is It Safe to Hurt in Church?

Today's Better Life

Thomas Nelson Publishers, monthly, $20.00, for counselees

Description Popular level, magazine format. Deals with a wide variety of counseling, recovery, fitness and health, and stage of life issues from a Christian perspective. Formerly *Christian Psychology for Today.* Published under the direction of the Minirth-Meier Clinics.

Legal and Ethical Issues

Legal Issues and Religious Counseling
Ronald K. Bullis and Cynthia S. Mazur

Westminster/John Knox Press, 1993, $11.99, paper, 127 pp., for counselors

Description A brief, readable book dealing with the three types of legal issues most encountered by religious counselors.

Authors Ronald K. Bullis is associate pastor, Tuckahoe Presbyterian Church, Richmond, Va. He is a licensed professional counselor and certified sex educator. Cynthia S. Mazur is a United Church of Christ minister currently working in disaster assistance as an attorney at the Federal Emergency Management Agency in Washington, D.C.

Contents *1.* The first amendment and religious counseling: a legal exegesis *2.* Tort law: clergy negligence, clergy malpractice, and the duty to protect the counselee *3.* The expanding vulnerability of religious counselors to legal action: sexual misconduct, and the duty to protect third parties *4.* State regulation of religious counselors *5.* Privileged communication for religious counselors *6.* Laws limiting clergy privilege *7.* General trends and patterns of religious counseling liability *8.* A legal audit for religious counselors

How to Start and Manage a Counseling Business *A Guide for Churches, Ministers, and Professionals,* Kathie Erwin

Word Publishing, 1993, $15.99, cloth, 253 pp., for counselors

Description This book aims at demystifying business development concepts for Christian counselors and pastors who are starting or managing counseling centers. Emphasis is placed on how to apply effective planning and budgeting and how to maximize marketing at low costs. The reader is guided through a simplified business plan. Basics of structure for corporations, partnerships, sole practitioners, and church-related counseling centers are presented along with business tax issues. The overall goal is to demonstrate that good ministry and good management are complementary. Here is the perfect minicourse in administration and marketing for counselors with business anxieties.

Author Dr. Kathie Erwin is a clinical psychotherapist in private practice in Florida. She has an M.A. in counseling psychology from Liberty University and an M.B.A. and a Ph.D. in management from California Coast University. She is a national certified counselor and a licensed mental health counselor.

Contents *1.* The three R's of a counseling practice *2.* Developing your business plan *3.* Structuring your counseling practice *4.* The church-linked counseling practice *5.* The people behind your business *6.* How to maximize marketing impact with minimal cost *7.* Budgeting your finances and your time *8.* Identifying sources of income *9.* Business tax issues *10.* Business ethics for counseling *11.* Finding referral services

The Christian Counselor's Legal Protection Kit Douglas R. Flather

American Association of Christian Counselors, 1995, $59.95, software

Description A new software project from the AACC. Aimed specifically at those providing counseling services who have never had a course on professional practice. A series of interactive modules walks the user through eight critical areas enabling them to confidently manage risk in their ministry or practice. Includes the custom forms generator "FastForms" and other useful tools (see Contents). Requires Microsoft Windows 3.1 and 5 mb hard disk space.

Author Douglas R. Flather is the resources coordinator for the American Association of Christian Counselors. He is adjunct professor of psychology at Washington Bible College, and the editor of this project, *Resource Guide for Christian Counselors.*

Contents *Module 1*—How to use the software *Module 2*—Ethics *Module 3*—High risk practices *Module 4*—Insurance *Module 5*—FastForms! Custom forms generator *Module 6*—Referrals (includes database) *Module 7*—Tough calls *Module 8*—Counselor self-care *Module 9*—More help *Module 10*—Annotated bibliography

Christian Ministries and the Law *What Church and Para-Church Leaders Should Know,* H. Wayne House

Baker Book House, 1992, $15.99, paper, 246 pp., for counselors

Description Almost every question that has come up involving church and state is covered by a lawyer. House covers such matters as counseling, taxation, and zoning.

Author H. Wayne House holds a law degree from O. W. Coburn School of Law and theological degrees from Western Conservative Baptist and Concordia Seminaries. He is a member of the American Bar Association and the American Trial Lawyers Association.

Contents *Part 1:* The American legal system *1.* A biblical view of law and government *2.* The origins of the Anglo-American law *3.* An introduction to the American legal system *4.* Church and state in America *5.* A look at the First Amendment *Part 2:* Counseling, church discipline, and conflict resolution *6.* The minister as counselor *7.* Church discipline and the right of privacy *8.* Reconciling disputes among Christians *Part 3:* Incorporation, Christian schools, property taxes, and political activity *9.* Should the church incorporate? *10.* Legal considerations for Christian schools *11.* Church property and zoning ordinances *12.* The IRS and church finances *13.* Tax planning for religious workers *14.* Charitable giving: funding the Christian challenge *15.* Clergy and political activity *Part 4:* Counseling church members regarding the law *16.* Should Christians sue? *17.* Is bankruptcy ethical for the Christian? *18.* The Christian leader's guide to criminal law *19.* Benefits of preventive lawyering

Legal Defense Handbook for Christians in Ministry *What You Need to Know Now about the Increasing Litigation against Churches,* Carl F. Lansing

NavPress, 1992, $15.00, paper, 271 pp., for counselors

Description A crucial resource for anyone in organized ministry. Written by a Christian lawyer, it offers invaluable advice on how to prevent costly and damaging lawsuits through legal wisdom in ministry practices. Includes practical guidelines for laypeople on legal issues in ministry.

Author Carl F. Lansing (J.D., Pepperdine University) practices law in Denver, Colo., with an emphasis in business law and litigation. He serves as corporate legal counsel to a diverse group of public and private companies and nonprofit ministries.

Contents *Part 1:* A legal storm brewing for ministries *1.* The changing legal winds for ministries *2.* The litigation avalanche hits ministries *Part 2:* The perilous course of the legal system *3.* The storm system: understanding legal origins *4.* Enterprise liability theory: opening deep pockets *5.* The Christian response thus far: in the world but not of it *6.* Could a killer lawsuit happen to you? *Part 3:* Guides through the storm: lawyers and the law *7.* The legal playing field *8.* "L.A. Law" is not the law *9.* Lawyers: friend or foe? *10.* Professor Kingsfield revisited: lawyers education, and ethics *11.* 10 Commandments for working with lawyers, part 1 *12.* 10 commandments for working with lawyers, part 2 *Part 4:* Dodging hailstones: substantive legal ministry issues *13.* Corporate law: structuring to avoid personal liability *14.* Real estate law: commonly overlooked basics *15.* Get it in writing and keep a copy *16.* Warnings about insurance coverage *17.* Counseling liabilities 101 *18.* Protecting counseling ministries from legal attack *19.* Counseling confidentiality and transference

Christian Counseling and the Law Steve Levicoff

Moody Press, 1991, $13.99, cloth, 203 pp., for counselors

Description Discusses the growing trend in litigation against pastors and Christian counselors. Written in easy-to-understand language that avoids "legalese," this book is a comprehensive guide to the legal ramifications of Christian counseling and how to avoid being sued. It is directed to both professionals and lay counselors in churches, counseling ministries, and private practice. Unlike most counseling law books which address the secular area, *Christian Counseling and the Law* focuses on issues particular to pastors and Christian counselors. Issues addressed include clergy malpractice, duty of care, counselor versus clergy confidentiality, child abuse reporting requirements, legal issues in church discipline, counseling cultists and their families, and biblical counseling in specialized situations such as medical ethics, conscientious objection, and abortion clinic protests.

Author Steve Levicoff is director of the Institute on Religion and Law in Ambler, Pa. He holds a Ph.D. in religion and law from the Union Institute, and his other books include *Name It and Frame It* (IRL) and *Street Smart: A Survival Guide to Personal Evangelism and the Law* (Baker).

Contents *1.* The dispensation of litigation? *2.* The explosive new area of law *3.* The first freedom *4.* What makes a counselor a counselor? *5.* Caveat emptor: let the buyer beware *6.* Anatomy of a church lawsuit *7.* Confidentiality and privileged communication *8.* Counseling malpractice and negligence *9.* Documenting the counseling relationship *10.* Church discipline and invasion of privacy *11.* Child abuse reporting: an ethical dilemma *12.* Counseling and medical issues *13.* Counseling and civil disobedience *14.* Counseling, conscientious objection, and sanctuary *15.* Counseling and the cults *16.* Christian conciliation: an alternative to litigation *17.* Legal resources for Christian counselors

Ministry of Reconciliation, A *A Survey of Christian Conciliation and Biblical Conflict Resolution,* Steve Levicoff

Moody Press, 1991, $24.95, cassette(s), 5 cassettes, for counselors

Description The United States has become the most lawsuit happy [sic] society in the world. Despite the guidelines of 1 Cor. 6:1–8, many of those suits involve Christians suing other Christians. *A Ministry of Reconciliation* shows us a better way, Christian conciliation—using biblical principles to mediate legal, interpersonal, and marriage and family disputes. Using biblical principles Levicoff discusses how conciliation can be used by pastors, counselors, and laypeople to resolve conflicts before they get to the stage of litigation. At a time when the People's Court admonishes us, "Don't take matters into your own hands, take them to court," this series discusses the biblical principles of mediating disputes. Subjects covered include the nature of conflict, principles of biblical resolution and mediation, how to implement the principles of Christian conciliation in both pastoral and professional counseling practices.

Author Steve Levicoff is director of the Institute on Religion and Law in Ambler, Pa. He holds a Ph.D. in religion and law from the Union Institute, and his other books include *Name It and Frame It* (IRL) and *Street Smart: A Survival Guide to Personal Evangelism and the Law* (Baker).

Name It and Frame It *New Opportunities in Adult Education and How to Avoid Being Ripped Off,* Steve Levicoff

Institute on Religion and Law, 1993, $29.95, paper, 172 pp., a reference or academic work

Description The most thorough guide available to nontraditional opportunities in higher education for Christians, *Name It and Frame It* includes chapters on professional credentialing for pastors and Christian counselors and profiles several counseling education programs and professional organizations, both good and bad. Includes comprehensive background information on related subjects such as accreditation, certification, and licensure. Covers undergraduate, graduate, doctoral, and professional programs and has been used as a resource tool by pastors, counselors, educational professionals, and prospective students seeking to pursue a higher education.

Author Steve Levicoff is director of the Institute on Religion and Law in Ambler, Pa. He holds a Ph.D. in religion and law from the Union Institute, and his other books include *Name It and Frame It* (IRL) and *Street Smart: A Survival Guide to Personal Evangelism and the Law* (Baker).

Contents *1.* So you want to have a ministry *2.* A bachelor to the beat of a different drummer *3.* A consumer's

257

guide to accreditation *4.* The wacky world of degree mills *5.* The ramifications of accreditation *6.* The wacky world of ordination mills *7.* A survey of accredited Christian correspondence courses and degree programs *8.* A survey of accredited graduate programs by extension *9.* "Christianizing" the secular option *10.* A survey of legitimate unaccredited Christian programs *11.* A survey of counseling programs, good and bad *12.* A survey of degree mills *13.* A survey of ordination mills *14.* Some closing epistles *15.* Further resources

Pastors, Counselors, and the Law . . .
How to Avoid Lawsuits in Your Pastoral or Christian Counseling Ministry, Steve Levicoff

Institute on Religion and Law, 1991, $39.95, cassette(s), 8 cassettes, for counselors

Description The American Bar Association has called litigation against churches, pastors, and Christian counselors "an explosive new area of law," and is now offering workshops for attorneys on how to sue churches and Christian ministries. This seminar is designed to equip pastors and counselors to avoid lawsuits before they occur.

Author Steve Levicoff is director of the Institute on Religion and Law in Ambler, Pa. He holds a Ph.D. in religion and law from the Union Institute, and his other books include *Name It and Frame It* (IRL) and *Street Smart: A Survival Guide to Personal Evangelism and the Law* (Baker).

Clergy Malpractice H. Newton Malony and Thomas L. Needham

Westminster/John Knox Press, 1986, paper, 185 pp., for counselors

Description A complex issue that has made newspaper headlines and that concerns every pastor is fully dealt with in this book, addressed to both students and practitioners. The authors bring together biblical, psychological, legal, and practical insights about malpractice and ministry in today's world and offer guidelines for future pastoral work. About to go out of print, but Westminster has a limited stock.

Authors H. Newton Maloney, Ph.D., is a clinical psychologist and United Methodist minister. He is also a professor and program director at Fuller Theological Seminary. Thomas L. Needham, Ed.D., is a marriage counselor and Baptist minister in Encino, Calif. He is an adjunct professor at Azuza Pacific University. Samuel Southard, Ph.D., is a pastoral counselor and Southern Bap-

tist minister. He is professor of pastoral theology in the School of Theology of Fuller Theological Seminary.

Contents *1.* Malpractice in the ministry *2.* What the law says—"clergy malpractice" Ramifications of a new theory—is the cloth unraveling? A first look at clergy malpractice *3.* Pastoral accountability in the Bible and theology *4.* Church discipline: handle with care *5.* Helping when the risks are great *6.* Confidentiality in the pastoral role *7.* Insurance protection for church and clergy *8.* The future of ministry in a changing world

Legal Guide for Day-to-Day Church Matters *A Handbook for Pastors and Church Members,* Cynthia S. Mazur and Ronald K. Bullis

The Pilgrim Press, 1994, $8.95, paper, 135 pp., for both counselors and counselees

Description Brief and to-the-point answers are offered for a multitude of legal issues facing churches and religious practitioners today.

Authors Cynthia S. Mazur received her master of divinity from Princeton Theological Seminary and her law degree from Georgetown and Syracuse Universities. Ronald K. Bullis received his master of divinity from Princeton Theological Seminary and his law degree from Syracuse University.

Contents *1.* Litigation *2.* Church procedures *3.* Government regulatory laws *4.* Copyright *5.* Personal injury *6.* Defamation *7.* Employment and labor law *8.* Contracts *9.* Agency *10.* Weddings *11.* Wills *12.* Church ownership and possession of property *13.* Money *14.* Tax laws *15.* How the church can obtain additional insurance

Law for the Christian Counselor *A Guidebook for Clinicians and Pastors,* George Ohlschlager and Peter Mosgofian

Word Publishing, 1992, $15.99, cloth, 365 pp., for counselors

Description This practical book describes the boundaries of legal liability, offers a synthesis of state laws in the field, and suggests guidelines for risk management. But since Christian therapy seeks to do more than avoid lawsuits, the authors outline the best biblical and clinical healing strategies for those suffering in delicate areas such as sexuality and suicide. They challenge Christian professionals to organize in order to set their own ethical guidelines instead of waiting until they are policed from without.

Authors George Ohlschlager is associate director and cofounder of the Redwood Family Institute. He holds an M.A. in counseling psychology from Trinity Evangelical Divinity School and an M.S.W. from the Graduate School of Social Work and J.D. from the College of Law of the University of Iowa. Peter Mosgofian is executive director and cofounder of the Redwood Family Institute. He is a graduate of Humbolt State University and holds an M.A. in theology and marriage and family therapy from Fuller Theological Seminary.

Contents *Part 1:* The grave new world of Christian counseling liability *1.* Introduction to law for the Christian counselor *2.* The legal regulation of Christian counseling *3.* Social and systemic trends in legal liability *4.* Nally and Smith: lessons from two landmark cases *Part 2:* Sexual misconduct in Christian counseling *5.* Wrongful sex and sexual misconduct crisis *6.* Legal liability for sexual misconduct in counseling *Part 3:* Confidentiality and its many exceptions *7.* Confidentiality and privileged communication *8.* Child and elder abuse reporting and intervention *9.* The duty and practice of suicide prevention *10.* Protecting third persons from client violence *Part 4:* The counseling process: managing liability risk *11.* A good start: informed consent and counseling *12.* Improper treatment and high risk counseling practices *13.* Dual relationships: undue influence, and conflict of interest *14.* Failure to consult or refer, abandonment, and wrongful termination *15.* God or mammon? Fees and money issues in Christian counseling *Part 5:* Special counseling modes and controversial cases *16.* Marriage, family, and child therapy; divorce and group counseling *17.* Psychiatry and inpatient hospital ministry *18.* Counseling in cases of abortion, AIDS, and cult programming *Part 6:* Corporate risks and counseling credentials *19.* The counseling pastor: competent counseling, referral, and leadership *20.* Professional Christian counselors: issues in training and licensure *21.* Supervision and consultation in private and agency practice *22.* Expert courtroom testimony by the Christian counselor *Part 7:* The maturation of the Christian counseling profession *23.* Protecting the profession: defending Christian counselors *24.* Organizing the profession: a call to maturity

Confidentiality and Clergy *Churches, Ethics and the Law,* William W. Rankin

Morehouse Publishing, 1990, $8.95, paper, 144 pp., for counselors

Description Written out of the author's personal experience and research, this work is a focused resource on the ethics and law of confidentiality for the clergy.

Author William W. Rankin writes and lectures widely on the subject of ethics and on global issues. He is currently rector of St. Stephen's Episcopal Church, Belvedere, Calif.

Contents *1.* The ethos of the church and the ethics of its clergy *2.* The confession: its characteristics and development through the Church of England *3.* Confession in the Episcopal church *4.* Pastoral counseling: confidentiality versus the duty to divulge, the duty to care, and others *5.* Ethics and the limits of confidentiality *6.* Professional ethics and the law *7.* Managing yourself and parish under the impact of litigation

Pastoral Care and Counseling Never Involves Sex John Kie Vining

Institute for Pastoral Care, 1992, $4.00, paper, 36 pp., for counselors

Description This highly-readable, soon-to-be formally published paper is an outstanding introduction to sexual ethics for pastoral counselors.

Author John Kie Vining holds a doctor of ministry degree from Columbia Theological Seminary. He is a licensed professional counselor in Georgia and Tennessee.

Contents Includes discussion on definitions, codes of ethics in the professional community, boundaries, ministerial neediness, pitfalls to avoid, the impact of ministerial sexual misconduct, transference and nontherapeutic counter-transference, referrals, and more.

The Minister's Hotline for Counseling Assistance

Rapha Resources, for counselors

Association of Christian Conciliation Services

Association of Christian Conciliation Services. An organization

Description A nationwide membership organization established to equip and assist people to deal with conflict. Offers a variety of educational resources designed to equip Christians to resolve conflict in a biblically faithful manner. Makes referrals.

The Christian Legal Society

The Christian Legal Society. An organization

Description A referral/networking organization for attorneys within the Christian community.

The National Legal Foundation

The National Legal Foundation. An organization

Description Maintains a Christian attorney referral service.

The Rutherford Institute

The Rutherford Institute. An organization

Description A legal and educational organization that defends First Amendment rights, such as freedom of religion, freedom of speech, and the sanctity of all human life. A nonprofit organization that does not charge for its services. Potentially helpful to church-based counseling centers and practitioners in defining/refining practices.

Zenas Ministries

Zenas Ministries. An organization

Description Provides free, legal information to churches and pastors on a variety of issues. Call or write for details. Also produces a newsletter dealing with various church-related legal issues.

Professional Associations

American Association of Christian Counselors, The

The American Association of Christian Counselors, founded 1986. An organization

Description The AACC seeks to promote excellence and unity in Christian counseling by providing professional, pastoral, and lay counselors with information, educational resources, liability insurance, conferences, and other benefits. Tools for counselors include the quarterly *Christian Counseling Today* magazine, the *Counseling Connection* newsletter, and a quarterly audio cassette tape of counseling information. The AACC is committed to the integration of biblical theology with the principles of counseling; to assist members in the development of excellence in their own counseling theory and practice to stimulate interaction and mutual encouragement between counselors; to inspire the highest levels of counselor training; to contribute to the strengthening of families; and to bring honor to Jesus Christ. Beginning in 1994, AACC will sponsor a number of regional conferences. $65.00/year membership.

American Association of Pastoral Counselors

American Association of Pastoral Counselors, founded 1963. An organization

Description Ecumenical organization that offers certification for pastoral counselors and helps pastoral counselors locate and evaluate various training resources. Publishes the AAPC newsletter which contains information pertinent to pastoral counselors and other professionals in the mental health field in areas such as politics, policy, conferences, workshops, research, job listings, and more. $35.00/year membership.

Association for Clinical Pastoral Education

Association for Clinical Pastoral Education, founded 1967. An organization

Description Clinical Pastoral Education (CPE) is theological and professional education for ministry. Conceived as a method of learning pastoral practice in a clinical setting under supervision, CPE developed into an effort to integrate into pastoral practice a knowledge of medicine, psychology, and behavioral sciences. In CPE, supervised students minister to people in crisis situations. Essential elements in CPE include an accredited CPE center ready to receive students, certified CPE supervisors to promote pastoral supervision, a small group of peers engaged in a common learning experience providing pastoral care to people in crisis, detailed reporting of pastoral practice, a specific time period, and an individual learning contract. The CPE sponsors an annual conference, usually in the spring. About 3,600 members, annual budget of $700,000, 7 on staff.

Association of Christian Therapists

Association of Christian Therapists. An organization

Description A nonprofit health care organization that seeks to help professionals in the medical and mental health care fields integrate the Holy Spirit into their personal and professional lives. Sponsors the *Journal of Christian Healing,* and national and regional conferences.

Association of Mental Health Clergy, The

Association of Mental Health Clergy. An organization

Description The Association of Mental Health Clergy (AMHC) is an interfaith organization for ministers, priests, rabbis, and other religious leaders professionally concerned with the mental health dimensions of religious ministry. The AMHC offers professional fellowship; a channel for exchanging new information on the challenges and opportunities of mental health ministry; a means for disseminating understandings and methods in the application of religion to the problems of persons with mental and emotional disorders; and an opportunity to formulate standards for more effective pastoral services—including certification demonstrating competence. Sponsors an annual meeting and *Cura Animarum* (translated the cure of souls), their official journal.

Christian Association for Psychological Studies, The

The Christian Association for Psychological Studies, founded 1956. An organization

Description The Christian Association for Psychological Studies (CAPS) is a nonprofit, charitable association of Christians in the psychological and pastoral professions, plus students and interns, integrating their faith and professions. The original purposes in founding CAPS in 1956 are still relevant today, more than a third of a century later. They have ongoing meaning in the lives of Christians in the psychological and pastoral professions and in the lives of the persons we serve, whether as clinicians, pastors, teachers, researchers, or students and interns in preparation. That is, CAPS is involved with: (1) integrating, perhaps reconciling, professional training and Christian faith through developing and communicating theoretical and applied relationships between Christianity and the helping professions; (2) fellowshipping with other Christians who are dealing with both professional and personal issues; (3) providing educational opportunities for members of the Christian community; and (4) sharing Christian values and professional experiences with colleagues and persons in our communities, both with Christians and non-Christians. Produces the *Journal of Christianity and Psychology* and sponsors an annual conference. Regional associations are also in existence. Membership of 2,300, 15 part-time staff, annual budget of $150,000.

Christian Chaplain Services

Christian Chaplain Services, founded 1926. An organization

Description Offers fellowship and professional training opportunities for chaplains. Call for a descriptive brochure.

Narramore Christian Foundation

Narramore Christian Foundation, founded 1958. An organization

Description The Narramore Christian Foundation (NCF) is a charitable, nonprofit educational, training, and counseling organization ministering primarily to the Christian community. The NCF ministries integrate a thoroughly biblical theology with a practical, professional psychology, while also recognizing the physiological causes of behavior. Jesus Christ is presented as Savior and Lord, and the application of God's Word is emphasized. Membership of 13,000; 35 serve on staff; annual budget—$1,700,000. $15.00 year/membership.

National Association for Christians in Recovery, The

The National Association for Christian Recovery, founded 1991. An organization

Description The NACR is a membership organization designed for people who want to be distinctively Christian about their recovery. The NACR publishes a quarterly newsletter and a quarterly mini-magazine (*STEPS*). In addition, an annual conference draws the membership together for education, training, and fellowship in recovery. Regional networks are in the process of being formed. The NACR sponsors a clergy network for pastors and other religious professionals in recovery and a mental health professional network for therapists and others interested in recovery issues. Membership of 4,200, 2 full-time staff, annual budget of $285,000. $20.00–60.00 year/membership.

National Association of Nouthetic Counselors

National Association of Nouthetic Counselors, founded 1975. An organization

Description The National Association of Nouthetic Counselors (NANC) is a fellowship of Christian pastors and laymen who have banded together to promote and develop biblical counseling. NANC exists to (1) certify counselors and counseling centers who are biblical and exemplary in their ministries; (2) stimulate and maintain high standards of ethics and proficiency in ministry; (3) maintain a referral network of trustworthy counselors and institutions; (4) provide continuing education. Sponsors an annual conference and the *Biblical Counselor Newsletter.* Membership of 136. $50.00 year/membership.

North American Association of Christians in Social Work

North American Association of Christians in Social Work. An organization

Description Networking organization that seeks to assist social workers in the process of integrating their faith into their occupation. Sponsors the *Journal of Christians in Social Work.*

Pathways to Promise *Interfaith Ministries and Prolonged Mental Illness*

Pathways to Promise. An organization

Description An ecumenical networking organization that seeks to assist those in the religious community involved with care to the mentally ill. Sponsors an annual conference, an extensive database of resources, and a forum on the Internet called Ministry and Mental Illness.

Psychologists Interested in Religious Issues

American Psychological Association, founded 1948. An organization

Description One of the subcategories of the American Psychological Association. Focuses on the effects of religion on the therapeutic process.

Reference Works for Professionals

New Dictionary of Christian Ethics and Pastoral Theology David J. Atkinson, David F. Field, Arthur Holmes, and Oliver O'Donovan

InterVarsity Press, 1994, $39.99, cloth, 944 pp., for counselors

Description *NDCEPT* is organized in two parts. In the first part, 18 extended articles, arranged in theological order, introduce readers to the main themes of Christian ethics and pastoral theology. In the second part, over 700 articles, arranged alphabetically, flow like tributaries from

those main themes. An easy-to-use reference system enables quick transition from the first to the second part and back again. Encompasses a wide range of subjects. It includes articles on traditional subjects like atonement, the kingdom of God, suffering, death and dying, and heaven and hell. Includes articles on timely issues like reproductive technology, transplant surgery, health and health care, economic and social justice, prison and prison reform, psychotherapy, family therapy, and more.

Editors David J. Atkinson is chancellor of Southwark Cathedral in London, England. He was formerly fellow and chaplain of Corpus Christi College, Oxford University. Editor David F. Field is director of professional ministry with the Church Pastoral Aid Society in Warwick, England. He was formerly vice principal of Oak Hill College in London, England. Consulting editor Arthur Holmes is professor of philosophy at Wheaton College in Wheaton, Ill. Consulting editor Oliver O'Donovan is regius professor of moral and pastoral theology at Oxford University.

Baker Encyclopedia of Psychology David G. Benner

Baker Book House, 1985, $39.99, cloth, 1,223 pp., a reference or academic work

Description This important encyclopedia presents information on all the major theories and concepts of contemporary psychology. Each of the main entries also includes an evaluation of the subject matter from a Christian perspective. This encyclopedia provides a comprehensive treatment of psychology from a Christian point of view, many articles being written with an explicit biblical or theological perspective. In addition, it factually presents major current findings and theories in the field. The focus is on the areas of personality, psychopathology, psychotherapy and other treatment approaches, major systems and theories of psychology, and the psychology of religion. There is also some consideration given to the areas of social, developmental, and general experimental psychology.

Editor Dr. David G. Benner (general editor) is a clinical psychologist currently serving as professor and chair of the Department of Psychology at Redeemer College and adjunct professor of psychology and Christianity at the University of Toronto (St. Michael's College). He has written and edited nine books and remains active in clinical work, specializing in the treatment of dissociative disorders.

The First Book of Self-Help Tests Rich Buhler and Gaylen Larson

Janet Thoma (a division of Thomas Nelson), 1993, $7.99, paper, 192 pp., for both counselors and counselees

Description Intriguing self-quizzes help you gain insight into why you behave the way you do. Anyone who suspects that they might have an obsessive-compulsive addiction or an emotional problem will learn to draw a link among behavior, motivating feelings, and historical root causes.

Authors Rich Buhler is the host of the nationally syndicated radio counseling program *Table Talk* that is broadcast nationally. Dr. Gaylen Larson is the founder/director of Alpha Counseling Center, southern California's largest professional counseling service.

A Minister's Handbook of Mental Disorders Joseph W. Ciarrochi

Paulist Press, 1993, $12.95, paper, 218 pp., for counselors

Description Part of the Integration series from Paulist Press. This book will assist pastoral counselors and clergy in recognizing the array of common health problems, to become familiar with standard explanations and treatment of these problems, and to discover helpful strategies for pastoral care. The book is a practical guide, yet it provides an up-to-date understanding of mental illness. It will allow the reader to be knowledgeable and comfortable in pastoral care and to participate collegially with mental health professionals in cases of referral. Topics include depression, anxiety, addictions, sexual dysfunctions, schizophrenia, and personality disorders.

Author Joseph W. Ciarrochi is associate professor of pastoral counseling at Loyola College in Maryland. A clinical psychologist, he also holds a master's degree in theology. His treatment and research interests lie in the area of compulsive behaviors.

Contents *1.* Pastoral care and abnormal psychology *2.* Theories of abnormal behavior *3.* Pastoral assessment *4.* Anxiety and related disorders *5.* Mood disorders *6.* Addictive disorders *7.* Schizophrenia *8.* Sexual problems *9.* Personality disorders

Christian Counseling A Comprehensive Guide—Revised Edition, Gary R. Collins

Word Publishing, 1988, $18.99, paper, 700 pp., for counselors

Description This proven "course" in pastoral counseling has been extensively expanded and revised by the author to include recent developments and research, new resources, and attention to newly urgent needs such as AIDS and eating disorders. Written with clarity and warmth, this volume also reflects the author's professional qualifications as a Christian psychologist and his practical experience in the field.

Author Dr. Gary R. Collins is a licensed psychologist with a Ph.D. in clinical psychology from Purdue University. He teaches on a part-time basis at Trinity Evangelical Divinity School and is the executive director of the Association of Christian Counselors.

Contents *Part 1:* Introductory issues *1.* The church and counseling *2.* The counselor and counseling *3.* The core of counseling *4.* The community and counseling *5.* The crises in counseling *Part 2:* Personal issues *6.* Anxiety *7.* Loneliness *8.* Depression *9.* Anger *10.* Guilt *Part 3:* Developmental issues *11.* Child rearing and parental guidance *12.* Adolescence *13.* Young adulthood *14.* Middle life *15.* The later years *Part 4:* Interpersonal issues *16.* Interpersonal relationships *17.* Sex apart from marriage *18.* Sex within marriage *19.* Homosexuality *20.* Violence and abuse *Part 5:* Identity issues *21.* Inferiority and self-esteem *22.* Physical illness *23.* Grief *24.* Singleness *25.* Choosing a marriage partner *Part 6:* Family issues *26.* Premarital counseling *27.* Marital problems *28.* Pregnancy issues *29.* Family problems *30.* Divorce and remarriage *Part 7:* Other issues *31.* Mental disorders *32.* Alcoholism *33.* Addictions *34.* Financial counseling *35.* Vocational counseling *Part 8:* Concluding issues *36.* Spiritual issues *37.* Other problems *38.* Counseling the counselor

Dictionary of Pastoral Care and Counseling Rodney J. Hunter

Abingdon Press, 1990, $59.95, cloth, 1,346 pp., a reference or academic work

Description A large, comprehensive reference work that contains both practical and theoretical articles on virtually every aspect of pastoral care and counseling related topics. State-of-the-art articles on prayer and pastoral care, the Bible

263

and the pastoral interpretation of Scripture, moral guidance, are among the hundreds of well-focused topics in this book. Excellent bibliographies. Extensive cross referencing. Authored by over 600 authorities from a wide variety of religious backgrounds and theological perspectives. "Book of the Year" Award from the Academy of Parish Clergy and the "International Angel" Award from Religion in Media.

Author Rodney J. Hunter is professor of pastoral theology at the Candler School of Theology, Emory University, Atlanta, Ga. An ordained Presbyterian minister, Dr. Hunter did his basic and graduate theological work at Princeton Theological Seminary, writing his doctoral dissertation under the direction of Seward Hiltner.

Quick Scripture Reference for Counseling John G. Kruis

Baker Book House, 1994 (11th ed.), $7.99, spiral, 160 pp., for counselors

Description Designed to meet the specific needs of those who wish to use the Scriptures in counseling. Scripture passages and texts are listed under more than 50 different topics. Arranged so that the reader can immediately see the primary thrust of the passage. It allows for the quick compilation of an agenda for counseling, homework, or meditation. Typical entries: adultery, bitterness, comfort, divorce, forgiveness, lying, training children, etc.

Author John G. Kruis holds a B.A. from Calvin College and a B.D. from Calvin Theological Seminary. Ordained in 1959, certified member of the National Association of Nouthetic Counselors since 1977. Presently directs the Biblical Counseling Center in Jenison, Mich.

The Complete Life Encyclopedia *A Minirth-Meier New Life Family Resource,* Frank Minirth, Paul Meier, and Stephen Arterburn

Thomas Nelson Publishers, 1995, $29.99, cloth, 600 pp.

Description Based on information from the collected works of the doctors at the Minirth-Meier New Life Clinics, this encyclopedia is organized alphabetically and distilled for easy reading.

Authors Psychiatrists Frank Minirth and Paul Meier are senior officers of the Minirth-Meier Clinic in Richardson, Tex. Stephen Arterburn has 17 years' experience in psychiatric health care.

The Turning Point *How Persons of Conscience Brought About Major Change,* Alex Sareyan

Herald Press, 1995, $16.95, paper, 314 pp.

Description The most comprehensive chronicle of contributions made by conscientious objectors who volunteered for service in America's mental hospitals and state institutions for the developmentally disturbed during WWII.

Author Since 1953 Alex Sareyan has led the Mental Health Materials Center, which develops and distributes publications and educational materials on mental illness to a wide variety of environments.

Contents *1.* Conscientious objectors in the U.S.: 1775 to WWII *2.* Out of sight, out of mind *3.* A view from the lion's den *4.* Agents for social change: part 1 *5.* Agents for social change: part 2 *6.* Perceptions and misperceptions *7.* The turning point *8.* Plan for action becomes a reality *9.* Minnesota joins the crusade *10.* The Mennonite mental health story *11.* Legacies of the civilian public service mental hospital program *12.* Looking back

Psychology and Theology in Western Thought, 1672–1965 Hendrika VandeKemp

Kraus International Publications, 1984, $75.00, cloth, 367 pp., a reference or academic work

Description This historical bibliography is a major reference work that annotates 1,000 English language books relevant to the integration of psychology and theology/religion. Books published prior to 1965 are sorted into seven major categories and 27 subcategories for easy retrieval, with books in each major section appearing in chronological order. English translations of foreign books as well as major book and monograph series are also included. There is a small section of information about organizations devoted to integration. The bibliography has section introductions and author, title, institution, and subject indices. This annotated bibliography is divided into the following subject sections: historical and philosophical bases for integration; biblical and theological bases for integration; the psychology of religion; psychology and theology; theological perspectives on personality theory and psychology; psychiatric and psychoanalytic perspectives, and others.

Author Hendrika VandeKemp, who is professor of psychology at Fuller Theological Seminary, was educated at Hope College (B.A.) and the University of Massachusetts/Amherst (M.S., Ph.D.). She has published extensively in the theory and history of psychology, with a special interest in the history of psychology/theology interface.

Counselor's Guide to the Brain and Its Disorders *Knowing the Difference between Sin and Disease,* Edward T. Welch

Zondervan Publishing House, 1990, $15.99, paper, 320 pp., for counselors

Description A handbook for counselors on brain functions and disorders to aid in diagnosis and treatment from a thoroughly biblical perspective. Contrasts the biomedical and moral models of psychopathology.

Author Dr. Edward T. Welch is a counselor with the Christian Counseling and Education Foundation and lecturer in practical theology at Westminster Theological Seminary in Philadelphia, Pa. He holds an M.Div. from Biblical Theological Seminary and a Ph.D. from the University of Utah. He is a member of the APA and is a licensed psychologist in the state of Pennsylvania.

Contents *1.* Worlds in collision *Part 1:* Biblical and medical background *2.* Biblical foundations *3.* Biological foundations *4.* The brain and behavior *5.* Diagnostic instruments *Part 2:* Diseases that affect intellect, mood, and behavioral capabilities *6.* "Must know" diseases—Alzheimer's disease and dementia—multiple sclerosis—Parkinson's disease and related disorders—seizures and epilepsy—stroke—brain tumors—head injury—diabetes—female hormonal changes *Part 3:* Misdiagnosis: counseling problems with medically treatable causes *7.* The no. 1 culprit: licit and illicit drugs *8.* Common deceptive problems: depression, anxiety, schizophrenia, and mania *9.* Other "masquerading" symptoms *10.* Avoiding misdiagnosis *11.* Conclusion: sin or sickness?

32. Psychology and Christianity, Integration

Christian Counselor's Casebook, The
Jay E. Adams

Zondervan Publishing House, 1986, $10.99, paper, 224 pp., for counselors

Description This companion volume to *Competent to Counsel* and *The Christian Counselor's Manual* is designed to help the user assimilate and apply the principles of nouthetic counseling.

Author Dr. Adams is the author of numerous books on Christian counseling. He has served on a seminary faculty (Westminster Theological) and in the pastorate. He is founder of Christian Counseling and Educational Foundation in Laverock, Pa., and visiting professor of practical theology at two seminaries.

Contents Contains many short case studies with interactive questions the counselor is to work through.

Christian Counselor's Manual, The *The Practice of Nouthetic Counseling,* Jay E. Adams

Zondervan Publishing House, 1986, $19.99, cloth, 496 pp., for counselors

Description A companion and sequel volume to *Competent to Counsel*. Indexes, a detailed table of contents, and many diagrams and forms make this one of the best reference books for Christian counselors.

Author Dr. Adams is the author of numerous books on Christian counseling. He has served on a seminary faculty (Westminster Theological) and in the pastorate. He is founder of Christian Counseling and Educational Foundation in Laverock, Pa., and visiting professor of practical theology at two seminaries.

Contents *Part 1:* The persons *1.* The persons involved in counseling *2.* The Holy Spirit is the principal person *3.* The human counselor *4.* The counselee *Part 2:* The presuppositions and principles *5.* Presuppositions and principles basic to counseling *6.* Hope *7.* Prayer *8.* The reconciliation/discipline dynamic *9.* Reconciliation *10.* Presuppositions and methodology *11.* Technique *Part 3:* The practice and the

process *12.* The language of counseling *13.* The language of emotion and action *14.* Sin is the problem *15.* Love in counseling *16.* Support, sympathy, and empathy *17.* The motivation for change *18.* Effecting biblical change *19.* Elements of dehabituation and rehabituation *20.* Getting started *21.* Goals and terminal dates *22.* The commitment of the counselee *23.* Is there a problem? *24.* Two basic approaches *25.* Ways of gathering data *26.* Asking questions *27.* Helping through homework *28.* An analysis of homework *29.* Ways of using homework *30.* Gifts that differ *31.* How to handle anger *32.* Dealing with envy, brooding, fretting, and self-pity *33.* Helping depressed persons *34.* Helping the "schizophrenic" *35.* Resolving sexual difficulties *36.* Helping those who fear *37.* Counseling those who fear they have committed the unpardonable sin

Competent to Counsel *Introduction to Nouthetic Counseling,* Jay E. Adams

Zondervan Publishing House, 1986, $17.99, cloth, 320 pp., for counselors

Description This classic text has helped thousands of pastors, students, laypeople, and Christian counselors develop both a general approach to Christian counseling and a specific response to particular problems.

Author Dr. Adams is the author of numerous books on Christian counseling. He has served on a seminary faculty (Westminster Theological) and in the pastorate. He is founder of Christian Counseling and Educational Foundation in Laverock, Pa., and visiting professor of practical theology at two seminaries.

Contents *1.* Christianity and psychiatry today *2.* The Holy Spirit and counseling *3.* What is wrong with the mentally ill? *4.* What is nouthetic counseling? *5.* The pastor as nouthetic counselor *6.* Nouthetic and Rogerian counseling *7.* Confess your sins *8.* Solving problems nouthetically *9.* Some principles of nouthetic technique *10.* Communication and multiple counseling *11.* Christian school teachers as nouthetic counselors

Theology of Christian Counseling, A
More Than Redemption, Jay E. Adams

Zondervan Publishing House, 1986, $15.99, paper, 352 pp., a reference or academic work

Description Connects biblical doctrine with practical living. The reader gains an insight into the rich theological framework that supports and directs a biblical approach to counseling.

Author Dr. Adams is the author of numerous books on Christian counseling. He has served on a seminary faculty (Westminster Theological) and in the pastorate. He is founder of Christian Counseling and Educational Foundation in Laverock, Pa., and visiting professor of practical theology at two seminaries.

Contents *1.* The need for theology in counseling *2.* Theology and counseling *3.* Counseling and special revelation—the doctrine of the Scriptures *4.* Counseling and man's basic environment—the doctrine of God *5.* God's name and counseling—the doctrine of God, continued *6.* Counseling and prayer—the doctrine of God, continued *7.* Counseling and the Trinity—the doctrine of God, continued *8.* Counseling and human life—the doctrine of man *9.* Counseling and human sin—the doctrine of man, continued *10.* Counseling and habit—the doctrine of man, continued *11.* How sin affects thinking—the doctrine of man, continued *12.* More than redemption—the doctrine of salvation *13.* Forgiveness in counseling—the doctrine of salvation, continued *14.* Counseling and the newness of life—the doctrine of sanctification *15.* Counseling and the Spirit's fruit—the doctrine of sanctification, continued *16.* Counseling and radical amputation—the doctrine of sanctification, continued *17.* Counseling and perseverance—the doctrine of sanctification, continued *18.* Counseling and suffering—the doctrine of sanctification, continued *19.* Counseling and the church—the doctrine of the church *20.* Counseling and new converts—the doctrine of the church, continued *21.* Counseling and church discipline—the doctrine of the church, continued *22.* Counseling and works of mercy—the doctrine of the church, continued *23.* Counseling, death and dying—the doctrine of the future *24.* Counseling and judgment—the doctrine of the future, continued

Christian Perspectives on Human Development LeRoy Aden, David G. Benner, and J. Harold Ellens

Baker Book House, 1988, $11.99, paper, 250 pp., a reference or academic work

Description Believing that no one theory of human development fully accounts for the dynamics of how a person passes through the stages of life, this book elaborates on several views that together show psychology's life-cycle theories in Christian perspective. The primary concern of this book is with life-cycle theories, with seeing people as historical creatures by recognizing that they go through certain stages of development. The book is a compilation of a number of different perspectives on human development.

Authors LeRoy Aden is professor of pastoral care, Lutheran Theological Seminary in Philadelphia. He has edited three other books in Baker's Psychology and Christianity series. David G. Benner, editor of four books and author of several others, taught psychology for ten years at Wheaton College. He now teaches at Redeemer College in Ontario, Canada. J. Harold Ellens is executive director emeritus of CAPS and is a psychotherapist in private practice. He is author of several books and many articles on pastoral care and counseling.

Contents *Part 1:* Developmental theory and faith *1.* Faith and the developmental cycle *2.* Adult faith development and ministry *3.* Adulthood and the development of lived religion *4.* Faith and cognitive development *5.* Anonymous faith and the psychology of identity *6.* Moments of doubt and growth in faith *Part 2:* Developmental theory and the mature self *7.* A model of relational maturity *8.* Religious maturities of the adult *9.* The unfolding Christian self *10.* Grace and the importance of the self *11.* The passive Christian and the mature self *12.* Spirituality in personality and psychotherapy *13.* The self as gift and promise *Part 3:* Developmental theory in specific situations *14.* Women in mid-life crisis *15.* Religious ritual and the excommunication of Ann Hibbens *16.* Life cycle theory and the dismissal of Jonathan Edwards *17.* Jesus and the age thirty transition

Counseling and the Human Predicament
A Study of Sin, Guilt, and Forgiveness, LeRoy Aden and David G. Benner

Baker Book House, 1992, $14.99, paper, 274 pp., a reference or academic work

Description Sin, guilt, and forgiveness form one of the most fertile intersections of psychology and theology. Our understanding of the dynamics of both the human predicament and the hope for healing are greatly enhanced as we allow the perspectives of psychology and theology to interact in the way in which they do in this book. Twelve authors show how the dialogue between psychology and theology has deepened our understanding of humankind's plight and rescue. Part 1 examines the integrity of the theological concepts of sin in relation to the psychological concept of sickness. Part 2 clarifies the nature, types, and origin of guilt; assesses the place of guilt in the human predicament; and draws out the implications of guilt in pastoral care. Part 3 explores the dynamics of forgiveness and its wholesome effect in human relationships. The book constitutes an ideal supplementary text for advanced pastoral counseling courses, theological and psychological studies of humankind, and human development courses.

Editors LeRoy Aden is professor of pastoral care, Lutheran Theological Seminary in Philadelphia. He has edited three other books in Baker's Psychology and Christianity series. David G. Benner, editor of four books and author of several others, taught psychology for ten years at Wheaton College. He now teaches at Redeemer College in Ontario, Canada. Aden and Benner serve as editors of this volume.

Contents *Part 1:* Sin *1.* Sin: theological and psychological perspectives *2.* A psychospiritual view of sin *3.* Sin and sickness in clinical practice *4.* Sin and sickness: the nature of human failure *5.* Psychopathology and the problem of guilt, confession, and expiation *6.* O. Hobart Mowrer: a psychological and theological critique *Part 2:* Guilt *7.* Pastoral counseling and the problem *8.* Psychoanalytic contributions to the Christian view of guilt *9.* Shame and the human predicament *10.* Pastoral counseling and human self-justification *11.* Counseling and the development of responsibility *Part 3:* Forgiveness *12.* Punitive and reconciliation models of forgiveness *13.* Forgiveness and human relationships *14.* Forgiveness and the healing of the family

Christians Who Counsel Ray S. Anderson

Zondervan Publishing House, 1990, $17.99, paper, 256 pp., for counselors

Description To help Christians who counsel see the nature of the task and understand theologically the shape of their distinctive vocation.

Author Ray S. Anderson is professor of theology and ministry at Fuller Theological Seminary in Pasadena, Calif.

Contents *Part 1:* Foundations for Christian counseling *1.* Integrative counseling *2.* Counseling the whole person *3.* The counselor as growth promoter *Part 2:* Spiritual dynamics in counseling *4.* The kingdom of God as therapeutic context *5.* The grace of God as therapeutic intervention *6.* The Word of God as empowerment for change *7.* The healing praxis of prayer *Part 3:* Counseling in a Christian mode *8.* Counseling as a Christian calling *9.* Counseling as Christian ministry *10.* Counseling as a professional practice *11.* The counselor as moral advocate *12.* Dynamics of pastoral care in counseling praxis

Learning to Tell Myself the Truth *A 12 Week Guide,* William Backus

Bethany House Publishers, 1993, $13.99, paper, 184 pp., for both counselors and counselees

Description A 12-week course toward freedom from anger, anxiety, depression, and perfectionism that utilizes the powerful principles of truth therapy.

Author William Backus is a widely published psychologist. He is respected for his efforts to integrate the valuable aspects of cognitive therapy with the truths of the gospel.

Telling Yourself the Truth William Backus and Marie Chapian

Bethany House Publishers, 1980, $8.99, paper, 182 pp., for both counselors and counselees

Description Backus and Chapian assert that the Bible is indeed correct when it says, "As a man thinks in his heart, so is he." Wrong thinking produces wrong emotions, reactions, and behavior—and unhappiness. Learning to deal with your thoughts is the first step on the road to healthy thinking. Explaining the life-changing method the authors call "Misbelief Therapy," they set out to demonstrate that three basic steps lead to satisfying living: locate your misbeliefs, remove your misbeliefs, replace your misbeliefs with the truth. Backus and Chapian integrate rational emotive/cognitive therapy with Christian theology at a popular level. They are careful to replace unbiblical aspects of the former with the foundational truth of Scripture. Highly readable. Places an emphasis on aligning self-talk with scriptural principles without minimizing the issues at hand. The book addresses fundamental issues of a variety of emotional disturbances.

Authors William Backus is a licensed clinical psychologist and an ordained Lutheran clergyman. He is founder and director of the Center for Christian Psychological Services, St. Paul, Minn., and an associate pastor of a large Lutheran church. Marie Chapian is a well-known speaker, author, and psychotherapist. She has also collaborated with Dr. Backus on *Why Do I Do What I Don't Want to Do?*

Contents *1.* What is misbelief? *2.* Do we really want to be happy? *3.* Misbelief in self-talk *4.* Misbelief in depression *5.* Misbelief in anger *6.* Misbelief in anxiety *7.* Misbelief in lack of self-control *8.* The misbelief of self-hate *9.* Misbelief in fear of change *10.* Misbelief in never taking a chance *11.* Misbelief in our relationships with others *12.* More misbeliefs guaranteed to make you miserable *13.* What must I do to be miserable—or—when the truth does not set us free

Christian Counseling and Psychotherapy David G. Benner

Baker Book House, 1987, $12.99, paper, 266 pp., for counselors

Description This edited volume introduces foundational and theoretical considerations involved in developing a Christian psychotherapy. The 28 contributors present specific approaches to and techniques of therapy useful for the Christian psychotherapist. They offer case studies to illustrate the concepts and methods discussed. The book is divided into three main sections. Part 1 devotes six chapters to outlining general strategies for developing and practicing Christian psychotherapy. The six chapters in part 2 examine specific techniques and approaches that can be employed by the Christian therapist. The third part consists of the 19 case studies that present varying theoretical orientations and approaches to Christian counseling.

Author Dr. David G. Benner is a clinical psychologist currently serving as professor and chair of the Department of Psychology at Redeemer College and adjunct professor of psychology and Christianity at the University of Toronto (St. Michael's College). He has written and edited nine books and remains active in clinical work, specializing in the treatment of dissociative disorders.

Contents *Part 1:* General issues and approaches *1.* Therapy with theological constructs and tactics *2.* Biblical themes in psychological theory and practice *3.* Toward an integral mode of psychotherapy *4.* Christian counseling and human needs *5.* Hope in psychotherapy *6.* The concept of the ideal—therapy for Christians *Part 2:* Specific therapies and techniques *7.* Basic biblical counseling *8.* Assertiveness training *9.* The encounter with the family of origin *10.* Hypnosis and theology *11.* Meditation and altered states of consciousness *12.* Preventing and reversing marital burnout *13.* A terrible swift sword: Christ imagery in therapy *14.* Treatment of multiple personality *15.* Developmental pacing of theology in therapeutic process *16.* Anger, denial, and healing of memories *17.* Hal and Gina—theological reflections on a clinical case *18.* The dream of the magician—a case of parataxic distortion *19.* Psychoanalysis and religious experience *20.* Working through resistance by prayer and the gift of knowledge *21.* A peace that passes understanding *22.* Earthly father, heavenly Father *23.* Fathers, provoke not your children *24.* Cognitive therapy with spiritual dimensions *25.* Postconversion symptom regression *26.* A case of congregational healing *27.* A Christian dimension to holistic care *28.* Starting over: what to do when a bad marriage gets worse *29.* A tardy pilgrim *30.* Andrew's anxiety *31.* Dependent personality disorder: a case conference

Healing Emotional Wounds David G. Benner

Baker Book House, 1990, $7.99, paper, 137 pp., for counselors

Description Though emotional pain is an inevitable part of life, Benner insists it can be healed. This book brings together what both psychology and the Bible have to say about undeserved hurt. The author's extensive training experience in counseling, and numerous case studies add to the depth of the book. Under consideration are the emotional, intellectual, and volitional aspects of emotional pain. The author provides steps that the readers can follow to help themselves and others experience this healing. This work is an attempt to understand the psychodynamic of emotional injury and healing. The book has two main divisions. Part 1 looks at the sorts of experiences that cause hurt and then traces the inner course of emotional events that follow. The author considers some of the ways in which we attempt to cope with this hurt. Part 2 is a review of what psychologists have come to understand about emotional healing. Each part presents concrete steps that can be taken to aid in the process of healing emotional wounds.

Author Editor David G. Benner is a clinical psychologist currently serving as professor and chair of the Department of Psychology at Redeemer College and adjunct professor of psychology and Christianity at the University of Toronto (St. Michael's College). He has written and edited nine books and remains active in clinical work, specializing in the treatment of dissociative disorders.

Contents *Part 1:* The context of emotional wounds *1.* The hurts we don't deserve *2.* The psychology of emotional pain *Part 2:* The context of emotional healing *3.* Re-experiencing the pain *4.* Reinterpreting the hurt *5.* Releasing the anger / *Conclusion:* Redemptive possibilities in suffering

Psychology and Religion David G. Benner

Baker Book House, 1993, $12.99, paper, for counselors

Description Fifty readings address the psychological roots of religion, the mind and faith, and the psychological aspects of sinful persons in relation to God.

Author Dr. David G. Benner is a clinical psychologist currently serving as professor and chair of the Department of Psychology at Redeemer College and adjunct professor of psychology and Christianity at the University of Toronto (St. Michael's College). He has written and edited nine books and remains active in clinical work, specializing in the treatment of dissociative disorders.

Psychotherapy and the Spiritual Quest
Examining the Links between Psychology and Spiritual Health, David G. Benner

Baker Book House, 1988, $13.95, cloth, 173 pp., for counselors

Description This book identifies the religious roots of psychotherapy, critiques the common psychological views of spirituality, and reviews the history and understanding of spirituality in a variety of Christian traditions. Presents a model of personality that relates psychological and spiritual dynamics, arguing that the human personality is a "psychospiritual unity." Examines the ways in which spiritual longings may be expressed through psychological strivings. It concludes with a discussion of the relation of psychotherapy and spiritual direction. This book explores the relation between psychological and spiritual aspects of persons. It argues that the two dimensions of persons are inextricably interconnected. Furthermore, it argues that psychotherapy necessarily addresses problems and issues that are spiritual in nature, not merely psychological, and it explores the implications of this assertion.

Author Dr. David G. Benner is a clinical psychologist currently serving as professor and chair of the Department of Psychology at Redeemer College and adjunct professor of psychology and Christianity at the University of Toronto (St. Michael's College). He has written and edited nine books and remains active in clinical work, specializing in the treatment of dissociative disorders.

Death in the Midst of Life *Perspectives on Death from Christianity and Depth Psychology,* Lucy Bregman

Baker Book House, 1992, $12.99, paper, 247 pp.

Description Lucy Bregman explores the landscape of Christian and secular perspectives, tracing the teachings of Scripture and comparing views of Christians with their secular counterparts throughout the world. She also reflects on the personal accounts of death, dying, and near-death experiences. This study will help readers see how Christianity and depth psychology are employed to critique materialistic understandings of death and dying.

Author Lucy Bregman is associate professor of religion at Temple University and author of *Through the Landscape of Faith.* Her Ph.D. is from the University of Chicago Divinity School.

Contents *1.* Testimonies *2.* Elisabeth Kübler-Ross: an ethical naturalist's approach to death and dying *3.* Depth psychologies of death: three legacies *4.* Contemporary depth psychologies of death *5.* Psychology's farther reaches *6.* Death in Christian theology today *7.* Biblical resources: the roles of death in the landscape of faith *8.* Encountering death: Christian resources *9.* A Christian critique of contemporary depth psychologies of death *10.* A Christian perspective on death

Why Do Christians Shoot Their Wounded? *Helping (Not Hurting) Those with Emotional Difficulties,* Dwight L. Carlson

InterVarsity Press, 1994, $10.99, paper, 180 pp., for both counselors and counselees

Description Physician Dwight L. Carlson marshals recent clinical evidence to demonstrate that many emotional hurts are just as biologically based as diabetes, cancer, and heart disease. For those who hurt, here is powerful liberation from guilt. For counselors and caregivers, here is vivid proof that people in pain deserve compassion, not condemnation.

Author Dr. Dwight Carlson, M.D., is a specialist in both internal medicine and psychiatry. He has an active psychiatry practice and is assistant clinical professor at UCLA.

Contents *Part 1*—How and why we shoot the wounded *1.* Don't shoot! I'm already wounded! *2.* Why we wound *3.* Can a Spirit-filled Christian have emotional wounds? *Part 2*—What causes emotional illness? *4.* It's not necessarily all in your mind *5.* It's not necessarily all in your mind continued *6.* How childhood experiences and stress cause emotional illness *7.* What about personal choice? *8.* Putting it all together *Part 3*—How shall the wounded be mended? *9.* The church, business, school, or hospital? *10.* How the strong can help—not shoot—the wounded *11.* What the wounded can do while the bullets are flying / *Appendix:* Are drugs of the devil or tools for healing?

Case Studies in Christian Counseling
Gary R. Collins

Word Publishing, 1991, $15.95, cloth, 272 pp., for counselors

Description A piercing, insightful text depicting several examples of Christian counseling at work. Part of the Resources for Christian Counselors series from Word.

Author Gary R. Collins is a licensed clinical psychologist with a Ph.D. from Purdue University.

Contents *1.* What is Christian counseling? *2.* A case of sexual obsessions *3.* Cognitive therapy with a depressed client *4.* Marriage counseling with Christian couples *5.* Counseling another counselor *6.* The use of hypnotherapy in counseling a Christian *7.* Counseling a fundamentalist family with a son who has AIDS *8.* An inpatient assessment with a severely depressed hospitalized patient *9.* A case of ritualistic abuse *10.* Counseling for panic disorder with agoraphobia

Excellence and Ethics in Christian Counseling Gary R. Collins

Word Publishing, 1991, $15.99, cloth, 228 pp., for counselors

Description The final volume in the Resources for Christian Counseling series from Word. Begins with a close look at excellence in Christian counseling and ends with future directions.

Author Gary R. Collins is a licensed clinical psychologist with a Ph.D. in clinical psychology from Purdue University.

Contents *1.* Excellence in Christian counseling *2.* Ethics in Christian counseling *3.* Liability in Christian counseling *4.* Theory in Christian counseling *5.* Effectiveness in Christian counseling *6.* Growth and training in Christian counseling *7.* Trends in Christian counseling *8.* Future directions in Christian counseling / A letter to Christian counselors / A code of ethics for Christian counselors / Informed consent: a sample

Basic Principles of Biblical Counseling
Meeting Counseling Needs through the Local Church, Larry Crabb

Zondervan Publishing House, 1975, $14.99, cloth, 112 pp., for counselors

Description Looks toward a counseling model that neither overlooks sin nor is reduced to a simplistic model of confrontation and exhortation.

Author Dr. Crabb is director of biblical counseling and chairman of the Department of Biblical Counseling at Colorado Christian University in Morrison, Colo. He earned his Ph.D. in clinical psychology from the University of Illinois in 1970.

He is the author of numerous books on self-understanding and counseling technique.

Contents *1.* Broadening our vision *2.* Confusion in counseling *3.* Floating anchors *4.* An aerial view *5.* Understanding our deepest needs 1 *6.* Understanding our deepest needs 2 *7.* Where problems start *8.* Weaving tangled webs *9.* Hold your client responsible: for what? *10.* The mood and goal of counseling

Effective Biblical Counseling *A Model for Helping Caring Christians Become Capable Counselors,* Larry Crabb

Zondervan Publishing House, 1977, $14.99, cloth, 208 pp., for counselors

Description Seeks to think through a model of counseling that can be integrated into the functioning of the local church.

Author Dr. Crabb is director of biblical counseling and chairman of the Department of Biblical Counseling at Colorado Christian University in Morrison, Colo. He earned his Ph.D. in clinical psychology from the University of Illinois in 1970. He is the author of numerous books on self-understanding and counseling technique.

Contents *Part 1:* A few preliminaries *1.* The goal of counseling—what are we trying to do? *2.* Christianity and psychology: enemies or allies? *Part 2:* Basic concepts: what do you need to know about people in order to effectively counsel? *3.* Personal needs: what do people need to live effectively? *4.* Motivation: why do we do what we do? *5.* Personality structure: taking apart the watch to see what makes it tick *Part 3:* Basic strategy: how to understand and deal with personal problems *6.* How problems develop 1 *7.* How problems develop 2 *8.* What do you try to change? *9.* A simple model for counseling *Part 4:* Developing a counseling program in the local church *10.* Counseling in the Christian community *11.* Chart index

Who We Are and How We Relate *The IBC Approach to Understanding What Makes People Tick,* Larry Crabb

NavPress, 1992, $7.00, paper, 87 pp., for both counselors and counselees

Description Ideal for use with the series or as a stand-alone resource, *Who We Are and How We Relate* will serve as an invaluable tool to help you understand what it is within you that shapes the ways you relate to God, others, and yourself.

Author Dr. Larry Crabb is the founder and director of the Institute of Biblical Counseling and the chairman of the Department of Biblical Counseling at Colorado Christian University in Morrison, Colo. He is the author of numerous books.

Healing for the City *Counseling in the Urban Setting,* Craig W. Ellison and Edward S. Maynard

Zondervan Publishing House, 1991, $14.99, paper, 320 pp., for counselees

Description Offers counselors a perspective on what life in the city requires of counseling and provides a multicultural perspective on common counseling concerns.

Authors Dr. Craig W. Ellison is professor of counseling and urban studies at the Alliance Theological Seminary. He is the author of five books. Dr. Edward S. Maynard is professor of humanities at the City University of New York, where he teaches African-American studies, anthropology, sociology, and psychology. He also has a private counseling practice in Manhattan.

Wisdom and Humanness in Psychology *Prospects for a Christian Approach,* Stephen C. Evans

Baker Book House, 1989, $8.99, paper, 161 pp., a reference or academic work

Description Contains an argument for the development of a distinctively Christian psychology, built around a biblical concept of wisdom, providing the condition for psychological knowledge and the basis of psychological health. Such a psychology would do justice to the distinctive qualities of human persons by seeing them as fundamentally constituted by their relation to God. This psychology would be committed to empirical research but would free itself from the dogmas of philosophical empiricism.

Author Stephen C. Evans is professor of philosophy and curator of the Hong Kierkegaard Library at St. Olaf College in Minn. Evans received his B.A. at Wheaton College and his Ph.D. from Yale University. He is the author of nine books.

Wholehearted Integration *Harmonizing Psychology and Christianity through Word and Deed,* Kirk. E. Farnsworth

Baker Book House, 1985, $6.99, paper, 160 pp., a reference or academic work

Description Evangelical psychologists talk much about integrating psychology with Christianity, but they say little about how to do it. Farnsworth is one of the few who do. In this book he proposes for psychology a human-science methodology and offers a method for validating religious experience. He describes in detail two completely different integration techniques: critical and embodied.

Author Professor of psychology at Wheaton College, holds the Ph.D. degree from Iowa State University.

The Recovery of Self *Regression and Redemption in Religious Experience,* Kevin Fauteux

Paulist Press, 1994, $18.95, paper, 256 pp., for counselors

Description Examines the psychological regression that takes place in religious experience. Drawing on, but ultimately disagreeing with the work of Freud, the author demonstrates that some forms of regressions to primitive states of consciousness can be healing. Fauteux argues that religious experience that restores a sense of unity to the individual and the cosmos can be positive and redemptive, thereby leading to psychological and spiritual growth. Discusses the "inner child" and asks the questions: Is regression pathological or not? and how do we know?

Author Kevin Fauteux, who holds a Ph.D. from the Graduate Theological Union in conjunction with the University of California, Berkeley, is a psychologist.

Contents I. Regression and religious experience *1.* Regression and religious experience *2.* Ego regression and purgation *3.* Instinctual regression and religious experience *4.* Symbiotic regression: the experience of unity II. Religious experience and regression in service of the ego *5.* Regression and adaptation *6.* Adaptation in ego-regressive "dying to self" *7.* Illumination and adaptive regression in the service of the ego *8.* Regressive restoration and reparation of symbiotic unity *9.* Elaboration of religious experience / *Conclusion*

Souls Are Made of Endurance *Surviving Mental Illness in the Family,* Stewart D. Govig

Westminster/John Knox Press, 1994, $10.99, paper, 110 pp., for both counselors and counselees

Description Govig gives a personal account of his family's struggle with their son's mental illness. After his son was diagnosed with schizophrenia, the family faced not only the personal anguish of finding medical care and therapy, but also the personal anguish and the questioning of faith and of God that often accompany such a crisis.

Author Stewart D. Govig is professor of religion, Pacific Lutheran University.

Contents *Part 1:* Finding out *1.* Rage in the rec room *2.* A domestic Chernobyl *3.* Of cuckoos nests and loony bins *Part 2:* Holding on *4.* Faith and frenzy *5.* Give us this day our daily meds *6.* Exodus on main street *7.* Care in focus *Part 3:* Letting go *8.* Giving sorrow words *9.* Reframing *10.* Cheating winter

The Tree of Healing *Psychological and Biblical Foundations of Counseling and Pastoral Care,* Roger F. Hurding

Zondervan Publishing House, 1991, $17.99, paper, 464 pp., a reference or academic work

Description A handbook that acquaints Christians with a relevant field of study that needs the best minds we have.

Author Dr. Roger F. Hurding holds two degrees from Cambridge University. He teaches at Trinity College, Bristol, England, and leads a training program for counselors at Network, a Christian counseling center in Bristol.

Contents *Part 1:* The rise of secular psychologies *1.* Introduction to the tree of pastoral care *2.* What is counseling? *3.* Behaviorism—man as machine *4.* Psychoanalysis: man and his instincts *5.* Psychoanalysis: man and society *6.* Personalism: man and self—humanistic psychology *7.* Personalism: man and self—existential psychology *8.* Transpersonalism: man beyond self *9.* The new therapies *Part 2:* Christian reaction and response *10.* Sinkers, swimmers, and strugglers *11.* Route finding in the forest *12.* Reaching to the word *13.* Reaching out: relationship counseling *14.* Reaching in: the inward journey *15.* Reaching back: healing the past *16.* The wonderful counselor

A Christian's Guide to Mental Wellness *How to Balance, Not Choose between, Psychology and Religion,* Richard P. Johnson

Ligouri Publications, 1994, $7.95, paper, for both counselors and counselees

Description Blends psychology and religion to offer a way to achieve optimum mental, emotional, and spiritual health.

Author Richard Johnson, Ph.D., is director of behavior sciences in the Department of Family Practice at St. John's Mercy Hospital, St. Louis, Mo.

Contents *1.* Are you asleep? *2.* What is mental illness? *3.* Attitudes: the foundations of personality *4.* Event: what you believe is what you perceive *5.* Evaluation: what you judge is what you get *6.* Feelings: making sense out of them *7.* Decision: choosing love *8.* Action: what people do *9.* Using the motivational model

When Counseling Is Not Enough *Biblical Answers to Those Who Still Hurt,* J. Kirk Johnston

Discovery House Publishers, 1994, $10.99, paper, 256 pp., for both counselors and counselees

Description A comprehensive volume that includes an analysis of counseling, the limits of Christian counseling, views on the sufficiency of Scripture. Offers advice on what to do when counseling is needed, and how to find a counselor.

Author Dr. Kirk Johnston is a student of psychology and has a Th.M. and Th.D. in Bible and theology. He has served as a pastor and pastoral counselor for a number of years in a large rural church.

Contents *1.* When counseling is not enough *2.* The issue of physical problems *3.* Emotional and spiritual problems *4.* The sufficiency of Scripture in counseling *5.* The use of Scripture in counseling *6.* Spiritual warfare *7.* Emotional trauma and discipleship *8.* From disappointment to discovery *9.* Victory in the midst of struggle *10.* The need for counseling *11.* Finding a counselor *12.* Depression *13.* Addiction *14.* Fear and pressure *15.* Anger *16.* Forgiveness *17.* Self-esteem *18.* Abuse *19.* Marital problems

Modern Psychotherapies *A Comprehensive Christian Appraisal,* Stanton L. Jones and Richard E. Butman

InterVarsity Press, 1991, $24.99, cloth, 425 pp., a reference or academic work

Description The authors survey and evaluate the most significant psychotherapies now in use, including Freudian analysis, behavior modification, existential therapy, family therapy, Jungian therapy, and six others.

Authors Stanton L. Jones (Ph.D., Arizona State University) is chairman of the Department of Psychology at Wheaton Graduate School. Richard E. Butman (Ph.D., Fuller Theological Seminary) is associate professor of psychology at Wheaton College.

Contents *Introduction 1.* The integration of Christianity and psychology *2.* A Christian view of persons The dynamic psychologies *3.* Classic psychoanalysis *4.* Contemporary psychodynamic psychotherapies *5.* Jungian therapy / Behavioral psychologies *6.* Behavior therapy *7.* Rational emotive therapy *8.* Cognitive behavioral therapy *9.* Alderian and reality therapies / The humanistic psychologies *10.* Person centered therapy *11.* Existential therapy *12.* Gestalt therapy *13.* Transactional analysis The family system psychologies *14.* Family therapy toward Christian psychologies *15.* Responsible eclecticism *16.* Christian psychotherapy

Biblical Concepts for Christian Counseling *A Case for Integrating Psychology and Christianity,* William T. Kirwan

Baker Book House, 1984, $9.99, paper, 230 pp., a reference or academic work

Description Does more than sound a clarion call for integration. Kirwan demonstrates that it can be done.

Author William T. Kirwan is a licensed psychologist at Psychiatric Associates as well as an ordained minister for an evangelical Presbyterian church. He holds two doctoral degrees, a D.Min. from Union Theological Seminary and a Ph.D. from St. Louis University.

Contents *Part 1:* Christianity and psychology *1.* The four basic counseling positions *2.* The biblical perspective *3.* A proper perspective for today *Part 2:* The loss and restoration of personal identity *4.* The loss of personal identity *5.* The restoration of personal identity *Part 3:* The essentials of Christian counseling *6.* A Christian model for counseling: imparting a sense of belonging *7.* A Christian model for counseling: edification and service *8.* Diagno-sis: type of personality and idealized image *9.* The counsel of God

Looking Back, Moving On *Applying Biblical Principles of Freedom to Your Life,* Boyd Luter

NavPress, 1992, $10.00, paper, 191 pp., for both counselors and counselees

Description Forced by personal circumstances to look at the biblical legitimacy of the recovery movement, Boyd Luter carefully examines the scriptural examples of recovery. He shows how even some of the most spiritually mature characters in the Bible—particularly Daniel and Paul—dealt with unhealthy or traumatic pasts and were able to move on toward emotional and spiritual wholeness. He addresses how one goes about forgetting what lies behind, how spiritually mature believers need to consider issues of recovery, and how to biblically evaluate the various approaches to recovery.

Author Dr. Boyd Luter (Th.M. in historical theology/Th.D. in New Testament theological studies, Dallas Theological Seminary) was associate editor of the *Life Recovery Bible.* He serves as chairman of the Department of Bible at Talbot Theological Seminary.

Contents *1.* Who needs recovery? *Part 1:* A prayer for recovery *2.* Better late than never *3.* Biblical study and deep recovery *4.* Getting beyond a shameful situation *5.* Back to the future, biblically *6.* Another chance—thank God! *Part 2:* A process of recovery *7.* Surviving a crisis at mid-life *8.* Getting beyond the good front *9.* Garbage in, garbage out *10.* Dying to live again *11.* Looking back, then moving on *12.* Living it up . . . or down? / *Appendix A:* Marks of safe-haven and not so safe churches / *Appendix B:* Preaching a teaching biblical recovery: a basic checklist

Truthful Living *What Christianity Really Teaches About Recovery,* Boyd Luter and Kathy McReynolds

Baker Book House, 1994, $10.99, paper, 200 pp.

Description The authors establish principles needed to maintain truth in recovery. They urge groups and counselors to welcome the authority of Scripture and accountability to the larger body of believers.

Authors A. Boyd Luter, associate professor of Bible exposition at Talbot School of Theology, and Kathy McReynolds, adjunct professor at Talbot team teach a course in recovery and the Bible.

Contents *1.* The delicate balance between truth and love *2.* The authoritative handbook for recovery *3.* The "father-figure" of biblical recovery *4.* The biblical basis of recovery *5.* The indwelling Counselor in recovery *6.* Biblical self-image *7.* The harsh reality behind dysfunctional living *8.* The process of biblical recovery *9.* The unseen conflict *10.* Teammates in biblical recovery *11.* Biblical recovery over the long haul

The Psychology of Religion for Ministry
H. Newton Malony

Paulist Press, 1995, $11.95, paper, 160 pp.

Description Provides ministers, church professionals, and others with a readable summary of contemporary findings of psychology about religion. An amazingly comprehensive work that is jargon and statistic free and exceptionally user-friendly.

Author H. Newton Maloney holds a Ph.D. in clinical psychology from George Peabody of Vanderbilt University. A licensed psychologist as well as an ordained minister in the United Methodist Church, he is senior professor at the Graduate School of Psychology, Fuller Theological Seminary.

Contents *1.* Being religious—a psychological point of view *2.* Boys and girls, black and white, young and old: do people differ in the way they are religious? *3.* Really believing: is there such a thing as mature faith? *4.* Religion and morals: does faith make a better person? *5.* Can religion make you well? Religion and mental health *6.* Are sermons better than sleeping pills?—the boon and bane of preaching *7.* What makes good clergy good?—being an effective minister *8.* Today's "Damascus roads"—the when, where, and how of religious experience

Counseling Options Robert S. McGee

Rapha Resources, no charge, paper, 12 pp., for both counselors and counselees

Description This booklet identifies all the possible resources and treatment options available to someone who is hurting. A great reference for someone who needs help but isn't sure where to start.

Author Robert McGee is founder and president of Rapha, a health care organization that provides in-hospital and outpatient care, with a Christ-centered perspective, for adults and adolescents suffering from psychiatric and substance abuse problems.

Cognitive Therapy Techniques in Christian Counseling Mark R. McMinn

Word Publishing, 1991, $15.99, cloth, 265 pp., for counselors

Description A relatively new development in counseling practice, cognitive therapy differs from traditional psychotherapy in that it attempts to understand clients' conscious thoughts and underlying core beliefs without looking for hidden meanings. Highly structured and goal-directed, cognitive therapy helps clients understand their problems in new ways and introduces new methods for coping with life's perplexities. This book blends contemporary cognitive therapy with Christian principles in providing specific ways counselors can help clients cope with anxiety, depression, eating disorders, stress, and anger.

Author Mark McMinn is professor of psychology at George Fox College in Newberg, Oreg. He received his Ph.D. in psychology from Vanderbilt University in 1983 and is a licensed psychologist in Oregon. He is the author of three other books dealing with counseling.

Contents *Part 1:* Concepts of cognitive therapy *1.* Choosing a road map *2.* An overview of cognitive therapy *3.* Christianity and cognitive therapy *Part 2:* The process of cognitive therapy *4.* The first interview *5.* Finding automatic thoughts *6.* Disputing automatic thoughts *7.* Finding core beliefs *8.* Changing core beliefs *9.* Maintenance *Part 3:* Applying cognitive therapy *10.* Depression *11.* Anxiety *12.* Stress and anger *13.* Other applications / *Appendix:* Client information forms / Homework forms

Bruised and Broken Understanding and Healing Psychological Problems, Paul D. Meier, Frank B. Minirth, and Donald E. Ratcliff

Baker Book House, 1992, $16.99, cloth, 256 pp., a reference or academic work

Description An introduction to abnormal psychology helps counselors, family, and the suffering individual understand illnesses, treatments, and personality types.

Authors Paul D. Meier and Frank Minirth are vice president and president, respectively, of the Minirth-Meier Psychiatric Clinic, Richardson, Tex. Donald E. Ratcliff is assistant professor of psychology and sociology at Toccoa Falls College.

Contents *1.* What is abnormal? *2.* What causes psychological problems? *3.* Depression and extreme moods *4.* Problems with stress adjustment *5.* Anxiety disorders *6.* Psychosis *7.* Physical problems *8.* Addictions and impulse control *9.* Sexual problems *10.* Child and adolescent disorders *11.* Personality disorders *12.* Healing and preventing problems

Introduction to Psychology and Counseling *Christian Perspective and Applications,* Paul D. Meier, Frank B. Minirth, et al.

Baker Book House, 1982, 1991, $26.99, cloth, 367 pp., a reference or academic work

Description This standard introduction to Christian psychology has been refined, updated, and reorganized with more information on counseling and ministry applications.

Authors Paul D. Meier and Frank Minirth are vice president and president, respectively, of the Minirth-Meier Psychiatric Clinic, Richardson, Tex. Frank Wichern is a family psychologist and adjunct professor of psychology and counselor training at Amber University, Dallas, Tex. Donald E. Ratcliff, the primary reviser for this edition, teaches psychology at Toccoa Falls College in Georgia.

Contents *1.* Introduction to psychology *2.* The biological basis of behavior *3.* Sensation and perception *4.* Emotions *5.* Motivation *6.* Learning *7.* Memory, cognition, and self esteem *8.* Intelligence *9.* Social psychology *10.* Child development *11.* Adolescent and adult development *12.* Personality *13.* The psychology of religion *14.* Abnormal psychology *15.* Psychotherapy and personal counseling *16.* Group and family counseling

Counseling and the Nature of Man
Frank B. Minirth and Paul D. Meier

Baker Book House, 1982, $5.99, paper, 82 pp., a reference or academic work

Description A concise overview of counseling theories and the various schools of psychology, this overview of counseling theory explains medical terms and includes summaries and valuable charts.

Authors Paul D. Meier and Frank Minirth are vice president and president, respectively, of the Minirth-Meier Psychiatric Clinic, Richardson, Tex. They have authored numerous books on Christian psychiatry and counseling.

Contents *1.* Man without Christ *2.* The comprehensive nature of man *3.* The diagnosis of psychological problems *4.* The mechanisms of defense *5.* The Christian comprehensive approach *6.* An analysis of several key topics *7.* Skills of the Christian counselor *8.* Putting it all together

Linked to Someone in Pain *Connecting with Your Loved Ones in Recovery,* Joyce Moccero and Cheryl Sanfacon

Victor Books, 1993, $7.99, paper, 192 pp., for counselees

Description Watching a loved one wrestle with emotional pain can leave one feeling bewildered and alone. But here is a helpful resource for those who observe loved ones in recovery. It provides advice for finding ways to get one's own needs met and reflects the experiences of many who have already gone through the process.

Authors Cheryl Sanfacon is a psychiatrist and assistant clinical professor at the Medical College of Pennsylvania. Joyce Magnin Moccero is a freelance writer and mother who lives in Philadelphia.

Contents *Part 1: 1.* Facing facts *2.* Code crazy *3.* Hidden colors *4.* A relationship of trust *Part 2: 5.* Being real and feeling important *6.* Shhh, don't tell, it's a secret! *7.* Change . . . is for better or worse *8.* Staying close by keeping your distance *9.* What do I tell the kids? *10.* Every home needs supports *Part 3: 11.* When therapy is over *12.* Just when you thought it was safe to hold hands again *13.* David's story five years later

Christian Perspectives on Being Human
A Multidisciplinary Approach to Integration, J. P. Moreland and David Ciocchi

Baker Book House, 1993, $11.99, paper, 306 pp., a reference or academic work

Description Thoughts on maturity, right-to-life issues, ethics, and other subjects are approached from viewpoints of anthropology, philosophy, psychology, and theology and the Bible. A series of articles by experts in their fields followed by several responses by others.

Editors J. P. Moreland is professor of philosophy of religion at Talbot School of Theology, Biola University. He holds a Ph.D. from the University of Southern California. Coeditor David M. Ciocchi is associate professor at Biola. His Ph.D. is from Fuller Theological Seminary.

Contents *Part 1:* Understanding human nature: the theological perspective *1.* Theology of human nature *Part 2:* Basic questions about human nature: Christian perspectives from philosophy *2.* A defense of a substance dualist view of the soul—response—response *3.* Human freedom—response—response *Part 3:* Accounting for human complexity: Christian perspectives from anthropology *4.* Mind, emotion, culture, and the person: perspectives from cultural anthropology and Scripture—response—response 5. On being human: a psychoanalytic perspective—response—response 6. The nature of human mental life—response—response Part 4: Understanding the moral/spiritual dimension of being human: Christian perspectives from New Testament studies, medical ethics, and education 7. The apostle Paul's view of the "sin nature/new nature" struggle—response—response 8. Views of human nature at the edges of life: personhood and medical ethics—response—response 9. Conscience: moral sensitivity and moral reasoning—response—response / Conclusion

The Integration of Psychology and Theology *An Introduction,* Bruce S. Narramore and John D. Carter

Zondervan Publishing House, 1979, $10.99, paper, 139 pp., a reference or academic work

Description Examines the relationship of psychology to theology and discusses whether they contradict each other or integrate with each other. Reference listing, annotated bibliography.

Authors John D. Carter holds the M.A. and Ph.D. degrees from the New School for Social Research. Bruce S. Narramore holds the M.A. degree from Pepperdine University and the Ph.D. degree from the University of Kentucky. He was the founding dean of the Rosemead Graduate School of Psychology.

Contents *1.* The encounter *2.* Barriers to integration *3.* The scope of integration *4.* The against model *5.* The of model *6.* The parallels model *7.* The integrates model *8.* The process of integration

The Psychology of Counseling *Professional Techniques for Pastors, Teachers, Youth Leaders . . . ,* Clyde M. Narramore

Zondervan Publishing House, 1960, $16.99, cloth, 303 pp., for counselors

Description Presents the basic concepts and techniques of counseling with appropriate illustrations. Discusses the effective use of Scripture in counseling. Contains a glossary and bibliography.

Author Dr. Clyde M. Narramore is the founder, director, and president of the Narramore Christian Foundation, an international organization specializing in counseling and the training of leaders. He is also the founder and first president of the Rosemead Graduate School of Psychology.

Contents *Part 1:* Basic concepts and techniques of counseling *1.* The importance of counseling *2.* To whom do they turn? *3.* The counselor *4.* Professional ethics *5.* Counseling arrangements *6.* The counseling process *7.* The best bet

8. The value of decision *9.* Accepting the counselee *10.* Waiting for the real problem *11.* Recognizing the therapeutic process *12.* The significance of pauses *13.* Problems and their settings *14.* Tracing the origins *15.* Physical causes *16.* Multiple perspective *17.* Motives for discussion *18.* Focusing on the client's problem *19.* Encouraging self-reliance *20.* Handling direct questions *21.* Involvement *22.* Responsibility for referrals *23.* Extending your counseling ministry *24.* The great physician *25.* Success in counseling *26.* Growing professionally *Part 2:* Special areas of counseling *27.* Counseling with teenagers *28.* The mentally and emotionally ill *29.* Basic guidelines in marriage counseling *30.* Problems of sex *Part 3:* The use of Scripture in counseling / *Appendix* / *31.* The use of Scripture in counseling *32.* Terms *33.* Books and recordings

Religion and Prevention in Mental Health *Research, Vision, and Action,* Kenneth I. Pargament

The Haworth Pastoral Press, 1994, $54.95, cloth, 333 pp., for counselors

Description Here is the first book that highlights the unique resource of religion in the field of prevention. Until now, religious systems have been largely an untapped resource of talent, energy, care, and physical and financial assets. Lays the foundation for preventive work in the religious arena.

Contents Religion as a resource for preventive action / Religious perspectives on prevention: the role of theology / A sociological overview: mental health implications of religio-cultural megatrends in the U.S. / Review of religion and mental health: prevention and the enhancement of psychosocial functioning / Religious factors in physical health and the prevention of illness / Religion and prevention of illness in later life / The religious dimension of coping: implications for prevention and promotion / Religious aspects in the resolution of parental grief: solace and support / Toward a psychosocial conceptualization of religion as a resource in cancer care and prevention / Prevention theory and action from the religious perspective / Healing and empowering through community narrative / The African-American church: a source of empowerment, mutual help, and social change / Reciprocal ministry: a transforming vision of help and leadership / Congregational consultation / Networking between agencies and black churches: the lay health advisor model / Preventing homelessness: religious organizations and housing development

Pathways to Understanding *A Manual and Videotape on Ministry and Mental Illness*

Pathways to Promise, 1995, $20.00–30.00, 3 ring, 77 pp.

Description A new series developed for seminary students, clergy in continuing education, faith group staffs, and lay people involved in caring ministries. A manual and videotape for those who require technical knowledge about chronic mental illness and how the religious community can respond to it. A manual for instructors and students and an accompanying video cassette allows a wide range of options for use.

Pathways to Promise is an ecumenical networking organization that seeks to assist those in the religious community involved with care to the mentally ill. Three seminaries (Aquinas Institute, Concordia, and Eden) in St. Louis worked with Pathways to develop this resource.

Contents *1.* The history of the faith community's response to mental illness *2.* Information about mental illness *3.* A theological perspective on ministry with people with a mental illness *4.* Pastoral care and mental illness *5.* The pastor's role with the person who is ill and with the family *6.* When to counsel, when to refer *7.* What to do in a crisis situation *8.* Information about community resources *9.* How to work with mental health services and providers *10.* Housing, legal, and insurance issues *11.* Faith group statements on mental illness *12.* Information on faith group networks, professional organizations, and advocacy and support groups

A Life of Wholeness *Reflections on Abundant Living,* Ann Raber

Herald Press, 1993 (revised), $7.95, paper, 160 pp., for both counselors and counselees

Description Challenges the (secular) concept that abundant life is connected with material possessions. This book suggests that we can live abundantly, if our definition of abundance changes. True abundance involves right relating to our bodies, each other, our environment, and our God. These right relationships affect how we handle many important areas in life. Ann Raber served as revision editor to this work that stirred significant discussion when first published in 1983.

Editor Ann Raber is the wellness program director of Mennonite Mutual Aid and revised this book as part of that role.

Contents *1.* A life of wholeness *2.* The body—God's temple *3.* Sexuality *4.* Nutrition *5.* Physical fitness *6.* Mental health *7.* Stress *8.* Deterrents to wholeness *9.* The global environment *10.* Toward spiritual wholeness *11.* Responsibility for wholeness *12.* Wholeness through the church

Taking the Word to Heart *Self and Other in an Age of Therapies,* Robert C. Roberts

Wm. B. Eerdmans Publishing Co., 1993, $16.99, paper, 315 pp., a reference or academic work

Description Christians today are besieged by various ideas about what it means to be a whole person, a happy and fulfilled person. While modern psychologies offer insights and practices that can be adapted for Christian use, they sometimes contradict and even displace true Christianity—often without anybody noticing what has happened. This situation calls for two things: a careful examination of the major psychological "models" that influence our thinking about persons and the development of a distinctively Christian psychology, so we won't be held captive by ideas that are alien to the Christian tradition.

Author Robert C. Roberts teaches psychology and philosophy at Wheaton College. He was educated at Wichita State, Yale, Oxford, and Princeton Theological Seminary. He is the author of four other books. Part 1 deals with six therapies: Rogerian, rational emotive, assertiveness training, contextual (family) therapy, Jungian analysis, and Kohut's psychoanalysis. Each therapy is examined as to the kind of character it would promote if maximally successful, and this is compared with Christian counterpart virtues, thus enabling us to see very clearly what can be adapted from the therapy. Part 2 offers a distinctively Christian psychology of relationships.

Contents *Part 1:* Therapy as heart-forming word *2.* Unconditional acceptance *3.* The truth will make you free *4.* Assert yourself! *5.* Between give and take *6.* Healing from the eternal *7.* Empathy and the formation of a self *Part 2:* Relating to one another *8.* Playing at competition *9.* Stamping out envy *10.* Forgiveness as therapy *11.* Reconcilable differences *12.* Children: who needs them? *13.* Welcome to the Kingdom *14.* Friends with God *15.* Belonging to the church *16.* Conclusion—Christianity as psychotherapy

The Miracle of Therapy *A Layperson's Guide to the Mysteries of Christian Psychology,* Georgiana G. Rodiger

Word Publishing, 1989, $12.99, cloth, 177 pp., for both counselors and counselees

Description Casebook format. Psychology that comes from a Christian perspective and a world view is a relatively new emphasis in the field of psychological study. To Dr. Rodiger, the Christian psychologist is positioned to combine the best of the healing arts with the power of God's own divine therapy. For anyone who wants to learn more about how faith and medicine can affect well-being and wholeness, this volume is must reading.

Author Georgiana G. Rodiger, Ph.D. (Fuller Graduate School of Psychology), is head of the Georgiana Rodiger Center, a nonprofit corporation, and has been previously associated with Pasadena Community Counseling Center and the psychiatric division of Children's Hospital in Los Angeles.

Contents *1.* Jeanie: it's fun to be sane *2.* David: back off sexually *3.* Marcie: you have a right to harmony *4.* Max: be a man *5.* Ann: enjoy being single *6.* Jonathan: go play golf *7.* Thea: you may not see your grandchild *8.* Ray: find new ways of relating *9.* Francie: you want to kill your mother *10.* Heidi: give me your child *11.* Robin: you've got to help me *12.* Philip: let him die joyfully

Integrative Therapy *A Comprehensive Approach,* Darrell Smith

Baker Book House, 1990, $13.99, paper, 242 pp., a reference or academic work

Description Various theories of the mind are set alongside the Bible's understanding for evaluation. The author then seeks a synthesis of usable tools for Christian therapy drawn from the therapeutic models.

Author Darrell Smith is professor of counseling psychology at Texas A & M and a part-time counselor. He received his Ph.D. from Purdue University. He has contributed to numerous journals.

Contents *Part 1:* Foundations of integrative therapy *1.* Historical perspective *2.* The person in a Judeo-Christian world view *Part 2:* Human development and behavior *3.* Personality *4.* Problems in living *5.* Theory of personality and behavior change *Part 3:* Process and procedures of integrative therapy *6.* Therapeutic relationship *7.* Problem analysis and goal statements *8.* Contemporary modes of intervention (1) *9.* Contemporary modes of intervention (2) *10.* Integrative therapy in practice / *Appendix: A.* Ethical principles of psychologists *B.* Pre-therapy questionnaire *C.* Informed consent *D.* Twelve steps to wholeness

Theology and Therapy *The Wisdom of God in a Context of Friendship,* Samuel Southard

Word Publishing, 1989, $18.99, cloth, 270 pp., a reference or academic work

Description Seeks to correlate the importance of listening and compassion with reference points for the application of spiritual power or wisdom to specific difficulties. Offers a theological base for Christian therapy with a practical orientation. States the significance of a theological system for Christian counsel. Demonstrates how those who help people can work from a solid base of understanding essential doctrines of Christianity. Also addresses counselor–counselee relationships.

Author Samuel Southard is professor of pastoral theology at Fuller Theological Seminary and author of more than 15 books. He holds the Ph.D. from Southern Baptist Theological Seminary. He is also on staff at Church of the Savior, West Hollywood, Calif.

Contents *Part 1:* Wisdom *1.* The significance of a theological system *2.* The Trinity: the self-revealing fellowship *3.* The incarnation: divine attitudes in human actions *4.* The image of God *5.* General revelation *6.* Cases of conscience *7.* Sin and atonement *8.* The will of God and our will *9.* The power of the Spirit *10.* The community of faith *11.* The Christian hope *Part 2:* Friendship *12.* Restrictive and redemptive choices *13.* Invitations to sharing *14.* The communication of virtue *15.* The blessing of a wise balance

Biblical Counseling with African-Americans *Taking a Ride in the Ethiopian's Chariot,* Clarence Walker

Zondervan Publishing House, 1992, $9.99, paper, 144 pp., for counselors

Description Sets forth the challenges and techniques useful for those who counsel black Americans today.

Author Clarence Walker is a licensed marriage and family counselor who holds a Ph.D. in counseling from Trinity Theological Seminary and an M.S.W. from Temple University.

Contents *Part 1:* Counseling issues with black counselees *1.* Ethnicity issues *2.* Gender issues *3.* Sexual issues *4.* Power issues *5.* Socio-economic issues *6.* Environmental issues *7.* Religious issues *Part 2:* The counseling process and black counselees: ten biblical principles *8.* Directive engaging *9.* Affective joining *10.* Active listening *11.* Explorative questioning *12.* Correlative beginning *13.* Integrative witnessing *14.* Objective proceeding *15.* Effective counseling *16.* Cooperative involving *17.* Positive terminating *Part 3:* Counseling interventions and black counselees *18.* Couple and individual approaches

Changing on the Inside John White

Servant Publications/Vine Books, 1991, $8.99, paper, 210 pp., for both counselors and counselees

Description White looks closely at the relationship between repentance and emotional health. He examines the nature of healthy, lasting change—not superficial adjustments, not new resolutions, or outward conformity, but real change that results in peace, intimacy, and a vital connection with God. Explores the psychology and theology of change.

Author Dr. John White is a psychiatrist and writer with a worldwide ministry. He is author of several other books.

Contents *1.* An inner revolution *2.* Anatomy of an earthquake *3.* Coming to ourselves: facing up to reality *4.* The beast in the basement: evil and reality *5.* Swimming with the tide: how repentance works *6.* The psychology of conscience *7.* Emotions befitting and earthquake *8.* Turning your own life around: journeying toward change *9.* Ongoing change: the emergence of the real person *10.* Persuasion or manipulation *11.* A new life for old

Psychotherapy and Religious Values
Everett L. Worthington Jr.

Baker Book House, 1993, $15.99, paper, 291 pp., a reference or academic work

Description Twenty-three contributors, among them David Benner, Newton Malony, Stan Jones, and others examine the issues surrounding the use and abuse of religious values in psychotherapy. Several of the articles were previously published in the *Journal of Psychology and Christianity,* but the present volume contains new material. The book will help professionals and students explore the complex issue of religious values in psychotherapy. The book is organized to parallel the therapeutic counseling process. Chapters cover critical issues, values in secular theories, factors predicting use of various counselors, the effects of pre-therapy information and diagnosis by the counselor, models of values in counseling, ethics, lay counseling, personality theory, future issues, and an analysis of Christian counseling.

Author Everett Worthington holds a Ph.D. in counseling from the University of Missouri–Columbia and has worked at Virginia Commonwealth University since 1978. As a licensed clinical psychologist, he has directed a community counseling agency, supervised others, and maintained a part-time private practice.

Contents *Introduction to the series / Preface:* Values and psychotherapy: not "whether," but "which" and "how" / *Introduction:* Critical issues in the study of psychotherapy and religious values *Part 1:* Definitions, the context of counseling, and theories of counseling *1.* Religious values in secular theories of psychotherapy *Part 2:* Before counseling begins *2.* Psychiatric factors predicting the use of clergy *3.* Values, pre-therapy information, and informed consent in Christian counseling *4.* The relevance of "religious diagnosis" for counseling *Part 3:* During counseling and psychotherapy *5.* Psychotherapy and religious values, an update *6.* Boundary areas of religious clients' values: target for therapy / *Appendix:* Surveys of therapists' religious values *Part 4:* Use of and training in Christian therapy techniques *7.* Self-reported professional practices of Christian psychotherapists *8.* Practitioners, religion, and the use of forgiveness in the clinical setting *9.* Training in the use of Christian disciplines as counseling techniques within Christian graduate training programs *Part 5:* An eye to the future *10.* Christian ethics and psychological explanations of "religious values" in therapy: critical connections *11.* Religious values and interventions in lay Christian counseling *12.* Proposed agenda for a spiritual strategy in personality and psychotherapy *13.* Psychology and the Christian faith: 20th and 21st centuries

Self-Talk, Imagery and Prayer in Counseling H. Norman Wright

Word Publishing, 1986, $15.99, cloth, 204 pp., for counselors

Description The author describes the elements of cognitive therapy, good counseling practices, and the importance of self-talk for both counselor and client.

Author H. Norman Wright is a licensed marriage, family, and child therapist. Formerly a professor at Biola University, he is author of more than 50 books.

Contents *1.* The most important element in counseling *2.* Hazards in counseling *3.* Thought life—the foundation for counseling *4.* The inner conversation approach to counseling *5.* Helping people change their thought lives *6.* The use of imagery in counseling *7.* The untapped resource of counseling—prayer *8.* Practical applications / *Appendix:* Suggested methods for controlling thoughts

33. Relationships

Bold Love *The Courageous Practice of Life's Ultimate Influence,* Dan Allender and Tremper Longman III

NavPress, 1992, $12.00, paper, 318 pp., for both counselors and counselees

Description Deals with the complexities of relating on a deep level with people in our lives. Shows how genuine love (not just politeness and ignoring offense) can bring restoration to even the most destructive relationships. A study guide is also available.

Authors Dr. Dan B. Allender (M.Div., Westminster Theological Seminary; Ph.D. Michigan State University) teaches in the biblical counseling department at Colorado Christian University. He travels extensively in his seminar ministry and teaches counselor training courses. Coauthor Tremper C. Longman III is professor of Old Testament at Westminster Theological Seminary. He received his M.Div. from Westminster Theological Seminary and his Ph.D. in ancient Near East studies from Yale University.

Contents *Introduction:* Forgiveness—an intricate mystery *Part 1:* The battlefield of the heart *1.* Mixed feelings about love *2.* Taking our hatred out of the closet *3.* Stunned into silence *4.* Facing a war of hearts *5.* Our divine warrior *Part 2:* Strategy for the war of love *6.* Resumé of a warrior *7.* Hungering for restoration *8.* Revoking revenge *9.* Giving good gifts *Part 3:* Combat for the soul *10.* Loving an evil person *11.* Loving a fool *12.* Loving a normal sinner / *Epilogue:* Bold love

Bold Love—A Discussion Guide Based on the Book *The Courage Practice of Life's Ultimate Influence,* Dan Allender and Tremper Longman III

NavPress, 1992, $5.00, paper, 71 pp., for both counselors and counselees

Description A study guide to enhance the understanding and application of the book of the same title.

Authors Dr. Dan B. Allender (M.Div., Westminster Theological Seminary; Ph.D. Michigan State University) teaches in the biblical counseling department at Colorado Christian University. He travels extensively in his seminar ministry and teaches counselor training courses. Coauthor Tremper C. Longman III is professor of Old Testament at Westminster Theological Seminary. He received his M.Div. from Westminster Theological Seminary and his Ph.D. in ancient Near East studies from Yale University.

When You Are Alone William V. Arnold and Margaret Anne Fohl

Westminster/John Knox Press, 1994, $9.99, paper, 118 pp., for counselees

Description Integrating religious and psychological perspectives and a variety of personal experiences, this problem and solution book looks at the positive values of solitude as well as the negative problems of loneliness.

Authors William V. Arnold is professor of pastoral counseling and dean of the faculty at Union Theological Seminary in Richmond, Va. Margaret Anne Fohl is associate pastor for pastoral care at Bryn Mawr Presbyterian Church in Bryn Mawr, Pa.

Contents *1.* Looking at aloneness *2.* When you are lonely *3.* When you seek solitude *4.* Moving between aloneness and community *5.* Aloneness and our Christian faith *6.* Aloneness from a human perspective

Addicted to Love *Recovering from Unhealthy Dependencies in Love, Romance & Sex,* Stephen Arterburn

Servant Publications/Vine Books, 1992, $12.99, paper, 288 pp., for both counselors and counselees

Description Stephen Arterburn discusses the many forms this type of addiction can take—from romance novels, relationships, spouse abuse, and sexual acting out. Like drug addicts, "love" addicts get their high from sex and romance, develop a tolerance for it, and need ever-greater doses to keep it going. Arterburn points the way to psychological and spiritual healing, to enable men and women to enjoy real and lasting intimacy.

Author Stephen Arterburn is president of New Life Treatment Centers, Inc., providers of psychiatric treatment for drug and alcohol abuse and other addictions.

Contents *1.* Marisa's story *2.* Hooked on romance *3.* Hooked on relationships *4.* Hooked on sex *5.* Origins of people addictions *6.* What keeps the addict addicted? *7.* Living with addiction *8.* Recovery, from the bottom up *9.* Healthy love

Telling Each Other the Truth William Backus

Bethany House Publishers, 1985, $8.99, paper, 189 pp., for counselees

Description A guide to the art of true communication—knowing what to say, how to say it, and when the time is right. Helps readers improve interpersonal relationships by learning to develop the habit of truthful speech. Various behavior modification and cognitive restructuring models are discussed in the light of God's Word.

Author William Backus is a licensed clinical psychologist and an ordained Lutheran clergyman. He is founder and director of the Center for Christian Psychological Services, St. Paul, Minn., and an associate pastor of a large Lutheran church.

Contents *1.* Say what you want to say *2.* Nothing's wrong with saying "I" *3.* Attacking and defending vs. speaking the truth in love *4.* Manipulation by guilt *5.* Ask and it shall be given unto you—how to make requests *6.* Free to say "no" *7.* Dealing with critical people *8.* How Matt. 18:15 keeps you from blowing up *9.* "If he listens to you": the loving art of listening *10.* Wrapping the truth in love *11.* Telling the truth in social talk—small talk

Untwisting Twisted Relationships *How to Restore Close Ties with Family and Friends,* William Backus and Candace Backus

Bethany House Publishers, 1988, $7.99, paper, 175 pp., for counselees

Description Whether with family, friends, or associates, personal relationships are a major source of concern for everyone—even for those who would rather pretend life can go on very well without other people. Tangles and twists have

great potential for affecting close relationships and seem to cause a large share of life's miseries and pain. The authors help the reader see that the only way to strong, secure, intimate relationships is through honestly facing these fallacies and replacing them with truths from God's Word.

Authors William Backus is a licensed clinical psychologist and an ordained Lutheran clergyman. He is founder and director of the Center for Christian Psychological Services, St. Paul, Minn., and an associate pastor of a large Lutheran church. Candace Backus is a counselor and vice president of Minnesota Psychtests, Inc.

Contents *1.* Twisted relationships *2.* How relationship misbeliefs develop *3.* Some "agreed" patterns on twisted relationships *4.* The radical misbeliefs of loneliness *5.* The way out of loneliness *6.* Childhood trauma and the "right person" misbelief *7.* Jealousy *8.* People-pleasers *9.* The controllers *10.* A crash course in friendship

Personal Relationships with Others David Batty

Turning Point Ministries, Inc., $5.00, spiral, for both counselors and counselees

Description Part of the Group Studies for New Christians support group materials from Turning Point Ministries. A leader's guide is also available.

Friends Forever *The Art of Lifetime Relationships,* Janet Chester Bly

Aglow Publications, 1991, $9.95, paper, 150 pp., popular level/general trade

Description Discusses why we need lifetime relationships, how to cope with negative behaviors, how to translate anger into positive action, and how to restore broken relationships. Ideas and practical suggestions are given to help you understand the dynamics of strong friendships. Included are five types of friendships, nine signs of a gracious friend, six steps to restoring relationships, and four essentials of friendships with children. Guidelines provided for leading a support group.

Author Janet Chester Bly is a freelance writer and speaker, cofounder with her husband, Stephen, of Welcome to the Family Seminars. She has published 13 books, including *How to Be a Good Mom.*

Contents Why love a lifetime? / It takes all kinds / If you do that once more I'll . . . / Somebody help! I'm so angry / Making the most of broken relationships / The long road home and back again / The ultimate, permanent invasion of privacy / A little child will lead them / A friend for life and eternity

When You Need to Take a Stand Carolyn Stahl Bohler

Westminster/John Knox Press, 1994, $9.99, paper, 116 pp., for counselees

Description Interpersonal relationships can be enhanced when you speak up for what you believe in. Drawing upon her counseling experience as well as her struggles in her own relationships as a mother, wife, pastor, and teacher, Carolyn Stahl Bohler presents guidelines for deciding when and how to take stands and finding strength to do so.

Author Carolyn Stahl Bohler is associate professor of pastoral theology and counseling, Union Theological Seminary.

Contents *1.* Speaking up in relationships *2.* When you are afraid of conflict *3.* When you are not sure where you stand *4.* When you don't think you have enough power *5.* When and how to speak *6.* Empowering others to speak *7.* Giving and receiving speech

Why Be Lonely? *A Guide to Meaningful Relationships,* Les Carter, Paul D. Meier, and Frank B. Minirth

Baker Book House, 1982, $8.99, paper, 169 pp., for counselees

Description Why do I feel lonely? What can I do to find love? These are the questions answered with case histories, self-examination tools, and compassionate counsel.

Authors Les Carter, Paul D. Meier, and Frank B. Minirth are associates in the Minirth-Meier Clinic. Using the facilities of the Richardson Medical Center, the clinic treats patients from all over the world.

Contents *Part 1:* A portrait of loneliness *1.* Intimacy and how to avoid it! *2.* A personal struggle *3.* A personal evaluation *Part 2:* The causes and consequences of loneliness *4.* The river runs deep *5.* Me against the world *6.* The sin factor—the ultimate origin of loneliness *7.* The victims of loneliness—from young to old *8.* The children of loneliness *9.* The cousins of loneliness *Part 3:* The overcoming of loneliness *10.* Enemies of loneliness *11.* Realistic thinking *12.* Do something about it *13.* Learning from biblical characters *14.* A final thought

Boundaries *When to Say Yes; When to Say No to Take Control of Your Life,* Henry Cloud and John Townsend

Zondervan Publishing House, 1992, $17.99, cloth, 256 pp., for counselees

Description This book presents a biblical treatment of boundaries, identifies how boundaries are developed and how they become injured, shows Christian misconceptions of their function and purpose, targets areas in our lives that have boundary conflicts, and gives a program for developing and maintaining healthy, biblical limits. Also available on audio and video.

Authors Dr. Henry Cloud and Dr. John Townsend are codirectors of the Minirth-Meier Clinic West, a group of treatment centers headquartered in Newport Beach, Calif. They both earned their Ph.D. degrees at Rosemead Graduate School of Psychology.

Contents *Part 1:* What are boundaries? *1.* A day in a boundariless life *2.* What does a boundary look like? *3.* Boundary problems *4.* How boundaries are developed *5.* Ten laws of boundaries *6.* Common boundary myths *Part 2:* Boundary conflicts *7.* Boundaries and your family *8.* Boundaries and your friends *9.* Boundaries and your spouse *10.* Boundaries and your children *11.* Boundaries and your work *12.* Boundaries and your self *13.* Boundaries and your God *Part 3:* Developing healthy boundaries *14.* Resistance to boundaries *15.* How to measure success with boundaries *16.* A day in the life with boundaries

Safe People *How to Find Relationships That are Good for You,* Henry Cloud and John Townsend

Zondervan Publishing House, 1995, $15.95, cloth, 199 pp.

Description *Safe People* will help you recognize 20 traits of relationally untrustworthy people. You'll discover how to avoid unhealthy entanglements, things about yourself that jeopardize your relational security. And, you'll find out what not to do to develop a balanced, healthy approach to relationships. A companion workbook is also available.

Authors Dr. Henry Cloud and Dr. John Townsend are codirectors of the Minirth-Meier Clinic West, a group of treatment centers headquartered in Newport Beach, Calif. They both earned their Ph.D. degrees at Rosemead Graduate School of Psychology.

Contents *Part 1*—Unsafe people *1*. What is an unsafe person? *2*. Personal traits of unsafe people *3*. Interpersonal traits of unsafe people *4*. How we lost our security *Part 2*—Do I attract unsafe people? *5*. Do I have a "safety deficit"? *6*. Why do I choose unsafe relationships? *7*. False solutions *8*. Why do I isolate myself from others? *Part 3*—Safe people *9*. What are safe people? *10*. Why do we need safe people? *11*. Where are the safe people? *12*. Learning how to be safe *13*. Should I repair or replace?

The Power of Love *Overcoming the Love of Power in Your Relationships,* David Congo and Janet Congo

Moody Press, 1993, $16.95, cloth, 224 pp., for counselees

Description Readers will learn how to overcome the need for control and build the kind of responsible, interdependent relationships that are the foundation for true fulfillment.

Making Real Friends in a Phoney World
Jim Conway

Zondervan Publishing House, 1989, $8.99, paper, 216 pp., for counselees

Description Focuses on skills that are necessary to develop long-term friendships.

Author Jim Conway holds five degrees in psychology and theology and is the author of many books. With his wife, Sally Conway, they own and operate Mid-Life Dimensions/Christian Living Resources, a nonprofit organization ministering to people at various stages of life through a variety of media formats.

Contents *Part 1:* Getting ready for friendships *1*. Listen to me *2*. This is going to be fun! *Part 2:* Qualities that draw friends to you *3*. Why we like people, why they like us *4*. What do I think of myself *5*. The maturing person *6*. Qualities that build friendships *Part 3:* Skills for deep and lasting friendships *7*. Attending: focusing on your friend *8*. Listening: one part of communication *9*. Talking: another part of communication *10*. Empathy: caring enough to send your very best *11*. Genuineness: being real in a phoney world *12*. Affirmation: passing on a blessing

Sexual Harassment No More Jim Conway and Sally Conway

InterVarsity Press, 1993, $9.99, paper, 220 pp., for counselees

Description Sexual harassment occurs and has been documented in the workplace, on dates, in marriage, in education, and in religion. The focus of this book is to help people understand the pervasiveness of sexual harassment and then

to specifically coach men and women how to deal with and avoid sexual harassment. The book concludes with a chapter on "values" to help men and women truly respect each other.

Authors Jim Conway holds five degrees in psychology and theology and is the author of many books. His wife, Sally Conway, holds an M.S. in human development. Together they own and operate Mid-Life Dimensions/Christian Living Resources, a nonprofit organization ministering to people at various stages of life through a variety of media formats.

Contents *Part 1:* Harassment in America *1*. It's real and it's pervasive *2*. Sexual harassment in the workplace *3*. Why do women put up with it? *4*. Guidelines for the harassed person *5*. Sexual harassment on dates *6*. Sexual harassment in marriage *7*. Sexual harassment in education *8*. Sexual harassment in religion *Part 2:* Insights for men and for the women who want to help them *9*. Why men harass *10*. "Male pattern ignorance" *11*. What men don't know will hurt them *12*. What men need to know about women *13*. A woman's sexual agenda *14*. To do and not to do *Part 3:* Insights for women to reduce harassment *15*. What women need to know to reduce harassment *16*. What women need to be to reduce harassment *17*. What women need to do to reduce harassment *Part 4:* Values that enable people to rise above harassment *18*. What you believe will change your life

How to Deal with Difficult People
Andrew Costello

Liguori Publications, 1994, $4.95, paper, 127 pp., for counselees

Description Discusses personality types, communication, expectations, and ways to look below the surface to improve personal relationships.

Contents *1*. Awareness and decision *2*. Flight or fight? *3*. Seeking help *4*. What do we expect? *5*. Roles people play *6*. Different folks, different strokes *7*. Enter, Jesus Christ *8*. Starting with ourselves *9*. Importance of dialogue *10*. From the top of the mountain

Understanding People *Deep Longings for Relationship,* Larry Crabb

Zondervan Publishing House, 1987, $16.99, cloth, 224 pp., for both counselors and counselees

Description Dr. Crabb examines one of the most crucial problems in Christian counseling today: the use and abuse of the Bible. He illustrates two common weaknesses of biblical counselors: They often "spiritualize" problems and limit questions to those for which they can find a prooftext, or they regard the Bible as more or less irrelevant when grappling with the hard questions people ask. It is with these unsatisfactory alternatives in mind that Dr. Crabb develops a model for biblical counseling that is grounded on the authority and sufficiency of the Scriptures. The aim is to help readers at all levels answer the question: "How do I use Scripture in helping others?"

Author Dr. Crabb is director of biblical counseling and chairman of the Department of Biblical Counseling at Colorado Christian University in Morrison, Colo. He earned his Ph.D. in clinical psychology from the University of Illinois in 1970. He is the author of numerous books on self-understanding and counseling technique.

Contents *Part 1:* A sufficient Bible—finding answers in Scripture *1.* How do we know what to believe? *2.* The Bible warrants our confidence *3.* Does the Bible speak meaningfully to every problem? *4.* The Bible is a sufficient guide for relational living *Part 2:* Understanding people—a tarnished image and broken relationships *5.* How can people truly change? *6.* People bear the image of God *7.* Dependent beings—people are personal *8.* Foolish thinkers: people are rational *9.* The beginning of change—repentance *10.* Free to choose: people are volitional *11.* Feeling the impact of life: people are emotional *Part 3:* Growing toward maturity *12.* The evidence of maturity: love *13.* The essence of maturity: realized dependency

Alone but Not Lonely Karen Dockrey

New Hope, 1992, $1.95, paper, 22 pp., for counselees

Description Gives an overview of the problem of loneliness, how teenagers can help their friend overcome the problem, and a Christian response to coping with the problem. This booklet is another in the Between Friends series.

Author Karen Dockrey works with youth at Bluegrass Baptist Church in Hendersonville, Tenn.

When You're Feeling Lonely Charles Durham

InterVarsity Press, 1984, $8.99, paper, 186 pp., for counselees

Description Helping readers conquer feelings of loneliness, Charles Durham shows how to reach out to others and discusses how to develop intimacy in new relationships.

Author Charles Durham is pastor of Prairie View Church of the Brethren in Friend, Kans.

Contents *Part 1:* What is loneliness? *1.* What is loneliness? *2.* The dangers of loneliness *Part 2:* Meeting our needs for companionship *3.* God *4.* Family *5.* Mate *6.* Intimacy and romance *7.* Community *8.* Solitude *Part 3:*

Reaching out *9.* Reaching for a friend *10.* Being a friend *11.* Reaching out to the lonely

How to Overcome Loneliness Elisabeth Elliot

NavPress, 1991 (3d printing), $2.00, paper, 23 pp., for counselees

Description Loneliness is not incurable. It can make life seem empty, meaningless, and unbearable. It isn't the kind of thing you can shake "once and for all." But loneliness can be overcome. So whether you've been ignoring a nagging emptiness, or feeling desperately alone, Elisabeth Elliot will show you how to transform your loneliness into expectancy, joy, and peace.

Making Friends (And Making Them Count) Em Griffin

InterVarsity Press, 1992, $10.99, paper, 223 pp., for counselees

Description Exploring the art of friendship, Griffin discusses what attracts one person to another. Includes how self-concept affects relationships, how people form first impressions, and how the right ingredients make for lasting friendships.

Author Em Griffin is professor of speech communication at Wheaton College and the author of *The Mind Changers.*

Contents *1.* The rules of the game *2.* Self-concept *3.* Motivation *4.* Perception *5.* Listening to language *6.* Nonverbal communication *7.* Interpersonal attraction *8.* Trust and transparency *9.* Accountability and forgiveness *10.* The friendship mandate

Longing for Company Judy Hamlin

Victor Books, 1993, $4.99, paper, 64 pp., for counselees

Description Part of the Searching for Answers series from Victor. Everyone is lonely at times, but women do not always recognize when loneliness has become an acute condition. The studies in this book will help women see the condition clearly and find answers through support of God and friends. These six sessions look at the difference between being lonely and loneliness, how loneliness affects one's personality, how satisfactory relationships can rescue one from loneliness, and how to achieve hope and victory, rather than defeat.

Author Dr. Judy Hamlin (Ph.D. in adult education/University of Southern Mississippi) is an authority on small groups and women's ministry.

Through the Wilderness of Loneliness
Tim Hansel

Chariot Family Publishing, $12.99, cloth, 128 pp., for counselees

Description Shows readers how to turn the desperation of loneliness into the delight of solitude. Reminds that God is always with us, no matter how alone we feel.

Thanks for Being My Friend Lois Walfrid Johnson

NavPress, 1988, $7.00, paper, 178 pp., for counselees

Description Part of the Let's Talk-About-It Stories for Kids series from NavPress. A series of short stories followed by discussion questions. Well-written, Christ-centered, and easy for young people to understand. This title deals with the issues associated with making and keeping friends. Does not prescribe simplistic solutions. Would be helpful in teaching friendship building skills to troubled children and preadolescents.

Author Lois Walfrid Johnson is the author of 19 books. She leads seminars and retreats and speaks at churches and conferences throughout the United States.

How to Get Along with Difficult People
Florence Littauer

Harvest House Publishers, 1991, $7.99, paper, for counselees

Description Littauer gives her most unique insights into dealing with the difficult personalities we all encounter at home or work. Over 170,000 copies in print.

Author Florence Littauer is the president of CLASS Speakers, Inc. Her books have won numerous awards and have sold over 100,000 copies.

Contents *1.* Who are the difficult people? *2.* What hope is there for understanding others? *3.* How can we deal with difficult people? *4.* How do the difficult people see us? *5.* How did Paul handle a difficult situation? *6.* How can we handle a difficult situation?

Getting beyond "How Are You?" *Learning to Connect in a Disconnected World,* David Mains and Melissa Mains Timberlake

Victor Books, 1992, $3.95, paper, 106 pp., for counselees

Description This refreshing and honest resource invites you to enjoy closer connections with your family, friends, and casual contacts. You will learn how to bring healing to your own soul and touch the lives of others.

Author David Mains is director and his daughter, Melissa Mains Timberlake, is program director at *The Chapel of the Air,* a 15-minute radio broadcast heard more than 500 times daily throughout North America.

Contents *1.* The value of asking good questions *2.* Questions that get beyond the obvious *3.* Listening skills *4.* Questions I wish others would ask *5.* Asking questions in the family *6.* Asking questions of people Jesus sends our way *7.* How questions help in a setting of polarization *8.* Questions to ask non-Christians *9.* More ways asking questions can benefit the church

Win-Win Relationships *9 Strategies for Settling Personal Conflicts Without Waging War,* H. Newton Malony

Broadman and Holman Publishers, 1995, $15.99, cloth, 179 pp.

Description Before Christians can successfully deal with problems at home, church, or work, they must first manage the conflict within themselves. This book written by a clinical psychologist, offers nine techniques for dealing with conflict, plus exercises to help readers apply strategies in their own circumstances.

Author H. Newton Maloney holds a Ph.D. in Clinical Psychology from George Peabody of Vanderbilt University. A licensed psychologist as well as an ordained minister in the United Methodist Church, he is senior professor at the Graduate School of Psychology, Fuller Theological Seminary.

Contents *1.* Conflicts exist inside people, not between them *2.* Conflicts are a threat to self-esteem *3.* Conflicts exist in many colors *4.* Conflicts can be reduced *5.* Conflict reduction begins with you *6.* Conflict resolution calls for analysis and action *7.* Conflicts can be prevented *8.* Self-control: the key to personal conflict prevention *9.* Peace is illusory; peacemaking is not

Learning to Love People You Don't Like
How to Develop Love and Unity in Every Relationship, Floyd McClung

Youth with a Mission Publishing, $6.99, paper, for counselees

Description Challenging and practical answers for achieving productive, lasting relationships.

Don't Let the Jerks Get the Best of You
Advice for Dealing with Impossible People, Paul D. Meier

Janet Thoma (a division of Thomas Nelson), 1993, $16.99, cloth, 256 pp., for counselees

Description A respected psychologist teaches the fine art of psychological self-defense with down-to-earth humor and personal anecdotes about "jerkiness" or the ability to be blindly selfish in our dealings with other human beings.

Author Paul Meier received an M.A. from the University of Arkansas College of Medicine and completed his psychiatry residency at Duke University. He also received an M.A. in biblical studies from Dallas Theological Seminary. Dr. Meier is cofounder of the national chain of Minirth-Meier Clinics and has coauthored more than 30 books.

Contents *Part 1:* Welcome to a world of jerks—and masochists *1.* It's a jungle out there, and it's full of jerks *2.* What does a first degree jerk look like? *3.* Careful! Second-degree jerks can be anywhere *4.* Society's sociopaths, nth degree jerks *5.* But why are we such pushovers for the predatory jerks? *Part 2:* Six steps out of masochism to maturity *6.* Meet the enemy, he is definitely us *7.* Are mom and dad still parenting you? *8.* Why not sing your own song? *9.* You can't stuff your anger forever *10.* Why keep running the rat race? *11.* Moving on toward maturity

Love in Action *Dealing with Conflict in Your Church,* Robert Moeller

Questar Publishing, 1995, $10.95, paper, 274 pp.

Description Find out how to deal with trouble in your congregation before it does irreparable damage, and learn how members and leaders can bond together to exalt Christ and glorify God.

Author Robert Moeller is a full-time author and writer, frequent guest speaker, and contributing editor to *Leadership Journal.* He is also an ordained pastor in the Evangelical Free Church of America.

Contents *Part 1*—When the family feuds *1.* A father's will *2.* How to break a father's heart *3.* The dig *4.* How to split the church *5.* The gallery *Part 2*—How to heal family ties *6.* How pastors can bring unity *7.* A tale of two parishes *8.* Getting it into your system *9.* What prayer and fasting can accomplish *10.* The value of saying "I'm sorry" *11.* A pastor is a terrible thing to waste *12.* When it's time to call 911 *13.* Taming your animal instincts *14.* On earth as it is in heaven

Building Bridges to Others *How to Get People to Like You,* Clyde M. Narramore

Narramore Christian Foundation, $19.99, video, for both counselors and counselees

Description One of the greatest joys in life is relating well to other people. This video shows what to do and not to do. Excellent for all ages.

Author Dr. Clyde M. Narramore is a licensed psychologist and the president and founder of the Narramore Christian Foundation—a charitable, nonprofit educational, training, and counseling organization ministering primarily to the Christian community. He is also the founder of the Rosemead School of Psychology and author of 29 books.

Guarding Your Self Esteem *How and Why We Defend Ourselves—What to Do about It,* Clyde M. Narramore

Narramore Christian Foundation, $19.95, video, for both counselors and counselees

Description Fourteen methods of guarding your self-esteem (defense mechanisms) are presented. Dr. Narramore explains why we use them, their effect, and how to resolve them.

Author Dr. Clyde M. Narramore is a licensed psychologist and the president and founder of the Narramore Christian Foundation—a charitable, nonprofit educational, training, and counseling organization ministering primarily to the Christian community. He is also the founder of the Rosemead School of Psychology and author of 29 books.

Love's Unseen Enemy *How to Overcome Guilt to Build Healthy Relationships,* Les Parrott

Zondervan Publishing House, 1994, $14.95, cloth, 221 pp., for counselees

Description A decade of research reveals how guilt secretly sabotages our relationships: step-by-step plans for becoming a genuinely loving person; visual features portray "compulsive love," "convenient love," "reluctant love," and "authentic love"; practical steps for overcoming the shame of toxic guilt; tips for building dynamic friendships, marriages, parent–child relationships, etc. Includes self-tests and personal inventories—great for small-group discussion.

Author Dr. Parrott is associate professor of psychology and director of the Center for Relationship Development at Seattle Pacific University. His education includes the M.A. in theology and Ph.D. in clinical psychology from Fuller Theological Seminary and a postdoctoral fellowship at the University of Washington School of Medicine. His other books include *Helping the Struggling Adolescent.*

Contents *Part 1:* Exposing the unseen enemy *1.* Identifying the unseen enemy: a self-test *2.* Coping with guilt *3.* Conscience: your internal thermostat *4.* What's shame got to do with it? *5.* Godly sorrow *6.* Overcoming false guilt *Part 2:* Unmasking love's counterfeits *7.* Identifying your relational style *8.* Compulsive love: the pleaser *9.* Convenient love: the controller *10.* Reluctant love: the withholder *11.* Authentic love: the lover *Part 3:* Building healthy relationships *12.* That's what friends are for *13.* Making love last a lifetime *14.* Raising healthy kids *15.* It's not just a job, it's a relationship *16.* Relating to God

Talking Back to Sexual Pressure *What to Say . . . ,* Elizabeth Powell

CompCare Publishers, 1991, $12.95, paper, 255 pp., for counselees

Description Best Self-Help Book of the Year (MBA Award winner). Clinical psychologist Elizabeth Powell offers ways to deal with difficult and uncomfortable sexual situations.

Author Elizabeth Powell, M.S., M.A., is a professor in a large urban community college district, where she teaches human sexuality and chairs the AIDS task force.

Contents *Part 1:* How to become assertive about sex *1.* Breaking the silence *2.* Understanding assertiveness *3.* Taking charge of your thoughts *Part 2:* How to respond to persuasion *4.* Standing up to verbal pressure *5.* Speaking up to avoid disease and pregnancy *Part 3:* How to cope with intrusion and force *6.* Resisting sexual harassment *7.* Avoiding acquaintance rape *8.* Responding to other sexual intrusion *Part 4:* How to speak up for your society *9.* Searching for the causes *10.* Becoming a witness

Friendship . . . the Basis for Love *Building a Quality Relationship That Will Last a Lifetime,* Dick Purnell

Thomas Nelson Publishers, 1994, $10.99, paper, 312 pp., for counselees

Description Includes a leader's guide. Readers are given practical ideas for building relationships with the opposite sex that could form the foundation for marriage. Single adults and students will learn biblical principles for understanding the opposite sex.

Author Dick Purnell is the director of Single Life Resources as well as being an author, speaker, and counselor.

Emotional Dependency Lori Rentzel

InterVarsity Press, 1990, $.99, paper, 31 pp., for counselees

Description With anecdotes, spiritual counsel, and readable clinical information, the author traces the roots of emotional dependency and outlines steps to severance of unhealthy relationships.

Recovery from Broken Relationships Dale Ryan and Juanita Ryan

InterVarsity Press, 1992, $4.99, paper, 60 pp., for both counselors and counselees

Description This Bible study is part of a series of 16 volumes on various recovery themes. Each book contains studies on six biblical texts. Leader's notes are provided for group study.

Authors Dale Ryan is the executive director of the Recovery Partnership, the parent organization to the National Association for Christian Recovery. Juanita Ryan is a counselor in private practice in Hacienda Heights, Calif.

Contents Recovering from broken relationships *Part 1:* Facing reality *1.* Grieving the hurts (Ps. 55:1–8, 12–17) *2.* Seeking forgiveness from God (Ps. 130) *Part 2:* Healing *3.* Accepting God's grace (John 4:6–19) *4.* Experiencing God's faithfulness (Isaiah 49:13–16) *Part 3:* Risking love again *5.* Growing in the capacity to love (1 Corinthians 13:1–7) *6.* Nurturing new relationships (Colossians 3:12–17)

The Peacemakers *A Biblical Guide to Resolving Personal Conflict,* Ken Sande

Baker Book House, 1991, $12.99, paper, 246 pp.

Description An essential for Christian lawyers interested or involved in conciliation. Provides the tools we need to accomplish unity and harmony.

Author Ken Sande is executive director of the Institute for Christian Conciliation. He regularly conciliates business, family, employment, and church disputes and serves as consultant to pastors and attorneys as they work to resolve conflicts outside the courtroom.

Contents *Part 1*—Glorify God *1.* Conflict provides opportunities *2.* Live at peace *3.* Trust in the Lord and do good *Part 2*—Get the log out of your eye *4.* Is this really worth fighting over? *5.* Examine yourself *6.* Free yourself from sin *Part 3*—Go and show your brother his fault *7.* Restore the sinner gently *8.* Speak the truth in love *9.* Take one or two others along *Part 4*—Go and be reconciled *10.* Forgive as God forgave you *11.* Look also to the interests of others *12.* Overcome evil with good / *Appendixes*

Loneliness Elizabeth Skoglund

InterVarsity Press, 1975, $.99, paper, 32 pp., for counselees

Description Provides biblical and practical help for overcoming loneliness.

Overcoming Shyness M. Blaine Smith

InterVarsity Press, 1993, $9.99, paper, 285 pp., for counselees

Description Blaine Smith has learned a lot about how to handle his shyness. Now he shares his insights and counsel with others who struggle with the pain of shyness and who see it as holding them back socially, in the workplace—and even spiritually. This very honest and practical book will help you make your shyness work for you rather than against you. It will give you courage to take new steps of assertiveness that don't violate your basic personality. And it will show you what it means to trust God at the most personal level.

Author M. Blaine Smith, a Presbyterian resource pastor, is director of Nehemiah Ministries. He is author of several books. He holds the doctor of ministry degree from Fuller Theological Seminary.

Contents *Part 1:* Understanding shyness *1.* A common experience *2.* The roots of shyness *3.* The benefits of shyness *4.* The drawback of shyness—catastrophizing *Part 2:* Taking control—one-half step at a time *5.* Staring fear down *6.* Breaking the panic cycle *7.* Praying for courage *8.* Asking for help *Part 3:* Awakening your social life *9.* Seeing the possibilities *10.* Putting yourself in the right context *11.* Warming up to conversation *12.* Knowing what to say *Part 4:* Asserting yourself—and your life *13.* Faith and assertiveness *14.* Taking initiative *15.* Learning optimism / *Appendixes* A. Facing the crowd—tips for confronting an audience *B.* Playing a role—and staying whole—overcoming impostor feelings

Trusting Learn Who and How to Trust, Pat Springle

Servant Publications/Vine Books, 1994, $8.99, paper, 232 pp., for counselees

Description Offers readers solid biblical counsel for rebuilding damaged trust and developing perceptive trust. These astute insights, borne from the author's years of research and counseling, will help readers break down the isolating barriers, take risks again, and experience true intimacy with God and others.

Author Pat Springle, former vice president of Rapha, is the president of Baxter Press, a publisher of Christian psychology literature. Springle is the author of several other books related to codependency issues.

Contents *Part 1:* What is trust? *1.* Intangible glue *2.* Retracing your steps *3.* The shattering of trust *4.* The erosion of trust *Part 2:* The twists and turns of trust *5.* Perceiving is believing *6.* Don't take any wooden nickels *7.* Getting away or giving in *8.* Charm and venom *9.* "Turbo trust" *Part 3:* Growing in trust *10.* Prognosis for change *11.* Learning to trust perceptively *12.* Hobbled by unbelief *13.* If you can't trust yourself *14.* Whom can you trust? *15.* Becoming worthy of trust

That's Not What I Meant In Every Relationship There Are Words That Hurt and Words That Heal, Tim Stafford

Zondervan Publishing House, 1995, $10.99, paper, 157 pp.

Description Offers a biblical perspective on the power of words and shows how to change personal patterns and habits of speaking. Instead of using words to abuse and harm, we can use them to build more honest, intimate, and satisfying relationships.

Author Tim Stafford is a noted freelance writer and journalist. He is a consulting editor for *Christianity Today.*

Contents *Introduction:* Pictures of the power of words *1.* Outside in: a way to change your life *2.* Taking inventory *3.* Toxic talk: harsh words and lies *4.* The power of praise *5.* Conversational junk food: flattery, bragging, and gossip *6.* Talking about trouble *7.* The right word at the right time / *Appendix:* Selected Scriptures in words

How to Fill the Emptiness Woodie J. Stevens

Beacon Hill Press of Kansas City, $1.95, paper, for counselees

289

Description Part of the Christian Living series from Beacon Hill. Briefly describes ways to overcome loneliness.

Hiding from Love *How to Change the Withdrawal Patterns That Isolate and Imprison You,* John Townsend

NavPress, 1991, $11.00, paper, 288 pp., for counselees

Description When you experience emotional injury, fear, shame, or unhealthy pride, your first impulse is to hide the hurting parts of yourself deep inside—so that God, others, and even you won't see them. Whatever hiding patterns you use, God wants you to be free from the isolation of your soul. Dr. Townsend will help you thoroughly explore and identify the hiding patterns you've developed—and guide you toward the healing grace and truth that God has built into safe, connected relationships with himself and others.

Author Dr. John Townsend (Th.M., Dallas Theological Seminary; Ph.D., Rosemead Graduate School of Psychology) is the codirector of the Minirth-Meier Clinic West in southern Calif. A clinical psychologist and a private marriage, family, and child counselor, he is a popular speaker and specialist on such topics as developmental models of spiritual and emotional growth and the integration of Scripture and psychology.

Contents *Part 1:* The hiding dilemma *1.* Jenny's story *2.* Our two biggest problems *3.* "This wasn't plan A" *4.* Our need for attachment *5.* Our need for separateness *6.* Our need for resolving good and bad *7.* Our need for authority and adulthood *Part 2:* Helpful and harmful hiding *8.* Helpful hiding: dealing with suffering *9.* Helpful hiding: preparing for relationship *10.* Harmful hiding: six critical stages *11.* Harmful hiding: the results *12.* The cost of harmful hiding *Part 3:* Hope for those in hiding *13.* Hiding from attachment *14.* Hiding from separateness *15.* Hiding from our good and bad selves *16.* Hiding from authority and adulthood *17.* Coming out of hiding

Hiding from Love—A Discussion Guide Based on the Book *How to Change the Withdrawal Patterns That Isolate and Imprison You,* John Townsend

NavPress, 1991, $6.00, paper, 91 pp., for both counselors and counselees

Description A companion guide to the book of the same title for use in discussion groups and support groups. Intended for leaders to guide discussion.

Author Dr. John Townsend (Th.M., Dallas Theological Seminary; Ph.D., Rosemead Graduate School of Psychology) is the codirector of the Minirth-Meier Clinic West in southern Calif. A clinical psychologist and a private marriage, family, and child counselor, he is a popular speaker and specialist on such topics as developmental models of spiritual and emotional growth and the integration of Scripture and psychology.

Contents *1.* What is hiding and why do we hide? *2.* How do I know if I'm hiding? *3.* Helpful hiding *4.* Harmful hiding *5.* The needs we hide from *6.* Patterns of harmful hiding *7.* The results of harmful thinking *8.* How to come out of harmful hiding

Loneliness Tom Varney

NavPress, 1992, $5.00, paper, 63 pp., for counselees

Description In this IBC discussion guide, you'll learn how to meaningfully reflect on and respond to the familiar life experience of loneliness—not react to it as a despised enemy. You'll look at such issues as: how to recognize the various dimensions of loneliness, how to profit from facing loneliness, how to respond to loneliness, how to embrace and help others and yourself when faced with loneliness.

Author Dr. Tom Varney is a private counselor, professor of counseling in the Colorado Christian University graduate program, and an associate of the Institute of Biblical Counseling.

Contents *Session 1:* Facing the reality of loneliness *Session 2:* Responding to loneliness *Session 3:* Learning from loneliness *Session 4:* Helping others in their loneliness / Help for leaders

Speaking Your Mind without Stepping on Toes *A Christian Approach to Assertiveness,* Henry A. Virkler

Victor Books, 1991, $8.99, paper, 204 pp., for counselees

Description Suggests that Christian assertiveness is a style of living, a healthy way of interacting. Christian assertiveness includes two basic sets of skills: relationship enhancement (developing relationships) and self-protective skills (ability to deal with conflict). They are skills that enable us to express our thoughts, feelings, beliefs, and desires in direct, honest, appropriate ways that do not violate the needs, rights, and self-esteem of others. A leader's guide designed for 12 90-minute group sessions (as in counseling centers) or 12 50-minute group sessions (possibly Sunday school) is available from the author for $15.00.

Author For 15 years, Virkler was involved in Christian counseling in the Atlanta area. During the same period he taught at the Psychological Studies Institute, a Christian counselor-training program. He presently teaches in the psychology and counseling programs at Liberty University.

Understanding How Others Misunderstand You *A Unique and Proven Plan for Strengthening Personal Relationships,* Ken Vogues and Ron Braund

Moody Press, 1992, $9.99, paper, 284 pp., for counselees

Description Two experts have taken the study of personalities to a new level of practical application. Using the pioneering DiSC profile, this book teaches in clear terms how to build closer, more understanding relationships at home, work, and church. A companion workbook is also available.

Authors Ken Vogues and Dr. Ron Braund have successfully incorporated the Carlson Learning Company's DISC system to fit biblical principles.

Contents *1.* People are different *2.* A common language for understanding behavior *3.* Expectations and environments *4.* The DiSC personality styles in daily living *5.* Understanding the dominant style *6.* Responding to the needs of the dominant personality *7.* Understanding the influencing style *8.* Responding to the needs of the influencing personality *9.* Understanding the steadiness style *10.* Responding to the needs of the steadiness personality *11.* Understanding the compliant style *12.* Responding to the needs of the compliant personality *13.* Transformation within personality styles

God, Where Is Love? *Break Free from the Pain of Codependency,* Claire W.

Zondervan Publishing House, 1993, $8.99, paper, 128 pp., for counselees

Description For singles or marrieds who struggle with the pain of codependency, here is a guide for improving relationship and communication skills. Part of the God, Help Me series from Zondervan. These self-help books are designed, not only to explain the recovery process, but to guide

and support the reader throughout that process. Emotional and spiritual healing are promoted through Bible verses, questions for reflection, writing assignments, and the personal examples of the author and other people who have experienced recovery.

Author Claire W. draws on her Ph.D. training in clinical psychology and her work as a counselor as she writes for Christians in recovery.

Contents *Part 1:* How do I learn to love and be loved? *1.* The problem of codependency *2.* The work of recovery *3.* Understanding, healing, and growth *4.* Communication and intimacy *5.* Communication and problem solving *Part 2:* How can I tell if it's love? *6.* Intimacy *7.* Sex *8.* Expectations *9.* Commitment *10.* Lynn and Steve in recovery

When You Feel Like Nobody Cares Dan Webster

NavPress, 1991, $2.00, paper, 18 pp., for counselees

Description Targets teenagers dealing with loneliness. Part of the Student Survival series from NavPress. Largely anecdotal with several reflection questions.

Author Dan Webster is the director of student ministries at Willow Creek Community Church in South Barrington, Ill.

Love Gone Wrong *What to Do When You Are Attracted to the Wrong Person Over and Over,* Thomas Whiteman and Randy Petersen

Oliver Nelson (a division of Thomas Nelson), 1994, $10.99, paper, 228 pp., for both counselors and counselees

Description Excellent for people in unhealthy relationships as well as people who want to help them, such as counselors, pastors, and discussion group leaders. Teaches readers how to develop balanced, happy relationships.

Authors Thomas A. Whiteman, Ph.D., is founder and director of Life Counseling Services in Pennsylvania, and president of FreshStart Seminars. Randy Petersen is a freelance writer.

Contents *1.* The group *2.* Types of addictive relationships *3.* Case study: Sally *4.* Characteristics of addictive relationships *5.* Test yourself *6.* Case study: Scott *7.* The roots of addictive behavior *8.* Case study: Bonnie *9.* Breaking the addictive cycle *10.* The canyon *11.* Case study: Laurie *12.* Best friends *13.* Balance *14.* Boundaries *15.* Case study: Christine *16.* Addiction within marriage *17.* Addiction in a same-sex relationship *18.* Family relationships

Dealing with Difficult People

Abbey Press, 1994, $.50 each, paper, 8 pp., for counselees

Description Part of the New CareSteps series from Abbey Press. Each CareStep pamphlet (three-panel) is filled with insightful advice and quotes from respected leaders in the helping professions. Very useful during the early stages of recovery. The underlying message in all CareSteps pamphlets is the emphasis on using all one's resources—emotional, physical, mental, social, and spiritual—to cope with life's biggest challenges. This title emphasizes trying gentle confrontation, preventing verbal abuse, giving anger a voice, taking responsibility for one's feelings, and practicing forgiveness.

Edge TV—Loneliness

NavPress, 1992, $24.95, video with leader's guide, 60 minutes, for both counselors and counselees

Description For youth workers who want to steer their group away from "church appropriate" discussions and get them talking about what's really going on in their lives. *Edge TV* (a video magazine for church youth groups) is the place to start. Created in partnership with Youth Specialties and IMS Productions, each episode of *Edge TV* is packed with high energy visuals, no-holds-barred drama, startling interviews, Christian music videos, captivating humor—and an honest approach to Jesus Christ that will get kids asking some very interesting questions.

Feeling Rejected *When the One You Love Doesn't Love You Back*

Abbey Press, 1993, $.50 each, paper, 8 pp., for counselees

Description Part of the CareNotes for Teens series from Abbey Press. CareNotes are 5 x 7 booklets designed to offer strength and help to (young) people in crisis. Each CareNote gently introduces an issue, then encourages a person to take appropriate steps toward resolution. Over 20 million CareNotes have been sold.

Learning to Live Alone

Abbey Press, $.50 each, paper, 8 pp., for counselees

Description Part of the CareNotes series from Abbey Press. CareNotes are short booklets that help readers identify issues and begin the process of seeking resolution. Anecdotal and uplifting. Beautiful photographs grace the covers. Over 20 million CareNotes have been sold in just over five years. Can be used as an alternative to a greeting card or in conjunction with pastoral care visits.

Loneliness *When It's Really Getting to You*

Abbey Press, 1993, $.50 each, paper, 8 pp., for counselees

Description Part of the CareNotes for Teens series from Abbey Press. CareNotes are 5 x 7 booklets designed to offer strength and help to (young) people in crisis. Each CareNote gently introduces an issue, then encourages a person to take appropriate steps toward resolution. Over 20 million CareNotes have been sold.

Loneliness

Ligouri Publications, $.75, paper, 24 pp., for both counselors and counselees

Description Points out that loneliness, for the most part, can be controlled and virtually eliminated with the right mind and attitude. Helps readers form positive attitudes and make the proper effort to keep them.

34. Self-Esteem

Self Esteem *Key to Happiness,* Russell M. Abata

Ligouri Publications, 1994, $3.95, paper, 63 pp., for counselees

Description Takes readers on a journey of self-discovery—helps readers look at themselves as a whole person in the same light as the pearl of great price Jesus speaks of in the Gospels. Covers how others think of you and more importantly how you think of yourself. A gospel-inspired road to self-esteem and true happiness. A great resource for counseling.

Beauty to Last a Lifetime *A Step-by-Step Guide to Inner and Outer Beauty for Teenage Girls,* Ken Abrams and Kim Boyce

Chariot Family Publishing, 1992, $14.99, paper, 208 pp., for counselees

Description Kim Boyce speaks to young teenage girls about inner beauty found through a healthy relationship with Jesus Christ and the importance of proper self-esteem and physical care. Experienced teen devotional author Ken Abrams reinforces Kim's balanced, positive biblical approach to beauty for teens with entertaining stories and text.

Author Kim Boyce is a nationally recognized recording artist and former beauty queen.

The Biblical View of Self-Esteem, Self-Love, and Self-Image Jay E. Adams

Harvest House Publishers, 1986, $6.99, paper, 143 pp., for both counselors and counselees

Description Now well-known biblical counselor and noted author Jay Adams brings much-needed clarification to the area of self-esteem and offers the church and every believer a truly biblical view of self.

Author Dr. Adams is the author of numerous books on Christian counseling. He has served on a seminary faculty (Westminster Theological) and in the pastorate. He is founder of Christian Counseling and Educational Foundation in Laverock, Pa., and visiting professor of practical theology at two seminaries.

Contents *1.* What's going on? *2.* A demand for change *3.* What brought this on? *4.* Let's test it biblically *5.* More about "need" *6.* Love . . . as yourself? *7.* Of infinite worth *8.* Worthy of salvation? *9.* Passages often overlooked *10.* What does the Bible teach? *11.* An accurate self-image *12.* Real life

Self-Care *A Theology of Personal Empowerment and Spiritual Healing,* Ray S. Anderson

Victor Books, 1995, $15.99, paper, 276 pp.

Description In this book, the author sensitively discusses what it means to view the self as God views it, as he created it, and how to experience self-worth, emotional health, and a strong, vital faith in the face of life's pain.

Author Ray S. Anderson is professor of theology and ministry at Fuller Theological Seminary.

Contents *Part 1*—Becoming an empowered self *1.* The growth of the self: a developmental process *2.* The social self: a relational model *3.* The subjective self: a theology of emotion *4.* The responsible self: the wisdom of the heart *5.* The worth of the self: positive self-esteem *Part 2*—Healing the wounded self *6.* Abuse: why people who hate themselves often hurt others *7.* Shame: letting go of emotional self-abuse *8.* Betrayal: an irreparable tear in the fabric of friendship *9.* Tragedy: an invisible tear in the eye of God *10.* Grief: from mourning's night to morning's light *11.* From overcoming to becoming: living on the growing edge

Who Am I? *A Woman's Guide to Self Acceptance,* Elizabeth Baker

Janet Thoma (a division of Thomas Nelson), 1994, $14.99, paper, 256 pp., for counselors

Description A workbook that helps women discover the mystery and beauty of what God uniquely created them to be. Includes worksheets and journaling exercises covering topics such as family background, temperament, memories, choices, and who we are in Christ.

Author Elizabeth Baker is a licensed counselor in private practice with the Center for Church Renewal in Plano, Tex. She holds a master's degree in counseling from Liberty University.

Contents *Part 1:* How did I lose myself? *1.* Symptoms of a lost self *2.* Throwing away the pieces *3.* Does God want me to search for myself? *Part 2:* Genetics, the biological stuff *4.* My link in the family chain *5.* My body, my personality *6.* Did God really choose to make me? *Part 3:* Environment, self molded by time and circumstances *7.* Can I trust my memories? *8.* My life's story *9.* Why did God allow my circumstances? *Part 4:* Choice, self damaged through will and decision *10.* Nonmoral choice: a gift of self-freedom *11.* Moral choice: the stain and the pain *12.* Forgiving others, forgiving myself *Part 5:* Seeing myself through God's eyes *13.* The truth about self *Part 6:* Accepting myself *14.* Answering the question of who I am

Dear Diary *The Secret Feelings of a Junior High Girl,* Pat Baker

Tyndale House Publishers, 1990, $4.95, paper, 142 pp., for counselees

Description Written for adolescent girls, this thoughtful, warmhearted book is an in-depth look at the many physical and emotional changes young girls experience. Comments and questions from junior high girls are sprinkled throughout.

Author Pat Baker is the mother of three daughters, a speaker in churches and at retreats, and the author of several books. She and her husband live in Bolivar, Mo.

Contents Secrets / Secret feelings about yourself / Secret feelings about having periods / Secret feelings about boys / Secret feelings about friends / Secret feelings about teachers / Secret feelings about parents

Love and Accepting Myself David Batty

Turning Point Ministries, Inc., $5.00, spiral, for counselees

Description Part of the Group Studies for New Christians support group materials from Turning Point Ministries. A leader's guide is also available.

You Are Very Special *A Biblical Guide to Self Worth,* Verna Birkey

Fleming H. Revell, 1977, $7.99, paper, 160 pp., for counselees

Description An exciting program that helps women know and follow God's pattern for successful, fulfilled womanhood. A practical, workable plan to help women realize their highest level of God-given potential.

Author Verna Birkey holds a master's degree from the Columbia Seminary and Graduate School of the Bible. She has been involved in teaching workshops since 1969.

Contents Ways you can use this book *1.* You are someone very special *2.* You are deeply loved *3.* You are fully known, yet fully accepted *4.* You are a person in progress *5.* You are God's redeemed child *6.* You are a person of value *7.* You are uniquely designed *8.* You are designed for purpose *9.* You are given an assignment *10.* You are continually sustained *11.* You are accompanied by God *12.* You are God's responsibility *13.* You are under God's constant care

Counseling and Self-Esteem David E. Carlson

Word Publishing, 1988, $15.99, cloth, 267 pp., for counselors

Description The author offers specific ways to build healthy self-esteem without denying our sinfulness or resorting to self-congratulation.

Author David E. Carlson is president of Arlington Counseling Associates in Arlington Heights, Ill.

Contents *1.* Self-esteem: a psycho-theological definition *2.* Self-esteem: a psycho-theological process *3.* Teaching people to build self-esteem: a 12-step process *4.* Teaching people their sensory process in developing self-esteem *5.* Teaching counselors the sensory process: a counseling situation *6.* Teaching parents to build self-esteem in their children *7.* Teaching people to be their own nurturing parents *8.* Teaching counselees to nurture themselves through recognizing and accepting feelings *9.* Teaching counselees to experience God as their nurturing parent *10.* Teaching the church to build self-esteem in its troubled families *11.* Helping people change: the answer is not the solution / *Appendix:* Definitions of self-esteem

The Performance Illusion *Why Do We Try So Hard to Be Liked?* Chap Clark

NavPress, 1993, $10.00, paper, 180 pp., for counselees

Description In *The Performance Illusion,* Chap Clark takes us not through a book but on an adventure. He brings us face-to-face with our most common terror—the terror of feeling we are not performing well enough for our parents, our wives or husbands, our children, our work, and sadly, even our God. In doing so, he exposes the tyranny of expectation that debilitates so many of us. As a result, we spend our lives exhausted by our dizzying activity, paralyzed by our fear of a poor performance. Then, just as we have lost hope, Chap shatters this "illusion of performance" by bringing us face-to-face with God's staggering love—a love that transcends our expectations and frees us from everyone else's.

Author Chap Clark is chairman of the Youth Ministries Department at Denver Seminary, an associate staff of Youth Specialties, and on the Young Life staff in the training department. He is the author of six books.

Contents *Part 1:* What's gone wrong? *1.* "I've been had!" *2.* In the name of love *3.* "If they could see me now!" *4.* Trust and obey *5.* The "blaming" syndrome—"It's not my fault!" *6.* "I did it my way!": the deity of loneliness *7.* What's gone wrong? *Part 2:* What must I do to be saved? *8.* Amazing grace *9.* What does grace look like? *10.* What must I do to be saved? *Part 3:* Performing for God versus responding to God's love *11.* What do I believe? *12.* Responding to God's love in my faith *13.* Responding to God's love in my family *14.* Responding to God's love in my friendships *15.* Responding to God's love in the tasks of life *16.* Carrying on the fight of freedom

Boundaries *When to Say Yes; When to Say No to Take Control of Your Life,* Henry Cloud and John Townsend

Zondervan Publishing House, 1992, $17.99, cloth, 256 pp., for counselees

Description This book presents a biblical treatment of boundaries, identifies how boundaries are developed, and how they become injured. Shows Christian misconceptions of their function and purpose, targets areas in our lives that have boundary conflicts, and gives a program for developing and maintaining healthy, biblical limits. Also available on audio and video.

Authors Dr. Henry Cloud and Dr. John Townsend are codirectors of the Minirth-Meier Clinic West, a group of treatment centers headquartered in Newport Beach, Calif. They both earned their Ph.D. degrees at Rosemead Graduate School of Psychology.

Contents *Part 1:* What are boundaries? *1.* A day in a boundariless life *2.* What does a boundary look like? *3.* Boundary problems *4.* How boundaries are developed *5.* Ten laws of boundaries *6.* Common boundary myths *Part 2:* Boundary conflicts *7.* Boundaries and your family *8.* Boundaries and your friends *9.* Boundaries and your spouse *10.* Boundaries and your children *11.* Boundaries and your work *12.* Boundaries and your self *13.* Boundaries and your God *Part 3:* Developing healthy boundaries

14. Resistance to boundaries *15.* How to measure success with boundaries *16.* A day in the life with boundaries

Curing the Self-Hate Virus Karen Dockrey

New Hope, 1992, $1.95, paper, 22 pp., for counselees

Description Targets teenagers. Gives advice on how to help a friend who has a poor self-image build self-confidence. This booklet is valuable for both friends and yourself in providing a Christian response to coping with the problem. It is a part of the Between Friends series.

Author Karen Dockrey works with youth at Bluegrass Baptist Church in Hendersonville, Tenn.

Self-Esteem Joan Lloyd Guest

InterVarsity Press, 1989 (5th ed.), $.99, paper, 32 pp., for counselees

Description The author examines the issue of self-esteem from Christian and clinical perspectives, discovering how low self-esteem originates in our childhood experiences and affects our adult lives. Suggestions are offered for improving our self-esteem, including gaining a concept of God's grace, seeking internal forgiveness, getting tuned in to one's feelings, and building supportive relationships.

Author Joan Guest (M.A., Northern Illinois University; M.S.W., George Williams College of Social Work, Aurora University) is a licensed social worker and family therapist at a psychiatric hospital. She has experience in both outpatient and inpatient settings and is also the author of *Forgiving Your Parents* and many magazine articles.

You're Better Than You Think Madeline Harris

NavPress, 1990, $3.95, paper, 80 pp., for both counselors and counselees

Description The purpose of this study guide is to allow women to examine the issue of low self-esteem and to offer realistic steps for recovery. Because self-esteem affects every area of life—personal happiness, peace of mind, family and other relationships, rearing children, job performance, and influencing others—the goal of this undertaking is to investigate the causes, effects, and recommendations for possible corrective measures.

Author Madeline Harris (B.A., Colorado Christian University) is the founder and president of Colorado Christian Communicators in Colorado Springs, Colo. As a freelance writer, she has published four books and speaks frequently at women's retreats and conferences.

Contents *Introduction:* The problem with low self-esteem / Crisis point: hidden self-portraits / Evaluation: the big cover-up / Bible lessons *1.* God doesn't carry a big stick *2.* Don't hold yourself hostage *3.* Searching for roots *4.* Oh, those little hurts *5.* One day at a time / Discussion: getting better together / Resources for recovery

Me, Myself, and I *How Far Should We Go in Our Search for Self-Fulfillment?* Archibald D. Hart

Servant Publications/Vine Books, 1992, $10.99, paper, 253 pp., for both counselors and counselees

Description Is it biblical or appropriate to pursue self-esteem? Psychologist Archibald D. Hart charts a biblical and balanced course through the tangled web of self-image, self-esteem, and self-denial to arrive at God's answer: healing, salvation, genuine esteem, and the grace to change for ourselves.

Author Archibald D. Hart is dean of the Graduate School of Psychology at Fuller Theological Seminary.

Contents *Part 1:* The problem with the self *1.* Sick of ourselves? *2.* Stuck with ourselves *3.* Four mistakes Christians make about the self *4.* Beneath the tip of the iceberg *Part 2:* Probing the self *5.* The damage prone self *6.* The disordered self *7.* Sin leads to dysfunction *8.* Made in the image of God *Part 3:* Healing the self *9.* Grace heals evil within *10.* The healthy self *11.* The gospel of self-esteem *12.* Reaching your potential in Christ

Overcoming the Rating Game Paul A. Hauck

Westminster/John Knox Press, 1991, $9.99, paper, 101 pp., for counselees

Description The similarity between inferiority feelings and low self-esteem is emphasized in this book. Diagnostic criteria are listed, three methods for overcoming inferiority are listed, performance-based self evaluations are discouraged, self-discipline is presented as a primary mental health strategy, and assertiveness is discussed.

Author Paul A. Hauck has been a full-time clinical psychologist in private practice in Rock Island, Ill., since 1968. He received his Ph.D. in

1953 from the University of Utah. In 1987 he was honored with the Distinguished Psychologist Award in Illinois. He travels widely, speaking and disseminating his views. He has over 30 articles published as well as 12 books. His writings have sold about 400,000 copies.

Contents *1.* How to recognize low self-esteem *2.* How bad is this pattern? *3.* The first step: never rate yourself or others *4.* The second step: develop performance confidence *5.* The third step: make people respect you *6.* What can you do?

You're Worth More Than You Think Lois Walfrid Johnson

NavPress, 1988, $7.00, paper, 178 pp., for counselees

Description Part of the Let's-Talk-About-It Stories for Kids series from NavPress. A series of short stories followed by discussion questions. Well-written, Christ-centered, and easy for young people to understand. This title deals with the struggles associated with developing appropriate self-esteem.

Author Lois Walfrid Johnson is the author of 19 books. She leads seminars and retreats and speaks at churches and conferences throughout the United States.

She Is Worthy *Encounters With Biblical Women,* Marjorie L. Kimbrough

Abingdon Press, 1995, $9.95, paper, 144 pp.

Description Examines women of the Bible who in the author's view exhibit positive self-esteem. To inspire today's Christian woman, Kimbrough shows how many biblical women were able to reach beyond the limits of their environment to touch the hand of God.

Author Marjorie L. Kimbrough is an instructor in religion and philosophy at Clark Atlanta University.

Contents *1.* Eve *2.* Sarah *3.* Leah *4.* Jochebed *5.* Miriam *6.* Deborah *7.* Samson's mother *8.* Ruth *9.* Hannah *10.* Abigail *11.* The woman of Abel *12.* The widow of Zarephath *13.* The widow with inexhaustible oil *14.* The Shunamite woman *15.* Naaman's maid *16.* Huldah *17.* Jehoshabeath *18.* Esther *19.* Judith *20.* Susana *21.* The Canaanite woman *22.* Pilate's wife *23.* The woman with the issue of blood *24.* The widow who gave all *25.* Elizabeth *26.* Mary *27.* Anna *28.* The anointing woman *29.* Mary of Bethany *30.* Martha *31.* The persistent widow *32.* Mary Magdalene *33.* Dorcas *34.* Mary, John Mark's mother *35.* Lydia *36.* Priscilla *37.* Phoebe/ *Conclusion*

Responsible Christian Assertiveness

Becoming the Person God Wants You to Be,
David Mathison

Narramore Christian Foundation, $19.99, video,
for counselees

Description Explains successful ways of handling
confrontations and differences. This frees people
to have good and honest relationships with each
other.

Author Dr. David Mathison is a licensed psychologist associated with the Narramore Christian
Foundation—a charitable, nonprofit educational,
training, and counseling organization ministering primarily to the Christian community.

Christ Esteem *Where the Search for Self-Esteem Ends,* Don Matzat

Harvest House Publishers, 1990, $7.99, paper,
207 pp., for counselees

Description Going against the tide of modern psychology, Matzat says to forget self-esteem and
instead learn to love, honor, and esteem Christ
Jesus.

Author Don Matzat, a pastor of 25 years, is currently pastor at Messiah Lutheran Church in St.
Louis, Mo. He is the author of two other books
and an experienced speaker who has appeared
on many national radio and television shows.

Contents *1.* A challenging generation *2.* An irrelevant
gospel? *3.* Knowing yourself *4.* The right diagnosis *5.* Identified with Adam *6.* Turning away from self *7.* Identified
with Christ *8.* Everything in Christ *9.* The conflict *10.* Looking unto Jesus *11.* Confessing the truth *12.* Rejoice in the
Lord *13.* Jesus is the life! *14.* Christians under construction *15.* The identity of the Christian community

Skin Deep *The Powerful Link between Your Body Image and Your Self Esteem,* Mary Ann Mayo

Servant Publications/Vine Books, 1992, $14.99,
cloth, 226 pp., for both counselors and counselees

Description Confronts unrealistic expectations
people tend to have regarding body image. Invites readers to look at what has shaped their attitude toward their body and how this attitude
was nurtured in childhood, confirmed in early
social interactions, circumscribed by certain re-

ligious teachings, and later reinforced by every
area of adult life.

Author Mary Ann Mayo is a marriage, family, and
child therapist and the author of a number of
books.

Contents *Part 1:* This sacred garment *1.* Beauty is in
the eye of the beholder *2.* What's hot, what's not *3.* The
illusive ideal *Part 2:* Mirror, mirror, on the wall *4.* Sex appeal *5.* Gender in question *6.* The battle of the bulge *7.* No
perfect couple *Part 3:* Body image redefined *8.* Accepting
who we are *9.* Painful lessons *10.* The overlooked answer

Building Your Self Image Josh McDowell

Tyndale House Publishers, 1984, $4.99, paper,
19 pp., for counselees

Description Practical answers to help readers overcome their fears, anxieties, and lack of self-
confidence. This book will show them how God's
higher image of who they are can take root in
their heart and mind.

Author Josh McDowell is a popular speaker and
author of over 30 best-selling books. He finished
graduate school magna cum laude with degrees
in languages and theology.

Contents *1.* Self-image: what is it? *2.* A new name for
a biblical concept *3.* Results of a poor self-image *4.* How
you decided who you are *5.* Growing up with mom and
dad *6.* Stories of childhood *7.* The case of the vanishing
father *8.* Self-image: resting on a three-legged stool *9.* Restructuring the foundation *10.* A new sense of belonging
11. A new sense of worthiness *12.* A new sense of competence *13.* The process of re-parenting *14.* Moving toward his image *15.* Self-image with a purpose

Search for Significance Robert S. McGee

LifeWay, 1992, $9.95, paper, 223 pp., for both
counselors and counselees

Description Part of the LifeWay Support Group
Ministry commissioned by the Southern Baptist
Convention. This title is for "approval addicts,"
"self-blamers," the "perpetually shamed," and
those caught in "performance traps." Designed
for individual and discovery-group study.
The book provides self-paced, interactive study
and resources for the 12 weekly sessions. A
leader's guide is also available ($4.95) that pro-
vides administrative guidance and suggested activities for the weekly discovery-group sessions.

Author Robert McGee is founder and president of
Rapha, a health care organization that provides
in-hospital and outpatient care, with a Christ-
centered perspective, for adults and adolescents

suffering from psychiatric and substance abuse problems.

Contents About the author / *Introduction* / *Unit 1:* Beginning the search *Unit 2:* The performance trap *Unit 3:* Justification *Unit 4:* Approval addict *Unit 5:* Reconciliation *Unit 6:* The blame game *Unit 7:* Propitiation *Unit 8:* Shame *Unit 9:* Major obstacles in growth *Unit 10:* Our source of change *Unit 11:* Renewing our minds *Unit 12:* The trip in

The Search for Significance Robert S. McGee and Dawson McAllister

Word Publishing, 1993 (13th printing), $9.99/12.99, paper, 102/492 pp., for both counselors and counselees

Description Dealing with the foundational principles of biblically based self-esteem, this book teaches us how to base our self-worth upon the love, forgiveness, and acceptance that comes through Jesus Christ. Discover why the desperate quest for personal success, status, beauty, and wealth does not bring lasting happiness. Learn how to be intense and ambitious about the right things, Christ and his cause, and how to be free to enjoy his love. Learn through self-analysis exercises to focus your attention on Christ and not yourself. Gain new skills for getting off the performance treadmill.

Author Robert S. McGee is a professional counselor and lecturer. He is also the founder and president of Rapha, a nationally recognized health care organization that provides in-hospital psychiatric care and substance abuse treatment, from a Christian perspective, in hospitals and treatment centers across the United States.

Contents *1.* Turning on the light *2.* Our search for significance *3.* The origin of the search *4.* The saving solution vs. Satan's stones *5.* The process of hope and healing *6.* The performance trap *7.* Approval addict *8.* The blame game *9.* Shame *10.* Obstacles to growth *11.* The Holy Spirit: our source of change *12.* Renewing the mind *13.* The weapons of our warfare *14.* Guilt vs. conviction *15.* The search concluded

The Search for Significance Devotional Robert S. McGee

Rapha Resources, $8.99, paper, for counselees

Description A 90-day guide with a different topic for every day. Reflection questions and weekly journals to help you apply these devotions to your life.

Author Robert McGee is founder and president of Rapha, a health care organization that provides in-hospital and outpatient care, with a Christ-centered perspective, for adults and adolescents suffering from psychiatric and substance abuse problems.

Don't Let the Jerks Get the Best of You
Advice for Dealing with Impossible People, Paul D. Meier

Janet Thoma (a division of Thomas Nelson), 1993, $16.99, cloth, 256 pp., for counselees

Description A respected psychologist teaches the fine art of psychological self-defense with down-to-earth humor and personal anecdotes about "jerkiness" or the ability to be blindly selfish in our dealings with other human beings.

Author Paul Meier received an M.A. from the University of Arkansas College of Medicine and completed his psychiatry residency at Duke University. He also received an M.A. in biblical studies from Dallas Theological Seminary. Dr. Meier is cofounder of the national chain of Minirth-Meier Clinics and has coauthored more than 30 books.

Contents *Part 1:* Welcome to a world of jerks—and masochists *1.* It's a jungle out there, and it's full of jerks *2.* What does a first degree jerk look like? *3.* Careful! Second-degree jerks can be anywhere *4.* Society's sociopaths, nth degree jerks *5.* But why are we such pushovers for the predatory jerks? *Part 2:* Six steps out of masochism to maturity *6.* Meet the enemy, he is definitely us *7.* Are mom and dad still parenting you? *8.* Why not sing your own song? *9.* You can't stuff your anger forever *10.* Why keep running the rat race? *11.* Moving on toward maturity

Building a Healthy Self Concept Frank B. Minirth and Paul D. Meier

Christian Family Video, 1991, $19.95, video, 60 minutes, for counselees

Description Part of the Minirth-Meier Church Counseling Video Library. The series is designed to enhance the counseling process as clients take the videos home for viewing. This title outlines factors for developing a healthy and balanced self-concept, from infancy through adulthood.

Authors Doctors Minirth and Meier have gained national prominence for their successful blending of biblical principles with proven clinical and medical treatment. They are nationally recognized authors of over 60 biblically based books on common psychological issues with over three million in copies in print.

Don't Put a Period Where God Put a Comma *Self-Esteem for Christians,* Nell W. Mohney

Abingdon Press, 1993, $7.50, paper, for counselees

Description Biblically based suggestions for developing a positive self-image, with helpful exercises and questions for reflection.

Self-Image James "Trip" Moore

NavPress, 1992, $5.00, paper, 64 pp., for counselees

Description In this IBC discussion guide, you'll look at what self-image is really all about, including: stories from your past that emotionally fuel your self-image, what you get out of a poor self-image that keeps you clinging to it, the unhealthy control that self-image can exert over your daily life, and how to pursue change that goes deeper than telling yourself you're OK.

Author James "Trip" Moore has a full-time counseling ministry in Quebec City, Canada. He also gives conferences and workshops in French and English and has spoken in the United States, Canada, and Europe on the topics of relationships and personal growth.

Contents *Session 1:* Fleeing from anguish—how self-image develops *Session 2:* A useful tool—how not liking myself works for me *Session 3:* A relational style—the result of a bad self-image *Session 4:* The path to change *Session 5:* The process of change / *Help for leaders*

A New Biblical Self-Image Clyde M. Narramore

Narramore Christian Foundation, $19.99, video, 60 minutes, for counselees

Description We all develop a self-image while growing up. However, a born-again Christian can have a new biblically based self image.

Author Dr. Clyde M. Narramore is a licensed psychologist and the president and founder of the Narramore Christian Foundation—a charitable, nonprofit educational, training, and counseling organization ministering primarily to the Christian community. He is also the founder of the Rosemead School of Psychology and author of 29 books.

Three Cheers for Big Ears Mary Rose Pearson

Tyndale House Publishers, 1992, $2.99, paper, 48 pp., for counselees

Description Children will grasp important lessons about accepting themselves and others in *Three Cheers for Big Ears.* When the neighborhood children ridicule Joshua about his big ears, he begins to wonder why God made him that way. But Joshua soon discovers that God can use him just the way he is—it's what he is like on the inside that counts. With sensitivity and insight, this book helps children learn to be thankful for who they are, and it reminds us all that God wants us to be kind to everyone—even those who are unkind to us.

Author Mary Rose Pearson has taught children in church classes for over 56 years. She has authored 12 books for ministry to children.

God's Remedy for Rejection Derek Prince

Creation House, 1993, $3.99, paper, 62 pp., for counselees

Description Prince proposes that rejection is at the root of many emotional and behavioral problems. Reconciliation with others and God is the answer to the wounds caused by rejection. Strong emphasis on Scripture throughout.

Author Dr. Derek Prince is recognized internationally as one of the leading Bible expositors of our time. His daily radio broadcast reaches more than half the globe, with translations into Arabic, five Chinese languages, Spanish, Russian, Mongolian, and Tongan.

Contents *1.* The nature of rejection *2.* Causes of rejection *3.* Betrayal and shame *4.* Results of rejection *5.* The ultimate rejection *6.* How to apply the remedy *7.* Acceptance among God's people *8.* Divine love

When You Feel Insecure John P. Reed

Westminster/John Knox Press, 1994, $9.99, paper, 131 pp., for counselees

Description Reed offers help to those who feel insecure about their lives and shows how they can identify and rid themselves of destructive behavior that causes insecurity.

Author John P. Reed is executive director of the Kilgore Samaritan Counseling Center in Louisville, Ky. He is a former church pastor and seminary instructor.

Contents *1.* Where are you Norman Rockwell? *2.* Fear and the danger of attachment *3.* The high cost of defense *4.* Opening the way to security *5.* Trust and the security of attachment *6.* The secure life

Emotional Dependency Lori Rentzel

InterVarsity Press, 1990, $.99, paper, 31 pp., for counselees

Description With anecdotes, spiritual counsel, and readable clinical information, the author traces the roots of emotional dependency and outlines steps to severance of unhealthy relationships.

Recovery from Distorted Images of Self
Dale Ryan and Juanita Ryan

InterVarsity Press, 1992, $3.95, paper, 60 pp., for both counselors and counselees

Description This Bible study is part of a series of 16 volumes on various recovery themes. Each book contains studies on six biblical texts. Leader's notes are provided for group study.

Authors Dale Ryan is the executive director of the Recovery Partnership, the parent organization to the National Association for Christian Recovery. Juanita Ryan is a counselor in private practice in Hacienda Heights, Calif.

Contents *1.* Seeing myself as loved *2.* Seeing myself as valued *3.* Seeing myself as capable *4.* Seeing myself as wonderfully made *5.* Seeing myself as repairable *6.* Seeing myself as human / *Leader's notes*

Stand Tall *Learning How to Really Love Yourself,* Bill Sanders

Fleming H. Revell, 1992, $7.99, paper, 164 pp., for counselees

Description Written specifically for teenagers. Within the pages of *Stand Tall* is counsel that will provide the hope and encouragement young people need to overcome negative thoughts and influences. Bill Sanders offers sure-fire strategies for building self-confidence, changing what they don't like about themselves, and appreciating their God-given uniqueness. His biblically based counsel is supported by a number of interesting, practical tools, including Bible study questions, self-evaluation quizzes, guidelines for keeping a journal, and checklists.

Author Bill Sanders continues to make a dynamic impact on the lives of young people through his nationwide outreach and popular books, including *Life, Sex, and Everything in Between* and two devotionals for guys and girls: *Outtakes* and *Goal Posts.* He has also written *School Daze* for parents and teachers.

Contents *Part 1:* What it means to have self-esteem *1.* Who am I—really? *2.* What influences self-esteem? *3.* Improving on what you've got *Part 2:* Building on your house of self-esteem *4.* Building blocks of self-esteem *5.* Me, wise? I'm too dumb! *6.* What fills my mental bucket? *7.* How does my stature measure up? *8.* Looking at myself from the inside out *9.* Am I what I do? *10.* What's in my name? *11.* God who? *12.* If God is so big, why am I so bad? *13.* Living inside a family *14.* What's it like in my family? *15.* Mean what you say communication *16.* Looking good, feeling good

Sometimes I Don't Like Myself *Repairing a Damaged Self-Image,* Candice Schap

Pacific Press, 1992, $7.95, paper, 96 pp., for counselees

Description An intensely personal look into the author's pursuit of a love and respect she feared would never be hers—and how she found it. With honesty and vulnerability, she explores reasons we suffer from poor self-esteem; how to overcome insecurity; the liberating discovery of God's unconditional acceptance and love; and how to see ourselves as we really are—and like what we see. The value of the book is in its personal approach, written for those who think they are alone in the world in their feelings of rejections and inadequacy.

Author Homemaker and mother of four. Speaker for women's groups and retreats of all denominations, Bible study and workshop leader, approved speaker for the Christian Women's Clubs evangelistic outreach of Stonecroft Ministries.

Contents *1.* The not-good-enoughs *2.* Knowing the enemy *3.* The tunnel *4.* Fear of rejection *5.* Lessons along the way *6.* Hurting others *7.* Pretending *8.* Voices

Overcoming Shyness M. Blaine Smith

InterVarsity Press, 1993, $9.99, paper, 285 pp., for counselees

Description Blaine Smith has learned a lot about how to handle his shyness. Now he shares his insights and counsel with others who struggle with the pain of shyness and who see it as holding them back socially, in the workplace—and even spiritually. This very honest and practical book will help you make your shyness work for you rather than against you. It will give you courage to take new steps of assertiveness that don't violate your basic personality. And it will show you what it means to trust God at the most personal level.

Author M. Blaine Smith, a Presbyterian resource pastor, is director of Nehemiah Ministries. He is author of several books. He holds the doctor of ministry degree from Fuller Theological Seminary.

Contents *Part 1:* Understanding shyness *1.* A common experience *2.* The roots of shyness *3.* The benefits of shyness *4.* The drawback of shyness—catastrophizing *Part 2:* Taking control—one-half step at a time *5.* Staring fear down *6.* Breaking the panic cycle *7.* Praying for courage *8.* Asking for help *Part 3:* Awakening your social life *9.* Seeing the possibilities *10.* Putting yourself in the right context *11.* Warming up to conversation *12.* Knowing what to say *Part 4:* Asserting yourself—and your life *13.* Faith and assertiveness *14.* Taking initiative *15.* Learning optimism / *Appendixes A.* Facing the crowd—tips for confronting an audience *B.* Playing a role—and staying whole—overcoming impostor feelings

Design for Wholeness *Dealing with Anger, Learning to Forgive, Building Self-Esteem,* Loughlan Sofield et al.

Ave Maria Press, 1990, $6.95, paper, 152 pp., for counselees

Description In a clear and readable style the authors present a model and case study for understanding and dealing with anger; offer a thorough discussion of forgiveness as the most effective way to deal with anger; propose a model for understanding and increasing self-esteem that is fundamental to effective, life-giving relationships; and promote dialogue as a way for people to resolve their problems with others and more thoroughly live their Christian lives to the fullest.

Authors Brother Loughlan Sofield, S.T., is senior editor of *Human Development* magazine and conducts workshops around the world on topics of ministry and psychology. He is the author of several books. Coauthor Sister Carroll Juliano, S.H.C.J., is director of Life Planning for Ministry in Summit, N.J., and has conducted workshops in North America, Europe, and Africa on life planning, ministry, and personal development. Coauthor Sister Rosine Hammett, C.S.C., Ph.D., is codirector of the Consultation Center for the Congregation of the Holy Cross. As a therapist

and lecturer, communications consultant, and facilitator of personal growth groups, she has worked with individuals all over the world.

Contents *1.* Anger: a threat to life *2.* Anger: a case study *3.* Forgiveness: new life *4.* Self-esteem: the path to life *5.* Dialogue: the key to growth

Building Self-Esteem *A Workbook for Teens,* Jerome Trahey

Resource Publications, Inc., 1992, $14.95, paper, 167 pp., for counselees

Description An activity-oriented book that encourages the development of positive self-esteem.

Author Jerome Trahey has done social work with the elderly, worked as a counselor, and is a former Irish Christian Brother. His degrees are in psychology and ministry.

Contents *1.* Identity: acceptance and development *2.* Barriers to self-esteem: construction and destruction *3.* Jesus: human, teenager, companion *4.* Values formation: choices and decision making *5.* Self-esteem and morality: genuineness and commitment

Becoming Your Own Best Friend *How to Love, Affirm, and Support Yourself,* Thomas A. Whiteman and Randy Petersen

Oliver Nelson (a division of Thomas Nelson), 1994, $12.99, cloth, 192 pp., for counselees

Description Shows how to win the battle over low self-esteem by overcoming the hurdles thrown in our way by our parents, our relationships, and even our churches. Does not merely offer pep talks or pop culture strategies to make you feel better. Instead it shows precisely what you must understand and do to empower your life by achieving a truly balanced, healthy self-esteem—one solidly based on how God sees you.

Authors Thomas Whiteman is the president of FreshStart Seminars and director of Life Counseling Services in Pennsylvania. Randy Petersen is a freelance writer.

Contents *1.* Best friends *2.* The balancing act *3.* Going slowly *4.* Taking stock of yourself *5.* Finding the villains *6.* Confronting the villains *7.* Self-image and God-image *8.* You can beat the system *9.* Exercising your gifts *10.* The human touch *11.* Keeping your balance

Does God Really Love Me? *Turning God's Love Loose in Your Life,* Earl D. Wilson

InterVarsity Press, 1986, $4.99, paper, 96 pp., for counselees

Description Helping readers overcome feelings of guilt, inferiority, and fear, Earl D. Wilson shows how to recognize and appreciate God's love.

Author Earl D. Wilson (Ph.D., University of Oregon) is associate professor of clinical and counseling psychology at Western Conservative Baptist Seminary and director of Lake Psychological and Counseling Services in Oregon.

Contents *1.* Why all this talk about love? *2.* God's extravagant love *3.* Savoring: the secret to feeling loved *4.* A sinner looks at love *5.* Understanding the source of love *6.* Love as a lifestyle *7.* Does love have a price tag? *8.* Why does God love us anyway?

Body Image *When You Don't Like the Way You Look*

Abbey Press, 1993, $.50 each, paper, 8 pp., for counselees

Description Part of the CareNotes for Teens series from Abbey Press. CareNotes are 5 x 7 booklets designed to offer strength and help to (young) people in crisis. Each CareNote gently introduces an issue, then encourages a person to take appropriate steps toward resolution. Over 20 million CareNotes have been sold.

Building Up Your Self-Esteem

Abbey Press, 1994, $.50 each, paper, 8 pp., for counselees

Description Part of the New CareSteps series from Abbey Press. Each CareStep pamphlet (three panel) is filled with insightful advice and quotes from respected leaders in the helping professions. Very useful during the early stages of recovery. The underlying message in all CareSteps pamphlets is the emphasis on using all one's resources—emotional, physical, mental, social, and spiritual—to cope with life's biggest challenges. This title emphasizes speaking well of oneself, talking to a friend, finding a way to measure progress, and considering outside support.

Edge TV—Body Image

NavPress, 1992, $24.95, video with leader's guide, 60 minutes, for both counselors and counselees

Description For youth workers who want to steer their group away from "church appropriate" discussions and get them talking about what's really going on in their lives. *Edge TV* (a video magazine for church youth groups) is the place to start. Created in partnership with Youth Specialties and IMS Productions, each episode of *Edge TV* is packed with high energy visuals, no-holds-barred drama, startling interviews, Christian music videos, captivating humor—and an honest approach to Jesus Christ that will get kids asking some very interesting questions.

35. Sexual Abuse

Sexual Abuse of Children—Prevention/Response

Child Sexual Abuse *A Handbook for Clergy and Church Members,* Lee W. Carlson

Judson Press, 1992, $6.95, paper, for counselors

Description How churches can respond to the victims of child abuse, the offenders, and their families. A holistic approach of repentance, forgiveness, and reconciliation are the goals of this healing ministry. Discusses signs of abuse, offender characteristics, reporting procedures, professional intervention, and education.

Sexual Abuse Prevention *A Study for Teenagers,* Marie M. Fortune

The Pilgrim Press, 1986 (3d printing), $6.95, paper, 32 pp., for counselees

Description A five-session course of study that has been tested with approximately 800 adolescents and over 80 adult leaders and parents, representing a wide cross-section of the population.

Author Marie Marshall Fortune is an ordained minister of the United Church of Christ. She is founder and director of the Center for Prevention of Sexual and Domestic Violence.

Sexual Abuse in Christian Homes and Churches Carolyn Holderread Heggen

Herald Press, 1993, $9.95, paper, 208 pp., for both counselors and counselees

Description Fills an important gap in sexual abuse literature. It examines the reality of sexual abuse in Christian homes and churches. An important book for those who want to understand the complex dynamics of abuse and want to work to end it. Explains the meaning of abuse, the resultant issues for survivors, families, and congregations. Includes practical ways in which congregations can respond to victims and perpetrators. It offers helpful suggestions on ways Christians can

work to prevent abuse and encourage the development of healthy sexual attitudes and behaviors among individuals and congregations.

Author Dr. Heggen is a psychotherapist, a university professor, and a pastoral elder in her congregation. Her clinical practice has primarily been with Christian victims and perpetrators of sexual abuse. She has published numerous articles about sexual abuse and about the relationship between religious beliefs and mental health.

Contents *1.* Sexual abuse: what it is and what to do about it *2.* The victim and resultant issues *3.* Denial, incidence, and factors related to abuse *4.* The perpetrator *5.* Religious beliefs and abuse *6.* Pastoral abuse *7.* Repentance, restitution, forgiveness, and reconciliation *8.* Congregational responses to abuse *9.* Making worship sensitive to survivors *10.* Preventing sexual abuse *11.* Congregational role in developing healthy sexuality

Stolen Childhood *What You Need to Know about Sexual Abuse,* Alice Huskey

InterVarsity Press, 1990, $8.99, paper, 181 pp., for both counselors and counselees

Description The author tells her own story and provides much needed information and reasoned counsel for all who are concerned about child sexual abuse.

Author Alice Huskey has been helping people with abusive backgrounds for many years. She works as a charge nurse on the adolescent psychiatric unit of Good Samaritan Hospital in Downer's Grove, Ill. Her work has also appeared in numerous magazines.

Contents *1.* A painful introduction *2.* What is sexual abuse? *3.* Scapegoats for abuse *4.* The climate for abuse *5.* Characteristics of abusers *6.* Characteristics of the abused *7.* The dilemma of disclosure *8.* The other victims *9.* Healing for the abused *10.* Healing for abusers and families *11.* What you can do / *Appendix:* Further reflections for those who have been abused

Sexual Abuse *Let's Talk about It,* Margaret O. Hyde

Westminster/John Knox Press, 1984, $10.00, cloth, for counselors

Description Designed to be read to children. Margaret O. Hyde deals with child abuse, suicide, drug abuse, runaways, and many other subjects in a clear, concise manner. She helps children recognize what sexual abuse is, where to go for help, and not to be ashamed to speak of it.

Author Margaret O. Hyde is author of many sensitive books about problems that affect young people.

Contents *1.* What is sexual abuse? *2.* Touching can be fun *3.* Some kinds of secrets should be told *4.* Who would do such a thing *5.* Binny's story *6.* Bob's secret *7.* When the secret is told *8.* Helping prevent sexual abuse

Sins of the Father *The Story of a Predatory Child Molester & the People Who Wouldn't Believe It,* Marianne Morris

Pacific Press, 1993, $9.95, paper, 224 pp., for both counselors and counselees

Description Marianne Morris (a pen name) chose to write anonymously about the devastating effects of child molestation in her family. This story was written with a desire to appeal to Christians to protect children from this silent plague.

Preventing Child Sexual Abuse *Ages 5–8,* Kathryn Goering Reid

The Pilgrim Press, 1994, $11.95, paper, 160 pp., for counselors

Description A companion guide to the book of *Preventing Child Sexual Abuse—Ages 9–12.* This project takes the message to a younger audience. This curriculum can help parents and those who work with children to deal with this difficult issue in the context of a religious education program. It draws on excellent secular materials while using basic biblical resources and confronts misinterpretations of Scripture that have been used to support abusive relationships.

Author Kathryn Goering Reid is pastor of Austin Mennonite Church and a curriculum writer for her denomination.

Preventing Child Sexual Abuse—Ages 9–12 Kathryn G. Reid and Marie M. Fortune

The Pilgrim Press, 1989, $9.95, paper, 125 pp., for counselors

Description This course provides information about sexual abuse and prevention to children between the ages of 9 and 12 (grades 4–6) in the context of a religious education program. The 13 sessions fit into a typical Sunday morning church school program but can also be used for summer vacation church school, after school programs, camping programs, and a variety of other children's group events.

Authors The Rev. Kathryn Goering Reid is an ordained minister in the Church of the Brethren and is currently serving at the Epworth United Methodist church in Berkeley, Calif. Marie Marshall Fortune is an ordained minister of the United Church of Christ. She is founder and director of the Center for Prevention of Sexual and Domestic Violence.

Contents *Introduction* (purpose, theology and sexual abuse prevention) / Planning for this course *1.* Each child is a child of God *2.* God's gift of feelings *3.* The rights of children *4.* God wants you to be safe *5.* Good touch/bad touch/confusing touch *6.* God cares about us *7.* What about the family *8.* Saying "no!" *9.* No more secrets *10.* Justice and forgiveness: responding to harm *11.* Peer pressure *12.* Advertising/males and females in media *13.* Wrapping it up with a positive self-image / *Appendix A:* Sexual abuse fact sheet *Appendix B:* Indicators of sexual abuse in children *Appendix C:* How to help a child victim of sexual abuse *Appendix D:* Reporting child sexual abuse *Appendix E:* What happens when a report is made *Appendix F:* Reporting child abuse: an ethical mandate for ministry / *Resources on sexual violence*

Facing the Brokenness *Meditations for Parents of Sexually Abused Children,* K. C. Ridings

Herald Press, 1991, $8.95, paper, 196 pp., for counselees

Description Parents of sexually abused children will find this devotional guide/workbook a source of strength and hope for dealing with the emotional pain of sexual abuse. Thirty-one days' worth of interactive questions, anecdotes, and Scripture readings address the various aspects of coping with this difficult problem.

Author K. C. Ridings lives with her husband and children in Mesa, Ariz. She is a freelance writer and speaks on the topic of sexual abuse.

Do You Have a Secret? *How to Get Help for Scary Secrets,* Pamela Russel and Beth Stone

CompCare Publishers, $6.95, paper, for counselees

Description This book helps adults talk with children about the difficulty of sexual abuse. Youngsters are encouraged to share their scary secrets and find the help they have been afraid to ask for. It helps kids know they are not the only ones who have experienced abuse. Without scaring a child who is not a victim, the book also gives valuable information every child needs in order to talk about things that are troubling.

I Can't Talk about It *A Child's Book about Sexual Abuse,* Doris Sandford and Graci Evans

Gold 'n' Honey Books (Questar), 1993, $7.99, cloth, 24 pp., for counselees

Description Part of the Hurts of Childhood series from Gold 'n' Honey. The series was developed for children ages 5–11 who have experienced deep and tragic hurts. The books deal gently and compassionately with children's delicate feelings when they're forced to handle burdens far too big for them to carry.

Something Must Be Wrong with Me *A Boy's Book about Sexual Abuse,* Doris Sandford and Graci Evans

Gold 'n' Honey Books (Questar), 1993, $7.99, cloth, 24 pp., for counselees

Description Part of the Hurts of Childhood series from Gold 'n' Honey. The series was developed for children ages 5–11 who have experienced deep and tragic hurts. The books deal gently and compassionately with children's delicate feelings when they're forced to handle burdens far too big for them to carry.

Sexual Misconduct in the Local Church *A Guide to Prevention and Healing*

The Life in Jesus Community, 1994, $100.00, video, 8 hours, 4 VHS, for counselors

Description An eight-hour video series with guidebook. The threefold purpose of the series is to (1) inform and aid the local church and church school in understanding the issues associated with sexual abuse and sexual harassment, (2) suggest ways churches can provide ongoing pastoral care for both victims and perpetrators, and (3) provide a plan by which congregations can demonstrate to insurance carriers their intent to act responsibly on this issue and thereby avoid needless expensive litigation.

Author This series is produced by the Life in Jesus Community, Rev. Philip C. Zampino (rector) and the Christian Counseling Center of Annapolis (Md.), Inc. Featured presenters include three clergy members, six Christian therapists, and one Christian attorney representing various denominations.

Contents Topics included in the series include: biblical and historical overview of sexual misconduct, legal issues, personal boundaries, clinical profile and treatment of sexual abusers, psychological impact on victims of sexual abuse, treatment and healing of children and adult victims, pastoral concerns, interviews with victims at various stages of healing, individual and corporate healing and restoration

Adult Recovery from Childhood Sexual Abuse

The Wounded Heart *Hope for Adult Victims of Childhood Sexual Abuse,* Dan B. Allender

NavPress, 1992 (6th printing), $9.99, paper, 255 pp., for both counselors and counselees

Description One of the most widely recognized works on recovery from sexual abuse. Going well beyond the solutions discussed in other books, *The Wounded Heart* is a next step for those who have begun the healing process and a safe place to start for others. Reaches deep into the wounded heart of someone you know, exploring the secret lament of the soul damaged by sexual abuse—and laying hold of the hope buried there by the one whose unstained image we all bear. A companion workbook for personal or group use is also available.

Author Dr. Dan B. Allender (M.Div., Westminster Theological Seminary; Ph.D., Michigan State University) teaches in the Biblical Counseling Department at Colorado Christian University. He travels extensively in his seminar ministry and teaches counselor training courses.

Contents *Part 1:* The dynamics of abuse *1.* The reality of a war: facing the battle *2.* The enemy: sin and shame *3.* Deflection: the clash with contempt *4.* The war zone: strategies for abuse *Part 2:* The damage of abuse *5.* Powerlessness *6.* Betrayal *7.* Ambivalence *8.* Secondary symptoms *9.* Style of relating *Part 3:* Prerequisites for growth *10.* The unlikely route to joy *11.* Honesty *12.* Repentance *13.* Bold love

The Wounded Heart—A Companion Workbook for Personal or Group Use
Hope for Adult Victims of Childhood Sexual Abuse, Dan B. Allender

NavPress, 1992 (3d printing), $14.99, paper, 189 pp., for both counselors and counselees

Description A companion guide to the book of the same name. Designed to be used either individually or in a group format. Includes helpful guidelines, worksheets, and instructions for the learner and leader. Special sections for men and ideas for groups.

Author Dr. Dan B. Allender (M.Div., Westminster Theological Seminary; Ph.D., Michigan State University) teaches in the Biblical Counseling Department at Colorado Christian University. He travels extensively in his seminar ministry and teaches counselor training courses.

Haunted Marriage *Overcoming the Ghosts of Your Spouse's Childhood Abuse,* Clark E. Barshinger, Lojan E. LaRowe, and Andreas Tapia

InterVarsity Press, 1995, $10.99, paper, 192 pp.

Description There are many books that describe how to find healing from past sexual abuse. Here is one of the first to identify the emotional, spiritual, and practical challenges faced by a man or woman whose spouse (or fiancé) has been abused.

Authors Clark Barshinger, Ph.D., and Lojan LaRowe, Ph.D., a husband–wife team are psychotherapists at Cherry Hill Counseling Center in Lake Zurich, Ill. They have 25 years of experience counseling individuals, married couples, and families. Andreas Tapia is senior news writer for *Christianity Today.*

Contents *Section 1*—Walking on eggshells (or why does she cry every time we make love?) *1.* Where did all this pain come from? *Section 2*—Becoming a responsive spouse *2.* The big picture *3.* Committing (emotionally, spiritually, financially) to the healing process *4.* Shadow boxing *5.* Active listening and careful feedback *6.* Protecting your turf sensitively *7.* When to act, when to wait *8.* Finding support *9.* The place of faith: seeing God in a new way *Section 3*—Paying for the sins of the father *10.* Sex *11.* Relating to family and friends *12.* Children and parenting tasks *13.* Managing workplace and home responsibilities in the midst of emotional chaos *14.* Divorce and separation—how to survive without leaving *Section 4*—Thriving alone and together *15.* Getting back to basics *16.* Power

marriage / *Appendixes: A.* Checklist for symptoms of abuse in a spouse's life *B.* Therapy techniques *C.* False memory movement

What to Do When You Find Out Your Wife Was Sexually Abused John Courtright and Sid Rogers

Zondervan Publishing House, 1994, $10.99, paper, 160 pp., for counselees

Description This book is written for the husbands of sexual abuse victims—men who are trying to cope with the fear, pain, confusion, and anger in living with a woman who is recovering from past sexual abuse.

Authors John Courtright is a sales director for Anderson Consulting. Dr. Sid Rogers is pastor of Grace Evangelical Free Church and adjunct professor at Talbot School of Theology. Both have dealt with past sexual abuse in their own marriages and now lead seminars for husbands of sexual abuse victims.

Contents *1.* When the past crashes into the present *2.* Early warning signs *3.* Ripples of chaos in a life of calm *4.* When her crisis becomes your crisis *5.* Have I become the enemy? *6.* Finding the emerald city *7.* A friend for all seasons *8.* Understanding the recovery process *9.* "You are the man" *10.* Playing your position *11.* Communicating terms of peace *12.* Doing what comes naturally

A House Divided *The Secret Betrayal—Incest,* Katherine Edwards

Zondervan Publishing House, 1990, $8.99, paper, 160 pp., for counselees

Description Author-victim Katherine Edwards gives us a first-person account of incest, its trauma, and its tragedy as well as its lingering effects. She offers hope for victims of incest as well as a clear warning for us all. The book is based on her award-winning story from *Campus Life* magazine.

Released to Love *Healing the Barriers That Hinder Sexual Intimacy and Fulfillment,* Alfred H. Ells

Oliver Nelson (a division of Thomas Nelson), 1994, $10.99, paper, 228 pp., for both counselors and counselees

Description Offers hope to those who are dealing with the effects of past or present sexual abuse, compulsions, and/or problems. Readers learn how to recover from sexual dysfunctions, overcome shame and painful memories, face their abuser, and allow God to restore the innocence they thought was lost forever.

Author Alfred H. Ells is a marriage and family counselor, seminar speaker, and best-selling author. He founded Samaritan Counseling Services in Scottsdale, Ariz.

Restoring Innocence Alfred H. Ells

Thomas Nelson Publishers, 1992, $10.99, paper, 228 pp., for counselees

Description Explaining how family influence and past experiences can hinder sexual intimacy, Ells helps the reader overcome the memories and shame, recover from sexual problems, face someone who's abused you, and live with a spouse who's been hurt too. A sensitive questionnaire inventory helps guide your healing.

Author Alfred H. Ells is a marriage and family counselor, seminar speaker, and best-selling author. He founded Samaritan Counseling Services in Scottsdale, Ariz.

In the Voice of a Child One Woman's Journey to Healing from Sexual Abuse, Judy Emerson

Janet Thoma (a division of Thomas Nelson), 1994, $12.99, paper, 276 pp., for counselors

Description A powerfully moving story taken from the personal journal of an incest victim. Offers hope for breaking the multigenerational chain of family shame and demystifies therapy and "inner work" by portraying it realistically and in Christian context.

Author Judy Emerson is a recovering survivor of childhood sexual abuse and is presently working toward becoming a therapist.

Contents *1.* What was it like growing up? *2.* Past halfway *3.* Just say no? How do you do that? *4.* Who is God anyway? *5.* Going back *6.* Mama *7.* My brother wasn't the only one *8.* Current events *9.* Declaration of independence *10.* Rock throwing *11.* Letting go *12.* Transference? Not me! *13.* Healing the shame *14.* Aftershocks *15.* Full circle

Light through the Dark Glass Esther's Child

Pacific Press, 1992, $9.95, paper, 192 pp., for counselees

Description Esther's Child was severely abused by the men in her life. She struggled year after

year with the heavy burden of low self-esteem. Yet she repeatedly reached out to God. This book is the heart wrenching true story of a young woman who finds glorious triumph through the Lord.

Author Esther's Child chose to write anonymously about her turbulent life experiences. She is a woman of strength and courage who lives a life of personal ministry to others.

Survivor Prayers Talking with God about Childhood Sexual Abuse, Catherine J. Foote

Westminster/John Knox Press, 1994, $8.99, paper, 96 pp., for both counselors and counselees

Description Prayers and meditations included here address spiritual issues faced by survivors. Foote calls for a community of faith in which children are heard, pain is honored, and healing can happen. She invites survivors to consider talking to God about their abuse as a way to break the silence. She invites the reader to bring to God all the struggles of healing and growing after a childhood of assault and to discover the power of survivor spirituality. A short (prose) chapter introduces a series of poems in each section.

Author Catherine J. Foote is minister to adolescents and their families, First Congregational Church, San Jose, Calif. She is founder of "Brake the Cycle," a cross-country bicycle ride that promotes action against child abuse.

Contents Introduction: a spiritual journey moving toward wholeness / God who walks with us / The long walk home / Conclusion: the journey goes on

When Victims Marry Building a Stronger Marriage by Breaking Destructive Cycles, Don Frank and Jan Frank

Thomas Nelson Publishers, 1991, $9.99, paper, 208 pp., for counselees

Description Help and hope for couples struggling in their marriages due to victimization in their past. Specific steps to rebuild the marriage foundation and enhance intimacy.

Authors Jan Frank holds a master's degree in marriage, family, and child counseling and is the author of the best-selling *A Door of Hope*. Don Frank, her husband, is a high school teacher and gifted communicator.

307

Contents *1.a.* Faulty foundations—Jan *1.b.* Faulty foundations—Don *2.* Preparing the soil *3.* Who needs an architect? Or blueprints? *4.* Periodic inspections *5.* Plumbing check *6.* Repairing the foundation *7.* Framing the house *8.* Walls of support/walls of division *9.* Insulation vs. isolation *10.* Is the roof leaking? *11.* Homeowner's insurance *12.* Stumbling blocks to unity *13.* Dwelling in unity

A Door of Hope *Recognizing and Resolving the Pains of the Past,* Jan Frank

Thomas Nelson Publishers, 1993, $9.99, paper, 196 pp., for counselees

Description An incest victim, now an experienced counselor, provides hope for victims of childhood trauma and shares ten steps for healing. An effective group therapy tool.

Author Jan Frank holds a master's degree in marriage, family, and child counseling and is the author of the best-selling *When Victims Marry.*

Contents *1.* Healing emotional wounds *2.* Step 1—face the problem *3.* Step 2—recount the incident *4.* Step 3—experience the feelings *5.* Step 4—establish responsibility *6.* Step 5—trace behavioral difficulties and symptoms *7.* Step 6—observe others and educate yourself *8.* Step 7—confront the aggressor *9.* Step 8—acknowledge forgiveness *10.* Step 9—rebuild self-image and relationships *11.* Step 10—express concern and empathize with others *12.* Restoration—his redeeming work

Child Sexual Abuse *A Hope for Healing,* Maxine Hancock and Karen Burton Mains

Harold Shaw Publishers, 1987, $8.99, paper, 197 pp., for both counselors and counselees

Description Written for adult victims and those who care about them, this book offers practical steps toward healing, restoration, and forgiveness from the effects of childhood sexual abuse. The book seeks to faithfully report and respond to the voices of people within the church whose lives have been touched by child sexual abuse. Each chapter begins with a verbatim first-person account presenting the personal chaos and recovery of a survivor (and in chapter 11, of a perpetrator) of child sexual abuse. After an analysis of the prevalence of child sexual abuse and the severity of its consequences, the book presents a therapy program that includes "something you can do right now" activities that can be carried out on a self-help basis, in a group, or under the supervision of a counselor or therapist. Fully indexed with notes and bibliography and program of action for survivors, helping friends, and church leaders.

Authors Maxine Hancock and Karen Burton Mains are both widely recognized writers, speakers, and counselors. Both authors have studied and counseled adults who have suffered the scars of child sexual abuse.

Contents *1.* The nature of child sexual abuse *2.* The physical and emotional aftermath *3.* Behavioral and relational problems *4.* The shadowed spirit *5.* Claiming the past *6.* The freedom of forgiveness *7.* The journey toward healing *8.* Seeing God as he really is *9.* Self-forgiveness—self-acceptance *10.* Understanding the abuser *11.* Portrait of an abuser *12.* The mother of the abused *13.* Renewing relationships *14.* The helpers *15.* Turning wounds into ministry *16.* Behold, I make all things new

Helping Victims of Sexual Abuse *A Sensitive, Biblical Guide for Counselors, Victims, and Families,* Lynn Heitritter and Jeanette Vought

Bethany House Publishers, 1989, $8.99, paper, 272 pp., for both counselors and counselees

Description Written from a background of over 20 years of collective experience, this work has a three-fold purpose. Primarily, it is to provide the Christian counselor with a better understanding of the victim's experience and to be a tool in the recovery process. Secondly, it is to help victims understand some of the effects of their abuse, to see the need to participate in their own recovery, and to be encouraged that recovery and a successful life is possible. Thirdly, it is a help to friends, relatives, and loved ones who have been victims. Awarded Top Five Final Nominee, the Gold Medallion Book Awards, 1990: Christianity and Society Category by the Evangelical Christian Publishers Association.

Authors Lynn Heitritter is a licensed parent/family educator, founder/former director of BE-COMES Sexual Abuse Support Group Program, and seminar speaker. She is presently pursuing her Ph.D. in family social science at the University of Minnesota. Coauthor Jeanette Vought is former director of New Life Homes and Family Services, a Christian social service agency licensed by the state of Minnesota. She holds a Ph.D. in counseling psychology and is a licensed marriage and family therapist and a clinical social worker.

Contents *Part 1:* Understanding the abused child *1.* Messages *2.* Through the eyes of a child *3.* Symptoms, signals, and effects *4.* Spiritual change *Section 2:* Understanding the abusive family *5.* Incest: the ultimate betrayal *6.* Intervention in incest *7.* Sexual abuse offenders: brethren, this ought not to be *Section 3:* Helping the adult victim *8.* Becomers: an introduction *9.* Step 1: realizing powerlessness *10.* Step 2: acknowledging victory in Christ *11.* Step 3: experiencing freedom from shame and guilt *12.* Step 4: discovering self-identity *13.* Step 5: sharing feelings *14.* Step 6: accepting responsibility *15.* Step 7: forgiving *16.* Step 8: maturing in relationship with God and others *17.* Step 9: ministering to others

Beyond the News *Sexual Abuse,* Jerry L. Holsopple

Mennonite Media Productions, 1993, $19.99, video, 60 minutes, for both counselors and counselees

Description This video resource includes five segments that encourage discussion around the various aspects of sexual abuse. It features true stories told by actors of people who have both survived and perpetrated sexual abuse. The video also includes an interview with Carolyn Holderread Heggen, Ph.D., a psychotherapist and author of *Sexual Abuse in Christian Homes and Churches.* She talks openly about her counseling experiences with survivors of sexual abuse, many of whom came from "very religious" homes.

Author Jerry L. Holsopple is an award-winning video producer as well as a writer, musician, and theologian. He has produced video appearing on all three major TV networks. His video curriculum Shalom Lifestyle's WHOLE PEOPLE EARTH has reached record numbers of young people. Holsopple received his masters of divinity from Associated Mennonite Biblical Seminaries in 1987.

Stolen Childhood *What You Need to Know about Sexual Abuse,* Alice Huskey

InterVarsity Press, 1990, $8.99, paper, 181 pp., for both counselors and counselees

Description The author tells her own story and provides much needed information and reasoned counsel for all who are concerned about child sexual abuse.

Author Alice Huskey has been helping people with abusive backgrounds for many years. She works as a charge nurse on the adolescent psychiatric unit of Good Samaritan Hospital in Downer's Grove, Ill. Her work has also appeared in numerous magazines.

Contents *1.* A painful introduction *2.* What is sexual abuse? *3.* Scapegoats for abuse *4.* The climate for abuse

5. Characteristics of abusers *6.* Characteristics of the abused *7.* The dilemma of disclosure *8.* The other victims *9.* Healing for the abused *10.* Healing for abusers and families *11.* What you can do / *Appendix:* Further reflections for those who have been abused

Healing from Sexual Abuse Kathleen

InterVarsity Press, 1991, $.99, paper, 29 pp., for both counselors and counselees

Description Anecdotal. Describes the pain and gradual, yet eventual, recovery process of a woman from the Midwest. Written from her own experience. Describes what kinds of help proved most valuable to her.

A Winter's Song *A Liturgy for Women Seeking Healing from Sexual Abuse in Childhood,* Jane A. Keene

The Pilgrim Press, 1991, $4.95, paper, 48 pp., for both counselors and counselees

Description Provides a framework for survivors of childhood sexual abuse in dealing directly with questions of faith and one's relationship with God. In liturgical format. It uses both masculine and feminine images for God.

Author Jane A. Keene is a writer and liturgist specializing in feminist theology.

Beyond the Darkness *Healing for Victims of Sexual Abuse,* Cynthia Kubetin and James D. Mallory

Rapha Resources, $8.99, paper, for both counselors and counselees

Description The author draws from personal experience and is joined by Dr. Mallory as they detail the trauma of abuse and the difficult road to recovery. They share that each victim can learn to grieve, let go, and reclaim trust, control, and intimacy. Readers will learn that through the Word of God a victim can move from survivor to thriver. Contains a small group leader's guide.

Learning More about Sexual Abuse Cynthia Kubetin

Rapha Resources, $2.50, paper, for both counselors and counselees

Description Traces the path from survivor to thriver. The author exposes false beliefs about abuse and points the way beyond the victim's past to regaining trust, control, and intimacy.

309

Shelter from the Storm *Hope for Victims of Sexual Abuse,* Cynthia Kubetin and James D. Mallory

LifeWay, 1994, $9.95, paper, 222 pp., for counselees

Description Part of the LifeWay Support Group Ministry commissioned by the Southern Baptist Convention. This title helps individuals understand the trauma and devastation of sexual abuse and helps them find the road to recovery as God, speaking through his Word, shows the path from victim to survivor to thriver. Designed for both individual and discovery-group study. The book provides self-paced, interactive study and resources for the 12 weekly sessions. A leader's guide is also available ($4.95) that provides administrative guidance and suggested activities for the weekly discovery-group sessions.

Authors Cynthia A. Kubetin is codirector of the Houston Christian Counseling Center, an affiliate with Rapha. James D. Mallory Jr., M.D., is the corporate medical director of Rapha and director of the Atlanta Counseling Center.

Contents *Unit 1:* A foundation for recovery *Unit 2:* Discovering hope *Unit 3:* Tell yourself the truth *Unit 4:* Out of the darkness into the light *Unit 5:* The family in the storm *Unit 6:* Letting go of shame and guilt *Unit 7:* Feeling anger and hurt *Unit 8:* Healing loneliness and fear *Unit 9:* Beginning to trust again *Unit 10:* The process of forgiveness *Unit 11:* Confronting the perpetrator *Unit 12:* Intimacy in relationships

From Victim to Victor *A Biblical Recipe for Turning Your Hurting into Healing,* Yvonne Martinez

Recovery Publications, Inc., 1993, $9.95, paper, 128 pp., for counselees

Description Uses biblical principles and Scripture to guide the reader through prayer, journaling, and daily devotional exercises. Martinez offers six important "Ingredients for Healing" as a foundation for recovery from victimization: learning who Jesus is and who you are in him, facing the secrets of your past, facing your sins, surrendering your guilt by trusting in God, understanding forgiveness, and trusting Jesus to win the spiritual battle. Christians dealing with issues of abuse will find *From Victim to Victor* an empowering tool for building an authentic healing relationship with God.

Author Yvonne Martinez is a counselor and lecturer. She lives in Hermosa Beach, Calif.

Contents Beginning the journey from victim to victor / Portrait of a victim / Healing ingredient 1: learning who Jesus is and who we are in him (relationship with God) / Healing ingredient 2: facing my secrets (self-examination) / Healing ingredient 3: facing my sins (self-examination) / Healing ingredient 4: surrender / Healing ingredient 5: understanding forgiveness / Healing ingredient 6: recognizing the enemy / The victor—the end is a beginning

Free to Forgive *Daily Devotions for Adult Children of Abuse,* Paul D. Meier and Frank B. Minirth

Janet Thoma (a division of Thomas Nelson), 1991, $7.99, paper, 372 pp., for counselees

Description Part of the Serenity Meditation series—365 inspirational messages written specifically for adult children of abuse. Brings the healing truths of Scripture into the recovery process.

Authors Doctors Minirth and Meier have gained national prominence for their successful blending of biblical principles with proven clinical and medical treatment. They are nationally recognized authors of over 60 biblically based books on common psychological issues with over three million in copies in print.

Memories Frank B. Minirth and Paul D. Meier

Christian Family Video, 1992, $19.95, video, 60 minutes, for both counselors and counselees

Description Part of the Minirth-Meier Church Counseling Video Library. The series is designed to enhance the counseling process as clients take the videos home for viewing. This title is designed for those struggling with their past. Presents practical counsel on dealing with memories from painful experiences.

Authors Doctors Minirth and Meier have gained national prominence for their successful blending of biblical principles with proven clinical and medical treatment. They are nationally recognized authors of over 60 biblically based books on common psychological issues with over three million in copies in print.

A Safe Place *Beyond Sexual Abuse—Especially for Teens,* Jan Morrison

Harold Shaw Publishers, 1990, $7.99, paper, 202 pp., for both counselors and counselees

Description Teen victims of sexual abuse are encouraged to work through fear, shame, hatred, and terrifying memories to discover real love. A look at God's love and the way he intended love and sexuality to be will help young people gain courage and trust.

Author Jan Morrison spends hours with abused teens, one-on-one. She speaks to church groups and works in high schools in three states educating school personnel and presenting programs for students on the effects of sexual abuse. Morrison is the director of Tree of Rest, Inc., a non-profit service organization for adolescent victims and survivors of sexual abuse.

Contents Getting acquainted *1.* Just the facts *2.* The real, true, inside you *3.* Angie's childhood *4.* Angie grows up *5.* A bag full of garbage / Sorting through the truth *6.* Scared to death *7.* I'm so confused! *8.* I feel so guilty *9.* Struggling with shame *10.* I hate you! *11.* Innocence lost *12.* Who can I trust? Acting it out *13.* The control game *14.* Sex without love *15.* The great escape *16.* Life at home *17.* Especially for guys / Getting together, learning the truth *18.* Support groups *19.* The awesome truth about God *20.* The real truth about love *21.* The wonderful truth about sex / Moving ahead *22.* The end of the story

Recovering from Childhood Sexual Abuse Victor M. Parachin

Ligouri Publications, 1994, $1.00, paper, for counselees

Description Professional counselor Victor M. Parachin outlines ten powerful strategies used by others who have reclaimed their lives. Includes how to recognize sexual abuse, how to use the power of prayer, and much more.

From Victim to Victor *Prescriptions from a Child Abuse Survivor,* Phil E. Quinn

Abingdon Press, 1994, $12.95, paper, 240 pp., for both counselors and counselees

Description Completes a trilogy including *Cry Out!* and *Renegade Saint* (both also available from Abingdon). Focuses on relieving pain and reclaiming the rest of life through healing and recovery. Includes practical suggestions from an abuse survivor.

Author Quinn is a writer and child advocate and founder of an organization dedicated to the prevention and elimination of child abuse. He holds a doctorate in ministry from Vanderbilt University.

Recovery from Abuse Dale Ryan and Juanita Ryan

InterVarsity Press, 1992, $4.99, paper, 60 pp., for both counselors and counselees

Description This Bible study is part of a series of 16 volumes on various recovery themes. Each book contains studies on six biblical texts. Leader's notes are provided for group study.

Authors Dale Ryan is the executive director of the Recovery Partnership, the parent organization to the National Association for Christian Recovery. Juanita Ryan is a counselor in private practice in Hacienda Heights, Calif.

Contents *1.* A prayer of doubt *2.* A prayer of helplessness *3.* A prayer of anguish *4.* An inarticulate prayer *5.* A prayer to God who shares our anger *6.* A prayer to the Father of compassion / *Leader's notes*

Please Somebody, Love Me! *Surviving Abuse and Becoming Whole,* Jillian Ryan and Joseph Ryan

Baker Book House, 1992, $9.99, paper, 60 pp., for counselees

Description Recording artist Jillian Ryan shares her own childhood pain, giving hope to struggling teens and adults who were abused as children and understanding to those who love them.

Healing Victims of Sexual Abuse Paula Sandford

Victory House Publishing, 1988, $8.95, paper, 164 pp., for counselors

Description A heart-to-heart communication from a veteran counselor to all those who work with sexual abuse victims, Sandford writes with clarity and compassion on a variety of topics including: depths of devastation, suppression, regression, frigidity, forgiveness, etc. She paves the way to healing through personal sharing, scriptural insights, love, and openness. Many agencies that deal with the abused have found this book to be a source of practical help. Sandford writes from an inner healing perspective.

Author With her husband, Paula Sandford has written four classics in the field of inner healing.

Contents *1.* Eyes to see and ears to hear *2.* The depths of devastation *3.* Suppression, regression, and frigidity *4.* A garland for ashes, the healing process *5.* Counselors who devour the afflicted *6.* Profile of an abuser *7.* Trouble and healing in the family / *Appendix of Scriptures*

The Healing Path *A Guide for Women Rebuilding Their Lives after Sexual Abuse,* John P. Splinter

Thomas Nelson Publishers, 1993, $12.99, paper, 256 pp., for both counselors and counselees

Description Blends personal experience stories with practical information and includes questions for journaling and action plans for personal growth. Readers will learn how to understand their behaviors, express their feelings, and gain a stronger self-esteem. Segments written by Annette, Maggie, Debbie, and Leona Mary.

Editor John P. Splinter is an associate pastor of Central Presbyterian Church, where he directs a large ministry and counseling center for single adults.

The Thorn of Sexual Abuse *The Gripping Story of a Family's Courage and One Man's Struggle,* Beth Sterling

Fleming H. Revell, 1994, $8.99, paper, 178 pp., for counselees

Description Here is the powerful account of one man's bondage to sexual addiction and the courageous family who ministers to him. "Paul's" journey to recovery illustrates that healing both the offender and the victim is possible.

Contents *1.* How can we help? *2.* He hugs me "funny" *3.* Stranger in our midst *4.* A matter of trust *5.* Cheese and nonsense *6.* The friend with many faces *7.* Filthy rags *8.* Tears and forgiveness *9.* Sexual addiction—what is it? *10.* Child molestation *11.* The arraignment *12.* Excuses and symptoms *13.* Diagnosis *14.* Marie's search for herself *15.* The sentencing *16.* Rebuilding a marriage *17.* The treatment *18.* In recovery / Epilogue / A professional perspective / Sources of help / Notes

My Father's Love *How God Replaces Sexual Abuse with Authentic Love,* Jim Talley and Jane Carlile Baker

Here's Life Publishers (c/o Thomas Nelson), 1992, $9.99, paper, 224 pp., for counselees

Description The gripping story of a woman whose father was an alcoholic and whose stepfather molested her. It outlines the steps she took to free herself from her past and includes a self-assessment section for victims of abuse.

Authors Dr. Jim A. Talley, a licensed marital and family therapist, is in private practice in Oklahoma. Jane Carlile Baker is director of communications at First Baptist Church of Modesto,

Calif. With her husband, she serves as coordinator of support group ministries at the church.

Contents *1.* What's wrong with this picture? *2.* The light at the end of the tunnel *3.* Which way is up? *4.* Wake me when it's over *5.* It's not a secret anymore *6.* The truth shall set you free *7.* A silk purse out of a sow's ear *8.* Not to have what it takes *9.* Names changed to protect the innocent *10.* All you can do is enough *11.* Out of the closet—now what? *12.* Into the second generation

Surviving the Secret *Healing the Hurts of Sexual Abuse,* Pamela Vredevelt and Kathryn Rodriguez

Description Provides compassion, help, and hope for those who have suffered sexual abuse. The writers assure that with God's love it is possible to recover completely. This is an updated and expanded edition.

Authors Pamela Vredevelt is director of Christian Counseling Services in Portland, Oreg. Dr. Kathy Rodriguez is a licensed clinical psychologist at Christian Counseling Services.

Contents *Part 1*—Victimization *1.* "I thought I was the only one" *2.* "How do I know if I'm a victim?" *Part 2*—Offending *3.* Recognizing offender behavior *4.* Recognizing offender thinking *5.* How do offenders groom their victims? *Part 3*—Rescuing *6.* "Why didn't anyone try to save me?" *7.* Surviving the betrayal of childhood *Part 4*—Moving beyond victimization *8.* Giving yourself the right to grieve *9.* Airing the wounds *10.* Getting the big picture *11.* The road of healing *Part 5*—Responsible caring *12.* Counsel for loved ones *13.* What about the Christian offender? / *Appendixes*

Recovering from Childhood Sexual Abuse

Abbey Press, $.50 each, paper, 8 pp., for counselees

Description Part of the CareNotes series from Abbey Press. CareNotes are short booklets that help readers identify issues and begin the process of seeking resolution. Anecdotal and uplifting. Beautiful photographs grace the covers. Over 20 million CareNotes have been sold in just over five years. Can be used as an alternative to a greeting card or in conjunction with pastoral care visits.

Sexual Misconduct in the Local Church *A Guide to Prevention and Healing*

The Life in Jesus Community, 1994, $100.00, video, 8 hours, 4 VHS, for counselors

Description An eight-hour video series with guidebook. The threefold purpose of the series is to

(1) inform and aid the local church and church school in understanding the issues associated with sexual abuse and sexual harassment, (2) suggest ways churches can provide ongoing pastoral care for both victims and perpetrators, and (3) provide a plan by which congregations can demonstrate to insurance carriers their intent to act responsibly on this issue and thereby avoid needless and expensive litigation.

Author This series is produced by the Life in Jesus Community, Rev. Philip C. Zampino (rector) and the Christian Counseling Center of Annapolis (Md.), Inc. Featured presenters include three clergy members, six Christian therapists, and one Christian attorney representing various denominations.

Contents Topics in the series include: biblical and historical overview of sexual misconduct, legal issues, personal boundaries, clinical profile and treatment of sexual abusers, psychological impact on victims of sexual abuse, treatment and healing of children and adult victims, pastoral concerns, interviews with victims at various stages of healing, individual and corporate healing and restoration

Incest Survivors Anonymous

Incest Survivors Anonymous. An organization

Description An international, self-help, mutual help recovery program for men, women, and teens. Spiritual in nature, adapted from the 12 steps of Alcoholics Anonymous. The organization assists in the establishment of incest survivor recovery groups and produces literature.

Incest Survivors Anonymous Information Exchange

Incest Survivors Anonymous. An organization

Description An information clearinghouse.

Life After Assault League, Inc.

Life After Assault League, Inc. An organization

Description A nonprofit Christian organization that offers free Christian counseling and direction (telephone and mail) to assist sexually abused adults and children. A referral resource for both Focus on the Family and the 700 Club.

Survivors of Incest Anonymous

Survivors of Incest Anonymous. An organization

Description An international support organization that provides literature, pen pal service, and referrals to hundreds of existing 12-step support groups throughout the United States. Spiritually oriented.

36. Sexuality and Related Issues

Abstinence, Sexual Purity

Sexual Temptation *How Christian Workers Can Win the Battle,* Randy Alcorn

InterVarsity Press, 1989, $2.99, paper, 32 pp., for counselors

Description In a world that makes sex an idol, we are fooling ourselves if we think society's lure will have no effect on us. Randy Alcorn, author of *Christians in the Wake of the Sexual Revolution,* explains how it is possible with God's help to live sexually pure lives.

Author Randy Alcorn codirects Eternal Perspective Ministries. He is a graduate of Multnomah School of the Bible, a college and seminary professor, and frequent conference speaker.

A Way of Escape Neil T. Anderson and Russell Rummer

Harvest House Publishers, 1994, $9.99, paper, 236 pp., for counselees

Description *The Bondage Breaker* helped believers understand Satan's assault on their hearts and minds. Now *A Way of Escape* equips Christians to fight and win in one of the most sensitive and vulnerable areas: their sexual thoughts and actions. Compassionate, yet uncompromising the truth, Anderson and coauthor Russ Rummer guide people in practical, biblical steps that lead to breaking the power of sin and experiencing true freedom in Christ.

Authors Neil T. Anderson is the president of Freedom in Christ Ministries. He is a highly sought counselor and conference speaker. Coauthor Russell Rummer is a licensed marriage, family, and child counselor.

Contents *1.* There is a way out *Part 1:* Detours in the darkness *2.* The lure of a sex-crazed world *3.* Pathways to sexual bondage *4.* The pimp in your mind *5.* The phony and the genuine *6.* The harvest of sinful deeds *7.* The dark dead end of bondage *Part 2:* The way of escape *8.* Beliefs that open prison doors *9.* Behaving must follow believing

10. Rethink how you think *11.* Recovery in Christ / *Appendix: A.* Steps to freedom in Christ *B.* Presenting a healthy view of sex and sexuality to your children.

Sex and the Christian Teen Jim Auer

Ligouri Publications, 1994, $3.95, paper, 64 pp., for counselees

Description Auer is not afraid to tackle tough questions teenagers ask such as: Whose business is my sex life? Why sex? What are we looking for? The reality of being sexually active, What happens when sex goes wrong, and more.

Author Jim Auer is a junior high schoolteacher who truly relates to today's teenager.

Contents *1.* Sex—where are we? Where are you? *2.* Whose business is my sex life? *3.* Sex—what are we looking for? *4.* A few pieces of you-know-what about being sexually active *5.* But how wrong? *6.* Starting over *7.* Fallout *8.* Sex gone very wrong *9.* Homosexuality *10.* A grab bag of good news

Intimate Deception *How to Escape the Trap of Sexual Impurity,* P. Roger Hillestrom

Multnomah Books (Questar), 1989, $7.99, paper, 156 pp., for counselees

Description Confronts today's relaxed sexual attitudes and the difficulties associated with them. This book provides practical steps for preventing harmful sexual patterns and gives hope to those who have already become enmeshed in false intimacy.

Author P. Roger Hillestrom is a marriage and family therapist with the Crista Counseling Service of Seattle, Wash. He holds professional degrees in psychology from Bethel College in St. Paul, Minn., and in family therapy from Biola University.

Contents *1.* The balancing act *2.* The intimacy trap *3.* The illicitness trap *4.* The technical virginity trap *5.* The abstinence trap *6.* The double-edged trap *7.* Sexual addiction *8.* The genius of Scripture *9.* Disengaging the traps

314

Living with No Regrets *Happy Healthy Relationships in Love, Sex and Marriage,* B. Charles Hostetter

Choice Books, 1988 (2d printing), $2.95, paper, 96 pp., for counselees

Description For teenagers it pays to honor the biblical blueprint for healthy, happy dating experiences and marriage—now more than ever. This easy-to-understand book helps young adult readers understand the power of sexual attraction and what to do about it before it creates the disasters we hear about every day. Deals frankly and biblically with sexual restraint vs. sexually transmitted diseases, the rewards of integrity vs. promiscuity. Helps the reader appreciate the value of intimacy in marriage.

Author B. Charles Hostetter provides biblical background and practical illustrations from his years as pastor, counselor, evangelist, and radio speaker.

Contents *1.* Thinking right about sex *2.* What the Bible says *3.* Judgment for impurity *4.* Sexual responsibility *5.* Turning life around *6.* The rewards of integrity *7.* Life without sex? *8.* Courting for marriage *9.* Are you in love? *10.* Now that you are engaged *11.* Holy matrimony

Sex, Guilt and Forgiveness Josh McDowell

Tyndale House Publishers, 1990, $2.99, paper, 89 pp., for counselees

Description This book offers practical counsel on learning to forgive oneself and others following sexual experiences outside of marriage. Readers can learn how to regain "spiritual virginity" in God's sight. A pocket-sized book.

Author Josh McDowell is a popular speaker and author of over 30 best-selling books. He finished graduate school magna cum laude with degrees in languages and theology.

Free to Love Again *Coming to Terms with Sexual Regret,* Dick Purnell

Thomas Nelson Publishers, 1994, $9.99, paper, 192 pp., for counselees

Description Nationally known speaker and counselor Dick Purnell helps readers find healing from sexual regret and develop healthy relationships with the opposite sex. Gives readers practical, biblical advice through following the seven steps to freedom.

Author Dick Purnell is the director of Single Life Resources as well as being an author, speaker, and counselor.

Contents *Part 1:* Sexual regrets *1.* A treasure chest of hope *2.* Closing Pandora's box *3.* The emotional tug of war *4.* The _____ made me do it *5.* On the road to restoration *6.* The way of restoration *Part 2:* Steps to freedom *Step 1:* Accept God's forgiveness *Step 2:* Forgive yourself *Step 3:* Expect powerful changes *Step 4:* Guard your mind *Step 5:* Dissolve immoral relationships *Step 6:* Purify your passions *Step 7:* Focus your future / *Epilogue:* You can do it!

Sex and Singles *Reasons to Wait,* Paul C. Reisser

Focus on the Family, 1992, $.35, paper, 15 pp., for counselees

Description Encourages sexual purity in straightforward language; uses logic and reason as well as anecdotes to persuade.

Author Paul Reisser, M.D., a family physician in southern Calif., serves on the Physician's Advisory Council for Focus on the Family.

Sex and the Teenager *Choices and Decisions,* Kieran Sawyer

Ave Maria Press, 1990, $3.95/$13.95 student/leader, paper/spiral, 112/168 pp., for counselees

Description Specifically designed to help young Catholics think through the many choices and decisions they must make in order to develop healthy, loving relationships. The program has a clear, straightforward goal: to encourage teens to say "no" to premarital sexual intercourse and to avoid such serious problems as teen pregnancy and sexually transmitted diseases.

Author Kieran Sawyer is widely known and respected for her work among teens. She is the director of the Tyme Out Youth Ministry Center in Milwaukee where she gives youth retreats and prepares adults for youth ministry work.

Contents *1.* Today's teens and their choices *2.* L.I.F.E. choices *3.* Dating choices *4.* The choice: to do or not to do *5.* The un-choice—teenage pregnancy *6.* No easy choices *7.* Contraception: is it a safe choice? *8.* Setting limits—a personal choice *9.* A criminal choice: sexual abuse *10.* A non-choice: sexual orientation *11.* Forgiveness: a healing choice *12.* Love choices

Sex: It's Worth Waiting For Greg Speck

Moody Press, 1992, $59.95, video, for both counselors and counselees

315

Description A former case worker with troubled youth teaches God's standards for physical and spiritual well-being during the adolescent years. A four-video set based on the book by the same title, also available from Moody Press.

Author Greg Speck (B.A., Bethel College) is the former president of Youth Ministries International. He is currently youth specialist with the Moody Bible Institute.

Contents *1.* Some straight talk about sex *2.* Petting, pinching, peer pressure *3.* Why not? *4.* Perversion and prevention

Edge TV—Sexual Decisions

NavPress, 1992, $24.95, video with leader's guide, 60 minutes, for both counselors and counselees

Description For youth workers who want to steer their group away from "church appropriate" discussions and get them talking about what's really going on in their lives. *Edge TV* (a video magazine for church youth groups) is the place to start. Created in partnership with Youth Specialties and IMS Productions, each episode of *Edge TV* is packed with high energy visuals, no-holds-barred drama, startling interviews, Christian music videos, captivating humor—and an honest approach to Jesus Christ that will get kids asking some very interesting questions.

Sex: When the Choices Are Confusing

Abbey Press, 1993, $.50 each, paper, 8 pp., for counselees

Description Part of the CareNotes for Teens series from Abbey Press. CareNotes are 5 x 7 booklets designed to offer strength and help to (young) people in crisis. Each CareNote gently introduces an issue, then encourages a person to take appropriate steps toward resolution. Over 20 million CareNotes have been sold.

Respect, Inc.

Respect, Inc. An organization

Description A Catholic support organization dedicated to providing information and educational materials that encourage abstinence from sex outside of marriage. Targets teenagers.

Teen-AID

Teen AID. An organization

Description A (secular) organization that develops, promotes, and provides family life education materials that focus on premarital abstinence and parent/teen communication. Call for their catalog.

Homosexuality and Lesbianism

Setting Love in Order *One Man's Journey into Wholeness,* Mario Bergner

Baker Book House, 1995, $11.99, paper, 208 pp., for counselees

Description Strongly challenges secular wisdom about the causes and treatment of homosexuality and reaffirms the biblical understanding of human sexuality. Bergner not only shares his personal history; he also describes the causes of and offers solutions for the plight of homosexuality.

Author Mario Bergner is a theological student at Trinity Seminary and a member of Leanne Payne's Pastoral Care Ministries staff.

Contents *1.* "Choose!" *2.* Coming out of denial *3.* Disordered love *4.* Setting love in order *5.* Christ in us *6.* Loving the same sex *7.* The hatred of woman *8.* Loving the other sex

Pursuing Sexual Wholeness *How Jesus Heals the Homosexual,* Andrew Comiskey

Creation House, 1992, $7.99, paper, 207 pp., for both counselors and counselees

Description Imparts extraordinary depth and breadth in understanding homosexual behavior and sexual brokenness in general. The author describes the journey out of homosexuality and into heterosexuality via a relationship with Jesus Christ. Discusses the roots and resolve of homosexuality and includes case histories of men and women who have found healing through the Living Waters program and being a vital part of the church.

Author Andrew Comiskey received his M.Div. from Fuller Theological Seminary where he studied theology and marriage and family therapy. He is an ordained minister and copastors in Los Angeles. He is the founder and director of Desert Streams Ministries, a multifaceted outreach to the sexually broken, with a focus on homosexual strugglers. Comiskey, a former homosexual, is married and has four children.

Pursuing Sexual Wholeness—Workbook
How Jesus Heals the Homosexual, Andrew Comiskey

Creation House, 1992, $10.99, paper, 216 pp., for counselees

Description Provides a Christ-centered step-by-step program for those who want to be free from homosexuality. The guide forms the syllabus for Andrew Comiskey's Living Waters program and can be worked through by an individual or group. The Pursuing Sexual Wholeness Guide examines each of the key areas that must be addressed by those seeking freedom from homosexuality. The combination of teaching, prayer, resources, and articles comprises the effective format for those seeking change.

Author Andrew Comiskey received his M.Div. from Fuller Theological Seminary where he studied theology and marriage and family therapy. He is an ordained minister and copastors in Los Angeles. He is the founder and director of Desert Streams Ministries, a multifaceted outreach to the sexually broken, with a focus on homosexual strugglers. Comiskey, a former homosexual, is married and has four children.

Homosexual No More William Consiglio

Victor Books, 1991, $8.99, paper, 204 pp., for counselors

Description A must-read book for counselors, pastors, and all who are concerned for the homosexual. Draws on counseling experience to provide an excellent practical guide to psychological and spiritual growth. The author calls his thoroughly biblical approach "reorientation therapy." Through this program, overcomers deal not only with the habits that reinforce homosexuality, but with the blocked emotional development that diverted them from God's heterosexual design in the first place. Includes strategies for coping with sexual temptation and suggestions for the counselor.

Author Founder/director of HOPE Ministries of Connecticut, which offers supportive educational and counseling services for Christians overcoming homosexuality. It is part of Exodus International, a parent organization for 80 ministries sharing the belief that homosexuality is learned behavior that can be changed. He is an associate professor of social work at Southern Connecticut State University.

Contents *1.* Reorientation therapy, a way out of homosexuality *2.* Answer these four questions, 10 facts about homosexuality *3.* All things work together for good, a spiritual renewal *4.* I never chose to be homosexual *5.* What do I have to do to change? *6.* It begins to hurt, you begin to heal *7.* Putting away childish things, conversations with God *8.* Conversations with the inner parent *9.* Train up a child, conversations with the inner child *10.* In due season, we shall reap—a Bible study summary *11.* Homosexual no more, David's testimony

Desires in Conflict *Answering the Struggle for Sexual Identity,* Joe Dallas

Harvest House Publishers, 1993 (2d printing), $9.99, paper, 288 pp., for both counselors and counselees

Description Written to the individual who is struggling with homosexuality. It addresses the personal struggle experienced by the man or woman who is homosexual but does not want to be. Written in an informal style, *Desires in Conflict* walks the reader through the phases of growth common to people overcoming homosexuality and draws heavily on the experiences of the many the author has worked with over the years. Chapters written directly to parents, family members, and the church are included. Both clinical and biblical data are supplied.

Author Joe Dallas has served as the president of Exodus International and has addressed the subject of homosexuality on innumerable secular and Christian broadcasts. He is currently training for the California Marriage and Family and Child License, and his articles have been featured in *Christianity Today, Cornerstone* magazine, and the *Christian Times.*

Coming Out of Homosexuality *New Freedom for Men and Women,* Bob Davies and Lori Rentzel

InterVarsity Press, 1994, $9.99, paper, 202 pp., for both counselors and counselees

Description Bob Davies (executive director of Exodus International) and Lori Rentzel (author of *Emotional Dependency*) offer a practical handbook for recovery and growth that examines the issues of sexual identity. Here are strategies for healing that have been developed and used by people all over the country.

317

Authors Bob Davies is executive director of Exodus International and Lori Rentzel is a freelance writer and editor in San Rafael, Calif.

Contents *1.* Can homosexuals really change? *2.* Biblical and scientific evidence for change *3.* The dynamics of change *4.* Exposing the roots *5.* Saying goodbye *6.* Breaking addictive patterns *7.* What's on your mind? *8.* Change in self-identity *9.* Forming healthy friendships *10.* Making peace with your abusive past *11.* Dating and romance *12.* Getting ready for marriage *13.* Growing in marital intimacy *14.* A vision for the future / *Appendix A:* Answers to common pro-gay arguments *Appendix B:* For further reading *Appendix C:* Resources for additional help

Out of Egypt *A Journey from Lesbianism to God's Healing Love,* Jeannette Howard

Jan Dennis (a division of Thomas Nelson), 1994, $10.99, paper, 218 pp., for counselees

Description When Howard became a Christian, she realized she had to leave her homosexual lifestyle. This book is the result of her five-year journey to freedom. A personal, honest story that will help women who have desired release from lesbianism but have not known how or even that it was possible. Jeanette Howard is the director of Reconciliation Ministries. She is a popular speaker and is well known among reparative ministries for homosexuals.

Homosexual Struggle Nancy

InterVarsity Press, 1978, $.35, paper, 27 pp., for counselees

Description A young woman, writing under a pseudonym, tells her story and gives others hope and practical suggestions for bringing their sexuality under the lordship of Christ.

Emotional Dependency Lori Rentzel

InterVarsity Press, 1990, $.99, paper, 31 pp., for counselees

Description With anecdotes, spiritual counsel, and readable clinical information, the author traces the roots of emotional dependency and outlines steps to severance of unhealthy relationships.

Counseling the Homosexual *A Compassionate and Biblical Guide for Pastors and Counselors,* Michael Saia

Bethany House Publishers, 1988, $8.99, paper, 240 pp., for counselors

Description This book will help equip members of Christ's body to effectively approach, support, and counsel those who struggle with homosexuality by giving practical, step-by-step, principle-oriented information. Saia presents both direction and encouragement to help them discover freedom and stability in their lives.

Author Michael Saia has had an extensive teaching ministry with Youth with a Mission for the past 15 years. This book is the result of his ministry to the homosexual community.

Contents *Part 1:* Development of the homosexual orientation *1.* We need a change *2.* An important distinction *3.* Theories, theories *4.* What went wrong? *5.* What does the Bible say? *Part 2:* Counseling the homosexual *6.* Coming out of the lifestyle *7.* Knowing God *8.* Self-understanding *9.* Fighting the unseen enemy *10.* Relating to the body of Christ *11.* A word to the struggler / *Appendix A:* Emotional dependency *Appendix B:* Witnessing to the homosexual *Appendix C:* Suggested reading/listening list *Appendix D:* Ministry referral list

Parents of the Homosexual David K. Switzer and Shirley Switzer

Westminster/John Knox Press, 1980, $9.99, paper, 118 pp., for counselees

Description How can parents—particularly Christian parents—accept the fact that their son or daughter is homosexual? David and Shirley Switzer, having counseled with homosexuals and their parents, present enlightening insights from persons who have struggled to make sense out of this emotionally charged issue. Advocates a tolerant view of homosexuality.

Authors David K. Switzer is associate professor of pastoral care and counseling at Perkins School of Theology. Shirley Switzer is a counselor in private practice in Dallas, Tex.

Contents *1.* "Oh no!" *2.* "We've lost our child!" *3.* Is our child really gay? *4.* Where does the fault belong? *5.* Where did we go wrong? *6.* If he or she "only loved us . . ." *7.* What will people think? *8.* What is homosexuality anyway? *9.* But doesn't the Bible condemn homosexuality? *10.* What does our child want of us?

Counseling and Homosexuality Earl D. Wilson

Word Publishing, 1988, $15.95, cloth, 225 pp., for counselors

Description Covers a wide variety of theoretical and practical issues associated with counseling homosexuals.

Author Earl Wilson is professor of clinical and counseling psychology at Western Conservative Baptist Seminary in Portland, Oreg.

Contents *1.* The new wave of uncertainty *2.* Confronting your own values *3.* Biblical controversies regarding homosexuality *4.* Causes of homosexuality *5.* Lesbianism and sexual confusion *6.* Special counseling considerations *7.* Assessing counselee needs *8.* Conducting the assessment interview *9.* Helpful models: verbal and visual *10.* Transference, countertransference, and other key issues *11.* Confronting homophobia *12.* AIDS, the dreaded killer *13.* Mobilizing the forces of the church *14.* Putting it into perspective / *Appendix:* Resources for dealing with AIDS counselees

Regeneration Books

For both counselors and counselees

Description Regeneration Books is probably the best and most comprehensive resource specializing in books on different aspects of overcoming homosexuality and lesbianism. You may call them for a free catalog of resources.

When Someone You Care about Is Gay

Abbey Press, $.50 each, paper, 8 pp., for counselees

Description Part of the CareNotes series from Abbey Press. CareNotes are short booklets that help readers identify issues and begin the process of seeking resolution. Anecdotal and uplifting. Beautiful photographs grace the covers. Over 20 million CareNotes have been sold in just over five years. Can be used as an alternative to a greeting card or in conjunction with pastoral care visits.

Exodus International

Exodus International. An organization

Description If you come across a counseling issue associated with homosexuality, the first thing you should do is contact Exodus International. A Christian ministry dedicated to helping men and women overcome homosexual bondage through a relationship with Jesus Christ. Sponsors an annual conference and regional seminars, maintains one of the most comprehensive referral listings in existence, provides various training opportunities for counseling homosexuals, and publishes various materials. Deals with issues and materials at all clinical levels and maintains strong spiritual content without being reductionistic.

Love in Action

Love in Action. An organization

Description With over 20 years of research and experience, Love in Action has gained worldwide recognition as a leading authority on healing for the homosexual. Provides information, and telephone counseling, networks support groups, sponsors a live-in counseling program, publishes an extensive reading list and booklets dealing with homosexuality and lesbianism. Love in Action is used as a referral by ministries such as Focus on the Family and the 700 Club.

Manhood, Male Sexual Identity

The Real Man Inside *How Men Can Recover Their Identity and Why Women Can't Help,* Verne Becker

Zondervan Publishing House, 1992, $14.99, cloth, 224 pp., for counselees

Description This timely book helps clarify men's issues for both men and women. It also serves as an excellent introduction to the growing "men's movement." Also available on two 60-minute audio tapes.

Author Verne Becker is a professional freelance writer and author of six books. He has previously served in editorial positions at several magazines.

Contents *1.* The passive man *2.* Men and the wound *3.* A movement among men *4.* Breaking the trance *5.* Snagging the self *6.* The myth-ing link *7.* Living on purpose

Men and Women *Enjoying the Difference,* Larry Crabb

Zondervan Publishing House, 1991, $15.99, paper, 240 pp., for both counselors and counselees

Description Men and women share a deadly problem that kills good relating. The problem is this: We are committed, first of all, to ourselves. Each of us, without blushing, holds fast to an overriding concern for our own well-being. Giving numerous examples from his counseling and speaking ministry, Crabb explores how we can turn away from ourselves and toward each other, how we can become what he calls "other-centered." Dr. Crabb maintains that we are different in important ways that, if understood and honored, can lead to a deep enjoyment of one another, an enjoyment that can last forever.

Author Dr. Crabb is director of biblical counseling and chairman of the Department of Biblical Counseling at Colorado Christian University in Morrison, Colo. He earned his Ph.D. in clinical psychology from the University of Illinois in 1970. He is the author of numerous books on self-understanding and counseling technique.

Contents *Part 1:* Why relationships don't work: the problem men and women share *1.* What's wrong with our marriage? *2.* Facing ourselves honestly *3.* The real problem *4.* Surely I'm not that bad! *5.* Change is possible *6.* Celebrating forgiveness *Part 2:* How relationships do work: the difference men and women can enjoy *7.* A tough question *8.* Is there really a difference? *9.* Masculinity and femininity *10.* Unique ways to freely love *11.* Relating as men and women *12.* Enjoying the difference

Sexual Character *Beyond Technique to Intimacy,* Marva J. Dawn

Wm. B. Eerdmans Publishing Co., 1993, $12.99, paper, 192 pp., for counselors

Description Offers a clear, fresh biblical perspective on sexuality. Dawn explains the importance of distinguishing between social and genital sexuality, discusses the forces in our technical society that jeopardize true intimacy, and outlines the "ethics of character" that forms the basis for discussion in the rest of the book. Holding to a positive biblical vision for sexual character leads Dawn to raise many provocative questions that apply to such issues as friendship, marriage, divorce, teenage dating, homosexuality, and abortion. Dawn ends the book by putting forth a hopeful vision of "sexual shalom" for individuals and Christian communities.

Author Marva J. Dawn is a theologian, author, and teacher working with Christians Equipped for Ministry, based in Vancouver, Wash.

Purity and Passion *Authentic Male Sexuality,* Rick Ghent and Jim Childerston

Moody Press, 1994, $16.99, cloth, 188 pp., for counselees

Description Constantly bombarded with misleading images, many men find themselves disillusioned and disappointed, unsure what it means to be a genuinely sexual male. This book offers practical, take-action insights that produce confident Christian men.

Authors Rick Ghent (M.A. in counseling from Denver Seminary) is a clinical therapist with South-

west Counseling Associates in Littleton, Colo. James K. Childerston (Ph.D. in clinical psychology from Fuller Theological Seminary) is a licensed psychologist in private practice in Hagerstown, Md.

Contents *1.* Sex is great *2.* The hollywood man *3.* The church man *4.* Men in hiding *5.* The biblical man *6.* The spiritual man *7.* Man to man *8.* The single man *9.* Sexual addiction *10.* Sexual dysfunction *11.* Man to child *12.* Man to woman

The Sexual Male *The Hart Report,* Archibald D. Hart

Word Publishing, 1993, $17.99, cloth, 256 pp., a reference or academic work

Description Our ideas about male sexuality have changed drastically over the past 30 years. This radical change has left many men with only a vague idea of their true role and identity in today's society. Based on extensive interviews and nationwide research, *The Sexual Male* addresses such issues as: what men need from sex; what satisfies them; what is normal and what is not; and why things go wrong.

Author Dr. Archibald Hart is professor of psychology and dean of the Fuller Graduate School of Psychology in Pasadena, Calif.

Reclaiming Manhood *A 12 Step Journey to Becoming the Man God Meant You to Be,* David Hawkins and Ross Tunnell

Victor Books, 1992, $13.95, paper, 166 pp., for both counselors and counselees

Description This book is designed for men who want to explore pertinent issues in a 12-step format. This interactive workbook explores issues such as marriage, sex and intimacy, work, ethics, money, power, and friendship. Individuals will see through the lens of Scripture God's design for men. The book is designed to be used individually or in a support group format.

Authors David B. Hawkins, A.C.S.W., Ph.D., is director of Pacific Psychological Associates and has been in private practice since 1979. Trained at Western Conservative Baptist Seminary, he has a master's degree in social work and a Ph.D. in clinical psychology. He leads a 12-step men's group at his church in Longview, Wash. Ross Tunnell III has a master's degree in divinity and theology from Western Conservative Baptist Seminary, where he was an instructor from 1969 to 1976. He has owned and operated Portland Counseling Services as well as presented numerous seminars on marriage and family life. He has had numerous articles published as well as this book.

Contents *1.* Men: coming of age *2.* Discussion on power/image *3.* Discussion on faith *4.* Discussion on family of origin *5.* Discussion on friendships/support *6.* Discussion on work *7.* Discussion on ethics *8.* Discussion on empathy *9.* Discussion on money *10.* Discussion on reconciliation *11.* Discussion on prayer/meditation *12.* Discussion on fitness / Glossary / Forming a men's Christian 12-step group / Recommended reading / Seminar announcement

The Masculine Journey *Understanding the Six Stages of Manhood,* Robert Hicks

NavPress, 1993, $15.00, cloth, 192 pp., for both counselors and counselees

Description Robert Hicks clearly outlines the six stages of masculinity—drawn from the six Hebrew terms for manhood—and reveals the vast resources God has invested in you as a man. By identifying which landmarks to watch for along the way, *The Masculine Journey* will help you discover where you currently stand in the process, how and why you arrived at your current stage, how to grow comfortable with your unique identity, how to move closer to God and experience genuine camaraderie with other men, how to move on toward the ultimate expression of manhood. A study guide is also available.

Author Robert Hicks is professor of pastoral theology at Seminary of the East in Dresher, Pa. A regular speaker on men's issues at conferences and seminars around the country, Hicks has been featured on over 150 radio and TV programs.

Contents *1.* An uneasy men's movement *2.* Creation male—Adam: the noble savage *3.* The phallic male—Zakar: mysterious taskmaster *4.* The warrior—Gibbor: the glorious hero *5.* The wounded male—Enosh: a painful incongruency *6.* The mature man—Ish: the reborn ruler *7.* The sage—Zaken: the fulfilled man *8.* A new male journey

You Are Wonderfully Made! Lois Walfrid Johnson

NavPress, 1988, $7.00, paper, 185 pp., for counselees

Description Part of the Let's Talk-About-It Stories for Kids series from NavPress. A series of short stories followed by discussion questions. Well-written, Christ-centered, and easy for young people to understand. This title deals with the emerging sexuality of young adolescents and the inevitable choices they will make.

Author Lois Walfrid Johnson is the author of 19 books. She leads seminars and retreats, and speaks at churches and conferences throughout the United States.

Men under Construction *Rebuilding the Way to Healthy Sexuality, Relationships and Identity,* Donald Joy

Victor Books, 1993, $8.99, paper, 204 pp., for counselees

Description Sometimes men have unique needs and concerns that are hidden beneath a facade of control and attempts at appearing "macho." The author responds to the secular men's movement from a Christian perspective. Deals with nurturing masculinity. Includes guidelines for conducting a men's support group.

Author Donald M. Joy is professor of human development at Asbury Theological Seminary in Wilmore, Ky. He is noted for his writing and speaking in the areas of sexual integrity and bonding.

Contents *1.* Design: maleness and manhood *2.* Deformity: father to son? *3.* Default: hi mom! *4.* Disorientation: in search of self? *5.* Bonding: who could love me as I am? *6.* Competing: scoring and other rewards *7.* Surviving: toughness that protects *8.* Meltdown: recovering security *9.* Celebration: my place in full-spectrum masculinity

The Man in the Mirror *Solving the 24 Problems Men Face,* Patrick M. Morley

Thomas Nelson Publishers, 1992, $17.99, cloth, 320 pp., for both counselors and counselees

Description Over 200,000 in print. These powerful strategies for gaining authentic manhood have given men the secrets of conquering 24 of the greatest problems they battle with every day.

Author Patrick Morely is a successful real estate developer. He graduated with honors from the University of Central Florida, which selected him as its outstanding alumnus of 1984. He regularly speaks to men's groups and teaches a weekly Bible study.

Contents *Part 1:* Solving our identity problems *1.* The rat race *2.* Leading an unexamined life *3.* Biblical Christian or cultural Christian? *4.* Significance: the search for meaning and purpose *5.* Purpose: why do I exist? *6.* The secret of job contentment *Part 2:* Solving our relationship problems *7.* Broken relationships *8.* Children: how to avoid regrets *9.* Wives: how to be happily married *10.* Friends: risks and rewards *Part 3:* Solving our money problems *11.* Money: a biblical point of view *12.* The four pillars of financial strength *Part 4:* Solving our time problems *13.* Decisions: how to make the right choice *14.* Priorities: how to decide what's important *15.* Time management: doing God's will *Part 5:* Solving our temperament problems *16.* Pride *17.* Fear *18.* Anger *19.* The desire to be independent *20.* Avoiding suffering *Part 6:* Solving our integrity problems *21.* Integrity: what's the price? *22.* Leading a secret thought life *23.* Accountability: the missing link *Part 7:* Conclusion *24.* How can a man change?

Eros Redeemed *Breaking the Stranglehold of Sexual Sin,* John White

InterVarsity Press, 1993, $17.99, cloth, 264 pp., for both counselors and counselees

Description Covers a wide range of issues associated with sexual dysfunction. In three sections White examines the causes and consequences of sexual sin, offers a biblical study of human sexuality and what it means to be a man or woman in Christ, and describes how to minister to those in need of healing, forgiveness, and hope. Covers topics such as the connections between promiscuity and violence, sexual sin within the leadership of the church, homosexuality, occult sexual abuse, gender stereotypes and differences, and issues of sexuality that confront singles.

Author John White is the author of many books including *Eros Defiled.* He is trained as a medical doctor and psychiatrist. He works with Vineyard Christian Fellowship in Vancouver, British Columbia.

Sexual Adjustment/Technique in Marriage

Family Planning *A Guide for Exploring the Issues,* Charles Balsam and Elizabeth Balsam

Ligouri Publications, 1994, $1.95, paper, 48 pp., for counselees

Description Offers the most up-to-date information on all family planning methods as well as a down-to-earth discussion of related aspects of family life. Includes a worksheet that allows couples to discuss family planning, their sexual relationship, and their expectations within the context of Christian marriage.

Authors Charles Balsam has been the director of the Office of Family Life Ministry for the diocese of Beaumont since 1979. Elizabeth Balsam is Natural Family Planning Coordinator and Respect Life Liaison for the diocese of Beaumont.

Restoring Innocence Alfred H. Ells

Thomas Nelson Publishers, 1994, $10.99, paper, 228 pp., for counselees

Description Explaining how family influence and past experiences can hinder sexual intimacy, Ells helps the reader overcome the memories and shame, recover from sexual problems, face someone who's abused you, and live with a spouse who's been hurt too. A sensitive questionnaire inventory helps guide your healing.

Author Alfred H. Ells is a marriage and family counselor, seminar speaker, and best-selling author. He founded Samaritan Counseling Services in Scottsdale, Ariz.

Sex in the Christian Marriage Richard Meier, Lorraine Meier, and Paul D. Meier

Baker Book House, 1988, $5.99, paper, 155 pp., for both counselors and counselees

Description Psychological and physical dimensions of romantic love and sexual fulfillment are applied to Christian marriage.

Authors Richard Meier, D.Min., a former pastor with 23 years' experience, is now a marriage counselor and popular seminar speaker. Lorraine Meier, Richard's wife, began counseling women during her many years as a pastor's wife. Paul D. Meier and Frank Minirth are vice president and president, respectively, of the Minirth-Meier Psychiatric Clinic, Richardson, Tex.

Contents *1.* Case studies of rekindled marriages *2.* Rekindling the flame *3.* How wrong emotions can affect sex *4.* Three phases of romantic sex *5.* Wives and orgasm *6.* Husbands and erection *7.* Husbands' problem plaguers *8.* Wives' problem plaguers *9.* The role of nutrition, weight, and exercise in sexuality *10.* Frequently asked questions and answers

To Have and to Hold *How to Achieve Life-Long Sexual Intimacy and Satisfaction,* Robert Moeller

Questar Publishing, 1995, $8.99, paper, 223 pp.

Description Moeller unmasks "fast lane" sexual fulfillment as a myth and teaches how husbands and wives can develop fulfilling sexual relationships by following biblical principles of love, fidelity, and monogamy.

Author Robert Moeller is a full-time author and writer, frequent guest speaker, and contributing editor to *Leadership* journal. He is also an ordained pastor in the Evangelical Free Church of America.

Contents *Part 1*—Creative bonding: establishing a healthy sexual relationship *1.* Who's having the best sex anyhow? *2.* Love isn't made, it's given *3.* Good sex begins in the Bible *4.* Aren't my needs your needs? *Part 2*—Sustained pleasure: preserving the satisfaction of married sex *5.* Time will let you *6.* Keep the grease pit drained *7.* What you do when no one is watching *8.* Divorce is the problem, not the solution *Part 3*—You don't send me flowers anymore: restoring the passion *9.* How to reconnect a disconnected sex life *10.* The trial was an error: the anticlimax of premarital sex *11.* Recovering from visual adultery *12.* Can you heal a broken heart? *13.* A modest proposal to rekindle your love life

Sex Problems—Their Causes and Cures
Clyde M. Narramore

Narramore Christian Foundation, $.50, paper, for both counselors and counselees

Description One of the many booklets available from the Narramore Christian Foundation. Designed to be handed to a person beginning to come to grips with a problem in living.

Author Dr. Clyde M. Narramore is a licensed psychologist and the president and founder of the Narramore Christian Foundation—a charitable, nonprofit educational, training, and counseling organization ministering primarily to the Christian community. He is also the founder of the Rosemead School of Psychology and author of 29 books.

Counseling for Sexual Disorders
Clifford L. Penner and Joyce J. Penner

Word Publishing, 1990, $15.99, cloth, 321 pp., for counselors

Description This husband and wife team provides guidelines for dealing with a wide range of sexual areas and conflicts. Part of the Resources for Christian Counselors series from Word.

Authors Joyce and Clifford Penner are sexual therapists in southern Calif. They are the authors of *The Gift of Sex* and conduct marriage seminars throughout the United States.

Contents *Part 1:* The framework for sexual counseling *1.* Sex is hard to talk about *2.* The therapist: are you comfortable with your sexuality? *3.* The Christian component—it sets you apart *4.* The marriage: sex provides the lubrication—not the fuel *5.* The body: sexual anatomy and the physical response *6.* What is sexual therapy? *7.* Why sexual therapy? *8.* Assessment *9.* Sexual therapy *Part 2:* Diagnosis and treatment *10.* Treating problems due to couple dissatisfaction *11.* Treating problems of sexual desire *12.* Treating problems of sexual arousal *13.* Treating problems of sexual release *14.* Treating problems of intercourse *15.* Understanding and treating sexual addictions *16.* The results of sexual therapy

52 Ways to Have Fun, Fantastic Sex *A Guidebook for Married Couples,* Clifford L. Penner and Joyce J. Penner

Janet Thoma (a division of Thomas Nelson), 1994, $7.99, paper, 144 pp., for both counselors and counselees

Description Offers a collection of ideas for building an active, exuberant sex life. Addressing both "cautious types" and "risk takers," the authors help couples rekindle lost or lagging passion. Included are tips on making sexual "appointments," increasing anticipation, discovering new ways to please one another, and more.

Authors Dr. Clifford and Joyce Penner are well-known sex therapists and authors of numerous titles on sexuality.

The Gift of Sex *A Guide to Sexual Fulfillment,* Clifford L. Penner and Joyce J. Penner

Word Publishing, 1981, $11.99, paper, 352 pp., for both counselors and counselees

Description Over 200,000 copies sold. A professional, sensitive guide to the physical and spiritual aspects of sex. This book has grown from the Penners' popular marriage and counseling seminar. Designed for any Christian couple, newlywed, or the long-term married couple who are interested in learning all they can about their God-given gift of sexuality. Sensitively illustrated with a strong biblical base. Also available on cassette and video formats.

Authors Clifford L. Penner is a clinical psychologist with Associated Psychological Services in Pasadena, Calif. Joyce Penner is a registered nurse who holds an M.N. in nursing from UCLA. Together, the Penners conduct sexual enhancement seminars around the country as well as work as sexual therapists.

Contents Introductory chapters *1.* Is this book for me? *2.* Why all the confusion? A biblical perspective *3.* Sexuality is a gift from God *4.* What the Bible says about our sexuality / The physical dimension *5.* Bodies *6.* Discovering and sharing our bodies *7.* How our bodies work *8.* Sexual response—four phases / The total experience *9.* Getting interested *10.* Having fun *11.* Initiating *12.* Meshing with each other's worlds *13.* Pleasuring *14.* Special treats that add pleasure *15.* Stimulating *16.* By invitation only *17.* Letting go *18.* Affirmation time *19.* Cleaning up *20.* Enhancing the sexual response / Moving past sexual barriers *21.* I'm not interested *22.* Differing sexual needs *23.* Never enough time *24.* You want to do what? *25.* Excluding God from the bedroom—a Christian dilemma *26.* I don't love him anymore *27.* Birth control gets in the way / Resolving technical difficulties *28.* Why sexual problems? *29.* Too soon—too fast *30.* Not enough when you need it—impotence *31.* No arousal or no release—some women's frustrations *32.* Pain reduces pleasure / Finding help *33.* Getting ourselves together *34.* Going for help *35.* Questions and answers *36.* Some final words

Making Love *A Christian Marriage Manual,* Douglas E. Rosenau

Oliver Nelson (a division of Thomas Nelson), 1994, $19.99, cloth, 384 pp., for counselees

Description A certified sex therapist combines training in counseling and in theology to give Christian couples both skills and attitudes for enjoying God's gift of married sex. Blends a conservative biblical viewpoint with honest, open discussion of love, romance, and sexual intimacy. Illustrated.

Author Dr. Douglas E. Rosenau is a licensed psychologist and marriage and family therapist. He received his Th.M. from Dallas Theological Seminary and an M.S.Ed. and Ed.D. from Northern Illinois University.

Contents *Part 1:* Setting the scene *1.* A biblical celebration *2.* The world's greatest lover *3.* Your erogenous zones *4.* The lovemaking cycle *5.* Minimizing the muss *Part 2:* Enhancing your pleasure *6.* Natural aphrodisiacs and creating a mood *7.* The joy of fantasy *8.* Sexual communication *9.* Sensuous massage *10.* Making love with clothes on *Part 3:* Delighting in each other *11.* Mutual pleasuring *12.* Creative intercourse *13.* Making love to your wife *14.* Making love to your husband *15.* Making love when you have a disability *16.* Sex after forty *Part 4:* Jumping common hurdles *17.* "I'm not very sexy" *18.* Women becoming more easily orgasmic *19.* "We haven't in six months" *20.* Relational ruts *21.* Dealing with infertility *Part 5:* Resolving problems *22.* Male malfunctioning *23.* Women and painful intercourse *24.* Survivors of sexual abuse *25.* Extramarital affairs *26.* Sexual short circuits

Body and Soul—A Married Couple's Guide *To Discovering and Understanding Unique Sexual Personalities,* Duane Storey and Sandford Kulkin

Questar Publishers, 1995, $10.99, paper, 256 pp.

Description Helps couples understand the relationship between personality type and physical and emotional intimacy. Combining helpful self-tests with seasoned counsel, the authors show how partners can develop a relationship that is deeply fulfilling—both physically and emotionally.

Authors Duane Storey is founder of Resources for Communication Concepts, an organization focused on helping individuals improve communication skills through the use of the DiSC system. Sandford Kulkin, Ph.D., is director of Creative Corporate Consulting and president of the Institute for Motivational Living.

Contents *Part 1*—Personality and sexuality: designed for intimacy *1.* Restoring Eden *2.* What is good communication? *3.* Discovering your personality type *4.* The dominant director *5.* The influencer *6.* The steady relator *7.* The conscientious thinker *8.* The gender gap *Part 2*—Counsel from the heart of a pastor *9.* Tending to the marriage garden: developing intimacy *10.* Do you respect me? *11.* Affair-proofing your marriage *12.* Encouragement and togetherness

Intended for Pleasure *Sex Technique and Sexual Fulfillment in Marriage,* Ed Wheat and Gaye Wheat

Fleming H. Revell, 1981 (revised), $15.99, cloth, 243 pp., for both counselors and counselees

Description A complete sexual manual, with basic information, illustrations, and frank discussion of all facets of human sexuality. Common sexual problems are described and techniques to solve them are presented.

Author Ed Wheat, M.D., a family physician from 1952—1988, now retired and disabled. Widely known for his work in marriage and family issues. Author of 4 other books.

Contents *1.* Intended for pleasure *2.* Finding God's design *3.* What if I'm not in love? How do I fall in love? *4.* Understanding the basics *5.* One flesh—the techniques of lovemaking *6.* Solutions to common problems *7.* For the preorgasmic wife—fulfillment ahead *8.* For the impotent husband— fulfillment again *9.* The power of sexual intimacy *10.* The "perfect" wife—by Gaye Wheat *11.* Planning and achieving parenthood *12.* Sex during pregnancy *13.* Sex after 60 . . . 70 . . . 80 *14.* Answers to your questions *15*. All love, all liking, all delight *16*. Your marriage: a private little kingdom

Fulfilled Sexually *How to Find Help and Hope for Difficulties,* Harold Wahking and Gene Zimmerman

Baker Book House, 1994, $8.99, paper, 127 pp.

Description The authors apply Scripture and psychological insights to the nature of sexuality as integral to personhood and help parents instill a healthy sexual identity in their children. They show that sexual intimacy is a "godly delight" of marriage as couples become aware of their own sexual issues and learn the dynamics of male–female communication. Singles likewise can find personal fulfillment and godly sexual identity.

Authors Harold Wahking is director of the Network of Christian Counseling Centers, Inc., and is a minister of counseling in St. Petersburg, Fla. Gene Zimmerman has served numerous pastorates and is a missions speaker and superintendent for the St. Petersburg District, United Methodist Church.

Contents *1.* Facing sexual problems faithfully *2.* Biblical foundations for understanding and fulfilling our sexuality *3.* God's design of masculine and feminine *4.* Sexual difficulties, past and present *5.* Sexual disharmony stemming from relationship disharmony *6.* Help and hope for men's sexual problems *7.* Help and hope for women's sexual problems *8.* Christian sex education in the home *9.* The Christian ideal, singles, and sexuality *10.* Christian hope for survivors of sexual abuse *11.* Homosexuality in Christian perspective *12.* Now is the time—this is the day!

Sexual Issues *A Short-Term Structured Model,* Harold Wahking and Gene Zimmerman

Baker Book House, 1994, $17.99, cloth, 197 pp.

Description Helps counselors gain enough confidence to encourage trust and openness in discussion of emotion-laden problems. Written for students or practicing pastoral counselors, each problem is adapted to the five-session Strategic Pastoral Counseling model developed by David G. Benner. A companion book of the Strategic Christian Living series, *Fulfilled Sexuality,* is available as a counselee handout or self-help resource.

Authors Harold Wahking is director of the Network of Christian Counseling Centers, Inc., and is a minister of counseling in St. Petersburg, Fla. Gene Zimmerman has served numerous pastorates and is a missions speaker and superintendent for the St. Petersburg District, United Methodist Church.

Contents *Part 1:* Foundations: counseling people with sexual problems *1.* Strategies for adding to your pastoral counseling skills *2.* Biblical foundations for counseling persons with sexual problems *3.* Specific aspects of the pastoral counseling relationship *Part 2:* Applications: specific sexual problems and Christian responses *4.* Gender differences in resolving sexual problems *5.* Sexual difficulties, past and present *6.* Sexual disharmony revealing relationship disharmony *7.* Parents and sexually active teens *8.* The Christian ideal: singles and sexuality *9.* Strategic pastoral counseling with survivors of sexual abuse *10.* Strategic pastoral counseling with homosexuals and their families *11.* Caring for God's people

One Flesh *God's Gift of Passion—Love, Sex & Romance in Marriage,* Bob Yandian

Pillar Books & Publishing Company, 1992, $14.95, cloth, 240 pp., for counselees

Description Yandian's insights into God's plan for intimacy will help readers see their own blind spots and misconceptions about sex, marriage, and love. More than a sexual handbook, *One Flesh* gives God's perspective on sex as it touches all areas of life for both single and married believers. There is a wealth of practical information on dating, mate selection, the honeymoon, compatibility in marriage, and training children about sexual purity.

Author Bob Yandian has pastored Grace Fellowship since 1980. Under his leadership, the church has earned a reputation for excellence and integrity.

Contents *1.* In the beginning, there was godly passion *2.* A famous father speaks to his son about sex—what not to do *3.* A famous father speaks to his son about sex—the righteous way *4.* Husbands, love your wives *5.* Wives, submit to your husbands *6.* Are singles complete? *7.* The labor of love *8.* God has called you to peace *9.* The husband's heart—her signature

American Association of Sex Educators, Counselors, and Therapists

American Association of Sex Educators. An organization

Description A [secular] professional organization that seeks to develop competency and standards for sex educators, sex counselors, and sex therapists through training, education, and research.

Assists in developing human relations and sex curricula, training professionals, and other services. Sponsors annual conference for sex educators and therapists.

American Board of Sexology

American Board of Sexology. An organization

Description A [secular] professional organization that provides education for therapists, supervision, and certification. Maintains a listing of qualified sex therapists.

37. Singleness

Wholly Single *A Network Discussion Guide,* Julia Duin

Harold Shaw Publishers, 1991, $3.99, paper, 48 pp., for both counselors and counselees

Description These studies will help you tackle such issues as loneliness, celibacy, sexual purity, and intimacy from a biblical perspective. As you study, you'll focus on Jesus—who himself was single.

Author Julia Duin has worked for ten years as a newspaper journalist, most recently as religion writer for the *Houston Chronicle.* She has been the recipient of several journalism awards and is studying for a master's degree in religion.

Contents *1.* Loneliness *2.* Waiting *3.* Thought life *4.* Celibacy and service *5.* Sexual sin and purity *6.* A new beginning *7.* Unwillingly single *8.* Intimacy with Christ / *Leader's notes*

Single but Not Alone *Meditations for Christian Women,* Jane Graver

CPH Publishing, 1983, $2.99, paper, 64 pp., for counselees

Description With insight, hope, and joy, this book encourages single women to keep growing and learning.

A Party of One *6 Studies for Women on Being Wholly Single,* Judy Hamlin

Victor Books, 1992, $4.99, paper, 64 pp., for counselees

Description Part of the Searching for Answers series from Victor. This study explores how to meet one's own needs while reaching out to others, how to learn the art of vulnerability, how to relate to the opposite sex, how to live life to the fullest, and other issues. Uses an interactive format.

Author Dr. Judy Hamlin (Ph.D. in adult education, University of Southern Mississippi) is an authority on small groups and women's ministry.

Contents *1.* An encouraging word *2.* Acceptance, significance, and belonging (I) *3.* Acceptance, significance, and belonging (II) *4.* Obedience *5.* Single wholeness *6.* Promised land / *Leader's notes*

Fortysomething and Single Harold Ivan Smith

Victor Books, 1991, $9.99, paper, 167 pp., for counselees

Description Will help single adults come to terms with this new season of life as they learn to admit I am 40+, to assess the past, to position oneself for the future, to reexamine dreams, to question priorities and commitments. Exhorts singles to keep close to Christ during the tides and times of midlife and provides motivational goals that will help single adults take charge and tackle their dreams.

Author Harold Ivan Smith is president of a consulting firm that focuses on singles in the workplace. His doctoral research at Rice Seminary where he earned a D.Min. examined the history of single adults in American culture. He is the author of more than 20 books.

Contents *1.* Fortysomething and still single *2.* Every day . . . in every way . . . I'm getting older *3.* There's more to being 40 and single than waiting for the right one to show up *4.* Keep in the middle of the road *5.* Shaping a fortysomething faith *6.* Life is hard but God is good *7.* Marching off the map *8.* Beyond this point . . . there be dragons *9.* There's more to having it all than having it all! *10.* Heroes in an age of celebrities *11.* Where will you be when you get to where you are going?

Positively Single *Coming to Terms with Single Life,* Harold Ivan Smith

Victor Books, 1986, $8.99, paper, 189 pp., for counselees

Description Singleness should be a positive experience, but many single people see it as being negative. This book looks at the single life as a time of growth and learning by looking at the true measure of success.

Author Harold Ivan Smith is president of a consulting firm that focuses on singles in the workplace. His doctoral research at Rice Seminary where he earned a D.Min. examined the history of single adults in American culture. He is the author of more than 20 books.

Contents *1.* What does it mean to be an adult? *2.* Coming to terms with yourself *3.* Coming to terms with your body *4.* Coming to terms with your parents *5.* Coming to terms with your work *6.* Coming to terms with your friends *7.* Coming to terms with your anxiety *8.* Coming to terms with guilt *9.* Coming to terms with resentment *10.* Coming to terms with Jesus *11.* Coming to terms with death *12.* Coming to terms with ministry / *Epilogue*

Reluctantly Single Harold Ivan Smith

Abingdon Press, 1994, $10.95, paper, 128 pp., for counselees

Description Challenges the notion that life begins after marriage. Smith calls for single adults to recognize the opportunity to be significantly single—to use this position in life to make a difference.

Author Harold Ivan Smith is well known for his combined ministries of writing, speaking, and counseling, especially in the area of singles ministries in the church.

Contents *1.* Single and reluctant *2.* Single and floating, fighting, and navigating *3.* Single and shattered *4.* Single and belonging *5.* Single and relevant *6.* Single and remembered / *Epilogue:* A king and a pauper

Common Mistakes Singles Make Mary Whelchel

Fleming H. Revell, 1989, $7.99, paper, 158 pp., for counselees

Description A candid discussion of the frustrations and stress of being single in a world built for couples. Addresses pressures singles receive from church communities, common mistakes singles make in accepting their singleness. Also covers mistakes married people make in their attitudes toward singles.

Author Mary Whelchel is a single professional woman who understands the Christian single from first-hand experience and ministry to singles. She is speaker and founder of the *Christian Working Woman* radio program, heard on over 400 Christian stations, and has authored five books.

Contents *1.* Common mistakes in our attitudes toward marriage *2.* Common mistakes in relating to the opposite sex *3.* Common mistakes men make in relationships with females *4.* Common mistakes women make in relationships to males *5.* Common mistakes in relating to our friends *6.* Common mistakes in relating to married people *7.* Common mistakes in relating to family members *8.* Common mistakes in our lifestyles *9.* Common mistakes in financial and career matters *10.* Common mistakes in our commitment to Jesus Christ *11.* Common mistakes others make in their attitudes toward singles

Beyond Singleness *Lifelines for the Separated, Divorced, Widowed, and Unmarried,* Helena Wilkinson

Marshall Pickering/Zondervan, 1995, $8.99, paper, 192 pp.

Description A conspiracy of silence surrounds singleness. The real issues (loneliness, sexuality, longing, and loss) are often left unaddressed—particularly in church. The author draws from her counseling work to show how singles can become vibrantly alive.

Author Helena Wilkinson is a trained counselor, author, and speaker.

38. Spiritual Counseling

General Works on Spiritual Counseling

How to Overcome Evil Jay E. Adams

P & R Publishing, 1977, $4.95, paper, 116 pp., for counselees

Description Intended for distribution to counselees struggling with their own propensity toward evil. Helps readers overcome temptation with God's help.

Author Dr. Adams is the author of numerous books on Christian counseling. He has served on a seminary faculty (Westminster Theological) and in the pastorate. He is founder of Christian Counseling and Educational Foundation in Laverock, Pa., and visiting professor of practical theology at two seminaries.

Contents *1.* Are you a winner? *2.* You can be a winner *3.* The evil you fight *4.* You are in a war *5.* Battle orders for today *6.* Is aggression Christian? *7.* The weapons of your warfare *8.* Your mouth is a problem *9.* How to manage your mouth *10.* You can't fight alone *11.* You are part of God's army *12.* No exceptions allowed *13.* Plan with finesse *14.* Make war, make peace *15.* Three ways to be a trouble maker *16.* Christian vigilantes *17.* Make room for God *18.* Meet your enemy's need *19.* Pour on the coals *20.* Epilogue

The Bondage Breaker *Overcoming Negative Thoughts, Irrational Feelings, and Habitual Sins,* Neil T. Anderson

Harvest House Publishers, 1991, $8.99, paper, 197 pp., for both counselors and counselees

Description *The Bondage Breaker* helps believers understand Satan's assault on their hearts and minds. Discusses the position of the believer, the vulnerability of the believer, and steps to freedom in Christ. A companion study guide is available as well as a version especially for young adults. Over 370,000 copies in print.

Author Neil T. Anderson is the president of Freedom in Christ Ministries. He is a highly sought counselor and conference speaker.

Contents *Part 1:* Take courage! *1.* You don't have to live in the shadows *2.* Finding your way in the real world *3.* You have every right to be free *4.* Confronting the rebel prince *5.* Jesus has you covered *Part 2:* Stand firm! *6.* Dealing with evil in person *7.* The lure of knowledge and power *8.* Enticed to do it your way *9.* Don't believe everything you hear *10.* Appearances can be deceiving *11.* The danger of losing control *Part 3:* Walk free! *12.* Steps to freedom in Christ *13.* Helping others find freedom in Christ

The Hidden Rift with God William Backus

Bethany House Publishers, 1990, $7.99, paper, 191 pp., for both counselors and counselees

Description Backus candidly deals with those seasons of life when God gives no hint of being near; when tragedy or painful difficulties pound in while prayers remain unanswered; when a person's life is shattered even though God could have prevented it. Both from his own experience and from his counseling practice, he shows the reader that the only way to heal the rift with God is through discovering the truth. Step-by-step, the reader is shown the way back to God. Unbalanced emotions, improper reactions, and inappropriate behavior may represent rifts with God. Rather than accepting God's view of what is good for them, people disagree and rift themselves from his love and care. God's truth alone can restore and reclaim. This is not a ten-steps-to-wholeness book, but is intended to help the reader go through the necessary steps to find inner wholeness—which is peace with God at the deepest level.

Author William Backus is a licensed clinical psychologist and an ordained Lutheran clergyman. He is founder and director of the Center for Christian Psychological Services, St. Paul, Minn., and an associate pastor of a large Lutheran church.

Contents *1.* Running from the one who loves us *2.* When the pain won't quit *3.* Spiritual drift *4.* The big distractions *5.* Is God wrong about the good? *6.* The point of contention *7.* The awful thing *8.* Where the rift leaves you *9.* Who does God think he is? *10.* Agreeing with God *11.* Sermons from science *12.* The healed rift

Why Do I Do What I Don't Want to Do?
William Backus and Marie Chapian

Bethany House Publishers, 1984, $6.99, paper, 141 pp., for both counselors and counselees

Description The sequel to *Telling Yourself the Truth*. The principles of misbelief therapy are now applied specifically in the areas of persistent sins and temptations. These are categorized under the headings: pride, envy, greed, sloth, lust, and gluttony. Without using the usual theological or clinical terminology, the authors show how to identify misbeliefs relating to specific issues, renounce those misbeliefs, and replace them with truth.

Authors William Backus is a licensed clinical psychologist and an ordained Lutheran clergyman. He is founder and director of the Center for Christian Psychological Services, St. Paul, Minn., and an associate pastor of a large Lutheran church. Marie Chapian is a well-known author, speaker, and psychotherapist. She also collaborated with Dr. Backus on *Telling Yourself the Truth*.

Contents *1.* Whose fault is it? *2.* Welcome to freedom *3.* God, make me willing *4.* What goes up usually comes down *5.* Why can't I be satisfied? *6.* The angry heart *7.* When more is never enough *8.* Laziness, the blues, and depression *9.* Romance and sexuality *10.* The problem of overeating *11.* Dead to sin

Baby Boomer Blues *Understanding and Counseling Baby Boomers and Their Families,* Gary R. Collins and Timothy Clinton

Word Publishing, 1992, $15.99, cloth, 272 pp., for counselors

Description Part of the new Contemporary Christian Counseling series from Word. Provides an analysis of the baby boomer phenomenon. Addresses the timeless Christian values that challenge every population segment while indicating how boomers can adjust their dreams to reality and move into midlife with the axis of biblical principles of growth.

Editors Dr. Gary Collins, a licensed psychologist, is editor for both this series and for Resources for Christian Counseling. Former professor of psychology at Trinity Evangelical Divinity School, he is also executive director of the American Association of Christian Counselors. Dr. Timothy

Clinton is associate dean at Liberty Baptist University.

Contents *Part 1:* Understanding baby boomers *1.* Who are the baby boomers? *2.* Baby boomer careers *3.* Baby boomer values *4.* Baby boomer families *5.* Baby boomer religion *6.* Baby boomer followers: the baby busters *Part 2:* Counseling baby boomers *7.* Connecting with baby boomers *8.* Counseling approaches with baby boomers *9.* Marriage counseling with baby boomers *10.* Personal counseling with baby boomers *11.* Spiritual counseling with baby boomers *Part 3:* Reaching the baby boomers *12.* Helping baby busters and the children of baby boomers *13.* Helping parents of baby boomers *14.* The future of baby boomers

Inside Out *Real Change Is Possible—If You're Willing to Start from the Inside Out,* Larry Crabb

NavPress, 1992, $10.00, paper, 224 pp., for both counselors and counselees

Description "You don't have to pretend you've got it all together . . . when you don't. You don't have to pretend your best relationship deeply satisfies . . . when it doesn't. You don't have to pretend your struggle with sin is a thing of the past . . . when it isn't." If you want a more vital union with God, a richer relationship with others, and a deeper sense of personal wholeness, let Larry Crabb help you look inside yourself. And discover how God works real, liberating change when you live from the inside out.

Author Dr. Larry Crabb (Ph.D. in clinical psychology, University of Illinois) is the founder and director of the Institute of Biblical Counseling. He is widely known for his work in the area of biblical counseling.

Contents *Part 1:* Looking beneath the surface of life *1.* Real change requires an inside look *2.* An inside look can be frustrating *3.* Knowing what to look for *Part 2:* We're thirsty people *4.* "If anyone is thirsty . . ." *5.* Springs of water? Then why so much pain? *6.* Becoming aware of our thirst *Part 3:* Digging broken wells *7.* Looking in all the wrong places *8.* The problem of demandingness *9.* Exposing wrong directions *Part 4:* Changing from the inside out *10.* Defining the problem *11.* The power of the gospel *12.* What it takes to change deeply / *Epilogue*—The high cost of change

Inside Out—Study Guide *A Study Guide Based on the Best-Selling Book,* Larry Crabb

NavPress, 1988, $6.00, paper, 107 pp., for both counselors and counselees

Description A chapter-by-chapter study guide with interactive questions to enhance the understanding and application of the book of the same title.

Author Dr. Larry Crabb (Ph.D. in clinical psychology, University of Illinois) is the founder and director of the Institute of Biblical Counseling. He is widely known for his work in the area of biblical counseling.

A Counselor's Prayer Book *Integrating Faith into Counseling,* Kathleen Fischer and Thomas Hart

Paulist Press, 1994, $9.95, paper, 160 pp., for counselors

Description A collection of 75 prayers and rituals for both counselor and client. The prayers help center the counselor on the work for the day, while helping the client learn to appreciate God's action within his or her life. Three sections contain: prayers for the counselor alone; prayers to be used with a client that deal with specific topics such as family instability, addictions, depressions, sexual abuse, and more; and finally a section containing various rituals such as saying goodbye to a loved one, bringing good out of evil, and strengthening family bonds. Included are centering prayers, psalms of praise, meditations, prayers of petition, litanies, and the prayerful use of the imagination.

Authors Drs. Kathleen Fischer and Thomas Hart are theology professors and therapists in Seattle.

Sometimes It's Hard to Love God *How Your Past Affects Your Relationship with God Now,* Dennis Guernsey

InterVarsity Press, 1989, $8.99, paper, 171 pp., for counselees

Description Designed to help readers overcome the inner barriers of family background, cultural values, and emotional makeup that can keep us from growing closer to God. Based on the Lord's prayer.

Author Dr. Dennis Guernsey is associate dean and director of the Institute for Marriage and Family Ministries at Fuller Theological Seminary in Pasadena, Calif.

Contents *1.* When we feel like spiritual failures *2.* When we're not what we pretend to be *3.* When our understanding of God is still that of a child *4.* When our earthly experiences are too painful *5.* When we have trouble with authority *6.* When our minds are confused *7.* When our

lives are directionless *8.* When we don't know how to ask *9.* When we feel lonely *10.* When our world is confusing *11.* When we live with unforgiveness *12.* When we struggle with sin *13.* A closing hymn

How to Pray When Life Hurts *Experiencing the Power of Healing Prayer,* Roy Lawrence

InterVarsity Press, 1992, $7.99, paper, 129 pp., for both counselors and counselees

Description As a hospital, school, and army chaplain, Lawrence has spent many years praying with people in the midst of crisis. In this book he offers practical counsel and biblical wisdom for all who want to know how to pray when it hurts.

Author Roy Lawrence is presently vicar of the churches of St. Stephen and St. Alban in Prenton and advisor in Christian healing to the bishop of Chester in England.

Contents *1.* The healing power of prayer *2.* How do you pray when you feel guilty or ashamed? *3.* How do you pray when you are angry or depressed? *4.* How do you pray when life has hurt you? *5.* How do you pray when you are anxious or fearful? *6.* How do you pray when you are busy or stressed? *7.* How do you pray when you feel jealous or envious? *8.* How do you pray when you or others are ill? *9.* How do you pray when you are not getting better? *10.* How do you pray in bereavement? *11.* The Lord's own method of prayer *12.* Jesus makes a difference

Caring for Spiritual Needs Phyllis J. Le Peau

InterVarsity Press, 1993, $4.99, paper, 62 pp., for counselors

Description Part of the seven-title Caring People Bible Studies from InterVarsity Press. Seven study guides and an introductory handbook cover all the basics of caregiving—from developing the character traits of caring to dealing with tough needs like depression, grief, and illness. Perfect for churches starting a caregiving program, groups ministering in hospitals and to shut-ins, or laypeople helping a friend through a crisis.

Author Phyllis J. Le Peau is a registered nurse and a former Nurses Christian Fellowship staff member. Currently, she is assistant program director for Wellness, Inc.

Contents *1.* What are spiritual needs? (Ps. 38) *2.* Recognizing spiritual needs (Matt. 9:1–13) *3.* The need for a relationship with God (Rom. 5:1–11) *4.* The need for meaning and purpose (1 Pet. 1:1–16) *5.* The need to be loved and belong (1 Jn. 4:7–21) *6.* The need for assurance

(Rom. 8:18–39) *7.* The need to persevere (Jas. 1:2–18) *8.* Caring for those who doubt (Luke 7:18–30) *9.* Caring for those in spiritual warfare (Eph. 6:10–20)

Counsel Yourself and Others from the Bible *The First Place to Turn for Tough Issues,* Bob Moorehead

Multnomah Books (Questar), 1994, $16.99, cloth, 284 pp., for both counselors and counselees

Description Focuses on the 33 most common questions and problems for which Christians seek counsel, including depression, marriage problems, bitterness, anger, and anxiety. Includes the most relevant Bible passages as part of the book text as well as additional scriptural references.

Author Dr. Bob Moorehead is senior pastor of Overlake Christian Church in Kirkland, Wash., one of the largest churches in the Pacific Northwest. He holds the Ph.D. from the California Graduate School of Theology.

Silent Pain *Finding God's Comfort for Your Hidden Heartache,* Kathy Olsen

NavPress, 1992, $10.00, paper, 251 pp., for counselees

Description What happens when we view God as tolerant of our distress rather than deeply sympathetic? Caught in this dilemma, many women suffer for years in silence, not sensing God's compassion, and feeling ashamed that they are not spiritual enough to experience his healing. This book speaks to this issue, helping us realize that there's more to the Christian life than grinning and bearing it. By treating our minds and hearts to new perspectives on God's character, the author explores how mourning allows us to deeply experience God's tender mercy and provides new hope, relief, and a return to peace—with God and ourselves.

Author Kathy Olsen is a freelance writer, Bible study leader, and conference speaker. She lives with her husband and two sons in Tyler, Tex.

Contents *Part 1:* Hurting *1.* Silent pain—a low-grade fever of the heart *2.* Why the pain won't go away *3.* The special needs of women in pain *Part 2:* Healing *4.* When God's heart breaks: discovering his compassion *5.* The paradox of sovereignty and compassion *6.* Barricades of the needy heart *7.* How God reaches us in our silence *8.* Finding life in the pain *Part 3:* Helping *9.* Building a compassionate community *10.* Compassion as energy

Praying Our Goodbyes Joyce Rupp

Ave Maria Press, 1993, $6.95, paper, 183 pp., for counselees

Description About the experience of leaving behind and moving on, the stories of union and separation that are written in all of our hearts. Focusing on the spirituality of change, this is a book for anyone who has experienced loss, whether it be a job change, end of a friendship, death of a loved one, financial struggle, midlife crisis, or an extended illness. It is designed to help in the healing process. Each chapter concludes with probing questions. The book ends with 24 prayer experiences incorporating images, symbols, and rituals as sources of strength and stepping stones toward healing.

Author Joyce Rupp (O.S.M.) holds a master's degree in religious education, is a trained spiritual director, and has given retreats for 20 years. Along with writing, speaking at conferences, and giving retreats, she currently is engaged in graduate studies in transpersonal psychology.

Freedom from the Performance Trap *Letting Go of the Need to Achieve,* David A. Seamands

Victor Books, 1988, $9.99, paper, 204 pp., for both counselors and counselees

Description No matter how hard performance-oriented Christians try, they never feel like they're accomplishing all they should. David Seamands shows how the grace of God can free believers from the performance trap.

Author David Seamands is professor emeritus of pastoral ministries and counselor in residence at Asbury Theological Seminary in Wilmore, Ky.

Contents *1.* The miracle of grace *2.* Barriers to grace *3.* Parental grace—or disgrace *4.* How it all began *5.* The bad news *6.* The consequences of disgrace *7.* The good news *8.* Grace and guilt *9.* Grace and emotions *10.* Grace and self-esteem *11.* Grace and negative emotions *12.* The panorama of God's grace

Putting Away Childish Things David A. Seamands

Victor Books, 1982, $7.99, paper, 144 pp., for counselees

Description We all have childish behavior patterns that hold us back from reaching spiritual and emotional maturity and hinder us from growing up spiritually. But you can move toward the maturity God desires for you if you follow the seasoned, biblical advice of this best-selling author and counselor who claims God can reprogram old, childish ways and lead you into Christian adulthood. More than 250,000 copies in print. A leader's guide is also available.

Author David Seamands is professor emeritus of pastoral ministries and counselor in residence at Asbury Theological Seminary in Wilmore, Ky.

Contents *1.* The hidden child in all of us *2.* The healing of memories *3.* A childhood motto which destroys adults *4.* Another childhood motto *5.* Childish ideas of love and marriage *6.* Childish ideas of God and his will *7.* Childish ideas of prayer *8.* Childhood confusion versus adult distinctions *9.* Childish dependency on feelings *10.* Childish concepts of self and self-surrender *11.* The ultimate crisis of life *12.* Reprogramming grace

Spiritual Dimensions of Mental Health
Judith Allen Shelly

InterVarsity Press, 1983, $8.99, paper, 179 pp., for counselors

Description Several mental health professionals discuss how caregivers can identify the spiritual needs of their clients and offer appropriate and effective help.

Author Judith Allen Shelly, associate director of resource development for Nurses Christian Fellowship, has written or contributed to many books on spiritual aspects of nursing. Sandra D. John, a former staff nurse, has taught in a psychiatric mental-health setting and has been a chaplain to psychiatric patients. She is now a family therapist.

Contents *Section 1:* What is mental health? *1.* Mental health: a personal struggle *2.* What is human? A context for defining mental health *3.* Toward a psychology of believing *4.* Interpretations of wholeness *5.* Evaluating holistic health modalities *Section 2:* Spiritual care and the psychiatric client *6.* What are spiritual needs? *7.* Healthy and unhealthy religious beliefs *8.* Assessing spiritual needs *9.* Meeting spiritual needs *10.* Prayer in a psychiatric setting *11.* Use of Scripture *12.* Clergy as colleagues *Section 3:* Personal mental health: how to keep your own sanity *13.* Qualities of a Christian counselor *14.* Caring for your colleagues *15.* Are my beliefs unbalanced? *16.* Burnout! *17.* When the helper needs help *18.* When the hurting hits home *19.* Psychiatric nursing: an opportunity for growth

Gems and Jargon *A Glossary of Terms Used in Sharing the Exchanged Life,* Charles R. Solomon

Grace Fellowship International, 1980, $1.95, paper, 30 pp., a reference or academic work

Description A glossary of terms which affords the thinking believer the opportunity to unlock some of the passages that could have been a mystery before.

Author Dr. Solomon is president and founder of Grace Fellowship International in Denver, Colo. God called him to the ministry of counseling in 1967, and he developed an approach that is biblical, Christ-centered, and cross-centered.

GFI Basic Conference Video Tapes
Charles R. Solomon

Grace Fellowship International, 1990, $200.00, video, 4 VHS w/books, for counselors

Description The video conference contains lectures by Dr. Solomon on the basics of spirituotherapy. The material is covered in more detail in his books. The video conference will give the viewer an overview of the approach to helping others as well as a challenge to personal appropriation of the believer's identity in Christ.

Author Dr. Solomon is president and founder of Grace Fellowship International in Denver, Colo. God called him to the ministry of counseling in 1967, and he developed an approach that is biblical, Christ-centered, and cross-centered.

Contents Identity, the rejection syndrome, the wheel and line, paths to the cross, faith is the victory, the precious blood, choosing and refusing

Handbook to Acceptance *Healing the Pain of Rejection through Experiencing Christ's Love,* Charles R. Solomon

Tyndale House Publishers, 1992, $6.99, paper, 140 pp., for counselors

Description Provides a systematic treatment of the effects of human rejection, intrapersonally and interpersonally, and the healing power of God's acceptance. Throughout the book, the constructs of acceptance and identity are juxtaposed. The Holy Spirit is shown to be the one who is able to renew the mind and transform the life as a believer appropriates the reality of being "accepted in the beloved."

Author Dr. Solomon is president and founder of Grace Fellowship International in Denver, Colo. God called him to the ministry of counseling in

1967, and he developed an approach that is biblical, Christ-centered, and cross-centered.

Contents *1.* Setting the stage *2.* The syndrome in operation *3.* Crisis and the cross *4.* Rejection—results of the fall *5.* Accepted in the beloved *6.* The effect of rejection on identity *7.* Living to succeed—identity through doing *8.* Succeeding to live—identity through dying *9.* Man: dichotomy or trichotomy *10.* The church, the college, and counseling *11.* God's answer to a rejecting society

Handbook to Happiness and You *A Spiritual Clinic,* Charles R. Solomon

Exchanged Life Foundation, 1991, $9.95, paper, 216 pp., for both counselors and counselees

Description Part 1 of the book is arranged in the form of a workbook that enables a person to have a sort of counseling interview with Dr. Solomon by proxy in the privacy of his own living room—a personal spiritual clinic. It draws on the diagrams from chapter 2 of *Handbook to Happiness* and is very similar to a first interview with Dr. Solomon. Part 2 is a spiritual clinic for the church. The truths taught in *Handbook to Happiness* and Dr. Solomon's other books are applied in the corporate setting. A lay counseling format is presented as well.

Author Dr. Solomon is president and founder of Grace Fellowship International in Denver, Colo. God called him to the ministry of counseling in 1967, and he developed an approach that is biblical, Christ-centered, and cross-centered.

Contents *Part 1:* A personal spiritual clinic *1.* Background information *2.* The diagnosis *3.* Spiritual surgery *Part 2:* A spiritual clinic for your church *1.* The church and I—a sentimental journey *2.* The work of the church—ministering in a selfish and sin-sick society *3.* The state of the church—a post-mortem *4.* Attempts to resuscitate the church *5.* Revival in the church—life out of ashes *6.* A plan for edifying the church *7.* A challenge to the church

The Ins and Outs of Rejection Charles R. Solomon

Grace Fellowship International, 1991, $6.95, paper, 226 pp., for both counselors and counselees

Description Shows the role rejection plays in the development of mental and emotional symptoms of which depression is perhaps the most common. The latter half of the book concentrates on the dynamics of spirituotherapy and is a sequel to *Handbook to Happiness.*

Author Dr. Solomon is president and founder of Grace Fellowship International in Denver, Colo.

God called him to the ministry of counseling in 1967, and he developed an approach that is biblical, Christ-centered, and cross-centered.

Contents *Part 1:* The ways in or the rejection syndrome *1.* Rejection—a family thing *2.* The aftermath of rejection *3.* Rejection in the church *4.* The message of the church *Part 2:* The way out or the cross *1.* A life in turmoil *2.* Crucified with Christ *3.* "I will bring the blind . . ." *4.* Dynamics of distress *5.* The perils of the well adjusted *6.* Dynamics of deliverance *7.* Dynamics of death/resurrection *8.* Dynamics of discipleship *9.* Dealing with regression and the adversary *10.* Therapy: bane or blessing? *11.* An open challenge to God's tattered army

Spiritual Gifts Assessment Bob Tippie

Maret Software International, $99.99, software, for both counselors and counselees

Description An assessment tool designed for the evaluation of the "practical" gifts such as wisdom, knowledge, faith, helps, government, prophecy, teaching, exhortation, giving, mercy, and service.

Author Bob Tippie is an ordained Baptist minister with an active counseling and consulting practice. He holds a bachelor's degree in psychology and a master's in pastoral counseling.

Designed for Dependency *Biblical Keys to Intimacy and Recovery,* Lori A. Varick

Emerald Books, 1993, $8.99, paper, for counselees

Description Through abuse and neglect, chronic physical, emotional, and spiritual problems occur. Healing is available as we see that we were designed to be not independent, but dependent on the living, creator God.

Jesus and Addiction *A Prescription to Transform the Dysfunctional Church & Recover Authentic Christianity,* Don Williams

Recovery Publications, Inc., 1993, $9.95, paper, 224 pp., for counselors

Description Williams argues convincingly that we must look at dysfunctional behavior within our culture, our churches, and ourselves in order to develop an authentic Christianity that can transform the church.

Author Don Williams is pastor of Vineyard Christian Fellowship of the Coast in La Jolla, Calif., and the author of several books.

Contents *Part 1:* The dysfunctional church *1.* Naming addiction in the church *2.* Getting at the root of our addictions *3.* Grace, grace, grace *4.* At home with the father *Part 2:* The one fully functioning person *5.* Living with the fearless Jesus *6.* Living with the free Jesus *7.* Living with the self-giving Jesus *Part 3:* Becoming a functional person *8.* Giving up fear *9.* Getting free *10.* Giving yourself away *Part 4:* A functional fellowship *11.* A fearless church *12.* A freeing church *13.* A self-giving church

Enneagram Spirituality *From Compulsion to Contemplation,* Suzanne Zuercher

Ave Maria Press, 1992, $8.95, paper, 176 pp., for counselors

Description A fresh, deep, and advanced discussion of enneagram theory with a spiritual emphasis absent in similar works.

Author Suzanne Zuercher is a graduate of Loyola University of Chicago. She also earned her master's degree in clinical psychology and is a licensed psychologist in Illinois.

Contents *1.* The first task of life *2.* The second task of life *3.* Vice and virtue *4.* The story of Mary Magdalene *5.* The story of Thomas *6.* The story of Peter *7.* The meaning of incarnation *8.* The present moment *9.* The contemplative attitude and discernment *10.* The way to contemplation *11.* The enneagram: a help to contemplation

Confronting Spiritual Doubt

Abbey Press, $.50 each, paper, 8 pp., for counselees

Description Part of the CareNotes series from Abbey Press. CareNotes are short booklets that help readers identify issues and begin the process of seeking resolution. Anecdotal and uplifting. Beautiful photographs grace the covers. Over 20 million CareNotes have been sold in just over five years. Can be used as an alternative to a greeting card or in conjunction with pastoral care visits.

When Your Prayers Go Unanswered

Abbey Press, $.50 each, paper, 8 pp., for counselees

Description Part of the CareNotes series from Abbey Press. CareNotes are short booklets that help readers identify issues and begin the process of seeking resolution. Anecdotal and uplifting. Beautiful photographs grace the covers. Over 20 million CareNotes have been sold in just over five years. Can be used as an alternative to a greeting card or in conjunction with pastoral care visits.

When Your Spiritual Life Seems Empty

Abbey Press, $.50 each, paper, 8 pp., for counselees

Description Part of the CareNotes series from Abbey Press. CareNotes are short booklets that help readers identify issues and begin the process of seeking resolution. Anecdotal and uplifting. Beautiful photographs grace the covers. Over 20 million CareNotes have been sold in just over five years. Can be used as an alternative to a greeting card or in conjunction with pastoral care visits.

Repairing Distorted Images of God

Finding God *Moving through Your Problems Toward . . . ,* Larry Crabb

Zondervan Publishing House, 1993, $17.99, cloth, 234 pp., for counselees

Description Most of us come to a point in life where we know that God is all that we have. But we don't know him well enough for him to be all that we need. This book will appeal to people who realize the psychology revolution stops short of restoring a deeply personal relationship with God. Too often, we think that we are the final point. Nothing matters more than our problems, so we angrily demand that God change our lives to suit our tastes. Radically rethinking the Christian life, *Finding God* leads the way to real freedom and joy by insisting that looking for God in the middle of our problems rather than requiring God to provide solutions to our problems is the path to life.

Author Dr. Crabb is director of biblical counseling and chairman of the Department of Biblical Counseling at Colorado Christian University in Morrison, Colo. He earned his Ph.D. in clinical psychology from the University of Illinois in 1970. He is the author of numerous books on self-understanding and counseling technique.

Contents *Part 1:* The importance of finding God *1.* A personal journey *2.* There's more to life than merely living *3.* Natural passions *4.* Supernatural passions *Part 2:* The obstacle to finding God *5.* Something is seriously wrong *6.* When God won't let us find him *7.* The foundation of the fallen structure: doubting God *8.* Why God won't let us find him *9.* The foundation of a solid structure: trusting God *10.* First floor: I need you *11.* Second floor: I hate you *12.* Third floor: I hate me *13.* Fourth floor: I will survive *14.* Fifth floor: here's how I will survive *Part 3:* The pathway to finding God *15.* Darkness before light *16.* Mistakes people make *17.* Understanding our passions, good and bad *18.* The nature of good and bad passions: toward disrupting the bad and releasing the good

19. Telling our stories *20.* Stories that disrupt and entice *21.* Coming home again

The Father I Never Knew *Finding the Perfect Parent in God,* Phil Davis

NavPress, 1991, $10.00, paper, 221 pp., for counselees

Description Painful memories or inadequate parenting examples can rob you of a healthy, biblical understanding of what it means to be God's child. Phil Davis presents God as the perfect heavenly parent—a view that is essential to a healthy spiritual and emotional life. In the process, he exposes what often distorts your perception of God.

Author Phil Davis is a husband, father of three, and the founding pastor of Lake Mary Community Church in Orlando, Fla. He earned his M.Div. from Trinity Evangelical Divinity School.

Contents *Part 1:* The search for an ideal parent *1.* A secret yearning *2.* God is dad too! *3.* Abba, father *4.* Parental hangover *Part 2:* Learning to see God as he is *5.* A father with his heart on his sleeve *6.* Father knows best *7.* This is going to hurt me more than it hurts you *8.* My dad's bigger than your dad *9.* The breadwinner and the bread of life *10.* A father who never lets go *Part 3:* Learning to see how God is parenting you *11.* Growing pains *12.* The weaning process (part 1) *13.* The weaning process (part 2) *14.* Full partnership / *Conclusion:* In my father's footsteps

Sometimes It's Hard to Love God *How Your Past Affects Your Relationship with God Now,* Dennis Guernsey

InterVarsity Press, 1989, $8.99, paper, 171 pp., for counselees

Description Designed to help readers overcome the inner barriers of family background, cultural values, and emotional makeup that can keep us from growing closer to God. Based on the Lord's prayer.

Author Dr. Dennis Guernsey is associate dean and director of the Institute for Marriage and Family Ministries at Fuller Theological Seminary in Pasadena, Calif.

Contents *1.* When we feel like spiritual failures *2.* When we're not what we pretend to be *3.* When our understanding of God is still that of a child *4.* When our earthly experiences are too painful *5.* When we have trouble with authority *6.* When our minds are confused *7.* When our lives are directionless *8.* When we don't know how to ask *9.* When we feel lonely *10.* When our world is confusing *11.* When we live with unforgiveness *12.* When we struggle with sin *13.* A closing hymn

Your View of God, God's View of You *Inspirational Devotions for Women,* Kathy Collard Miller

Beacon Hill Press of Kansas City, 1992, $9.95, paper, 133 pp., for counselees

Description How do we really see God? Do we fully comprehend his character and grace? In this devotional written uniquely for women, Miller captures the heart of God, revealing our misconceptions of God and his view of us.

Author Kathy Collard Miller is an author and speaker at conferences and retreats. She has authored several books.

When You're Angry at God William Rabior

Ligouri Publications, 1989, $.75, paper, 24 pp., for counselees

Description Is it wrong to be angry at God? How can a person let go of such anger? This booklet answers these questions and explains that God accepts anger, even when it is directed at him.

Recovery from Distorted Images of God Dale Ryan and Juanita Ryan

InterVarsity Press, 1992, $4.99, paper, 60 pp., for both counselors and counselees

Description This Bible study is part of a series of 16 volumes on various recovery themes. Each book contains studies on six biblical texts. Leader's notes are provided for group study.

Authors Dale Ryan is the executive director of the Recovery Partnership, the parent organization to the National Association for Christian Recovery. Juanita Ryan is a counselor in private practice in Hacienda Heights, Calif.

Contents *1.* Distortion: the God of impossible expectations *2.* Distortion: the emotionally distant God *3.* Distortion: the disinterested God *4.* Distortion: the abusive God *5.* Distortion: the unreliable God *6.* Distortion: the God who abandons

How We See God John Sandford and Paula Sandford

Elijah House, 1993, $23.95, video, 90 minutes, for counselees

Description John and Paula Sandford uncover the process of a personal perception of God—how the parents of an individual directly affect that perception. Methods and direction for healing those perceptions are given.

Authors John and Paula Sandford have written or coauthored nine books, including *Transformation of the Inner Man,* a classic in the field of inner healing that has sold over 500,000 copies.

Divine or Distorted? *God As We Understand God,* Jerry Seiden

Recovery Publications, Inc., 1993, $7.95, paper, 128 pp., for counselees

Description Those in recovery as well as those just beginning their search for an authentic relationship with God will find this book an empowering tool to heal their distortions and a catalyst for personal reflection and change.

Author Jerry Seiden (M.A., Southern California College) has been a pastor (Assemblies of God) and Christian school administrator for more than 12 years. He is also the anonymous author of other recovery books.

Contents *Part 1:* God: distorted by parents—defined in Christ *1.* Acceptance/Roger and Daisy *2.* Significance/listen to me! *3.* Competence/what's wrong with you? *4.* Virtue/locked out *5.* Power/the boy who could do anything *Part 2:* God: distorted by church—described in law *6.* Difference/different but loved *7.* Fairness/daily bread *8.* Jubilee/fresh start *9.* Disadvantages/winners *10.* Redeemers/Cora *Part 3:* God: distorted by fear—depicted in Exodus *11.* Rescue/eyes to see *12.* Provision/missionary manna *13.* Protection: birthdays lost *14.* Victory/victory at sea *15.* Promise/rainbow

Stupid Ways, Smart Ways to Think about God Michael Shevack and Jack Bemporad

Ligouri Publications, 1993, $13.95, paper, 126 pp., for counselees

Description Arranged in two parts, the first surveys the ten stupidest ways many adults think about God and helps us discard ideas that cause guilt, confusion, or frustration. The second part seeks to correct them.

Please Let Me Know You God *How to Restore a True Image of God and Experience His Love Again,* Larry D. Stephens

Janet Thoma (a division of Thomas Nelson), 1992, $15.99, cloth, 256 pp., for counselees

Description Helps readers identify the distortions in their image of God by exploring ten common distortions and how they are developed. See and

feel God's true image through intimate letters from him based on the Psalms and Scriptures. Includes a 30-day devotional program.

Author Dr. Larry D. Stephens is a marriage and family therapist and a certified alcohol and drug abuse counselor with the Minirth-Meier Clinic in Dallas, Tex. For his Ph.D. dissertation, he conducted a survey of how Christians develop their image of God.

Contents *Part 1:* The distorted image / An open letter from God *1.* The distorted image *Part 2:* Assessing our image of God *2.* Symptoms of distortions in our image of God *3.* Diagnosing our distortions *4.* Where distortions begin *Part 3:* Who does God say he is? *5.* The four-dimensional image *6.* God's true image *7.* Spiritual decontamination *8.* Reparented by God *Part 4:* Knowing God intimately *9.* Obstacle to knowing God intimately *10.* Giving your children a hug from God / A letter to God / The 30-day image of God restoration program

Will the Real God Please Stand Up? *Healing Our Dysfunctional Images of God,* Carolyn Thomas

Paulist Press, 1991, $4.95, paper, 76 pp., for both counselors and counselees

Description A step-by-step handbook for members of dysfunctional families to help heal their images of God as angry and unfriendly.

Author Dr. Carolyn Thomas, a Sister of Charity of Nazareth, holds an M.A. in theology, an S.T.M. in Old Testament, and a Ph.D. in New Testament. She teaches at college and seminary levels and is presently professor of biblical studies at Brescia College, Ky.

Contents *1.* The challenge *2.* God is faithful in loving us *3.* God is faithful in forgiving us *4.* God is faithful in caring for us *5.* God is faithful in consoling us *6.* God calls us to personal growth

Disappointment with God *Three Questions No One Asks Aloud,* Philip Yancey

Zondervan Publishing House, 1988, $9.99, paper, 260 pp., for counselees

Description This book won the ECPA Gold Medallion Award and was voted the Book of the Year by readers of *Christianity Today* in 1990. *Disappointment with God* deals with the issues that discourage or disillusion people in their personal relationship with God. It considers three questions—Is God Silent? Is God Unfair? and Is God Hidden? The first part of the book presents a survey of the entire Bible, examining how God interacted with human history. The second part gets more personal, addressing the questions in an honest, struggling way. It faces the struggles Christians have in maintaining faith in the midst of adversity. Ideal for counselees who are struggling with doubt, self-image problems, unanswered prayer, personal and family disappointments.

Author Philip Yancey earned graduate degrees in communications and English from Wheaton College Graduate School and the University of Chicago. He joined the staff of *Campus Life* magazine in 1971 and worked there as editor for eight years. Since 1978 he has primarily concentrated on freelance writing. More than 600 of his articles have appeared in 80 different publications. Five of his 11 books have received Gold Medallion Awards from the Evangelical Christian Publishers Association.

Contents *Book 1:* God within the shadows *Part 1:* Hearing the silence *1.* A fatal error *2.* Up in smoke *3.* The questions no one asks aloud *4.* What if *5.* The source *Part 2:* Making contact: the father *6.* Risky business *7.* The parent *8.* Unfiltered sunlight *9.* One shining moment *10.* Fire and the word *11.* Wounded lover *12.* Too good to be true *Part 3:* Drawing closer: the son *13.* The descent *14.* Great expectations *15.* Divine shyness *16.* The postponed miracle *17.* Progress *Part 4:* Turning it over: the spirit *18.* The transfer *19.* Changes in the wind *20.* The culmination *Book 2:* Seeing in the dark *21.* Interrupted *22.* The only problem *23.* A role in the cosmos *24.* Is God unfair? *25.* Why God doesn't explain *26.* Is God silent? *27.* Why God doesn't intervene *28.* Is God hidden? *29.* Why Job died happy *30.* Two wagers, two parables

Making Peace with God after Losing a Child

Abbey Press, $.50 each, paper, 8 pp., for counselees

Description Part of the CareNotes series from Abbey Press. CareNotes are short booklets that help readers identify issues and begin the process of seeking resolution. Anecdotal and uplifting. Beautiful photographs grace the covers. Over 20 million CareNotes have been sold in just over five years. Can be used as an alternative to a greeting card or in conjunction with pastoral care visits.

Inner Child/Inner Healing

Emotionally Free Rita Bennett

Fleming H. Revell, 1982, $8.99, paper, 254 pp., for counselees

Description Teaching on how to experience healing of deep hurts and painful memories emerges from Rita and Dennis Bennett's seminars into a book about psychological renewal and healing in Christ.

Author Rita Bennett is known internationally for her ministry of teaching, writing, and Healing the Whole Person Seminars with her husband.

How to Pray for Inner Healing for Yourself and Others Rita Bennett

Fleming H. Revell, 1984, $6.99, paper, 126 pp., for both counselors and counselees

Description A guide for effective prayer counseling. The author carefully discusses the preparation for prayer healing ministry and gives detailed instructions for dealing with the various kinds of emotional traumas that people experience.

Author Rita Bennett is known internationally for her ministry of teaching, writing, and Healing the Whole Person Seminars with her husband.

Contents *1.* What's in it for you? *2.* A starting point *3.* Have you heard the call? *4.* His presence for your journey *5.* When you pray *6.* Helps along the way *7.* Journey to life's beginning *8.* You don't travel alone

Inner Wholeness through the Lord's Prayer Rita Bennett

Chosen Books, 1991, $8.99, paper, 228 pp., for both counselors and counselees

Description In an affirming devotional style, the author encourages readers to meditate on each phrase of the Lord's prayer and receive its healing truths. Complete with a study guide for individual or group use.

Author Rita Bennett is known internationally for her ministry of teaching, writing, and Healing the Whole Person Seminars with her husband.

Making Peace with Your Inner Child Rita Bennett

Fleming H. Revell, 1987, $8.99, paper, 192 pp., for counselees

Description Helps the reader find true peace in life through the Scripture-based process of soul healing. She reveals how to receive inner healing through case studies, prayer sessions, and specific instruction for seeking help.

Author Rita Bennett is known internationally for her ministry of teaching, writing, and Healing the Whole Person Seminars with her husband.

Contents *1.* Making peace with your hurt inner child *2.* Marty makes peace with Martha *3.* A gift of peace for you *4.* Making peace with your inner parents *5.* Peace with your mother *6.* Beth makes peace *7.* Beth makes peace 2 *8.* Peace with your father *9.* Peace with your Heavenly Father

The Child in Each of Us *Healing the Wounds of Childhood That Hinder Our Growth As Adults,* Richard W. Dickinson and Carole Gift Page

Victor Books, 1992, $8.99, paper, 180 pp., for both counselors and counselees

Description You have an inner child in you who wants to live freely and to express your inner longings and needs—a child who wants to be understood and loved, who wants to reach spontaneously for life. The child in you has so often been stifled, so often discouraged, hemmed in, so often ignored that you can almost forget about that most vital part of your life. Jesus is the lover of your inner child. He desires to nurture and care for it, so that you can become a whole person and nurturer of those in your care.

Authors Dr. Richard Dickinson is a clinical psychologist in private practice and owner of Interface Psychological Service in Los Alamitos, Calif. He is professor of psychology at El Camino Community College and director of IDAK , a midlife career transitional service for Los Angeles and Orange County. He received his Ph.D. from Rosemead School of Psychology, Biola University. Carole Gift Paige has authored 29 books and hundreds of short stories and articles. She is a frequent speaker at writers' conferences.

Contents Introduction / Discovering the inner child / Abuses of the inner child / The many masks we wear / Why we feel so alone with others / Why marriages often fail / Creating children in our own image / Creating our own stress / Releasing your inner child / Developing a caring inner parent / Suggestions for people helpers

The Child in Each of Us—Workbook
Healing the Wounds of Childhood That Hinder Our Growth As Adults, Richard W. Dickinson, Carole Gift Page, and Beth Funk

Victor Books, 1992, $15.95, paper, 238 pp., for both counselors and counselees

Description Companion guide to the book. The workbook provides you with the tools to heal the wounds of your childhood, break the cycle of your negative thoughts and actions, recover your self-esteem in Christ, change destructive patterns in your parenting, feel a freedom and aliveness you may not have felt in a long time. Contains the entire text of *The Child in Each of Us,* journaling exercises, prayer exercises, Scripture meditation and memorization, small group study guide, recovery resources.

Authors Dr. Richard Dickinson is a clinical psychologist in private practice and owner of Interface Psychological Service in Los Alamitos, Calif. He is professor of psychology at El Camino Community College and director of IDAK , a midlife career transitional service for Los Angeles and Orange County. He received his Ph.D. from Rosemead School of Psychology, Biola University. Carole Gift Paige has authored 29 books and hundreds of short stories and articles. She is a frequent speaker at writers' conferences. Beth Funk has been involved with recovery groups for four years. She is director of recovery groups and single ministry at Ocean Hills Community Church in San Juan Capistrano, Calif.

Contents *Part 1:* Discovering the inner child / Abuses of the inner child / The many masks we wear / Why we feel so alone with others / Why marriages often fail / Creating children in our own image / Creating our own stress / Releasing your inner child / Developing a caring inner parent / Suggestions for people helpers *Part 2: Appendix 1:* Group study format, group guidelines, personal journey summary sheets *Appendix 2:* Support group resources, specialized reading resources *Appendix 3:* Supplemental journaling pages

Inner Healing *A Handbook for Helping Yourself and Others,* Mike Flynn and Doug Gregg

InterVarsity Press, 1993, $9.99, paper, 192 pp., for both counselors and counselees

Description This straightforward handbook shows readers how God can set a new course in their lives. The authors take an approach to inner healing that stresses the principles and models provided by Scripture while correcting common myths and misunderstandings. They offer readers all the necessary tools for embarking on their own healing journey.

Authors Mike Flynn is rector of St. Jude's Episcopal Church in Burbank, Calif. Doug Gregg is copastor of Faith United Presbyterian Church in Highland Park, Calif., and adjunct professor of spiritual formation and development at Fuller Theological Seminary.

Contents *1.* What is the mystery of inner healing? *2.* How we became involved in inner healing *3.* Theological underpinnings *4.* Using the Bible in inner healing *5.* Jesus' healing authority *6.* Jesus' healing love *7.* Praying for oneself *8.* Praying for others *9.* Psychological factors *10.* Frequent mistakes *11.* Working with the Spirit *12.* Spiritual warfare *13.* Wider dimensions of inner healing

New Clothes from Old Threads *12-Step Messages for the Child in Each of Us,* Sally Hill

Recovery Publications, Inc., 1991, $9.95, paper, 440 pp., for both counselors and counselees

Description A variety of childhood favorites are interwoven with 12-step reflections to form a rich tapestry of insights for daily living. This charming book helps us look at life through the eyes of our inner child.

Author Sally Hill has been using the 12 steps in her life "one day at a time" for nine years. She is a student in the doctoral program in counseling psychology at Texas Woman's University in Denton, Tex.

Contents Introduction / January—Rapunzel / February—Rumpelstilzkin, Cinderella / March—Prince Charming / April—Snow White / May—The 12 dancing princesses / June—The emperor's new clothes, The ugly duckling / July—Cinderlad / August—East of the sun / September—Prince Hyacinth, Hansel and Gretel / October—The fir-tree / November—Beauty and the beast / December—The fisherman and his wife, The selfish giant

Inner Healing for Broken Vessels *Seven Steps to a Woman's Way of Healing,* Linda H. Hollies

Abingdon Press, 1992, $8.95, paper, 112 pp., for both counselors and counselees

Description The seven steps to inner healing described in this book are steps the author learned through much pain and struggle as she has made her journey from childhood wounds to wholeness. Each chapter weaves the story of a present-day woman's struggle with that of a woman from the Bible. Biblical principles for help are included, and at the end of each chapter are questions and suggestions for growth in the healing process.

Author Linda H. Hollies is pastor of Richards Street United Methodist Church in Joliet, Ill. She is

founder and executive director of Woman to Woman Ministries, Inc.

Play Therapy Michael Joseph

Abbey Press, 1990, $3.95, paper, 80 pp., for counselees

Description Do you know how to play anymore? The delightful pages of *Play Therapy* are a practical strategy for reclaiming the gift of joy, which is your birthright. Discovering the wonder of your inner child is not only good therapy but a response to the ancient wisdom call to "become as a little child." Format: A series of about 30 short sayings, proverbs, and admonitions accompanied by whimsical cartoons on every page.

Deep Wounds, Deep Healing *Discovering the Vital Link between Spiritual Warfare and Inner Healing,* Charles H. Kraft

Servant Publications/Vine Books, 1994, $9.99, paper, for both counselors and counselees

Description In seeking healing for deep wounds like the trauma of incest or the pain of divorce, Charles H. Kraft believes that Christians often overlook the powerful link between spiritual warfare and inner healing. Many times professional counseling by itself is simply not enough. Deep healing requires an understanding of the spiritual roots of emotional wounds in order to bring about lasting freedom and wholeness to the sufferer. A complete guide to inner healing, for both the sufferer and those who minister to them.

Author Charles H. Kraft, who has been involved in a healing ministry for eight years, is professor of anthropology and intercultural communication at Fuller Theological Seminary in Pasadena, Calif.

Contents *Part 1:* An introduction to deep-level healing *1.* It's about freedom *2.* What is deep-level healing? *3.* Who needs deep-level healing? *4.* An orientation for the one who ministers *5.* How to do deep-level healing *6.* Helpful techniques in ministering *Part 2:* Issues and problems in deep-level healing *7.* Our reactions are usually the main problem *8.* Healing our wounded self-image *9.* Healing from infected wounds from the past *10.* Healing from the loss of death and divorce *11.* Ministry of the inner family *12.* Demonization and deep-level healing

Unlocking the Secrets of Your Childhood Memories Kevin Leman and Randy Carlson

Janet Thoma (a division of Thomas Nelson), 1994, $14.99, paper, 288 pp., for counselees

Description A workbook based on the best-selling book of the same title. An innovative program to help you understand why you do the things you do, turn negative memories into positive ones, and make your best memories work for you. Allows readers to tap into their childhood memories, analyze them, relieve a little stress, gain a little acceptance, alleviate some of their pain.

Authors Dr. Kevin Leman is the author of 13 books on family and marriage, a psychologist, and host of the syndicated radio program *Parent Talk*. Randy Carlson is the president of Today's Family Life, Inc. and the vice president of the Family Life Radio Network.

Freeing Your Mind from Memories That Bind *How to Heal from the Hurts of the Past,* Fred Littauer and Florence Littauer

Janet Thoma (a division of Thomas Nelson), 1988, $10.99, paper, 304 pp., for both counselors and counselees

Description In four sections, the authors set forth a biblical basis for inner healing through Jesus Christ. The authors explore emotional dysfunction and the childhood experiences that potentially lead to it through an extensive series of 94 brief chapters.

Authors Fred Littauer is a graduate of New York University and the director of CLASS ministries. With his wife, he travels to seminars and speaking engagements in the United States and abroad. Florence Littauer is a popular speaker and best-selling author.

The Power of Memories *How to Use Them to Improve Your Health and Well-Being,* Frank Minirth

Thomas Nelson Publishers, 1995, $18.99, cloth, 256 pp.

Description Understanding how memories work, realizing their effect on someone, then acting on that understanding can help readers reshape their lives and futures. An amazing number of health problems can be reduced by examining memories, according to Minirth.

Author Frank Minirth, M.D., is cofounder and co-CEO of the Minirth-Meier New Life Clinics, one

of the largest mental health care providers in the United States.

Contents *Part 1*—When memory works for us *1.* The power of memories *2.* Our mind's amazing power to remember *3.* The changing world inside our memories *4.* Memories—a mirror of who we are *Part 2*—When memory works against us *5.* Can our memories be distorted? *6.* Unhappy memories—all of us have some *7.* Preparing to mend memories *8.* Healing unhappy memories *9.* When memories will not heal *Part 3*—When children remember *10.* Shaping young kids' memories *11.* Shaping teen memories *12.* Meeting a child's special memory needs *Part 4*—When memories build the future *13.* Building good family memories *14.* Blessed memories

Scripture Pathways to Inner Healing
Victor M. Parachin

Ligouri Publications, 1994, $6.95, paper, for counselees

Description A ten-week program of daily meditations and prayers based on the stages of inner healing. Without resorting to "recovery" jargon, Parachin brings a uniquely Christian element to the popular concept of inner healing. Each day's reflection begins with an appropriate Scripture passage and concludes with a prayer and affirmation.

Contents *1.* From hesitation to hope *2.* From fear to faith *3.* From tears to trust *4.* From victim to victor *5.* From pain to peace *6.* From adversity to advantage *7.* From cynicism to celebration *8.* From grieving to growing *9.* From hurting to healing *10.* From callousness to compassion

Deliverance and Inner Healing *A Comprehensive Guide,* John Sandford and Mark Sandford

Chosen Books, 1992, $11.95, paper, 380 pp., for counselors

Description The first of its kind, this book reconciles the deliverance and inner healing fields of Christian ministry. Offering balanced biblical teaching, the Sandfords show how both inner healing and deliverance are valuable and necessary if people are to grow in Christ. They correct some of the misunderstandings and abuses in both fields and present new directions for the fields to work in harmony.

Authors John Sandford (M.Div., Chicago Theological Seminary) served as pastor for 21 years before founding Elijah House and is the author or coauthor of seven other books. Coauthor Mark Sandford, (M.Div., Denver Theological Seminary) served as a counselor in private practice in Florida

341

and now serves on the counseling staff of Elijah House in north Idaho.

Contents *Section 1:* The relationship between deliverance and inner healing *1.* Deliverance and inner healing—both-and; not either-or *2.* A sensible view of deliverance *3.* What inner healing is *4.* What inner healing is not *5.* A Christian can be demonized *6.* Deliverance and inner healing meet at the armor *7.* The do's and don'ts of deliverance *8.* A balanced attitude about mental illness *9.* When deliverance and inner healing are inappropriate *Section 2:* Deliverance and inner healing from types and functions of demons *10.* Delivering places *11.* Delivering animals and objects *12.* Demonic specialists *13.* Strongholds, individual and corporate *Section 3:* The relationship of occultism, spiritism, and cults to demons, deliverance, and inner healing *14.* Occult involvement and demons *15.* Spiritualism, delusion, and cults

Healing the Wounded Spirit John Sandford and Paula Sandford

Victory House Publishing, 1983, $11.95, paper, 473 pp., for counselors

Description Sequel to *The Transformation of the Inner Man.* A book of inner healing therapy, it covers topics faced by counselors such as anorexia, dyslexia, schizophrenia, child abuse, depression, death wishes, occult involvement, spiritual adultery, idolatry, generational sin, grief, etc. This is a book for counselors and others who suffer from hidden hurts—past or present. Through the Sandfords' unique teaching style, one learns to discern a wounded spirit in self and others.

Authors John Sandford is a veteran counselor with over 35 years' experience. He is author/coauthor of more than seven best-selling titles that relate to recovery and inner healing. He travels extensively. With her husband, Paula Sandford has written four classics in the field of inner healing.

Contents *Section 1:* Incarnational wounds and sins *1.* The forgotten functions of our spirit *2.* In utero encounters *3.* Wounds from feeling rejected *4.* Anorexia, dyslexia, schizophrenia, child abuse *Section 2:* Sickness and sinful conditions of the spirit *5.* The slumbering spirit *6.* Spiritual imprisonment *7.* Depression *8.* Defilements, devils, and death wishes *9.* Identification and shirkism *Section 3:* Spiritual sins *10.* Occult involvement *11.* Spiritualism and exorcism *12.* Spiritual adultery and idolatry *Section 4:* Things which impinge upon and wound our spirits *13.* Generational sin *14.* Burden bearing—and leeches *15.* Grief, frustration, and loss *16.* Dwelling within a sinful group

The Transformation of the Inner Man
The Most Comprehensive Book on Inner

Healing Today, John Sandford and Paula Sandford

Victory House Publishing, 1981, $11.95, paper, 412 pp., for counselors

Description One of the most comprehensive books on inner healing on the market today. Topics include: sanctification, performance orientation, forgiveness, the counselor's role, inner vows, hearts of stone, bitter-root judgments, sexual sins, homosexuality, individuation, parenting, the body of Christ, etc. Over 200,000 copies have been sold to date.

Authors John Sandford is a veteran counselor with over 35 years' experience. He is author/coauthor of more than seven best-selling titles that relate to recovery and inner healing. He travels extensively. With her husband, Paula Sandford has written four classics in the field of inner healing.

Contents *Section 1:* Foundations *1.* Sanctification and transformation *2.* The evangelical base of transformation *3.* Performance orientation *4.* The base of law *5.* The central power and necessity of forgiveness *6.* Breaking the cycle *7.* The role of a Christian counselor *Section 2:* Early life—hidden sins *8.* Crib time *9.* Toddling terrors *10.* From walking, to school *Section 3:* Six to twelve—most common and vitiating malformations of character *11.* Inner vows *12.* Hearts of stone *13.* Flight, control, burial, and possessiveness *14.* Bitter-root judgment and expectancy *Section 4:* Sexual sins and difficulties *15.* Fornication, adultery, inordinate desire, and aberrations *16.* Archetypes and homosexuality *17.* Parental inversion and substitute mates *Section 5:* Teens and marriage *18.* Individuation and destiny malaise *19.* Finding, leaving, and cleaving *20.* The problem of becoming one *Section 6:* The resurrection side *21.* Fathers and mothers in Christ *22.* Body ministry and fellowship

Healing for Damaged Emotions
Recovering from the Memories That Cause Our Pain, David A. Seamands

Victor Books, 1981, $9.99, paper, 144 pp., for both counselors and counselees

Description Just below the concealing, protective mask many individuals wear are recorded thoughts and emotions and memories that profoundly affect the way we look at life, God, others, and ourselves, and frequently need the healing touch of God and a process of recovery. Through Seamand's realistic, scriptural approach, countless numbers of individuals have learned to deal honestly and successfully with their inner hurts. First published in 1981, this work has over 750,000 copies in print.

Author David Seamands is professor emeritus of pastoral ministries and counselor in residence at Asbury Theological Seminary in Wilmore, Ky.

Contents *Part 1: 1.* Damaged emotions 2. Guilt, grace, and debt collecting 3. The wounded healer 4. Satan's deadliest weapon 5. Healing our low self-esteem 6. Healing our low self-esteem 2 *Part 2: 7.* Symptoms of perfectionism 8. The process of healing for perfectionism 9. Super you or real you? 10. Myths and truths about depression 11. Dealing with depression 12. Healed helpers

Healing for Damaged Emotions—Workbook *Recovering from the Memories That Cause Our Pain,* David A. Seamands

Victor Books, 1993, $15.99, paper, 237 pp., for both counselors and counselees

Description Victor Books is pleased to offer the *Healing for Damaged Emotions Workbook,* a new format that provides tools to examine what lies below the surface of life and to find healing for the painful scars that cripple one's emotions. This workbook contains: the entire text of *Healing for Damaged Emotions,* Scripture meditation and memorization, prayer exercises, journaling exercises, a small group guide, recovery resources.

Author David Seamands is professor emeritus of pastoral ministries and counselor in residence at Asbury Theological Seminary in Wilmore, Ky.

Contents *Part 1: 1.* Damaged emotions 2. Guilt, grace, and debt collecting 3. The wounded healer 4. Satan's deadliest weapon 5. Healing our low self-esteem 6. Healing our low self-esteem 2 *Part 2: 7.* Symptoms of perfectionism 8. The process of healing for perfectionism 9. Super you or real you? 10. Myths and truths about depression 11. Dealing with depression 12. Healed helpers *Part 2: Appendix 1:* Group study format—guidelines for group sharing—personal journaling summary sheets *Appendix 2:* Support group resources—specialized reading resources *Appendix 3:* Supplemental journaling pages

Healing of Memories David A. Seamands

Victor Books, 1985, $10.99, paper, 189 pp., for both counselors and counselees

Description The memory is a complex function that is often at the center of deep-rooted emotional problems. The memory is also where the Holy Spirit can begin the healing process. A great resource for anyone involved in counseling ministry.

Author David Seamands is professor emeritus of pastoral ministries and counselor in residence at Asbury Theological Seminary in Wilmore, Ky.

Contents *1.* The mystery of memory 2. What is healing of memory? 3. Why do some memories need healing? 4. Creating the atmosphere for healing 5. Biblical foundations for memory healing 6. Indications for the healing of memories 7. Distorted concepts of God 8. Difficulties from the distortions about God 9. Preparing for the prayer time 10. Conducting the prayer time 11. Healing memories of sexual trauma 12. Follow-up, cautions, and conclusions

Putting Away Childish Things David A. Seamands

Victor Books, 1982, $8.99, paper, 144 pp., for counselees

Description We all have childish behavior patterns that hold us back from reaching spiritual and emotional maturity and hinder us from growing up spiritually. But you can move toward the maturity God desires for you if you follow the seasoned, biblical advice of this best-selling author and counselor who claims God can reprogram old, childish ways and lead you into Christian adulthood. More than 250,000 copies in print. A leader's guide is also available.

Author David Seamands is professor emeritus of pastoral ministries and counselor in residence at Asbury Theological Seminary in Wilmore, Ky.

Contents *1.* The hidden child in all of us 2. The healing of memories 3. A childhood motto which destroys adults 4. Another childhood motto 5. Childish ideas of love and marriage 6. Childish ideas of God and his will 7. Childish ideas of prayer 8. Childhood confusion versus adult distinctions 9. Childish dependency on feelings 10. Childish concepts of self and self-surrender 11. The ultimate crisis of life 12. Reprogramming grace

Depth Healing and Renewal through Christ *Guided Meditations for Individuals or Groups,* Flora Slosson Wuellner

Abingdon Press, 1992, $10.95, cassette(s), for both counselors and counselees

Description This 90-minute cassette contains five recorded meditations on the following topics: listening to our bodies and bonding with Christ; healing our wounds of birth, early infancy, and inherited family wounds; healing a special memory; healing our central personality problem; healing for a future experience. Participants in these healing meditations are encouraged to remember always the continuing presence and tenderness of God experienced through the living Christ.

Author Flora Slosson Wuellner is an ordained United Church of Christ minister and the best-selling author of numerous books.

Recovery Devotionals

The Frazzled Mother's Guide to Inner Peace *A Practical Guide Divided into 10-Minute Readings,* Pat Baker

Tyndale House Publishers, 1992 (5th ed.), $6.95, paper, 175 pp., for counselees

Description The book includes every situation, hardship, or thought new mothers encounter. Addresses the nonstop responsibilities that accompany caring for a baby. It deals with the new mother's fears, frustrations, and fatigue with personal encouragement and support from God's Word and a great deal of compassion from the author.

Author Pat Baker is the mother of three daughters, a speaker in churches and at retreats, and the author of several books. She and her husband live in Bolivar, Mo.

Contents *Phase one:* Fears, frustrations, and fatigue *Phase two:* Some new breakthroughs *Phase three:* Better days . . . and nights *Phase four:* Four months and counting

Bible Promises for the Healing Journey Lana L. Bateman

Barbour and Company, 1989, $13.95/$8.95, cloth/paper, 119 pp., for counselees

Description If you are recovering from abuse, compulsive behavior, or codependency, here is help and hope from God's Word. *Bible Promises for the Healing Journey* is a collection of Bible verses appropriately arranged for the following five stages: preparation, provisions, the journey, obstacles, rewards. The passages chosen instill a sense of hope, security, and confidence in the Lord's ability to minister to the hurting heart.

Author Lana L. Bateman is the founder of Philippian Ministries, based in Dallas, Tex. She speaks throughout the United States and also in England and Canada.

Poems for the Healing Journey Lana L. Bateman

Barbour and Company, 1991, $9.97, cloth, 348 pp., for counselees

Description The five stages of inward healing toward emotional wholeness described in *Bible Promises for the Healing Journey* are now illuminated by the words of fellow travelers. Abuse and loss of many kinds and the ultimate victory over one's past, however traumatic, are poignantly recalled.

Author Lana L. Bateman is the founder of Philippian Ministries.

Create in Me a Clean Heart *Prayer and Scripture to Cleanse and Make Whole,* Ray Beeson

Thomas Nelson Publishers, 1995, $10.99, cloth, 160 pp.

Description Focusing on 20 biblical themes, this direct, helpful book aids readers in finding a deeper relationship with Christ through specific, directed prayer.

Author Ray Beeson is the founder of Overcomer's Institute and a minister, speaker, and author of numerous books.

Rhythms of the Heart *Readings That Connect Your Mood to God's Word,* Shelley Chapin

Victor Books, 1993, $8.99, paper, 512 pp., for counselees

Description This book is designed to provide you with daily insights and encouragement. Most devotional guides provide helpful support, but often the entry for the day does not coincide with the reader's felt need. This collection of over 200 readings explores our emotions and our responses to life. God's Word becomes the basis for insight into our hearts and experiences. Christian authors such as Jay Kesler, Max Lucado, Shelley Chapin, Ken Boa, and Boyd Luter help connect our moods to God's Word. The foreword is provided by Joni Eareckson Tada and a portion of all proceeds goes directly to Joni's ministry.

Author Editor Shelley Chapin is a family counselor, author, musician, teacher, and conference speaker. She holds a master's degree from Dallas Theological Seminary and is enjoying doctoral studies in the field of counseling.

Meditations for the Twelve Steps—A Spiritual Journey Friends in Recovery and Jerry S.

Recovery Publications, Inc., 1993, $6.95, paper, 176 pp., for counselees

Description A beautifully written devotional companion to the best-selling *The Twelve Steps—A Spiritual Journey Workbook,* based on the wisdom of the Bible and the spiritual truths of the 12 steps. Format: Scripture passage, anecdote, prayer.

Twelve Step Prayers for a Way Out
Friends in Recovery and Jerry S.

Recovery Publications, Inc., 1993, $7.95, paper, 128 pp., for counselees

Description This collection of prayers and inspirational readings was compiled to assist members of all 12-step fellowships with healing and spiritual progress. Can be used alone or with the companion volume: *The 12 Steps—A Way Out.* Designed to assist readers in seeking a more fulfilling spiritual connection with their higher power.

A Walk with the Serenity Prayer *Daily Devotions for People in Recovery,* Paul D. Meier, Frank B. Minirth, and Janet Congo

Thomas Nelson Publishers, 1991, $7.99, paper, 372 pp., for counselees

Description A daily devotional that takes readers through the seven key principles of the serenity prayer. Format: Scripture passage, several encouraging paragraphs, followed by a brief prayer.

Authors Doctors Minirth and Meier have gained national prominence for their successful blending of biblical principles with proven clinical and medical treatment. They are nationally recognized authors of over 60 biblically based books on common psychological issues with over three million copies in print.

Facing the Brokenness *Meditations for Parents of Sexually Abused Children,* K. C. Ridings

Herald Press, 1991, $8.95, paper, 176 pp., for counselees

Description Parents of sexually abused children will find this devotional guide/workbook a source of strength and hope for dealing with the emotional pain of sexual abuse. Thirty-one days' worth of interactive questions, anecdotes, and Scripture readings address the various aspects of coping with this difficult problem.

Author K. C. Ridings lives with her husband and children in Mesa, Ariz. She is a freelance writer and speaks on the topic of sexual abuse.

Rooted in God's Love *Biblical Meditations for People in Recovery,* Dale Ryan and Juanita Ryan

InterVarsity Press, 1993, $7.99, paper, 256 pp., for both counselors and counselees

Description This book is a series of meditations on biblical texts for people recovering from the most difficult of life's struggles. More than just a daily "positive affirmation," these meditations take the biblical text seriously as a resource for recovery.

Authors Dale Ryan is the executive director of the Recovery Partnership, the parent organization to the National Association for Christian Recovery. Juanita Ryan is a counselor in private practice in Hacienda Heights, Calif.

Contents *1.* Images of recovery *2.* Invitations *3.* Promises *4.* Honesty *5.* Spiritual distress in recovery *6.* God's help in tough times *7.* Seeing ourselves in new ways *8.* Living with limits *9.* Change *10.* Grief *11.* Healing *12.* Fellowship in recovery *13.* Taking in God's love *14.* Seeing God in new ways *15.* Rest *16.* Hope *17.* Joy

Handbook to Happiness in Verse
Charles R. Solomon

Solomon Publications, 1988, $4.95, paper, 59 pp., for counselees

Description This book contains the poems that were published in the first edition of *Handbook to Happiness* and some that were written since its publication. Since the poems were written out of pain, they have been used by God to strike a resonant chord in the lives of many hurting believers. Its strength is not so much in the technical perfections of the poetry but in the message that can be communicated by the Spirit from heart to heart.

Author Dr. Solomon is president and founder of Grace Fellowship International in Denver, Colo.

345

God called him to the ministry of counseling in 1967, and he developed an approach that is biblical, Christ-centered, and cross-centered.

Contents *1.* Poems *2.* The wheel and the line

The Jesus Person Pocket Promise Book
Over 800 Promises from the Word of God,
David Wilkerson

Regal Books, 1972, $2.99, paper, 83 pp., for both counselors and counselees

Description Verses are arranged by topic and need. Passages are quoted in full. Pocket-sized book.

Daily Meditations for Parenting Our Kids
Thomas Wright

Recovery Publications, Inc., 1993, $8.95, paper, 384 pp., for counselees

Description Written primarily for parents in recovery, this book includes 366 meditations and affirmations full of wisdom, insight, and comfort—poignant reflections for every parent facing the day-to-day challenges of raising kids.

Bible Promise Life Recovery Devotional, The

Tyndale House Publishers, 1993, $7.99, paper, 400 pp., for counselees

Description Each of the 360 readings is built around a Scripture promise and offers words of challenge for emotional and spiritual wholeness.

Day at a Time, A *Daily Reflections for Recovering People*

CompCare Publishers, 1976, $8.95, paper, 370 pp., for counselees

Description A best-selling inspirational. A longtime favorite among 12-step members with reflections and prayers to bring comfort and hope. Available in a variety of formats. Call publisher for details.

Life Recovery Bible. The *The Twelve Step Bible for People in Recovery*

Tyndale House Publishers, 1992, $19.99/$29.99, cloth/paper, for counselees

Description A study Bible specifically developed to help those who are hurting and in need of healing. Some of the features are: edited by Stephen Arterburn (New Life Treatment Centers) and David Stoop (Minirth-Meier-Stoop Clinic); uses *Living Bible* text throughout; 84 12-step devotionals interspersed throughout; serenity prayer devotionals, more than 50 Bible-based recovery devotionals; key Bible characters are profiled with important recovery lessons drawn from their lives, and a topical index and user's guide.

Recovery Bible—NIV

Zondervan Publishing House, 1993, $19.99, paper, 1472 pp., for counselees

Description A day-by-day guide connecting 12-step programs with the principles of God's Word. Including the full NIV Bible text, the *Recovery Bible* also includes 400 in-text life connections, 365 daily meditations, book introductions, reading plans, articles, and a 12-step index. People in all stages of recovery will benefit from this Bible.

39. Stress

Women under Stress *Preserving Your Sanity,* Randy Alcorn and Nanci Alcorn

Multnomah Books (Questar), 1986, $9.99, paper, 147 pp., for counselees

Description Deals with tensions and stresses unique to women. Demonstrates ways God can use such stresses to strengthen and teach you. Proposes a biblical lifestyle that honors God and respects the limits of your resources.

Authors Randy and Nanci Alcorn codirect Eternal Perspective ministries. They are both graduates of Multnomah School of the Bible. Randy Alcorn is a college and seminary professor and frequent conference speaker.

Contents *1.* Special stress on today's woman *2.* Stress: what's it all about? *3.* Stress, your circumstances, and your perspective *4.* How God uses stress for your good and his glory *5.* How to cope with stress *6.* Getting on top of your emotions *7.* Guilt, God, and self-esteem *8.* Are you meant to be wonder-wife and super-mom? *9.* Managing your time and tasks before they manage you *10.* How exercising right relieves stress *11.* How eating right relieves stress *12.* Your health and hormones *13.* Discovering the lost art of relaxation / *Conclusion:* Pace your race

Survival for Busy Women *Establishing Efficient Home Management,* Emilie Barnes

Harvest House Publishers, 1993, $8.99, paper, 271 pp., for counselees

Description This expanded 160,000-copy bestseller provides the practical plan to help active women organize their homes and live more balanced, stress-free lives. In this newly revised edition, noted home management expert Emilie Barnes gives step-by-step directions to help busy women evaluate priorities, eliminate clutter, and save time by planning ahead.

Author Emilie Barnes is the best-selling author of 11 books with sales of nearly 700,000 copies.

Contents *Part 1:* Survival through an organized you *1.* A thought for the woman of the nineties *2.* Recipe for beating stress *3.* Establishing the target *4.* Priorities—what comes first? *5.* On your way to the organized you! *6.* What

to do with all the paper *7.* Making time your friend *Part 2:* Survival through an organized home *8.* From total mess to total rest *9.* Saving time and money by meal planning *10.* Planning an efficient pantry and kitchen *11.* Washing and caring for our clothes *12.* Cleaning and organizing the garage *13.* Sewing and crafts solutions *Part 3:* Survival through organized children *14.* Child-proof safety in the home *15.* Family conference time *16.* Babysitting survival guide *17.* Teach your children about money *18.* Smart ideas for parents—that work! *Part 4:* Survival through organized moving *19.* You're moving . . . again? *20.* Let's have a garage sale! *Part 5:* Survival through organized vacations and travel *21.* Organizing a memorable vacation *22.* Travel smart—automobile organization *23.* Travel for less *24.* Family cruises can be fun *Part 6:* Survival through organized finances *25.* Record-keeping made simple *26.* Cheaper can be better *27.* Super energy—money saving tips *28.* Money management means money saved

Battle Fatigue Joe B. Brown

Broadman and Holman, 1995, $14.95, cloth, 226 pp.

Description This book highlights specific sources of stress that challenge almost everyone and presents a detailed guide to the biblical approach for defusing even the worst of stresses.

Author Joe B. Brown is senior pastor of Hickory Grove Baptist Church in Charlotte, N.C.

Contents *Part 1*—Walking when wounded *1.* Walking the distance *2.* Running the marathon *3.* Flying on eagle's wings *Part 2*—Winning the daily battles *4.* Developing personal priorities *5.* Building a magnificent marriage *6.* Prospering in a profession *7.* Firming up relationships, through forgiveness *8.* Surviving when your brook dries up *Part 3*—Gaining the ultimate victory *9.* Rebuilding broken altars *10.* Realizing it is never too late / *Conclusion:* Remember the best

Jumping Hurdles, Hitting Glitches, Overcoming Setbacks Steve Brown

NavPress, 1993, $15.00, cloth, for counselees

Description This collection of parables, anecdotes, and real-life stories delivers a message of hope and perseverance to anyone under pressure. If you're in need of a bit of understanding, some humor, or some down-to-earth encouragement, you'll find it here.

347

Author Steve Brown, a former Presbyterian minister, is an exceptional speaker.

Nam Vet *Making Peace with Your Past,* Chuck Dean

Multnomah Books (Questar), 1988, $8.99, paper, 156 pp., for counselees

Description Chuck Dean suggests how veterans can permanently break free from self-destructive behaviors and make lasting peace with their past.

Author Chuck Dean is executive director of Point Man International, a nonprofit support organization dedicated to healing the war wounds of Vietnam veterans.

Contents *1.* When I get home *2.* Living for DEROS *3.* A different kind of war *4.* The price still being paid *5.* "It don't mean nuthin" *6.* Nightmares *7.* Survival, guilt, and things I've done *8.* Outbursts of rage *9.* PTSD and the veteran's family *10.* Self-meditation *11.* My story *12.* How I made peace with my past *13.* Making peace with your past

Acceptance Therapy Lisa Engelhardt

Abbey Press, 1991, $3.95, paper, 70 pp., for counselees

Description Inspired by the multimillion selling booklet by Vincent Collins, *Acceptance Therapy* conveys the same liberating message of "let go and let God" for a new generation learning to be free from compulsions. The proven self-help blend of inspiring text and engaging illustrations gently guides the reader on a spiritual journey toward a life-affirming, health-giving outlook that remarkably touches at the very heart of recovery and wellness. An ideal gift book.

You've Got What It Takes *6 Studies for Women Who Have More Than They Can Handle,* Judy Hamlin

Victor Books, 1992, $4.99, paper, 64 pp., for counselees

Description Part of the Searching for Answers series from Victor. This study explores how to make good decisions, put life in balance, get finances in order, bring the best in relationships. Includes other topics for bringing a biblical, healthy balance to one's life. Uses an interactive format.

Author Dr. Judy Hamlin (Ph.D. in adult education, University of Southern Mississippi) is an authority on small groups and women's ministry.

Contents *1.* Remapping your priorities *2.* You can make good decisions *3.* Life out of balance *4.* Financial smarts *5.* How to begin the process of worship *6.* A gift worth receiving

Adrenalin and Stress *The Exciting New Breakthrough That Helps You Overcome Stress Damage,* Archibald D. Hart

Word Publishing, 1991, $8.99, paper, 208 pp., for counselees

Description This groundbreaking book explains the role played by adrenalin—the hormone dumped into our systems by stress—in either helping or hurting the way we cope with life's demands. It shows the dangers of coming to depend upon the excitement of life in the fast lane. And it shows the advantage of depending instead on God and the built-in mechanisms he has given us for stress control.

Author Archibald D. Hart is dean of the Graduate School of Psychology and professor of psychology at Fuller Theological Seminary. A skilled psychotherapist and committed Christian, Dr. Hart brings to this book the same combination of professional knowledge and personal concern that has made his other works successful.

Contents *Part 1:* Adrenalin arousal—the essence of stress disease *1.* Understanding the nature of stress *2.* How stress does its damage *3.* Stress as "hurry sickness" *4.* Stress and the spirit *Part 2:* Diagnosing your adrenalin arousal *5.* The symptoms of distress *6.* Are you an adrenalin addict? *7.* Adrenalin and cholesterol *8.* Finding the source of your stress *9.* How to monitor your adrenalin arousal *Part 3:* Healing your hurry sickness *10.* Managing your adrenalin *11.* The secret of sleep *12.* Learning to relax *13.* Changing your type-A behavior *14.* Creativity and stress *15.* Spiritual antidotes for stress / *Study guide*

Scripture-Based Solutions to Handling Stress Pat King

Ligouri Publications, 1990, $4.95, paper, 143 pp., for counselees

Description Combines scriptural advice and professional research to help readers take charge of their lives and defeat the feelings of helplessness and exhaustion. Includes journaling and Scripture-based exercises.

Contents "I've been there too"—the author's story *Part 1:* Defining the problem *1.* Our bodies under stress *2.* The stress of not being appreciated 3. Difficult transitions 4. Continuing stress *Part 2:* Finding solutions 5. Setting priorities 6. The eight-part plan for taking care of your body 7. Energy levels 8. The importance of saying "no" 9. Friends, the ultimate support system 10. Making peace through reconciliation 11. Letting go of the past through forgiveness 12. The secret of energy / Continuing on—helps for further progress / The I-gain-control-of-my-life chart

Life after Vietnam *How Veterans and Their Loved Ones Can Heal the Psychological Wounds of War,* Delores A. Kuenning

Paragon House Publishers, 1991, $22.95, cloth, 320 pp., for counselees

Description A recovery manual aimed at Vietnam's living casualties: those plagued with post-traumatic stress disorder and their relatives. The author sketches the historical background, then through personal interviews tells the powerful, moving stories of emotionally and/or physically ravaged veterans—men/women, soldiers, POWs, MIAs, Amerasians, and Agent Orange victims. Is currently being used in Vet centers throughout the United States. The author uses sound psychological and spiritual principles to help veterans understand and recover from compounded grief associated with post-traumatic stress disorder. Kuenning offers essential communication guidelines for their spouses, family, friends, and clergy. Each chapter and three appendixes list detailed resources, making this the most complete and caring guide available to veterans and those who share their lives. The author capably blends psychology with Bible teachings. Her extensive research, clear writing, and sound advice on resolving grief and guilt is both state-of-the-art psychology and the compassionate essence of most religions.

Author Delores A. Kuenning is the wife of a United Church of Christ clergyman and has been a freelance writer for more than 25 years and has written extensively on social, medical, and spiritual issues.

Contents *Part 1:* Understanding the war in Vietnam 1. How and why the U.S. got involved 2. Why Vietnam was a different war *Part 2:* Coping with the pain of wartime memories 3. They came home changed—what is post-traumatic-stress syndrome? 4. Women—the forgotten veterans 5. Overcoming the emotional scars of physical wounds 6. Warrior's women—living with a Vietnam veteran 7. The enduring wounds of agent orange 8. When loved ones did not come home 9. POWs/MIAs then and now 10. Amerasians—a legacy of war *Part 3:* Spiritual

healing 11. Where was God in Vietnam? 12. Coming to terms with the guilt of war 13. Unfinished business and steps through grief 14. The healing of memories *Part 4:* Other therapy 15. Delayed parades 16. The wall of tears 17. Veterans speak out / *Appendix:* A. The church's historical approach to war B. Devotional readings C. A word to the church D. Communication guidelines for pastors E. How to help POWs/MIAs

Everybody's Breaking Pieces off Me *Stress Relieving Devotions for Women,* Susan Lenzkes

Discovery House Publishers, 1992, $7.99, paper, 128 pp., for counselees

Description Any woman who is handling stress on a daily basis will appreciate these short, easy-to-read, yet powerful devotions.

Four Ways to Deal with Stress Daniel L. Lowery

Ligouri Publications, 1987, $.75, paper, 24 pp., for counselees

Description Helps readers better understand and deal with stress in their lives. Considers a variety of stress-reducing practices and focuses on four positive, personal, prayerful ways to cope.

Women and Stress *A Practical Approach to Managing Tension,* Jean Lush with Pam Vredevelt

Fleming H. Revell, 1992, $14.99, cloth, 272 pp., for counselees

Description Writing in an informative style, the authors explore the causes of stress, cite typical responses to tension, and offer proven strategies for managing emotions and alleviating stress.

Authors Jean Lush has written several best-selling books. She is the director of Christian Counseling Services and a licensed professional counselor. Pam Vredevelt is a professional counselor.

Contents *Part 1:* What makes us tense 1. Anger 2. Painful emotions 3. Low self-esteem 4. Grief 5. Rehabilitation 6. Job stress 7. Unmet needs 8. Parenting pressures 9. Hormonal pressures 10. Menopause *Part 2:* Typical responses to tension 11. The role of early conditioning 12. Our storage pot 13. Mrs. Flight 14. Mrs. Fight 15. Mrs. Sit Tight *Part 3:* Secrets to taming your tensions 16. Do away with disorder 17. Diversions 18. More ways to discharge your tension 19. Don't look back

Stress Management *Finding the Balance,* Keith Madsen

Serendipity, 1992, $6.95, paper, 94 pp., for both counselors and counselees

Description A 7- or 14-week course utilizing Scripture and discussion questions. Designed for anyone interested in learning how to manage stress.

Contents *1.* The many faces of stress *2.* Setting our own pace *3.* Listening to body language *4.* Keeping our focus *5.* Just say "thanks" *6.* A little help from my friends *7.* Restoring the soul

Stress Mary Dell Miles

Abingdon Press, 1994, $4.95, paper, 64 pp., for both counselors and counselees

Description Part of the LifeSearch series from Abingdon. Designed for use in small group settings, provides flexible format and a leader's guide. Deeper than most topical studies.

Author Mary Miles operates an ecumenical film cooperative. She also works as a Christian education consultant and as an adult fitness instructor.

Contents *1.* Welcome to lifesearch! *2.* QuickLead *3.* Icons *4.* Introduction *5.* Chapter 1—time to think about stress *6.* Chapter 2—just talking helps *7.* Chapter 3—no more stress in my relationships please *8.* Chapter 4—no one said life would be easy *9.* Chapter 5—minding the store *10.* Group resources

Slow-Down Therapy Linus Mundy

Abbey Press, 1990, $3.95, paper, 80 pp., for counselees

Description *Slow-Down Therapy* is not "35 steps to becoming mostly mellow." Rather what you will find are 35 concrete ideas for helping you discover something you already possess—time, enough time. Here you will find tips for discovering your own ways to a more peaceful, relaxed use of time. These ways are there for the finding, even in the busiest of lives. Format: a series of about 30 short sayings, proverbs, and admonitions accompanied by whimsical cartoons on every page.

Pressure Points Gary Jackson Oliver

Moody Press, 1993, $10.95, for counselees

Description Helps readers understand and deal with life's pressures.

Author Gary J. Oliver is a psychologist at Southwest Counseling Associates and visiting professor at Denver Seminary.

Teenage Stress and What to Do about It
Ralph Ranieri

Ligouri Publications, 1983, $.75, paper, 24 pp., for counselees

Description In this booklet, the author suggests some ways to handle five common causes of stress in a teenager's life such as change, the fear of being average, "putting your eggs in one basket," and peer pressure.

Stress Relief Randy Reynolds and David Lynn

Zondervan Publishing House, 1992, $4.99, paper, 96 pp., for both counselors and counselees

Description Part of the Recovery Discovery series of workbooks. This title offers help for those struggling with stress, exhaustion, burnout, relapse, compassion, fatigue, and compulsions by pointing them to God's purposes for the Sabbath.

How to Balance Competing Time Demands *Keeping the Five Most Important Areas of Your Life in Balance,* Doug Sherman and William Hendricks

NavPress, 1992, $9.00, paper, for counselees

Description Learn how to balance the five most important areas of your life—family, work, spiritual growth, church, and community.

Stress Steve Shores

NavPress, 1992, $5.00, paper, 64 pp., for counselees

Description In this IBC discussion guide, you'll look at how stress can both help and hinder you in your personal growth and relationships. You'll learn how to avoid meaningless stress and take advantage of stress that causes growth.

Author Steve Shores is a private practice counselor and writer in Hickory, N.C. Formerly he was assistant professor of pastoral ministries and director of counseling services at Dallas Theological Seminary.

Contents *Session 1*—The good news about stress—what stress is good for *Session 2*—The bad news about stress—stress and the pursuit of approval *Session 3*—Two strange roommates—stress and self-condemnation *Session 4*—Bringing the good and the bad together *Session 5*—Turning for home / *Conclusion* / Help for leaders

Horrific Traumata *A Pastoral Response to the Post-Traumatic Stress Disorder,* Duncan Sinclair

The Haworth Pastoral Press, 1993, $24.95, cloth, 116 pp., for counselors

Description Shares the stories of persons whose meaning, hope, and faith were ripped from them by others or by traumatic events. Duncan Sinclair presents a clear and workable understanding of the nature of PTSD that gives clergy and others involved direct insight into the causes of many behaviors.

Author Duncan Sinclair, M.Div., is an Episcopal priest and a licensed marriage and family therapist in Georgia.

Contents The nature of trauma / Results of trauma / Trauma delayed PTSD / Spiritual diagnosis / Very special cases / The victim and family / Pastoral counseling and the treatment process / Pastoral response—a view from Scripture

Margin *How to Create the Emotional, Physical, and Time Reserves You Need,* Richard A. Swenson

NavPress, 1992, $17.00, cloth, 275 pp., for counselees

Description Dr. Swenson provides a prescription against the danger of overloaded lives. Focusing on margin in four key areas—emotional energy, physical energy, time, and finances—he offers an overall picture of health that employs contentment, simplicity, balance, and rest.

Author Richard Swenson, M.D., holds an M.D. from the University of Illinois School of Medicine. He has spent five years in private practice and is currently an associate professor at the University of Wisconsin Medical School.

Contents *1.* Marginless living *Part 1:* The problem: pain *2.* The pain of progress *3.* The pain of problems *4.* The pain of stress *5.* The pain of overload *Part 2:* The prescription: margin *6.* Margin *7.* Margin in emotional energy *8.* Margin in physical energy *9.* Margin in time *10.* Margin in finances *Part 3:* The prognosis: health *11.* Health through contentment *12.* Health through simplicity *13.* Health through balance *14.* Health through rest *15.* Pain, margin, health, and relationship

How to Handle Stress D. D. Warrick

NavPress, 1991, $2.00, paper, 23 pp., for counselees

Description Although there are times when a certain amount of stress can be good, more often it comes as an undesirable blow to our system—just as unwelcome as the circumstances causing it. If you're looking for ways to reduce the amount of stress in your life, this booklet will help. You'll not only learn how stress works (an important part of overcoming it), but you'll discover what to do the next time you feel it creeping into your life.

Beyond Chaos *Stress Relief for the Working Woman,* Sheila West

NavPress, 1991, $15.00, cloth, 208 pp., for counselees

Description Targets career women. Designed to instruct and inspire in the art of purposeful living—a way of life that enables you to establish goals, make decisions, experience God's peace and fulfillment, even in the midst of chaos.

Author Sheila West is the cofounder, owner, president, and CEO of ACI Consolidated, Inc., an INC. 500 company in Monroe, Mich.

Contents *Part 1:* Setting the anchor that never shifts: the importance of purpose *1.* Take hold of something incredible *2.* Adjust your own sails *Part 2:* Planning for the journey: carrying out your purpose through vision *3.* Set your sights with action-vision *4.* Take care of yourself *5.* Nurture your relationships *6.* Take charge with change in the marketplace *Part 3:* Progress in the midst of chaos: achieving extraordinary results one step at a time *7.* Sync or sink: integrating your agenda with MINI steps *8.* Trade survival for excellence *Part 4:* Becoming a person in the marketplace: remembering what the journey is all about *9.* You can influence others through CEO leadership *10.* Success: hitting the right targets *11.* Stay on the completeness edge

Spirituality *God's Rx for Stress,* Neil B. Wiseman

Beacon Hill Press of Kansas City, 1992, paper, 250 pp., for counselees

Description *Spirituality* offers tremendous resources for substantially reducing stress. Author Neil Wiseman bridges the gap with understanding and relief for those bound by the pressures of life.

Author Neil B. Wiseman has served his denomination as pastor, professor, magazine editor, and academic dean. In career and family roles, he has both learned for himself and counseled others on stress management.

Easing the Burden of Stress

Abbey Press, $.50 each, paper, 8 pp., for counselees

Description Part of the CareNotes series from Abbey Press. CareNotes are short booklets that help readers identify issues and begin the process of seeking resolution. Anecdotal and uplifting. Beautiful photographs grace the covers. Over 20 million CareNotes have been sold in just over five years. Can be used as an alternative to a greeting card or in conjunction with pastoral care visits.

Easing the Stress in Your Life

Abbey Press, 1994, $.50 each, paper, 8 pp., for counselees

Description Part of the New CareSteps series from Abbey Press. Each CareStep pamphlet (three-panel) is filled with insightful advice and quotes from respected leaders in the helping professions. Very useful during the early stages of recovery. The underlying message in all CareSteps pamphlets is the emphasis on using all one's resources—emotional, physical, mental, social, and spiritual—to cope with life's biggest challenges. This title emphasizes making lists, confronting stress, taking care of oneself, reaching out to trusted people, and improving skills in specific areas to avoid stress.

Grades *When the Pressure Is Too Much*

Abbey Press, 1993, $.50 each, paper, 8 pp., for counselees

Description Part of the CareNotes for Teens series from Abbey Press. CareNotes are 5 x 7 booklets designed to offer strength and help to (young) people in crisis. Each CareNote gently introduces an issue, then encourages a person to take appropriate steps toward resolution. Over 20 million CareNotes have been sold.

Reaching the Vietnam Vet

Focus on the Family, 1988, $.35, paper, 10 pp., for counselees

Description Discusses PTSD and suggests several ways individuals and churches can help vets struggling with PTSD.

40. Suffering

Help for Pain and Suffering *Stories and Reflections,* Russell M. Abata

Ligouri Publications, 1991, $1.95, paper, 64 pp., for counselees

Description A priest/counselor consults Bible passages and examples from modern life to help readers continue to have faith even when relief is nowhere in sight.

Contents *1.* Looking for help *2.* Going to Jesus for help *3.* Consulting nature for help *4.* Bringing the teachings together *5.* Facing the mystery of evil *6.* Discovering peace despite pain *7.* Accepting the challenges of life and love

Christ and Your Problems Jay E. Adams

P & R Publishing, 1971, $1.50, paper, 32 pp., for counselees

Description Do you have problems that seem too great to bear? Do you wonder if there is a way out of the mess you are in? This helpful booklet was written to put such problems in perspective. Showing first that no one's problems are unique, Jay Adams offers genuine hope based on God's promise in 1 Cor. 10:13. Readers will gain the courage to take responsible action, knowing that a real solution is to be found in God's way.

Author Dr. Adams is the author of numerous books on Christian counseling. He has served on a seminary faculty (Westminster Theological) and in the pastorate. He is founder of Christian Counseling and Educational Foundation in Laverock, Pa., and visiting professor of practical theology at two seminaries.

How to Handle Trouble Jay E. Adams

P & R Publishing, 1982, $3.50, paper, 66 pp., for counselees

Description An exposition of Phil. 1:12–16 where Paul views his hardship as an opportunity to glorify Christ. Adams presents clear and biblical directives for discerning God's hand at work in bringing good out of troublesome circumstances, great or small.

Author Dr. Adams is the author of numerous books on Christian counseling. He has served on a seminary faculty (Westminster Theological) and in the pastorate. He is founder of Christian Counseling and Educational Foundation in Laverock, Pa., and visiting professor of practical theology at two seminaries.

Contents *Preface / Introduction / 1.* Paul's trouble at home *2.* God is in the trouble *3.* God is up to something *4.* God is up to something good *5.* You must get involved *6.* Effects of biblical involvement *7.* Preparing for trouble *8.* Handling self-inflicted trouble

Keeping Up Your Spirits Therapy Linda Allison-Lewis

Abbey Press, 1991, $3.95, paper, 80 pp., for counselees

Description Offers a series of delightfully illustrated reflections that are sure to help bolster the human spirit and be an affordable, uplifting attitude adjuster. Great for the hospitalized or home bound—as well as anyone who faces everyday suffering. Format: a series of about 30 short sayings, proverbs, and admonitions accompanied by whimsical cartoons on every page.

If God Is So Good, Why Do I Hurt So Bad? *An Understanding Look at the Journey from Pain to Wholeness,* David B. Biebel

NavPress, 1991, $8.00, paper, 175 pp., for counselees

Description An award-winning, honest-to-God, and somewhat earthy presentation of the pilgrimage through the mountains of pain. Especially geared to those with long-term, unresolved hurts. Using his own experience with the death of one son and the handicapping illness of another as a platform and point of identification with the reader, the author walks along with that person through the process of disintegration, re-

353

organization, and integration that must take place in order for broken pieces to become whole. Also useful for support and study groups.

Author David B. Biebel (M.T.S./D.Min., Gordon Conwell Theological Seminary) is ordained in the Evangelical Free Church of America. He has served in a variety of pastoral and parachurch roles including Focus on the Family, where he edited the *Physician Magazine.* He has written or collaborated on seven books.

Contents *1.* Educated at the university *Section 1:* When losses come, they can bring . . . *2.* Crisis—learning my limits *3.* Confusion—what's wrong with me? *4.* Fragmentation—when life's not fair *5.* Putting the pieces back together *Section 2:* When losses come, what do I know? *6.* God loves me—I can count on him *7.* Suffering has value—I can trust him *8.* Jesus wants me whole—alive from the inside out *Section 3:* When losses come, who do I know? *9.* Loving God in a new way *10.* Toward integration—real people in a plastic world *11.* Power from the pain—conclusions and new directions *12.* To kiss the joy—celebrating what it is

When Life Isn't Fair *Why We Suffer and How God Heals,* Dwight Carlson and Susan Carlson

Harvest House Publishers, $7.99, paper, for both counselors and counselees

Description The dramatic story of Susan Carlson's struggle with leukemia and her remarkable spiritual, emotional, and physical healing. Blending personal experience with medical and spiritual insight, *When Life Isn't Fair* is a deeply moving study of physical and emotional suffering.

Author Dr. Dwight Carlson, M.D., is a specialist in both internal medicine and psychiatry. He has an active psychiatry practice and is assistant clinical professor at UCLA.

Contents *Part 1:* The problem of suffering *1.* Oh no, Lord, not our daughter! *2.* Life's not fair *3.* Who is to blame? *4.* How can a loving God allow suffering? *Part 2:* The causes of suffering *5.* God's will and suffering *6.* Specific causes of suffering *Part 3:* God's sovereignty in suffering *7.* God's responsibility and purpose in suffering *8.* Promises to hold onto *9.* How God heals *Part 4:* Finding meaning in suffering *10.* Face your feelings *11.* Seek appropriate help *12.* The will to health *13.* We really need each other *14.* To accept the things I cannot change *15.* The healing power of hope *16.* Laughter, praise, and joy *17.* Suffering with purpose and meaning / *Appendixes*

Will the Pain Ever Go Away? Alice Lawson Cox

NavPress, 1991, $4.00, paper, 77 pp., for counselees

Description When you're in pain over the loss of someone or something you love, life can seem like an endless desert without water. Time itself won't heal your agony and listlessness. You need to grieve and confront the pain. In this book, Cox will guide you through your desert of pain by showing you how to: admit that you're hurting; deal with your anger, fear, and sadness; accept that life will never be the same again; face what it means and go on. Brief articles and interactive Bible study format.

Author Alice Lawson Cox is a freelance writer and student from Arlington, Va. She is the former editor for the Prison Fellowship regional newsletters.

Contents Introduction: stranded in the desert of pain / Question: will I ever be happy again? / Respite: prescription for pain relief / Lesson 1—Why me Lord? / Lesson 2—Does anybody really care? / Lesson 3—Can I be healed? / Lesson 4—Why should I hope? / Extras—When chocolate isn't enough / The positive side of pain / Good grief, bad grief / More than a myth / The choice is yours / Hope and help for sufferers

When God Doesn't Make Sense James Dobson

Tyndale House Publishers, 1993, $17.99, cloth, 288 pp., for counselees

Description Addressed with love to those who are experiencing this source of spiritual disillusionment and despair. It emphasizes that this kind of confusion is universal in human experience. However, the Lord has assured us of his constant care. We can trust him even when the circumstances swirling around us are beyond comprehension. In short, God makes sense even when he doesn't make sense.

Author Dr. James Dobson is a licensed psychologist and the president of Focus on the Family, a Colorado Springs based organization dedicated to the preservation of the home.

Contents *1.* When God doesn't make sense *2.* The betrayal barrier *3.* God doesn't make sense even when he does make sense *4.* Acceptance or despair *5.* "He will deliver us, but if not . . ." *6.* Questions and answers *7.* The adversity principle *8.* Faith must be tough *9.* The wages of sin *10.* More questions and answers *11.* Beyond the betrayal barrier

God's Presence in Time of Trouble John M. Drescher

Herald Press, 1989, $1.95, paper, 16 pp., for counselees

Description Short meditations to give assurance of God's care and provision during times of suffering and testing. Directed to specific personal needs. Designed to be given by pastors, chaplains, doctors, nurses, and all who share words of hope and faith at an appropriate moment.

Author Drescher has written over 30 books and more than 100 journal and magazine articles. He has served as pastor, bishop, editor, and seminary teacher.

Strength for Suffering John M. Drescher

Herald Press, 1969, $1.95, paper, 16 pp., for counselees

Description Directed to specific needs and designed to be given by pastors, chaplains, doctors, nurses, and all who share at the appropriate moment of hope and faith. Meditation to help the sufferers understand what can happen for good, even in difficult situations.

Author Drescher has written over 30 books and more than 100 journal and magazine articles. He has served as pastor, bishop, editor, and seminary teacher.

Suffering and God's Presence John M. Drescher

Herald Press, 1969, $1.95, paper, 16 pp., for counselees

Description Written to point people to the greatest resource of all—God. Although there may be no quick answers, there can be the quiet confidence that God knows our need and wants the best for us. To this truth untold multitudes have testified throughout time immemorial.

Author Drescher has written over 30 books and more than 100 journal and magazine articles. He has served as pastor, bishop, editor, and seminary teacher.

Where Is God When Bad Things Happen? Horace A. Duke

Abbey Press, 1991, $7.95, paper, 166 pp., for counselees

Description The author explores what he learned from people who survived childhood sexual abuse, lost family members to death, or who lived a time with a terminal prognosis. Out of the harsh realities of human experience, and in the tradition of Rabbi Harold Kushner and Philip Yancey, Duke has fashioned a practical theology that can provide the reader with new peace, understanding, and resolve.

Author Horace O. Duke is a pastoral counselor at Hope Ministries, West Linn, Oreg. He holds a doctor of ministry degree in pastoral counseling.

Contents 1. The question—"where was God when I was raped?" 2. The perplexity—wrong questions, wrong answers 3. The answers—"God was carrying me, God was in me" 4. The mystery—God, power, and powerlessness 5. The demand—God, grace, and gratuitousness 6. An incredible deduction—God is with us, God is in us 7. The secret—six times down, seven times up 8. The choice—if you get where you are going, where will you be?

Living with Stroke Episcopal Radio-TV Foundation, The

Morehouse Publishing, 1989, $12.95, cassette(s), 60 minutes, for counselees

Description Gives personal testimony of those who have suffered stroke and offers practical helps as to the recovery process. Discussion guide included with questions regarding one's own experience with stroke. A Good Neighbor Project distributed by Morehouse Publishing.

Meeting God in the Darkness Robert Hudnut

Regal Books, 1989, $12.99, cloth, 160 pp., for counselees

Description God has much to reveal to us in our dark hours if we will accept them with patience and grace.

Author Robert K. Hudnut is pastor of Winnetka Presbyterian Church in the Chicago suburb of Winnetka, Ill. A Phi Beta Kappa graduate of Princeton University, he is the author of ten books. He holds the M.Div. from Union Theological Seminary.

Contents Part 1: The darkness 1. My friend 2. What is a negative emotion? 3. The negative way 4. The way of the soul 5. The imitation of Christ Part 2: The treasures 6. The gift of conflict 7. The gift of denial 8. The gift of being out of control 9. The gift of anxiety 10. The gift of fear 11. The gift of temptation 12. The gift of guilt 13. The gift of anger 14. The gift of alienation 15. The gift of doubt 16. The gift of purposelessness 17. The gift of chance 18. The gift of illness 19. The gift of death 20. The gift of ego

21. The gift of pride *22.* The gift of sin *23.* The gift of despair / *Epilogue*

Sickness and Death in the Christian Family Peter Jeffrey

P & R Publishing, 1994, $4.99, paper, for counselees

Description Trials, problems, sufferings are not to surprise the Christian. The question for Christians is how we are to face them. Mary, Martha, and Lazarus were devoted and earnest Christians when sickness and death entered their family. Starting from this biblical case study, the author draws upon his own personal experience and that of great men in the past to show how we can find rest and encouragement in God even in times of great personal stress.

When You Ask Why *Dealing with the Questions and Agony of Hurting Hearts,* Daniel E. Johnson

New Leaf Press, 1992 (5th printing), $4.95, paper, 64 pp., for both counselors and counselees

Description Describes the various biblical responses to life's hurts.

Author Daniel E. Johnson is the executive director of Trans World Ministries, an organization dedicated to Bible teaching and missionary evangelism. He has held several pastorates.

Contents *1.* The trials of life *2.* The problem *3.* When you ask why *4.* Beyond understanding *5.* Dealing with grief *6.* The truth about heaven *7.* Getting on with life

When All Hell Breaks Loose *You May Be Doing Something Right,* Steven J. Lawson

NavPress, 1993, $17.00, cloth, 255 pp., for counselees

Description Suffering wears many masks. But one thing is usually sure. To its victim, it doesn't make sense. And so the question begins—"Why God?" As you move through this inspiring portrait of the life of Job, you'll not only draw strength from Dr. Lawson's many practical insights, but you'll come to fully understand Job's great themes, including: the sovereignty of God, the scope and purpose of spiritual warfare, the nature of angels and demons, and why good people suffer.

Author Dr. Steven J. Lawson has been the pastor of the Bible Church of Little Rock since 1981.

Dr. Lawson holds a Th.M. from Dallas Theological Seminary and a D.Min. from Reformed Theological Seminary. He is a featured speaker for the Billy Graham Evangelistic Association.

Contents *1.* Lightning rod in the storm *2.* The invisible war *3.* Living hell *4.* I just want to lie down and die *5.* With friends like these *6.* The four spiritual flaws *7.* I need you on my team, not on my back *8.* There's hope at the end of your rope *9.* Come in out of the pain *10.* It's time to take inventory *11.* Putting the pieces back together *12.* Speechless, spitless, and all shook up *13.* Nowhere to look but up

Make the Tough Times Count *How to Rise above Adversity,* Florence Littauer

Here's Life Publishers (c/o Thomas Nelson), $9.99, paper, for counselees

Description Insightful, practical, helpful ideas for turning difficult situations into valuable opportunities. Based on the author's life story.

Author Florence Littauer is the president of CLASS Speakers, Inc. Her books have won numerous awards and have sold over 100,000 copies.

Why Is God Silent When We Need Him the Most? *A Journey of Faith into the Articulate Silence of God,* James Long

Zondervan Publishing House, 1994, $11.95, cloth, 169 pp., for counselees

Description Invites readers to embark on a journey that every Christian must take if faith is to survive the challenges of life. Here is perceptive observation and guidance.

Author James Long is an award-winning writer and director of development for *Campus Life* magazine. He has held staff ministry positions at the denominational and local church levels.

Contents *Part 1:* The silence of God *1.* Silence: the sound of infinity *2.* Distraction: when life outshouts God *3.* Contradiction: conflicting voices *4.* Mystery: a whisper of purpose *5.* Language: translating the transcendent *Part 2:* The voice of God *6.* Creation: a muffled voice *7.* Scripture: a sure and certain voice *8.* Christ: the word became flesh *9.* Spirit: inside interpreter *10.* Spiritual insight: the mind of Christ *11.* The church: speaking the truth in love *12.* Perspective: teaching the silence to talk *Part 3:* The mystery of God *13.* Partial answers *14.* God's government: an incongruous kingdom *15.* God's will: the paradox of power *16.* Faith: beyond the shadow of doubt *17.* Fear: ultimate test of trust *18.* Prayer: monologues with God? *19.* Quiet: the articulate silence of God

Help Lord, My Whole Life Hurts Carole Mayhall

NavPress, 1992, $9.00, cloth, 180 pp., for counselees

Description The author carefully explores the measures God uses to "strip away" our dependence on other things so that we will learn to trust in him alone. She examines the despair, doubt, and numbness that often accompany his stripping processes and gently shares how to survive during these times.

Author Carole Mayhall (B.A., Wheaton College) is a popular conference speaker and author of numerous works.

Contents *1.* Abject failure: losing success *2.* Waiting in the fog *3.* When the props go: losing support *4.* Inexplicable incapacitation: losing strength *5.* Character assassination: losing self *6.* Aloneness: losing intimacy *7.* In the valley of the shadow: losing loved ones *8.* The coming of winter *9.* Desolation: losing the sense of God's presence *10.* Trials upon trials: losing understanding *11.* The reason for it all

Lord of My Rocking Boat Carole Mayhall

NavPress, 1992, $5.00, paper, 157 pp., for counselees

Description Discover how the Lord's clear voice can quiet the waves and bring you inner peace and strength even in the midst of life's greatest storms.

Author Carole Mayhall (B.A., Wheaton College) is a popular conference speaker and author of numerous works.

Contents *Part 1:* What rocks my boat? *1.* Problems *2.* People *3.* Priorities *4.* Pain *5.* Worthless things *6.* Personalities *7.* Prisons *8.* The tidal wave *9.* Leaks *10.* Soaring *Part 2:* Who then is this? *11.* The God of details *12.* The God of sunshine *13.* The God of delights

Suffering with God *Looking for Hope When Life Falls Apart,* Alister E. McGrath

Zondervan Publishing House, 1994, $12.99, paper, 128 pp., for counselees

Description "I can think of few things less helpful to someone going through pain than a sophisticated theological defense of the integrity of God or a gentle romp through the subtle logic of necessary evil . . . The real issue is not our defending God's honor and integrity, but making sense of our experience. How does God relate to our world of suffering?"

Author Alister E. McGrath is research lecturer at the University of Oxford; lecturer in Christian doctrine and ethics at Wycliffe Hall, Oxford; and research professor of systematic theology at Regent College, Vancouver, B.C.

How to Find Meaning in Suffering Leo E. Missinne

Ligouri Publications, 1990, $.75, paper, 24 pp., for counselees

Description Helps readers find meaning in suffering through real life examples of others who endured tremendous anguish and survived—even triumphed. Explores positive aspects of suffering.

Why Suffering? Paul W. Nisly

Herald Press, 1980, $1.95, paper, 16 pp., for counselees

Description Paul W. Nisly reviews the problem of suffering and helps readers trust the God who created us to care for us.

Through the Darkness *Glimmers of Hope,* Adolfo Quezada

Abbey Press, 1993, $7.95, paper, 259 pp., for counselees

Description Fifty-three brief meditations, arranged alphabetically, are at once practical and poetic. Blending psychological and spiritual insights, they offer grace-filled glimmers of hope for life's toughest times.

Author Adolfo Quezada is a writer and counselor in private practice in Tucson, Ariz., where he resides with his wife and three children.

Yet Will I Trust Him *Accepting the Sovereignty of God in Times of Need,* Peg Rankin

Regal Books, 1987, $7.99, paper, 178 pp., for counselees

Description It's easy to accept God's will when life is going well—but what about the hard times? Here is a compassionate guide for yielding to God's sovereignty and remembering his promise to never leave us or forsake us.

Author Former English teacher, now Bible teacher, layperson ministering to laypeople. In demand nationally and internationally, presenting up to 250 lectures annually on a variety of topics. Author of two other books.

Contents *Part 1:* Who is God? *1.* The God of Scripture *2.* The King of kings *3.* The first cause of actions *4.* A master of creativity *Part 2:* Where is God? *5.* A biblical view of crisis *6.* A personal crisis *7.* Universal crises *8.* Precious promises *Part 3:* Why must we have crises? *9.* Snakes and lions *10.* Wrestling with God *11.* The problem of suffering *12.* God's sovereignty in healing *13.* Claiming God's best *14.* Acknowledging his sovereignty *15.* From curse to blessing *Part 4:* What do crises accomplish? *16.* The glory of suffering *17.* Rooted in Christ *18.* Nothing but leaves *19.* The believer's choice *20.* The fruit of the Spirit *Part 5:* How can I have victory? *21.* Emotion or action *22.* A widow's victory *23.* Active passivity *24.* Stages of suffering *25.* The upward spiral *26.* Identification with Christ *27.* Personal thoughts

When Servants Suffer *Finding Purpose in Pain,* Ron Rhodes

Harold Shaw Publishers, 1989, $3.99, paper, 80 pp., for counselees

Description This Fisherman Bible Study guide cuts through some of the confusion surrounding human pain and suffering. It deals with questions like: Do you sometimes feel as if God is ignoring your pain? Do you wonder if your faith is deficient because no miracle has come? Do you secretly doubt that God is truly all-powerful and all loving? The study guide helps counselees understand how sin, Satan, the world, and God's discipline fit into the problem of suffering. There is also a section entitled "When God Says No."

Author Ron Rhodes holds a Th.D. and Th.M. degree, both from Dallas Theological Seminary. He is author of a variety of books and study guides. He is presently affiliated with the Christian Research Institute (Irvine, Calif.) and is co-host of the national *Bible Answer Man* radio broadcast.

To Run and Not Grow Tired Fran Sciacca

NavPress, 1991, $5.00, paper, 90 pp., for both counselors and counselees

Description If you've sustained some inner wounds and you're not sure how to heal them, take some time to restore your soul by looking at the lives of men and women who struggled to keep running when they were faced with adversity. A series of 12 inductive Bible studies.

Author Fran Sciacca holds an M.A. in systematic theology from Denver Theological Seminary. He and his wife are coauthors of the Lifelines series of Bible studies for young adults.

Contents *1.* Hannah—coping with criticism *2.* Peter—failing someone you love *3.* Sarah—misplaced hope *4.* Cain—self-pity: a doorway to destruction *5.* Jezebel—the appetite for control over others *6.* Paul—dealing with your past *7.* Martha—the threat of resentment *8.* King Saul—the desire for notoriety *9.* The ten spies—the corrosive power of negativism *10.* Joseph—victim or victor? *11.* Jesus—facing the death of someone you love *12.* The Holy Spirit—a misunderstood "counselor"?

Crisis *Crucible of Praise,* Latayne C. Scott

Howard Publishing Company, 1992, $7.95, paper, 144 pp., for counselees

Description First-person account of crisis and the effect of praise and prayer in an individual's life. Solid scriptural base and integration of Bible passages and narrative. Praised by reviewers for its honesty and intimate writing style. Good for a person in the midst of a crisis.

Author An ex-cult member who wrote several books on cults and involvement with them. Contributor to many Christian periodicals.

Contents *Part 1:* Principles of praise *1.* A crisis begins *2.* A crisis concludes *3.* Praise: who is our God? *4.* Praise: what he's done in the past *5.* Praise: what he will do in the future *Part 2:* Praise and prayer in multiple /sustained crises *6.* The rubber meets the road *7.* Dealing with the aftermath of a sustained crisis *8.* The relationship of praise to prayer *9.* Prayer in crisis

Up From the Ashes *How to Survive and Grow through Personal Crisis,* Karl Slaikeu and Steve Lawhead

Zondervan Publishing House, 1987, $9.99, paper, 256 pp., for counselees

Description Outlines four strategies for putting life together again: taking care of your body, managing painful feelings, changing your mind, and adjusting your behavior. Provides help when other solutions have failed.

Authors Dr. Karl A. Slaikeu has worked for two decades in the field of crisis management and has a clinical consulting practice in Austin, Tex. Steve Lawhead is a professional writer.

Contents *1.* Danger and opportunity *2.* Anatomy of a crisis *3.* Giving yourself psychological aid *4.* A blueprint for growth *5.* Taking care of your body *6.* Managing painful feelings *7.* Changing your mind *8.* Door openers *9.* Adjusting your behavior *10.* Making changes *11.* A child in crisis: how adults can help *12.* Putting it all together / *Appendixes*

No Longer a Victim Malcolm Smith

Pillar Books & Publishing Company, 1992, $3.95, paper, 64 pp., for counselees

Description Deals with self pity, guilt, and a "victim mindset." Helps individuals see suffering from a godly perspective.

Author Malcolm Smith is involved in a teaching ministry based in Texas.

Joy through the Night *Biblical Resources for Suffering People,* Aida Spencer and William Spencer

InterVarsity Press, 1993, $11.99, paper, 252 pp., for both counselors and counselees

Description The Spencers combine their theological training, ministry expertise, and personal experiences to offer biblical resources for coping with suffering. A valuable handbook for those who suffer as well as counselors, pastors, and caregivers. The Spencers are both working pastors who teach at Gordon Conwell Theological Seminary.

Authors Aida Spencer is professor of New Testament at Gordon Conwell Theological Seminary. Her husband, William, is a pastor, adjunct professor of theology, and author.

Contents *1.* World of pain *2.* Response to a world of pain *3.* Punishment for sin *4.* Advancement of God's reign: persecution *5.* Advancement of God's reign: testing *6.* Responding to suffering by promoting God's reign *7.* Mystery *8.* Joy in the midst of suffering *9.* Encouraging one another *10.* The joy of morning

The Upside of Down *Finding Hope When It Hurts,* Joseph M. Stowell

Moody Press, 1991, $8.99, paper, 202 pp., for counselees

Description For people who have felt fear, anger, and confusion in all kinds of calamities, yet desire to discover that good things can occur in the midst of them all. By applying the biblical principles Joseph Stowell systematically outlines, you can do the seemingly impossible: consider every trial a thing of joy.

Author Joseph M. Stowell (D.D., the Master's College) is president of the Moody Bible College Institute of Chicago and a frequent speaker at churches, conferences, and events throughout the United States and Canada.

Contents *1.* The upward, inward look *2.* Who's to blame? *3.* The terms of engagement *4.* What is going on? *5.* Counting it joy *6.* Truths that hold us steady *7.* The purpose of bringing about what is good *8.* Capable and usable *9.* God-sufficient *10.* Platforming his power *11.* Job's unusual task *12.* Why do the wicked prosper? *13.* Keep on keeping on

In God's Waiting Room *Learning through Suffering,* Lehman Strauss

Moody Press, 1985, $3.75, paper, 102 pp., for counselees

Description Dr. Strauss's willingness to bare his own feelings and his expert exposition of key Scriptures on suffering will encourage every suffering Christian.

Encourage Me *Caring Words for Heavy Hearts,* Charles Swindoll

Zondervan Publishing House, 1982, $3.95, paper, 87 pp., for counselors

Description Written to provide encouragement to those hurting. In his unique, Scripture-based style, Swindoll skillfully combines the Bible and anecdotes to provide help to the discouraged. A series of short, devotional readings.

Author Charles Swindoll is president of Dallas Theological Seminary, host of the radio program *Insight for Living,* and a best-selling author.

Glorious Intruder *God's Presence in Life's Chaos,* Joni Eareckson Tada

Multnomah Books (Questar), 1994, $10.99, paper, 240 pp., for counselees

Description Devotional style book that proclaims God is involved in the tiniest details of our lives. Joni shows how God can bring peace and healing in the midst of difficult circumstances. The first paper edition of the 1990 Gold Medallion winner.

Author Joni Eareckson Tada is the director of JAF Ministries, a ministry that brings together the church and disabled people through evangelism, encouragement, inspiration, and practical service.

Finding God in the Dark *Rays of Hope for Life's Difficult Days,* David Walls

Victor Books, 1993, $9.99, paper, 192 pp., for counselees

Description Written for people who may feel the emotional and spiritual pain that comes with a deep, gnawing feeling that everything seems to be going the wrong way. From his own life and the experience of others, David Walls offers some answers that will help readers wrap their security around the truths of God's Word. Convinced that adversity will make us better persons if we go through the experience with God, Walls gives the reader practical, biblical advice.

Author David Walls is senior pastor of the 3,000-member Church of the Open Door in Elyria, Ohio. He has also served congregations in a number of other locations.

Contents *1.* Surprised by suffering *2.* When you can't hide the pain *3.* When the bottom falls out *4.* When trouble is near *5.* Running scared *6.* When you want to run away *7.* When you can't stop crying *8.* Wisdom for difficult days *9.* When you have to keep going *10.* When the heat is on *11.* When God lets you fall

Heart of Healing, Heart of Light

Encountering God, Who Shares and Heals Our Pain, Flora Slosson Wuellner

Abingdon Press, 1992, $8.95, paper, 128 pp., for counselees

Description A warm invitation to search again for the heart and love of God, which is always there, but which we sometimes forget. Offers ways to move toward healing of pain, toward acceptance of God's forgiveness, and toward reconciliation with others. Scripturally based meditations form a substantive part of this new volume from a well-known, internationally respected prayer leader.

Author Flora Slosson Wuellner is an ordained United Church of Christ minister and the best-selling author of numerous books.

Disappointment with God *Three Questions No One Asks Aloud,* Philip Yancey

Zondervan Publishing House, 1988, $9.99, paper, 260 pp., for counselees

Description This book won the ECPA Gold Medallion Award and was voted the Book of the Year by readers of *Christianity Today* in 1990. *Disappointment with God* deals with the issues that discourage or disillusion people in their personal relationship with God. It considers three questions—Is God Silent? Is God Unfair? and Is God Hidden? The first part of the book presents a survey of the entire Bible, examining how God in-

teracted with human history. The second part gets more personal, addressing the questions in an honest, struggling way. It faces the struggles Christians have in maintaining faith in the midst of adversity. Ideal for counselees who are struggling with doubt, self-image problems, unanswered prayer, personal and family disappointments.

Author Philip Yancey earned graduate degrees in communications and English from Wheaton College Graduate School and the University of Chicago. He joined the staff of *Campus Life* magazine in 1971 and worked there as editor for eight years. Since 1978 he has primarily concentrated on freelance writing. More than 600 of his articles have appeared in 80 different publications, five of his 11 books have received Gold Medallion Awards from the Evangelical Christian Publishers Association.

Contents *Book 1:* God within the shadows *Part 1:* Hearing the silence *1.* A fatal error *2.* Up in smoke *3.* The questions no one asks aloud *4.* What if *5.* The source *Part 2:* Making contact: the father *6.* Risky business *7.* The parent *8.* Unfiltered sunlight *9.* One shining moment *10.* Fire and the word *11.* Wounded lover *12.* Too good to be true *Part 3:* Drawing closer: the son *13.* The descent *14.* Great expectations *15.* Divine shyness *16.* The postponed miracle *17.* Progress *Part 4:* Turning it over: the spirit *18.* The transfer *19.* Changes in the wind *20.* The culmination *Book 2:* Seeing in the dark *21.* Interrupted *22.* The only problem *23.* A role in the cosmos *24.* Is God unfair? *25.* Why God doesn't explain *26.* Is God silent? *27.* Why God doesn't intervene *28.* Is God hidden? *29.* Why Job died happy *30.* Two wagers, two parables

Where Is God When It Hurts? Philip Yancey

Zondervan Publishing House, 1990, $8.99, paper, 285 pp., for counselees

Description Centers on the problem of physical pain. If God is love, why does he allow his children to suffer? This book shows how even the deepest pain can be filled with spiritual promise. A best-seller (500,000 copies) since its publication in 1976, the book was extensively revised and expanded in 1990 with more than 100 pages added. *Where Is God When It Hurts?* should speak to anyone for whom life just doesn't make sense. It is written for the person in pain as well as the one who wants to reach out and help but just doesn't know how. Won the ECPA Gold Medallion Award as best Inspirational Book the year it was published.

Author Philip Yancey earned graduate degrees in communications and English from Wheaton College Graduate School and the University of Chicago. He joined the staff of *Campus Life* magazine in 1971 and worked there as editor for eight years. Since 1978 he has primarily concentrated on freelance writing. More than 600 of his articles have appeared in 80 different publications. Five of his 11 books have received Gold Medallion Awards from the Evangelical Christian Publishers Association.

41. Suicide

When Someone Wants to Die S. J. Anderson

InterVarsity Press, 1988, $2.99, paper, 32 pp., for counselees

Description Offers help and hope for those who want to die as well as their family and friends.

The Fierce Goodbye *Hope in the Wake of Suicide,* G. Lloyd Carr and Gwendolyn C. Carr

InterVarsity Press, 1990, $7.99, paper, 158 pp., for both counselors and counselees

Description This book deals with the aftermath of death by suicide on those who are left and is written by a biblical scholar. The personal, historical, biblical, and theological aspects on the subject of suicide are woven throughout. An appendix of primary sources is included for the interested. The accompanying poems express the poet's own grieving and healing process. Those dealing with loss and grieving will find hope through sorrow and through poems, painful but real. This informative book touches humanity, giving the kind of help that says "this is how it is . . . but we go on." Interspersed sections: Section 1—Chronological poetry. Section 2—Issues associated with suicide. Section 3—Scripture and church positions on suicide. Appendix: Historical perspectives on suicide (church fathers).

Authors G. Lloyd Carr (Ph.D., Boston University) is professor of biblical and theological studies at Gordon College. He is the author of *Song of Solomon,* a Tyndale Old Testament Commentary. Gwendolyn Carr has been widely published in magazines and anthologies and is the author of *Stars and Songs.*

Teenage Suicide *Facts, Myths, and Prevention,* Richard S. DeBlassie

Ligouri Publications, 1989, $.75, paper, 24 pp., for counselees

Description Explains the myths about suicide as well as what to do when dealing with a suicidal person. Also discusses the role of parents and schools in preventing suicide.

Please Help Me Hold On Charles Dickson

New Hope, 1992, $1.95, paper, 20 pp., for counselees

Description Helps young people become aware of the issues associated with teen suicide. Provides life and spiritual suggestions for assisting a friend who might be suicidal.

Author Charles Dickson is a counselor and teacher in Hickory, N.C.

After Suicide John H. Hewett

Westminster/John Knox Press, 1980, $10.99, paper, 119 pp., for counselees

Description This constructive guide offers much-needed information and clinically tested advice for those struggling to cope in the aftermath of a suicide. Written in clear, everyday language, it presents the facts and demonstrates how to deal with feelings of guilt, anger, bewilderment, and shame. Presents positive steps that can help family and friends find strength together as they readjust and return to healthy productive living.

Author John H. Hewett is pastor, First Baptist Church, Asheville, N.C.

Contents *1.* Getting the facts straight *2.* Coping with acute grief: what to expect *3.* A family of survivors *4.* Helping your children in the aftermath *5.* Suicide and your faith *6.* Living as a suicide survivor *7.* Anniversary memorial service

That Nothing Be Wasted *My Experience with the Suicide of My Son,* Mary Langford

New Hope, 1988, $2.95, paper, 56 pp., for counselees

Description Mary Langford's world shattered when she learned that her son James had committed suicide. In simple, yet moving language, she recounts her family's journey through grief and into healing in the days and months following his death. Through all the pain and questioning, their faith in God enabled them not only to survive, but to bring good out of tragedy. John Hewett, author of *After Suicide,* has provided suggestions on how to cope with a loved one's suicide; they are found at the back of the book.

Author Mary Langford earned her master's degree in marriage and family counseling from Southwestern Baptist Theological Seminary in Fort Worth, Tex.

A Reason to Live *Help Out of Depression, Even Self-Destructive Thoughts and into Life!* Donalyn Powell

Bethany House Publishers, 1989, $6.99, paper, 144 pp., for counselees

Description Written for teenagers. Holds attention while helping them let go of the dream and reality that's not matching up with what they think life should be. It gives them reasons for why they feel the way they do with godly answers they can apply to their lives. Successful as a discussion book for youth groups or for anyone close to one who is suicidal. Composed of collections of letters from young people.

Author Donalyn Powell is an award-winning photographer and designer. She has 20 years' experience working with youth within the church and inner cities. She is a special speaker for numerous events.

Contents *1.* Suicide is forever *2.* A God of second chances *3.* Something worth living for *4.* Reaching for God *5.* Someone to walk with us *6.* Open arms *7.* A mother's prayer *8.* In the middle *9.* The promise *10.* Buried secrets *11.* "Dear father" *12.* A hiding place *13.* A reason to live *14.* The colors of your heart *15.* A letter just for you *16.* A final word: the facts about suicide

Bearing the Special Grief of Suicide

Abbey Press, $.50 each, paper, 8 pp., for counselees

Description Part of the CareNotes series from Abbey Press. CareNotes are short booklets that

help readers identify issues and begin the process of seeking resolution. Anecdotal and uplifting. Beautiful photographs grace the covers. Over 20 million CareNotes have been sold in just over five years. Can be used as an alternative to a greeting card or in conjunction with pastoral care visits.

Dealing with Suicidal Feelings

Abbey Press, $.50 each, paper, 8 pp., for counselees

Description Part of the CareNotes series from Abbey Press. CareNotes are short booklets that help readers identify issues and begin the process of seeking resolution. Anecdotal and uplifting. Beautiful photographs grace the covers. Over 20 million CareNotes have been sold in just over five years. Can be used as an alternative to a greeting card or in conjunction with pastoral care visits.

Suicide: When It Happens to Someone You Know

Abbey Press, 1993, $.50 each, paper, 8 pp., for counselees

Description Part of the CareNotes for Teens series from Abbey Press. CareNotes are 5 x 7 booklets designed to offer strength and help to (young) people in crisis. Each CareNote gently introduces an issue, then encourages a person to take appropriate steps toward resolution. Over 20 million CareNotes have been sold.

National Suicide Assistance 24-Hour Hotline

National Suicide Assistance Hotline. An organization

Description National crisis intervention hotline.

National Teen Crisis Hotline

National Teen Crisis Hotline. An organization

Description Offers phone counseling, crisis intervention, and other helpful resources to teenagers in crisis.

42. Support Groups and Twelve-Step Resources

The Workbook on Christians under Construction and in Recovery Maxie Dunnam

> Abingdon Press, 1993, $6.95, paper, 160 pp., for both counselors and counselees
>
> **Description** For anyone who has experienced problems with perfectionism, procrastination, codependency, trust, and vulnerability, self-esteem, guilt and shame, and compulsions to rescue, control, or be a victim. A seven-week program with daily readings that include Scripture, reflecting, and recording, as well as suggestions for living out the lesson. Includes leader's instructions.
>
> **Author** Maxie Dunnam has been senior pastor of Christ United Methodist Church in Memphis, Tenn., since 1982. He has authored more than two dozen books.
>
> **Contents** *Week one*—Getting ourselves off our hands *Week two*—When being good is bad for you *Week three*—Growing in self-esteem *Week four*—Overcoming the destructive "don'ts" that have shaped our lives *Week five*—Dealing with guilt and shame *Week six*—Getting ourselves out of hock *Week seven*—Pay attention to yourself

A Walk with Your Shepherd *The 23rd Psalm and the Twelve Steps to Recovery,* William Gaultiere

> Moody Press, 1992, $17.99, cloth, 349 pp., for counselees
>
> **Description** A 12-step manual for people seeking to recover from destructive behavior or emotional trauma. It is based on Psalm 23, which includes a dozen biblical and psychological recovery principles similar to those employed in AA.
>
> **Author** William Gaultiere (Ph.D., International University) is a clinical psychologist at the Minirth-Meier Clinic West in Orange, Calif.
>
> **Contents** 52 weekly readings that include prose and interactive questions

Living Free *A Guide to Forming and Conducting a Recovery Ministry,* Ron Halvorson and Valerie Deilgat

> Recovery Publications, Inc., 1992, $5.95, paper, 96 pp., for counselors
>
> **Description** Practical guidance, resources, and field-tested materials to help pastors and church leaders reach out to members in need. Offers a simple and effective program to guide church leaders in helping people who are troubled by the lingering effects of addictive or dysfunctional upbringing. The Christ-centered ministry outlined here offers a vital way to bring recovery more fully into the church.
>
> **Author** Ron Halvorson is an experienced counselor and author of several recovery books.
>
> **Contents** *1.* Restoring the church as primary caregiver *2.* The 12 steps and their relationship to Christianity *3.* Recovery support group ministries *4.* Forming a recovery ministry *5.* The living free program *6.* Organizing and conducting the living free program *7.* Working with a recovery partner

Life Support Leader's Handbook *Your Church's Lifeline to Hurting People,* Johnny Jones

> LifeWay, 1993, $9.95, paper, 224 pp., for both counselors and counselees
>
> **Description** Part of the LIFE Support Group Ministry commissioned by the Southern Baptist Convention. This collection of strategic helps is designed for every leader and facilitator of LIFE support groups. Includes: how to organize the ministry and develop leadership; group dynamics; mechanics of how a group functions; dealing with challenging situations; and making referrals.
>
> **Author** Johnny Jones is the LIFE support project coordinator at the Baptist Sunday School Board in Nashville, Tenn.

364

Contents *Introduction* / *1.* Calling churches to the ministry of Jesus *2.* Small groups in the church *3.* LIFE support ministries in the church *4.* Organizing the ministry and developing leadership *5.* Foundational concepts *6.* Understanding group dynamics *7.* The mechanics of a group *8.* Sharing Jesus with unsaved members *9.* Dealing with challenging situations *10.* Making referrals *11.* Training for LIFE support ministry *12.* Experiencing small groups

Twelve Steps to a New Day *An Interactive Recovery Workbook for Spiritual Growth,* Ron Keller

Janet Thoma (a division of Thomas Nelson), 1993, $12.99, paper, 224 pp., for counselees

Description Takes the reader on a personalized journey through the 12 steps. For those recovering from obsessive-compulsive behavior or drug/alcohol addiction. A small group leader's resource manual is included.

Author Ron Keller has done extensive work with the 12-step process through many organizations.

Contents The twelve steps for life in Christ / How to use this book / *1.* I admit that I am powerless *2.* I can't change myself—but God can *3.* Surrender leads to serenity *4.* Know yourself to love yourself *5.* Free at last *6.* Ready *7.* Asking for healing *8.* Sharing the healing *9.* Making amends *10.* Daily review *11.* My most important daily appointment *12.* I will reach out to others / 12-step process / Group leader's resource manual

The Twelve Steps *The Church's Challenge and Opportunity,* Charles T. Knippel

CPH Publishing, 1994, $9.99, paper, 96 pp., for counselors

Description Looks at the 12 steps of recovery from a biblical perspective, identifies ministry opportunities, and provides a Christian version for goal-directed spiritual growth. One of the best evaluations of the 12 steps from an evangelical perspective on the market.

Author Charles T. Knippel is a parish pastor with extensive experience working with chemical dependency. He holds a doctorate from St. Louis University.

Contents *Part 1:* The twelve steps—their origin and meaning *1.* A sketch of Bill W's life *2.* Bill W's preparation of the twelve steps *3.* Influences of the Oxford group on the twelve steps *4.* Bill W's explanation of each step *Part 2:* The twelve steps—challenge for the church *5.* The challenge for a biblical response *6.* A biblical evaluation of the twelve steps *7.* Biblical conclusions about the twelve steps *Part 3:* The twelve steps—opportunity for the church *8.* The opportunity for sharing the gospel with twelve step

practitioners *9.* The opportunity for enriching Christian growth

Living Free! *A Christ-Centered 12 Step Program,* Jimmy Ray Lee

Baker Book House, 1993, $7.99, paper, 171 pp., for counselors

Description A self-help Bible study in workbook format that uses the successful program of Turning Point Seminars in helping persons with addictions and life-controlling problems. Includes a group leader's guide.

Author Jimmy Ray Lee is president of Turning Point Ministries and founder of Project 714, both based in Chattanooga, Tenn. A former pastor, he serves on the national board of Teen Challenge.

Contents *Part 1:* A personal guide / *Introduction* / *Session 1*—Admitting my powerlessness *Session 2*—Acknowledging my belief in Jesus Christ *Session 3*—Affirming my need for the care of God *Session 4*—Auditing my life *Session 5*—Accounting for my actions *Session 6*—Agreeing with God *Session 7*—Abandoning my sins *Session 8*—Amending my ways *Session 9*—Acting on my amends *Session 10*—Analyzing my walk with Christ *Session 11*—Anchoring my walk with Christ *Session 12*—Advancing my faith in Christ / Follow-up: where do I go from here? *Part 2:* A facilitator's group guide *Part 3:* Resources / Selected Scriptures / Phases of life-controlling problems / Communication by care-fronting / Sharing questions / Friend search / Enabling / Personal boundaries / How to receive Christ / Suggested readings

Meeting Needs through Support Groups *How to Sponsor a Support Group . . . ,* Sara Hines Martin

New Hope, 1992, $5.95, paper, 96 pp., for counselors

Description An outstanding resource for anyone beginning a recovery ministry. Provides valuable help in understanding the issues and steps involved in establishing and operating a wide variety of support group ministries. Well organized and documented.

Author Sara Hines Martin (M.A., Georgia State University) is a counselor in private practice in Marietta and Acworth, Ga. She specializes in working with adult children of alcoholics. She teaches seminars internationally on ACOA topics.

Contents *1.* Foundations *2.* Guidelines for leaders of support groups and growth groups *3.* Kinds of groups *4.* Family issue-related *5.* Growth groups and support groups *6.* Addiction-related support groups *7.* Grief-related support groups *8.* AIDS-related support groups *9.* Rape-

and incest-related support groups *10*. Support groups for families of prisoners *11*. Support groups for women who have had abortions *12*. Churches with support groups *13*. Suggestions for other growth groups and support groups / *Resources*

Life in Process *Moving beyond the Things That Hinder, Moving toward the Love That Heals,* Dennis D. Morgan

Victor Books, 1993, $9.95, cloth, 192 pp., for counselees

Description Effectively balancing the 12-step model with the Word of God, this book helps the reader evaluate his or her present and to revisit one's past. While processing this self-discovery, the reader can discover how it impacts his or her future. Written in a nonclinical style. The 16 chapters are followed by a "process time" where the reader can interact with the material read.

Author Dennis Morgan, Psy.D., is now a senior psychologist with Tennessee Christian Medical Center near Nashville. He was formerly in private practice with Christian Counseling Centers in the San Francisco Bay area.

Contents *Part 1:* Early steps *1*. Life unmanageable *2*. Powerlessness *3*. Belief in someone greater than myself *4*. Renewed sanity *5*. Turning to God *6*. The life inventory *7*. Admitting *8*. Committing and desiring for God to remove patterns *Part 2:* Further steps *9*. Humbly asking God to renew our minds *10*. Renewing sick and sinful patterns *11*. Transforming into patterns of righteousness *12*. Willing to amend *13*. Amending *14*. The inventory continued and admissions promptly made *15*. Seeking growth with Jesus *16*. Carrying the message

The Complete Handbook for Recovery Ministry in the Church *A Practical Guide to Establishing Recovery Support Groups within Your Church,* Bill Morris

Thomas Nelson Publishers, 1993, $15.99, paper, 192 pp., for counselors

Description Anyone wanting to start church recovery or support groups will find a complete strategy for organizing and maintaining support groups in the church. Practical, Bible-based recovery programs.

Contents *Section 1:* Developing a philosophy: why the church needs a recovery ministry *1*. The statistical reality *2*. The biblical mandate *3*. The Mount Paran experience *4*. New life or new age? *Section 2:* Defining the purpose: what it means to be a Christ-centered support group *5*. Definition and purpose *6*. Distinctive characteristics *7*. Goals and expectations *Section 3:* Determine a strategy *8*. Starting a group *9*. Developing a group meeting format

10. Establishing guidelines *11*. The group meeting *12*. Congregational acceptance of a recovery ministry *Section 4:* Deciding on a structure: maintaining a recovery ministry *13*. Group traditions *14*. Group problems, group principles, and group conscience *15*. Group leadership *16*. Servanthood and sponsorship *17*. The twelve steps *18*. Family of choice *Section 5:* Personal stories *19*. The stories of those who know

Power Life Journal Mike S. O'Neil and Charles E. Newbold Jr.

Sonlight Publishing, 1993, $15.00, spiral, 170 pp., for counselees

Description On these open dated pages are a saying and a Scripture for each week that provide food for thought. Pages for recording prayer requests are included as well as a section on goal setting. One year's worth of pages, unobtrusively bound in black with a plastic comb binder that lays open for ease of writing.

Authors Mike O'Neil is the architect of the Power Life Recovery System and founder of Power Life Resources. An experienced presenter, clinician, hospital administrator, and consultant, he attended Central State University of Oklahoma and is a nationally certified addiction counselor and certified alcohol and other drug abuse counselor. Coauthor Charles E. Newbold (M.Div., Christian Theological Seminary) is an experienced pastor, counselor, teacher, and writer. He is the author of several books.

Power Life Small Group Support Ministry *Training and Implementation Manual,* Mike S. O'Neil

Sonlight Publishing, 1993, $30.00, three-ring, 145 pp., for counselors

Description This manual has specific instructions for starting small support groups that take the 12 steps using the *Power to Choose: 12 Steps to Wholeness* book. It shows in detail how to conduct small groups, outline and teach 12-step educational choices, set up and conduct support groups, and utilize the Power Life Resources to begin and maintain a growing recovery ministry. Designed primarily for churches, this material works equally well in counseling centers and other recovery services. Part 1 deals with the needs and defines recovery terms. Part 2 explains the value of the support group ministry in general. Part 3 details how the Power Life Recovery System is structured and provides step-by-step procedures for implementation. Shows how to conduct the various support group meetings.

Author Mike O'Neil is the architect of the Power Life Recovery System and founder of Power Life Resources. An experienced presenter, clinician, hospital administrator, and consultant, he attended Central State University of Oklahoma and is a nationally certified addiction counselor and certified alcohol and other drug abuse counselor.

Contents *Section 1:* Dysfunctional family systems / Why the 12 steps in the church? / Functional and dysfunctional family systems / Addictions / Progression of dependency / Codependency means . . . / Enabling behaviors / Care taking / Adult children of dysfunctions / The family roles / The family rules *Section 2:* Small support group ministry / The small support group ministry / Disciplines for a successful group experience / Group conscience / The group facilitator / Small group facilitation / Twelve steps to reconciliation / Overview of the 12 steps / Church needs assessment *Part 3:* Power Life Christian Recovery System / Church leadership orientation / Power Life Recovery System / Stages for implementing the system / Resolution to implement the Power Life System / Small group support ministry leadership authority / Planning table for implementation / Power Life Resources— when and how to use them / Promotional campaign / Starting the initial PTC leaders group / New PTC leadership orientation and training

Power to Choose *Twelve Steps to Wholeness,* Mike S. O'Neil

Sonlight Publishing, 1993 (2d printing), $19.95, paper, 209 pp., for counselees

Description The author, in street-wise language, explains the 12 steps and guides one through the actual taking of the steps through the use of questions and exercises. This solution-oriented book is not for the substance abuse addict alone. Presents basic principles that enhance recovery from codependency and other obsessive-compulsive behaviors such as addictions to sex, food, work, relationships, religion, gambling, abusiveness, etc. It is a helpful tool for anyone who simply wants to grow in their relationship with God. Especially effective with small groups. Brief instructions on how to use the book both individually and in a small support group are followed by an overview of the 12 steps. Each step has a workbook section with questions and instructions.

Author Mike O'Neil is the architect of the Power Life Recovery System and founder of Power Life Resources. An experienced presenter, clinician,

hospital administrator, and consultant, he attended Central State University of Oklahoma and is a nationally certified addiction counselor and certified alcohol and other drug abuse counselor.

12 Steps *The Path to Wholeness,* Richard Peace

Serendipity, 1990, $6.95, paper, 96 pp., for both counselors and counselees

Description A 7- or 14-week course designed for those wanting to become a support group while discussing what is involved in recovery from addictions via 12-step programs. Seeks to understand the spiritual foundation of the 12-step process. It is not a 12-step program in itself but more of an introduction. Designed to complement 12-step programs that focus on specific addictions.

Contents *1.* Twelve steps to wholeness *2.* Going beyond denial *3.* Naming the higher power *4.* Coming to God *5.* The practice of confession *6.* The dynamics of repentance *7.* An addiction-free lifestyle

Parables for Personal Growth *Tales for Your Healing Journey,* Melinda Reinicke

Recovery Publications, Inc., 1993, $12.95, paper, 160 pp., for counselees

Description These parables not only help us see our wounds, they show us how to mend the brokenness. A prince desperately tries to stop riding an addictive dragon when he realizes he is becoming a beast himself. An enchanted mirror leads a princess to believe she is grotesquely ugly until she finds her true identity. A distraught painter learns how to reclaim a beautiful canvas that has been slashed and stained. They all find help from their compassionate king as he wisely guides them on the healing journey. Personal reflection experiences follow each parable. Can be used for individual journaling or group discussion.

Author Clinical psychologist Dr. Melinda Reinicke counsels from a Christian perspective with adults from dysfunctional families and sexual abuse survivors. Popular speaker and workshop leader. Graduate of Rosemead, Biola University.

Support and Recovery Group Training Manual Linda Ross and Sandy Kline

Serendipity, 1992, $6.95, paper, 64 pp., for counselors

Description A training manual for those already involved in leading support/recovery type groups, for those considering leading a group, and for the supervisors and trainers of group leaders. This manual is unique in that it is directed toward the special needs of leading a support/recovery group and to the special needs within this group.

Authors Sandy Kline, M.Ed., is a counselor at Renewal Counseling Center in Tucson, Ariz., who specializes in the treatment of codependency and addictions. She leads Christian recovery groups, trains group leaders, and develops group materials. Coauthor Linda Ross, M.Ed., is a graduate of the University of Arizona. She is a counselor/therapist with Renewal Counseling Center, a Christian agency offering services to families, couples, and individuals. She is a consultant and developer for the Christian Action Council's Post-abortion program.

Contents *1.* Why we need support and recovery groups in the church *2.* Are you ready to lead a group? *3.* Who's responsible? *4.* Group rules *5.* Leadership techniques and interventions *6.* How to start your groups

Recovery: A Lifelong Journey Dale Ryan and Juanita Ryan

InterVarsity Press, 1992, $4.99, paper, 60 pp., for both counselors and counselees

Description This Bible study is part of a series of 16 volumes on various recovery themes. Each book contains studies on six biblical texts. Leader's notes are provided for group study. This title expands on steps 10 through 12, showing how recovery is a lifelong journey.

Authors Dale Ryan is the executive director of the Recovery Partnership, the parent organization to the National Association for Christian Recovery. Juanita Ryan is a counselor in private practice in Hacienda Heights, Calif.

Contents *1.* Practicing self awareness (Ps. 139:23–24) *2.* Continuing confession (Hosea 14:1–2, 4) *3.* Seeking God (Ps. 119:25–37) *4.* Asking for guidance (Ps. 143:7–11) *5.* Carrying the message to others (2 Corinthians 5:17–20) *6.* Practicing the principles (Galatians 5:13–23)

Twelve Steps to Spiritual Wholeness *A Christian Pathway,* Philip St. Romain

Ligouri Publications, 1993, $2.95, paper, 96 pp., for counselees

Description Applies the 12 steps of Christian spirituality to help readers break free from the negative and sinful influences in their lives.

Contents *1.* Admitting our powerlessness *2.* Trusting in a higher power *3.* Centering in God *4.* Knowing ourselves *5.* Admitting our wrongs *6.* Eliminating our character defects *7.* Letting go, letting God *8.* Making peace in relationships *9.* Making amends and forgiveness *10.* Living one day at a time *11.* Meeting God through prayer *12.* Walking the walk

Courage to Change *The Christian Roots of the 12-Step Movement,* Samuel M. Shoemaker

Revell, 1994, $9.99, paper, 223 pp.

Description Presents the biblical roots behind Alcoholics Anonymous in the words of the man who first conceived of "twelve steps" toward a renewed life.

Author Samuel M. Shoemaker (1893–1963), an influential pastor and writer, helped develop the twelve steps of Alcoholics Anonymous. This book is adapted from his writings.

Contents *1.* Estrangement from God *2.* Came to believe *3.* The decision to surrender *4.* Self-examination and confession *5.* Willingness to change and humbly seeking rebirth *6.* Reconciliation and setting things right *7.* Walking with God in daily life *8.* The guiding guidance of God *9.* The experience of Christ—passing it on *10.* Shoemaker's Christian lifelines *11.* How to know the will of God *12.* Shoemaker touches the life of an alcoholic *13.* The way to find God *14.* The turning point *15.* The three levels of life *16.* What the church has to learn from alcoholics *17.* What is conversion? *18.* Those twelve steps as I understand them

Rapha's Handbook for Group Leaders Pat Springle

Rapha Resources, $8.00, paper, for counselors

Description Focuses on the use of the 12-step model, family influences, healing emotional wounds, and more. Includes formats, checklists, Q&A about small groups—the nuts and bolts of starting and running an effective small group ministry.

Author Pat Springle is currently senior vice president, Church and Family Resources for Rapha, Inc. He served on the staff of Campus Crusade for Christ for 18 years. He is the author of several other recovery-oriented works.

The Twelve Step Life Recovery Devotional David Stoop and Stephen Arterburn

Tyndale House Publishers, $7.99, paper, 384 pp., for counselees

Description A daily devotional guide that helps people understand and apply the biblical principles found in the 12 steps of recovery. There are 30 meditations for each step.

Authors David Stoop, Ph.D., is the clinical director of the Minirth-Meier-Stoop Clinics in southern Calif. Stephen Arterburn is the founder of New Life Treatment Centers, now merged with the Minirth-Meier Clinics.

Anyone Anonymous Tim Timmons

Revell, $8.99, paper, for both counselors and counselees

Description Twelve steps to freedom from compulsive behavior, habits, or addictions. Leads the reader step-by-step through a biblically sound program to a lifestyle of recovery.

Power Recovery *The Twelve Steps for a New Generation,* James Wiley

Paulist Press, 1995, $7.95, paper, 172 pp.

Description Designed to be a companion volume to the A.A. Big Book. Drawing on the candid life stories of 148 young people in recovery, the author offers a welcome guide that includes a Work Plan for each of the steps.

Author James Wiley is an active member of A.A. He has sponsored 26 alcoholics/addicts. He is also vice president and editorial director of American Home Magazine Publishing Company and public relations director for Burlington Industries.

Contents *Part 1*—Hook in, power up, and get well/ *Introduction/* Crashing and burning / Beginning to heal / Connecting to the power / Who you really are / Dumping your garbage / Beating a dead horse / Cutting loose / Users, hurters, and dumpers / Repairing the damage / Scoping out trouble / Powering up / Reaching out / *Part 2*—A twelve step workshop / Work Plan for each of the 12 steps

43. Unhealthy Religion

Involvement in Cults, the Occult, or Satanism

The Occult Brooks Alexander

InterVarsity Press, 1983, $.99, paper, 32 pp., for counselees

Description Discussing the current popularity of occult beliefs and practices, Brooks Alexander presents biblical guidelines for dealing with false spirits and satanic activity.

Adversary, The *The Christian Versus Demon Activity,* Mark I. Bubeck

Moody Press, 1975, $7.99, paper, 160 pp., for counselees

Description Bubeck covers the subject from a mature, biblical perspective. Specific guidelines for dealing with the devil and demonic powers. Clear explanations that have helped thousands of Christians recognize their victory in the spiritual world. More than 260,000 copies in print.

Author Mark I. Bubeck (D.Min., Talbot Theological Seminary) is pastor of Central Baptist Church, Sioux City, Iowa.

Overcoming the Adversary *Warfare Praying against Demonic Activity,* Mark I. Bubeck

Moody Press, 1984, $7.99, paper, 139 pp., for counselees

Description Companion to the classic, *The Adversary.* Further practical help on how to walk in victory amidst the spiritual war.

Author Mark I. Bubeck (D.Min., Talbot Theological Seminary) is pastor of Central Baptist Church, Sioux City, Iowa.

Contents *1.* Satan is not invincible *2.* Keeping a sovereign perspective *3.* The believer's union with Christ *4.* The person of the Holy Spirit and his mighty power *5.* The whole armor of God: the belt of truth *6.* The whole armor of God: the breastplate of righteousness *7.* The whole armor of God: the shoes of peace *8.* The whole armor of God: the shield of faith *9.* The whole armor of God: the helmet of salvation *10.* The whole armor of God: the sword of the Spirit *11.* The allness of prayer *12.* Invincible prayer in action

Counseling and the Demonic Rodger K. Bufford

Word Publishing, 1988, $15.99, cloth, 223 pp., for counselors

Description Part of Word Publishing's Resources for Christian Counseling series. An overview of satanic and demonic influence is provided, mental illness and demonic influence are compared and contrasted, guidelines for detecting the presence of demonic influence and distinguishing from mental illness are offered, and strategies for spiritual and psychological interventions are suggested. Persons are viewed as wholes in which spiritual, psychological, and physical factors interact; thus coordinated care in all domains is recommended.

Author Graduate: the King's College and University of Illinois; professor/chair, Graduate School of Clinical Psychology, George Fox College; licensed psychologist. Contributor to *Baker's Encyclopedia of Psychology* and *Dictionary of Pastoral Care and Counseling;* and contributing editor, the *Journal of Psychology and Theology.*

Contents *1.* The devil made me do it *2.* Satan is alive and active *3.* Biblical accounts of satanic activity *4.* Faulty thinking: separating the spiritual and the physical *5.* Mental illness *6.* Mental disorders *7.* Demon possession *8.* Demonic influence and mental disorders *9.* Assessment and diagnosis of demonic influence *10.* Spiritual interventions *11.* Counseling approaches *12.* Summary and conclusion

How to Respond to Satanism Bruce G. Frederickson

CPH Publishing, 1988, $2.79, paper, 40 pp., for both counselors and counselees

Description Provides clear, detailed information on Satanism. Compares teachings to those of the Bible and suggests ways to share Christ.

Contents *1.* Introduction *2.* The enemy and his footprints *3.* The whispers of God *4.* Satan visible—religious satanists *5.* On the margin of the visible—satanic cults *6.* Do-it-yourself satanists *7.* From a Christian perspective

Unmasking the Cults Alan W. Gomes

Zondervan Publishing House, 1995, $4.99, saddleback, 92 pp.

Description The introductory volume in the Zondervan *Guide to Cults and Religious Movements.* Gomes defines the characteristics of cults, and why such groups subvert the search for spiritual truth. He explains the emotional and spiritual appeal of cults, who is susceptible, and techniques cult leaders use to attract members. An exceptional overview of issues associated with understanding cults and their attraction.

Author Alan W. Gomes, Ph.D. serves as general editor to the entire series. He is associate professor of historical theology at Talbot School of Theology, Biola University.

Contents *1.* What is a cult? *2.* Statistics on cults *3.* Theological characteristics of cults *4.* Sociological and psychological perspective on cults and false religions *5.* Why do people join cults? *6.* Keeping people out of cults

Cults and the Occult Edmond C. Gruss

P & R Publishing, 1994, $8.99, paper, 232 pp., for both counselors and counselees

Description Cults and the Occult. What are they saying? Why do they attract so many people? And how can you respond? Edmond G. Gruss answers those questions and more in this helpful introduction and exposé of the leading cults and the Occult.

Cults and the Family Florence Kaslow

The Haworth Pastoral Press, 1982, $37.95, cloth, 190 pp., for counselors

Description An anthology dealing with a wide variety of issues associated with families and cult involvement. Not written from a religious perspective.

Contents *1.* The cult phenomenon: historical, sociological, and familial factors contributing to their development and appeal *2.* The dynamics of mass conversion *3.* The typology of family responses to a new religious movement *4.* Cults, culture, and community *5.* Cults versus families: a case of misattribution of cause? *6.* Families and cults *7.* Perfect families: visions of future in a new religious movement *8.* Our involvement with a cult *9.* The cult phenomenon: behavioral science perspectives *10.* Ther-

apeutic community and the danger of the cult phenomenon *11.* Information search strategies: cults and the family

Dictionary of Cults, Sects, Religions and the Occult George A. Mather, Larry A. Nichols, and Alvin J. Schmidt

Zondervan Publishing House, 1993, $24.99, cloth, 376 pp., a reference or academic work

Description A complete dictionary of sects, cults, and religions. Probably the most significant reference book on the subject to be published in recent decades.

Authors Rev. George Mather is a noted authority on cults and the occult. He is the founder and director of the New England Institute of Religious Research. Rev. Larry A. Nichols is an ordained minister in the Lutheran church. He is a full-time pastor and part-time college chaplain and professor. Dr. Alvin J. Schmidt is a professor of sociology at Illinois College.

Demon Possession John Warwick Montgomery

Bethany House Publishers, 1976, $12.99, paper, 384 pp., for both counselors and counselees

Description The uncanny phenomenon, seen through the eyes of doctors, psychiatrists, historians, anthropologists, and theologians. A variety of essays.

Author John Warwick Montgomery (Ph.D., University of Chicago) is professor of law and theology at the International School of Law, Washington, D.C.

Contents *Part 1:* Demonology in the Bible *1.* The demythologization of the demonic in the Old Testament *2.* Response *3.* Jesus and the unclean spirits *4.* Response *Part 2:* Demonology in history and law *5.* The occult revival in historical perspective *6.* Not suffering witches to live *Part 3:* Demonology in literature *7.* The cosmocrats: diabolism in modern literature *Part 4:* Demonology in anthropological perspective *8.* Spirit possession as it relates to culture and religion *9.* Possession, trance state, and exorcism in two East African communities *Part 5:* Demonology on the mission field *10.* Demonism on the mission field *11.* Demonism on the mission field—the problem of communicating a difficult phenomenon *Part 6:* Demonology viewed psychiatrically *12.* Hysteria and demons, depression and oppression, good and evil *13.* Commentary on "hysteria and demons" (above article) *14.* Psychological observations on demonism *15.* Commentary on "psychological observations" (above article) *16.* Reflections on the demonic: a psychiatric perspective *17.* Taste and see *Part 7:* Demonology and pastoral care *18.* Problems and procedures in exorcism *19.* Victims become victors *Part 8:* Demonology and theology *20.* Demonology today *21.* Response *22.* Satan and demons—a theological perspective *23.* Criteria for discerning of spirits *24.* Satan and demonology in eschatologic perspective

Principalities and Powers *A New Look at the World of the Occult,* John Warwick Montgomery

Bethany House Publishers, 1973, $10.99, paper, 224 pp., a reference or academic work

Description A book that covers the entire subject of the occult. Grounded in serious literature on the subject . . . not hearsay or nonsense. Majors on interpretation of the phenomena rather than simple reporting. Does not cater to either the occult left or religious right.

Author John Warwick Montgomery (Ph.D., University of Chicago) is professor of law and theology at the International School of Law, Washington, D.C.

Contents *1.* But is it real? *2.* A bit of hidden history *3.* Cabala and Christ *4.* The stars and the hermetic tradition *5.* The land of modor *6.* God's devil: a ghost story with a moral / *Epilogue:* Before you close the creaking door *Appendixes: A.* The early church's concept of demonic activity *B.* A Reformation-era letter on demon possession *C.* The gospel according to LSD *D.* Suggested readings

Cults and Brainwashing Clyde M. Narramore

Narramore Christian Foundation, $.50, paper, for counselees

Description One of the many booklets available from the Narramore Christian Foundation. Designed to be handed to a person beginning to come to grips with a problem in living.

Author Dr. Clyde M. Narramore is a licensed psychologist and the president and founder of the Narramore Christian Foundation—a charitable, nonprofit educational, training, and counseling organization ministering primarily to the Christian community. He is also the founder of the Rosemead School of Psychology and author of 29 books.

Exorcism *Fact or Fiction?* Ken Olsen

Thomas Nelson Publishers, 1992, $10.99, paper, 256 pp., for both counselors and counselees

Description A look at the secret world of the exorcist and a fascinating study of the truths and myths surrounding exorcism. Helps readers understand today's spiritual warfare and how human souls can be reclaimed for Jesus Christ.

Author Ken Olsen is a nationally known speaker and author of five books. He is a clinical psychologist and Lutheran minister. He received his Ed.D. in counseling psychology from Arizona State University.

Contents *Part 1:* Spiritual warfare *1.* My name is legion *2.* Worldviews at war *3.* Who is the devil? *Part 2:* The left-hand path *4.* Subtle snares *5.* Witchcraft: the lust for power *6.* Satanism *7.* Satanic ritual abuse *Part 3:* Exorcism *8.* The abc's of possession *9.* Preparing for exorcism *10.* Anatomy of an exorcism *Part 4:* Freedom *11.* The heal and set free *12.* The story of Lou Ann *13.* Healing ritual abuse survivors *14.* A call to arms

Battling the Occult Russ Parker

InterVarsity Press, 1990, $7.99, paper, 155 pp., for counselees

Description Helping ordinary people recognize and defeat occult activity, Russ Parker discusses superstition, fortune telling, magic, demonic presences, deliverance ministry, and more.

Author Russ Parker is vicar of Christ Church, Coalville, and St. Peter's Bardon Hill (both in Great Britain). He is a member of the Leicester Diocesan Deliverance Advisory Group.

Contents *1.* The occult explosion *2.* Know your enemy *3.* Occult doors 1—superstitions and fortune telling *4.* Occult doors 2—spiritism and magic *5.* The occult attraction *6.* Why the occult works *7.* Signals of distress: discernment before ministry *8.* Preparing for ministry *9.* Christian deliverance ministry *10.* Praying for deliverance *11.* Signs of deliverance

Satanism Bob Passantino and Gretchen Passantino

Zondervan Publishing House, 1995, $4.95, saddleback, 92 pp.

Description Part of Zondervan *Guides to Religious Cults and Movements.* The author shows how in the midst of prevailing attitudes of skepticism and disbelief, Satanism has made unprecedented inroads into our society.

Authors Bob and Gretchen Passantino are the directors of Answers in Action, an organization in Costa Mesa, Calif., dedicated to Christian discipleship and a Christian worldview.

Contents *1.* Introduction *2.* History *3.* Misconceptions about Satanism *4.* Theology *5.* Witnessing tips *6.* Selected bibliography *7.* Parallel comparison chart *8.* Glossary

How to Rescue Your Loved One from Mormonism David A. Reed and John R. Farkas

Baker Book House, 1994, $8.99, paper, 203 pp.

Description Cult authorities Reed and Farkas affirm that with the proper strategy you can rescue your loved one from Mormonism. Of great value also to anyone who has felt flatfooted when a Mormon missionary approaches them.

Authors John R. Farkas is president of Berean Christian Ministries and a former Mormon. David A. Reed, a former Jehovah's Witness Elder and presiding minister, has also written *Jehovah's Witness Answered Verse by Verse.*

Contents *1.* "Rescue" from a religion? *2.* Don't delay—act today! *3.* Overall strategy *4.* Techniques that work *5.* Tools to use *6.* Step by step *7.* Archaeology—does it support the Book of Mormon? *8.* God's and goddesses *9.* The fruits of Mormonism *10.* God's "prophet" *11.* "Restored" then changed again *12.* Scripture changes *13.* Strange teachings *14.* Providing alternatives *15.* Can this family stay together? *16.* Warning: the life you save may be your own *17.* Afterwork: gradual rehabilitation

How to Rescue Your Loved One From the Watchtower David A. Reed

Baker Book House, 1989, $8.99, paper, 168 pp.

Description Tells exactly what to do. Helps people plan a strategy, collect convincing evidence, present material in a convincing way, and become familiar with the tools you'll need.

Author David A. Reed, a former Jehovah's Witness Elder and presiding minister, has also written *Jehovah's Witness Answered Verse by Verse.*

Contents *1.* "Rescue" from a religion? *2.* Don't delay—act today! *3.* Overall strategy *4.* Techniques that work *5.* Tools to use *6.* Step by step *7.* God's "prophet" *8.* A changing "channel" *9.* Doctoring medical doctrines *10.* Strange ideas taught in God's name *11.* "God's Visible Organization" *12.* Providing an alternative *13.* Can this marriage be saved? *14.* When children are involved *15.* Warning: the life you save may be your own *16.* Afterwork: gradual rehabilitation

Breaking the Circle of Satanic Ritual Abuse *Recognizing and Recovering from Hidden Trauma,* Daniel Ryder

CompCare Publishers, 1992, $15.95, paper, 265 pp., for both counselors and counselees

Description Cult survivor and counselor Daniel Ryder brings to light the traumatic reality of this insidious threat. He explores the following: what Satanism is and how people are drawn to it; how to recognize symptoms of ritual abuse; how survivors can recover through a combination of therapy; 12-step, "inner child" work; and integration of multiple personalities. Anecdotes are also included.

Author Daniel Ryder is a journalist who is also a certified chemical dependency counselor and licensed social worker.

Contents *1.* "What the hell was that?" *2.* Satanism *3.* Recruitment *4.* What therapists are seeing *5.* It isn't "only a dream" *6.* Other clues *7.* Mind control *8.* You're getting warmer *9.* Primers *10.* Reactions to violence *11.* Threats and infiltration *12.* The inner child *13.* Uncovering advanced clues *14.* Support for survivors *15.* Twelve step ritual abuse groups *16.* Twelve step applications for abuse survivors *17.* MPD *18.* Drugs *19.* New messages *20.* Demons: real or imagined *21.* To family and friends *22.* Fighting back

Don't Make Me Go Back, Mommy *A Child's Book about Ritual Abuse,* Doris Sandford and Graci Evans

Gold 'n' Honey Books (Questar), 1993, $7.99, cloth, 24 pp., for counselees

Description Part of the Hurts of Childhood series from Gold 'n' Honey. The series was developed for children ages 5–11 who have experienced deep and tragic hurts. The books deal gently and compassionately with children's delicate feelings when they're forced to handle burdens far too big for them to carry.

After Mormonism What? Latayne C. Scott

Baker Book House, 1994, $7.95, paper, 139 pp., for counselors

Description A book for aftercare of ex-Mormons. Scott discusses the major problem for ex-Mormons—the collapse of their belief system—and describes how to help them think through Christian doctrine while anchoring their faith in the Word of God.

Author An ex-cult member who wrote several books on cults and involvement with them. Contributor to many Christian periodicals.

Contents *Part 1:* The territory *1.* The problem illustrated, the collapse of a belief system *Part 2:* The tools *2.* Foundational strategies *3.* Assessing Mormon world view *4.* The four epistemologies—how we know what we know *5.* The Christian epistemology—faith *6.* Symbolism and contrast: tools of the fifth epistemology

7. Tainted symbols *Part 3:* The teaching: assessment, contrast, and symbolism *Lesson 1*—Redefining the Godhead *Lesson 2*—Redefining salvation and the church *Lesson 3*—Redefining the role of Scripture *Lesson 4*—Redefining obedience and trust in others

Why We Left a Cult *Six People Tell Their Stories,* Latayne C. Scott

Baker Book House, 1993, $9.99, paper, 206 pp., for counselees

Description First-person accounts of two Jehovah's Witnesses, two Christian Scientists, and two New Agers who lived their group's teaching faithfully and then left to become Christians. Also includes their answers to specific questions on reaching cult members and nurturing them. Glossary included.

Author An ex-cult member who wrote several books on cults and involvement with them. Contributor to many Christian periodicals.

Contents *Part 1:* Personal testimonies and points of departure *Part 2:* Identifying factor in leaving the cult and effective nurture of ex-cultists / Personal costs and compensations / Opposition from the cult / Mistakes made by Christians in witnessing / What I miss / Changed view of God and the Bible / The role of demonic elements / Current religious life / Changed attitudes toward leaders / Advice for concerned Christians / Teaching techniques / Helpful resources in the decision making / Helpful resources for spiritual growth / Advice to parents about cults / Effective nurturing

Why We Left Mormonism *Eight People Tell Their Stories,* Latayne C. Scott

Baker Book House, 1990, $7.99, paper, 166 pp., for counselees

Description First-person accounts of eight people who were faithful Mormons as well as their answers to specific questions about witnessing to Mormons and discipling the new ex-Mormon believer. Reviewers called this book "important and innovative" and "an excellent resource" and "must get."

Author An ex-cult member who wrote several books on cults and involvement with them. Contributor to many Christian periodicals.

Contents *Part 1:* Personal testimonies *1.* RS—former bishop who left Mormonism at a high cost *2.* DW—drifted away from his ancestors' religion *3.* CB—changed from a super Mormon to dedicated Christian missionary *4.* SG— won to Jesus by a loving Christian husband *5.* TG—pioneering for the real Jesus *6.* KB—plagued by doubts while serving as a Mormon missionary *7.* ST—Brigham Young's great-great granddaughter *8.* LS—former BYU scholarship

student now and ex-Mormon writer *Part 2:* Identifying factors involved in leaving Mormonism and effective nurture of ex-Mormons *9.* Personal costs and compensations *10.* Opposition from the Mormon church *11.* Mistakes Christians make *12.* Toward an easier transition *13.* Current worship experiences *14.* Advice for concerned Christians *15.* Helpful books for decision making *16.* Helpful resources for nurturing *17.* Effective nurturing techniques

Bob Larson Ministries

Bob Larson Ministries. An organization

Description Bob Larson is the host of the syndicated radio talk show *Talk Back,* a hard-hitting show that deals directly with difficult issues teenagers deal with— particularly involvement with the occult. Sponsors a national referral service to Christians skilled in dealing with such issues and has produced books, videos, and cassettes such as the following:—*In the Name of Satan* (Ritual Abuse)—*Satanism*—*The Seduction of America's Youth*—*Larson's New Book of Cults* (Reference work)

Cult Awareness Network

Cult Awareness Network. An organization

Description A nonprofit organization comprised of former cult members, mental health professionals, lawyers, clergy, and law enforcement officers. Founded to educate the public about the harmful effects of mind control as used by destructive cults. Provides assistance to former cult members, heads FOCUS support groups for former cult members, hosts an annual conference, publishes a monthly newsletter with significant legal updates, book reviews, and articles by cult experts. Also maintains a book catalog with very specific titles (published by both Christian and non-Christian publishers).

International Cult Education Program

International Cult Education Program. An organization

Description A national organization composed of professionals and lay experts that seeks to educate staff and youth in colleges, universities, high schools, churches, synagogues about cults and psychological manipulation. ICEP is a program of the American Family Foundation. Produces/distributes materials for families of cult members, counselors, and others. Members of the religious community should note that many of the resources produced/distributed by the ICEP are written from a secular (though not necessarily antireligious) perspective. Sample titles: Cultic Studies Journal / The Cult Observer / Cults: What Parents Should Know / Recovery from Cults / Satanism and Occult-Related Violence

Shield of Faith Ministries

Shield of Faith Ministries. An organization

Description Resources for recovery from cult, occult, or New Age experiences.

Spiritual Counterfeits Project

Spiritual Counterfeits Project. An organization

Description Since 1973, SCP has been a frontline ministry confronting the occult, the cults, and the New Age movement. Grounded in the conservative evangelical faith, SCP is also an information broker and gives advice by telephone through its ACCESS line (510-540-5767). Maintains an extensive library and files on cults, the occult, and "new religious movements."

Religious Abuse in Churches

Faith That Hurts, Faith That Heals

Understanding the Fine Line between Healthy Faith and Spiritual Abuse, Stephen Arterburn and Jack Felton

Oliver Nelson (a division of Thomas Nelson), 1991, $10.99, paper, 320 pp., for both counselors and counselees

Description This one-of-a-kind guide shows people how to free themselves from an artificial and misguided faith that serves human ego rather than God.

Authors Stephen Arterburn is the founder and chairman of New Life Treatment Centers, Inc. He is the author/coauthor of 14 books. Jack Felton is an ordained minister and licensed therapist at New Hope Christian Counseling Center, Inc., and is minister of outreach and staff therapist at LifeCare Christian Therapy Centers.

Contents *1.* The extremes of faith that hurts *2.* What is faith that hurts and religious addiction? *3.* Twenty-one harmful beliefs of a faith that hurts *4.* When religion becomes an addiction *5.* Religious addiction: the progression *6.* Ten characteristics of a harmful faith system *7.* The roles of harmful faith *8.* Ten rules of a harmful faith sys-

tem *9.* Treatment and recovery *10.* Seventeen characteristics of a helpful faith

Healing Spiritual Abuse *How to Break Free from Bad Church Experiences,* Ken Blue

InterVarsity Press, 1993, $8.99, paper, 168 pp., for both counselors and counselees

Description Includes discussions on the following: what spiritual abuse is and how to recognize it; examples, stories, and illustrations; a strong statement of the gospel of grace; help for churchgoers on finding healing from past abuse; and help for pastors and church leaders on how to avoid or correct patterns that may lead to spiritual abuse.

Author Ken Blue is pastor of Foothills Church in San Diego, Calif.

Contents *1.* An invitation to freedom *2.* The seat of Moses—the power to abuse *3.* Sniffing out the yeast of the Pharisees *4.* Heavy loads *5.* They do it for show *6.* Majoring on minors and missing the point *7.* Who gets hooked and why *8.* Healed by grace *9.* Healthy church leadership *10.* Healthy church discipline

Never Good Enough *How to Break the Cycle of Codependence & Addiction for the Next Generation,* Carol Cannon

Pacific Press, 1993, $10.95, paper, 256 pp., for counselees

Description Takes a look at the reasons behind addictive and codependent behavior. Experiences are told by the victims of those problems. Understanding that these behaviors can begin during childhood and that they are a no-fault disease, those struggling to win their battles can begin recovery.

Author Carol Cannon is the program director at the Bridge, which provides extended care for dependency disorders, specializing in the treatment of hidden addictions along with chemical dependency.

Contents *Part 1:* The impact of codependence on Christian families *1.* Will the real codependent please stand up? *2.* When "knowing better" isn't enough *3.* Sin, the ultimate addiction *4.* Anesthesia for wounded spirits *5.* Addiction as a no-fault disease *6.* Why conservative Christians are at high risk for addiction *Part 2:* Hidden addictions among Christians *7.* Officially approved addictions *8.* The abandonment of self *9.* Trying too hard to do the right thing *10.* Using religion as a mood modulator *11.* Confessions of a churchaholic *12.* The hurry disease *13.* The making of a martyr *Part 3:* The anatomy of a dysfunctional family *14.* Shattered dreams, wounded hearts, broken toys

15. Shot down by friendly fire *16.* Robes of righteousness, coats of shame *17.* Who's in control—you or your feelings? *18.* Do Christians have to be boundariless to be selfless? *19.* What we didn't learn in kindergarten *20.* Can the church be a dysfunctional family? *Part 4:* Thrice born: recovery from codependence *21.* Pardon, your symptoms are showing *22.* Sanctified white-knuckling *23.* Healing for adult children of Pharisees and publicans *24.* When the Holy Spirit came to Akron *25.* Rejoicing in the Lord and in recovery

Letters to a Devastated Christian Gene Edwards

Tyndale House Publishers, 1989, $5.99, paper, 56 pp., for counselees

Description In exploring the aspects of Christian groups who emphasize submission and authority, the author offers hope to followers left with bitterness and resentment.

Author Gene Edwards, for many years a pastor and evangelist, is a beloved storyteller and the author of 11 books.

Churches That Abuse *Help for Those Hurt by Legalism, Authoritarian Leadership, Manipulation . . . ,* Ronald M. Enroth

Zondervan Publishing House, 1993, $5.99, paper, 272 pp., for both counselors and counselees

Description Warns and informs readers about the psychologically and spiritually abusive churches and groups that are all too prevalent today— based on such traits as control-oriented leadership, spiritual elitism, manipulation of members, and perceived persecution.

Author Ronald M. Enroth is a leading scholar and national resource on cults and cultism. He is professor of sociology at Westmont College and the author of many books on cults and new religions.

Contents *1.* Introduction: abusive churches, a view from within *2.* Fringe and fanaticism: abusive churches can go over the edge *3.* Past and present: abusive churches are not new *4.* Authority and power: abusive churches misuse spiritual authority *5.* Manipulation and control: abusive churches use fear, guilt, and threats *6.* Elitism and persecution: abusive churches see themselves as special *7.* Life-style and experience: abusive churches foster rigidity *8.* Dissent and discipline: abusive churches discourage questions *9.* Exit and adjustment: abusive churches make leaving painful *10.* Discernment and response: abusive churches present a warning *11.* Challenge and change: abusive churches will always exist

Recovering from Churches That Abuse
Help for Those Hurt by Legalism,

Authoritarian Leadership, Manipulation . . . , Ronald M. Enroth

Zondervan Publishing House, 1994, $15.99, paper, 224 pp., for both counselors and counselees

Description Follow-up book to *Churches That Abuse.* Responds to the problems encountered in the previous title and points the way to spiritual and emotional recovery. Will help not only those abused, but also counselors, relatives, and friends who want to help restore broken lives. Specific topics include: dispelling emotional confusion, relating to friends in spiritually abusive environments, making decisions and other life adjustments, anticipating backlash after exit, renewing a personal relationship with God, finding the strength of forgiveness, and more.

Author Ronald M. Enroth is a leading scholar and national resource on cults and cultism. He is professor of sociology at Westmont College and the author of many books on cults and new religions.

Fundamentalistic Religion Eva Jayaprakash and Joshi Jayaprakash

InterVarsity Press, 1994, $4.99, paper, 48 pp., for both counselors and counselees

Description Part of the Global Issues Bible Studies from InterVarsity Press. Designed for individuals and groups, each guide contains introductory material and guidelines for leaders. This title examines Shi'ite, Marxist, Hindu, and Christian fundamentalistic movements.

Authors Eva and Joshi Jayaprakash are staff workers in Calcutta with the Union of Evangelical Students (IVP's sister movement in India).

Contents Introducing fundamentalistic religion *1.* The Christian fundamentals *2.* The heart of the law *3.* The radical demands of the gospel *4.* Freedom versus bondage *5.* Preaching the good news *6.* Growing as disciples

The Subtle Power of Spiritual Abuse
Recognizing and Escaping Spiritual Manipulation & False Spiritual Authority, David Johnson and Jeff VanVonderen

Bethany House Publishers, 1991, $9.95, paper, 240 pp., for both counselors and counselees

Description Defines spiritual abuse and describes steps to be taken by one presently in an abusive situation or even for one who has recently left one.

Authors The authors have worked together for nearly a decade at Church of the Open Door in Minneapolis, Minn.

Contents *Part 1:* Spiritual abuse and its victims introduction *1.* "Help me!" *2.* Spiritual abuse is not new *3.* Abused Christians *4.* The pre-abuse set-up *5.* Identifying the abusive system *6.* When you cannot leave *7.* Abuse and Scripture *8.* Revictimizing victims *Part 2:* Abusive leaders and why they are trapped introduction *9.* "Because I'm a pastor, that's why!" *10.* "You can trust me" *11.* Image is everything *12.* Straining gnats, swallowing camels *13.* The weight of religion *14.* "No admittance" *15.* Spreading "the gospel" *16.* The people get devoured *Part 3:* Post-abuse recovery introduction *17.* How to escape a spiritual trap *18.* Renewing the mind *19.* Recovering right focus *20.* One response—flight *21.* A second response—fight / *Appendix:* A message to abusers

Healing Spiritual Abuse and Religious Addiction Sheila Matthew and Dennis Linn Matthew

Paulist Press, 1994, $8.95, paper, 176 pp., for both counselors and counselees

Description With an engaging mix of theory, practicality, and self-disclosure, the authors explore the dynamics of the problem, then offer true ways to find healing. In no way antichurch, the book shows how to become deeply connected to the healthiest dimensions of Christian tradition while remaining absolutely true to one's self.

Authors The authors work together writing, teaching, giving retreats, and providing spiritual direction. They've taught courses in over 30 countries and in many universities, including a course to doctors accredited by the AMA.

Contents *1.* Spiritual abuse and spiritual reparenting *2.* Sexual abuse and God the mother *Introduction to chapters 3–7:* Four roles that make us vulnerable to spiritual abuse and religious addiction *3.* The responsible Pharisee *4.* The rebel Samaritan *5.* The lost Essene *6.* The distractor Sadducee *7.* Generational healing of spiritual abuse *Introduction to chapters 8–9:* What does Jesus say and what would Jesus do? *8.* Scripture and spiritual abuse *9.* What would Jesus do?

Breaking Free! *Rescuing Families from the Clutches of Legalism,* David R. Miller

Baker Book House, 1992, $9.99, paper, 176 pp., for counselors

Description *Breaking Free!* points the way to freedom and renewal, not by throwing out authority but by rejecting human ideas and sticking to God's standards. The author is a "recovering legalist" himself and has seen his family come out of legalism and into the true freedom found only in Jesus Christ. Filled with case studies and personal examples, the author presents a biblically based and psychologically verifiable method of recovery.

Author David R. Miller, married for more than three decades and a father and grandfather, earned his doctorate in counseling psychology from the University of South Carolina in 1981. Dr. Miller is a licensed counselor in Virginia, has authored seven books, and is a frequent seminar leader for singles and stepparents. Dr. Miller is professor of counseling and psychology at Liberty University in Lynchburg, Va.

Contents *1.* The irrationality of legalism *2.* Liberty lost: legalism and the family *3.* Children: legalism's casualties *4.* Legalistic and nonlegalistic families, how they differ *5.* Legalism and family violence *6.* Legalism and child discipline *7.* The child acquires an identity *8.* Legalism and person-to-person interaction *9.* Psycho-spiritual aspects of legalism *10.* The bondage of legalism

Behind the Masks *Personality Disorders in Religious Behavior,* Wayne Oates

Westminster/John Knox Press, 1989, $10.99, paper, 139 pp., for counselors

Description One of America's leading pastoral counselors draws on the most recent psychological insights to describe in everyday language common personality disorders that make human interaction so difficult. Proposing pastoral care approaches that combine understanding with empathy and firmness, Dr. Oates discusses how the resources of the Christian faith can unmask these disorders so the real person can emerge.

Author Wayne E. Oates is professor of psychiatry and behavioral sciences, University of Louisville School of Medicine, and senior professor of psychology of religion, Southern Baptist Theological Seminary.

Contents *1.* The mask of dependence *2.* The mask of the packaged personality *3.* The mask of self-assurance *4.* The mask of hostility and aggression *5.* The mask of passive aggression *6.* The mask of too many scruples *7.* The mask of detachment from life *8.* Persons on the edge of chaos *9.* After the masks are gone

When You're Angry at the Church William Rabior

Ligouri Publications, 1989, $.75, paper, 24 pp., for counselees

Description Explores the reasons people become angry at the church. Helps readers judge whether or not their anger is justified and suggests healthy ways to reconcile themselves with the church.

Recovery from Spiritual Abuse Dale Ryan and Juanita Ryan

InterVarsity Press, 1992, $4.99, paper, 60 pp., for both counselors and counselees

Description This Bible study is part of a series of 16 volumes on various recovery themes. Each book contains studies on six biblical texts. Leader's notes are provided for group study.

Authors Dale Ryan is the executive director of the Recovery Partnership, the parent organization to the National Association for Christian Recovery. Juanita Ryan is a counselor in private practice in Hacienda Heights, Calif.

Contents *1.* Resisting pretense—the struggle for honesty *2.* Resisting self-righteousness—the struggle to acknowledge our needs *3.* Resisting the quick-fix—the struggle to persevere *4.* Resisting performance—the struggle for freedom and grace *5.* Resisting judgmentalism—the struggle for compassion *6.* Resisting legalism—the struggle for love / *Leader's notes*

Growing Up Fundamentalist *Journeys in Legalism and Grace,* Stefan Ulstein

InterVarsity Press, 1995, $12.99, paper, 240 pp.

Description Many who grew up in fundamentalist Christian homes look back with appreciation on their childhood. But others battle with a way of life they now consider legalistic, rigid, and filled with more guilt than with grace. Some of these have left the church altogether; others hold a robust, if altered faith. Stefan Ulstein's probing interviews will help you learn how your friends, your children, and maybe those you hope to evangelize perceive the complicated way of life often called fundamentalism.

Author Stefan Ulstein is the author of *Pastors Off the Record.* A freelance journalist based in Belle-

vue, Wash., he is a regular contributor to *Christianity Today.*

Contents *Preface:* Fundamentalism defined *Part 1*—Life in the church: the separated life revisited *1.* Our sense of right can close us off from others *2.* Colorful vegetables and the secret food bank *3.* Their theology wasn't bad, just immature *4.* Does anyone stay in fundamentalism? *5.* Each point of view contains its own duality *6.* If God exists, and he's good, that's enough *Part 2*—The life of the mind: intellect, heart, and soul *7.* I didn't have to untie all the Gordian knots *8.* Nudes, cadavers, and a 900 foot Jesus *9.* Sometimes I avoid the big questions *10.* They jump on bandwagons *11.* Veering off the sawdust trail *12.* Mao, the ivy league, and blacks who like Rush Limbaugh *Part 3*—Sexuality: from abuse to ecstasy *13.* The girl in the basement *14.* I left my tribe when I came out as a lesbian *15.* God loves me more than he loves his own rules *16.* I killed the Barbie doll he gave me *17.* I want to feel his pleasure *Part 4*—Family values *18.* Sin was what other people did *19.* Creeping fundamentalism *20.* We apologized to our kids *21.* I want to be honest *22.* Grace breaks the cycle of abuse

Tired of Trying to Measure Up Jeff VanVonderen

Bethany House Publishers, 1993, $7.99, paper, 192 pp., for both counselors and counselees

Description Written to point the way to freedom for Christians who live under an unwritten religious code of expectations and rules that shame them and drain them of spiritual strength.

Staying Faithful When the Church Lets You Down

Abbey Press, $.50 each, paper, 8 pp., for counselees

Description Part of the CareNotes series from Abbey Press. CareNotes are short booklets that help readers identify issues and begin the process of seeking resolution. Anecdotal and uplifting. Beautiful photographs grace the covers. Over 20 million CareNotes have been sold in just over five years. Can be used as an alternative to a greeting card or in conjunction with pastoral care visits.

44. Violent Crime

Counseling Victims of Violence Sandra L. Brown

American Association for Counseling and Development, 1991, $27.95, paper, 241 pp., for counselors

Description A powerful guide for mental health professionals and others who work with crime victims. Full of practical ways to help victims of specific crimes at each stage of recovery—what the victim is concerned about, how to intervene at the crisis, which social services are needed, short-term counseling issues, long-term counseling issues.

Author Sandra L. Brown is founder and executive director of Bridgework Ministries, Inc., an educational and counseling resource for victims of violence. In addition to teaching about traumatology, she has produced and hosted an award-winning cable television show on the needs of victims of violence, *A Voice for Victims*.

Contents *1.* A victim's story *2.* Psychodynamics of trauma *3.* Effective therapies for trauma victims *4.* Victims of robbery *5.* Assault—elder abuse—ethnic violence—hate/gay violence *6.* Domestic violence *7.* Sexual trauma—rape—intrafamilial sexual abuse (incest) *8.* Violence against children—physical abuse—treating the sexually abused child *9.* Murder *10.* Cult, satanic, and ritual victims *11.* Conclusion: crime fighters or crime repairers

Sexual Violence—The Unmentionable Sin *An Ethical and Pastoral Perspective,* Marie M. Fortune

The Pilgrim Press, 1983, $10.95, paper, 240 pp., for counselors

Description Sexual violence has long been an unmentionable sin. Marie Fortune courageously examines a subject too long surrounded by silence, a silence she has the courage to break.

Author Marie Marshall Fortune is an ordained minister of the United Church of Christ. She is founder and director of the Center for Prevention of Sexual and Domestic Violence.

Contents *Part 1:* An ethical perspective *1.* Definitions of sexual violence *2.* Confusing sexual activity and sexual violence *3.* Reframing ethical questions *4.* Consensual sex and a new sexual ethic *5.* Rape is an unnatural act *Part 2:* A pastoral perspective *6.* Role of the minister *7.* Responding to rape victims *8.* Responding to child sexual abuse *9.* Responding to sex offenders *10.* Religious concerns and pastoral issues *11.* Community of faith *12.* Strategies for action

The Dancer *One Woman's Journey from Tragedy to Triumph,* Susan Lee

Baker Book House, 1991, $7.99, paper, 101 pp., for counselees

Description Some suggest that as many as one of three women in a lifetime will be raped. The prognosis for recovery is dismal. This book is Susan Lee's story. It describes the story of both physical and mental recovery from a brutal rape, and on another level a spiritual rebirth—a painful odyssey from a self-centered, egotistical individual to a woman of compassion.

Author Lee is an author, speaker, and the director of marketing and public relations for Prison Fellowship. She is also the founder of "The Joy Dancers," a prison dance ministry that teaches aerobics and uses dance as a way to reach inmates with the message of the gospel.

Contents *1.* Dancing in the dark *2.* Prima in pieces *3.* Break dance *4.* The dancer returns *5.* The dance of anger *6.* Forgiveness: his signature of peace *7.* New steps for a new life *8.* Enter the joy dancers *9.* Tales of the dance *10.* Wounded healer in a dance symphony

Talking Back to Sexual Pressure *What to Say . . . ,* Elizabeth Powell

CompCare Publishers, 1991, $12.95, paper, 255 pp., for counselees

Description Best Self-Help Book of the Year (MBA Award Winner). Clinical psychologist Elizabeth Powell offers ways to deal with difficult and uncomfortable sexual situations.

Author Elizabeth Powell, M.S., M.A., is a professor in a large urban community college district, where she teaches human sexuality and chairs the AIDS task force.

Contents *Part 1:* How to become assertive about sex *1.* Breaking the silence *2.* Understanding assertiveness *3.* Taking charge of your thoughts *Part 2:* How to respond to persuasion *4.* Standing up to verbal pressure *5.* Speaking up to avoid disease and pregnancy *Part 3:* How to cope with intrusion and force *6.* Resisting sexual harassment *7.* Avoiding acquaintance rape *8.* Responding to other sexual intrusion *Part 4:* How to speak up for your society *9.* Searching for the causes *10.* Becoming a witness

Out of Ashes *Nightmare in an Urban Neighborhood,* Helen Wells Quintela

Herald Press, 1991, $8.95, paper, 160 pp., for counselees

Description This is a painful story of the effects of abuse and violence on its victims. It explores the power of evil but also speaks of hope and tells of the rebuilding of lives broken by hatred and despair. The story will not be new to urban dwellers. For those whose lives are not touched by such violence, Helen Wells Quintela's story of her family's experience may be shocking. Yet it is a story the church must hear and deal with.

Author Helen Wells Quintela attended Harvard Graduate School of Education. She is the founding pastor of the St. Paul Mennonite Fellowship, begun in 1984.

She Said No Kay Rizzo

Pacific Press, 1994, $10.95, paper, 192 pp., for counselees

Description Deals with date rape. The subject matter of this book may seem shocking to Christians, yet the characters involved in this sad tale are young people who attend a Christian college and have made a commitment to Christ. The no-nonsense message to both young men and women regarding their choices and responsibility for their actions is worth the price of the book alone.

Sexual Assault *Will I Ever Feel Okay Again?* Kay Scott

Bethany House Publishers, 1993, $8.99, paper, 192 pp., for counselees

Description One woman's personal journey to wholeness and a guide for other victims, their families, and friends. The author was brutally raped at age 19. She speaks forthrightly but taste-

fully to all the scenarios familiar to other rape victims, including the years it took to overcome the sexual adjustment in her marital relationship. Includes counseling information as well as listing organizations that can help. This work was originally released under the title *Raped.* This version has been revised and updated with current information on the subject of sexual assault.

Author Kay Scott is a writer and homemaker who graduated from Hope College. She has spoken out on television and radio about her experience and has had a one-on-one ministry with survivors of rape.

Contents *Part 1:* The story *1–15.* Rape and recovery *16.* Ten years after the rape *17.* Twenty four years after the rape *Part 2:* Common questions *18.* Why do they blame me? *19.* What about date rape? *20.* What can family and friends do about rape? *21.* How can I help support the woman I love? *22.* How do I overcome the fear? *23.* When I pray, why do I feel like God's not there? *24.* Why can't I find comfort in the Bible? *25.* Do I need counseling? *26.* Where's the church? *27.* What about abortion in the case of rape? *28.* Why should I forgive? / *Appendix:* Facts, statistics, and further information / Stages of recovery / Common feelings following sexual violence / *Recommended reading*

Staying Safe *Prison Fellowship's Guide to Crime Prevention,* Beth Spring

Zondervan Publishing House, 1994, paper, for counselees

Description Finding a better way to protect your family is more than a better idea; it's a necessity. Beth Spring will tell you what convicts say would have stopped them from breaking the law. The book covers protection on the street, in cars, and in homes.

Finding Healing after Rape

Abbey Press, 1993, $.50 each, paper, 8 pp., for counselees

Description Part of the CareNotes series from Abbey Press. CareNotes are 5 x 7 booklets designed to offer strength and help to people in crisis. Each CareNote gently introduces an issue, then encourages a person to take appropriate steps toward resolution. Over 20 million CareNotes have been sold.

National Victim's Center

National Victim's Center. An Organization

Description A networking organization that offers information for crime victims, counseling resources, and referrals to qualified professionals and support services.

National Organization for Victim Assistance

National Organization for Victim Assistance. An organization

Description (Secular) organization that provides a variety of services to victims of crime, including written materials and referrals to local counselors skilled in assisting victims.

National Victim's Resource Center

National Victim's Resource Center. An organization

Description A (secular) research clearinghouse that disseminates information on criminal justice, statistics, and victim assistance. Maintains a national referral service for organizations dedicated to helping victims of crime.

45. Women's Issues

Women under Stress *Preserving Your Sanity,* Randy Alcorn and Nanci Alcorn

Multnomah Books (Questar), 1986, $9.99, paper, 147 pp., for counselees

Description Deals with tensions and stress unique to women. Demonstrates ways God can use such stresses to strengthen and teach you. Proposes a biblical lifestyle that honors God and respects the limits of your resources.

Authors Randy and Nanci Alcorn codirect Eternal Perspective ministries. They are both graduates of Multnomah School of the Bible. Randy Alcorn is a college and seminary professor and frequent conference speaker.

Contents *1.* Special stress on today's woman *2.* Stress: what's it all about? *3.* Stress, your circumstances, and your perspective *4.* How God uses stress for your good and his glory *5.* How to cope with stress *6.* Getting on top of your emotions *7.* Guilt, God, and self-esteem *8.* Are you meant to be wonder-wife and super-mom? *9.* Managing your time and tasks before they manage you *10.* How exercising right relieves stress *11.* How eating right relieves stress *12.* Your health and hormones *13.* Discovering the lost art of relaxation / *Conclusion:* Pace your race

The Rage of Hormones *Help and Understanding for Women and the Men Who Love them,* Holly Anderson

Thomas Nelson Publishers, 1995, $12.99, paper, 252 pp.

Description For women who suffer from hormonal imbalances, including premenstrual syndrome and postpartum depression, menopause, and more. Emphasizes women don't need to accept out of control hormones that threaten their emotional, spiritual, and mental equilibrium.

Author Holly Anderson is founder and director of the Premenstrual Syndrome Treatment Clinic.

Survival for Busy Women *Establishing Efficient Home Management,* Emilie Barnes

Harvest House Publishers, 1993, $8.99, paper, 271 pp., for counselees

Description This expanded 160,000 copy bestseller provides the practical plan to help active women organize their homes and live more balanced, stress-free lives. In this newly revised edition, noted home management expert Emilie Barnes gives step-by-step directions to help busy women evaluate priorities, eliminate clutter, and save time by planning ahead.

Author Emilie Barnes is the best-selling author of 11 books with sales of nearly 700,000 copies.

Contents *Part 1:* Survival through an organized you *1.* A thought for the woman of the nineties *2.* Recipe for beating stress *3.* Establishing the target *4.* Priorities—what comes first? *5.* On your way to the organized you! *6.* What to do with all the paper *7.* Making time your friend *Part 2:* Survival through an organized home *8.* From total mess to total rest *9.* Saving time and money by meal planning *10.* Planning an efficient pantry and kitchen *11.* Washing and caring for our clothes *12.* Cleaning and organizing the garage *13.* Sewing and crafts solutions *Part 3:* Survival through organized children *14.* Child-proof safety in the home *15.* Family conference time *16.* Babysitting survival guide *17.* Teach your children about money *18.* Smart ideas for parents—that work! *Part 4:* Survival through organized moving *19.* You're moving . . . again? *20.* Let's have a garage sale! *Part 5:* Survival through organized vacations and travel *21.* Organizing a memorable vacation *22.* Travel smart—automobile organization *23.* Travel for less *24.* Family cruises can be fun *Part 6:* Survival through organized finances *25.* Record-keeping made simple *26.* Cheaper can be better *27.* Super energy—money saving tips *28.* Money management means money saved

Love, Laughter, and a High Disregard for Statistics *Surviving Breast Cancer with Your Sense of Humor and Sexuality Intact,* Sue Buchanan

Janet Thoma (a division of Thomas Nelson), 1994, $10.99, paper, 192 pp., for counselees

Description Buchanan shares her personal experience of breast cancer with heart and humor that will encourage and inspire women with similar experiences. Provides informative, practical answers to a breast cancer patient's everyday questions, from diagnosis to reconstructive surgery.

Author Sue Buchanan has recovered from breast cancer and speaks on the topic for the American Cancer Society.

Contents *1.* Red and pink and purple *2.* Tomorrow is just a day away *3.* No mastectomy? *4.* The wonders of pink play-dough *5.* Chemotherapy and my cat, Ya *6.* Statistics? I'm the only me! *7.* Some words should be whispered *8.* When it rains it pours *9.* Celebrating your faith *10.* The green frog of Christmas *11.* Celebrating your friends *12.* If it's broken, fix it *13.* Milestones—a vacation, a party, and a wedding *14.* A yellow convertible and a pink and black Ford *15.* A quest for the nobel prize *16.* Dandruff, cobwebs, and lizard spit

Dying to Live Georgia Comfort

Tyndale House Publishers, 1992, $8.99, paper, 131 pp., for counselees

Description The inspiring story of one woman's courageous fight against breast cancer. Going beyond clinical facts, Georgia Comfort presents the human side of coping with a disease that could be called a national epidemic. From the initial diagnosis to the trauma of a bone marrow transplant, *Dying to Live* testifies to the author's faith and the prayers of others who gave her strength and determination to live.

Author Georgia Comfort lives with her husband, Philip, and their three sons in Carol Stream, Ill. She is an accomplished pianist.

Contents *1.* "You have cancer" *2.* The disease spreads *3.* The disease spreads even further *4.* My three sons *5.* My friend Barb *6.* Struggling with mortality *7.* A bleak prognosis *8.* Preparing for bone marrow transplant *9.* The big blast *10.* Life out of death *11.* After death comes resurrection *12.* My last week in the hospital *13.* Going home *14.* An alien in my own world *15.* Trying to make a comeback *16.* Determined to live *17.* Overcoming despair *18.* I believe the true report

Sexual Harassment No More Jim Conway and Sally Conway

InterVarsity Press, 1993, $9.99, paper, 220 pp., for counselees

Description Sexual harassment occurs and has been documented in the workplace, on dates, in marriage, in education, and in religion. The focus of this book is to help people understand the pervasiveness of sexual harassment and then to specifically coach men and women how to deal with and avoid sexual harassment. The book

concludes with a chapter on "values" to help men and women truly respect each other.

Authors Jim Conway holds five degrees in psychology and theology and is the author of many books. His wife, Sally Conway, holds an M.S. in human development. Together they own and operate Mid-Life Dimensions/Christian Living Resources, a nonprofit organization ministering to people at various stages of life through a variety of media formats.

Contents *Part 1:* Harassment in America *1.* It's real and it's pervasive *2.* Sexual harassment in the workplace *3.* Why do women put up with it? *4.* Guidelines for the harassed person *5.* Sexual harassment on dates *6.* Sexual harassment in marriage *7.* Sexual harassment in education *8.* Sexual harassment in religion *Part 2:* Insights for men and for the women who want to help them *9.* Why men harass *10.* "Male pattern ignorance" *11.* What men don't know will hurt them *12.* What men need to know about women *13.* A woman's sexual agenda *14.* To do and not to do *Part 3:* Insights for women to reduce harassment *15.* What women need to know to reduce harassment *16.* What women need to be to reduce harassment *17.* What women need to do to reduce harassment *Part 4:* Values that enable people to rise above harassment *18.* What you believe will change your life

Menopause *Help and Hope for This Passage,* Sally Conway

Zondervan Publishing House, 1990, $9.99, paper, 240 pp., for counselees

Description A well-documented and researched book that translates the medical jargon and research into laywoman's language. The book is used in a number of clinics around the country as a complete informational tool for the menopausal woman. It is useful in helping women feel hopeful and take charge of their health at this crucial life stage.

Author Sally Conway holds an M.S. in human development. Together with her husband, they own and operate Mid-Life Dimensions/Christian Living Resources, a nonprofit organization ministering to people at various stages of life through a variety of media formats.

Contents *Part 1:* Encounter with menopause *1.* You are here *2.* First-time changes with you *3.* Our foremothers *Part 2:* Old wives' tales, new wives' tales, and facts *4.* Your wonderful body *5.* Now that reproduction is over *6.* The estrogen question *7.* Hysterectomy—pro and con *8.* The joy, or pain, of sex *9.* Osteoporosis—the silent thief *10.* Combating heart attacks and other assaults *11.* It's not just your imagination *Part 3:* Surviving and thriving *12.* The doctor connection *13.* A place for you *14.* Setting your course *15.* For husbands and children only

Understanding Menopause James Dobson

Focus on the Family, 1991, $.35, paper, 12 pp., for counselees

Description Chapter reprint from Dr. Dobson's best-selling *What Wives Wish Their Husbands Knew about Women.* Describes experiences, symptoms, and other issues associated with menopause.

Author James C. Dobson, Ph.D., is founder and president of Focus on the Family. A licensed psychologist, he has authored 12 best-selling books on the family, including *The Strong Willed Child, Love Must Be Tough, Parenting Isn't for Cowards,* and the *New Dare to Discipline.*

Healing for the Empty Heart Marion Duckworth

Bethany House Publishers, 1993, $7.99, paper, 208 pp., for counselees

Description "Why do I feel this emptiness, numbness . . . as if something is wrong—when nothing is wrong? If Jesus promised to be with me always—why do I feel so lonely inside?" An honest, biblical view of what Jesus meant when he said he had come to heal the brokenhearted. Written in a warm, easy-to-read style.

Author Marion Duckworth is an award-winning author with ten books, numerous curriculum materials, and more than 400 published articles to her credit.

Contents *Part 1:* The starting place *1.* Running on empty *2.* Learn how to trust *3.* Damaged women speak *Part 2:* The healing journey *4.* Find human help *5.* Support groups *6.* The healing word of God *7.* Open up in prayer *8.* Worship: touching hearts *9.* Discover yourself through journaling *10.* The church as family *11.* Tough times are teaching times *Part 3:* Now and then *12.* When it hurts most *13.* Celebrate and anticipate

Women: The Misunderstood Majority
Contemporary Concerns in Counseling Women, M. Gay Hubbard

Word Publishing, 1992, $15.99, cloth, 274 pp., for counselors

Description The author's stated goal is "to provide practical information for both women clients and their counselors to better understand women's gender-distinctive needs and characteristics and the social reality of women's life ex-

periences, and then to be able to act on this information."

Author Dr. M. Gay Hubbard is a psychologist with a Ph.D. from the University of Pittsburgh. Dr. Hubbard serves as a counseling associate in private practice at Christian Counseling Associates, Inc.

Contents *1.* Women as consumers of counseling services *2.* Mental health and the mythology of women *3.* The new mythology *4.* The mythology of the therapist *5.* The complexities of gender research *6.* Sex differences *7.* Gender and developmental differences *8.* Women in transition *9.* Unique individuals in the common bond of womanhood

Celebrate-Your-Womanhood Therapy
Karen Katafiasz

Abbey Press, 1992, $3.95, paper, 80 pp., for counselees

Description Rejoices in the unique experience and manifold gifts of half the human family. Timely and relevant, this enchantingly illustrated "self-help" book is bubbling over with an affirming and empowering message for women of all ages and life situations.

Contents A series of about 30 short sayings, proverbs, and admonitions accompanied by whimsical cartoons on every page.

Help for Women with Too Much to Do
Pat King

Ligouri Publications, 1993, $3.95, paper, 127 pp., for counselees

Description A writer, speaker, and mother of ten helps other women cope with life's demands with renewed vigor.

Contents *1.* The day I ran out of energy *2.* Nonreciprocity: what it means to be unappreciated *3.* High ambiguity situations: when the available solutions don't solve the problems *4.* High-stress situation: when life lets you down *5.* Difficult transitions: why change is never easy *6.* Our bodies under stress and how we avoid the symptoms *7.* Creating a new lifestyle *8.* Sixteen ways to say no *9.* The ultimate in energy: getting to know Christ

The Pleasers *Women Who Can't Say No and the Men Who Control Them,* Kevin Leman

Spire Books, $4.99, paper, for counselees

Description Deals with assertiveness and self-confidence.

Author Dr. Kevin Leman is the author of 13 books on family and marriage, a psychologist, and host of the syndicated radio program *Parent Talk.*

Emotional Phases of a Woman's Life Jean Lush and Patricia H. Rushford

Fleming H. Revell, 1987, $8.99, paper, 220 pp., for counselees

Description Do hormones really impact your emotions? In this upbeat and informative book, the authors discuss the relationship between your emotions and your changing physiology, both monthly and lifelong. Writing in an easy-to-read style, they help you prepare for each phase of your life and at the same time provide insights and counsel for such intriguing topics as having an affair—with your husband, creating an aura of mystique, weathering your emotional storms, and growing older, growing better.

Authors Jean Lush, M.A., is a counselor and speaker in the Seattle area and has appeared often on *Focus on the Family* with James Dobson. Patricia H. Rushford, R.N., M.A. in counseling, has written numerous articles and 14 books. She is a contributing editor to *Christian Parenting Today* and adjunct professor at Western Evangelical Seminary.

Contents *Part 1:* Entering womanhood *1.* On being a woman *2.* The emotional side of things *3.* The nature of a woman *4.* Sometimes it hurts . . . *5.* The good news is . . . *Part 2:* The romantic phase *6.* Great expectations *7.* Distressing news: postpartum blues *8.* Premenstrual syndrome and you *9.* PMS: making it better *Part 3:* Midlife mistakes *10.* Is this all there is? *11.* Could it be my hormones? *12.* Managing mid-life malaise *13.* A woman of mystique *Part 4:* The menopause *14.* The season of change *15.* Managing menopause *Part 5:* Postmenopause *16.* The last for which the first was made

Women and Stress A Practical Approach to Managing Tension, Jean Lush with Pam Vredevelt

Fleming H. Revell, 1992, $14.99, paper, 272 pp., for counselees

Description Writing in an informative style, the authors explore the causes of stress, cite typical responses to tension, and offer proven strategies for managing emotions and alleviating stress.

Author Jean Lush has written several best-selling books. She is the director of Christian Counseling Services and a licensed professional counselor.

Contents *Part 1:* What makes us tense *1.* Anger *2.* Painful emotions *3.* Low self-esteem *4.* Grief *5.* Rehabilitation *6.* Job stress *7.* Unmet needs *8.* Parenting pressures *9.* Hormonal pressures *10.* Menopause *Part 2:* Typical responses to tension *11.* The role of early conditioning *12.* Our storage pot *13.* Mrs. Flight *14.* Mrs. Fight *15.* Mrs. Sit Tight *Part 3:* Secrets to taming your tensions *16.* Do away with disorder *17.* Diversions *18.* More ways to discharge your tension *19.* Don't look back

Women and Their Emotions Miriam Neff

Moody Press, 1983, $7.99, paper, 150 pp., for counselees

Description From experience as a counselor and counselee, Miriam Neff combines biblical truths and psychological insights to help women understand and master their emotions.

Author Miriam Neff holds a degree in counseling from Northwestern University. She is a homemaker, Bible study teacher, and a freelance writer.

Contents *1.* Who's in charge? *2.* It's good to feel *3.* Anger *4.* Fear *5.* Empathy *6.* Envy *7.* Love *8.* Anxiety *9.* Discouragement *10.* Depression *11.* Grief *12.* Bitterness and hatred *13.* Guilt *14.* Breaking emotional habits

Sometimes I Feel Like Running Away from Home Simple Ways That Will Renew Your Spirit and Save Your Sanity, Elizabeth Newenhuyse

Bethany House Publishers, 1993, $7.99, paper, 208 pp., for counselees

Description Christian women often feel caught in the tug-of-war amid life's demands. One voice inside says, "You must be the servant of all. It's selfish to want time and space for your own needs." Another voice says "I feel like I'm losing it—burning out . . . I just need a little time for myself." Where does this fight come from? How can a woman—wife and mother—win? The author suggests that taking time out for yourself is not selfish, but a God-given requirement for being restored and renewed in one's inner spiritual life.

Author Elizabeth Newenhuyse is a writer whose byline has appeared dozens of times in Christian periodicals and on two previous books. Formerly senior editor of *Marriage Partnership.*

Contents *1.* The care and feeding of souls *2.* A bad case of the "I shoulds" *3.* Attack of the killer "To-do" list *4.* How to be the perfect mother and other big laughs *5.* The state of your unions *6.* Yes, you too can be thin *7.* On the matter of resourcefulness *8.* Give me some space and get out of my face 9. How do you find the time to spend with God? 10. Sometimes I feel like running away from my demanding self 11. How to fall apart and pick yourself up again 12. Take your dreams out of the closet 13. Making peace with where you've been, looking forward to where you're going

Women Facing Life's Demands
A Workbook for Handling the Pressure Points in Your Life, Gary Jackson Oliver, H. Norman Wright, and Rita Schweitz

Moody Press, 1993, $12.99, paper, 117 pp., for counselees

Description This workbook will help you analyze your strengths and weaknesses, take stock of your roles and true goals in life, evaluate the effectiveness of the ways you express anger, and learn to use anger in recognizing the need for, and path to, change. Utilizes an inductive, fill-in-the-blank format.

Authors Gary J. Oliver (Ph.D., University of Nebraska) is a psychologist at Southwest Counseling Associates. He is also visiting professor at Denver Seminary. H. Norman Wright (M.R.E., Fuller Seminary) is a licensed marriage, family, and child therapist. Rita Schweitz is currently completing her doctorate at Oxford Graduate School. She has worked closely with prominent Christian psychiatrists and psychologists on books to heal and deepen relationships with God and others.

Contents *Part 1:* Facing life's demands *Part 2:* Pressure from your projects, roles, and work load *Part 3:* Pressure from people

Talking Back to Sexual Pressure *What to Say . . . ,* Elizabeth Powell

CompCare Publishers, 1991, $12.95, paper, 255 pp., for counselees

Description Best Self-Help Book of the Year (MBA Award Winner). Clinical psychologist Elizabeth Powell offers ways to deal with difficult and uncomfortable sexual situations.

Author Elizabeth Powell, M.S., M.A., is a professor in a large urban community college district, where she teaches human sexuality and chairs the AIDS task force.

Contents *Part 1:* How to become assertive about sex 1. Breaking the silence 2. Understanding assertiveness 3. Taking charge of your thoughts *Part 2:* How to respond to persuasion 4. Standing up to verbal pressure 5. Speak-

ing up to avoid disease and pregnancy *Part 3:* How to cope with intrusion and force 6. Resisting sexual harassment 7. Avoiding acquaintance rape 8. Responding to other sexual intrusion *Part 4:* How to speak up for your society 9. Searching for the causes 10. Becoming a witness / *Appendix:* Where to get and give help

Coming of Age *Personal Insights on Menopause,* Lois Mowday Rabey

Thomas Nelson Publishers, 1995, $12.99, cloth, 192 pp.

Description An informative, well-researched examination of the midlife change women sometimes find difficult to cope with. Includes a serious discussion of the issues as well as anecdotes from the humorous side. Offers guidance from a Christian perspective.

Author Lois Mowday Rabey is the former director of public relations for Evangelism Explosion International and is a frequent speaker at women's seminars and conferences.

What You Need to Know about Menopause *Answers to the Questions Women Ask Most,* Paul Reisser and Teri Reisser

Servant Publications/Vine Books, 1994, $8.99, paper, 211 pp., for counselees

Description Addresses the physical issues of menopause as well as the related topics of women's health, aging, and the emotional and sexual responses we make to the process. Women will find sound medical information, easy-to-understand answers, and honest discussions about the issues that affect them and their bodies.

Authors Paul Reisser, M.D., a family physician in southern Calif., serves on the Physician's Advisory Council for Focus on the Family. Teri Reisser, M.S., is presently director of services for the Right to Life League of southern Calif.

Contents 1. Who wants to read about aging? 2. What's going on or off at menopause? 3. How do I get ready?—physical preparations 4. How do I get ready?—relational, intellectual, emotional, and spiritual preparation 5. Taming depression, anxiety, and other beasts 6. The "E" word: should I use estrogen? 7. How do I detect trouble? 8. Is there (sex) life after 50? 9. Is the best yet to come?

PMS *What It Is And What You Can Do about It,* Sharon M. Sneed and Joe S. McIlhaney Jr.

Baker Book House, 1988, $6.99, paper, 150 pp., for both counselors and counselees

Description Combines good advice and real help from an experienced, sympathetic gynecologist and a dietitian/nutritionist who herself suffers from PMS. The result is a complete, easy-to-understand discussion of PMS and suggestions for treatment.

Authors Sharon Sneed, Ph.D., R.D., L.D., has been a practicing dietitian and nutritionist for more than ten years. Joe S. McIlhaney Jr., M.D., began his obstetrical/gynecological practice in Austin, Tex., in 1968.

Contents *Part 1:* Recognizing PMS *1.* Sharon's story *2.* Case studies of women with PMS *3.* History, causes, and incidence of PMS *Part 2:* Diagnosing PMS *4.* Identifying your symptoms *5.* The menstrual cycle—a physiological review *6.* Talking with your doctor about PMS *7.* Accepting your PMS diagnosis *Part 3:* Treating PMS *8.* Treatment options *9.* Exercise and PMS *10.* Diet and PMS *11.* Drugs and PMS *Part 4:* Living with PMS *12.* Family, friends, lifestyle, and PMS *13.* Stress and PMS *14.* Other options *15.* Your spiritual life and PMS

In God's Hand *One Woman's Experience with Breast Cancer,* Becky Lynn Wecksler and Michael Wecksler

Herald Press, 1989, $5.95, paper, 104 pp., for counselees

Description This is the story of a young woman with breast cancer. Overnight she realizes how precious her God-given life is as she and her family struggle to cope with the disease. She thought she had faith. But when she knows she cannot control her destiny, only then does she truly grasp the meaning of trusting the Lord.

Author Becky Lynn Wecksler continues her nursing career working part-time in the recovery room for a rural trauma center.

Menopause and Midlife Robert G. Wells and Mary C. Wells

Tyndale House Publishers, 1993, $14.99, paper, 162 pp., for counselees

Description A fresh, medically up-to-date, balanced look at the subject of menopause in the setting of midlife stresses. The authors show how one affects the other and offers to the reader ways to successfully cope during these midlife years.

Authors Robert G. Wells, M.D., is an obstetrician and gynecologist with a thriving practice in southern Calif. A fellow of the American College of Obstetricians and Gynecologists, he is an expert in the field of menopause and its management. Coauthor Mary Wells is both patient coordinator and lay counselor at the Menopause Center of Long Beach, which she and Dr. Wells founded in 1987.

Contents *1.* Taking control of your menopause and midlife *2.* Menopause, emotions, and midlife stresses *3.* Understanding menopause *4.* Hormone replacement therapy *5.* A matter of choice *6.* Estrogen and the cardiovascular system *7.* Estrogen and osteoporosis *8.* Surviving menopause: Mary's story *9.* Sexuality in midlife *10.* Maximizing your health in midlife *11.* Making the most of midlife *12.* A word to husbands *13.* Answers to your questions about menopause and midlife

Questions Women Ask in Private *Trusted Counsel on the Most Compelling Issues Women Face Today,* H. Norman Wright

Regal Books, 1993, $17.99, cloth, 350 pp., for both counselors and counselees

Description This comprehensive book contains more than 120 questions compiled from a wide variety of counselors. Includes questions on topics such as: intimacy, marriage, communication, sexuality, abuse, loneliness, wounds from the past, forgiveness, female issues, divorce and remarriage, blended families, single motherhood, and much more. Designed for professional and pastoral counselors as a "give-to" resource for women. Includes a comprehensive appendix listing caring professionals and organizations for personal follow-up.

Author Dr. H. Norman Wright is one of America's best known Christian marriage and family counselors at the Family Counseling and Enrichment Center in Tustin, Calif. He is author of more than 50 books. He has also served on the faculty of Talbot School of Theology and the Graduate School of Marriage Counseling of Biola University.

Contents *Introduction:* Why men and women are different *Section 1:* Women's issues *2.* Self-esteem *3.* Self-improvement *4.* Being single *5.* Stress *6.* Depression *7.* Health issues *8.* Spiritual issues and healing the past *Section 2:* Marriage issues *9.* Sex, intimacy, and romance *10.* How can I understand my husband? *11.* Unfaithfulness in marriage *12.* Communication in marriage *13.* How to save your marriage *14.* Anger and control in marriage *15.* Abusive husband *16.* Marriage and hot buttons: finances, alcoholism, and in-laws *Section 3:* Family issues *17.* Dealing with your parents *18.* Dealing with aging parents *19.* Codependency within the family *20.* Dysfunctional families *21.* Dealing with childhood sexual abuse *22.* Grieving a loss *Section 4:* Parenting issues *23.* Parenting problems *24.* Parenting hot buttons: anger, frustration, rebellion, drugs *25.* Single parents *Section 5:* Divorce and remarriage *26.* Divorce and remarriage *27.* Blended families

Recovering after a Mastectomy

Abbey Press, $.50 each, paper, 8 pp., for counselees

Description Part of the CareNotes series from Abbey Press. CareNotes are short booklets that help readers identify issues and begin the process of seeking resolution. Anecdotal and uplifting. Beautiful photographs grace the covers. Over 20 million CareNotes have been sold in just over five years. Can be used as an alternative to a greeting card or in conjunction with pastoral care visits.

PMS Access—A Division of Madison Pharmacy Association

PMS Access. An organization

Description You are invited to call for a free information packet on PMS that includes helpful details on diet, exercise, stress management, and vitamin therapies for dealing with PMS. Also maintains a question line to pharmacists skilled in dealing with questions about PMS. (Secular)

46. Youth/Adolescence

No Youthworker Is an Island Ridge Burns and Pam Campbell

Victor Books, 1992, $8.95, paper, 210 pp., for counselors

Description Based on a survey of 100 youth workers, this book offers practical, time-tested advice in key areas for youth workers.

Authors Ridge Burns is president of the Center for Student Missions. He is a graduate of Trinity Evangelical Divinity School. Pam Campbell is an editor and freelance writer. She has 15 years of youth ministry experience and is a graduate of Wheaton Graduate School.

Contents *1.* Students *2.* School and community *3.* Church staff and congregation *4.* Parents *5.* Personal issues *6.* Programs *7.* Youth groups *8.* Family *9.* Competition *10.* The future

The Angry Teenager *Why Teens Get So Angry and How Parents Can Help,* William Lee Carter

Thomas Nelson Publishers, 1995, $10.99, paper, 264 pp.

Description For parents of teenagers, a book that will help them understand anger—the most common, yet one of the most misunderstood emotions their teens will express. No other book addresses so thoroughly the topic of teenage anger, assessing the different types of anger, and explaining how to deal with each type.

Author Dr. William Lee Carter is a licensed psychologist in family practice who specializes in counseling children and adolescents.

Is My Family Crazy or Is It Me? Joseph McLean Hesh

NavPress, 1990, $4.00, paper, 52 pp., for counselees

Description Part of the Crossroad series from NavPress. Designed for junior high students who

want to know more about the challenges, options, and decisions they'll face in the years ahead. Provides format and ideas for lively discussions with youth. This title deals with improving relationships within the family.

Contents *1.* Playing tennis without a net—the importance of rules *2.* Hey, where's the steering wheel to this car?—the importance of making good choices *3.* Conversations with a television set—learning to listen *4.* Adventures in food color—getting along with brothers and sisters *5.* When your genes don't seem to fit—accepting your family heritage *6.* Would somebody please turn this family off!—finding calm in the middle of the storm

Swimming for Shore in a Sea of Sharks Joseph McLean Hesh

NavPress, 1990, $4.00, paper, 54 pp., for counselees

Description A discussion guide for junior high teens who want to know more about the challenges, options, and decisions they'll face in the years ahead. This title is aimed at helping youth establish a sense of purpose in life.

Contents *1.* Everybody have fun tonight—getting beyond the pursuit of pleasure *2.* Just a little bit more—getting beyond the material world *3.* Mirror, mirror on the wall—getting beyond a focus on self *4.* A real cool disease—getting beyond superficial faith *5.* Apocalypse tomorrow—getting beyond despair and rebellion *6.* Go against the flow—getting beyond shifting values

Helping the Struggling Adolescent *A Guide to 30 Common Problems for Parents, Counselors and Youth Workers,* Les Parrott

Zondervan Publishing House, 1993, $12.99, paper, 144 pp., for counselors

Description A reference guide for parents and all who counsel or work with teenagers, identifying the most common struggles and how to deal with them.

Author Dr. Parrott is associate professor of psychology and director of the Center for Relationship Development at Seattle Pacific University. His education includes the M.A. in theology and

Ph.D. in clinical psychology from Fuller Theological Seminary and a postdoctoral fellowship at the University of Washington School of Medicine. His other books include *Helping the Struggling Adolescent.*

Contents *Part 1:* Effective helping *1.* Adolescence: a struggle for identity *2.* Characteristics of effective helping: a self-inventory *3.* The heart of helping *4.* A parent's guide to professional help *Part 2:* The struggles of adolescents / Abuse / Anger / Anxiety / Body image / Depression / Drugs and alcohol / Eating disorders / Forgiveness / God's will / Grief / Guilt / Homosexuality / Inferiority / Loneliness / Masturbation / Obsessions and compulsions / Panic attacks / Parents / Peer pressure / Phobias / Pornography / Promiscuity and premarital sex / Schizophrenia / School work / Shyness / Siblings / Sleep disturbances / Spiritual doubt / Stuttering / Suicide

Helping the Struggling Adolescent
A Counseling Guide, Les Parrott

Zondervan Publishing House, 1993, $12.99, paper, 154 pp., for counselors

Description A companion guide to the book by the same title that deals with 30 common problems teenagers are coping with today, from abuse to suicide. This new companion book puts together under one cover a wide range of assessment tools so that those who counsel can gauge the presence and severity of particular issues in their adolescent clients.

Author Dr. Parrott is associate professor of psychology and director of the Center for Relationship Development at Seattle Pacific University. His education includes the M.A. in theology and Ph.D. in clinical psychology from Fuller Theological Seminary and a postdoctoral fellowship at the University of Washington School of Medicine. His other books include *Helping the Struggling Adolescent.*

Contents *Part 1:* Special issues in counseling *1.* Common pitfalls in counseling adolescents *2.* Legal and ethical issues related to counseling *3.* Avoiding counselor burnout: a survival kit *Part 2:* Rapid assessment tools / Using and interpreting rapid assessment tools / List of instruments cross-referenced by problem area / Rapid assessment instruments—Anger situations form—Are you dying to be thin?—Bulimia test—Checklist for making a major decision—Child's attitude toward mother—Child's attitude toward father—Clinical anxiety scale—Cognitive slippage scale—Compulsive eating scale—Compulsiveness inventory—Concern over weight and dieting scale—Dysfunctional attitude scale—Eating attitudes scale—Family adaptability and cohesion evaluation scale—Fear questionnaire—Fear survey—Schedule 2—Generalized contentment scale—Goldfarb fear of fat scale—Guilt scale—Hare self-esteem scale—Index of self-esteem—In-

tense ambivalence scale—Internal versus external control of weight scale—Inventory of religious beliefs—Michigan alcoholism screening test—Mobility inventory for agoraphobia—Novacco anger scale—Obsessive compulsive scale—Reasons for living inventory—Restraint scale—Revised UCLA loneliness scale—Self-efficacy scale—Self-rating depression scale—Skills for classroom success checklist—Skills for study success checklist—Stanford shyness survey—State—Trait anger scale—Teen alert questionnaire—Tough turf peer pressure quiz

Adolescents in Turmoil, Parents under Stress *A Pastoral Ministry Primer,* Richard D. Parsons

Paulist Press, 1987, $7.95, paper, 145 pp., for counselors

Description A Christian, value-based approach to the understanding of and caring for the adolescent in turmoil and their parents under stress.

Author Dr. Richard D. Parsons is professor of psychology in the Graduate Department of Pastoral Counseling at Neumann College, Aston, Pa. He maintains a private practice and is recognized as an expert in the field of problems of adolescents.

Contents *1.* Working with the adolescent—a special challenge *2.* Adolescence: storm and stress *3.* Communications *4.* Moving toward independence and the art of letting go *5.* Sex and the adolescent: an issue broader than the birds and the bees *6.* Drugs: use and abuse *7.* Nurturing the adolescent through school and other inconveniences *8.* Loneliness and alienation: adolescent without connection *9.* Suicide: the darkest of all moments

Pastoral Care with Adolescents in Crisis
G. Wade Rowatt Jr.

Westminster/John Knox Press, 1989, $13.99, paper, 168 pp., for counselors

Description Drawing upon personal experience, clinical knowledge, social research, and interviews, Wade Rowatt outlines the pressures that today's young people experience and offers principles and methods for responding. He focuses on five major areas of adolescent crises: family problems, sexual problems, substance abuse, school pressures, and depression and suicide.

Author G. Wade Rowatt Jr. is professor of psychology of religion and associate dean of the School of Theology, Southern Baptist Theological Seminary, Louisville, Ky. He is a coauthor of *The Two Career Marriage* and has written many other books and articles.

Contents *1.* Adolescents in crisis *2.* Developmental issues and crises *3.* Principles of caring *4.* Methods of pastoral care and counseling 5. Family problems 6. Sexual problems 7. Peer and academic problems 8. Depression and suicide 9. Substance abuse 10. The churches respond

Reaching Out to Troubled Youth Dwight Spotts and David Veerman

Victor Books, 1987, $11.95, paper, 248 pp., for counselors

Description A handbook for caring Christian adults that helps them reach troubled teenagers. Offers facts, figures, and case studies. It takes readers step-by-step through the whys and hows of a ministry that can change lives.

Authors Dwight H. Spotts (M.A., University of Illinois) has been helping troubled young people for over 20 years. He has started guidance programs in 23 states and overseas. David R. Veerman is a veteran youth worker and author of over 25 books. He is the former national Campus Life director for Youth for Christ/USA.

Contents 1. Should you be working with troubled youth? 2. Understanding troubled youth 3. Communicating with troubled youth 4. Disciplining troubled youth 5. Handling problem situations 6. Communicating the gospel to troubled youth 7. Teaching the Bible to troubled youth 8. Teaching pro-social skills 9. Getting troubled youth into the church 10. Working with parents of troubled youth 11. Working with community services 12. Working with institutional youth 13. Handling special problems

Advanced Peer Counseling in Youth Groups *Equipping Kids to Help Each Other with the Tough Issues,* Joan Sturkie and Siang-Yang Tan

Zondervan Publishing House, 1993, $14.99, paper, 160 pp., for counselors

Description An advanced training program for peer counselors that deals with all the major issues that teenagers face: sexuality, drugs and alcohol, family problems, and more.

Authors Joan Sturkie is a peer counseling consultant and trainer to teachers and students across the United States. She has written five other books on peer counseling. Siang-Yang Tan is director of the doctor of psychology program and associate professor in the Graduate School of Psychology, Fuller Theological Seminary.

Contents *Section 1:* Leader's guide to advanced peer counseling *Section 2:* The advanced peer counseling course 1. Crisis counseling 2. Peer pressure 3. School-related issues 4. Family issues 5. Child abuse 6. Drugs and alcohol 7. Sexuality 8. Pregnancy 9. AIDS 10. Eating disorders 11. Codependency 12. Death and loss 13. Suicide 14. War 15. Spiritual problems 16. Cults 17. The occult *Section 3:* Resources

Peer Counseling in Youth Groups *Equipping Your Kids to Help Each Other,* Joan Sturkie and Siang-Yang Tan

Zondervan Publishing House, 1992, $12.99, paper, 176 pp., for counselors

Description Everything you need to build a peer counseling program in your church to help teens minister to each other.

Authors Joan Sturkie is a peer counseling consultant and trainer to teachers and students across the United States. She has written five other books on peer counseling. Siang-Yang Tan is director of the doctor of psychology program and associate professor in the Graduate School of Psychology, Fuller Theological Seminary.

Youth Enrichment Survey Bob Tippie

Maret Software International, 1991, $99.99, software, for counselors

Description Designed for use by counseling youth ministers. Measures depression, anxiety, moral attitudes toward parents and others, and psychological distress.

Author Bob Tippie is an ordained Baptist minister with an active counseling and consulting practice. He holds a bachelor's degree in psychology and a master's in pastoral counseling.

Intensive Care *Helping Teenagers in Crisis,* Rich VanPelt

Zondervan Publishing House, 1988, $12.99, paper, 290 pp., for counselors

Description Whether you're a church or parachurch youth worker, teacher, counselor, parent, or friend, now is the time to develop the skills you need to assist teenagers and their families in times of crisis. This book offers such skills.

Index of Publishers and Organizations

AARP Widowed Persons Service
1909 K. St. NW
Washington, DC 20049
Ph. 202-728-4370

Abbey Press
One Caring Place
St. Meinrad, IN 47577
Ph. 800-325-2511

Abingdon Press/Upper Room Books
201 Eighth Avenue South
P.O.Box 801
Nashville, TN 37202
Ph. 800-251-3320

Adult Children of Alcoholics (ACOA)
2225 Sepulveda Blvd
Suite 200
Torrance, CA 90505
Ph. 213-302-7240

Aglow Publications
P.O. Box 6000
Colorado Springs, CO 80934
Ph. 800-366-7788

AIDS Information Ministries
P.O. Box 136116
Fort Worth, TX 76136
Ph. 817-237-0230

AIDS Resource Ministry
12488 Venice Boulevard
Los Angeles, CA 90066-3804
Ph. 310-572-0140

Al-Anon/Alateen Family Group Headquarters
P.O. Box 862
Midtown Station
New York, NY 10018-0862
Ph. 800-344-2666

Alcohol and Drug Abuse Hotline
Ph. 800-252-6465

Alcoholics Anonymous
P.O. Box 459
Grand Central Station
New York, NY 10163
Ph. 212-870-3400

Alcoholics For Christ
1316 N. Campbell Rd.
Royal Oak, MI 48067
Ph. 800-441-7877

Alzheimer's Association, Inc.
919 North Michigan Ave.
Suite 1000
Chicago, IL 60611
Ph. 800-621-0379

Alzheimer's Disease & Related Disorder Association
Ph. 800-272-3900

Alzheimer's Disease Education and Referral
P.O. Box 8250
Silver Spring, MD 20907-8250
Ph. 800-438-4380

American Association of Christian Counselors
P.O. Box 739
Forest, VA 24551-9969
Ph. 800-526-8673

American Anorexia/Bulimia Association
418 East 76th Street
New York, NY 10021
Ph. 212-734-1114

American Association for Counseling
5999 Stevenson Ave.
Alexandria, VA 22304

American Association of Homes for the Aging
90 E Street NW
Suite 500
Washington, DC 20004
Ph. 202-783-2242

American Association of Retired Persons
1909 K. St. NW
Washington, DC 20049
Ph. 202-434-2277

American Association of Sex Educators
435 N. Michigan Ave.
Suite 1717
Chicago, IL 60611
Ph. 312-644-0828

American Association of Suicidology
Box 2459 S. Ash
Denver, CO 80222
Ph. 303-692-0985

American Board of Sexology
1929 18th St. NW
Suite 1166
Washington, DC 20009
Ph. 202-462-2122

American Cancer Society
Ph. 800-227-2345

American Fertility Society
1209 Montgomery Ave.
Birmingham, AL 35216-2809

American Fertility Society, The
2140 11th Ave. South
Suite 200
Birmingham, AL 35205
Ph. 205-933-8494

American Victims of Abortion
419 7th Street NW
Suite 500
Washington, DC 20004
Ph. 202-626-8800

Americans for a Sound AIDS/HIV Policy
P.O. Box 17433
Washington, DC 20041
Ph. 703-471-7350

AMG Publishers
P.O. Box 22000
6815 Shallowford Rd.
Chattanooga, TN 37422
Ph. 800-251-7260

Answers in Action
P.O. Box 2067
Costa Mesa, CA 92628
Ph. 714-957-0249

Anxiety Disorders Association of America
6000 Executive Blvd.
Ste. 200
Rockville, MD 20852
Ph. 301-321-8368

Association of Christian Conciliation
1537 Ave. D.
Suite 352
Billings, MT 59102
Ph. 406-256-1583

Ave Maria Press
Notre Dame, IN 46556
Ph. 219-287-2831

Baker Book House
P.O. Box 6287
Grand Rapids, MI 49516-6287
Ph. 800-877-2665

Barbour and Company
P.O. Box 719
Uhrichsville, OH 44683
Ph. 800-852-8010

Barnabas Center, The
P.O. Box 3875
San Rafael, CA 94912-3875

Batterers Anonymous
1269 N. "E" St.
San Bernadino, CA 92405
Ph. 714-884-6809

Beacon Hill Press of Kansas City
P.O. Box 419527
616 Walnut Avenue
Kansas City, MO 64141
Ph. 800-821-2890

Bethany Christian Services
901 Eastern, NE
Grand Rapids, MI 49503
Ph. 800-238-4269

Bethany House Publishers
11300 Hampshire Ave. S.
Minneapolis, MN 55438
Ph. 800-328-6109

Beyond Rejection Ministries, Inc.
P.O. Box 1667
Cottonwood, CA 96022
Ph. 800-966-2437

Bob Larson Ministries
P.O. Box 360
Denver, CO 80236
Ph. 303-985-4673

Bridge Publishing
2500 Hamilton Boulevard
South Plainfield, NJ 07080
Ph. 800-631-5802

Broadman Holman Publishers
127 Ninth Ave N.
Nashville, TN 37234
Ph. 800-251-3225

Cancer Information Hotline
Ph. 800-525-3777

Candlelighters Childhood Cancer Foundation
7910 Woodmont Ave.
Suite 460
Bethesda, MD 20814
Ph. 800-366-2223

Care Net
101 W. Broad Street
Suite 500
Falls Church, VA 22046
Ph. 703-237-2100

Chariot Family Publishing
20 Lincoln Ave.
Elgin, IL 60120
Ph. 800-437-4337

Child Find of America, Inc.
Ph. 800-426-5678

Childhelp USA
6463 Independence Ave.
Woodland Hills, CA 91637
Ph. 800-422-4453

Children of the Night
Ph. 800-551-1300

Children With Attention Deficit Disorder Association
1859 N. Pine Island Rd.
Ste. 185
Plantation, FL 33322
Ph. 305-587-3700

Children's Hospice International
901 N. Washington Street
Alexandria, VA 22314
Ph. 703-684-0226

Choice Books
5044 16th St. NE
Hickory, NC 23601

Chosen Books
P.O. Box 6287
Grand Rapids, MI 49516-6287
Ph. 800-877-2665

Christian Action Council
101 Broad St.
Suite 500
Falls Church, VA 22040
Ph. 703-237-2100

Christian AIDS Services Alliance
P.O. Box 3612
San Rafael, CA 94912-3612

Christian Counseling and Education
3495 College Ave.
San Diego, CA 92115
Ph. 619-582-5554

Christian Family Video
2077 North Collins Boulev
Suite 202
Richardson, TX 75080
Ph. 800-231-0095

Christian Financial Concepts
601 Broad Street SE
Gainesville, GA 30501
Ph. 800-722-1976

Christian Helplines International
P.O. Box 10855
Tampa, FL 33679
Ph. 813-874-5509

Christian Legal Society, The
P.O. Box 1492
Merrifield, VA 22003
Ph. 703-642-1070

Christian Publications
3825 Hartzdale Drive
Camp Hill, PA 17011
Ph. 800-233-4443

Co-Dependents Anonymous, Inc.
P.O. Box 33577
Phoenix, AZ 85067-3577
Ph. 602-277-7991

Codependents of Sex Addicts
P.O. Box 14537
Minneapolis, MN
Ph. 612-537-6904

College Press
223 West 3rd
Joplin, MO 64801
Ph. 800-289-3300

Committe on Disability Concerns
2850 Kalamazoo Ave. SE
Grand Rapids, MI 49560-0001

Compassionate Friends, The
P.O. Box 1347
Oak Brook, IL 60521
Ph. 708-990-0010

CompCare Publishers
3850 Annapolis Lane
Suite 100
Minneapolis, MN 55447
Ph. 800-328-3330

Cornerstone Press
4707 N. Malden
Chicago, IL 60640
Ph. 312-989-2080

Covenant House
Ph. 800-999-9999

CPH Publishing
3558 South Jefferson Ave.
Saint Louis, MO 63118-3968
Ph. 800-325-3040

Creation House
190 N. Westmonte Drive
Altamonte Springs, FL 32714
Ph. 800-451-4598

Cult Awareness Network
2421 West Pratt Boulevard
Suite 1173
Chicago, IL 60645
Ph. 312-267-7777

Cult Information Service
1541 Northcrest Ave.
Columbus, OH 43220
Ph. 614-459-0634

DD-Anon-Group One
P.O. Box 4017
Appleton, WI 54915

Debtors Anonymous General Service Board
P.O. Box 20322
New York, NY 10025-9992
Ph. 212-969-0710

Depression After Delivery
P.O. Box 1282
Morrisville, PA 19067
Ph. 800-944-4773

Discovery House Publishers
Elm Hill Pike & Nelson Pl
PO Box 141000
Nashville, TN 37214-1000
Ph. 800-251-4000

E.Power Associates
P.O. Box 236
Brentwood, TN 37024-2346
Ph. 615-371-1320

Elijah House
P.O. Box 6287
Grand Rapids, MI 49516-6287
Ph. 800-877-2665

Emerald Books
P.O. Box 635
Lynnwood, WA 98046
Ph. 800-922-2143

Exchanged Life Foundation
P.O. Box 27315
Denver, CO 80227
Ph. 303-980-0003

Exodus International
P.O. Box 2121
San Rafael, CA 94912-2121
Ph. 415-454-1017

FIND
Guideposts Outreach Ministries
P.O. Box 855
Carmel, NY 10512-9971
Ph. 914-225-3681

Fleming H. Revell
P.O. Box 6287
Grand Rapids, MI 49516-6287
Ph. 800-877-2665

Focus On The Family
Colorado Springs, CO 80995
Ph. 719-531-3400

Foundation for Children with AIDS, The
1800 Columbus Ave.
Boston, MA 02119
Ph. 617-442-7442

Gam-Anon/Gamateen
P.O. Box 157
Whitestone, NY 11357
Ph. 718-352-1671

Gamblers Anonymous
P.O. Box 17173
Los Angeles, CA 90017
Ph. 213-386-8789

Gilgal Publications
P.O. Box 3386
Sunriver, OR 97707
Ph. 503-593-8418

Gold 'N' Honey Books (Questar)
P.O. Box 1720
Sisters, OR 97759
Ph. 800-929-0910

Gospel Light Publishing
2300 Knoll Drive
Ventura, CA 93003
Ph. 805-644-9721

Gospel Light Video
P.O. Box 3875
Ventura, CA 93006
Ph. 800-4-GOSPEL

Grace Fellowship International
P.O. Box 27315
Denver, CO 80227
Ph. 303-980-0003

H.A.N.D. of Santa Clara County
P.O. Box 341
Los Gatos, CA 95031
Ph. 408-732-3228

Harold Shaw Publishers
P.O. Box 567
Wheaton, IL 60189
Ph. 800-742-9782

Harper and Row
1160 Battery Street
San Francisco, CA 94111-1213
Ph. 415-477-4400

HarperCollins
10 East 53rd Street
New York, NY 10022-5299

Harvest House Publishers
1075 Arrowsmith
Eugene, OR 97402
Ph. 800-547-8979

Haworth Pastoral Press, The
10 Alice Street
Binghamton, NY 13904
Ph. 800-342-9678

Health Communications
(Order from) 4313 Canyons
Austin, TX 78731-2858
Ph. 512-338-4821

Heart to Heart
2115 S.E. Adams
Milwaukee, OR 97222-7773
Ph. 503-654-3870

Hendrickson Publishers
P.O. Box 3473
Peabody, MA 01961-3473
Ph. 800-358-3111

Herald Press
616 Walnut Ave.
Scottsdale, PA 15683-1999
Ph. 412-887-8500

Here's Life Publishers
(c/o Thomas Nelson Publishers)
Elm Hill Pike & Nelson Pl
P.O. Box 141000
Nashville, TN 37214-1000
Ph. 800-251-4000

Holt International Children's Services
P.O. Box 2880
Eugene, OR 97402
Ph. 503-687-2202

Hospice Education Institute
Five Essex Square
P.O. Box 713
Essex, CT 06426
Ph. 800-331-1620

Howard Publishing Company
2430 Juan Tabo, NE
Ste. 178
Albuquerque, NM 87112
Ph. None

Incest Survivors Anonymous
P.O. Box 17245
Long Beach, CA 90807-7245

Incest Survivors Anonymous
P.O. Box 3399
New Haven, CT 06515
Ph. 203-780-3951

Institute for Pastoral Care
234 Bald Eagle Drive
Cleveland, TN 37312

Institute on Religion and Law
820 North LaSalle Dr
Chicago, IL 60610
Ph. 800-678-8812

INTERCHRISTO Christian Placement Network
Ph. 800-426-1342

International Cult Education Program
P.O. Box 1232
Gracie Station
New York, NY 10028
Ph. 212-439-1550

International Society for the Study
5700 Old Orchard Road,
First Floor
Skokie, IL 60077-1024

InterVarsity Press
P.O. Box 1400
5206 Main Street
Downer's Grove, IL 60615
Ph. 800-843-9487

Jan Dennis (A division of Thomas Nelson Publishers)
Elm Hill Pike & Nelson Place
P.O. Box 141000
Nashville, TN 37214-1000
Ph. 800-251-4000

Janet Thoma (A division of Thomas Nelson Publishers)
Elm Hill Pike & Nelson Place
P.O. Box 141000
Nashville, TN 37214-1000
Ph. 800-251-4000

Joni and Friends
P.O. Box 3333
Agoura Hills, CA 91301
Ph. 818-707-5664

Judson Press
P.O. Box 851
Valley Forge, PA 19482-0851
Ph. 215-768-2118

Kraus International Publications
Fuller Theological Seminary
Pasadena, CA 91101

Last Harvest Ministries
Ph. 800-422-4582

Liberty Godparent Home
1000 Villa Rd.
Lynchburg, VA 24503
Ph. 800-542-4453

Life After Assault League, Inc.
1336 W Lindberg
Appleton, WI 54914
Ph. 414-739-4489

Life in Jesus Community, The
P.O. Box 40
Libertytown, MD 21762
Ph. 410-795-4869

LifeSkills
Ph. 916-366-9444

LifeWay
The Sunday School Board -
127 Ninth Ave. N
Nashville, TN 37203-9982
Ph. 800-458-2772

Ligouri Publications
One Ligouri Drive
Ligouri, MO 63057-9999
Ph. 800-325-9521

Lion Publishing
20 Lincoln Ave.
Elgin, IL 60120
Ph. 800-447-5466

Love and Action
3 Church Circle
Annapolis, MD 21401
Ph. 410-268-3442

Love in Action
Ph. 415-454-0960

MAP International
P.O. Box 50
Brunswick, GA 31521-0050
Ph. 912-265-6010

Maret Software International
3813 W. 214th St.
Mattson, IL 60443
Ph. 708-748-1188

Marshall Pickering/Zondervan
5300 Patterson SE
Grand Rapids, MI 49530
Ph. 800-727-1309

Mennonite Media Productions
1251 Virginia Ave
Harrisonburg, VA 22801
Ph. 703-434-6701

Missing Children Help Center
Ph. 800-872-5437

Moody Press
820 North LaSalle Dr.
Chicago, IL 60610
Ph. 800-678-8812

Morehouse Publishing
P.O. Box 1321
Harrisburg, PA 17105
Ph. 800-877-0012

Multnomah Books (Questar)
P.O. Box 1720
Sisters, OR 97759
Ph. 800-929-0910

Narcotics Anonymous, World Service
16155 Wyandotte St.
Van Nuys, CA 91406
Ph. 818-780-3951

Narramore Christian Foundation
P.O. Box 5000
Rosemead, CA 91770
Ph. 800-543-3337

National AIDS Hotline
Ph. 800-342-2437

National AIDS Information Clearinghouse
P.O. Box 6003
Rockville, MD 20849-6003
Ph. 800-458-5231

399

National Association for Children of Alcoholics

31582 Coast Highway
Suite 201
South Laguna, CA 92667
Ph. 714-449-3889

National Association of Adult Children

P.O. Box 463
Fond du Lac, WI 54935

National Association of Anorexia Nervosa

P.O. Box 7
Highland Park, IL 60035
Ph. 708-831-3438

National Center for Missing and Exploited Children

1835 K. St. NW
Suite 700
Washington, DC 20006
Ph. 800-843-5678

National Clearinghouse for Alcohol and Substance Abuse

P.O. Box 2345
Rockville, MD 20847
Ph. 800-729-6686

National Committee for the Prevention of Child Abuse

332 S. Michigan Ave.
Suite B
Chicago, IL 60604
Ph. 312-663-3520

National Council on Compulsive, The

445 West 59th Street
New York, NY 10019
Ph. 800-522-4700

National Council on Sexual Addiction

P.O. Box 20249
Wittenburg, AZ 85358
Ph. 800-321-2066

National Depressive & Manic Depressive Illness Foundation

730 North Franklin
Suite 501
Chicago, IL 60610
Ph. 800-826-3632

National Domestic Violence Hotline

Huntington Woods, MI 48070
Ph. 202-638-6388

National Drug Abuse Information & Referral

Ph. 800-662-4357

National Foundation for Depressive

Ph. 800-248-4344

National Hospice Organization

Suite 901
1901 N. Moore St.
Arlington, VA 22209
Ph. 703-243-5900

National Institute of Mental Health

5600 Fisher's Lane
Room 7-99
Rockville, MD 20857
Ph. 800-647-2642

National Institute on Aging

P.O. Box 8057
Gaithersburg, MD 20890
Ph. 800-222-2225

National Legal Foundation, The

P.O. Box D
Chesapeake, VA 23320-0020
Ph. 804-424-4242

National Network of Runaway and You

905 6th St. SW
Suite 612
Washington, DC 20006
Ph. 202-488-0739

National Office of Post-abortion Reconcilliation

7818 Chapel Cove
Laurel, MD 20707

National Organization for Victim Assistance

1757 Park Road N.W.
Washington, DC 20010

National Runaway Switchboard
Ph. 800-621-4000

National Sexual Addiction Hotline
P.O. Box 20249
Wittenburg, AZ 85358
Ph. 800-321-2066

National Suicide Assistance Hotline
Ph. 800-333-4444

National Teen Crisis Hotline
Ph. 800-621-4000

National Victim's Center
2111 Wilson Blvd
Ste. 300
Arlington, VA 22201
Ph. 800-394-2255

National Victim's Resource Center
Ph. 800-627-6872

NavPress / Piñion Press
P.O. Box 35001
Colorado Springs, CO 80935
Ph. 800-955-3336

New Hope
P.O. Box 12065
Birmingham, AL 35202-2065
Ph. 205-991-4933

New Leaf Press
P.O. Box 311
Green Forest, AR 72638
Ph. 800-643-9535

Nurturing Network, The
910 Main Street Suite 360
P.O. Box 2050
Boise, ID 83701
Ph. 800-866-4666

Oliver Nelson (A division of Thomas Nelson Publishers)
Elm Hill Pike & Nelson Pl
PO Box 141000
Nashville, TN 37214-1000
Ph. 800-251-4000

Open Arms
P.O. Box 1056
Columbia, MO 65205
Ph. 314-449-7672

Operation Lookout National Center
12128 Cyrus Way
Building B, Suite 40
Mukilteo, WA 98275-5706
Ph. 800-782-7335

Overcomers Outreach
2290 West Whittier Blvd
Suite A/D
La Habra, CA 90631
Ph. 213-697-3994

Overeaters Anonymous, Inc.
World Service Office
PO Box 92870
Los Angeles, CA 90009
Ph. 800-743-8703

P & R Publishing
P.O. Box 817
Phillipsburg, NJ 08865
Ph. 800-631-0094

Pacific Press
P.O. Box 7000
Boise, ID 83707
Ph. 800-447-7377

Paragon House Publishers
90 Fifth Ave.
New York, NY 10011
Ph. 212-620-2820

Pathways to Promise
5400 Arsenal Street
St. Louis, MO 63139
Ph. 314-644-8400

Paulist Press
997 MacArthur Boulevard
Mahwah, NJ 07430
Ph. 800-836-3161

Penner Publications
2 North Lake Ave.
Suite 610
Pasadena, CA 91101
Ph. 818-449-2525

Pilgrim Press, The
700 Prospect Ave. East
Cleveland, OH 44115-1100
Ph. 800-537-3394

Pillar Books & Publishing Company
P.O. Box 471692
Tulsa, OK 74147-1692
Ph. 800-542-2665

Piñion Press
P.O. Box 35007
Colorado Springs, CO 80935
Ph. 800-955-3336

PMS Access
Ph. 800-222-4767

Post Abortion Ministries
P.O. Box 3092
Landover Hills, MD 20784-0092
Ph. 301-773-4630

Project Rachel
3501 S. Lake Drive
P.O. Box 07477
Milwaukee, WI 53207-0477
Ph. 414-483-4141

Pure Life Ministries
P.O. Box 345
Crittendon, KY 41030
Ph. 800-635-1866

Pyranee Books / Zondervan
5300 Patterson Ave. SE
Grand Rapids, MI 49530
Ph. 800-727-3480

Questar Publishers
P.O. Box 1720
Sisters, OR 97759

Rainbows for All God's Children, Inc.
1111 Tower Rd.
Schaumberg, IL 60173
Ph. 708-310-1880

Rapha Resources
12700 N. Featherwood Dr.
Suite 250
Houston, TX 77034-4436
Ph. 800-460-4673

Recovery Publications, Inc.
1201 Knoxville St.
San Diego, CA 92110-3718
Ph. 800-873-8384

Regal Books
2300 Knoll Drive
Ventura, CA 93003
Ph. 800-446-7735

Regeneration Books
P.O. Box 9830
Baltimore, MD 21284
Ph. 410-661-0284

RESOLVE
1310 Broadway
Somerville, MA 02144-1731
Ph. 617-623-0744

Resource Publications, Inc.
160 E. Virginia St.
Suite 290
San Jose, CA 95112-5876
Ph. 408-286-8505

Respect, inc.
P.O. Box 349
Bradley, IL 60915
Ph. 815-932-8389

Rutheford Institute, The
P.O. Box 7482
Charlottsville, VA 22906-7482
Ph. 804-978-3888

Serendipity
P.O. Box 1012
Littleton, CO 80160
Ph. 800-525-9563

Servant Publications / Vine Books
P.O. Box 8617
Ann Arbor, MI 48107
Ph. 800-458-8505

Sex Addicts Anonymous
P.O. Box 3038
Minneapolis, MN 55403
Ph. 612-871-1520

Sex and Love Addicts Anonymous
P.O. Box 119
New Town Branch
Boston, MA 02258
Ph. 617-332-1845

Sexaholics Anonymous
P.O. Box 300
Simi Valley, CA 93062
Ph. 805-851-3343

SHARE: Pregnancy and Infant Loss Support
St. Joseph's Health Center
300 First Capitol Dr
St. Charles, MO 63301-2893
Ph. 314-947-6164

Shield of Faith Ministries
P.O. Box 19367
Denver, CO 80219

SIDS Alliance
10500 Little Patuxent Par
Suite 420
Columbia, MD 21044
Ph. 800-221-7437

Society for Young Victims
Ph. 800-999-9024

Solomon Publications
Ph. 303-980-0003

Sonlight Publishing
P.O. Box 110512
Nashville, TN 37222-0512
Ph. 615-331-0691

South Oakes Hospital
Ph. 800-732-9808

Spender Menders
P.O. Box 15000-156
San Francisco, CA 94115
Ph. 415-773-9754

Spire Books
P.O. Box 6287
Grand Rapids, MI 49516-6287
Ph. 800-877-2665

Spiritual Counterfeits Project
P.O. Box 4380
Berkeley, CA 94704
Ph. 415-540-5767

Stephen Ministries
8016 Dale Ave.
St. Louis, MO 63117
Ph. 314-645-5511

Stepping Stones
2900 N. Rock Rd.
Wichita, KS 67226-1198

Sudden Infant Death Syndrome Alliance
Ph. 800-638-7437

Survivors And Victims Empowered
P.O. Box 10756
Lancaster, PA 17605-0756
Ph. 717-569-3636

Survivors of Incest Anonymous
P.O. Box 21817
Baltimore, MD 21222-6817
Ph. 410-433-2365

Teen Aid
Ph. 509-328-2080

Thomas Nelson Publishers
Elm Hill Pike & Nelson Pl
P.O. Box 141000
Nashville, TN 37214-1000
Ph. 800-251-4000

Tough Love
P.O. Box 1069
Doylestown, PA 18901
Ph. 800-333-1069

Turning Point Ministries, Inc.
P.O. Box 22127
Chattanooga, TN 37422-2127
Ph. 800-879-4770

Tyndale House Publishers
351 Executive Drive
Box 80
Wheaton, Il 60189-0080
Ph. 800-323-9400

Victor Books
1825 College Avenue
Wheaton, IL 60187-4498
Ph. 800-323-9409

Victory House Publishing
P.O. Box 700238
Tulsa, OK 74170
Ph. 918-747-5009

Vine Books
1143 Highland Dr.
Suite E
Ann Arbor, MI 48108
Ph. 313-677-6490

W.A.T.C.H. Network
P.O. Box 12638
El Paso, TX 79913
Ph. 915-581-2011

WEBA
P.O. Box 268
Venus, TX 76084
Ph. 214-366-3600

Wellspring Retreat and Resource Center
P.O. Box 67
Albany, OH 45710
Ph. 614-698-6277

WESCOM Inc.
P.O. Box 46312
Chicago, IL 60646
Ph. 312-792-7034

Westminster/John Knox Press
100 Witherspoon Street
Room 1620
Louisville, KY 40202-1396
Ph. 800-523-1631

Wm. B. Eerdmans Publishing Co.
255 Jefferson S.E.
Grand Rapids, MI 49503
Ph. 800-253-7521

Word Publishing
5221 N. O'Conner Blvd.
Irving, TX 75039
Ph. 800-933-9673

Workaholics Anonymous
Westchester Comm. College
AAB 75 Grasslands Rd
Valhalla, NY 10595
Ph. 914-347-3620

Youth With a Mission Publishing
P.O. Box 55787
Seattle, WA 98155
Ph. 800-922-2143

Zenas Ministries
P.O. Box 20043
Panama City, FL 32407
Ph. 904-769-4938

Zondervan Publishing House
5300 Patterson Ave. S.E.
Grand Rapids, MI 49530
Ph. 800-727-3480

404

Index of
Extended Topics

Couldn't find your topic in the table of contents? Try looking here.

Index of Extended Topics